BIBLIOGRAPHY

BIBLIOGRAPHY

of

HISTORICAL WRITINGS

published in

GREAT BRITAIN AND THE EMPIRE

1940 - 1945

By LOUIS B. FREWER

EDITED FOR THE BRITISH NATIONAL COMMITTEE OF THE
INTERNATIONAL COMMITTEE OF HISTORICAL SCIENCES

GREENWOOD PRESS, PUBLISHERS
WESTPORT, CONNECTICUT

Library of Congress Cataloging in Publication Data

Frewer, Louis Benson.
   Bibliography of historical writings published in
Great Britain and the Empire, 1940-1945.

     Reprint of the 1947 ed. published by B. Blackwell,
Oxford.
     1. History--Bibliography. 2. Great Britain--Im-
prints. I. International Committee of Historical
Sciences. British National Committee. II. Title.
Z6201.F7 1974   016.9 ,   74-12628
ISBN 0-8371-7735-9

Originally published in 1947 by Basie Blackwell, Oxford

Reprinted with the permission of Louis B. Frewer

Reprinted in 1974 by Greenwood Press,
a division of Williamhouse-Regency Inc.

Library of Congress Catalog Card Number 74-12628

ISBN 0-8371-7735-9

Printed in the United States of America

PREFACE

THIS Bibliography has been produced with the approval of the British National Committee of the International Committee of Historical Sciences in view of the fact that publication of the *International Bibliography of Historical Sciences* covering the years of the War will in any event not be possible for some years. It is felt that there is urgent need among scholars in all fields of history for bibliographical aids to the historical work that has appeared during the War. It proved possible to continue during the War the preparation of the British material for the *International Bibliography* in the same manner as before the War. In consequence the British National Committee considered that it was highly desirable that this material should be made available as soon as possible in the form of a single volume containing a list of historical writings (books, articles and reviews) published in the years 1940–1945 in Great Britain and the British Commonwealth. The agreement of Dr. Waldo Leland, President of the International Committee of the Historical Sciences, was obtained. When the publication of the *International Bibliography* is resumed, it will be possible to utilize in it the material in this volume. This Bibliography is prepared in the same way as the *International Bibliography* and, with a few slight modifications, classified according to the same subject headings. Any shortcomings or errors are, we hope, outweighed by the advantages of speedy publication and availability to historical scholars and students in all countries who have been cut off from recent historical work for so many cruel and severing years. Publication of this volume has been made possible by a grant from the British Academy.

As compiler and editor of this volume we have been fortunate enough to secure the expert services of Mr. L. B. Frewer, M.A., Superintendent of Rhodes House Library, Oxford, who was responsible for the British material in the pre-war volumes of the *International Bibliography*. The British National Committee are much indebted to Mr. B. H. Sumner, Warden of All Souls College, Oxford, who made the necessary arrangements on their behalf for the publication of this volume and contributed most valuable assistance to the final stages of its preparation.

F. M. POWICKE,

Chairman, International Bibliography Commission of the International Committee of Historical Sciences.

CHARLES K. WEBSTER,

Chairman, British National Committee of the International Committee of Historical Sciences.

April, 1947.

EDITORIAL NOTE

THIS volume has been prepared as far as possible in the same manner and format as the *International Bibliography of Historical Sciences*. It is a selective compilation of historical writings, covering all aspects of history down to the beginning of the second World War, published in Great Britain and the Commonwealth between 1940 and 1945 inclusive, together with articles from some one hundred and twenty periodicals published in Great Britain and the Commonwealth, and reviews of such works which have appeared in these periodicals. There are included in this Bibliography books published in the United States by certain American universities which are also published in Great Britain by the Oxford and Cambridge University Presses. The selection has been made from Whitaker's *Cumulative Book List for Great Britain* and from books mentioned in bibliographies and reviews in the above-mentioned periodicals.

A list of these periodicals, with the abbreviations adopted, will be found on pages ix–xii. These abbreviations accord with those in use in the *World List of Historical Periodicals and Bibliographies*. It will be seen from this list that, in accordance with the pre-war practice in the *International Bibliography*, no attempt has been made to cover systematically the transactions and proceedings of local societies in Great Britain, so that local history, as regards articles, is represented for the most part only by those articles which appeared in more general periodicals.

The method of classification follows that of the *International Bibliography*, with as few modifications as possible.

Bibliographies that come under the heading of a section or a sub-section will be found at the beginning of the relative section or sub-section, otherwise in B 1 *a* and B 1 *b*. Sub-sections B 6 to B 13 contain writings covering in time or subject matter a wider range than those covered by any one of the other headings. History of the Middle Ages (I) is taken to cover chronologically from about A.D. 500 to 1450, and Modern History since the late fifteenth century in the case of K, M, N and O, and since the Reformation, inclusive, in the case of L.

Material falling under headings L to P is to be found under those headings and not under K 2, countries. Entries are not duplicated.

In general, all items concerning solely the countries covered by Q, R, S, and T, are placed under these headings, and not under other subject headings, *e.g.* Indian economic history will be found under Q 3 not N 3, Chinese art under Q 5 not under B 10 or M 8. Exceptions to this are material relating to the East India Company, which will be found in P 2 *c*, and material relating to Australia and New Zealand since 1787 which will be found in P 2 *g* or, if relating to the 20th century, in K 2 Australia, K 2 New Zealand, or under the subjects covered by L, M, N and O. Reference can be made to the Index of Places which includes all items relating *e.g.* to Australia and New Zealand.

Certain sections which contain no material at all have been included as an indication that nothing has appeared during the years under review on the subjects they cover. Every effort has been made to render all entries complete in every detail, but a few have proved elusive, and in these cases certain information is lacking, *e.g.* number of pages or price.

In conclusion, I desire to make most grateful acknowledgment of the expert guidance, advice and ready co-operation in the planning and publication of this work by Mr. B. H. Sumner, Warden of All Souls College, Oxford; of the assistance rendered by Mr. J. J. Jones, M.A., of the National Library of Wales, and Mr. J. G. Edwards, M.A., of Jesus College, Oxford, in the matter of the Welsh contributions; of help in the laborious task of classifying and indexing so ably rendered by Miss L. F. Leake, B.A., and Mr. T. G. England, M.A.; and of the work in typing original entries carried out by Mr. T. A. T. Cox and Mr. E. A. Dyer.

Oxford,   L.B.F.
April, 1947.

I am grateful to a correspondent for having brought to my notice certain minor misprints in the earlier edition: these have now been corrected.

November, 1947.   L.B.F.

LIST OF PERIODICALS

Africa	Africa
African Affairs	African Affairs (*formerly* Journal of the Royal African Society)
African Stud.	African Studies (*formerly* Bantu Studies)
A. Archaeol. Anthrop.	Annals of Archaeology and Anthropology
A. Sci.	Annals of Science
Antiq. J.	Antiquaries Journal
Antiquity	Antiquity
Archaeologia	Archaeologia
Archaeol. aeliana	Archaeologia Aeliana
Archaeol. cambrensis	Archaeologia Cambrensis
Archaeol. cantiana	Archaeologia Cantiana
Archaeol. J.	Archaeological Journal
Archives Y.B.S. Afr. Hist.	Archives Year Book for South African History
Army Quar.	Army Quarterly
Art in Australia	Art in Australia
Arts in N. Zealand	Arts in New Zealand
Asiatic R.	Asiatic Review
Austral. Law J.	Australian Law Journal
Austral. Nat. R.	Australian National Review
Austral. Quar.	Australian Quarterly
Bantu Stud.	Bantu Studies (*afterwards* African Studies)
Baptist Quar.	Baptist Quarterly
B.Y.B.I.L.	British Year Book of International Law
B. Rech. hist.	Bulletin des Recherches historiques
B. Board celtic Stud.	Bulletin of the Board of Celtic Studies
B. Imp. Inst.	Bulletin of the Imperial Institute
B. Inst. hist. Research	Bulletin of the Institute of Historical Research
B. John Rylands Library	Bulletin of the John Rylands Library
B. Publ. Archives Nova Scotia	Bulletin of the Public Archives of Nova Scotia
B. Uganda Society	Bulletin of the Uganda Society (*afterwards* Uganda Journal)
Burlington Mag.	Burlington Magazine
Cambridge hist. J.	Cambridge Historical Journal
Canad. Art	Canadian Art
Canad. Bar R.	Canadian Bar Review
Canad. Cath. hist. Assoc. Rept.	Canadian Catholic Historical Association Report

Canad. hist. Assoc. Rept.	Canadian Historical Association Annual Report .
Canad. hist. R.	Canadian Historical Review
Canad. J. Econ. pol. Sci.	Canadian Journal of Economics and Political Science
Class. Quar.	Classical Quarterly
Class. R.	Classical Review
Congreg. hist. Soc. Trans.	Congregational Historical Society Transactions
Congreg. Quar.	Congregational Quarterly
Dalhousie R.	Dalhousie Review
J. West. Austral. hist. Soc.	Early Days: journal of the Western Australia Historical Society
Econ. Hist.	Economic History
Econ. Hist. R.	Economic History Review
Econ. J.	Economic Journal
Econ. Record	Economic Record
Economica	Economica
Eng. hist. R.	English Historical Review
Geogr. J.	Geographical Journal
Geography	Geography
Greece and Rome	Greece and Rome
Grotius Soc. Trans.	Grotius Society Transactions
Hibbert J.	Hibbert Journal
Hist. Stud. Australia N.Z.	Historical Studies, Australia and New Zealand
History	History
Int. Affairs	International Affairs
Int. J.	International Journal
Int. R. Missions	International Review of Missions
Iraq	Iraq
Irish hist. Stud.	Irish Historical Studies
Jamaican hist. R.	Jamaican Historical Review
J. comp. Legisl. int. Law	Journal of Comparative Legislation and International Law
J. Documentation	Journal of Documentation
J. hell. Stud.	Journal of Hellenic Studies
J. public Admin. N.Z.	Journal of Public Administration, New Zealand
J. rom. Stud.	Journal of Roman Studies
J. Barbados Museum	Journal of the Barbados Museum
J. archaeol. Assoc.	Journal of the British Archaeological Association
J. Friends hist. Soc.	Journal of the Friends Historical Society
J. hist. Soc. presb. Church Wales	Journal of the Historical Society of the Presbyterian Church of Wales

J. polynesian Soc.	Journal of the Polynesian Society
J. presb. hist. Soc.	Journal of the Presbyterian Historical Society
J. Roy. African Soc.	Journal of the Royal African Society (*afterwards* African Affairs)
J. anthrop. Inst.	Journal of the Royal Anthropological Institute
J. asiatic Soc.	Journal of the Royal Asiatic Society
J. central asian Soc.	Journal of the Royal Central Asian Society
J. Roy. statist. Soc.·	Journal of the Royal Statistical Society
J. Soc. Bibl. nat. Hist.	Journal of the Society for the Bibliography of Natural History
J. Soc. Army hist. Research	Journal of the Society of Army Historical Research
J. welsh bibliogr. Soc.	Journal of the Welsh Bibliographical Society
L.Q.R.	Law Quarterly Review
Library	Library
Man	Man
Mariner's Mirror	Mariner's Mirror
Med. and Renaissance Stud.	Mediaeval and Renaissance Studies
Med. Stud.	Mediaeval Studies, Toronto
Med. Ævum	Medium Ævum
Mod. Language R.	Modern Language Review
Musical Times	Musical Times
Nat. Library Wales J.	National Library of Wales Journal
National R.	National Review
N.Z. Geogr.	New Zealand Geographer
19th Century	Nineteenth Century
Nova Scotia hist. Soc. Coll.	Nova Scotia Historical Society Collections
Numism. Chron.	Numismatic Chronicle
Oceania	Oceania
Ontario hist. Soc. Pap.	Ontario Historical Society Papers and Records
Philosophy	Philosophy
Pol. Quar.	Political Quarterly
Proc. british Academy	Proceedings of the British Academy
Proc. prehist. Soc.	Proceedings of the Prehistoric Society
Quar. Dept. Antiq. Palestine	Quarterly of the Department of Antiquities, Palestine
Quar. R.	Quarterly Review
Queen's Quar.	Queen's Quarterly
Rhodes-Livingstone Inst. J.	Rhodes-Livingstone Institute Journal
Roy. Austral. hist. Soc. J.	Royal Australian Historical Society Journal

Sci. Progress	Science Progress
Scottish geogr. Mag.	Scottish Geographical Magazine
Slavonic R.	Slavonic Review
Sociol. R.	Sociological Review
South African J. Econ.	South African Journal of Economics
South African Law J.	South African Law Journal
Sudan Notes and Records	Sudan Notes and Records
Theology	Theology
Trans. Proc. Japan Soc.	Transactions and Proceedings of the Japan Society
Trans. Carmarthenshire Antiq. Soc.	Transactions of the Carmarthenshire Antiquarian Society
Trans. Soc. Cymmr.	Transactions of the Hon. Society of Cymmrodorion
Trans. Newcomen Soc.	Transactions of the Newcomen Society
Trans. philol. Soc.	Transactions of the Philological Society
Trans. Roy. hist. Soc.	Transactions of the Royal Historical Society
Trans. Roy. Soc. Canad.	Transactions of the Royal Society of Canada
Trans. R. Soc. S. Australia	Transactions of the Royal Society of South Australia
Trans. Unitarian hist. Soc.	Transactions of the Unitarian Historical Society
Uganda J.	Uganda Journal (*formerly* Bulletin of the Uganda Society)
United Empire	United Empire

CONTENTS

A
AUXILIARY SCIENCES
(No. 1 – 226)

B
MANUALS, GENERAL WORKS
(No. 227 – 772)

C

PRE-HISTORY
(No. 773 – 914)

D

THE ANCIENT EAST
(No. 915 – 1021)

E

GREEK HISTORY
(No. 1022 – 1112)

F

HISTORY OF ROME AND ANCIENT ITALY
(No. 1113 – 1242)

G

EARLY HISTORY OF THE CHURCH TO GREGORY THE GREAT
(No. 1243 – 1269)

H

BYZANTINE HISTORY (SINCE JUSTINIAN)
(No. 1270 – 1275)

I

HISTORY OF THE MIDDLE AGES
(No. 1276 – 1842)

K

MODERN HISTORY, GENERAL WORKS
(No. 1843 – 2617)

L

MODERN RELIGIOUS HISTORY
(No. 2618 – 2933)

M

HISTORY OF MODERN CULTURE
(No. 2934 – 3693)

N

MODERN ECONOMIC AND SOCIAL HISTORY
(No. 3694 – 4259)

O

MODERN LEGAL AND CONSTITUTIONAL HISTORY
(No. 4260 – 4416)

P

HISTORY OF COLONIAL, IMPERIAL AND INTERNATIONAL RELATIONS
(No. 4417 – 4959)

Q
ASIA
(No. 4960–5184)

R

S

T

A

AUXILIARY SCIENCES

§ 1. Palaeography

1. CLARK (K. W.). Eight American praxapostoloi. London, Cambridge Univ. Press, 41, in-8, 204 p., (plates), 12s. R : G. D. Kilpatrick, *J. hell. Stud.*, 42 (43), vol. 62, p. 113.

2. KER (Neil R.). William of Malmesbury's handwriting. *Eng. hist. R.*, 44, vol. 59, p. 371-376.

3. LAIRD (Charlton). Palatinus Latinus 1970, a composite MS. *Mod. Language R.*, 43, vol. 38, p. 117-121.

4. WILLOUGHBY (H. R.) and COLWELL (E. C.). The Elizabeth Day McCormick Apocalypse. London, Cambridge Univ. Press, 40, 2 vols. in-8, 625, 206 p., (plates), 165s. R : P.P.A., *J. hell. Stud.*, 42 (43), vol. 62, p. 112-113.

§ 2. Diplomatic

§ 3. History of the Book

5. FITZWILLIAM MUSEUM, CAMBRIDGE. Catalogue. An exhibition of printing at the Fitzwilliam Museum, Cambridge. London, Cambridge Univ. Press, 40, in-8, xi-136 p., 1s. R : F. C. Francis, *Library*, 40/41, vol. 21, p. 339-345.

6. BAIKIE (J.). The English Bible and its story. New ed. London, Seeley Service, 43, in-8, 320 p., (illus.), 6s.

7. BAIN (D. C.). Some notes on the printing of the " Summa de Exemplis ", 1499. *Library*, 40, vol. 21, p. 192-198.

8. BAIN (J. S.). A bookseller looks back : the story of the Bains. London, Macmillan, 40, in-8, xvi-304 p., (illus.), 15s.

9. BALD (R. C.). The foul papers of a revision. *Library*, 45, vol. 26, p. 37-50.

10. BEATTIE (William). A hand-list of works from the press of John Wreittoun at Edinburgh, 1624-c.1639. (Edinb. bibliogr. soc. trans., vol. 2, pt. 2, 1939-40). Edinburgh, 1941.

11. BESTERMAN (Theodore). Early printed books to the end of the 16th century. London, Quaritch, 40, in-8, 309 p., 21s.

12. BOLITHO (Hector). A Batsford centenary : record of a hundred years of publishing and bookselling, 1843-1943. London, Batsford, 43, in-8, viii-148 p., (plates), 10s. 6d. R : *National R.*, 44, vol. 122, p. 261-262. F. C. Francis, *Library*, 43/44, vol. 24, p. 95-96.

13. BÜHLER (Curt F.). Some documents concerning the Torresani and the Aldine Press. *Library*, 44/45, vol. 25, p. 111-121.

14. BUSHNELL (George H.). Patrick Bower. *Library*, 42, vol. 23, p. 23-30.

15. BUTLER (Pierce). The origin of printing in Europe. London, Cambridge Univ. Press, 41, in-8, 156 p., (plates), 9s. R : V. Scholderer, *Library*, 43, vol. 24, p. 89-91.

16. CLARKE (W. J.). Early Nottingham printers and printing. Nottingham, Forman, 42, in-8, 79 p., privately pr. R : G. E. Flack, *Library*, 43/44, vol. 24, p. 202-204.

17. GARRETT (Christina). " The Resurreccion of the Masse ", by Hugh Hilarie, or John Bale (?). *Library*, 40, vol. 21, p. 143-159.

18. GREG (W. W.). The two John Busby's. *Library*, 43, vol. 24, p. 81-86.

19. GREG (W. W.). The copyright of *Hero and Leander*. *Library*, 43/44, vol. 24, p. 165-174.

20. GREG (W. W.). Entrance, licence, and publication. *Library*, 44, vol. 25, p. 1-22.

21. GUPPY (Henry). The evolution of the art of printing. *B. John Rylands Library*, 40, vol. 24, p. 198-233 ; Manchester, Univ. Press, 41, in-8, 45 p., 18 plates, 2s.

22. HANNEFORD-SMITH (William). Recollections of a half-century's association with the House of Batsford (1893-1943). London, 43, 31 p., printed for private circulation.

23. HAZEN (A. T.). A bibliography of the Strawberry Hill Press. London, Oxford Univ. Press, 43, in-4, 300 p., (facs.), 66s. 6d.

24. HERBERT (Robert). Limerick printers and printing. Part 1 of the catalogue of the local collection in the City of Limerick public library. Limerick, Public Libr., 42, in-8, 62 p., 2s. 6d. R : F. O'Kelley, *Irish hist. Stud.*, 43, vol. 3, p. 330-335.

25. HOBSON (G. D.) ed. English bindings, 1490-1940, in the library of J. R. Abbey. London, Chiswick Press, 40, privately printed.

26. HOBSON (G. D.). Blind-stamped panels in the English book-trade, c. 1485-1555. London, Oxford Univ. Press, 44, in-8, 111 p., members only. (Suppl., Bibliographical Soc. Trans., 17). R : E. P. Goldschmidt, *Burlington Mag.*, 45, vol. 86, p. 101.

27. HODGSON (S.). Papers and documents recently found at Stationers' Hall. *Library*, 44, vol. 25, p. 23-36.

28. HOUSEHOLDER (Fred W.). The first pirate. *Library*, 43, vol. 24, p. 30-46.

29. JOHNSON (A. F.). The italic types of Robert Granjon. *Library*, 40/41, vol. 21, p. 291-309.

30. JOHNSON (A. F.). An alphabet by Pieter Coecke Van Aelst. *Library*, 43, vol. 23, p. 195-197.

31. JOHNSON (A. F.). The supply of types in the 16th century. *Library*, 43, vol. 24, p. 47-65.

32. KRAMER (S.). A history of Stone & Kimball and Herbert S. Stone & Co., with a bibliography of their publications, 1893-1905. London, Cambridge Univ. Press, 40, in-8, 379 p., 24s.

33. A list of type specimens. *Library*, 42, vol. 22, p. 185-204.

34. MCMANAWAY (James G.). Latin title-page mottoes as a clue to dramatic authorship. *Library*, 45, vol. 26, p. 28-36.

35. MCMURTRIE (D. C.). The Gutenberg documents. London, Oxford Univ. Press, 42, in-8, 239 p., 21s.

36. MCMURTRIE (D. C.). The book : the story of printing and bookmaking. London, Oxford Univ. Press, 44, in-4, 708 p., (illus., figs.), 30s.

37. MORGAN (Charles). The House of Macmillan, 1843-1943. London, Macmillan, 43, in-8, 264 p., 8s. 6d. R : R. W. Chapman, *Eng. hist. R.*, 44, vol. 59, p. 276-277. O. Williams, *National R.*, 44, vol. 122, p. 78-83. G. B. H., *Queen's Quar.*, 44, vol. 51, p. 346. A. Robinson, *Econ. J.*, 44, vol. 54, p. 120-123.

38. MORISON (Stanley). ' Black-Letter ' text. London, Cambridge Univ. Press, 42, in-2, iv-39 p., 48 figs. (100 copies printed). R : S. H. Steinberg, *Library*, 42, vol. 23, p. 134-138.

39. MORISON (S.). Early humanistic script and the first Roman type. *Library*, 43, vol. 24, p. 1-29 and plates.

40. MORISON (S.). The typographic arts, past, present & future. Edinburgh, Thin, 44, in-8, 44 p., 3s. 6d. R : J. Wardrop, *Library*, 44/45, vol. 25, p. 194-196.

41. MOSS (William E.). Bindings from the library of Robt. Dudley, Earl of Leicester, 1533-1588. A new contribution to the history of English 16th-century gold-tooled bookbind-

ings. Crawley, Sussex, The Author, 40, 37s. 6d., privately printed.

42. NASH (Ray). Rastell fragments at Dartmouth. *Library*, 43, vol. 24, p. 66-73 & facs.

43. OLDHAM (J. Basil). Shrewsbury School library bindings : catalogue raisonné. Oxford, Clarendon Press, 43, in-2, 183 p., 44 plates, 63s. R : G. D. Hobson, *Library*, 43/44, vol. 24, p. 194-202.

44. PAIGE (Donald). An additional letter and booklist of Thomas Chard, stationer of London. *Library*, 40, vol. 21, p. 26-43.

45. POTTINGER (David Thomas). Printers and printing. London, Oxford Univ. Press, 41, in-8, viii-143 p., (illus.), 8s. 6d. R : H. Hope-Nicholson, *Burlington Mag.*, 43, vol. 82, p. 130.

46. ROTH (Cecil). The Marrano press at Ferrara, 1552-1555. *Mod. Language R.*, 43, vol. 38, p. 307-317.

47. SADLEIR (Michael). " Minerva Press " publicity : a publisher's advertisement of 1794. *Library*, 40, vol. 21, p. 207-215.

48. SCHOLDERER (Victor). The invention of printing. *Library*, 40, vol. 21, p. 1-25.

49. SHAABER (M. A.). The meaning of the imprint in early printed books. *Library*, 43/44, vol. 24, p. 120-141.

50. TAYLOR (A.) and ARLT (G. O.). Printing and progress : 2 lectures. London, Cambridge Univ. Press, 42, in-8, viii-68 p., 9s.

51. THOMAS (Henry). Copperplate engravings in early Spanish books. *Library*, 40, vol. 21, p. 109-142.

52. THOMAS (H.). An unknown impression by the printer of the first edition of the *Lusiadas*. *Library*, 40/41, vol. 21, p. 309-319.

53. ULLSTEIN (H.). The rise and fall of the House of Ullstein. London, Nicholson & Watson, 44, in-8, 256 p., 10s. 6d. R : A.G.W., *Int. Affairs*, 44, vol. 20, p. 577.

54. WEIL (E.). William Fitzer, the publisher of Harvey's *De Motu Cordis*, 1628. *Library*, 43/44, vol. 24, p. 142-164.

55. WILLARD (Oliver M.). The survival of English books printed before 1640 : a theory and some illustrations. *Library*, 43, vol. 23, p. 171-190.

56. WILLIAMS (William). The first three Welsh books printed in America. *Nat. Library Wales J.*, 42, vol. 2, p. 109-119.

57. WILLIAMS (W.). More about the first three Welsh books printed in America. *Nat. Library Wales J.*, 43, vol. 3, p. 19-22.

58. WILLOUGHBY (H. E.). The first authorised English Bible and the Cranmer preface. London, Cambridge Univ. Press, 43, in-8, x-50 p., (facs.), 6s. R : L. A. Sheppard, *Library*, 43, vol. 23, p. 199-200. H. A. K., *Queen's Quar.*, 43, vol. 50, p. 325-326.

59. WINSHIP (George Parker). Printing in the 15th century. London, Oxford Univ. Press, 40, in-8, xi-158 p., (illus.), 9s. (Penn. Univ., Rosenbach fellowship in bibliogr., publ. 7). R : V. Scholderer, *Library*, 41, vol. 22, p. 90-91.

§ 4. Chronology

60. KINCAID (C. A.). The romance of the Indian calendar. *J. asiatic Soc.*, 43, p. 255-259.

61. PARKER (R. A.). and DUBBERSTEIN (W. H.). Babylonian chronology, 626 B.C.-A.D. 45. London, Cambridge Univ. Press, 43, in-4, xiv-46 p., 5s. (Stud. in ancient oriental civilization).

62. POLLARD (A. F.). New Year's Day and Leap Year in English history. *Eng. hist. R.*, 40, vol. 55, p. 177-193.

63. POLLARD (A. F.). Chronology, synchronology and history. *History*, 40, vol. 25, p. 193-207.

64. PRAKKEN (D. W.). Studies in Greek genealogical chronology. London, Mitre Press, 44, in-8, 114 p., (tables), 12s. 6d.

65. THOMSON (George). The Greek calendar. *J. hell. Stud.*, 43, vol. 63, p. 52-65.

§ 5. Genealogy

66. BECKLES (Richard). Beckles of Barbados. *J. Barbados Mus.*, 44, vol. 12, p. 3-19.

67. BOWEN (Elizabeth). Bowen's Court. London, Longmans, 42, in-8, viii-341 p., 16s. R : R. D. Edwards, *Irish hist. Stud.*, 43, vol. 3, p. 416-417. T. W. Moody, *Eng. hist. R.*, 45, vol. 60, p. 264-265.

68. DOBBS (Margaret E.). Women of the Ui Dúnlainge of Leinster. *Irish Geneal.*, 40, vol. 1, p. 196-206.

69. FALK (B.). The Berkeleys of Berkeley Square. London, Hutchinson, 44, in-8, 284 p., (illus.), 18s.

70. HARVEY (John H.). Some notes on the family of Dampier. *Mariner's Mirror*, 43, vol. 29, p. 54-57.

71. HUGHES (G. H.). Y Dwniaid. (The family of Donne). *Trans. Soc. Cymmr.*, 41 (43), p. 115-149.

72. HUTCHINSON (H. G.). The Walronds, co-heirs of ancient barony. *J. Barbados Mus.*, 44, vol. 11, p. 89-95.

73. JAMES (G. F.). Pioneers or posterity ? *Hist. Stud. Australia N.Z.*, 43, vol. 2, p. 227-238.

74. JENKINS (R. T.). Rhai o deulu Mary Shelley. (Some of the family of Mary Shelley). *J. hist. Soc. presb. Church Wales*, 43, vol. 28, p. 96-113, 135-153.

75. KETTON-CREMER (R. W.). Norfolk portraits. London, Faber, 44, in-8, 180 p., (illus.), 15s.

76. MACLEOD (Roderick Charles). The book of Dunvegan : documents from the muniment room of the MacLeods of MacLeod at Dunvegan Castle, Isle of Skye. Vol. 2 : 1700-1920. Aberdeen, King's College, Third Spalding Club, 40, in-8, 179 p., 30s.

77. MALCHELOSSE (Gérard). Généalogie de la famille Mondelet. *B. Rech. hist.*, 45, vol. 51, p. 51-59.

78. MORIARTY (G. Andrews). The Turners of New England and Barbados. *J. Barbados Mus.*, 42, vol. 10, p. 7-14.

79. POWLEY (Edward B.). The house of de la Pomerai. London, Hodder & Stoughton ; Liverpool, Univ. Press, 44, in-8, xxvi-135 p., 42s. R : E. St. J. Brooks, *Irish hist. Stud.*, 44, vol. 4, p. 122-123. C. T. Clay, *Eng. hist. R.*, 45, vol. 60, p. 109-110.

80. ROY (P. G.). La famille de Berey des Essarts. *B. Rech. hist.*, 44, vol. 50, p. 310-317, 321-347, 353-373.

81. SCHRIFTGIESSER (K.). The amazing Roosevelt family, 1613-1942. London, Jarrolds, 43, in-8, 246 p., 15s.

82. WHITE (Geoffrey H.). The first House of Bellême. *Trans. Roy. hist. Soc.*, 40, vol. 22, p. 67-99.

§ 6. Sigillography and Heraldry

83. CARR (H. G.). Sledge-flags, their origin and development. *Mariner's Mirror*, 41, vol. 27, p. 5-13.

84. CARR (H. G.). Barge flags of the City livery companies of London. *Mariner's Mirror*, 42, vol. 28, p. 222-230.

85. COLLINS (S. M.). Some English, Scottish, Welsh and Irish arms in medieval continental rolls. *Antiq. J.*, 41, vol. 21, p. 203-210.

86. COLLINS (S. M.). Papworth and his Ordinary. *Antiq. J.*, 42, vol. 22, p. 3-16.

87. COLLINS (S. M.). The Grünen-berg Wappenbuch : some correc-tions. *Antiq. J.*, 44, vol. 24, p. 38-44 (illus.).

88. COUNCER (C. R.). Heraldic notices of the church of St. Martin, Herne. *Archaeol. cantiana*, 40 (41), vol. 53, p. 81-100.

89. DRIVER (G. R.). Seals from 'Amman and Petra. *Quar. Dept. Antiq. Palestine*, 44, vol. 11, p. 81-82.

90. EISEN (G. A.). Ancient Oriental cylinder and other seals. London, Cambridge Univ. Press, 40, in-8, 94 p., (plates, illus.), 30s.

91. ELLISTON-ERWOOD (F. C.). Two coats of arms from Kent in London. *Archaeol. cantiana*, 44, vol. 57, p. 44-50.

92. JENKINSON (Hilary). What hap-pened to the Great Seal of James II ? *Antiq. J.*, 43, vol. 23, p. 1-13 (illus.).

93. JONES (Evan John). Medieval heraldry : some 14th-century her-aldic works, ed. with an intr., Engl. transl. of the Welsh text, arms in colour, and notes, by E. J. Jones. Cardiff, Lewis, 43, in-8, lxvi-206 p., 42s.

94. REYNOLDS (E. E.). Introduc-tion to heraldry. London, Methuen, 40, in-8, ix-149 p., (illus.), 6s. 6d.

95. TAYLOR (F.). Selected Cheshire seals (12th-17th century) from the collections in the John Rylands Lib-rary. *B. John Rylands Library*, 41/42, vol. 26, p. 393-412 (plates).

96. TOMLINSON (H. Ellis). The heraldry of Manchester. *B. John Rylands Library*, 44, vol. 28, p. 207-227.

97. WAGNER (Anthony R.). A dic-tionary of British arms (heraldry). *Antiq. J.*, 41, vol. 21, p. 299-322 ; 43, vol. 23, p. 42-47.

98. WAGNER (A. R.). A seal of Strongbow in the Huntington Library. *Antiq. J.*, 41, vol. 21, p. 128-132.

§ 7. Numismatics

99. ALLEN (Derek F.). The Irish bracteates. *Numism. Chron.*, 42, p. 71-85.

100. ARKELL (A. J.). Forged Mahdi pounds. *Sudan Notes and Records*, 45, vol. 26, p. 43-49.

101. ASKEW (Gilbert). The mint of Bamburgh castle. *Numism. Chron.*, 40, vol. 20, p. 51-56.

102. BARAMKI (J.). Coin hoards from Palestine, 1-2. *Quar. Dept. Antiq. Palestine*, 44, vol. 11, p. 30-36, 86-90.

103. BELLINGER (Alfred R.). A tetradrachm of Hyspaosines. *Numism. Chron.*, 44, 6th ser., vol. 4, p. 58-59.

104. BELLINGER (A. R.). Crassus and Cassius at Antioch. *Numism. Chron.*, 44, 6th ser., vol. 4, p. 59-61.

105. BELLINGER (A. R.). Parthian drachmae of Orodes II and Phraates IV. *Numism. Chron.*, 44, 6th ser., vol. 4, p. 62-64.

106. CAHN (Herbert A.). A new Carian mint. *Numism. Chron.*, 42, p. 92-94.

107. CHITTENDEN (Jacqueline). Hermes-Mercury dynasts and em-perors. *Numism. Chron.*, 45, vol. 5, p. 41-57.

108. EVANS (Arthur). Notes on early Anglo-Saxon gold coins. *Num-ism. Chron.*, 42, p. 19-41.

109. GOODACRE (Hugh). Notes on some Byzantine coins. *Numism. Chron.*, 45, vol. 5, p. 34-40.

110. HAUGHTON (H. L.). The Shaikhano dheri hoard, March 1940. *Numism. Chron.*, 40, vol. 20, p. 123-126.

111. HAUGHTON (H. L.). A note on the distribution of Indo-Greek coins. *Numism. Chron.*, 43, p. 50-59.

112. HEMMY (A. S.). A summary of the application of statistical methods

to the determination of the weight-standards of Roman coins. *Numism. Chron.*, 42, p. 86-91.

113. KIRKMAN (J. S.). New varieties of Roman coins from the 1936-1938 excavations at Leicester. *Numism. Chron.*, 40, vol. 20, p. 24-31.

114. LAWRENCE (L. A.). On a hoard of plated Roman denarii. *Numism. Chron.*, 40 (41), vol. 20, p. 185-189.

115. MATTINGLY (Harold). Catalogue of coins of the Roman Empire in the British Museum. Vol. 4 : Antoninus Pius to Commodus. London, British Museum, 40, in-8, 964 p., 111 plates, 100s. R : J. M. C. Toynbee, *Numism. Chron.*, 40 (41), vol. 20, p. 203-212 ; *J. rom. Stud.*, 41, vol. 31, p. 198-201. C. H. V. Sutherland, *Class. R.*, 41, vol. 55, p. 93-95. C. Oman, *Eng. hist. R.*, 41, vol. 56, p. 106-109.

116. MATTINGLY (H.). The " little" talents of Sicily and the West. *Numism. Chron.*, 43, p. 14-20.

117. MATTINGLY (H.). " Aes " and " pecunia " : records of Roman currency down to 269 B.C. *Numism. Chron.*, 43, p. 21-39.

118. MATTINGLY (H.). Coinage of the Dark Age in Britain. *Antiquity*, 43, vol. 17, p. 162-166.

119. MATTINGLY (H.). Carausius, his mints and his money system. *Antiquity*, 45, vol. 19, p. 122-124.

120. MATTINGLY (H.). The first age of Roman coinage. *J. rom. Stud.*, 45, vol. 35, p. 65-77.

121. MILNE (J. G.). A group of coins attributable to the revolt of Naxos in 467. *Numism. Chron.*, 40, vol. 20, p. 76-88.

122. MILNE (J. G.). The mint of Kyme in the 3rd century B.C. *Numism. Chron.*, 40 (41), vol. 20, p. 129-137.

123. MILNE (J. G.). Notes on the Oxford collections, 6 : Phrygia to Galatia. *Numism. Chron.*, 40 (41), vol. 20, p. 213-254 (plates).

124. MILNE (J. G.). The *aes grave* of central Italy. *J. rom. Stud.*, 42, vol. 32, p. 27-32.

125. MILNE (J. G.). The Evans collection at Oxford : the Cretan coins. *Numism. Chron.*, 43, p. 73-91.

126. MILNE (J. G.). An exchange-currency of Magna Graecia. *J. rom. Stud.*, 44, vol. 34, p. 46-48 (illus.).

127. MILNE (J. G.). A hoard of Brettian bronze. *Numism. Chron.*, 44, 6th ser., vol. 4, p. 114-115.

128. MILNE (J. G.). *Bigati*. *J. rom. Stud.*, 44, vol. 34, p. 48-49.

129. NELSON (Philip). Some unpublished coins of Northumbria. *Numism. Chron.*, 44, 6th ser., vol. 4, p. 120-122.

130. O'NEIL (B. H. St. J.). Some overstrikes and other Roman coins from Maiden castle, Dorset. *Numism. Chron.*, 40 (41), vol. 20, p. 179-184.

131. PEARCE (Bertram W.). The coins from Richborough, a survey. *Numism. Chron.*, 40, vol. 20, p. 57-75.

132. PEARCE (J. W. E.). Issues of the solidi ' Victoria AVGG ' from Treveri. *Numism. Chron.*, 40 (41), vol. 20, p. 138-161.

133. PEARCE (J. W. E.). Barbarous overstrikes found in 4th-century hoards : some additional evidence from the East. *Numism. Chron.*, 40 (41), vol. 20, p. 162-163.

134. PEARCE (J. W. E.). Lugdunum: *siliqua*-coinage of Valentinian II and Eugenius. *Numism. Chron.*, 44, 6th ser., vol. 4, p. 45-57.

135. PEARCE (J. W. E.) and OMAN (Sir Charles). A find of *siliquae* from Colerne, Wiltshire. *Numism. Chron.*, 42, p. 97-104.

136. REIFENBERG (A.). A hoard of Tyrian and Jewish shekels. *Quar. Dept. Antiq. Palestine*, 44, vol. 11, p. 83-85.

137. ROBINSON (E. S. G.). The coinage of the Libyans and kindred Sardinian issues. *Numism. Chron.*, 43, p. 1-13.

138. ROBINSON (E. S. G.). Greek coins found in Cyrenaica. *Numism. Chron.*, 44, 6th ser., vol. 4, p. 105-113.

139. SCHWABACHER (Willy). Mesembria on the Aegean. *Numism. Chron.*, 42, p. 94-97.

140. SELTMAN (Charles). *Argentum Oscense* and *Bigati*. *Numism. Chron.*, 44, 6th ser., vol. 4, p. 77-82.

141. SKINNER (F. G.) and BRUCE-MITFORD (R. L. S.). A Celtic balance-beam of the Christian period. *Antiq. J.*, 40, vol. 20, p. 87-102 (illus.).

142. SMITH (W. Owston). Schlick of Bassano. *Numism. Chron.*, 40, vol. 20, p. 32-50.

143. SUTHERLAND (C. H. V.). A Theodosian silver hoard from Rams Hill. *Antiq. J.*, 40, vol. 20, p. 481-485 (illus.).

144. SUTHERLAND (C. H. V.). Roman imperial coins in the Oxford collection, 2 : Vespasian to Domitian. *Numism. Chron.*, 40 (41), vol. 20, p. 255-264.

145. SUTHERLAND (C. H. V.). C. Baebius and the coinage of (?) Dium under Tiberius. *J. rom. Stud.*, 41, vol. 31, p. 73-81.

146. SUTHERLAND (C. H. V.). Overstrikes and hoards : the movement of Greek coinage down to 400 B.C. *Numism. Chron.*, 42, p. 1-18.

147. SUTHERLAND (C. H. V.). Anglo-Saxon sceattas in England : their origin, chronology and distribution. *Numism. Chron.*, 42, p. 42-70.

148. SUTHERLAND (C. H. V.). The senatorial gold and silver coinage of 16 B.C. : innovation and inspiration. *Numism. Chron.*, 43, p. 40-49.

149. SUTHERLAND (C. H. V.). The date and significance of the ' candela-brum ' coins of Augustus. *Class. R.*, 44, vol. 58, p. 46-49.

150. SUTHERLAND (C. H. V.). The Evans collection at Oxford : Roman coins of the early Empire. *Numism. Chron.*, 44, 6th ser., vol. 4, p. 1-26.

151. SUTHERLAND (C. H. V.). The gold and silver coinage of Spain under Augustus. *Numism. Chron.*, 45, vol. 5, p. 58-78.

152. SYDENHAM (Edward A.). The date of Piso-Caepio. *Numism. Chron.*, 40 (41), vol. 20, p. 164-178.

153. SYDENHAM (E. A.). On Roman plated coins. *Numism. Chron.*, 40 (41), vol. 20, p. 190-202.

154. SYDENHAM (E. A.). The White Horse and ancient British coin-types. *Numism. Chron.*, 44, 6th ser., vol. 4, p. 65-76.

155. SYLLOGE NUMMORUM GRAECORUM. Sylloge nummorum Graecorum. Vol. 4 : Fitzwilliam museum. Leake and general collections, pt. 1 : Spain (Emporiae, Rhoda), Italy. London, Oxford Univ. Press, 40, in-2, 14 p., plates, 16s. R : H. Mattingly, *Greece and Rome*, 41, vol. 10, p. 141.

156. ── ── Vol. 3, pt. 3 : The Lockett collection. London, Oxford Univ. Press, 42, in-2, 12 plates, 17s.6d.

157. TOYNBEE (Jocelyn M. C.). A new bronze medallion of Antoninus Pius. *Numism. Chron.*, 40, vol. 20, p. 1-8.

158. TOYNBEE (J. M. C.). Two new gold medallions of the later Roman empire. *Numism. Chron.*, 40, vol. 20, p. 9-23.

159. TOYNBEE (J. M. C.). An early 18th-century forerunner of the modern numismatist. *Numism. Chron.*, 42, p. 108-110.

160. TOYNBEE (J. M. C.). Greek imperial medallions. *J. rom. Stud.*, 44, vol. 34, p. 65-73 (illus.).

161. TOYNBEE (J. M. C.). Roman medallions : their scope and purpose.

Numism. Chron., 44, 6th ser., vol. 4, p. 27-44.

162. WALKER (John). Catalogue of Arab-Sassanian coins in the British Museum. London, British Museum, 41, in-8, clxi-244 p., 42s. R : A.S.T., *J. central asian Soc.*, 41, vol. 28, p. 456-457.

163. WALSH (E. H. C.). Notes on the silver punch-marked coins, and the copper punch-marked coins, in the British Museum. *J. asiatic Soc.*, 41, p. 223-232.

164. WHITEHEAD (R. B.). Notes on the Indo-Greeks. *Numism. Chron.*, 40, vol. 20, p. 89-122.

165. WHITEHEAD (R. B.). The eastern satrap Sophytes. *Numism. Chron.*, 43, p. 60-72.

166. WHITEHEAD (R. B.). The dynasty of the general Aspavarma. *Numism. Chron.*, 44, 6th ser., vol. 4, p. 99-104.

167. WHITTON (C. A.). Additional notes on Edward III and Henry V. *Numism. Chron.*, 44, 6th ser., vol. 4, p. 116-120.

168. WÜTHRICH (G.). Celtic numismatics in Switzerland. *Numism. Chron.*, 45, vol. 5, p. 1-33.

§ 8. Linguistics

169. EAST (R. M.). A vernacular bibliography for the languages of Nigeria. Zaria, Literature Bureau, 41, in-8, 85 p., 1s. 3d. R : C. M. D(oke), *African Stud.*, 43, vol. 2, p. 74. I. C. Ward, *Africa*, 43, vol. 14, p. 99.

170. NICHOLS (M. W.). Bibliographical guide to materials on American Spanish. London, Oxford Univ. Press, 41, in-8, 126 p., 6s. 6d.

171. CRAIGIE (Sir W.) and HULBERT (J. R.) eds. A dictionary of American English on historical principles. 20 pts. London, Oxford Univ. Press, 36-44, in-4, 17s. ea.

172. CRAWFORD (D. S.). Greek and Latin : an introduction to the historical study of the classical languages. Cambridge, Heffer, 41, in-8, 332 p., 7s. 6d.

173. DOKE (C. M.). Bantu language pioneers of the 19th century. *Bantu Studies*, 40, vol. 14, p. 207-246.

174. DOKE (C. M.). The growth of comparative Bantu philology. *African Stud.*, 43, vol. 2, p. 41-64.

175. FIEDLER (H. G.). The oldest study of Germanic proper names. *Mod. Lang. R.*, 42, vol. 37, p. 185-192.

176. HALLOCK (R. T.). The Chicago Syllabary and the Louvre Syllabary A O 7661. London, Cambridge Univ. Press, 41, in-4, xiv-80 p., (plates), 24s. (Or. Inst. Assyr. Stud.).

177. HEYWORTH-DUNNE (J.). Printing and translations under Muhammad 'Ali of Egypt. The foundation of modern Arabic. *J. asiatic Soc.*, 40, p. 325-349.

178. HYATT (J. P.). The treatment of final vowels in early Neo-Babylonean. London, Oxford Univ. Press, 41, in-4, 69 p., 9s.

179. JEFFREYS (M. D. W.). Some historical notes on African tone languages. *African Stud.*, 45, vol. 4, p. 135-145.

180. LEWY (E.). On the distribution of the languages in the old Eurasian region. *Trans. philol. Soc.*, 43 (44), p. 5-13.

181. MARIN (G.). An old Pwo-Karen alphabet. *Man*, 43, vol. 43, p. 17-19.

182. MYRES (John L.). The order of the letters in the Greek alphabet. *Man*, 42, vol. 42, p. 110-114.

183. RAUM (O. F.). The African chapter in the history of writing. *African Stud.*, 43, vol. 2, p. 179-192.

184. RHYS (Morgan John). Letters to William Owen-Pughe, ed. by G. J. Williams. *Nat. Library Wales J.*, 42, vol. 2, p. 131-141.

185. SPEISER (E. A.). Introduction to Hurrian. London, Oxford Univ. Press, 43, in-8, 260 p., 15s. 6d. (Annual of the American Schools of Oriental Research, Vol. 20, 1940-41).

186. WELLS (J. E.). A manual of the writings in Middle English, 1050-1400, 8th suppl. London, Oxford Univ. Press, 42, in-8, 106 p., 7s.

187. WOOLF (H. B.). The old Germanic principles of name-giving. London, Oxford Univ. Press, 40, in-8, 311 p., 18s.

§ 9. Historical Geography

188. AVI-YONAH (M.). Map of Roman Palestine. London, Oxford Univ. Press, 40, in-4, 56 p., 3s.

189. BABER (F. T.). The historical geography of the iron industry of the Forest of Dean. *Geography*, 42, vol. 27, p. 54-62.

190. BALLARD (G. A.). Cape Horn. *Mariner's Mirror*, 45, vol. 31, p. 144-147.

191. BEARD (Charles Relly). An unrecorded map by Diogo Homem. *Mariner's Mirror*, 45, vol. 31, p. 51-55.

192. BESTON (Henry). The St. Lawrence. Toronto, Univ. Press, 42, in-8, xi-274 p., $3.00. (Rivers of America). R : J.A.R., *Queen's Quar.*, 43, vol. 50, p. 101-102.

193. BLAKE (John W.). New light on Diogo Homem, Portuguese cartographer. *Mariner's Mirror*, 42, vol. 28, p. 148-160.

194. BOWEN (E. G.). Wales, a study in geography and history. Cardiff, Univ. of Wales Press Bd., 41, in-8, 182 p., 3s. 6d. R : E.E.E., *Geography*, 41, vol. 26, p. 188. H. J. Randall, *Archaeol. cambrensis*, 41, vol. 96, p. 214-216.

195. CRONE (G. R.). 17th-century Dutch charts of the East Indies. *Geogr. J.*, 43, vol. 102, p. 260-265.

196. DARBY (H. C.). The medieval Fenland. London, Cambridge Univ. Press, 40, in-8, xvii-200 p., (plates, maps), 12s. 6d. (Cambr. stud. in econ. hist.). R : J.E.M., *Geography*, 41, vol. 26, p. 42.

197. DEACON (G. E. R.). The Sargasso sea. *Geogr. J.*, 42, vol. 99, p. 16-28.

198. DICKINSON (Robert E.). The development and distribution of the medieval German town, 1-2. *Geography*, 42, vol. 27, p. 9-21, 47-53.

199. FLEURE (H. J.). Notes on the evolution of Switzerland. *Geography*, 41, vol. 26, p. 169-177.

200. FOX (Sir Cyril). The boundary line of Cymru. London, Oxford Univ. Press, 41, in-8, 28 p., (maps), 3s. R : W.J.H., *Archaeol. cambrensis*, 41, vol. 96, p. 218.

201. GOLDSCHMIDT (E. P.). The Lesina Portolan chart of the Caspian sea. *Geogr. J.*, 44, vol. 103, p. 272-278.

202. GRUNDY (G. B.). The ancient highways of Somerset. *Archaeol. J.*, 39 (40), vol. 96, p. 226-297.

203. GUTHRIE (Douglas). The earliest continental guide-book (Dr. Andrew Boorde's 'Boke of Knowledge', 1542). *Scottish geogr. Mag.*, 43, vol. 59, p. 6-9.

204. HEAWOOD (Edward). A hitherto unrecorded MS. map of Northamptonshire by John Norden. *Geogr. J.*, 40, vol. 96, p. 368-369.

205. HEAWOOD (E.). An unrecorded Blaeu world map of c. 1618. *Geogr. J.*, 43, vol. 102, p. 170-175 (plate).

206. INGLETON (Geoffrey C.). A brief history of marine surveying in Australia. 2 pts. and appendices. *Roy. Austral. hist. Soc. J.*, 44, vol. 30, p. 1-44, 85-151, 259-288.

207. LAIDLER (George). The Nottawasaga portage, Simcoe county, Ontario : a historic line of communication between Lake Simcoe and the Georgian Bay. *Ontario hist. Soc. Pap.*, 43, vol. 35, p. 39-48.

208. LANDON (Fred). Lake Huron. Toronto, McClelland & Stewart, 44, in-8, 398 p., $4.50. (Amer. lakes ser.). R : W. B. Kerr, *Canad. hist. R.*, 44, vol. 25, p. 436-437.

209. LYNAM (Edward). British maps and map-makers. London, Collins, 44, in-8, 48 p., (plates), 4s. 6d. (Britain in pictures).

210. MARKHAM (S. F.). Climate and the energy of nations. London, Oxford Univ. Press, 42, in-8, x-220 p., (maps), 15s. R : V. G. Childe, *Antiquity*, 43, vol. 17, p. 103-106. J. L. Myres, *Class. R.*, 43, vol. 57, p. 48-49.

211. —— —— Rev. and enlarged ed. London, Oxford Univ. Press, 45, in-8, 236 p., (maps), 18s.

212. MONKHOUSE (F. J.). Some features of the historical geography of the German mining enterprise in Elizabethan lakeland. *Geography*, 43, vol, 28, p. 107-113.

213. Ó DOMHNAILL (Séan). The maps of the Down survey. *Irish hist. Stud.*, 43, vol. 3, p. 381-392.

214. POUNDS (N. J. G.). Lanhydrock Atlas. *Antiquity*, 45, vol. 19, p. 20-26.

215. QUAIFE (Milo M.). Lake Michigan. Toronto, McClelland, 44, in-8, 384 p., (plates), $4.50. (Amer. lakes ser.). R : W. S. Wallace, *Canad. hist. R.*, 45, vol. 26, p. 449.

216. RAYMOND (William O.). The river St. John, its physical features, legends, and history from 1604 to 1784. New ed., ed. by J. C. Webster. Sackville, N.B., Tribune Press, 43, in-8, xii-280 p., $3.00. R : A. G. Bailey, *Canad. hist. R.*, 43, vol. 24, p. 314-315.

217. SHERWIN-WHITE (A. N.). Geographical factors in Roman Algeria. *J. rom. Stud.*, 44, vol. 34, p. 1-10 (maps).

218. SMITH (Sir G. A.). Atlas of the historical geography of the Holy Land. New ed. London, Hodder & Stoughton, 42, in-8, xxvii-744 p., (maps), 63s.

219. TAYLOR (E. G. R.). Notes on John Adams and contemporary map makers. *Geogr. J.*, 41, vol. 97, p. 182-184.

220. TOGAN (A. Zeki Validi). Biruni's picture of the world. Delhi, Latifi Press, 41, in-8, 162 p., 12s. 6d. (Mem. of the Archaeol. Soc. of India, 53). R : R.B.S., *Geogr. J.*, 44, vol. 103, p. 284-295.

221. WANKLYN (H. G.). The eastern marchlands of Europe. London, Philip, 41, in-8, xxiii-356 p., (maps), 12s. 6d. R : W. O. Henderson, *Econ. Hist. R.*, 42, vol. 12, p. 105-106.

222. WHITAKER (Harold). A descriptive list of the printed maps of Cheshire, 1577-1900. Manchester, Chetham Soc., 42, in-8, xv-220 p., members only. (Remains, hist. and literary, n.s., vol. 106). R : E. H., *Geogr. J.*, 43, vol. 102, p. 85.

§ 10. Iconography

223. COLLINS (A. H.). The iconography of Darenth font. *Archaeol. cantiana*, 43, vol. 56, p. 6-10 (plates).

224. LOEWENSTEIN (John, prince). The swastika, its history and meaning. *Man*, 41, vol. 41, p. 49-55.

225. PANOFSKY (Erwin). Studies in iconology : humanistic themes in the art of the Renaissance. London, Oxford Univ. Press, 40, in-4, xxxiii-262 p., (plates), 15s. (Bryn Mawr college, Flexner lect. on the humanities 7). R : W. Stechow, *Burlington Mag.*, 41, vol. 78, p. 33.

226. WILLOUGHBY (Harold Rideout). Elizabeth Day McCormick Apocalypse. Vol. 1 : A Greek corpus of Revelation iconography, by H. R. Willoughby ; Vol. 2 : History and text, by E. C. Colwell. London, Cambridge Univ. Press, 40, 2 vols. in-8, 625, 206 p., (plates), 165s.

B

MANUALS, GENERAL WORKS

§ 1. Historical Bibliography

a. RETROSPECTIVE BIBLIOGRAPHY

227. BESTERMAN (Theodore). Early world bibliography of bibliographies. 2 vols. and index. London, Author, 39-40, 2 vols. in-4, 252s. R : J. Hennig, *Irish hist. Stud.*, 42, vol. 3, p. 222-224.

228. BESTERMAN (T.). Early printed books to the end of the 16th century. A bibliography of bibliographies. London, Quaritch, 40, in-8, 309 p., 21s. R : F. C. Francis, *Library*, 41, vol. 22, p. 91-97.

229. BLACKWELL (Henry). A bibliography of Welsh Americana. Ed. by W. Williams. Aberystwyth, National Library of Wales, 42, in-8, vii-92 p., 5s. (National Library of Wales Journ., Suppl., Ser. 3, no. 1).

230. BOOK-AUCTION RECORDS. Book-auction records, 1940-43 : a priced and annotated annual record of London, New York and Edinburgh book-auctions. Vol. 37-40. London, Stevens, 40-45, 4 vols. in-8, 42s. ea.

231. CANT (Ronald Gordon). The St. Andrews University theses, 1579-1747 : a bibliographical introduction. (Edinb. bibliogr. soc. trans., vol. 2, pt. 2, 1939-40). Edinburgh, 1941.

232. CROSS (T. P.) ed. Bibliographical guide to English studies. Rev. ed., 8th. London, Cambridge Univ. Press, 44, in-12, x-74 p., 6s. R : J. H. P. Pafford, *Library*, 44/45, vol. 25, p. 193.

233. HERMANNSSON (H.). Bibliographical notes. London, Oxford Univ. Press, 43, in-8, 99 p., (illus.), 13s. 6d. (Islandica ser.).

234. GAURY (Gerald de). An Arabian bibliography. *J. central asian Soc.*, 44, vol. 31, p. 315-320.

236. O'NEILL (E. H.). Biography by Americans, 1658-1936 : a subject bibliography. London, Oxford Univ. Press, 40, in-8, 465 p., 18s.

237. WORLD LIST. World list of historical periodicals and bibliographies. Ed. by P. Caron and M. Jaryc. London, Oxford Univ. Press, 40, in-8, 391 p., 30s.

238. YU (Shih Yu) and MIN (Liu Hsuan). Bibliography of oriento-logical contributions in 175 Japanese periodicals ; with indices. In Chinese. London, Luzac, 40, in-8, xliv-502 p., 45s. (Harvard-Yenching Inst., Sino-logical index ser., suppl., no. 13).

b. CURRENT BIBLIOGRAPHY

239. BESTERMAN (Theodore). A bibliography of the Bulletin of the Academy of Sciences of the U.S.S.R. *J. Documentation*, 45, vol. 1, p. 45-56.

240. BRIET (Suzanne). La documentation en France, 1940-5. *J. Documentation*, 45, vol. 1, p. 125-135.

241. BRITISH MUSEUM, Dept. of printed books. Subject index of the modern works added to the British Museum library, 1936-40. London, The Museum, 44, 2 vols. in-8, 1356, 1268 p., 315s. R : Th. B(esterman), *J. Documentation*, 45, vol. 1, p. 116-117.

242. Choix de bibliographies publiées en France, 1939-44. *J. Documentation*, 45, vol. 1, p. 148-150.

243. CUMULATIVE BOOK LIST. Five year Cumulative book list, 1939-1943. London, Whitaker, 45, in-4, xxxii-640 p., 80s.

244. FRANCIS (F. C.). A list of the writings of Ronald Brunlees McKerrow. *Library*, 40/41, vol. 21, p. 229-263.

§2. Archives, Libraries and Museums

245. ARCHIVES YEAR BOOK FOR SOUTH AFRICAN HISTORY. Ed. by C. G. Botha, C. Beyers, J. L. M. Franken, H. B. Thom. 2nd-5th year. Cape Town, Govt. Printer, 39[40]-43, 8 vols. in-4, 193, 205, 344, 242, 247, 255, 238, 272 p., 12s. 6d. ea. R (2nd, 4th year) : E. A. Walker, *Eng. hist. R.*, 41, vol. 56, p. 325-326 ; 45, vol. 60, p. 118-120.

246. ARMAJANI (M. E. M. Yahya). Descriptive catalogue of the Garrett collection of Persian, Turkish and Indic MSS., including miniatures in the Princeton University Library. London, Oxford Univ. Press, 40, in-8, 93 p., 34s.

247. BARNETT (L. D.). Catalogue of the Tod collection of Indian MSS. in the possession of the Royal Asiatic Society. *J. asiatic Soc.*, 40, p. 129-178.

248. BINNS (Kenneth). The publication of historical records in Australia. *Hist. Stud. Australia N.Z.*, 40, vol. 1, p. 91-96.

249. BRITISH MUSEUM, Natural History. Catalogue of the books, MSS., maps and drawings in the British Museum (Natural history). Vol. 8, suppl., P-Z. London, Oxford Univ. Press, 40, in-4, 512 p., 40s.

250. BROUGHTON (L. N.). The Wordsworth collection formed by Cynthia Morgan St. John, and given to Cornell University : suppl. to the catalogue. London, Oxford Univ. Press, 42, in-8, 96 p., 9s.

251. BROWN (George W.). The problem of public and historical records in Canada. *Canad. hist. R.*, 44, vol. 25, p. 1-5.

252. CANADA. The discussion of the problem of public and historical records in Canada, by the Archives Committee. *Canad. hist. Assoc. Rept.*, 44, p. 40-45.

253. CANADA. Libraries in Canada, 1938-40. Pt. 3 of the Biennial survey of education in Canada, 1938-40. Ottawa, Dominion Bur. of statistics, 41, in-8, 39 p., 35c. R : J. J. Talman, *Canad. hist. R.*, 42, vol. 23, p. 91.

254. CANADA. Report of the Public Archives for the year 1939-44. Ottawa, King's Printer, 40-45, 6 vols. in-8, 138, 108, 313, 186, 186, 154 p., 50c. ea. ; 1944, $1.00. R (1941) : I. Leeson, *Hist. Stud. Australia N.Z.*, 42, vol. 2, p. 125-126 ; (1942) : W. P. M(orrell), *Eng. hist. R.*, 45, vol. 60, p. 281.

255. CARLTON (W. J.). A descriptive catalogue of the library of Samuel Pepys. Pt. 4, Shorthand books. London, Sidgwick, 40, in-8, 125 p., 18s.

256. CASTANEDA (C. E.). and DABBS (J. A.) eds. Guide to the Latin American manuscripts of the University of Texas Library. London, Oxford Univ. Press, 40, in-8, 217 p., 12s. 6d.

257. CHABRIER (Madeleine). La Bibliothèque Nationale, 1940-4. *J. Documentation*, 45, vol. 1, p. 136-147.

258. CHARLTON (H. B.). The Folger Shakespeare memorial library. *B. John Rylands Library*, 42, vol. 27, p. 70-73.

259. COLLIER (J. D. A.). Library development in Tasmania. *Austral. Quar.*, 45, vol. 17, no. 3, p. 105-110.

260. CORPUS VASORUM ANTIQUORUM. Corpus vasorum antiquorum. U.S.A., fasc. 8 : Fogg Museum and Gallatin collections, by G. H. Chase and M. Z. Pease. London, Oxford Univ. Press, 42, in-8, 116 p., 64 plates, 30s. R : J.D.B., *J. hell. Stud.*, 42 (43), vol. 62, p. 99. O. Kurz, *Burlington Mag.*, 43, vol. 83, p. 234.

261. DAVIES (J. C.). Deposited collections, 14 : The Powis Castle collection, ii. Correspondence. *Nat. Library Wales J.*, 44, vol. 3, p. 138-150.

262. DAVIES (Sir W. Ll.) and ELLIS (Megan). Handlist of MSS. in the National Library of Wales. Pt. 4-7. Aberystwyth, National Library of Wales, 42-44, in-8, 2s. 6d., 5s. (National Library of Wales Journ., Suppl., Ser. 2, no. 4-7).

263. FINCH (Jeremiah S.). Sir Hans Sloane's printed books. *Library*, 41, vol. 22, p. 67-72.

264. GASKIN (L. J. P.). Centenary of the opening of George Catlin's North American Indian Museum and Gallery in the Egyptian Hall, Piccadilly. With a memoir of Catlin. *Man*, 40, vol. 40, p. 17-21.

265. GILES (L.). Six centuries at Tunhuang : a short account of the Stein collection of Chinese MSS. in the British Museum, ed. by W. P. Yetts. London, Luzac, 44, in-4, 50 p., (plates), 7s. 6d.

266. GOLDSCHMIDT (E. Ph.). Austrian monastic libraries. *Library*, 44, vol. 25, p. 46-65.

267. GRIMES (W. F.). Museums and the future. *Antiquity*, 44, vol. 18, p. 42-49.

268. HERBERT (Robert). Limerick printers and printing. Part 1 of the catalogue of the local collection in the City of Limerick public library. Limerick, Public Libr., 42, in-8, 62 p., 2s. 6d.

269. HILTON (R.). Handbook of Hispanic source materials and research organisations in the U.S. London, Oxford Univ. Press, 42, in-4, 457 p., 22s. 6d. R : A.M.F., *Queen's Quar.*, 42, vol. 49, p. 182. W. J. Entwistle, *Mod. Language R.*, 42, vol. 37, p. 521.

270. HIRSCH (Rudolf). The Philadelphia bibliographical center. *J. Documentation*, 45, vol. 1, p. 21-25.

271. HUTTON (R. S.). The origin and history of ASLIB. *J. Documentation*, 45, vol. 1, p. 6-20.

272. IVANOW (V.). Catalogue of the Arabic manuscripts in the collection of the Royal Asiatic society of Bengal prepared by V. Ivanow and revised and ed. by M. H. Hosain. Vol. 1. (Bib. Indica, Work no. 250, Issue no. 1,500). London, Luzac, 40, in-8, 17s. 6d.

273. JONES (E. D.). Manuscripts of Welsh-American interest in the National Library of Wales. *Nat. Library Wales J.*, 42, vol. 2, p. 154-170.

274. KIDD (Gwendolen M.). Historical museums in Canada. *Canad. hist. R.*, 40, vol. 21, p. 285-297.

275. LEESON (Ida L.). Archives in New South Wales. *Hist. Stud. Australia N.Z.*, 40, vol. 1, p. 96-99.

276. MURRAY (Florence B. and Elsie McLeod). Preliminary guide to the manuscript collection in the Toronto public libraries. Toronto, Public Libr., 40, in-8, 60 p., $1.00. R : I. Leeson, *Hist. Stud. Australia N.Z.*, 42, vol. 2, p. 125-126.

277. NATIONAL LIBRARY OF WALES. Handlist of manuscripts in the National Library of Wales. Pt. 1-2. Aberystwyth, Nat. Libr. of Wales, 40-41, in-8, 50, 63 p., 2s. 6d.

278. NATIONAL MUSEUM OF WALES. The Museum and its contents : a war-time guide. 2nd ed. Cardiff, National Museum of Wales, 42, in-8, 54 p., (illus.), 3d.

279. PECKHAM (H. H.). Guide to the manuscript collections in the William L. Clements Library. London, Oxford Univ. Press, 43, in-8, 420 p., (illus.), 28s.

280. PITT (E. R.). Archives in the Public Library of Victoria. *Hist. Stud. Australia N.Z.*, 40, vol. 1, p. 99-100.

281. PITT (G. H.). The South Australian archives. *Hist. Stud. Australia N.Z.*, 40, vol. 1, p. 46-56.

282. PITT (G. H.). Archives in South Australia. *Hist. Stud. Australia N.Z.*, 40, vol. 1, p. 101-102.

283. PLENDERLEITH (H. J.). Some aspects of museum laboratory work. *Antiquity*, 42, vol. 16, p. 97-112.

284. QUEBEC. Rapport de l'Archiviste de la Province de Québec pour 1939/40-1943/44. Québec, Imprimeur de S.M., 40-44, 5 vols. in-8, 486, 489, 515, 486, 482 p., $2.00 ea. R (1939/40) : M. H. Long, *Canad. hist. R.*, 41, vol. 22, p. 440-441. (1940/41, 1941/42) : J. J. Talman, *Canad. hist. R.*, 42, vol. 23, p. 329-330 ; 44, vol. 25, p. 209-210.

285. RINDGE (S. K. and A. H.). Willnits J. Hole art collection : illustrated catalogue of old masters collected and given to University of California, Los Angeles. London, Cambridge Univ. Press, 43, in-4, viii-46 p., (illus.), 3s.

286. ROBERTS (W. Wright). English autograph letters in the John Rylands Library (Manchester). *B. John Rylands Library*, 41, vol. 25, p. 119-136.

287. ROYAL ASIATIC SOCIETY. Catalogue of printed books, published before 1932, in the Library of the Royal Asiatic Society. London, Luzac, 40, in-4, vi-541 p., 63s. R : E. D. Maclagan, *J. asiatic Soc.*, 41, p. 381-382.

288. SCHROEDER (E.). Persian miniatures in the Fogg Museum of art. London, Oxford Univ. Press, 44, in-4, 168 p., (illus.), 28s. R : B. Gray, *Burlington Mag.*, 44, vol. 85, p. 232-233.

289. SELWOOD (E. H.). The Bibles and related books in the B.M.S. library. *Baptist Quar.*, 43, vol. 11, p. 156-159.

290. SERJEANT (R. B.). Handlist of Arabic, Persian and Hindustani MSS. of New College, Edinburgh. London, Luzac, 42, in-8, 16 p., 3s. 6d.

291. SHASTRI (Haraprasada). Descriptive catalogue of the Sanskrit manuscripts in the collection of the Royal Asiatic Society of Bengal. Revised and ed. by C. Chakravarti. Vol. 8, pt. 1, Tantra manuscripts. London, Luzac, 40, in-8, 3, 608 p., 17s. 6d.

292. SMITH (Anna H.). Catalogue of Bantu, Khoisan and Malagasy in the Strange collection of Africana. Johannesburg, Public Libr., 42, in-4, 232 p., typescript. R : C.M.D(oke), *African Stud.*, 42, vol. 1, p. 231. A. N. Tucker, *Africa*; 44, vol. 14, p. 479-480.

293. TAYLOR (F.). The Hatton Wood manuscripts in the John Rylands Library, Manchester. Manchester, Univ. Press, 41, in-8, 25 p., 1s. 6d.

294. TAYLOR (F.). The books and manuscripts of Scipio Le Squyer, deputy chamberlain of the exchequer (1620-59). *B. John Rylands Library*, 41, vol. 25, p. 137-164.

295. THOMPSON (J. W.). Ancient libraries. London, Cambridge Univ. Press, 40, in-8, 120 p., 12s.

296. TYSON (Moses). The first 40 years of the John Rylands Library (Manchester). *B. John Rylands Library*, 41, vol. 25, p. 46-66.

297. WHITE (H. L.). Trends in archival administration. *Hist. Stud. Australia N.Z.*, 40, vol. 1, p. 102-115.

298. WORRELL (W. H.) ed. Coptic texts in the University of Michigan collection. London, Oxford Univ. Press, 43, in-8, 394 p., (facs.), 28s.

299. YOUNG (P.). Catalogus librorum manuscriptorum Bibliothecae Wigorniensis, made in 1622-1623, ed. by I. Atkins and N. R. Ker. London, Cambridge Univ. Press, 44, in-8, vi-84 p., 15s. R : E. Ph. Goldschmidt, *Library*, 44/45, vol. 25, p. 188-189.

300. YOUSSEF (E.). Catalogue des MSS. persans et arabes de la Bibliothèque de la faculté de théologie et

de la philosophie de l'Iran.   In Persian and Arabic. Vol. 2. London, Luzac, 41, in-8, 795 p., 20s.

§ 3. History of Historical Sciences

a. GENERAL

301. BUTTERFIELD (H.). Tendencies in historical study in England. *Irish hist. Stud.*, 45, vol. 4, p. 209-223.

302. CLARK (G. N.). The origin of the ' Cambridge Modern History'. *Cambridge hist. J.*, 45, vol. 8, p. 57-64.

303. FRANCIS (F. C.). Recent bibliographical work. *Library*, 42, vol. 23, p. 108-126.

304. LANCTOT (Gustave).   Les historiens d'hier et l'histoire d'aujourd' hui. *Canad. hist. Assoc. Rept.*, 41, p. 5-14.

305. MANSOOR (M.). The story of Irish orientalism. London, Hodges, 44, in-8, 64 p., 5s. R : A. J. Arberry, *Asiatic R.*, 45, vol. 41, p. 318. E. D. Maclagan, *J. asiatic Soc.*, 45, p. 206.

306. THOMPSON (J. W.) and HALL (B. J.). A history of historical writing. London, Macmillan, 43, 2 vols. in-8, xvi-676 ; ix-674 p., 63s.

307. WELLEK (R.). The rise of English literary history. London, Oxford Univ. Press, 41, in-8, 275 p., 14s.

b. BIOGRAPHIES

308. JANÖSI (F. Engel de). The correspondence between Lord **Acton** and Bishop Creighton. *Cambridge hist. J.*, 40, vol. 6, p. 307-321.

309. DOUVILLE (Raymond). L'abbé Jos.-Elzéar **Bellemarre**, historien de la Baie-du-Febvre et de Nicolet. *Canad. Cath. hist. Assoc. Rept.*, 43-44, vol. 11, Fr. Sect., p. 163-175.

310. JACOB (E. F.). Charles **Bémont** and his services to English history. London, Oxford Univ. Press, 41, in-8, 10 p., 9d.

311. BAINTON (Roland H.). George Lincoln **Burr,** his life.   Selections from his writings, ed. by L. O. Gibbons.   London, Oxford Univ. Press, 43, in-8, 518 p., (illus.), 22s. 6d. R : G. P. G(ooch), *Eng. hist. R.*, 44, vol. 59, p. 286-287.

312. MOODY (T. W.). The writings of Edmund **Curtis**. *Irish hist. Stud.*, 43, vol. 3, p. 393-400.

313. FORSTER (E. M.). Goldsworthy Lowes **Dickinson** : a memoir. New ed. London, Arnold, 45, in-8, 288 p., 7s. 6d.

314. VENDRYES (Harry E.).   Bryan **Edwards**, 1743-1800. *Jamaican hist. R.*, 45, vol. 1, p. 76-82.

315. FREEMAN (A.) and PALMER (G. H.). An academic courtship, 1886-1887 : letters. London, Oxford Univ. Press, 42, in-8, 288 p., 12s. 6d.

316. CRONNE (H. A.).   Historical revision, no. 103 : Edward Augustus **Freeman**, 1823-1892. *History*, 43, vol. 28, p. 78-92.

317. ROSENTHAL (Erwin I. J.). Saadya **Gaon** : an appreciation of his Biblical exegesis. *B. John Rylands Library*, 42, vol. 27, p. 168-178.

318. GIBBON (Edward). The library of E. **Gibbon**, a catalogue of his books, ed. by G. Keynes. London, Cape, 40, in-8, 288 p., plates, 15s. R : J.E.N., *Library*, 40, vol. 21, p. 218-223.

319. LOW (D. M.). Edward **Gibbon**, 1734-1794. New ed. London, Chatto & Windus, 40, in-8, xiv-370 p., 8s. 6d.

320. NORTON (J. E.).   A bibliography of the works of Edward **Gibbon**.   London, Oxford Univ. Press, 40, in-8, 272 p., 21s. R : G. Jones, *Mod. Language R.*, 42, vol. 37, p. 381-382.

321. HENNIG (John). The historical work of Louis **Gougaud**. *Irish hist. Stud.*, 42, vol. 3, p. 180-186.

322. GUPPY (Henry). In honour of Henry **Guppy**. Bulletin of the John Rylands Library, Manchester, vol. 25, August 1941. Manchester, Univ. Press, 41, in-8, 239 p., 2s. 6d.

323. **Holdsworth** (Sir W.). In Memoriam. *L.Q.R.*, 44, vol. 60, p. 138-159.

324. DUNLOP (D. M.). The Spanish historian **Ibn Hubaish**. *J. asiatic Soc.*, 41, p. 359-362.

325. GOLDMAN (Eric F.). John Bach **McMaster** : American historian. London, Oxford Univ. Press, 43, in-8, 206 p., (illus.), 12s. R : G. P. G(ooch), *Eng. hist. R.*, 44, vol. 59, p. 429.

326. BRITTAIN (F.). Bernard Lord **Manning** : a memoir. Cambridge, Heffer, 42, in-8, vi-96 p., (plates, illus.), 7s. 6d. R : E. Ely, *Theology*, 43, vol. 46, p. 91.

327. MATTHEWS (A. G.). B. L. **Manning** the historian. *Congreg. hist. Soc. Trans.*, 43, vol. 14, p. 136-142.

328. WADE (Mason). Francis **Parkman,** heroic historian. Toronto, Macmillan, 42, in-8, xiv-466 p., $5.75. R : R. Flenley, *Canad. hist. R.*, 43, vol. 24, p. 196. G. Frégault, *B. Rech. hist.*, 43, vol. 49, p. 18-20.

329. **Références biographiques canadiennes**. *B. Rech. hist.*, 43, vol. 49, p. 59-64, 127-128, 193-200, 225-229, 256-263, 288-297 ; 44, vol. 50, p. 220-224, 247-256.

330. CROWFOOT (J. W.). George **Reisner** : an impression. *Antiquity*, 43, vol. 17, p. 122-128.

331. LEACH (A. J.). The Rev. G. N. **Smith,** a Pembrokeshire antiquary. *Archaeol. cambrensis*, 45, vol. 98, p. 248-254.

332. SMITH (L. A.). George Adam **Smith**. London, Hodder & Stoughton, 43, in-8, 272 p., (illus.), 8s. 6d.

333. MICKLEWRIGHT (F. H. Amphlett). Goldwin **Smith** : a liberal teacher. *Congreg. Quar.*, 42, vol. 20, p. 133-139.

334. POPE-HENNESSY (U.). Agnes **Strickland,** biographer of the queens of England, 1796-1874. London, Chatto & Windus, 40, in-8, 328 p., (illus.), 16s.

335. SYMONDS (John Addington). J. A. **Symonds** (1840-1893), the historian of the Renaissance. *Times lit. Supp.*, 40, p. 506, 510.

336. GOOCH (G. P.). Harold **Temperley**, 1879-1939. London, Oxford Univ. Press, 40, in-8, 41 p., 3s. 6d. (British Academy).

337. PENSON (L. M.). Harold **Temperley**, 1879-1939. *History*, 40, vol. 24, p. 121-124.

c. HISTORICAL CONGRESSES AND ORGANIZATIONS

338. BRITISH SCHOOL AT ATHENS. Annual. No. 39-40 : session 1938/39-1939/40. London, Macmillan, 42-43, 2 vols. in-4, 112, 87 p., (plates), 42s. ea.

339. CANADIAN HISTORICAL ASSOCIATION. Report of the annual meeting, 1940-45, with historical papers, ed. by R. G. Riddell, R. M. Saunders. Toronto, Univ. Press, 40-45, 6 vols. in-8, 134, 104, 132, 119, 125, 98 p., 10s. ea.

340. Conventions et congrès canadiens au Canada et aux États-Unis (1880-1933). *B. Rech. hist.*, 42, vol. 48, p. 54-60.

341. Newcomen Society for the study of the history of engineering and technology. Transactions. Vol. 19-21. 1938/39-1940/41. London, The Society, 40-43, 3 vols. in-4, 296, 184, 178 p., (plates), 20s. ea.

342. PARSLOE (G.). Guide to the historical publications of the societies of England and Wales. 11th-12th supplement, 1939-1941. *B. Inst. hist.*

Research, 40, suppl. no. 11 ; 43, suppl. no. 12, p. 1-18.

343. TILLEY (N. M.). The Trinity College Historical Society, 1892-1941. London, Cambridge Univ. Press, 42, in-8, x-134 p., (plates), 6s.

d. COLLECTED PAPERS

344. LEA (Henry Charles). Minor historical writings, etc., ed. A. C. Howland. London, Oxford Univ. Press, 43, in-8, 424 p., 21s. 6d. R : G. P. G(ooch), *Eng. hist. R.*, 45, vol. 60, p. 287.

345. MACNEILL (Eoin). Essays and studies presented to Professor Eoin MacNeill on the occasion of his 70th birthday, 1938, ed. by J. Ryan. Dublin, Sign of the Three Candles, 40, in-8, 593 p., 42s.

346. ROBINSON (H. Wheeler). Studies in history and religion presented to H. Wheeler Robinson on his 70th birthday, ed. by E. A. Payne. London, Lutterworth Press, 42, in-8, 272 p., 21s. R : A. C. Underwood, *Baptist Quar.*, 43, vol. 11, p. 181-185. W. B. Selbie, *Hibbert J.*, 43, vol. 41, p. 379-380.

§ 4. Methodology, Philosophy and Teaching of History

347. AUCHMUTY (James Johnston). The teaching of history. Dublin, Educ. Co., 40, in-8, 60 p., 1s. R : J. C. Beckett, *Irish hist. Stud.*, 41, vol. 2, p. 461-463.

348. BABA (Bay Nuzhet). Linguistic reform and historical research in the new Turkey. *Asiatic R.*, 44, vol. 40, p. 173-176.

349. BALDWIN (Martin). The exhibition as a medium for the study and teaching of history. *Canad. hist. Assoc. Rept.*, 41, p. 55-64.

350. BARZUN (J.), HOLBORN (H.) and others. The interpretation of history, ed. J. R. Strayer. London,

Oxford Univ. Press, 43, in-8, 192 p., 16s. 6d. (Princeton books in the humanities).

351. BEAGLEHOLE (J. C.). Some philosophies of history. *Hist. Stud. Australia N.Z.*, 42, vol. 2, p. 95-113.

352. BEAGLEHOLE (J. C.). The writing of imperial history. *Hist. Stud. Australia N.Z.*, 43, vol. 2, p. 129-140.

353. BEAN (C. E. W.). The technique of a contemporary war historian. *Hist. Stud. Australia N.Z.*, 42, vol. 2, p. 65-79.

354. BELOFF (Max). The study of contemporary history : some further reflections. *History*, 45, vol. 30, p. 75-84.

355. BELTON (Leslie). The deep roots of history. *Hibbert J.*, 43, vol. 41, p. 147-151.

356. BODIN (J.). Method for the easy comprehension of history, tr. from the Latin by B. Reynolds. London, Oxford Univ. Press, 45, in-8, 432 p., 40s. R : R. Flenley, *Canad. hist. R.*, 45, vol. 26, p. 438-440.

357. BURN (W. L.). The historian and the lawyer. *History*, 43, vol. 28, p. 17-36.

358. BUTTERFIELD (H.). The study of modern history. London, Bell, 45, in-8, 37 p., 2s.

359. CASE (S. J.). The Christian philosophy of history. London, Cambridge Univ. Press, 43, in-8, viii-221 p., 12s. R : H. H. Rowley, *Baptist Quar.*, 43, vol. 11, p. 188-191.

360. CLAPHAM (J. H.). The historian looks forward. London, Oxford Univ. Press, 43, in-8, 16 p., 1s.

361. CLARK (G. N.). Historical scholarship and historical thought. London, Cambridge Univ. Press, 44, in-8, 24 p., 1s. 6d.

362. CROCE (Benedetto). History as the story of liberty, tr. by S.

Sprigge. London, Allen & Unwin, 41, in-8, 324 p., 12s. 6d. R : G. M. Young, *Pol. Quar.*, 41, vol. 12, p. 333-336. H. Goad, *Int. Affairs*, 41, vol. 19, p. 267-268. A. Peel, *Congreg. Quar.*, 41, vol. 19, p. 262-263. *National R.*, 41, vol. 116, p. 738-739.

363. DAVIES (D. R.). The two humanities. An attempt at a Christian interpretation of history in the light of war. London, Clarke, 40, in-8, 256 p., 7s. 6d.

364. ' EXAMINER '. Is our Roman history teaching reactionary ? *Greece and Rome*, 43, vol. 12, p. 57-61.

365. FIELDHOUSE (H. N.). The failure of the historians. *Canad. hist. Assoc. Rept.*, 42, p. 52-70.

366. GILLIES (A.). Herder's approach to the philosophy of history. *Mod. Language R.*, 40, vol. 35, p. 193-206.

367. HART (B. H. L.). Why don't we learn from history ? London, Allen & Unwin, 44, in-8, 64 p., 2s. (P.E.N. Books ser.).

368. HENDERSON (G. B.). A plea for the study of contemporary history. *History*, 41, vol. 26, p. 51-55.

369. Historical research for university degrees in the United Kingdom, 1939-40. *B. Inst. hist. Research*, 40, Thesis suppl. no. 8.

370. HULME (Edward Maslin). History and its neighbours. London, Oxford Univ. Press, 42, in-8, x-197 p., 8s. 6d. R : R. Flenley, *Canad. hist. R.*, 44, vol. 25, p. 316-319. J. L. Myres, *Man*, 44, vol. 44, p. 78. G.R.C., *Geogr. J.*, 42, vol. 100, p. 272-273.

371. JEFFERYS (Charles W.). History in motion pictures. *Canad. hist. R.*, 41, vol. 22, p. 361-368.

372. LEE (N. E.). History and educational reform. *Hist. Stud. Australia N.Z.*, 44, vol. 3, p. 1-34.

373. LEON (Philip). Who makes history ? A study of Tolstoy's answer in ' War and Peace '. *Hibbert J.*, 44, vol. 42, p. 254-258.

374. McDONALD (A. H.). The study of the ancient background of history. *Hist. Stud. Australia N.Z.*, 40, vol. 1, p. 4-20.

375. MAINWARING (J.). The combination of history and geography in senior schools and the middle forms of secondary schools. *History*, 44, vol. 29, p. 58-67, 187-191.

376. MILLER (H.). History and science. London, Cambridge Univ. Press, 40, in-8, 201 p., 12s.

377. MITCHELL (R. Else). History in theory and practice, its study and sources. *Roy. Austral. hist. Soc. J.*, 40, vol. 26, p. 397-402.

378. OAKELEY (Hilda D.). Freedom or necessity in the making of history. *Hibbert J.*, 40, vol. 38, p. 442-448.

379. PHILLIPS (Charles E.). The teaching of international relations in Canada. *Canad. hist. Assoc. Rept.*, 45, p. 78-82.

380. PLEKHANOV (G. V.). The role of the individual in history. London, Lawrence & Wishart, 40, in-8, 64 p., 1s. 6d.

381. PRINCE (A. E.). The need for a wider study of military history. *Canad. hist. R.*, 44, vol. 25, p. 20-28.

382. ROBERTSON (Sir Charles Grant). The value of historical studies in time of war. *History*, 40, vol. 24, p. 289-294.

383. SCHMITT (Bernadotte E.). Some historians of modern Europe : essays in historiography by former students of the department of history of the University of Chicago. London, Cambridge Univ. Press, 42, in-8, x-533 p., 30s. R : H. N. Fieldhouse, *Canad. hist. R.*, 42, vol. 23, p. 210-213. E.J.K., *Queen's Quar.*, 42, vol. 49, p. 277-279.

384. SCHUYLER (Robert Livingston). History in a changing world. *Brit. Columbia hist. Quar.*, 41, vol. 5, p. 269-283.

385. SUMNER (B. H.). War and history. Edinburgh, Oliver & Boyd, 45, in-8, 28 p., 1s.

386. TEGGART (F. J.). Theory and processes of history. London, Cambridge Univ. Press, 41, in-8, xii-324 p., 21s.

387. THOMSON (David). The historian's contribution to contemporary thought. *History*, 43, vol. 28, p. 156-161.

388. TOYNE (S. M.). A history syllabus : thoughts on what to learn and how to learn it. *History*, 45, vol. 30, p. 159-172.

389. TREVELYAN (G. M.). History and the reader. London, Cambridge Univ. Press, 45, in-8, 40 p., 2s. 6d.

390. TROTTER (R. G.). Aims in the study and teaching of history in Canadian universities to-day. *Canad. hist. Assoc. Rept.*, 43, p. 50-62.

391. WALSH (W. H.). The intelligibility of history. *Philosophy*, 42, vol. 17, p. 128-143.

392. WARE (Caroline F.) ed. The cultural approach to history. London, Oxford Univ. Press, 40, in-8, ix-359 p., 17s. 6d. R : D. W. B(rogan), *Eng. hist. R.*, 41, vol. 56, p. 678-679.

393. WISDOM (J. O.). Hegel's dialectic in historical philosophy. *Philosophy*, 40, vol. 15, p. 243-268.

394. WRIGHT (C. J.). The humanisation of history. *Hibbert J.*, 43, vol. 41, p. 140-146.

§ 5. Ethnography, Anthropology and Folklore

395. MURDOCK (George P.). Ethnographic bibliography of North America, publ. for the Dept. of Anthrop., Yale Univ. London, Oxford Univ. Press, 41, in-4, xvi-168 p.,

9s. R : C.R.H.T., *J. polynesian Soc.*, 42, vol. 51, p. 142.

396. SCHAPERA (I.). Select bibliography of South African native life and problems. London, Oxford Univ. Press, 41, in-8, xii-249 p., 10s. 6d. (Inter-univ. comm. for Afr. studies). R : A. I. Richards, *Man*, 41, vol. 41, p. 137; *J. Roy. African Soc.*, 41, vol. 40, p. 377-378. M. Gluckman, *South African J. Econ.*, 41, vol. 9, p. 319-322.

---

397. BANKS (Mary MacLeod). British calendar customs : Scotland. Vol. 3. London, Glaisher, 41, in-8, 266 p., 15s. (Folk-lore soc. publ.). R : H. J. Rose, *Man*, 43, vol. 43, p. 94.

398. BRETT (S. Reed). Witchcraft. *Quar. R.*, 42, vol. 279, p. 206-217.

399. DRIVER (G. R.). Witchcraft in the Old Testament. *J. asiatic Soc.*, 43, p. 6-16.

400. ETTLINGER (Ellen). The invulnerable hero in Celtic legend. *Man*, 42, vol. 42, p. 43-45.

401. FLEURE (H. J.). Race and its meaning in Europe. *B. John Rylands Library*, 40, vol. 24, no. 2, p. 234-249.

402. FOGG (Walter). Villages, tribal markets, and towns : some considerations concerning urban development in the Spanish and international zones of Morocco. *Sociol. R.*, 40, vol. 32, p. 85-107.

403. FOGG (W.). A Moroccan tribal shrine and its relation to a nearby tribal market. *Man*, 40, vol. 40, p. 100-104.

404. HAILE (F. B.). Origin legend of the Navaho flintway. Text and transl. London, Cambridge Univ. Press, 43, in-4, xii-320 p., (illus.), 18s.

405. HILDBURGH (W. L.). Further notes on the uses in Spain of prehistoric stone implements as amulets. *Man*, 41, vol. 41, p. 13-18.

406. JENNESS (D.). The Eskimos : their past and future. *Queen's Quar.*, 44, vol. 51, p. 132-148.

407. JONES (J. J.). The Legend of Madoc. *Nat. Library Wales J.*, 42, vol. 2, p. 120-123.

408. MACDONALD (Gregory). The Kashubs on the Baltic. *Slavonic Y.B.* (*Slavonic R.*), 40, vol. 19, p. 265-275.

409. PEATE (Iorwerth C.). Mari Lwyd : a suggested explanation. [A pre - Christian horse - ceremony in Wales]. *Man*, 43, vol. 43, p. 53-58.

410. PEEL (R. F.). The Tibu peoples and the Libyan desert. *Geogr. J.*, 42, vol. 100, p. 73-87.

411. QUIGGIN (A. Hingston). Haddon the head-hunter : a short sketch of the life of A. C. Haddon. London, Cambridge Univ. Press, 42, in-8, xii-170 p., 7s. 6d.

412. RIDDELL (W. H.). Tiger and dragon. *Antiquity*, 45, vol. 19, p. 27-31 (illus.).

413. RIDDELL (W. H.). Concerning unicorns. *Antiquity*, 45, vol. 19, p. 194-202 (illus.).

414. SPECK (Frank G.). Penobscot man : the life history of a forest tribe in Maine. London, Oxford Univ. Press, 40, in-8, 325 p., (illus.), 18s. R : J. H. H., *Man*, 42, vol. 42, p. 18-19.

415. SPENCE (Lewis). The supernatural character of Robin Hood. *Hibbert J.*, 42, vol. 40, p. 280-285.

416. TREGAMETH (A.). Old Welsh customs : hen arferion Cymru. Welsh transl. by J. Pierce. Liverpool, Evans, 43, in-8, vi-48 p., (illus.), 6s.

417. WRIGHT (Arthur R.). British calendar customs : England. Vol. 3 : Fixed festivals, June-December, ed. by T. E. Lones. London, Glaisher, 41, in-8, 272 p., 21s. (Folk-lore soc. publ.).

§ 6. General History

a. PERIODICALS

See list of Periodicals at beginning of volume.

b. UNIVERSAL HISTORY

418. BRADY (C.). The legends of Ermanaric. London, Cambridge Univ. Press, 44, in-8, xii-342 p., 18s.

419. BURCKHARDT (J.). Reflections on history, tr. from the German by M. D. Hotinger. London, Allen & Unwin, 43, in-8, 219 p., 12s. 6d. *National R.*, 43, vol. 121, p. 240.

420. COBBAN (Alfred). Dictatorship : its history and theory. New ed. London, Cape, 43, in-8, 352 p., 12s. 6d. R : Sir A. McFadyean, *Int. Affairs*, 44, vol. 20, p. 112.

421. COBBAN (A.). The nation state. *History*, 44, vol. 29, p. 44-57.

422. COULTON (G. G.). Antisemitism : a chapter in world history. *Hibbert J.*, 44, vol. 42, p. 226-230.

423. EGHBAL (A.). Tarikh Umoomi wa Iran. History of Europe during the 15th to 17th centuries and history of Iran from Islam to Mongols. In Persian. London, Luzac, 40, in-8, 585 p., 13s. 6d.

424. Encyclopaedia of world history : ancient, medieval and modern, chronologically arranged. A revised and modern version of Ploetz's *Epitome*, ed. by W. L. Langer. London, Harrap, 41, in-4, xxxii-1155-lxvi p., (maps, tables), 25s. R : G. E. Morey, *Int. Affairs*, 41, vol. 19, p. 329-330.

425. FERRERO (G.). The principles of power : the great political crises of history, tr. by T. R. Jaeckel. London, Allen, 42, in-8, ix-333 p., 21s.

426. FISCHER (E.). The passing of the European age. London, Oxford Univ. Press, 44, in-8, 228 p., 14s.

427. FISHER (H. A. L.). History of Europe. New ed. London, Eyre &

Spottiswoode, 43, 2 vols. in-8, 1,333 p., 30s.

428. FLEURE (H. J.). Peasants in Europe. *Geography*, 43, vol. 28, p. 55-61.

429. FULLER (J. F. C.). Decisive battles : their influence upon history and civilization. Vol. 2 : From Napoleon the First to General Franco. London, Eyre, 40, in-8, 560 p., 16s. R : *Army Quar.*, 40, vol. 40, p. 379.

430. GRAEBNER (I.) and BRITT (S. H.). Jews in a Gentile world. London, Macmillan, 42, in-8, x-436 p., 18s.

431. HERTZ (F.). Nationality in history and politics, ed. by K. Mannheim. London, Kegan Paul, 44, in-8, 417 p., 25s. R : A. Cobban, *Int. Affairs*, 44, vol. 20, p. 408-409.

432. HOOK (S.). The hero in history, a study in limitation and possibility. London, Secker & Warburg, 45, in-8, 184 p., 8s. 6d.

433. HORNELL (James). Floats and buoyed rafts in military operations. *Antiquity*, 45, vol. 19, p. 72-79 (illus.).

434. JEDLICKI (M. B.). Germany and Poland through the ages : a lecture. Cambridge, Galloway & Porter, 42, in-8, 24 p., (maps), 1s.

435. KOHN (Hans). World order : in historical perspective. London, Oxford Univ. Press, 42, in-8, 370 p., 12s. 6d.

436. KOHN (H.). The idea of nationalism. London, Macmillan, 45, in-8, xiii-735 p., 36s. R : A.E.P., *Queen's Quar.*, 45, vol. 52, p. 101-102.

437. McCABE (J.). The golden ages of history. London, Watts, 40, in-8, xi-242 p., 10s. 6d.

438. McDONALD (A. H.). The study of world history from the Australian angle. *Roy. Austral. hist. Soc. J.*, 43, vol. 29, p. 1-20.

439. MATHESON (Colin). Man and bear in Europe. *Antiquity*, 42, vol. 16, p. 151-159.

440. MICHELET (Raymond). African empires and civilisation. Manchester, Panaf Service, 45, in-8, 39 p., 2s. (Int. African Service Bur., publ. 4). R : E. Huxley, *Int. Affairs*, 45, vol. 21, p. 554.

441. MITCHELL (Charles). A book of ships. London, Penguin, 41, in-8, 50 p., 1s. (King Penguin ser.). R : R.C.A., *Mariner's Mirror*, 42, vol. 28, p. 172.

442. NEHRU (J.). Glimpses of world history. London, L. Drummond, 42, in-8, 1016 p., (map), 12s. 6d.

443. OLSON (Alma Luise). Scandinavia, the background for neutrality. London, Lippincott, 40, in-8, 358 p., 14s.

444. Oxyrhynchus Papyri. Pt. 18, ed. by E. Lobel, C. H. Roberts and E. P. Wegener. London, Oxford Univ. Press, 42, in-4, 227 p., (plates), 63s. (Egypt exploration soc. Graeco-Roman memoirs).

445. PRIBICHEVICH (Stoyan). Living space, the story of south-eastern Europe. London, Heinemann, 40, in-8, viii-362 p., 15s. R : E. H. Carr, *Int. Affairs*, 40, vol. 19, p. 130.

446. RANDALL (Henry John). The creative centuries : a study in historical development. London, Longmans, 44, in-8, 420 p., 17s. 6d. R : V. G. Childe, *Antiquity*, 45, vol. 19, p. 107-108.

447. RICHMOND (H. W.). The objects and elements of sea power in history. *History*, 43, vol. 28, p. 1-16.

448. RODGERS (W. L.). Naval warfare under oars, 4th to 16th centuries : a study of strategy, tactics and ship design. London, Stevens & Brown, 40, in-8, xii-358 p., (illus., maps), 27s. R : R.C.A., *Mariner's Mirror*, 40, vol. 26, p. 322-323.

449. ROTH (C.). A short history of the Jewish people. Rev. ed. Oxford,

East & West Libr., 43, in-8, xii-447 p., 5s.

450. SCOTT (G. R.). The history of torture throughout the ages. London, Laurie, 40, in-8, 328 p., (illus.), 15s.

451. TEGGART (Frederick J.). Rome and China, a study of correlations in historical events. London, Cambridge Univ. Press, 41, in-8, xvii-283 p., (maps), 18s. R : P. M. Sykes, *J. central asian Soc.*, 41, vol. 28, p. 467-468. G. F. Hudson, *Philosophy*, 43, vol. 18, p. 87-89.

452. WEECH (W. N.) ed. History of the world. London, Odhams Press, 44, in-8, 960 p., (maps), 9s. 6d.

c. HISTORY, BY COUNTRIES

Africa

453. BATTEN (T. R.). Africa past and present. London, Oxford Univ. Press, 43, in-8, 108 p., 2s. R : A. J· Haile, *African Stud.*, 44, vol. 3, p. 149-150.

Cyprus

454. HILL (Sir George Francis). A history of Cyprus. Vol. 1 : to the conquest of Richard Lion Heart. London, Cambridge Univ. Press, 40, in-4, xviii-352 p., (plates, maps), 25s. R : S.S., *Antiq. J.*, 40, vol. 20, p. 512-514. M.M., *Geography*, 41, vol. 26, p. 96. A. H. M. Jones, *Eng. hist. R.*, 41, vol. 56, p. 304-305. R.M.D., *J. hell. Stud.*, 42 (43), vol. 62, p. 86.

455. LUKE (Sir Harry). Cyprus, an historical retrospect. *Asiatic R.*, 44, vol. 40, p. 417-423.

456. NEWMAN (P.). A short history of Cyprus. London, Longmans, 40, in-8, xix-235 p., 5s.

Czechoslovakia

457. SETON-WATSON (R. W.). A history of the Czechs and Slovaks. London, Hutchinson, 43, in-8, 413 p., 15s. R : A. J. P. T(aylor), *Eng. hist. R.*, 44, vol. 59, p. 431-432. H.G.S.,

Geogr. J., 44, vol. 103, p. 80-81. A.G.A.W., *Int. Affairs*, 44, vol. 20, p. 290-291. W. Taffs, *History*, 45, vol. 30, p. 104-105. W. Barker, *Slavonic R.*, 45, vol. 23, p. 173-174.

Denmark

458. BIRCH (J. H. S.). Denmark in history. New ed. London, Murray, 45, in-8, 444 p., 7s. 6d.

Egypt

459. BAZRAG (Mohammed Ali). Tarikh Miar wa Khandan. History of Egypt, in Persian. London, Luzac, 42, in-8, 212 p., (illus.), 12s. 6d.

France

460. DOORLY (E.). The story of France. London, Cape, 44, in-8, 274 p., (illus.), 8s. 6d.

461. MARRIOTT (Sir J. A. R.). A short history of France. London, Methuen, 42, in-8, 291 p., 15s. R : T. E. Utley, *Int. Affairs*, 43, vol. 19, p. 593.

462. —— —— New ed. London, Methuen, 44, in-8, 296 p., 15s.

Germany

463. HEARNSHAW (F. J. C.). Germany the aggressor—throughout the ages. London, Chambers, 40, in-8, 384 p., (maps), 7s. 6d. R : *National R.*, 40, vol. 114, p. 633-635.

464. MARVEY (S. M.). 1,000 years of German aggression. London, F. P. Agency, 43, in-8, 116 p., 5s. 6d.

465. OLIVEIRA (A. R.). A people's history of Germany, tr. from Spanish by E. E. Brooke. London, Gollancz, 42, in-8, 288 p., 7s. 6d.

466. STEINBERG (S. H.). A short history of Germany. London, Cambridge Univ. Press, 44, in-8, xii-304 p., (maps), 12s. 6d. R : R. Birley, *Int. Affairs*, 45, vol. 21, p. 281. *Pol. Quar.*, 45, vol. 16, p. 183-184. *Quar. R.*, 45, vol. 283, p. 121-122.

467. STERN-RUBARTH (Edgar). A short history of the Germans. London, Duckworth, 41, in-8, 159 p., (maps), 3s. 6d.

468. VERMEIL (Edmond). Germany's three Reichs, their history and culture, tr. by E. W. Dickes. London, Dakers, 45, in-8, 420 p., 18s. R : I. M. Massey, *Int. Affairs*, 45, vol. 21, p. 412-413.

Great Britain
(see also **Scotland**).

469. McDOUGALL (D. J.). Some recent books on English history. *Canad. hist. R.*, 44, vol. 25, p. 421-427.

470. MILNE (A. T.) ed. Writings on British history, 1936. London, Cape, 40, in-8, 392 p., 12s. 6d. R : L. Hanson, *Library*, 41, vol. 22, p.97-99. G.P., *B. Inst. hist. Research*, 41, vol. 19, p. 32.

———

471. ADDISON (W.). Epping forest. London, Dent, 45, in-8, 250 p., (illus.), 12s. 6d.

472. BALDWIN (Leland Dewitt). God's Englishman : the evolution of the Anglo-Saxon spirit. London, Cape, 43, in-8, 265 p., 12s. 6d.

473. CRAWFORD (O. G. S.). Southampton. *Antiquity*, 42, vol. 16, p. 36-50 (illus.).

474. DODD (A. H.). Welsh and English in East Denbighshire : a historical retrospect. *Trans. Soc. Cymmr.*, 40, p. 34-65.

475. DODDS (Madeleine Hope) ed. Northumberland county history. Vol. 15 : The parishes of Simonburn, Rothbury, Alwinton. Newcastle, Reed, 40, in-4, 526 p., (plates, illus.), 63s. R : H.E.D.B., *Eng. hist. R.*, 41, vol. 56, p. 153-154.

476. HOWSE (W. H.). Presteigne, past and present. Hereford, Jakeman, 45, in-8, 142 p., 7s. 6d.

477. HUGHES (R. Elfyn). Environment and human settlement in the Commote of Arllechwedd Isaf (Caernarvonshire). *Trans. Caern. hist. Soc.*, 40, p. 1-25 (illus.).

478. JENKIN (A. K. Hamilton). Cornwall and its people : Cornish seafarers, Cornwall and the Cornish, Cornish homes and customs. In 1 vol. London, Dent, 45, in-8, 500 p., (illus.), 12s. 6d.

479. JONES (E. D.). Some glimpses of Cardiganshire. *J. welsh bibliogr. Soc.*, 43, vol. 6, p. 5-27.

480. KINVIG (R. H.). History of the Isle of Man. London, Oxford Univ. Press, 44, in-8, 256 p., 5s. R : E.G.B., *Geography*, 45, vol. 30, p. 99-100.

481. KNIGHT (Charles B.). A history of the city of York. York, Herald Printing Works, 44, in-8, ix-774 p., 42s. R : S.C.F., *Scottish geogr. Mag.*, 44, vol. 60, p. 87.

482. LEWIS (F. R.). Welsh history from English archives, with some notes on John Morris and the expedition to Cartagena, 1740-41. *Trans. Soc. Cymmr.*, 39 (40), p. 29-54.

483. LLOYD (Sir J. E.). The early history of Lleyn (Caernarvonshire). *Trans. Caern. hist. Soc.*, 40, p. 26-34.

484. LLOYD (Sir J. E.). Golwg ar hanes Cymru. Cyfieithiad Cymraeg gan R. T. Jenkins. (A view of Welsh history. Welsh transl. by R. T. Jenkins). Aberystwyth, Gwasg Aberystwyth, 43, in-8, 88 p.

485. MANSERGH (Nicholas). Britain and Ireland. London, Longmans, 42, in-8, 96 p., 6d. (Longmans' pamph. on the British Commonwealth). R : D. Macardle, *Int. Affairs*, 42, vol. 19, p. 531.

486. MORRELL (J. B.). York monuments. London, Batsford, 44, in-4, viii-131 p., (illus.), 63s. (Arts and crafts in York). R : F. E. Hutchinson, *19th Century*, 45, vol. 137, p. 72-77.

487. MORTON (A. L.). A people's history of England. London, Central Books, 45, in-8, 563 p., (maps), 10s. 6d.

488. MUNRO (J.). Short history of Great Britain. Edinburgh, Oliver & Boyd, 42, in-8, 513 p., (map), 6s.

489. REDFORD (A.). The emergence of Manchester. *History*, 40, vol. 24, p. 32-49.

490. RICHARDS (T.). Sources of Caernarvonshire history, University College Library, Bangor. *Trans. Caern. hist. Soc.*, 40, p. 87-95.

491. ROTH (Cecil). A history of the Jews in England. London, Oxford Univ. Press, 41, in-8, 312 p., 15s. R : C. Johnson, *Eng. hist. R.*, 42, vol. 57, p. 495-496. J. Parkes, *Econ. Hist. R.*, 42, vol. 12, p. 98-99. L. B. Namier, *19th Century*, 42, vol. 132, p. 279-280. N. Sykes, *Hibbert J.*, 42, vol. 40, p. 398-399.

492. ROWSE (A. L.). The spirit of English history. London, Cape, 43, in-8, 150 p., (illus.), 7s. 6d. R : A.E.P., *Queen's Quar.*, 44, vol. 51, p. 339.

493. ROWSE (A. L.). The English spirit : essays in history and literature. London, Macmillan, 44, in-8, x-275 p., 12s. 6d.

494. SMITH (Frederick). Coventry : six hundred years of municipal life. Coventry, Coventry Evening Telegraph, 45, in-8, 210 p., 15s.

495. SMITH (R. A. Lendon). Bath. London, Batsford, 44, in-8, 118 p., (plates), 12s. 6d. R : *Quar. R.*, 45, vol. 283, p. 121. *Burlington Mag.*, 45, vol. 87, p. 208.

496. STEEGMANN (J.). Cambridge : as it was and as it is to-day. London, Batsford, 40, in-8, 128 p., (illus., maps), 10s. 6d.

497. Victoria history of the counties of England. Sussex. Vol. 7 : The rape of Lewes, ed. by L. F. Salzman.

London, Oxford Univ. Press, 40, in-8, 286 p., 42s. R : D. H. S. Cranage, *Eng. hist. R.*, 41, vol. 56, p. 116-117.

498. WILLIAMS (A. H.). An introduction to the history of Wales. Vol. 1 : Pre-historic times to 1063 A.D. Cardiff, Univ. of Wales Press Board, 41, in-8, x-192 p., 5s. R : D. Williams, *History*, 41, vol. 26, p. 142-144. E. Davies, *Archaeol. cambrensis*, 41, vol. 96, p. 211-214.

499. WILLIAMSON (J. A.). The evolution of England. 2nd ed. London, Oxford Univ. Press, 44, in-8, 506 p., (maps), 10s.

Greece

500. AGHNIDES (Thanassis). What ancient Greece means to the modern Greek. *B. John Rylands Library*, 43, vol. 27, p. 260-270.

501. ARGENTI (Philip P.). Bibliography of Chios from classical times to 1936. London, Oxford Univ. Press, 40, in-8, 836 p., 42s. R : W.M., *Eng. hist. R.*, 41, vol. 56, p. 351-352.

502. ARGENTI (P. P.). Chius vincta, or, The occupation of Chios by the Turks (1566) and their administration of the island (1566-1912) described in contemporary diplomatic reports and official despatches. London, Cambridge Univ. Press, 41, in-8, cclxxviii-264 p., (plates), 25s. R : C.W.C., *Eng. hist. R.*, 42, vol. 57, p. 397.

503. GIUSTINIANI (Hieronimo). History of Chios, ed. by P. P. Argenti. London, Cambridge Univ. Press, 42, in-8, xxxv-462 p., 42s. R : *J. hell. Stud.*, 43, vol. 63, p. 138-139. R. M. Dawkins, *Class. R.*, 44, vol. 58, p. 65-66.

Iceland

504. THÓRDARSON (Björn). Iceland, past and present, tr. by Sir W. Craigie. London, Oxford Univ. Press, 41, in-8, 46 p., 1s. R : B.B.R., *Geogr. J.*, 42, vol. 99, p. 103.

505. —— —— 2nd, rev. ed. London, Oxford Univ. Press, 45, in-8, 48 p., 2s. 6d.

506. TURVILLE-PETRE (G.). Notes on the intellectual history of the Icelanders. *History*, 42, vol. 27, p. 111-123.

Ireland

507. HENCHY (Patrick) and O'NEILL (T. P.). Writings on Irish history, 1944. *Irish hist. Stud.*, 45, vol. 4, p. 332-349.

508. McDOWELL (R. B.). Writings on Irish history, 1939, 40. *Irish hist. Stud.*, 41, vol. 2, p. 303-327; 42, vol. 3, p. 78-104.

509. CASSERLEY (D.). History of Ireland. Dublin, Talbot Press, 41, 2 vols. in-8, 168, 152 p., (illus.), 3s. R : J. N. Shearman, *Irish hist. Stud.*, 44, vol. 4, p. 113-114.

510. CLARKE (Randall). A short history of Ireland. London, Univ. Tutorial Press, 41, in-8, 156 p., 2s. 6d. R : J. N. Shearman, *Irish hist. Stud.*, 44, vol. 4, p. 113-114.

511. COOPER (A.). An eighteenth century antiquary, ed. by L. Price. Dublin, Falconer, 42, in-8, 128 p., (plates), 10s. 6d.

512. CURTIS (Edmund) and McDOWELL (R. B.). Irish historical documents, 1172-1922. London, Methuen, 43, in-8, 331 p., 18s. R : H. G. Richardson, *Irish hist. Stud.*, 45, vol. 4, p. 358-361.

513. MACALISTER (R. A. S.). The book of the taking of Ireland. Pt. 3. Dublin, Talbot Press, 40, in-8, 206 p., 16s. (Irish texts soc.).

514. MACALISTER (R. A. S.). Ancient Ireland. New ed. London, Methuen, 42, in-8, 307 p., (illus.), 11s. 6d.

515. PERRY (F. T.). The chronicles of Eri (the ancient Irish : who they were, and their connections with the coronation stone). London, Stockwell, 40, in-8, 160 p., 3s. 6d. R : R. A. S. Macalister, *Irish hist. Stud.*, 41, vol. 2, p. 335-337.

516. QUINN (David B.). Agenda for Irish history. *Irish hist. Stud.*, 45, vol. 4, p. 254-269.

Italy

517. HASSALL (W. O.). Special collections in England of use for Italian studies. *J. Documentation*, 45, vol. 1, p. 63-71.

518. SALVATORELLI (Luigi). A concise history of Italy from prehistoric times to our own day, tr. by B. Miall. London, Allen & Unwin, 40, in-8, 688 p., 21s. R : C. Petrie, *Int. Affairs*, 40, vol. 19, p. 54-55.

Japan

519. DILTS (M. N.). Pageant of Japanese history. London, Longmans, 42, in-8, 380 p., (illus.), 12s. 6d.

520. RICE (Stanley). The Japanese in the light of history. *Asiatic R.*, 42, vol. 38, p. 321-327.

Latin America

521. HUMPHREYS (R. A.). Latin America : bibliography. London, Roy. Inst. of Int. Affairs, 41, in-8, 36 p., 1s. 6d.

522. JAMES (P. E.). Latin America. London, Cassell, 43, in-8, 926 p., (plates, maps), 35s.

523. PECK (A. M.). Pageant of South American history. London, Longmans, 42, in-8, 405 p., (illus.), 12s. 6d.

Norway

524. BRØGGER (A. W.). From the Stone age to the motor age : a sketch of Norwegian cultural history. *Antiquity*, 40, vol. 14, p. 163-181 (illus.).

525. KEILHAU (Wilhelm). Norway in world history. London, MacDonald, 44, in-8, 208 p., 5s. (Cross

roads ser.). R : G.M.G.-H., *Int. Affairs*, 45, vol. 21, p. 279-280.

526. KOHT (Halvdan) and SKARD (Sigmund). The voice of Norway. London, Hutchinson, 44, in-8, 176 p., 4s. R : H.H.A., *Int. Affairs*, 45, vol. 21, p. 280.

Poland

527. BOHDANOWICZ (L.). The Muslims in Poland, their origin, history, and cultural life. *Asiatic R.*, 41, vol. 37, p. 646-656 ; *J. asiatic Soc.*, 42, p. 163-180.

528. GÓRKA (O.). Outline of Polish history, past and present. London, Faber, 42, in-8, 112 p., (maps), 5s.

529. —— —— 2nd, rev. and enlarged ed. London, Alliance Press, 45, in-8, 140 p., (maps), 8s. 6d.

530. HALECKI (O.). The history of Poland, an essay in historical synthesis, tr. by M. M. Gardner and M. Corbridge-Patkaniowska. London, Dent, 42, in-8, xvi-272 p., (plates), 15s. R : W.F.R., *History*, 43, vol. 28, p. 118-119.

531. LIGOCHI (E. E.). Legends and history of Poland. London, Nelson, 43, in-8, 120 p., (illus., map), 6s.

532. NEWMAN (B.). The story of Poland. London, Hutchinson, 43, in-8, 176 p., (illus., map), 7s. 6d.

533. PACEWICZ (K.). Polish armed forces through the ages, ed. by M. Kukiel. London, Orbis Ltd., 44, in-2, 72 p., (illus.), 30s.

534. SLOCOMBE (George). A history of Poland. Revised and enlarged ed. London, Nelson, 40, in-8, 375 p., 10s. 6d. R : D. Mitrany, *Pol. Quar.*, 40, vol. 11, p. 277-279. W. J. Rose, *Slavonic Y.B.* (*Slavonic R.*), 40, vol. 19, p. 337-338.

Rumania

535. GHYKA (Matila Costiescu). A documented chronology of Roumanian history from pre-historic times to the present day, tr. by F. G. Renier and A. Cliff. Oxford, Blackwell, 41, in-8, 135 p., 5s. R : W. Miller, *History*, 43, vol. 28, p. 216-217.

Scotland

536. BARTY (A. B.). The history of Dunblane. Stirling, Mackay, 44, in-4, 296 p., (illus.), 21s.

537. FORRESTER (D. M.). Logiealmond : the place and the people. London, Oliver & Boyd, 45, in-8, 254 p., 10s. 6d.

538. MACKENZIE (A. M.). The kingdom of Scotland. Edinburgh, Chambers, 40, in-8, 396 p., 12s. 6d.

539. MACKINTOSH (M.). A history of Dundee and the surrounding district of Angus. Dundee, Winter, 40, in-8, 7s. 6d.

540. MACKINTOSH (M.). A history of Inverness. Inverness, Highland News Ltd., 40, in-8, 7s. 6d.

541. MASSON (R.). Short history of Scotland the nation. London, Nelson, 42, in-8, 362 p., 3s. 6d.

542. SETON (Sir B. G.). The House of Seton : a study of lost causes. Edinburgh, Lindsay & Macleod, 41, 2 vols. in-4, 695 p., 70s.

Spain

543. TREND (J. B.). The civilization of Spain. London, Oxford Univ. Press, 44, in-16, 224 p., (maps), 3s. (Home Univ. libr.). R : G.D.E., *Int. Affairs*, 45, vol. 21, p. 129. O. Williams, *National R.*, 44, vol. 123, p. 167-171.

Union of Soviet Socialist Republics

544. ALLEN (W. E. D.). The Ukraine, a history. London, Cambridge Univ. Press, 40, in-8, xvi-404 p., (maps), 21s. R : B. H. Sumner, *Eng. hist. R.*, 42, vol. 57, p. 264-267. V. Conolly, *Econ. Hist. R.*, 42, vol. 12, p. 104-105. *Geogr. J.*, 41, vol. 97, p. 252-253.

545. DOROSHENKO (D.). History of the Ukraine, ed. by G. W. Simpson, tr. by H. Chikalenko-Keller. Saskatoon, Ukrainian Self-reliance League of Canada, 40, in-8, 686 p., $3.50. R : S. Davidovich, *Int. Affairs*, 41, vol. 19, p. 214. J.P.H.M., *Geogr. J.*, 41, vol. 97, p. 57-58.

546. HOWARD (Alexander) and NEWMAN (Ernest). Pictorial history of Russia from Rurik to Stalin. London, Hutchinson, 43, in-8, 215 p., (maps), 16s. R : *National R.*, 44, vol. 122, p. 172.

547. HRUSHEVSKY (Michael). A history of the Ukraine, ed. by O. J. Frederiksen. London, Oxford Univ. Press, 41, in-8, 629 p., 18s.

548. ISWOLSKY (Helen). Soul of Russia. London, Sheed, 44, in-8, xi-172 p., (plates), 10s. 6d. R : J. Degras, *Int. Affairs*, 45, vol. 21, p. 418-419.

549. KERNER (R. J.). The urge to the sea : the course of Russian history. London, Cambridge Univ. Press, 42, in-8, xvii-212 p., (maps), 15s. (North-eastern Asia seminar publ.). R : B. H. Sumner, *Eng. hist. R.*, 42, vol. 57, p. 508-509. E.H.M., *Geogr. J.*, 42, vol. 100, p. 87-88.

550. LOEWENSON (Leo). Some recent books on Russian history. *History*, 43, vol. 28, p. 207-215.

551. MILIUKOV (P.). Outlines of Russian culture, ed. by M. Karpovich. London, Oxford Univ. Press, 42, 3 vols. in-8, 234, 130, 160 p., 22s. 6d.

552. PRICE (Morgan P.). Russia through the centuries : the historical background of the U.S.S.R. London, Allen & Unwin, 43, in-8, 136 p., (maps), 5s. R : J. Maynard, *Pol. Quar.*, 44, vol. 15, p. 174-176.

553. SEELEY (Frank Friedeberg). Russia and the slave trade. *Slavonic R.*, 45, vol. 23, p. 126-136.

554. SEGAL (L.). Russia : a concise history from the foundation of the State to Hitler's invasion. London, Allen, 44, in-8, 262 p., (illus., map), 8s. 6d.

555. SHULGIN (Basil). Kiev, mother of Russian towns. *Slavonic Y.B.* (*Slavonic R.*), 40, vol. 19, p. 62-82.

556. SUMNER (B. H.). Survey of Russian history. London, Duckworth, 44, in-8, 464 p., (maps, illus.), 16s. R : R. M. Hodgson, *J. central asian Soc.*, 44, vol. 31, p. 325-326. *National R.*, 44, vol. 123, p. 435-436. M. Postan, *Econ. Hist. R.*, 44, vol. 14, p. 89-91. E. H. Carr, *Int. Affairs*, 44, vol. 20, p. 294-295. V. Minorsky, *Slavonic R.*, 45, vol. 23, p. 157-159.

557. VERNADSKY (George). Ancient Russia. London, Oxford Univ. Press, 43, in-8, 440 p., 33s. 6d.

558. VERNADSKY (G.). A history of Russia. Rev. ed. London, Oxford Univ. Press, 44, in-8, 532 p., (maps), 18s. 6d.

559. WOLFE (L.). A short history of Russia. London, Nicholson & Watson, 42, in-8, 160 p., 4s. 6d.

§ 7. Constitutional and Legal History

560. ANDERSON (R. B.) ed. A supplement to Beale's Bibliography of early English law books. London, Oxford Univ. Press, 44, in-4, 62 p., 14s.

561. FRIEDMANN (W.). Western and German legal thought. Community or cleavage ? *L.Q.R.*, 42, vol. 58, p. 257-264.

562. HAMBURGER (Max). The awakening of western legal thought, tr. by B. Miall. London, Allen & Unwin, 42, in-8, 167 p., 10s. 6d. R : O. Kahn-Freund, *Sociol. R.*, 42, vol. 35, p. 240-241.

563. HOLDSWORTH (Sir W.). The treaty-making power of the Crown. *L.Q.R.*, 42, vol. 58, p. 175-183.

564. LAWSON (F. H.). Notes on the history of tort in the civil law. *J. comp. Legisl. int. Law*, 40, vol. 22, p. 136-165.

565. M'MILLAN (A. R. G.). The evolution of the Scottish judiciary. Edinburgh, Green, 41, in-8, 81 p., 6s. R : W. S. Holdsworth, *Eng. hist. R.*, 41, vol. 56, p. 653.

566. POTTER (H.). An historical introduction to English law and its institutions. 2nd, rev. ed. London, Sweet & Maxwell, 43, in-8, x-588 p., 25s. R : C.A.W., *Canad. Bar R.*, 43, vol. 21, p. 333-334.

567. POTTER (H.). A short outline of English legal history. 4th, rev. ed. London, Sweet & Maxwell, 45, in-8, xvi-256 p., 17s. 6d.

568. WEINBAUM (Martin). British borough charters, 1307-1660, ed. by M. Weinbaum. London, Cambridge Univ. Press, 43, in-8, lxvii-241 p., 21s. R : J. Le Patourel, *Eng. hist. R.*, 44, vol. 59, p. 407-408.

569. WILLIAMS (G.). Language and the law. *L.Q.R.*, 45, vol. 61, p. 71-86, 179-195, 293-303, 384-406.

§ 8. Economic and Social History

570. MANN (D. de L.). List of books and articles on the economic history of Great Britain and Ireland. *Econ. Hist. R.*, 44, vol. 14, p. 208-213.

571. BRELSFORD (Vernon). Historical sociology : an introduction to social evolution and culture. London, Gifford, 43, in-8, 320 p., (tables), 8s. 6d. R : H.J.E.P., *Man*, 45, vol. 45, p. 116.

572. BROMEHEAD (C. E. N.). The early history of water-supply. *Geogr. J.*, 42, vol. 99, p. 142-151, 182-196.

573. BURKE (Thomas). The streets of London through the centuries, illustr. from prints, paintings, drawings and photographs. London,

Batsford, 40, in-8, viii-152 p., 10s. 6d. R : R. F. Jessup, *Antiq. J.*, 42, vol. 22, p. 147.

574. BURKE (T.). English night-life from Norman curfew to present blackout. London, Batsford, 41, in-8, ix-150 p., 81 plates, 10s. 6d. R : *National R.*, 42, vol. 118, p. 395.

575. BURKE (T.). Travel in England : from pilgrim and pack-horse to light car and plane. London, Batsford, 43, in-8, 154 p., 10s. 6d.

576. CLOUGH (Shepard Bancroft) and COLE (Charles Woolsey). Economic history of Europe. London, Harrap, 42, in-8, 842 p., (plates, maps), 18s. R : K. F. Helleiner, *Canad. J. Econ. pol. Sci.*, 42, vol. 8, p. 299-305.

577. DIETZ (Frederick C.). An economic history of England. Toronto, Clarke Irwin, 42, in-8, xii-616 p., $3.00. R : D. J. McDougall, *Canad. hist. R.*, 43, vol. 24, p. 300-301.

578. HOLE (Christina). English custom and usage. London, Batsford, 41, in-8, viii-151 p., (plates), 10s. 6d. R : P. J. Heather, *Man*, 43, vol. 43, p. 93-94.

579. LABOVITCH (M.). Clothes through the ages. London, Quality Press, 44, in-8, 128 p., (illus.), 10s.

580. LEEMING (J.). From barter to banking. The story of the world's coinage and money. London, Appleton, 40, in-8, xv-138 p., (illus.), 8s. 6d.

581. McCLINTOCK (H. F.). Old Irish and Highland dress, with notes on that of the Isle of Man. Dundalk, Tempest, 43, in-4, 188 p., (plates), 25s. R : G. S. Thomson, *Antiquity*, 45, vol. 19, p. 164-166. M. MacNeill, *Irish hist. Stud.*, 44, vol. 4, p. 117-119.

582. SCOTT (G. R.). The history of prostitution. London, Laurie, 41, in-8, 239 p., 12s. 6d.

583. SMITH (Robert Sidney). The Spanish guild merchant : a history of

the consulado, 1250-1700. London, Cambridge Univ. Press, 41, in-8, xii-168 p., 15s. R : R. Hammond, *Econ. Hist. R.*, 42, vol. 12, p. 97-98. J. H. Clapham, *Econ. J.*, 42, vol. 52, p. 75-76.

584. STARK (W.). The history of economics in its relation to social development, ed. by K. Mannheim. London, K. Paul, 44, in-8, 80 p., 7s. 6d.

585. TREVELYAN (G. M.). English social history : a survey of six centuries—Chaucer to Queen Victoria. London, Longmans, 44, in-8, 628 p., (maps), 21s. R : T. S. Ashton, *Econ. Hist. R.*, 44, vol. 14, p. 191-193. W.E.C.H., *Queen's Quar.*, 43, vol. 50, p. 211-213. D. J. McDougall, *Canad. hist. R.*, 43, vol. 24, p. 298-300. G. N. Clark, *Eng. hist. R.*, 45, vol. 60, p. 249-252. E. S. de Beer, *History*, 45, vol. 30, p. 99-102. J. Clapham, *Econ. J.*, 45, vol. 55, p. 82-83. D. Hudson, *National R.*, 45, vol. 124, p. 253-257.

586. USHER (Abbott Payson). The early history of deposit banking in Mediterranean Europe. Vol. 1. The structure and functions of the early credit system [&] Banking in Catalonia, 1240-1723. London, Oxford Univ. Press, 43, in-8, 672 p., 28s. R : E. V. Morgan, *Econ. J.*, 45, vol. 55, p. 269-271.

§ 9. History of Civilization, the Sciences and Education

587. COOPER (I. M.). Bibliography on educational broadcasting. London, Cambridge Univ. Press, 43, in-8, x-576 p., 30s.

588. GARRISON (Fielding H.). A medical bibliography : a check-list of texts illustrating the history of the medical sciences, revised by L. T. Morton. London, Grafton, 43, in-8, viii-412 p., 50s.

589. BOSSENBROOK (W. J.) and JOHANNSEN (R.). Foundations of western civilization. London, Heath, 40, in-8, xxi-695 p., (illus.), 12s. 6d.

590. CLARK (Grahame). Education and the study of man. *Antiquity*, 43, vol. 17, p. 113-121.

591. COLE (F. J.). A history of comparative anatomy : from Aristotle to the 18th century. London, Macmillan, 44, in-8, viii-524 p., (illus.), 30s.

592. COOLIDGE (J. L.). History of geometrical methods. London, Oxford Univ. Press, 40, in-8, 450 p., 30s.

593. DAMPIER (Sir W. C.). A history of science. Rev. ed. London, Cambridge Univ. Press, 42, in-8, xxiii-574 p., 25s. R : C. E. Raven, *Theology*, 42, vol. 45, p. 53-55. A. Wolf, *Philosophy*, 42, vol. 17, p. 368-369.

594. DAMPIER (Sir W. C.). A shorter history of science. London, Cambridge Univ. Press, 44, in-8, x-190 p., (plates, figs.), 7s. 6d.

595. DIRINGER (David). The origins of the alphabet. *Antiquity*, 43, vol. 17, p. 77-90 (illus.).

596. DRAPER (A.) and LOCKWOOD (M.). The story of astronomy. London, Allen & Unwin, 40, in-8, 394 p., (illus.), 12s. 6d.

597. ELKAN (Lucy). Lycurgus in the judgement of a German 18th-century humanist. *Greece and Rome*, 45, vol. 14, p. 82-86.

598. EMORY (Kenneth P.). Oceanian influence on American Indian culture. *J. polynesian Soc.*, 42, vol. 51, p. 126-135.

599. GARLICK (Phyllis L.). The wholeness of man : a study in the history of healing. James Long lectures for 1943. London, Highway Press, 43, in-8, 202 p., 10s. 6d. R : L. W. Grensted, *Int. R. Missions*, 43, vol. 32, p. 440-441. F. W. Camfield, *Theology*, 44, vol. 47, p. 139-140.

600. GUPPY (Henry). Human records : a survey of their history from the beginning. *B. John Rylands Library*, 42, vol. 27, p. 182-222.

601. GUTHRIE (Douglas). A history of medicine. London, Nelson, 45, in-8, 448 p., (illus.), 30s.

602. HARPER (N. D.). Some historical aspects of race and culture contact. *Hist. Stud. Australia N.Z.*, 44, vol. 3, p. 35-57.

603. JOHNSON (Humphrey J. T.). The Bible and the early history of mankind. London, Burns & Oates, 43, in-8, 69 p., 4s. 6d. R : A. R. Vidler, *Theology*, 43, vol. 46, p. 210-211.

604. KREMERS (E.) and URDANG (G.). History of pharmacy. London, Lippincott, 41, in-8, 466 p., (illus.), 25s.

605. LASKI (Harold J.). Faith, reason and civilisation : an essay in historical analysis. London, Gollancz, 44, in-8, 203 p., 6s. R : C. B. Macpherson, *Canad. J. Econ. pol. Sci.*, 45, vol. 11, p. 310-311.

606. LATIFF (Khan). A short history of the glorious Moslem civilization. Pt. 9-13 in 1 vol. London, Luzac, 42, in-8, iv-94 p., 10s. 6d. (Pearls of Sufistic lore).

607. MURPHY (John). The development of the civilized mind in the ancient civilizations. *Philosophy*, 42, vol. 17, p. 250-256.

608. MYRES (Sir John L.). Mediterranean culture. London, Cambridge Univ. Press, 43, in-8, 51 p., 3s. (Frazer lect., 1943). R : C. F. C. Hawkes, *Man*, 45, vol. 45, p. 116.

609. O'MALLEY (L. S. S.). Modern India and the West : a study of the interaction of their civilizations. London, Oxford Univ. Press, 41, in-8, xii-834 p., 36s. R : H.J.F., *Geography*, 42, vol. 27, p. 40. Sir R. Burn, *Int. Affairs*, 42, vol. 19, p. 380-382. C. R. Fay, *Econ. J.*, 42, vol. 52, p. 84-87.

610. PATZAK (V.). The Caroline university of Prague. *Slavonic Y.B.* (*Slavonic R.*), 40, vol. 19, p. 83-95.

611. PEATE (Iorwerth C.). The Welsh house : a study in folk culture. London, Hon. Soc. of Cymmrodorion, 40, in-8, xviii-232 p., (plates, maps), 15s. (Y Cymmrodor, vol. 47). R : A.E.R., *Man*, 41, vol. 41, p. 46-47. C. A. R. Radford, *Archaeol. cambrensis*, 41, vol. 96, p. 100-102. C. Fox, *Antiquity*, 40, vol. 14, p. 445-448.

612. PEATE (I. C.). Diwylliant gwerin Cymru. (The culture of the Welsh folk). Lerpwl, Evans, 42, in-8, xvi-154 p., (illus.), 7s. 6d.

613. ROBERTSON (Archibald). Morals in world history. London, Watts, 45, in-8, v-126 p., 8s. 6d. R : D. C. Somervell, *Int. Affairs*, 45, vol. 21, p. 525. H. D. Oakeley, *Hibbert J.*, 45, vol. 44, p. 92-93.

614. ROBINS (F. W.). The Ferry. *Antiquity*, 44, vol. 18, p. 123-129.

615. SINGER (Charles Joseph). A short history of science to the 19th century. London, Oxford Univ. Press, 41, in-8, 400 p., 8s. 6d.

616. SITWELL (S.). Primitive scenes and festivals. London, Faber, 42, in-8, 284 p., (illus.), 21s.

617. SUHR (E. G.). Two currents in the thought stream of Europe. London, Oxford Univ. Press, 42, in-8, 482 p., 22s. 6d.

618. TAYLOR (F. Sherwood). Science, past and present. London, Heinemann, 45, in-8, 284 p., (illus.), 10s. 6d.

619. THORNDIKE (Lynn). A history of magic and experimental science. Vol. 5-6. London, Oxford Univ. Press, 41, 2 vols. in-8, xxii-695, xviii-766 p., 133s. (Hist. of sci. soc., publ., n.s. 4). R : C. H. Desch, *Sociol. R.*, 43, vol. 35, p. 49-50.

620. TRIAL (G. T.). History of education in Iceland. Cambridge,

Heffer, 45, in-8, xii-96 p., (illus.), 10s. 6d.

621. WALKER (P. G.). An outline of man's history. Tillicoultry, N.C.L.C. Publ. Soc., 43, in-8, 272 p., (maps), 3s. (Outline ser.).

622. WOODWARD (A. M.). Greek history at the Renaissance. J. hell. Stud., 43, vol. 63, p. 1-14.

§ 10. History of the Arts and Archaeology

623. FARMER (Henry George). The sources of Arabian music. An annotated bibliography of Arabic manuscripts which deal with the theory, practice and history of Arabian music. Bearsden, Glasgow, The Author, 40, in-8, 100 p., (illus.), 10s. R : W.L., Musical Times, 40, vol. 81, p. 414-415. A. J. Arberry, J. asiatic Soc., 43, p. 133. B.L., J. central asian Soc., 43, vol. 30, p. 120.

624. ADAM (L.). Primitive art. London, Penguin, 40, in-8, 160 p., 6d. R : African Stud., 42, vol. 1, p. 155-156. R. Carline, Burlington Mag., 42, vol. 80, p. 51.

625. BATSFORD (H.) and FRY (C.). The cathedrals of England. New ed. London, Batsford, 42, in-8, 180 p., (illus.), 8s. 6d.

626. BIEBER (M.). Laocoon : the influence of the group since its discovery. London, Oxford Univ. Press, 42, in-4, 28 p., (illus.), 7s. 6d.

627. BLOM (Eric). Music in England. London, Penguin, 42, in-8, 220 p., 9d.

628. BROWN (C. K. F.). Treasures of the Surrey churches in the diocese of Guildford. Guildford, Biddles, 43, in-8, 76 p., 2s. 6d.

629. BUCHTHAL (Hugo). Indian fables in Islamic art. J. asiatic Soc., 41, p. 317-324 (plates).

630. BUCHTHAL (H.). The common classical sources of Buddhist and Christian narrative art. J. asiatic Soc., 43, p. 137-148 (plates).

631. CARLINE (Richard). The dating and provenance of negro art. Burlington Mag., 40, vol. 77, p. 115-123.

632. CHART (D. A.) ed. A preliminary survey of the ancient monuments of Northern Ireland. Belfast, H.M.S.O., 40, in-8, 268 p., 73 plates, 15s. R : W.H., Eng. hist. R., 40, vol. 55, p. 673.

633. CHILDE (V. G.). Progress and archaeology. London, Watts, 44, in-8, 96 p., 2s. 6d. (Thinker's libr.). R : C.T.S., African Stud., 45, vol. 4, p. 152-154.

634. COBB (G.). The old churches of London. London, Batsford, 42, in-8, 116 p., (plates), 15s. R : H. Hope-Nicholson, Burlington Mag., 42, vol. 81, p. 207-208. National R., 42, vol. 119, p. 89.

635. CROSSLEY (F. H.). English church craftsmanship, 1100-1800 A.D. London, Batsford, 41, in-8, viii-120 p., 224 plates, 8s. 6d. (Brit. heritage ser.).

636. CROSSLEY (F. H.). An introduction to the study of screens and lofts in Wales and Monmouthshire, with especial reference to their design, provenance and influence. Pt. 1 : General introduction. Archaeol. cambrensis, 43, vol. 97, p. 135-160 (illus.).

637. DANIEL (G. E.). The three ages : an essay on archaeological method. London, Cambridge Univ. Press, 43, in-8, 60 p., 3s. 6d.

638. EAST INDIAN SCULPTURE from the first century of our Christian era to the 18th century. London, Luzac, 40, in-8, 23 p., (illus.), 5s. (Toledo, Ohio, museum of art).

639. EVANS (Joan). Time and chance : the story of Arthur Evans and his forbears. London, Longmans, 43, in-8, xi-410 p., (illus.), 21s. R :

Quar. R., 43, vol. 281, p. 249-250. R.M.D., *J. hell. Stud.*, 43, vol. 63, p. 121. O. G. S. C[rawford], *Antiquity*, 43, vol. 17, p. 215-216.

640. FARMER (H. G.). Sa'adyah Gaon on the influence of music. London, Probsthain, 43, in-4, xi-109 p., (facs.), 21s.

641. FIELD (Henry) and PROSTOV (Eugene). Archaeology in the Soviet Union. *Antiquity*, 40, vol. 14, p. 404-426.

642. FLETCHER (B.). A history of architecture on the comparative method. Rev. ed. London, Batsford, 43, in-8, xxx-1,033 p., (illus.), 52s. 6d.

643. FOX (Aileen). The place of archaeology in British education. *Antiquity*, 44, vol. 18, p. 153-157.

644. FRERE (S. S. and D. H. S.). Archaeology and education. *History*, 42, vol. 27, p. 97-110.

645. FYFE (T.). Architecture in Cambridge. Examples of English architectural styles from Saxon to modern times. London, Cambridge Univ. Press, 42, in-8, xiv-120 p., (illus., figures), 8s. 6d.

646. GEIRINGER (Karl). Musical instruments, their history from the Stone age to the present day, tr. by B. Miall. London, Allen & Unwin, 43, in-8, 339 p., (illus.), 25s. (Phaidon Press art books).

647. GRAY (W. F.). Historic churches of Edinburgh. Edinburgh, Grant & Murray, 40, in-8, 184 p., 6s.

648. HAKE (H. M.). The English historic portrait : document and myth. London, Oxford Univ. Press, 44, in-8, 20 p., 2s. 6d.

649. JACOBSTHAL (Paul). Imagery in early Celtic art. London, Oxford Univ. Press, 42, in-8, 25 p., (illus.), 6s. (Sir John Rhys mem. lect.). R : J. M. de Navarro, *J. rom. Stud.*, 43, vol. 33, p. 112-113.

650. JACOBSTHAL (P.). Early Celtic art. London, Oxford Univ. Press, 44, 2 vols. in-2, 256 p., 279 plates, 210s. R : E. T. L(eeds), *Antiq. J.*, 45, vol. 25, p. 159-162.

651. JONES (E. A.). Catalogue of the plate of Oriel College, Oxford. London, Oxford Univ. Press, 45, in-4, 124 p., (illus.), 50s.

652. LIPMAN (Jean). American primitive painting. London, Oxford Univ. Press, 42, in-2, 158 p., (plates), 30s.

653. LONG (E. T.). An introduction to Dorset church architecture. *J. archaeol. Assoc.*, 39 (40), vol. 4, p. 1-38.

654. LONGFIELD (Ada K.). Some tapestry makers in Ireland. *Burlington Mag.*, 44, vol. 85, p. 250-257.

655. MANN (J. G.). The etched decoration of armour : a study in classification. London, Oxford Univ. Press, 44, in-8, 31 p., (plates, figs.), 9s. 6d.

656. MINNS (Sir Ellis H.). The art of the northern nomads. London, Oxford Univ. Press, 44, in-4, 54 p., 28 plates, 10s. 6d. (Brit. Acad., Hertz trust lect., 1942). R : J. L. Myres, *Class. R.*, 45, vol. 59, p. 22-23.

657. MOREY (C. R.). Early Christian art. London, Oxford Univ. Press, 42, in-4, 292 p., (illus.), 37s. 6d. R : H. Buchthal, *Class. R.*, 43, vol. 57, p. 121-124.

658. NEWMARCH (Rosa). The music of Czechoslovakia. London, Oxford Univ. Press, 42, in-8, 244 p., 8s. 6d.

659. NITCHIE (Elizabeth). The Reverend Colonel Finch. London, Oxford Univ. Press, 40, in-8, 109 p., (plates), 10s. R : E. J. Morley, *Mod. Language R.*, 41, vol. 36, p. 536-537.

660. PERKINS (J. B. Ward). Medieval and early Renaissance architecture in Malta. *Antiq. J.*, 42, vol. 22, p. 167-175 (illus.).

661. PERKINS (J. T.). The cathedrals of Normandy. New ed. London, Methuen, 42, in-8, 16 plates, 9s. 6d.

662. PEVSNER (N.). Academies of art, past and present. London, Cambridge Univ. Press, 40, in-4, xiv-323 p., (illus.), 23s.

663. PORTER (E.). Music : a short history. London, Hutchinson, 40, in-8, 254 p., (illus.), 10s. 6d.

664. POWELL-COTTON (P. H. G.) and PINFOLD (G. F.). The Beck find. Prehistoric and Roman site on the foreshore at Minnis Bay. Report and catalogue. *Archaeol. cantiana*, 39 (40), vol. 51, p. 191-203.

665. PRUNIÈRES (Henri). A new history of music : the Middle Ages to Mozart, tr. from the French by E. Lockspeiser. London, Dent, 43, in-8, 414 p., 21s.

666. PUYVELDE (Leo van). The Flemish drawings in the collection of His Majesty the King at Windsor Castle. London, Oxford Univ. Press, 42, in-4, 62 p., 108 illus., 17s. 6d. (Phaidon press art books). R : H. Hope-Nicholson, *Burlington Mag.*, 43, vol. 83, p. 181-182.

667. PUYVELDE (L. van). The Dutch drawings in the collection of His Majesty the King at Windsor Castle. London, Allen & Unwin, 44, in-4, 78 p., (illus.), 25s.

668. RACKHAM (Bernard). Catalogue of Italian maiolica in the Victoria and Albert Museum. Text and plates. London, H.M.S.O., 40, 2 vols. in-4, xxiii-485, xxvii-222 plates, 28s. 6d.

669. ROBERTSON (D. S.) A handbook of Greek and Roman architecture. 2nd ed. London, Cambridge Univ. Press, 43, in-8, xxvi-480 p., (plates, figs.), 18s.

670. RUSSELL (A. L. N.). Westminster Abbey : the story of its building and its life. London, Chatto & Windus, 43, in-8, 94 p., 1s. 6d.

671. SACHS (C.). History of musical instruments. London, Dent, 42, in-8, 504 p., (illus.), 36s.

672. ST. JOSEPH (J. K.). Air photography and archaeology. *Geogr. J.*, 45, vol. 105, p. 47-61.

673. SCHOLES (P. A.). A miniature history of music. London, Oxford Univ. Press, 42, in-8, 53 p., 1s. 6d.

674. SCHOLES (P. A.). The listener's history of music. 3rd ed. Vol. 3. London, Oxford Univ. Press, 43, in-8, 180 p., (illus.), 6s.

675. SIMPSON (William Douglas). The Province of Mar. Rhind lect. in archaeol., 1941. Aberdeen, Univ. Press, 43, in-4, xi-167 p., (plates), 10s. 6d. (Aberdeen Univ. stud., 121). R : W.P.H., *Eng. hist. R.*, 45, vol. 60, p. 267. A. Fox, *Archaeol. cambrensis*, 44, vol. 98, p. 148-150. I. A. Richmond, *Antiq. J.*, 44, vol. 24, p. 72-74.

676. SWIFT (E. H.). Hagia Sophia. London, Oxford Univ. Press, 41, in-2, xvii-265 p., (plates), 50s. R : T.F., *J. hell. Stud.*, 42 (43), vol. 62, p. 110-111.

677. TRENDALL (Arthur Dale). Guide to the casts of Greek and Roman sculpture, Nicholson Museum, University of Sydney. Sydney, Nicholson Museum, 41, in-8, 108 p., 2s. R : J. S. W. Webb, *Hist. Stud. Australia N.Z.*, 42, vol. 2, p. 62-63.

678. TSUI CHI. Chinese influence on English art. *Asiatic R.*, 43, vol. 39, p. 195-199.

679. VALE (Edmund). Ancient England, a review of monuments and remains in public care and ownership. London, Batsford, 41, in-8, viii-151 p., (plates), 10s. 6d. R : A. Graham, *Antiquity*, 42, vol. 16, p. 278-280.

680. VAYSON DE PRADENNE (A.). The early art of northern Europe. *Antiquity*, 40, vol. 14, p. 182-192.

681. WILENSKI (R. H.). A miniature history of European art. 2nd, rev. ed. London, Oxford Univ. Press, 45, in-8, 106 p., (illus.), 6s.

682. WOLF (A.). The Edward P. Greene collection of engraved portraits and drawings at Yale University, ed. by T. Sizer. London, Oxford Univ. Press, 42, in-4, 142 p., (plates), 22s. 6d.

683. WOODRUFF (H.). The index of Christian church art, ed. by C. R. Morey. London, Oxford Univ. Press, 42, in-8, 93 p., 4s. 6d.

§ 11. Religious History

a. GENERAL

684. ADDISON (James Thayer). The Christian approach to the Moslem, a historical study. London, Oxford Univ. Press, 42, in-8, 375 p., 18s. 6d. R : G. W. Broomfield, *Theology*, 45, vol. 48, p. 138-139.

685. ALINGTON (C. A.). Christianity in England : an historical sketch. London, Oxford Univ. Press, 42, in-8, 191 p., 4s.

686. ALLARD (S. L.). and CROSSE (G.). A dictionary of English church history. New ed. London, Mowbray, 43, in-8, 676 p., 15s.

687. BAKER (Archibald G.) ed. A short history of Christianity, by A. G. Baker (ed.), M. H. Shepherd, jr., J. T. McNeill, M. Spinka, W. E. Garrison, W. W. Sweet. London, Cambridge Univ. Press, 41, in-8, vii-279 p., 12s. R : K. S. Latourette, *Int. R. Missions*, 41, vol. 30, p. 264-266.

688. BETTENSON (H.) ed. Documents of the Christian church. London, Oxford Univ. Press, 43, in-8, 474 p., 3s. (World's classics).

689. BLAIKIE (W. G.). A manual of Bible history, rev. by C. D. Matthews. London, Nelson, 40, in-8, 432 p., 10s. 6d.

690. CADOUX (C. J.). The historic mission of Jesus, a constructive re-examination of the eschatological teaching in the synoptic Gospels. London, R.T.S., 41, in-8, xxiv-376 p., 21s. (Lutterworth libr., vol. 12). R : A. J. Grieve, *Congreg. Quar.*, 42, vol. 20, p. 260-261. H. H. Rowley, *Baptist Quar.*, 42, vol. 11, p. 60-63. H. G. Wood, *Hibbert J.*, 42, vol. 40, p. 393-395.

691. DAVIES (D. R.). Divine judgment in human history. London, S.P.C.K., 43, in-8, 64 p., 1s. 6d. (Christian newsletter ser.).

692. FARROW (John). Pageant of the Popes. London, Sheed & Ward, 43, in-8, 424 p., (illus.), 16s.

693. FOSTER (John). Then and now: the historic church and the younger churches, ed. by K. S. Latourette. London, Student Christian Movement, 42, in-8, 188 p., 6s. R : E. R. Morgan, *Int. R. Missions*, 42, vol. 31, p. 357-359.

694. GOODSPEED (E. J.). A history of early Christian literature. London, Cambridge Univ. Press, 42, in-8, xiv-324 p., 15s.

695. HANDASYDE (A. K.). God's book shelf : the history of faith and fear. London, Allenson, 43, in-8, 112 p., 3s. 6d.

696. HARDY (Edward Rochie) jr. Militant in earth; 20 centuries of the spread of Christianity. London, Oxford Univ. Press, 40, in-8, vii-255 p., (maps), 12s. 6d. R : K. S. Latourette, *Int. R. Missions*, 41, vol. 30, p. 264-266. C. S. Phillips, *Theology*, 41, vol. 43, p. 185-186.

697. HARDY (E. R.) jr. Christianity and history. *Theology*, 40, vol. 40, p. 14-25, 104-111.

698. HUGHES (P.). A popular history of the Catholic Church. London, Burns, Oates, 40, in-8, xiv-294 p., 7s. 6d.

699. HYMA (Albert). Christianity and politics, a history of the principles and struggles of church and state. London, Lippincott, 40, in-8, 331 p., 15s. R : N. Micklem, *Int. Affairs*, 41, vol. 19, p. 201-202.

700. KELLY (B.). Short survey of church history. London, Virtue, 44, in-8, 114 p., 2s. 6d.

701. KENYON (F.). The Bible and archaeology. London, Harrap, 40, in-8, 310 p., (illus.), 15s.

702. LATOURETTE (Kenneth Scott). Indigenous Christianity in the light of history. *Int. R. Missions*, 40, vol. 29, p. 429-440.

703. LEVONIAN (Lootfy). Studies in the relationship between Islam and Christianity, psychological and historical. London, Allen and Unwin, 40, in-8, 158 p., 6s. R : H. Gray, *Int. Affairs*, 40, vol. 19, p. 112-113. L. E. Browne, *Int. R. Missions*, 41, vol. 30, p. 149-150.

704. NUTTALL (Geoffrey F.). History and church history. *Congreg. Quar.*, 41, vol. 19, p. 125-131.

705. O'DOHERTY (J. F.). A history of the Catholic Church. Dublin, National Press, 44, in-8, xix-294 p., (maps), 3s. 9d.

706. OLMSTEAD (A. T.). Jesus in the light of history. London, Scribners, 42, in-8, 316 p., 10s. 6d. R : H. I. Bell, *J. asiatic Soc.*, 43, p. 274-277. S. Cave, *Congreg. Quar.*, 43, vol. 21, p. 73-74.

707. OTTO (Rudolf). The Kingdom of God and the Son of Man : a study in the history of religion, tr. by F. V. Filson and B. Lee-Woolf. New ed. London, Lutterworth Press, 43, in-8, 408 p., 18s. (Lutterworth libr., 9). R : G. O. Williams, *Theology*, 43, vol. 46, p. 161-162.

708. PAUL (Francis J.). Romanism and evangelical Christianity : a study of origins and development. London, Hodder, 40, in-8, 503 p., 16s. R : R. Cant, *Theology*, 40, vol. 41, p. 256.

709. PAYNE (E. A.) ed Studies in history and religion. Redhill, Lutterworth Press, 42, in-8, 272 p., 21s.

710. QUALBEN (L. P.). A history of the Christian church. London, Nelson, 40, in-8, 644 p., 12s. 6d.

711. SAMPSON (Ashley). Famous English sermons, 730-1939. London, Nelson, 40, in-8, 383 p., 5s. R : C. Smyth, *Theology*, 41, vol. 43, p. 251-252.

712. SMYTH (Charles). The art of preaching, 747-1939. London, S.P.C.K., 40, in-8, xii-257 p., 8s. 6d. R : A. C. Scupholme, *Theology*, 40, vol. 40, p. 310-311.

713. STANFORD (W. B.). Christianity and the classics. *Greece and Rome*, 44, vol. 13, p. 1-9.

714. SYKES (Norman). The study of ecclesiastical history. London, Cambridge Univ. Press, 45, in-8, 32 p., 1s. 6d. R : A. R. Vidler, *Theology*, 45, vol. 48, p. 261-262.

715. TEMPLE (William). Christianity as an interpretation of history. London, Longmans, 45, in-8, 22 p., 1s.

716. WATSON (E. W.). The Church of England. 2nd ed. London, Oxford Univ. Press, 44, in-8, 192 p., 3s. 6d. (Home Univ. libr.).

717. WATT (Margaret H.). History of the parson's wife. London, Faber, 43, in-8, 200 p., 8s. 6d. R : M. Maxse, *National R.*, 43, vol. 121, p. 77-81.

b. MONOGRAPHS

718. ARBERRY (A. J.). An introduction to the history of Ṣūfism. London, Longmans, 43, in-8, 84 p., 7s. 6d. (Sir A. Suhrawardy lectures for 1942). R : M. Smith, *J. central asian Soc.*, 43, vol. 30, p. 327-328.

719. BARKER (J.). Sacrificial priesthood : historical origins and development. London, Dacre Press, 41, in-8, 40 p., 1s. 6d.

720. BELLAMY (H. S.). The book of Revelation is history. London, Faber, 42, in-8, 204 p., 8s. 6d. R : P. de D. May, *Theology*, 42, vol. 45, p. 236-237. A. J. Grieve, *Congreg. Quar.*, 43, vol. 21, p. 74-75.

721. BEVAN (Edwyn). Holy images' an enquiry into idolatry and image-worship in ancient paganism and in Christianity. London, Allen and Unwin, 40, in-8, 184 p., 7s. 6d. R : A. C. Underwood, *Int. R. Missions*, 40, vol. 29, p. 402-404. E.P.B., *Archaeol. J.*, 39 (40), vol. 96, p. 304-305. E. O. James, *Man*, 41, vol. 41, p. 23. W. L. Knox, *Theology*, 41, vol. 42, p. 126-127.

722. BROWN (Arthur C. L.). The origin of the Grail legend. London, Oxford Univ. Press, 43, in-8, 488 p., 28s. R : W. J. Gruffydd, *Mod. Language R.*, 44, vol. 39, p. 202-203.

723. BUTTERWORTH (Charles C.). The literary lineage of the King James Bible, 1340-1611. London, Oxford Univ. Press, 41, in-8, xi-394 p., 16s. R : B. J. Roberts, *Mod. Language R.*, 43, vol. 38, p. 142-143.

724. CHENCHIAH (P.), CHAKKARAI (V.) and SUDARISANAM (A. N.). Asramas, past and present. Madras, Indian Christian Book Club, 41, in-8, Rs. 2. R : N. Macnicol, *Int. R. Missions*, 42, vol. 31, p. 130-132.

725. COUGHLIN (James F.). Ukrainians, their rite, history and religious destiny. *Canad. Cath. hist. Assoc. Rept.*, 43-44, vol. 11, Engl. Sect., p. 19-33.

726. CUTNER (H.). A short history of sex-worship. London, Watts, 40, in-8, xiii-222 p., 8s. 6d.

727. DARK (S.). Seven archbishops. London, Eyre & Spottiswoode, 44, in-8, 238 p., 12s. 6d. R : V. H. H. Green, *Theology*, 44, vol. 47, p. 259-261.

728. DAVIES (J. Conway). The records of the church in Wales. *Nat. Library Wales J.*, 45, vol. 4, p. 1-34.

729. DIX (Gregory). A detection of aumbries, with other notes on the history of reservation. London, Dacre, 42, in-8, 72 p., 3s. 6d. R : E. C. Ratcliff, *Theology*, 43, vol. 46, p. 14-16.

730. DUGMORE (C. W.). The influence of the synagogue upon the Divine office. London, Oxford Univ. Press, 44, in-8, ix-151 p., 10s. 6d.

731. EDWARDS (Douglas). The Virgin birth in history and faith. London, Faber, 43, in-8, 240 p., 12s. 6d. R : A. Richardson, *Theology*, 43, vol. 46, p. 160-161.

732. ENGLAND (H. G.). The godhood and manhood of Jesus : a positive re-statement of an historic dogma. *Hibbert J.*, 44, vol. 43, p. 55-62.

733. HENNING (W. B.). The Manichaean fasts. *J. asiatic Soc.*, 45, p. 146-164.

734. KRAEMER (Hendrik). The riddle of history : thoughts on Romans IX-XI. *Int. R. Missions*, 43, vol. 32, p. 78-87.

735. KRAUSS (Samuel). Two hitherto unknown Bible versions in Greek. *B. John Rylands Library*, 42, vol. 27, p. 97-105.

736. LANGTON (Edward). Good and evil spirits : a study of the Jewish and Christian doctrine, its origin and development. London, S.P.C.K., 42, in-8, xvi-324 p., 15s. R : C. Williams, *Theology*, 42, vol. 45, p. 232-234. W. A. L. Elmslie, *Int. R. Missions*, 43, vol. 32, p. 106-108.

737. MARETT (R. R.). Cave worship. *Hibbert J.*, 40, vol. 38, p. 298-306.

738. MORISON (Stanley). English prayer books, an introduction to the literature of Christian public worship. London, Cambridge Univ. Press, 43, in-8, viii-142 p., 6s. (Problems of Worship, vol. 1). R : R.S.K.S., *Queen's Quar.*, 45, vol. 52, p. 242. J. F. Gerrard, *Library*, 45, vol. 26, p. 204-206.

739. PERKINS (Jocelyn). Westminster Abbey, its worship and ornaments. Vol. 2. London, Oxford Univ. Press, 40, in-4, 215 p., (plates), 25s. (Alcuin Club coll., 34). R : A. S. G. Butler, *19th Century*, 40, vol. 128, p. 518-519. A. Oswald, *Burlington Mag.*, 40, vol. 76, p. 201.

740. RATCLIFF (E. C.). On the rite of the inthronization of bishops and archbishops. *Theology*, 42, vol. 45, p. 71-82.

741. REMBAO (Alberto). Prehispanic religion in modern Mexico. *Int. R. Missions*, 42, vol. 31, p. 163-171.

742. RIOS (Romanus). Monte Cassino, 529-1944. *B. John Rylands Library*, 45, vol. 29, p. 49-68.

743. ROBERTSON (Edward). The riddle of the Torah : suggesting a solution. *B. John Rylands Library*, 43, vol. 27, p. 359-383.

744. ROBINSON (H. Wheeler) ed. The Bible in its ancient and English versions. London, Oxford Univ. Press, 40, in-8, vii-337 p., 12s. 6d. R : C. S. Phillips, *Theology*, 41, vol. 42, p. 244. E. A. Payne, *Baptist Quar.*, 41, vol. 10, p. 290-291.

745. ROBINSON (H. W.). Redemption and revelation in the actuality of history. London, Nisbet, 42, in-8, 312 p., 12s. 6d. (Libr. of constructive theology). R : E. L. Mascall, *Theology*, 43, vol. 46, p. 42-44. L. A. Garrard, *Hibbert J.*, 43, vol. 41, p. 190-191.

746. ZUNTZ (G.). The ancestry of the Harklean New Testament. London, Oxford Univ. Press, 45, in-8, 128 p., 12s. 6d. (Brit. Acad., suppl. papers 7).

§ 12. History of Philosophy

747. BOGARDUS (E. S.). The development of social thought. London, Longmans, 40, in-8, viii-564 p., 18s.

749. ELLIS (William). The idea of the soul in western philosophy and science. London, Allen, 40, in-8, 314 p., 12s. 6d. R : *Baptist Quar.*, 40, vol. 10, p. 237-238.

750. FOSTER (Michael B.). Masters of political thought. Vol. 1 : Plato to Machiavelli. London, Harrap, 42, in-8, ix-302 p., 10s. 6d. R : *History*, 43, vol. 28, p. 110.

751. FURFEY (P. H.). A history of social thought. London, Macmillan, 43, in-8, xiii-468 p., 14s.

752. GILBERT (K. E.) and KUHN (H.). A history of esthetics. London, Macmillan, 40, in-8, xxii-582 p., 18s.

753. ROGERS (C. F.). Prediction in the light of history and religion. London, S.C.M., 42, in-8, 63 p., 1s. 3d.

§ 13. History of Literature

754. Cambridge bibliography of English literature, ed. by F. W. Bateson. London, Cambridge Univ. Press, 40, 4 vols. in-8, xxxvii-912; xviii-1003; xix-1098 ; 287 p., 147s. R : F. C. Francis, *Library*, 42, vol. 22, p. 250-255.

755. HARBAGE (Alfred). Annals of English drama, 975-1700. An analytical record of all plays, extant or lost, chronologically arranged and indexed by authors, titles, dramatic companies, &c. London, Oxford Univ. Press, 41, in-4, 264 p., 14s.

756. KENNEDY (A. G.). A concise bibliography for students of English. London, Oxford Univ. Press, 45, in-8, 170 p., 9s. 6d.

757. Arrom (J. J.). Historia de la literatura dramatica cubana. London, Oxford Univ. Press, 44, in-8, 144 p., 16s. 6d.

758. Bisson (L. A.). Des vers de France : a short history of French literature. Harmondsworth, Penguin, 43, 2 vols. in-8, 140, 160 p., 1s. 6d. R : L. W. Tancock and W. J. Entwistle, *Mod. Language R.*, 44, vol. 39, p. 302-304.

760. Chadwick (H. M. and N. K.). The growth of literature. Vol. 3. London, Cambridge Univ. Press, 40, in-8, xxvi-928 p., 35s. R : W. J. Entwistle, *Mod. Language R.*, 40, vol. 35, p. 547-549. H. J. Rose, *Man*, 40, vol. 40, p. 143.

761. Chambers (R. W.). Poets and their critics : Langland and Milton. London, Oxford Univ. Press, 42, in-8, 48 p., 3s. 6d.

762. Drinkwater (John). The outline of literature, rev. by H. Pollock and C. Nairne. London, Harrap, 42, in-8, 1010 p., (plates), 12s. 6d.

763. Entwistle (William J.) and Gillett (Eric). The literature of England, A.D. 500-1942. London, Longmans, 43, in-8, 292 p., 7s. 6d.

764. Evans (B. Ifor). Tradition and Romanticism. Studies in English poetry from Chaucer to W. B. Yeats. London, Methuen, 40, in-8, 213 p., 6s.

765. Gassner (John). Masters of the drama. Toronto, Macmillan, 40, in-8, xvii-804 p., $4.25. R : W.A., *Queen's Quar.*, 40, vol. 47, p. 484-485.

766. Grierson (H. J. C.) and Smith (J. C.). A critical history of English poetry. London, Chatto & Windus, 44, in-8, 528 p., 21s.

767. Martin (R. H.). The golden age and the cyclical theory in Greek and Latin literature. *Greece and Rome*, 43, vol. 12, p. 62-71.

768. Murphy (John). The primitive character of poetic genius. *Man*, 42, vol. 42, p. 37-41.

769. Sampson (George). The concise Cambridge history of English literature. London, Cambridge Univ. Press, 41, in-8, xiv-1094 p., 15s. R : B. G. Brooks, *19th Century*, 41, vol. 130, p. 300-301. E. C. Batho, *Mod. Language R.*, 42, vol. 37, p. 491-493.

770. Trevelyan (Humphrey). Goethe and the Greeks. London, Cambridge Univ. Press, 41, in-8, xvi-322 p., 18s. R : V. Ehrenberg, *J. hell. Stud.*, 42 (43), vol. 62, p. 92-93.

771. Waterhouse (Gilbert). A short history of German literature. London, Methuen, 42, in-8, 160 p., 6s. R : W. H. Bruford, *Mod. Language R.*, 43, vol. 38, p. 170.

772. Wellek (René). The rise of English literary history. London, Oxford Univ. Press, 41, in-8, vii-275 p., 18s. 6d. R : E. J. Sweeting, *Mod. Language R.*, 43, vol. 38, p. 359.

C

PRE-HISTORY

§ 1. General

773. CHILDE (V. Gordon). Prehistoric communities of the British Isles. London, Chambers, 40, in-8, 304 p., (illus.), 20s. R : C. F. C. Hawkes, *Man*, 41, vol. 41, p. 37-38. D. P. Dobson, *History*, 41, vol. 25, p. 357-358. M.D., *Geography*, 41, vol. 26, p. 94. E. C. Curwen, *Antiquity*, 41, vol. 15, p. 203-206. S. Piggott, *Proc. prehist. Soc.*, 41, vol. 7, p. 148-150. Sir C. Fox, *Antiq. J.*, 41, vol. 21, p. 165-168. G. Clark, *J. rom. Stud.*, 42, vol. 32, p. 140-142.

774. CHILDE (V. G.). War in prehistoric societies. *Sociol. R.*, 41, vol. 33, p. 126-138.

775. CHILDE (V. G.). What happened in history. London, Penguin, 42, in-8, 256 p., 9d. R : J. L. Myres, *Man*, 44, vol. 44, p. 27-28. B.D.M., *African Stud.*, 44, vol. 3, p. 148-149. O. G. S. C[rawford], *Antiquity*, 43, vol. 17, p. 101-103.

776. CHILDE (V. G.). Archaeology in the U.S.S.R., the forest zone. *Man*, 43, vol. 43, p. 4-9.

777. CHILDE (V. G.). Rotary querns on the continent and in the Mediterranean basin. *Antiquity*, 43, vol. 17, p. 19-26 (illus.).

778. CHILDE (V. G.). Recent excavations on prehistoric sites in Soviet Russia. *Man*, 44, vol. 44, p. 41-43.

779. CHILDE (V. G.). Directional changes in funerary practices during 50,000 years. *Man*, 45, vol. 45, p. 13-19.

780. CLARK (Grahame). Prehistoric England. London, Batsford, 40, in-8, 128 p., 8s. 6d. R : J. F. Nichols, *History*, 41, vol. 26, p. 70-71. *National R.*, 41, vol. 116, p. 495-496. M.D.,

Geography, 41, vol. 26, p. 148. A.D.L., *Antiq. J.*, 41, vol. 21, p. 349-350. P.C., *Geogr. J.*, 41, vol. 97, p. 254. C. W. Phillips, *Burlington Mag.*, 42, vol. 80, p. 52.

781. CLARK (G.). Horses and battleaxes. *Antiquity*, 41, vol. 15, p. 50-70 (illus.).

782. CLARK (G.). Bees in antiquity. *Antiquity*, 42, vol. 16, p. 208-215.

783. CLARK (G.). Water in antiquity. *Antiquity*, 44, vol. 18, p. 1-15.

784. CLARK (W. E. Le Gros). Pithecanthropus in Peking. *Antiquity*, 45, vol. 19, p. 1-5.

785. CLIFFORD (E. M.) and DANIEL (G. E.). The Rodmarton and Avening portholes. *Proc. prehist. Soc.*, 40, vol. 6, p. 133-165.

786. COLEMAN (A. P.). The last million years : a history of the pleistocene in North America, ed. by G. F. Kay. London, Oxford Univ. Press, 41, in-8, xii-216 p., (maps), 16s. R : O. T. Jones, *Geogr. J.*, 42, vol. 99, p. 267-271.

787. CURWEN (E. C.). The significance of the pentatonic scale in Scottish song. *Antiquity*, 40, vol. 14, p. 347-362.

788. DANIEL (Glyn E.). The dual nature of the megalithic colonisation of prehistoric Europe. *Proc. prehist. Soc.*, 41, vol. 7, p. 1-49 (illus.).

789. DANIEL (G. E.). The three ages : an essay on archaeological method. London, Cambridge Univ. Press, 43, in-8, 59 p., 3s. 6d.

790. DIKAIOS (P.). New light on prehistoric Cyprus. *Iraq*, 40, vol. 7, pt. 1, p. 69-83.

791. DIKSHIT (K. N.). Prehistoric civilization of the Indus valley. London, Luzac, 40, in-8, 60 p., (illus.), 4s. (Sir W. Meyer lecture, 1935).

792. ETTLINGER (Ellen). Omens and Celtic warfare. *Man*, 43, vol. 43, p. 11-17.

793. Fox (Sir Cyril). The personality of Britain : its influence on inhabitant and invader in prehistoric and early historic times. 4th ed., revised. Cardiff, National Museum of Wales, 43, in-8, 99 p., (maps, plates), 5s. R : E.E.E., *Antiq. J.*, 43, vol. 23, p. 165-166. E. G. R. Taylor, *Antiquity*, 44, vol. 18, p. 103.

794. GARNETT (Alice). The loess regions of Central Europe in prehistoric times. *Geogr. J.*, 45, vol. 106, p. 132-143.

795. GARROD (D. A. E.). Excavations at the cave of Shukbah, Palestine, 1928. With an appendix on the fossil mammals of Shukbah, by D. M. A. Bate. *Proc. prehist. Soc.*, 42, n.s., vol. 8, p. 1-20 (plates).

796. GRIMES (W. F.). Early man and the soils of Anglesey. *Antiquity*, 45, vol. 19, p. 169-174.

797. MATHIASSEN (Therkel). Prehistory in Denmark, 1939-1945. *Proc. prehist. Soc.*, 45, vol. 11, p. 61-65.

798. NEELY (G. J. H.). Excavations at Ronaldsway, Isle of Man. *Antiq. J.*, 40, vol. 20, p. 72-86 (illus.).

799. NORTH (F. J.). Paviland cave, the ' Red Lady ', the deluge, and William Buckland. *A. Sci.*, 42, vol. 5, p. 91-128.

800. OAKLEY (K. P.). A note on the late post-glacial submergence of the Solent margin. *Proc. prehist. Soc.*, 43, vol. 9, p. 56-59.

801. Ó RÍORDÁIN (Seán P.). Antiquities of the Irish countryside. Cork, Univ. Press, 42, in-8, 57 p., 5s. (Hist. and archaeol. papers, 4). R : K. B. Nowlan, *Irish hist. Stud.*, 45, vol. 4, p. 284-285.

802. PEAKE (Harold J. E.). The fencing of early tombs. *Man*, 44, vol. 44, p. 58-60.

802a. PERKINS (J. B. Ward). Problems of Maltese prehistory. *Antiquity*, 42, vol. 16, p. 19-35 (illus.).

803. PIGGOTT (Stuart). A trepanned skull of the Beaker period from Dorset and the practice of trepanning in prehistoric Europe. *Proc. prehist. Soc.*, 40, vol. 6, p. 112-132.

804. PIGGOTT (S. and C. M.). Excavations at Rams Hill, Uffington, Berks. *Antiq. J.*, 40, vol. 20, p. 465-480 (illus.).

805. PLANT (Edith). Man's unwritten past. London, Oxford Univ. Press, 42, in-8, 262 p., (illus.), 5s. (Realms of natural sci.). R : D. P. Dobson, *Antiquity*, 43, vol. 17, p. 109-110.

806. RICHARDSON (K. M.). Excavations at Poundbury, Dorchester, Dorset, 1939. *Antiq. J.*, 40, vol. 20, p. 429-448 (illus.).

807. ROUSE (I.). Prehistory in Haiti. London, Oxford Univ. Press, 40, in-8, 202 p., (plates), 11s. 6d.

808. SCHAEFFER (Claude F. A.). In the wake of the ' Argo '. *Man*, 44, vol. 44, p. 43-44.

809. TOCHER (J. F.). The Book of Buchan (jubilee volume), ed. by J. F. Tocher. Aberdeen, Buchan Club, 43, in-8, 21s. R : W. D. Simpson, *Antiquity*, 44, vol. 18, p. 163-164.

810. VARLEY (W. J.) and JACKSON (J. W.). Prehistoric Cheshire. Chester, Cheshire Rural Community Council, 40, in-8, 116 p., (maps), 4s. 6d. (Handbooks to the hist. of Cheshire 1). R : M.D., *Geography*, 41, vol. 26, p. 147.

811. VAYSON DE PRADENNE (A.). Prehistory, tr. E. F. Row. London, Harrap, 40, in-8, 239 p., 6s. R : V. G. Childe, *Antiquity*, 40, vol. 14, p. 451-452.

812. WAINWRIGHT (G. A.). Early tin in the Aegean. *Antiquity*, 44, vol. 18, p. 57-64.

814. WHEELER (R. E. M.). Maiden Castle, Dorset. London, Quaritch, 43, in-4, xx-399 p., (illus., maps), 30s. (Soc. of antiq. of London, research comm. repts., 12). R : C. F. C. Hawkes, *J. rom. Stud.*, 44, vol. 34, p. 155-157. W. F. Grimes, *Antiquity*, 45, vol. 19, p. 6-10.

§ 2. Palaeolithic and Mesolithic Ages

815. ARKELL (W. J.). Three Oxfordshire palaeoliths and their significance for pleistocene correlation. *Proc. prehist. Soc.*, 45, vol. 11, p. 20-31 (illus.).

816. BREUIL (H.), VAULTIER (M.) and ZBYSZEWSKI (G.). Les plages anciennes portugaises entre les Caps d'Espichel et Carvoliro et leurs industries paléolithiques. *Proc. prehist. Soc.*, 42, n.s., vol. 8, p. 21-25.

817. CHILDE (V. Gordon). The antiquity and function of antler axes and adzes. *Antiquity*, 42, vol. 16, p. 258-264 (illus.).

818. CHILDE (V. G.). Prehistory in the U.S.S.R. 1 : Palaeolithic and mesolithic. A. Caucasus and Crimea. B. The Russian plain. 2 : The copper age. *Man*, 42, vol. 42, p. 98-103, 130-136.

819. CHILDE (V. G.). The mesolithic and neolithic in northern Europe. *Man*, 43, vol. 43, p. 34-36.

820. CHILDE (V. G.). The cave of Parpalló and the upper palaeolithic age in southeast Spain. *Antiquity*, 44, vol. 18, p. 29-35 (illus.).

821. CURWEN (E. C.). Some food-gathering implements : a study in mesolithic tradition. *Antiquity*, 41, vol. 15, p. 320-336.

822. DUNNING (G. C.). A stone circle and cairn on Mynydd Epynt, Brecknockshire. *Archaeol. cambrensis*, 43, vol. 97, p. 169-194 (illus.).

823. HAWKES (C. F. C.). Two palaeoliths from Broom, Dorset. *Proc.* *prehist. Soc.*, 43, vol. 9, p. 48-52 (illus.).

824. MARETT (R. R.). Further excavation of La Cotte de St. Brelade, Jersey. *Antiq. J.*, 40, vol. 20, p. 460-464.

825. MOVIUS (Hallam L.). The Irish Stone age, its chronology, development and relationships. London, Cambridge Univ. Press, 42, in-8, xxiv-338 p., (figs., plates, tables), 30s. R : A.D.L., *Antiq. J.*, 43, vol. 23, p. 160-162. H. J. Fleure, *Man*, 44, vol. 44, p. 51.

826. PATERSON (T. T.). Core, culture and complex in the Old Stone Age. *Proc. prehist. Soc.*, 45, vol. 11, p. 1-19 (illus.).

827. PATERSON (T. T.) and FAGG (B. E. B.). Studies on the palaeolithic succession in England, 2 : The Upper Brecklandian acheul (Elveden). *Proc. prehist. Soc.*, 40, vol. 6, p. 1-29.

828. RIDDELL (W. H.). Dead or alive ? (A study of palaeolithic cave-drawings). *Antiquity*, 40, vol. 14, p. 154-162.

829. RIDDELL (W. H.). Palaeolithic paintings—Magdalenian period. *Antiquity*, 42, vol. 16, p. 134-150 (illus.).

830. RIDDELL (W. H.). Cave-paintings, Lescaux. *Antiquity*, 42, vol. 16, p. 359-360.

831. SELIGMAN (C. G.) and CATON-THOMPSON (Gertrude). An unusual flint implement from Egypt, in the Seligman collection. *Man*, 42, vol. 42, p. 108-110.

832. STEKELIS (M.). Note on some flint implements from the seven wells (Sab'a Biyar). *Quar. Dept. Antiq. Palestine*, 44, vol. 11, p. 44-46.

§ 3. Neolithic Age

833. BECKER (C. O.). The megalithic ruins at Cuzco, Peru. *Trans. Newcomen Soc.*, 40/41 (43), vol. 21, p. 129-138.

834. BULLING (A.). Neolithic symbols and the purpose of art in China. *Burlington Mag.*, 43, vol. 82, p. 91-101 (plates).

835. CLARK (Grahame). Farmers and forests in neolithic Europe. *Antiquity*, 45, vol. 19, p. 57-71.

836. DAVIES (Margaret). Types of megalithic monuments of the Irish Sea and North Channel coastlands : a study in distributions. *Antiq. J.*, 45, vol. 25, p. 125-144.

837. FORDE (Daryll). Multiple chambered tombs in north-western France. *Proc. prehist. Soc.*, 40, vol. 6, p. 170-176.

838. FRERE (D. H. S.). Late neolithic grooved ware near Cambridge. *Antiq. J.*, 43, vol. 23, p. 34-41 (illus.).

839. PEAKE (Harold J. E.). The earliest structure at Stonehenge. *Man*, 45, vol. 45, p. 74-78.

840. SCOTT (Sir Lindsay). Neolithic culture of the Hebrides. *Antiquity*, 42, vol. 16, p. 301-306.

§ 4. Bronze Age

841. CHITTY (L. F.). Bronze implements from the Oswestry region of Shropshire. *Archaeol. cambrensis*, 40, vol. 95, p. 27-35 (illus.).

842. CLARK (J. G. D.) and GODWIN (H.). A late Bronze age find near Stuntney, Isle of Ely. *Antiq. J.*, 40, vol. 20, p. 52-71. (illus.).

843. COGHLAN (H. H.). Some fresh aspects of the prehistoric metallurgy of copper. *Antiq. J.*, 42, vol. 22, p. 22-38 (illus.).

844. CURWEN (Eliot). An egg-shaped mace-head [found in Sussex]. *Antiq. J.*, 41, vol. 21, p. 337-341.

845. DIKAIOS (P.). The excavations at Vounous-Bellapais in Cyprus, 1931-2. *Archaeologia*, 40, vol. 88, p. 1-174 (illus.).

846. FIELD (J. O.). Bronze castings found at Igbo, Southern Nigeria. *Man*, 40, vol. 40, p. 1-6.

847. Fox (Sir Cyril). Stake-circles in turf barrows : a record of excavation in Glamorgan, 1939-40. *Antiq. J.*, 41, vol. 21, p. 97-127.

848. Fox (Sir C.). A datable ' ritual barrow ' in Glamorganshire. *Antiquity*, 41, vol. 15, p. 142-161 (illus.).

849. Fox (Sir C.). The non-socketed bronze sickles of Britain. *Archaeol. cambrensis*, 41, vol. 96, p. 136-162 (plates).

850. Fox (Sir C.) and Fox (Aileen). The Golden Mile barrow, in Colwinston parish, Glamorgan. *Archaeol. cambrensis*, 41, vol. 96, p. 185-192.

851. GRINSELL (L. V.). The Bronze age round barrows of Wessex. *Proc. prehist. Soc.*, 41, vol. 7, p. 73-113.

852. GRINSELL (L. V.). The boat of the dead in the Bronze age. *Antiquity*, 41, vol. 15, p. 360-370 (illus.).

853. GRINSELL (L. V.). The Kivik cairn, Scania. *Antiquity*, 42, vol. 16, p. 160-174.

854. HAWKES (C. F. C.). The Deverel urn and the Picardy pin : a phase of Bronze age settlement in Kent. *Proc. prehist. Soc.*, 42, n.s., vol. 8, p. 26-47 (plates).

855. NORTH (F. J.). A geologist among the cairns. (Notes on the value of cooperation). *Antiquity*, 40, vol. 14, p. 377-394.

856. ORY (J.). A late Bronze age tomb at Tell Jerishe. *Quar. Dept. Antiq. Palestine*, 40, vol. 10, no. 1, p. 55-57.

857. ORY (J.). A Middle Bronze age tomb at el-Jisr. *Quar. Dept. Antiq. Palestine*, 45, vol. 12, p. 31-42.

858. PHILLIPS (C. W.). Some recent finds from the Trent, near Nottingham. *Antiq. J.*, 41, vol. 21, p. 133-143.

859. Piggott (C. M.). Five late Bronze age enclosures in north Wiltshire. *Proc. prehist. Soc.*, 42, n.s., vol. 8, p. 48-61 (plates).

860. Piggott (C. M.). The Grim's Ditch complex in Cranborne Chase. *Antiquity*, 44, vol. 18, p. 65-71 (illus.).

861. Piggott (Stuart). Timber circles : a re-examination. *Archaeol. J.*, 39 (40), vol. 96, p. 193-222.

862. Savory (H. N.). A Middle Bronze age barrow at Crick, Monmouthshire. *Archaeol. cambrensis*, 40, vol. 95, p. 169-191 (illus.).

863. Savory (H. N.). Some unpublished late Middle Bronze age pottery from West Wales. *Archaeol. cambrensis*, 41, vol. 96, p. 31-48 (illus.).

864. Schaeffer (C. F. A.). Archaeological discoveries in Trialeti—Caucasus. *J. asiatic Soc.*, 44, p. 25-29 (plates).

865. Sheppard (T.). The Parc-y-Meirch hoard, St. George parish, Denbighshire. *Archaeol. cambrensis*, 41, vol. 96, p. 1-10 (illus.).

866. Sherwin (G. A.). A second bronze hoard of Arreton Down type found in the Isle of Wight. *Antiq. J.*, 42, vol. 22, p. 198-201 (illus.).

867. Stone (J. F. S.). The Deveral-Rimbury settlement on Thorny Down, Winterbourne Gunner, S. Wilts. *Proc. prehist. Soc.*, 41, vol. 7, p. 114-133 (illus.).

868. Stone (J. F. S.) and Hill (N. G.). A round barrow on Stockbridge Down, Hampshire. *Antiq. J.*, 40, vol. 20, p. 39-51 (illus.).

869. Wace (A. B.). The Treasury of Atreus. *Antiquity*, 40, vol. 14, p. 233-249 (illus.).

870. Williams (Audrey). Two Bronze age barrows on Fairwood Common, Gower, Glamorgan. *Archaeol. cambrensis*, 44, vol. 98, p. 52-63 (illus.).

871. Worsfold (F. H.). A report on the late Bronze age site excavated at Minnis Bay, Birchington, Kent, 1938-40. *Proc. prehist. Soc.*, 43, vol. 9, p. 28-47 (illus.).

§ 5. Iron Age

872. Bersu (Gerhard). Excavations at Little Woodbury, Wiltshire. Pt. 1 : The settlement as revealed by excavation. *Proc. prehist. Soc.*, 40, vol. 6, p. 30-111.

873. Bradford (J. S. P.). An early Iron age settlement at Standlake, Oxon. *Antiq. J.*, 42, vol. 22, p. 202-214 (illus.).

874. Brinson (J. G. S.). Two burial groups of Belgic age, Hothfield Common, near Ashford. *Archaeol. cantiana*, 43, vol. 56, p. 41-47.

875. Clarke (R. Rainbird). The Iron age in Norfolk and Suffolk, 2 : A revised estimate of the Sutton ' hut-urn '. *Archaeol. J.*, 39 (40), vol. 96, p. 1-113, 223-225.

876. Coghlan (H. H.). Prehistoric iron prior to the dispersion of the Hittite empire. *Man*, 41, vol. 41, p. 74-80.

877. Cotton (M. A.) and Richardson (K. M.). A Belgic cremation site at Stone, Kent. *Proc. prehist. Soc.*, 41, vol. 7, p. 134-141.

878. Dudley (Harold E.). The one-tree boat at Appleby, Lincolnshire. *Antiquity*, 43, vol. 17, p. 156-161 (illus.).

879. Fleure (H. J.) and Dunlop (Margaret). Glendarragh circle and alignments, the Braaid, I.O.M. *Antiq. J.*, 42, vol. 22, p. 39-53 (illus.).

880. Fox (Aileen) and Threipland (Leslie Murray). The excavation of two cairn cemeteries near Hirwaun, Glamorgan. *Archaeol. cambrensis*, 42, vol. 97, p. 77-92 (plates).

881. Fox (Sir Cyril). Life in Anglesey 2,000 years ago : an early Iron age discovery. *Antiquity*, 44, vol. 18, p. 95-97 (illus.).

882. Fox (Sir C.). An early Iron age discovery in Anglesey. *Archaeol. cambrensis*, 44, vol. 98, p. 134-138 (illus.).

883. Fox (Sir C.). A find of the early Iron age from Llyn Cerrig Bach, Anglesey. Cardiff, National Museum of Wales, 45, in-8, 72 p., (illus.), 7s. 6d. R : J. Hawkes, *Archaeol. cambrensis*, 45, vol. 98, p. 263-264. E. T. Leeds, *J. rom. Stud.*, 45, vol. 35, p. 147.

884. Fox (Sir C.). A shield-boss of the early Iron age from Anglesey with ornament applied by chasing tools. *Archaeol. cambrensis*, 45, vol. 98, p. 199-220 (illus.).

885. Frere (Sheppard). An Iron age site near Epsom. *Antiq. J.*, 42, vol. 22, p. 123-138 (illus.).

886. Graham (A.). A list of brochs and broch sites. *Antiq. J.*, 43, vol. 23, p. 19-25.

887. Gresham (Colin A.). Spettisbury rings, Dorset. *Archaeol. J.*, 39 (40), vol. 96, p. 114-131 (illus.).

888. Gresham (C. A.). Multiple ramparts. *Antiquity*, 43, vol. 17, p. 67-70.

889. Harding (Lankester). Two Iron age tombs from 'Amman. *Quar. Dept. Antiq. Palestine*, 44, vol. 11, p. 67-74.

890. Hawkes (C. F. C.) and Jacobsthal (Paul). A Celtic bird-brooch from Red Hill, near Long Eaton, Notts. *Antiq. J.*, 45, vol. 25, p. 117-124.

891. Hemp (W. J.) and Gresham (C. A.). Hut-circles in north-west Wales. *Antiquity*, 44, vol. 18, p. 183-196 (illus.).

892. Hogg (A. H. A.). Gwynedd and the Votadini. *Antiquity*, 45, vol. 19, p. 80-84 (illus.).

893. Hulme (E. Wyndham). Prehistoric and primitive iron smelting. Pt. 2 : The crucible processes of the East. *Trans. Newcomen Soc.*, 40/41 (43), vol. 21, p. 23-30.

894. Lowther (A. W. G.). Iron age pottery from Wisley, Surrey. *Proc. prehist. Soc.*, 45, vol. 11, p. 32-38 (illus.).

895. O'Neil (B. H. St. J.). Excavations at Ffridd Faldwyn camp, Montgomery, 1937-39. *Archaeol. cambrensis*, 42, vol. 97, p. 1-66 (plans, illus.).

896. O'Neil (B. H. St. J.). Grey Ditch, Bradwell, Derbyshire. *Antiquity*, 45, vol. 19, p. 11-29 (illus.).

897. Perkins (J. B. Ward). Excavations on Oldbury Hill, Ightham, 1938. *Archaeol. cantiana*, 39 (40), vol. 51, p. 137-181.

898. Perkins (J. B. W.). Two early linch-pins, from Kings Langley, Herts, and from Tiddington, Stratford-on-Avon. *Antiq. J.*, 40, vol. 20, p. 358-367 (illus.).

899. Stebbing (W. P. D.). Cherry Garden Hill tumulus, Folkestone. *Archaeol. cantiana*, 43, vol. 56, p. 28-33.

900. Wainwright (G. A.). The coming of iron to some more African peoples. *Man*, 43, vol. 43, p. 114-116.

901. Wheeler (R. E. M.). Hillforts of northern France : a note on the expedition to Normandy, 1939. *Antiq. J.*, 41, vol. 21, p. 265-270.

902. Wheeler (R. E. M.). Multiple ramparts : a note in reply. *Antiquity*, 44, vol. 18, p. 50-52.

903. Whitley (Margaret). Excavations at Charlbury Camp, Dorset, 1939. *Antiq. J.*, 43, vol. 23, p. 98-121 (illus.).

904. Williams (Audrey). The excavation of Bishopston Valley promontory fort. *Archaeol. cambrensis*, 40, vol. 95, p. 9-19 (illus.).

905. WILLIAMS (Audrey). A promontory fort at Henllan, Cardiganshire. *Archaeol. cambrensis*, 45, vol. 98, p. 226-240 (illus.).

§ 6. Origins of Civilization

906. HAWKES (C. F. C.). Race, prehistory, and European civilization. *Man*, 42, vol. 42, p. 125-130.

907. ROBERTSON (Edward). Early navigation : its extent and importance. *B. John Rylands Library*, 40, vol. 24, p. 285-306.

§ 7. Origins of the European Peoples outside Ancient Greece and Italy

908. GAUL (James H.). The Vadastra culture of the Lower Danubian area : some comments. *Man*, 40, vol. 40, p. 68-73.

909. GIMPERA (P. Bosch). Two Celtic waves in Spain. Sir John Rhys memorial lect., 1939. London, Milford, 42, in-8, 126 p., (maps, plates), 9s. 6d. (Proc. of the Brit. Academy, vol. 26). R : C. F. C. Hawkes, *Man*, 42, vol. 42, p. 118 ; *Archaeol. cambrensis*, 42, vol. 97, p. 127-128.

910. OSWALD (Felix). The origin of the Coritani. *Antiq. J.*, 41, vol. 21, p. 323-332.

911. SULIMIRSKI (T.). Scythian antiquities in central Europe. *Antiq. J.*, 45, vol. 25, p. 1-11 (map).

912. HAWKES (C. F. C.). The prehistoric foundations of Europe to the Mycenaean age. London, Methuen, 40, in-8, xv-414 p., (plates, maps), 21s. R : A. H. McDonald, *Hist. Stud. Australia N.Z.*, 41, vol. 1, p. 207-208. D. P. Dobson, *J. archaeol. Assoc.*, 40 (41), vol. 5, p. 119. G. Clark, *Antiquity*, 41, vol. 15, p. 388-390. S. Piggott, *Proc. prehist. Soc.*, 41, vol. 7, p. 150-152. V. G. Childe, *Antiq. J.*, 40, vol. 20, p. 394-398. C. Fox, *Archaeol. cambrensis*, 40, vol. 95, p. 94-96.

913. HAWKES (Jaquetta and Christopher). Prehistoric Britain. London, Penguin, 44, in-8, 136 p., (plates, figs.), 9d. (Pelican books). R : V. G. Childe, *Man*, 45, vol. 45, p. 118.

914. HORNELL (James). Sea-trade in early times. *Antiquity*, 41, vol. 15, p. 233-256 (illus.).

THE ANCIENT EAST

§ 1. General Antiquity

915. MYRES (Sir J. L.). Mediterranean culture. London, Cambridge Univ. Press, 43, in-8, 51 p., 2s. (Frazer lect., 1943). R : A. F. Giles, *Class. R.*, 44, vol. 58, p. 27.

916. SAVILE (L. H.). Ancient harbours. *Antiquity*, 41, vol. 15, p. 209-232 (illus.).

917. STEIN (Sir Aurel). On Alexander's route into Gedrosia : an archaeological tour in Las Bela. *Geogr. J.*, 43, vol. 102, p. 193-227.

§ 2. The Near East in General

918. AVI-YONAH (M.). Abbreviations in Greek inscriptions : the Near East, 200 B.C.-A.D. 1000. London, Oxford Univ. Press, 40, in-4, 125 p., 8s. (Quarterly of the Dept. of Antiquities in Palestine, suppl. to vol. 9). R : M. N. T(od), *J. hell. Stud.*, 42 (43), vol. 62, p. 89.

919. BEN-DOR (I.). Palestinian alabaster vases. *Quar. Dept. Antiq. Palestine*, 44, vol. 11, p. 93-112.

920. CATON-THOMPSON (Gertrude). The tombs and Moon temple of Hureidha (Hadhramaut). London, Quaritch, 44, in-4, xv-191 p., (plates), 21s. R : H. Ingrams, *Antiquity*, 45, vol. 19, p. 187-193 (illus.). H. St. J. B. Philby, *J. central asian Soc.*, 45, vol. 32, p. 101-104.

921. CLEMESHA (William Wesley). The early Arab thalassocracy. *J. polynesian Soc.*, 43, vol. 52, p. 110-131.

922. CROWFOOT (J. W.). Dura-Europos. *Antiquity*, 45, vol. 19, p. 113-121 (illus.).

923. HAMILTON (R. A. B.). Six weeks in Shabwa. *Geogr. J.*, 42, vol. 100, p, 107-123.

924. HAUGHTON (H. L.). Some archaeological gleanings from Gandhara on the North-West frontier of India. *J. central asian Soc.*, 45, vol. 32, p. 299-306.

925. LOUD (Gordon). The Megiddo ivories. London, Cambridge Univ. Press, 40, in-4, 25 p., (plates), 90s. R : K. R. Maxwell-Hyslop, *Antiquity*, 42, vol. 16, p. 87-88.

926. PFISTER (R.) and BELLINGER (L.). The excavations at Dura-Europos. Final report 4, pt. 2. London, Oxford Univ. Press, 45, in-4, 72 p., (illus.), 16s. 6d.

927. PHILBY (H. St. J. B.) and TRITTON (A. S.). Najran inscriptions. *J. asiatic Soc.*, 44, p. 119-129.

928. ROSTOVTZEFF (M. I.), BELLINGER (A. R.), BROWN (F. E.) and WELLES (C. B.) ed. The excavations at Dura-Europos. Prelim. report of 9th season, 1935-36. Pt. 1 : The Agora and Bazaar. London, Oxford Univ. Press, 45, in-4, 284 p., (illus.), 33s. 6d.

929. SAUNDERS (J. J.). The Orient and the Graeco-Roman world before Islam. *History*, 40, vol. 25, p. 161-170.

930. SCHAEFFER (C. F. A.). French archaeological excavations in Syria between the two wars. *J. central asian Soc.*, 42, vol. 29, p. 184-194.

931. SCHWABE (M.). Khirbat Mafjar : Greek inscribed fragments. *Quar. Dept. Antiq. Palestine*, 45, vol. 12, p. 20-30.

932. SMITH (Sidney). Alalakh and chronology. London, Luzac, 40, in-8, 52 p., 5s. R : J. L. Myres, *Man*, 41, vol. 41, p. 134-135.

933. STEIN (Sir Aurel). Surveys on the Roman frontier in Iraq and Trans-Jordan. *Geogr. J.*, 40, vol. 95, p. 428-438.

934. TARN (W. W.). Demetrias in Sind. *J. asiatic Soc.*, 40, p. 179-193.

935. TARN (W. W.). Two notes on Seleucid history. 1 : Seleucus' 500 elephants. 2 : Tarmita. *J. hell. Stud.*, 40 (41), vol. 60, p. 84-94.

936. TOLL (Nicholas). The excavations at Dura-Europos. Final report 4, pt. 1, fasc. 1 : The green glazed pottery. London, Oxford Univ. Press, 43, in-4, 100 p., (plates, illus.), 13s. 6d. R : J. W. Crowfoot, *Antiq. J.*, 45, vol. 25, p. 162-163.

937. WEILL (Raymond). Phoenicia and western Asia to the Macedonian conquest, tr. by E. F. Row. London, Harrap, 40, in-8, 208 p., 6s. R : A.M.W., *Burlington Mag.*, 42, vol. 80, p. 78. Lady Fowle, *Asiatic R.*, 41, vol. 37, p. 425.

938. WESTERMANN (W. L.), KEYES (C. W.) and LIEBESNY (H.) ed. Zenon papyri : business papers of the 3rd century B.C. dealing with Palestine and Egypt. Vol. 2. London, Oxford Univ. Press, 41, in-4, 231 p., (plates), 30s. (Columbia papyri, Greek ser., 4).

§ 3. **Egypt**

939. BALLARD (G. A.). The great obelisk lighter of 1550 B.C. *Mariner's Mirror*, 41, vol. 27, p. 290-306.

940. BREASTED (J. H.). A history of Egypt from earliest times to the Persian conquest. New ed. London, Hodder & Stoughton, 42, in-8, 200 p., 50s.

941. DAVIES (N. de G.). The tomb of the Vizier Ramose, based on preliminary work by T. E. Peet. London, Oxford Univ. Press, 41, in-2, 35 p., 57 plates, 63s. (Egypt explor. soc., Mond excavations at Thebes, 1).

942. GLANVILLE (S. R. K.). The legacy of Egypt. London, Oxford Univ. Press, 42, in-8, 444 p., (plates, figs.), 10s. R : G. A. Wainwright, *J. hell. Stud.*, 42 (43), vol. 62, p. 91-92.

J. L. Myres, *Class. R.*, 43, vol. 57, p. 39-42. M. H. Richmond, *Int. R. Missions*, 43, vol. 32, p. 216-218. G. D. Hornblower, *Man*, 45, vol. 45, p. 111-114.

943. GRINSELL (L. V.). Egyptian bronze-making again. *Antiquity*, 44, vol. 18, p. 100-102.

944. HOLSCHER (U.). The mortuary temple of Ramses III. Pt. 1. London, Cambridge Univ. Press, 42, in-2, xiv-88 p., (figs., plates), 96s. (Chicago univ., Or. inst. publ.).

945. HORNBLOWER (G. D.). Osiris and the fertility-rite. *Man*, 41, vol. 41, p. 94-103.

946. HORNBLOWER (G. D.). The Egyptian fertility-rite : postscript. *Man*, 43, vol. 43, p. 26-34.

947. HORNBLOWER (G. D.). The establishing of Osiris. *Man*, 45, vol. 45, p. 59-63.

948. HORNELL (James). The sailing ship in ancient Egypt. *Antiquity*, 43, vol. 17, p. 27-41 (illus.).

949. HORNELL (J.). The palm leaves on boats' prows of Gerzian age. *Man*, 45, vol. 45, p. 25-27.

950. LANGTON (N. and B.). The cat in ancient Egypt. London, Cambridge Univ. Press, 40, in-4, xi-92 p., (illus.), 25s.

951. MOND (Sir Robert) and MYERS (Oliver H.). Temples of Armant : a preliminary survey. London, Egypt Exploration Soc., 40, 2 vols. in-4, xii-223; 107 plates, 63s. (Excavation mem., Egypt exploration soc., no. 43). R : A. M. Blackman, *A. Archaeol. Anthrop.*, 40, vol. 27, p. 166-168.

952. NELSON (H. H.). Key plans showing locations of Theban temple decorations. London, Cambridge Univ. Press, 42, portfolio, xii-37 plates, 18s. (Chicago univ., Or. inst. publ., 56).

953. SEELE (K. C.). The coregency of Ramses II with Seti I and the date

of the Great Hypostyle Hall at Karnak. London, Cambridge Univ. Press, 41, in-4, xiv-96 p., 16s. 6d. (Stud. in ancient or. civilization).

954. SØLVER (Carl V.). The Egyptian obelisk-ships. *Mariner's Mirror*, 40, vol. 26, p. 237-255.

955. STEINDORFF (G.) and SEELE (K. C.). When Egypt ruled the East. London, Cambridge Univ. Press, 42, in-8, xvi-284 p., (illus.), 24s.

956. WAINWRIGHT (G. A.). Studies in the petition of Peteêsi. *B. John Rylands Library*, 44, vol. 28, p. 228-271.

957. WAINWRIGHT (G. A.). Rekhmirê's metal-workers. *Man*, 44, vol. 44, p. 94-98.

958. WEST (L. C.). Currency in Roman and Byzantine Egypt. London, Oxford Univ. Press, 45, in-8, 206 p., 20s.

959. WINLOCK (H. E.). Excavations at Deir el Bahri, 1911-1931. London, Macmillan, 43, in-8, x-235 p., (illus.), 30s. R : J. W. Crowfoot, *Antiquity*, 43, vol. 17, p. 167-168. S.S., *Antiq. J.*, 43, vol. 23, p. 162-163.

960. YOUTIE (H. C.) and PEARL (O. M.) ed. Tax rolls from Karanis. Pt. 2. London, Oxford Univ. Press, 40, in-8, 266 p., 17s. (Stud., Univ. of Michigan humanistic ser., 43).

§ 4. Cyrene

§ 5. Mesopotamia

961. ALBRIGHT (W. F.), KELSO (J. L.) and THORLEY (J. P.). Annual of American schools of oriental research. Vol. 21-22 : The excavation of Tell-Beit Mirsim, vol. 3. London, Oxford Univ. Press, 43, in-4, 256 p., (illus.), 24s.

962. ALEXANDER (J. B.) ed. Early Babylonian letters and economic texts. London, Oxford Univ. Press, 43, in-4, 40 p., (facs.), 33s. 6d.

963. BAQIR (Taha). Excavations at 'Aqar Qüf, 1942-1943. London, Oxford Univ. Press, 44, in-8, 16 p., (illus.), 7s. 6d. (Iraq, suppl., 1944).

964. —— —— —— 2nd interim rept., 1943-1944. (Iraq, suppl., 1945).

965. DELOUGAZ (P.). The temple oval at Khafajah. London, Cambridge Univ. Press, 40, in-4, 175 p., (plates, illus.), 60s.

966. DELOUGAZ (P.) and LLOYD (S.). Pre-Sargonid temples in the Diyala region. London, Cambridge Univ. Press, 43, in-4, xviii-320 p., (plates, figs.), 90s.

967. DRIVER (G. R.) and MILES (Sir John C.). Ordeal by oath at Nuzi. *Iraq*, 40, vol. 7, p. 132-138.

968. FAUST (D. E.). Contracts from Larsa dated in the reign of Rim-Sin. London, Oxford Univ. Press, 41, in-4, 47 p., 78 plates, 22s. 6d. R : S. Smith, *Antiquity*, 42, vol. 16, p. 371-372.

969. FISH (T.). Letters from the war front in ancient Mesopotamia. *B. John Rylands Library*, 41/42, vol. 26, p. 287-306.

970. FISH (T.). Food of the gods in ancient Sumer. *B. John Rylands Library*, 43, vol. 27, p. 308-322.

971. FISH (T.). The place of the small state in the political and cultural history of ancient Mesopotamia. *B. John Rylands Library*, 44, vol. 28, p. 83-98.

972. FRANKFORT (H.). More sculpture from the Diyala region. London, Cambridge Univ. Press, 44, in-4, xiv-50 p., (plates, map, figs.), 60s. (Chicago univ., Or. inst. publ., 60).

973. GADD (C. J.). Tablets from Chagar Bazar and Tall Brak. *Iraq*, 40, vol. 7, pt. 1, p. 22-66.

974. HILZHEIMER (M.). Animal remains from Tell Asmar. London,

Cambridge Univ. Press, 42, in-8, xiv-52 p., (illus., tables), 12s. 6d. (Chicago univ., Stud. in ancient or. civilization, 20).

975. KRAMER (S. N.). Lamentation over the destruction of Ur. London, Cambridge Univ. Press, 41, in-8, xii-100 p., (plates), 12s. (Or. Inst. Assyr. stud.).

976. LLOYD (Seton). Iraq government soundings at Sinjar. *Iraq*, 40, vol. 7, pt. 1, p. 13-21.

977. LLOYD (S.). Ruined cities of Iraq. London, Oxford Univ. Press, 44, in-8, 120 p., (plates), 3s. 6d.

978. MACKAY (Dorothy). Ancient river beds and dead cities. *Antiquity*, 45, vol. 19, p. 135-144 (illus.).

979. SPEISER (E. A.). The beginnings of civilization in Mesopotamia. *Antiquity*, 41, vol. 15, p. 162-175.

980. STEIN (Sir Aurel). The ancient trade route past Hatra and its Roman posts. *J. asiatic Soc.*, 41, p. 299-316.

981. STEPHENS (F. J.). Old Assyrian letters and business documents. London, Oxford Univ. Press, 45, in-4, 40 p., (illus.), 33s. 6d.

982. THOMPSON (R. Campbell). A selection from the cuneiform historical texts from Nineveh (1927-32). *Iraq*, 40, vol. 7, p. 85-131.

§ 6. Hittites

983. GELB (I. J.). Hittite hieroglyphic monuments. London, Cambridge Univ. Press, 40, in-4, 40 p., (plates), 60s. (Chicago Univ., or. inst. publ., vol. 45).

984. GELB (I. J.). Hittite hieroglyphs, 3. London, Cambridge Univ. Press, 43, in-8, xx-76 p., 10s. 6d. (Stud. in ancient or. civilization, 21).

985. GURNEY (O. R.). Hittite prayers of Mursili II. *A. Archaeol. Anthrop.*, 40, vol. 27, p. 4-163.

§ 7. Palestine. Jews and Semitic Races to the end of Antiquity

986. ALBRIGHT (W. F.). Archaeology and the religion of Israel. London, Oxford Univ. Press, 42, in-8, xii-238 p., 10s. 6d. (Colgate-Rochester divinity school, Ayer lect., 1941). R : H. H. Rowley, *Congreg. Quar.*, 43, vol. 21, p. 71-72. H.A.K., *Queen's Quar.*, 43, vol. 50, p. 422-423.

987. BELL (H. I.). Anti-Semitism in Alexandria. *J. rom. Stud.*, 41, vol. 31, p. 1-18.

988. BERKOVITS (E.). Towards historic Judaism. Oxford, East & West Libr., 43, in-8, 144 p., 5s.

989. CROWFOOT (J. W.), KENYON (Kathleen M.) and Sukenik (E. L.). The buildings at Samaria. London, Palestine Exploration Fund, 42, in-8, xvi-139 p., (plates), 40s. (Subscribers 21s.). R : A. W. Lawrence, *J. hell. Stud.*, 42 (43), vol. 62, p. 109. R. D. Barnett, *Antiquity*, 45, vol. 19, p. 219-220.

990. Excavations in Palestine and Trans-Jordan, 1938-9 : Jerusalem— The citadel (with) Bibliography. *Quar. Dept. Antiq. Palestine*, 41, vol. 9, p. 206-218.

991. GARSTANG (J. and J. B. E.). The story of Jericho. London, Hodder & Stoughton, 40, in-8, xv-200 p., (illus.), 8s. 6d. R : J.W.C., *Geogr. J.*, 41, vol. 97, p. 258-260.

992. GLUECK (N.). Annual of the American schools of oriental research. Vol. 18-19 : Explorations in eastern Palestine, 3. London, Oxford Univ. Press, 40, in-8, 287 p., (illus.), 11s. 6d.

993. GUILLAUME (A.). Magical terms in the Old Testament. *J. asiatic Soc.*, 42, p. 111-131.

994. HAMILTON (R. W.). Excavations against the north wall of Jerusalem, 1937-8. *Quar. Dept. Antiq. Palestine*, 40, vol. 10, no. 1, p. 1-54.

995. HAMILTON (R. W.). Khirbat Mafjar : stone sculpture, 1-2. *Quar. Dept. Antiq. Palestine*, 44, vol. 11, p. 47-66 & plates; 45, vol. 12, p. 1-19.

996. HENSCHEL-SIMON (E.). Note on the pottery of the 'Amman tombs. *Quar. Dept. Antiq. Palestine*, 44, vol. 11, p. 75-80.

997. HORSFIELD (G. and A.). Sela-Petra, the Rock, of Edom and Nabatene, 4 : The finds. *Quar. Dept. Antiq. Palestine*, 41, vol. 9, p. 105-205 (plates).

998. ILIFFE (J. H.). Imperial art in Trans-Jordan : figurines and lamps from a potter's store at Jerash. *Quar. Dept. Antiq. Palestine*, 44, vol. 11, p. 1-26 (plates).

999. ILIFFE (J. H.). A model shrine of Phoenician style. *Quar. Dept. Antiq. Palestine*, 44, vol. 11, p. 91-92.

1000. JARVIS (C. S.). To Petra from the west : a forgotten Roman highway. *Antiquity*, 40, vol. 14, p. 138-147.

1002. KIRKBRIDE (A. S.) and HARDING (Lankester). The seven wells of Beni Murra. *Quar. Dept. Antiq. Palestine*, 44, vol. 11, p. 37-43.

1003. MURRAY (M. A.) and ELLIS (J. C.). A street in Petra. London, Brit. School of Archaeol., 40, in-4, 38 p., 41 pl., 25s. (Publ. no. 62). R : W. J. Martin, *A. Archaeol. Anthrop.*, 40, vol. 27, p. 170.

1004. OESTERLEY (W. O. E.). The Jews and Judaism during the Greek period : the background of Christianity. London, S.P.C.K., 41, in-8, x-307 p., 10s. 6d. R : F. S. Marsh, *Theology*, 41, vol. 43, p. 242-243. H. Kosmala, *Int. R. Missions*, 42, vol. 31, p. 363-365.

1005. ROBERTSON (Edward). Temple and torah : suggesting an alternative to the Graf-Wellhausen hypothesis. *B. John Rylands Library*, 41, vol. 26, p. 183-205.

1006. ROBERTSON (E.). The priestly code : the legislation of the Old Testament and Graf-Wellhausen. *B. John Rylands Library*, 42, vol. 26, p. 369-392.

1007. ROBERTSON (E.). Samuel and Saul. *B. John Rylands Library*, 44, vol. 28, p. 175-206.

1008. ROWE (A.). The four Canaanite temples of Beth-Shan. Pt. 1 : The temples and cult objects. London, Oxford Univ. Press, 40, in-2, 101 p., (plates), 67s. 6d. (Pa. Univ. museum, publ. of Palestine sect.).

1009. SMITH (J. M. Powis). The prophets and their times. 2nd ed., revised by W. A. Irwin. London, Cambridge Univ. Press, 41, in-8, xviii-342 p., 15s. R : H. H. Rowley, *Baptist Quar.*, 42, vol. 11, p. 125-126.

1010. SPARKS (H. F. D.). The Lachish excavations and their bearing upon Old Testament study. *Theology*, 41, vol. 43, p. 17-27.

1011. TUFNELL (Olga), INGE (Charles H.) and HARDING (L.). Lachish II (Tell ed Duweir) : the Fosse Temple. Vol. 2 of the Wellcome-Marston archaeological research expedition to the Near East. London, Oxford Univ. Press, 40, in-2, 96 p., (plates), 25s. R : *J. Roy. african Soc.*, 41, vol. 40, p. 84. J. W. Crowfoot, *Antiquity*, 41, vol. 15, p. 45-49. K.M.K., *Antiq. J.*, 44, vol. 24, p. 156-157.

§ 8. Iran

1012. BAILEY (H. W.). Zoroastrian problems in the ninth century books. London, Oxford Univ. Press, 43, in-8, 243 p., 15s.

1013. GUZARISH-NAMA-IRAN. History of ancient Iran. In Persian. London, Luzac, 40, in-8, 272 p., 7s. 6d.

1014. HENNING (W. B.). The murder of the Magi. *J. asiatic Soc.*, 44, p. 133-144.

1015. HERZFELD (Ernst E.). Iran in the ancient East : archaeological studies presented in the Lowell lectures at Boston. London, Oxford Univ. Press, 41, in-2, 363 p., 131 plates, 252s. R : J. Marshall, *J. asiatic Soc.*, 43, p. 121-123. W. L. Hildburgh, *Burlington Mag.*, 43, vol. 82, p. 51-52. V. G. Childe, *Antiquity*, 42, vol. 16, p. 361-364.

1016. LANGSDORFF (A.) and Mc-COWN (D. E.). Tall-i-Bakun A : season of 1932. London, Oxford Univ. Press, 43, in-4, xii-84 p., (plates, figs.), 60s. (Chicago univ., Or. inst. publ., 59).

1017. McCOWN (Donald E.). The comparative stratigraphy of early Iran. London, Cambridge Univ. Press, 42, in-4, xvi-65 p., (plates), 15s. (Stud. in ancient or. civilization, 23). R : V. G. Childe, *Antiquity*, 42, vol. 16, p. 353-358.

1018. MINORSKY (V.). Some early documents in Persian, 2 : Persian documents from Bāmiyān. *J. asiatic Soc.*, 43, p. 86-99.

1019. PIGGOTT (Stuart). Dating the Hissar sequence—the Indian evidence. *Antiquity*, 43, vol. 17, p. 169-182 (illus.).

1020. PRZEWORSKI (S.). Luristān bronzes in the collection of Mr. Frank Savery. *Archaeologia*, 40, vol. 88, p. 229-269 (illus.).

1021. STEIN (Sir Aurel). Old routes of western Iran. Antiquities examined, described and illustrated with the assistance of Fred H. Andrews. London, Macmillan, 40, in-4, 432 p., (illus.), 42s. R : J. V. Harrison, *J. central asian Soc.*, 41, vol. 28, p. 94-96. E.O.L., *Geogr. J.*, 41, vol. 97, p. 329. P. M. Sykes, *J. asiatic Soc.*, 41, p. 367-371. A. D. H. Smith, *Asiatic R.*, 41, vol. 37, p. 426-427.

E

GREEK HISTORY

§ 1. Classical World in General

1022. ANDERSON (R. C.). Triremes and other ancient galleys. *Mariner's Mirror*, 41, vol. 27, p. 314-323.

1023. BLAIKLOCK (E. M.). Schoolboys of the ancient world. *Greece and Rome*, 42, vol. 11, p. 97-102.

1024. GIMPERA (P. Bosch). The Phokaians in the far west. *Class. Quar.*, 44, vol. 38, p. 53-59.

1025. CARY (M.) and HAARHOFF (T. J.). Life and thought in the Greek and Roman world. London, Methuen, 40, in-8, x-348 p., (plates, maps), 8s. 6d. R : H. H. Scullard, *Congreg. Quar.*, 41, vol. 19, p. 175-176. A.H.M.J., *Eng. hist. R.*, 41, vol. 56, p. 337. *History*, 41, vol. 26, p. 152-153. *Greece and Rome*, 41, vol. 10, p. 141.

1026. DIXON (Pierson). The Iberians of Spain and their relations with the Aegean world. London, Oxford Univ. Press, 40, in-8, xi-159 p., (maps), 8s. 6d. R : C. F. C. Hawkes, *Burlington Mag.*, 41, vol. 78, p. 166-167. J.P.H.M., *Geogr. J.*, 41, vol. 97, p. 123. M. I. Henderson, *J. hell. Stud.*, 40 (41), vol. 60, p. 100. C. F. C. Hawkes, *Antiquity*, 41, vol. 15, p. 391-393.

1027. FORSTER (E. S.). Dogs in ancient warfare. *Greece and Rome*, 41, vol. 10, p. 114-117 ; vol. 11, p. 34.

1028. JONES (A. H. M.). The Greek city from Alexander to Justinian. London, Oxford Univ. Press, 40, in-4, x-393 p., 21s. R : E. G. Turner, *J. rom. Stud.*, 44, vol. 34, p. 142-143. V. E., *J. hell. Stud.*, 42 (43), vol. 62, p. 98. A. N. Sherwin-White, *Class. R.*, 41, vol. 55, p. 43-45.

1029. JAEGER (Werner W.). Paideia: the ideals of Greek culture, 2-3, tr. by G. Highet. Oxford, Blackwell, 44, 2 vols. in-8, 442, 374 p., 45s. R : J. L. Myres, *Man*, 45, vol. 45, p. 115-116. *Greece and Rome*, 45, vol. 14, p. 93-95. J. Tate, *Class. R.*, 45, vol. 59, p. 54-56. F. Clarke, *Hibbert J.*, 45, vol. 43, p. 183-185.

1030. MOMIGLIANO (Arnaldo). 'Terra marique'. *J. rom. Stud.*, 42, vol. 32, p. 53-64.

1031. MORRISON (J. S.). The Greek trireme. *Mariner's Mirror*, 41, vol. 27, p. 14-44.

1032. MYRES (Sir J. L.). The ancient shape of Attica. *Greece and Rome*, 43, vol. 12, p. 33-42.

1033. PRENTICE (W. K.). The ancient Greeks. London, Oxford Univ. Press, 41, in-8, viii-254 p., 14s.

1034. RUSSELL (A. G.). The Greek as a mercenary soldier. *Greece and Rome*, 42, vol. 11, p. 103-112.

1035. SMITH (Sidney). The Greek trade at Al Mina : a footnote to Oriental history. *Antiq. J.*, 42, vol. 22, p. 87-112.

1036. TODD (F. A.). Some ancient novels. London, Oxford Univ. Press, 40, in-8, 152 p., 7s. 6d.

§ 2. Prehellenic Epoch

1037. PERSSON (A. W.). The religion of Greece in prehistoric times. London, Cambridge Univ. Press, 42, in-8, viii-190 p., (plates, figs.), 12s. (Sather lect., 17). R : E.J.F., *J. hell. Stud.*, 42 (43), vol. 62, p. 61.

§ 3. Sources and Criticisms of Sources

a. AUTHORS

1038. GOMME (A. W.). A historical commentary on Thucydides, vol. 1. London, Oxford Univ. Press, 45, in-8, 492 p., 20s.

1039. PEARSON (Lionel). Lost Greek historians judged by their fragments. *Greece and Rome*, 43, vol. 12, p. 43-56.

1040. WADE-GERY (H. T.). The Spartan Rhetra in Plutarch, *Lycurgus VI. Class. Quar.*, 43, vol. 37, p. 62-72; 44, vol. 38, p. 1-9, 115-126.

b. EPIGRAPHY

1041. HEICHELHEIM (R. E.). The Greek inscriptions in the Fitzwilliam Museum (Cambridge). *J. hell. Stud.*, 42 (43), vol. 62, p. 14-20.

1042. MERITT (B. D.). Epigraphica attica. London, Oxford Univ. Press, 40, in-8, xi-157 p., (plates), 10s. 6d. (Martin classical lect., vol. 9). R : A.M.W., *J. hell. Stud.*, 42 (43), vol. 62, p. 87-88.

1043. RAUBITSCHEK (A. E.). Some notes on early Attic stoichedon inscriptions. *J. hell. Stud.*, 40 (41), vol. 60, p. 50-59.

1044. TOD (Marcus N.). The progress of Greek epigraphy, 1939-1940. *J. hell. Stud.*, 42 (43), vol. 62, p. 51-83.

§ 4. Political History

a. GENERAL

1045. AGARD (W. R.). What democracy meant to the Greeks. London, Oxford Univ. Press, 42, in-8, 290 p., 14s.

1046. BALOGH (E.) and HEICHELHEIM (F. M.). Political refugees in ancient Greece, from the period of the tyrants to Alexander the Great. Johannesburg, Witwatersrand Univ. Press, 43, in-8, xvi-134 p., 7s. 6d. R : P. Treves, *J. hell. Stud.*, 43, vol. 63, p. 132-133. G. Murray, *B.Y.B.I.L.*, 44, vol. 21, p. 234-235. F.E.A., *J. comp. Legisl. int. Law*, 44, vol. 26, pt. 3/4, p. 82-83. M. P. Charlesworth, *Class. R.*, 45, vol. 59, p. 23-24.

1048. MEIGGS (Russell). The growth of Athenian imperialism. *J. hell. Stud.*, 43, vol. 63, p. 21-34.

1049. MOMIGLIANO (A.). Sea-power in Greek thought. *Class. R.*, 44, vol. 58, p. 1-7.

1050. PRENTICE (William Kelly). The Greek political experience : studies in honour of W. K. Prentice, by various contributors. London, Oxford Univ. Press, 41, in-8, x-252 p., (maps), 14s. R : P. Treves, *J. hell. Stud.*, 43, vol. 63, p. 131-132. A. W. Gomme, *Class. R.*, 43, vol. 57, p. 44-46.

b. MONOGRAPHS

1051. CARY (M.). The Peace of Callias. *Class. Quar.*, 45, vol. 39, p. 87-91.

1052. FREEMAN (Kathleen). Thourioi. *Greece and Rome*, 41, vol. 10, p. 49-64.

1053. HARLEY (T. Rutherford). ' A greater than Leonidas ' (Brasidas). *Greece and Rome*, 42, vol. 11, p. 68-83.

1054. LAST (Hugh). Thermopylae. *Class. R.*, 43, vol. 57, p. 63-66.

1055. McDONALD (William A.). The political meeting-places of the Greeks. London, Oxford Univ. Press, 43, in-8, 328 p., (plates), 30s. R : R.E.W., *J. hell. Stud.*, 43, vol. 63, p. 127-128. A.W.L., *Eng. hist. R.*, 45, vol. 60, p. 423. A.M.W., *Greece and Rome*, 44, vol. 13, p. 95-96. J. L. Myres, *Class. R.*, 44, vol. 58, p. 62-64. J. F. Dobson, *Antiquity*, 44, vol. 18, p. 164-165.

1056. PARKE (H. W.). The deposing of Spartan kings. *Class. Quar.*, 45, vol. 39, p. 106-112.

1057. STEIN (Sir Aurel). Notes on Alexander's crossing of the Tigris and the battle of Arbela. *Geogr. J.*, 42, vol. 100, p. 155-164.

1058. WADE-GERY (H. T.). Kritias and Herodes. *Class. Quar.*, 45, vol. 39, p. 19-33.

1059. WALBANK (F. W.). Olympichus of Alinda and the Carian expedition of Antigonus Doson. *J. hell. Stud.*, 42 (43), vol. 62, p. 8-13.

1060. WESTLAKE (H. D.). Timoleon and the reconstruction of Syracuse. *Cambridge hist. J.*, 42, vol. 7, p. 73-100.

1061. WESTLAKE (H. D.). Seaborne raids in Periclean strategy. *Class. Quar.*, 45, vol. 39, p. 75-84.

§ 5. History of Law and Institutions

1062. CALHOUN (George M.). Introduction to Greek legal science, ed. by F. de Zulueta. London, Oxford Univ. Press, 44, in-8, v-86 p., 5s. R : F.W.W., *Greece and Rome*, 45, vol. 14, p. 30.

1063. DINSMOOR (W. B.)., The Athenian Archon list in the light of recent discoveries. London, Oxford Univ. Press, 40, in-4, 274 p., 22s. 6d. R : W. W. Tarn, *Class. R.*, 40, vol. 54, p. 202-203.

1064. EHRENBERG (Victor). An early source of Polis-constitution. *Class. Quar.*, 43, vol. 37, p. 14-18.

1065. FORSTER (E. S.). Guilty or Not Guilty : four Athenian trials. *Greece and Rome*, 43, vol. 12, p. 21-27.

1066. HAMBURGER (Max). The awakening of western legal thought, tr. by B. Miall. London, Allen and Unwin, 42, in-8, xxiii-167 p., 10s. 6d. R : A. H. Campbell, *Class. R.*, 43, vol. 57, p. 50-51.

1067. HAMMOND (N. G. L.). The Seisachtheia and the Nomothesia of Solon. *J. hell. Stud.*, 40 (41), vol. 60, p. 71-83.

1068. HOPPER (R. J.). Interstate juridical agreements in the Athenian empire. *J. hell. Stud.*, 43, vol. 63, p. 35-51.

1069. MILNE (J. G.). The chronology of Solon's reforms. *Class. R.*, 43, vol. 57, p. 1-3.

1070. PERDICAS (Panajotis). On history and outlines of Greek maritime law. *Trans. Grotius Soc.*, 39 [40], vol. 25, p. 33-50.

1071. WYCHERLEY (R. E.). The Ionian agora. *J. hell. Stud.*, 42 (43), vol. 62, p. 21-32.

§ 6. Economic and Social History

1072. AUSTIN (R. G.). Greek board-games. *Antiquity*, 40, vol. 14, p. 257-271.

1073. DAY (John). An economic history of Athens under Roman domination. London, Oxford Univ. Press, 42, in-8, x-300 p., 23s. 6d. R : F.W.W., *Greece and Rome*, 43, vol. 12, p. 91-92. F. M. Heichelheim, *Econ. J.*, 43, vol. 53, p. 100-101 ; *J. hell. Stud.*, 43, vol. 63, p. 130-131. M. N. Tod, *J. rom. Stud.*, 43, vol. 33, p. 105-107.

1074. EHRENBERG (Victor). The people of Aristophanes : a sociology of old Attic comedy. Oxford, Blackwell, 43, in-8, xii-320 p., (plates), 25s. R : P.G.M., *Greece and Rome*, 44, vol. 13, p. 94. H. Michell, *Canad. J. Econ. pol. Sci.*, 44, vol. 10, p. 243-246. A. W. Pickard-Cambridge, *Class. R.*, 44, vol. 58, p. 19-21.

1075. GLOVER (T. R.). The challenge of the Greek, and other essays. London, Cambridge Univ. Press, 42, in-8, x-241 p., 12s. 6d. R : *J. hell. Stud.*, 42 (43), vol. 62, p. 92. C.H.W., *History*, 43, vol. 28, p. 109-110.

1076. MICHELL (H.). The economics of ancient Greece. London, Cambridge Univ. Press, 40, in-8, 415 p., 18s. R : W. J. Sartain, *Class. R.*, 43, vol. 57, p. 42-44. A. Robinson, *Econ. J.*, 41, vol. 51, p. 118-119. H. A. Thompson, *Canad. J. Econ. pol. Sci.*, 41, vol. 7, p. 583-588. F. M. Heichelheim, *Economica*, 41, vol. 8, p. 109-110. V. E., *Eng. hist. R.*, 42, vol. 57, p. 148-149.

1077. ROSTOVTZEFF (M.). The social and economic history of the Hellenistic world. London, Oxford Univ. Press, 41, 3 vols. in-8, 1779 p., (plates), 105s. R : D.M.M., *J. central asian Soc.*, 41, vol. 28, p. 451-453. V. G. Childe, *Antiquity*, 41, vol. 15, p. 395-398. W. W. Tarn, *J. rom. Stud.*, 41, vol. 31, p. 165-171. F. M.

Heichelheim, *J. hell. Stud.*, 43, vol. 63, p. 129-130. C. F. C. Hawkes, *Antiq. J.*, 43, vol. 23, p. 60-63. H. Michell, *Canad. J. Econ. pol. Sci.*, 42, vol. 8, p. 247-260. F. W. Walbank, *Class. R.*, 42, vol. 56, p. 81-84. F. M. Heichelheim, *Econ. J.*, 42, vol. 52, p. 59-61.

1078. WHITE (A. J.). Class distinctions in 5th-century Athens. *Greece and Rome*, 44, vol. 13, p. 15-25.

1079. WYCHERLEY (R. E.). Priene and modern planning. *Greece and Rome*, 45, vol. 14, p. 12-16.

§ 7. History of Literature, Philosophy and Science

1080. BATES (W. N.). Sophocles-poet and dramatist. London, Oxford Univ. Press, 40, in-8, 291 p., 16s.

1081. BOWRA (C. M.). Sophoclean tragedy. London, Oxford Univ. Press, 44, in-8, vi-384 p., 20s. R : A.N.W.S., *Greece and Rome*, 45, vol. 14, p. 92-93.

1082. CASSON (Stanley). Why Homer wrote the Odyssey. *Antiquity*, 42, vol. 16, p. 71-84.

1083. CHERNISS (H.). The riddle of the early Academy. London, Cambridge Univ. Press, 45, in-12, viii-104 p., 9s.

1084. CORNFORD (F. M.). Was the Ionian philosophy scientific ? *J. hell. Stud.*, 42 (43), vol. 62, p. 1-7.

1085. FORSTER (E. S.). Riddles and problems from the Greek anthology. *Greece and Rome*, 45, vol. 14, p. 42-47.

1086. HARDIE (Colin). Homer and the Odyssey : another point of view. (With a rejoinder by Stanley Casson). *Antiquity*, 42, vol. 16, p. 265-277.

1087. KNIGHT (W. F. J.). The Aeschylean universe. *J. hell. Stud.*, 43, vol. 63, p. 15-20.

1088. LITTLE (A. M. G.). Myth and society in Attic drama. London, Oxford Univ. Press, 42, in-8, vii-

95 p., (illus.), 7s. 6d. R : A. M. Dale, *J. hell. Stud.*, 43, vol. 63, p. 135-136. H. D. F. Kitto, *Class. R.*, 43, vol. 57, p. 112-114.

1089. MURRAY (Gilbert). Aeschylus. London, Oxford Univ. Press, 40, in-8, xi-242 p., 7s. 6d.

1090. MURRAY (G.). Ritual elements in the New Comedy. *Class. Quar.*, 43, vol. 37, p. 46-54.

1091. PRENTICE (W. K.). Those ancient dramas called tragedies. London, Oxford Univ. Press, 42, in-8, 204 p., (illus.), 12s. 6d.

1092. THOMAS (Ivor) transl. Selections illustrating the history of Greek mathematics. Vol. 2 : From Aristarchus to Pappus. London, Heinemann, 42, in-8, xi-683 p., 10s. R : D'A. W. Thompson, *Class. R.*, 42, vol. 56, p. 75-76.

1093. THOMSON (George). Aeschylus and Athens : a study in the social origins of drama. London, Lawrence and Wishart, 41, in-8, xii-476 p., 21s. R : W.F.J.K., *Greece and Rome*, 41, vol. 11, p. 46-48. J. L. Myres, *Man*, 42, vol. 42, p. 21-22. W. F. J. Knight, *J. hell. Stud.*, 42 (43), vol. 62, p. 96-97. A. W. Pickard-Cambridge, *Class. R.*, 42, vol. 56, p. 21-26.

1094. TODD (F. A.). Some ancient novels : Lucippe and Clitophon, Daphnis and Chloe, The satiricon, The golden ass. London, Oxford Univ. Press, 40, in-8, vi-144 p., 7s. 6d. R : H.D.F.K., *J. hell. Stud.*, 42 (43), vol. 62, p. 93.

1095. WEBSTER (T. B. L.). Greek interpretations. Manchester, Univ. Press, 42, in-8, viii-128 p., 5s. R : P. Treves, *J. hell. Stud.*, 43, vol. 63, p. 134-135.

1096. WEBSTER (T. B. L.). Forethoughts on later Greek comedy. *B. John Rylands Library*, 45, vol. 29, p. 143-159.

§ 8. Religion and Mythology

1097. COOK (Arthur Bernard). Zeus: a study in ancient religion. Vol. 3, pt. 1-2. London, Cambridge Univ. Press, 40, 2 pts. in-4, 168s.

1098. MAAS (P.). The Philinna papyrus. *J. hell. Stud.*, 42 (43), vol. 62, p. 33-38.

1099. NILSSON (Martin P.). Greek popular religion. London, Oxford Univ. Press, 40, in-8, xviii-166 p., (plates), 12s. 6d. (Amer. council of learned societies, lect. on the hist. of religions, n.s., 1). R : M. Braun, *Hibbert J.*, 41, vol. 40, p. 102-104. H.J.R., *J. hell. Stud.*, 42 (43), vol. 62, p. 90-91.

1100. PARKE (H. W.). The days for consulting the Delphic oracle. *Class. Quar.*, 43, vol. 37, p. 19-22.

1101. ROBINSON (David M.). Necrolynthia : a study in Greek burial customs and anthropology. London, Oxford Univ. Press, 42, in-4, 306 p., (plates), 67s. 6d. (Excavations at Olynthus, pt. 11 : Johns Hopkins Univ., stud. in archaeol., no. 32). R : J. L. Myres, *Man*, 43, vol. 43, p. 94-95. V. G. Childe, *Antiquity*, 43, vol. 17, p. 217-218. P. N. Ure, *Class. R.*, 43, vol. 57, p. 85-86. J.R.D., *Greece and Rome*, 43, vol. 12, p. 94-95.

§ 9. Archaeology and History of Art

1102. BAILEY (B. L.). The export of Attic black-figure ware. *J. hell. Stud.*, 40 (41), vol. 60, p. 60-70.

1103. BEAZLEY (J. D.). A marble lamp. *J. hell. Stud.*, 40 (41), vol. 60, p. 22-49.

1104. BEAZLEY (J. D.). Attic red-figure vase-painters. London, Oxford Univ. Press, 42, in-8, 1,200 p., 63s. R : T.B.L.W., *J. hell. Stud.*, 42 (43), vol. 62, p. 98-99. O. Kurz, *Burlington Mag.*, 43, vol. 83, p. 234. F. M. Heichelheim, *Econ. J.*, 43, vol. 53, p. 101-102. M. Robertson, *Class. R.*, 43, vol. 57, p. 38-39.

1105. GRACE (F. R.). Archaic sculpture in Boeotia. London, Oxford Univ. Press, 40, in-4, 86 p., (illus.), 21s. R : S. Benton, *J. hell. Stud.*, 40 (41), vol. 60, p. 106-107.

1106. MARKMAN (S. D.). The horse in Greek art. London, Oxford Univ. Press, 44, in-8, 232 p., (illus.), 30s.

1107. PAYNE (Humfry) and others. Perachora, the sanctuaries of Hera Akraia and Limenia : excavations of the British School of Archaeology at Athens, 1930-33. London, Oxford Univ. Press, 40, in-2, 286 p., (plates), 64s. R : M. Robertson, *J. hell. Stud.*, 40 (41), vol. 60, p. 101-102. W. L. Cuttle, *Class. R.*, 41, vol. 55, p. 41-43.

1108. RICHTER (G. M. A.). Archaic Attic gravestones. London, Oxford Univ. Press, 45, in-8, 176 p., (illus.), 14s.

1109. RICHTER (G. M. A. and I. A.). Kouroi : a study of the development of the Greek kouros from the late 7th to the early 5th century B.C. London, Oxford Univ. Press, 42, in-8, xxi-428 p., 208 plates, 84s. (Yale Univ., Martin A. Ryerson lect., 1938). R : G. F. Forsey, *Antiquity*, 44, vol. 18, p. 161-163.

1110. ROBERTSON (Martin). The excavations at Al Mina, Sueidia, 4 : The early Greek vases. *J. hell. Stud.*, 40 (41), vol. 60, p. 2-21.

1111. ROBINSON (David M.). Necrolynthia. Metal and minor miscellaneous finds. (Excavations at Olynthus, 9, 10). London, Oxford Univ. Press, 42, 2 vols. in-4, 307, xxvi-593 p., (plates), 67s. 6d., 90s. (Johns Hopkins Univ. stud. in archaeol., 31, 32). R : J.P.D., *Greece and Rome*, 42, vol. 11, p. 95-96. R.E.W., *J. hell. Stud.*, 42 (43), vol. 62, p. 103-104.

1112. TRITSCH (F. J.). The Harpy tomb at Xanthus. *J. hell. Stud.*, 42 (43), vol. 62, p. 39-50.

§ 1. The Peoples of Italy
§ 2. The Etruscans

1113. GOLDSCHEIDER (Ludwig) ed. Etruscan sculpture. London, Allen & Unwin, 41, in-4, 40 p., (plates), 12s. 6d. (Phaidon ser.). R : W. L. Hildburgh, *Burlington Mag.*, 44, vol. 85, p. 233-234.

1114. HILDBURGH (W. L.). Lunar crescents as amulets in Spain. *Man*, 42, vol. 42, p. 73-84.

1115. RICHTER (G. M. A.). Handbook of the Etruscan collection, Metropolitan Museum of Art, New York. London, Quaritch, 41, in-8, xxiv-86 p., (plates), 11s.

§ 3. Sources and Criticisms of Sources

a. AUTHORS

1116. FLETCHER (G. B. A.). Some certain or possible examples of literary reminiscence in Tacitus. *Class. R.*, 45, vol. 59, p. 45-50.

1117. RICHARDS (G. C.). Strabo, the Anatolian who failed of Roman recognition. *Greece and Rome*, 41, vol. 10, p. 79-90.

1118. SMITH (R. E.). Plutarch's biographical sources in the Roman Lives. *Class. Quar.*, 40, vol. 34, p. 1-10.

1119. SMITH (R. E.). The sources of Plutarch's Life of Titus Flaminius. *Class. Quar.*, 44, vol. 38, p. 89-95.

1120. THOMPSON (E. A.). Ammianus Marcellinus and the Romans. *Greece and Rome*, 42, vol. 11, p. 130-136.

1121. THOMPSON (E. A.). Olympiodorus of Thebes. *Class. Quar.*, 44, vol. 38, p. 43-52.

1122. TOYNBEE (J. M. C.). Two notes of Tacitus : 1, ' Coloniae et municipia ' in the Dialogus ; 2, ' urgentibus imperii fatis ', Germania 33. *Class. R.*, 44, vol. 58, p. 39-43.

1123. WOODWARD (Arthur M.). A manuscript of the Latin version of Appian's *Civil Wars*. *Library*, 45, vol. 26, p. 149-157.

b. INSCRIPTIONS

1124. O'BRIEN (J. L.). Augustus and the Monument of Ancyra. *Hist. Stud. Australia · N.Z.*, 45, vol. 3, p. 111-138.

1125. WARMINGTON (E. H.). Remains of old Latin. Vol. 4 : Archaic inscriptions. London, Heinemann, 40, in-8, 400 p., 10s. (Loeb class. libr.). R : H. Mattingly, *Class. R.*, 42, vol. 56, p. 34-35.

1126. WRIGHT (R. P.). New readings of a Severan inscription from Nicopolis, near Alexandria. *J. rom. Stud.*, 42, vol. 32, p. 33-38 (illus.).

§ 4. Political History

a. GENERAL

1127. ADCOCK (F. E.). The Roman art of war under the Republic. London, Oxford Univ. Press, 42, in-8, 148 p., 8s. 6d. R : F.W.W., *Greece and Rome*, 44, vol. 13, p. 30-31.

1128. BAYNES (Norman H.). The decline of the Roman power in western Europe : some modern explanations. *J. rom. Stud.*, 43, vol. 33, p. 29-35.

1129. HASKELL (H. J.). This was Cicero : modern politics in a Roman toga. London, Secker & Warburg, 43, in-8, 427 p., 15s. R : H. Last, *J. rom. Stud.*, 43, vol. 33, p. 93-97. A. F. Giles, *Class. R.*, 43, vol. 57, p. 117-118.

1130. McDONALD (A. H.). The rise of Roman imperialism. Sydney, Australasian Medical Publ. Co., 40, in-8, 18 p. R : A. F. Giles, *Class. R.*, 40, vol. 54, p. 216.

1131. MOORE (R. W.). The Roman commonwealth. London, Hodder, 42, in-8, 268 p., 15s. R : *Greece and Rome*, 43, vol. 12, p. 93. H. Mattingly, *Antiquity*, 43, vol. 17, p. 53-54.

1132. —— New ed. Bickley, Engl. Univ. Press, 43, in-8, 268 p., (plates, map), 15s.

1133. RADIN (M.). Marcus Brutus. London, Oxford Univ. Press, 40, in-8, 238 p., 11s. 6d.

1134. SALMON (E. T.). A history of the Roman world from 30 B.C. to A.D. 138. London, Methuen, 44, in-8, 363 p., 20s. R : H. Last, *J. rom. Stud.*, 45, vol. 35, p. 125-127.

1135. SCRAMUZZA (Vincent M.). The Emperor Claudius. London, Oxford Univ. Press, 40, in-8, 328 p., 16s. (Harvard hist. studies, 44). R : A. Momigliano, *J. rom. Stud.*, 42, vol. 32, p. 125-127. H. H. Scullard, *History*, 41, vol. 26, p. 141-142.

b. MONOGRAPHS

1136. ALFÖLDI (A.). The reckoning by the regnal years and victories of Valerian and Gallienus. *J. rom. Stud.*, 40, vol. 30, p. 1-10.

1137. CHARLESWORTH (M. P.). Pietas and Victoria : the emperor and the citizen. *J. rom. Stud.*, 43, vol. 33, p. 1-10.

1138. DUDLEY (D. R.). Blossius of Cumae. *J. rom. Stud.*, 41, vol. 31, p. 94-99.

1139. GREEN (Charles). Glevum and the Second Legion. 2 pts. *J. rom. Stud.*, 42, vol. 32, p. 39-52; 43, vol. 33, p. 15-28 (illus.).

1140. HENDERSON (M. I.). Julius Caesar and Latium in Spain. *J. rom. Stud.*, 42, vol. 32, p. 1-13.

1141. LAST (H.). ' Cinnae quater consulis '. *Class. R.*, 44, vol. 58, p. 15-17.

1142. LOADER (W. R.). Pompey's command under the Lex Gabinia. *Class. R.*, 40, vol. 54, p. 134-136.

1143. MCDONALD (A. H.). The Roman citizenship. *Hist. Stud. Australia N.Z.*, 43, vol. 2, p. 239-254.

1144. MCDONALD (A. H.). Rome and the Italian confederation (200-186 B.C.). *J. rom. Stud.*, 44, vol. 34, p. 11-33.

1145. MULLENS (H. G.). The women of the Caesars. *Greece and Rome*, 42, vol. 11, p. 59-67 ; 43, vol. 12, p. 28-29.

1146. REED (T. Dayrell). The battle for Britain in the fifth century : an essay in Dark age history. London, Methuen, 44, in-8, 205 p., 10s. 6d. R : J. N. L. Myres, *Antiq. J.*, 45, vol. 25, p. 81-85.

1147. RICHMOND (I. A.). Gnaeus Iulius Agricola. *J. rom. Stud.*, 44, vol. 34, p. 34-45 (illus.).

1148. ROGERS (Robert Samuel). Studies in the reign of Tiberius : some imperial virtues of Tiberius and Drusus Julius Caesar. London, Oxford Univ. Press, 43, in-8, ix-181 p., (plates), 12s. 6d. R : F.W.W., *Greece and Rome*, 44, vol. 13, p. 29-30.

1149. SCULLARD (H. H.). Charops and Roman policy in Epirus. *J. rom. Stud.*, 45, vol. 35, p. 58-64.

1150. SIMPSON (W. Douglas). Stilicho and Britain. *J. archaeol. Assoc.*, 42, vol. 7, p. 41-52.

1151. STARR (C. G.). The Roman imperial navy, 31 B.C.-A.D. 324. London, Oxford Univ. Press, 42, in-8, 246 p., (map), 11s. 6d. (Studies in classical philology ser.).

1152. WALBANK (F. W.). Philip V of Macedon. London, Cambridge Univ. Press, 40, in-8, xi-387 p., (plates, maps), 18s. (Hare prize essay, 1939). R : M. Cary, *History*, 41, vol. 26, p. 141.

1153. WALBANK (F. W.). A note on the embassy of Q. Marcius Philippus, 172 B.C. *J. rom. Stud.*, 41, vol. 31, p. 82-93.

1154. WALBANK (F. W.). Alcaeus of Messene, Philip V, and Rome. *Class. Quar.*, 42, vol. 36, p. 134-145 ; 43, vol. 37, p. 1-13 ; 44, vol. 38, p. 87-88.

1155. WALBANK (F. W.). Polybius, Philinus, and the first Punic war. *Class. Quar.*, 45, vol. 39, p. 1-18.

§ 5. **History of Law and Institutions**

1156. BUCKLAND (W. W.). Gaius, I, 166. 'Tutela parentis manumissionis'. *J. rom. Stud.*, 43, vol. 33, p. 11-14.

1157. BUCKLAND (W. W.). Alienation and manumission by one of Consortes. *L.Q.R.*, 42, vol. 58, p. 483-486.

1158. BUCKLAND (W. W.). The Interpretationes to Pauli Sententiae and the Codex Theodosianus. *L.Q.R.*, 44, vol. 60, p. 361-365.

1159. BUCKLAND (W. W.). Pauli Sententiae and the compilers of the Digest. *L.Q.R.*, 45, vol. 61, p. 34-48.

1160. HOWE (L. L.). The Pretorian prefect from Commodus to Diocletian (A.D. 180-305). London, Cambridge Univ. Press, 43, in-8, xiv-142 p., 12s. R: A. F. Giles, *Class. R.*, 43, vol. 57, p. 120-121.

1161. LAST (Hugh). The Fiscus : a note. *J. rom. Stud.*, 44, vol. 34, p. 51-59.

1162. LAST (H.). The Servian reforms. *J. rom. Stud.*, 45, vol. 35, p. 30-48.

1163. LEE (R. W.). The elements of Roman law : with a translation of the Institutes of Justinian. London, Sweet & Maxwell, 44, in-8, 488 p., 27s. 6d.

1164. LÉVY-BRUHL (H.). The Act 'Per Aes et Libram'. *L.Q.R.*, 44, vol. 60, p. 51-62.

1165. LUCAS (C.). Notes on the Curatores Rei Publicae of Roman Africa. *J. rom. Stud.*, 40, vol. 30, p. 56-74.

1166. PRINGSHEIM (F.). The character of Justinian's legislation. *L.Q.R.*, 40, vol. 56, p. 229-246.

1167. PRINGSHEIM (F.). Legal estate and equitable interest in Roman law. *L.Q.R.*, 43, vol. 59, p. 244-249.

1168. PRINGSHEIM (F.). The unique character of classical Roman law. *J. rom. Stud.*, 44, vol. 34, p. 60-64.

1169. RICHMOND (I. A.) and STEVENS (C. E.). The land-register of Arausio. *J. rom. Stud.*, 42, vol. 32, p. 65-77.

1170. SCHULZ (Fritz). Roman registers of births and birth certificates. *J. rom. Stud.*, 42, vol. 32, p. 78-91.

1171. WALBANK (F. W.). Polybius on the Roman constitution. *Class. Quar.*, 43, vol. 37, p. 73-89.

§ 6. **Economic and Social History**

1172. ADCOCK (F. E.). Women in Roman life and letters. *Greece and Rome*, 45, vol. 14, p. 1-11.

1173. CARCOPINO (Jérôme). Daily life in ancient Rome, ed. by H. T. Rowell, tr. by E. O. Lorimer. London, Routledge, 41, in-8, 342 p., 16s. 6d. (Yale Univ., O. B. Cunningham mem. publ. fund). R : O.B., *History*, 41, vol. 26, p. 153-154.

1174. CHILVER (G. E. F.). Cisalpine Gaul. Social and economic history from 49 B.C. to the death of Trajan. London, Oxford Univ. Press, 41, in-8, vi-235 p., (maps), 17s. 6d. R : M. P. Charlesworth, *Class. R.*, 43, vol. 57, p. 90-91. *Greece and Rome*, 42, vol. 11, p. 143-144. A. Momigliano, *J. rom. Stud.*, 42, vol. 32, p. 135-138.

1175. FRANK (Tenney). An economic survey of ancient Rome. Vol. 5 : Rome and Italy of the Empire, and General Index to vol. 1-5. London, Oxford Univ. Press, 40, 2 vols. in-8, 37s. 6d. R : M. P. Charlesworth, *Class. R.*, 41, vol. 55, p. 46-48.

1176. HUNT (H. K.). Population problems of the Roman Republic. 2 pts. *Hist. Stud. Australia N.Z.*, 41, vol. 1, p. 145-156, 213-224.

1177. KENNEDY (E. C.) and WHITE (G. W.). S.P.Q.R. : the history and social life of ancient Rome. London, Macmillan, 44, in-8, xii-278 p., (illus., map, diagram), 4s.

1178. YOUTIE (H. C.) and PEARL (O. M.). Papyri and astraka from Karanis. London, Oxford Univ. Press, 45, in-8, 276 p., 22s. 6d. (Stud., Humanistic ser., vol. 47; Michigan papyri, vol. 6). R : H. I. Bell, *J. rom. Stud.*, 45, vol. 35, p. 136-140; *Class R.*, 45, vol. 59, p. 74-76.

§ 7. History of Literature, Philosophy and Science

1179. KNIGHT (W. F. Jackson). Roman Vergil. London, Faber, 44, in-8, viii-348 p., 15s. R : L.J.D.R., *Greece and Rome*, 45, vol. 14, p. 30-31.

1180. MARTIN (J. M. K.). Seneca the satirist. *Greece and Rome*, 45, vol. 14, p. 64-71.

1181. MATHEW (Gervase). The character of the Gallienic renaissance. *J. rom. Stud.*, 43, vol. 33, p. 65-70.

1182. MOMIGLIANO (Arnaldo). Literary chronology of the Neronian age. *Class. Quar.*, 44, vol. 38, p. 96-100.

1183. MOMIGLIANO (A.). The Locrian Maidens and the date of Lycophron's *Alexandra. Class. Quar.*, 45, vol. 39, p. 49-53.

1184. RAND (E. K.). The building of eternal Rome. London, Oxford Univ. Press, 43, in-8, xi-318 p., 20s. R : H. Mattingly, *Class. R.*, 44, vol. 58, p. 23-24.

1185. REYNOLDS (R. W.). Criticism of individuals in Roman popular comedy. *Class. Quar.*, 43, vol. 37, p. 37-45.

1186. RICHARDSON (L.) jr. Poetical theory in Republican Rome. London, Oxford Univ. Press, 44, in-8, 186 p., 6s. 6d.

1187. THOMPSON (E. A.). The Emperor Julian's knowledge of Latin. *Class. R.*, 44, vol. 58, p. 49-51.

1188. TOYNBEE (Jocelyn M. C.). Dictators and philosophers in the first century A.D. *Greece and Rome*, 44, vol. 13, p. 43-58.

1189. WHATELY (S.). Noises off : some sound-effects in Virgil. *Greece and Rome*, 45, vol. 14, p. 17-28.

1190. WHITE (G. W.) and KENNEDY (E. C.). Roman history, life and literature. London, Macmillan, 42, .in-8, xiv-335 p., (illus., map), 6s.

§ 8. Religion and Mythology

1191. CORMACK (J. M. R.). High priests and Macedoniarchs from Beroea. *J. rom. Stud.*, 43, vol. 33, p. 39-44.

1192. WRIGHT (R. P.). The Whitley Castle altar to Apollo. *J. rom. Stud.*, 43, vol. 33, p. 36-38.

§ 9. Archaeology and History of Art

a. GENERAL

1193. BEAZLEY (J. D.). Groups of Campanian red-figure. *J. hell. Stud.*, 43, vol. 63, p. 66-111 (illus.).

1194. CURWEN (E. C.). The problem of early water-mills. *Antiquity*, 44, vol. 18, p. 130-146 (illus.).

1195. DOHAN (E. H.). Italic tombgroups in the University Museum, Pennsylvania. London, Oxford Univ. Press, 42, in-2, xii-113 p., (plates), 34s. R : J. D. Beazley, *Class. R.*, 44, vol. 58, p. 30-31. P. Jacobsthal, *J. rom. Stud.*, 43, vol. 33, p. 97-100.

1196. FREND (W. H. C.). The revival of Berber art. *Antiquity*, 42, vol. 16, p. 342-352.

1197. OSWALD (F.). Decorated ware from Lavoye. *J. rom. Stud.*, 45, vol. 35, p. 49-57.

1198. PRYCE (T. Davis). Roman decorated red-glazed ware. *J. rom. Stud.*, 42, vol. 32, p. 14-26 (plates).

1199. ROSTOVTZEFF (M.). 'Vexillum' and victory. *J. rom. Stud.*, 42, vol. 32, p. 92-106 (illus.).

1200. RYBERG (Inez Scott). An archaeological record of Rome, 7th to 2nd centuries, B.C. London, Christophers, 40, 2 pts. in-8, xiv-222; 223-247 p., (plates), 35s. (Stud. and documents, 13). R : M. L. Clarke, *Theology*, 40, vol. 41, p. 318-319.

1201. TILLY (Bertha). Vergilian cities of the Roman campagna. *Antiquity*, 45, vol. 19, p. 125-134.

1202. TRENDALL (A. D.). The Shellal mosaic, and other classical antiquities in the Australian War Memorial, Canberra. Canberra, Austral. War Memorial, 42, in-4, 27 p., (plates), 2s. 6d. R : A. H. McDonald, *Hist. Stud. Australia N.Z.*, 42, vol. 2, p. 121-122. D. Dettmann, *Austral. Quar.*, 42, vol. 14, no. 4, p. 101-102.

1203. WAR OFFICE, Archaeological Adviser. The war and classical remains in Italy. *Antiquity*, 44, vol. 18, p. 169-172 (illus.).

b. ROMAN BRITAIN

1204. ATKINSON (Donald). Report on excavations at Wroxeter (the Roman city of Viroconium) in the County of Salop, 1923-1927. London, Oxford Univ. Press, 42, in-8, 406 p., (plates, figures), 21s. R : E.D., *Archaeol. cambrensis*, 43, vol. 97, p. 239-240. K.M.K., *Antiq. J.*, 43, vol. 23, p. 66-67. I. A. Richmond, *J. rom. Stud.*, 43, vol. 33, p. 113-115. R.N., *Greece and Rome*, 43, vol. 12, p. 93-94.

1205. CORDER (Philip). Excavations at Elmswell, east Yorkshire, 1938. Hull, Univ. College Local Hist. Comm., 40, in-8, 62 p., 1s. R : M.K.C., *Antiq. J.*, 40, vol. 20, p. 401-403. I. A. Richmond, *Archaeol. J.*, 39 (40), vol. 96, p. 308-309.

1206. CORDER (P.). A Roman pottery of the Hadrian-Antonine period at Verulamium. *Antiq. J.*, 41, vol. 21, p. 271-298.

1207. CORDER (P.). Verulamium, 1930-40. *Antiquity*, 41, vol. 15, p. 113-124.

1208. CORDER (P.) and HAWKES (C. F. C.). A panel of Celtic ornament from Elmswell, East Yorkshire. *Antiq. J.*, 40, vol. 20, p. 338-357 (illus.).

1209. CORDER (P.) and RICHMOND (Ian A.). Petuaria. *J. archaeol. Assoc.*, 42, vol. 7, p. 1-30 (plates).

1210. CURWEN (E. C.). Roman lead cistern from Pulborough, Sussex. *Antiq. J.*, 43, vol. 23, p. 155-157.

1211. DAVIES (Ellis). The discovery of a ' nest ' of Roman patellae near Llanberis, Caernarvonshire. *Archaeol. cambrensis*, 44, vol. 98, p. 129-133 (illus.).

1212. DUNNING (G. C.). Two fires of Roman London. *Antiq. J.*, 45, vol. 25, p. 48-77 (illus.).

1213. FOX (Aileen). The Roman legionary fortress at Caerleon in Monmouthshire : report on the excavations carried out in Myrtle Cottage orchard in 1939. Cardiff, National Museum of Wales, 41, in-8, 56 p., (illus.), 1s. 6d.; *Archaeol. cambrensis*, 40, vol. 95, p. 101-152 (illus.).

1214. FOX (Sir Cyril). The reerection of Maen-Madoc, Ystradfellte, Breconshire. *Archaeol. cambrensis*, 40, vol. 95, p. 210-216 (illus.).

1215. FRERE (Sheppard). A Claudian site at Needham, Norfolk. *Antiq. J.*, 41, vol. 21, p. 40-55 (illus.).

1216. GOODCHILD (R. G.). Romano-British disc-brooches derived from Hadrianic coin-types. *Antiq. J.*, 41, vol. 21, p. 1-8 (illus.).

1217. GOODCHILD (R. G.). T-shaped corn-drying ovens in Roman Britain. *Antiq. J.*, 43, vol. 23, p. 148-163 (illus.).

1218. GUILLAUME (Alfred). The Phoenician graffito in the Holt collection of the National Museum of Wales. *Iraq*, 40, vol. 7, pt. 1, p. 67-69.

1219. HALL (A. F.). A three-tracked Roman road at Colchester : a description and a commentary from a layman's point of view. *J. archaeol. Assoc.*, 42, vol. 7, p. 53-70.

1220. HEMP (W. J.). A hill-fort problem. *Archaeol. cambrensis*, 42, vol. 97, p. 93-97.

1221. HOGG (A. H. A.). Native settlements of Northumberland. *Antiquity*, 43, vol. 17, p. 136-147 (illus.).

1222. KENYON (K. M.). Excavations at Viroconium, 1936-7. *Archaeologia*, 40, vol. 88, p. 175-227 (illus.).

1223. KIRKMAN (J. S.). Canterbury kiln site. The pottery. Sherd register. *Archaeol. cantiana*, 40 (41), vol. 5, p. 118-133.

1224. MACALISTER (R. A. S.). Corpus inscriptionum insularum Celticarum. Vol. 1. Dublin, Stationery Office, 45, in-8, 515 p., 42s. R: O. G. S. Crawford, *Antiquity*, 45, vol. 19, p. 207-209.

1225. MARPLES (M.). Sarn Helen : a Roman road in Wales. Newtown, Welsh Outlook Press, 40, in-8, 45 p., 2s. 6d.

1226. MYRES (J. N. L.). Wingham Villa and Romano-Saxon pottery in Kent. *Antiquity*, 44, vol. 18, p. 52-55 (illus.).

1227. O'NEIL (B. H. St. J.). Excavations at Porth Dafarch, Holyhead Island, Anglesey, 1939. *Archaeol. cambrensis*, 40, vol. 95, p. 65-74 (illus.).

1228. O'NEIL (B. H. St. J.). Grim's Bank, Padworth, Berkshire. *Antiquity*, 43, vol. 17, p. 188-195 (illus.).

1229. Ó RÍORDÁIN (Seán P.). The excavation of a large earthen ring-fort at Garranes, co. Cork. London, Williams & Norgate; Dublin, Hodges, Figgis, 42, in-8, 150 p., 7s. 6d. (Proc., R. Irish Acad., vol. 47). R : C. F. C. Hawkes, *Man*, 43, vol. 43, p. 69.

1230. OSWALD (Felix). Margidunum. *J. rom. Stud.*, 41, vol. 31, p. 32-62 (illus.).

1231. OSWALD (F.). The mortaria of Margidunum and their development from A.D. 50 to 400. *Antiq. J.*, 44, vol. 24, p. 45-63.

1232. PERKINS (J. B. W.). Roman Villa, Lockleys, Welwyn. *Antiquity*, 40, vol. 14, p. 317-320 (illus.).

1233. RICHMOND (I. A.). Ancient Rome and northern England : a historical summary. *Antiquity*, 40, vol. 14, p. 292-300.

1234. RICHMOND (I. A.). Recent discoveries in Roman Britain from the air and in the field. *J. rom. Stud.*, 43, vol. 33, p. 45-54 (illus.).

1235. RICHMOND (I. A.). Three fragments of Roman official statues from York, Lincoln, and Silchester. *Antiq. J.*, 44, vol. 24, p. 1-9 (illus.).

1236. RICHMOND (I. A.). The Sarmatae, *Bremetennacum Veteranorum* and the *Regio Bremetennacensis*. *J. rom. Stud.*, 45, vol. 35, p. 15-29 (illus.).

1237. RILEY (D. N.). Aerial reconnaissance of the Fen basin. *Antiquity*, 45, vol. 19, p. 145-153 (illus.).

1238. Roman Britain in 1940-44. *J. rom. Stud.*, 41, vol. 31, p. 128-148; 42, vol. 32, p. 107-119; 43, vol. 33, p. 71-81; 44, vol. 34, p. 76-91; 45, vol. 35, p. 79-92 (illus.).

1239. TAYLOR (M. V.). The Sidmouth bronze : legionary standard or tripod ? *Antiq. J.*, 44, vol. 24, p. 22-26 (illus.).

1240. WEBSTER (Graham). A Roman pottery kiln at Canterbury. *Archaeol. cantiana*, 40 (41), vol. 5, p. 109-116.

1241. WEBSTER (G.). A Roman pottery at South Carlton, Lincs. *Antiq. J.*, 44, vol. 24, p. 129-143 (illus.).

1242. WILLIAMS (Audrey). The excavation of High Penard promontory fort, Glamorgan. *Archaeol. cambrensis*, 41, vol. 96, p. 23-30 (illus.).

§ 1. Sources

1243. BÉVENOT (M.). A new Cyprianic fragment. *B. John Rylands Library*, 44, vol. 28, p. 76-82.

1244. MANSON (T. W.). The life of Jesus : a study of the available materials, 1-3. *B. John Rylands Library*, 43, vol. 27, p. 323-337; 44, vol. 28, p. 119-136, 382-403.

1245. SHELTON (H. S.). The authorship and date of the Gospels reconsidered; the origin of the Gospels. *Hibbert J.*, 43, vol. 41, p. 167-171; vol. 42, p. 71-76.

1245a. SHELTON (H. S.). The Gospels and the new papyri. *Hibbert J.*, 45, vol. 43, p. 157-162.

§ 2. General

1246. BARTLET (James Vernon). Church-life and church-order during the first four centuries, ed. by C. J. Cadoux. Oxford, Blackwell, 43, in-8, lxiv-207 p., 15s. (Trinity Coll., Cambridge, Birkbeck lect.). R : A. Peel, *Congreg. Quar.*, 43, vol. 21, p. 169-171. T. Jalland, *Theology*, 43, vol. 46, p. 89-90. C. C. J. Webb, *Hibbert J.*, 43, vol. 42, p. 90-93.

1247. BOAK (A. E. R.). Christianity and the fall of Rome : a reappraisal. *Queen's Quar.*, 43, vol. 50. p. 235-246.

1248. CADOUX (C. J.). The early Christian attitude to war. London, Allen & Unwin, 40, in-8, xxxii-272 p., 5s.

1249. COCHRANE (Charles Norris). Christianity and classical culture : a study of thought and action from Augustus to Augustine. London, Oxford Univ. Press, 40, in-8, vii-523 p., 30s. R : T. M. Parker, *Theology*, 41, vol. 42, p. 303-304. H. Mattingly, *Antiquity*, 42, vol. 16, p. 369-370.

1250. JALLAND (Trevor Gervase). The Church and the Papacy : a historical study. London, S.P.C.K., 44, in-8, xi-568 p., 25s. (Bampton lecture, 1942). R : C. Lattey, *Hibbert J.*, 44, vol. 43, p. 86-87. N. Sykes, *Theology*, 44, vol. 47, p. 227-232.

1251. KLAUSNER (Joseph). From Jesus to Paul, tr. by W. F. Stinespring. London, Allen, 44, in-8, xvi-624 p., 18s. R : W. L. Knox, *Theology*, 45, vol. 48, p. 90-91.

1252. KNOX (Wilfred L.). Some Hellenistic elements in primitive Christianity. London, Oxford Univ. Press, 44, in-4, 116 p., 7s. 6d. (British Acad., Schweich lect. on Biblical archaeol., 1942). R : S.M.G., *Queen's Quar.*, 45, vol. 52, p. 374. S. H. Mellone, *Hibbert J.*, 45, vol. 43, p. 286-288.

1253. LEBRETON (J.) and ZEILLER (J.). The history of the primitive church, tr. by E. C. Messenger. Vol. 1. London, Burns, Oates, 42, in-8, 269 p., 16s. R : H. E. Symonds, *Theology*, 42, vol. 45, p. 237-238. A. J. Grieve, *Congreg. Quar.*, 42, vol. 20, p. 361-362. Vol 2. London, Burns, Oates, 44, in-8, 503 p., 18s. R : H. E. Symonds, *Theology*, 45, vol. 48, p. 118-119.

1254. NILSSON (M. P.). The historical Hellenistic background of the New Testament. London, Oxford Univ. Press, 42, in-8, 31 p., 2s. 6d.

1255. RAYNER (A. J.). Christian society in the Roman Empire. *Greece and Rome*, 42, vol. 11, p. 113-123.

1256. RYLANDS (L. G.). The beginnings of gnostic Christianity. London, Watts, 40, in-8, viii-300 p., 15s.

1257. SANDERS (J. N.). The Fourth Gospel in the early Church, its origin and influence on Christian theology up to Irenaeus. London, Macmillan, 43, in-8, viii-92 p., 7s. 6d. (Kaye prize essay, 1939). R : R. H. Strachan, *Theology*, 43, vol. 46, p. 208-209.

1258. SCOTT (E. F.). The nature of the early Church. London, Scribner, 42, in-8, vii-245 p., 8s. 6d.

§ 3. Special Studies

1259. BARRETT (Helen M.). Boethius : some aspects of his times and work. London, Cambridge Univ. Press, 40, in-8, ix-179 p., 8s. 6d. R : J. M. L. Thomas, *Hibbert J.*, 41, vol. 39, p.,218-220. C. C. J. Webb, *Philosophy*, 41, vol. 16, p. 328-329. W.H.V.R., *Eng. hist. R.*, 41, vol. 56, p. 154.

1260. CROSS (F. L.). A study of St. Athanasius. Oxford, Clarendon Press, 45, in-8, 22 p., 2s. R : N. H. Baynes, *J. rom. Stud.*, 45, vol. 35, p. 121-124.

1261. CROWFOOT (J. W.). Early churches in Palestine. London, Oxford Univ. Press, 41, in-8, xiv-166p., (plates), 8s. 6d. (Brit. acad., Schweich lect., 1937). R : C. A. R. R(adford), *Antiq. J.*, 42, vol. 22, p. 78-79.

1262. FITZGERALD (G. M.). A sixth century monastery at Beth-Shan (Scythopolis). London, Oxford Univ. Press, 40, in-2, ix-19 p., (plates), 34s. (Univ. museum, publ., of the Palestine section, vol. 4).

1263. JALLAND (Trevor). The life and times of St. Leo the Great. London, S.P.C.K., 41, in-8, viii-542 p., 21s. R : C. J. Cadoux, *Congreg. Quar.*, 41, vol. 19, p. 364-365. S. L. Greenslade, *Theology*, 41, vol. 43, p. 189-191.

1264. MANSON (T. W.). St. Paul in Ephesus, 3 : the Corinthian correspondence. B. *John Rylands Library*, 41/42, vol. 26, p. 101-120, 327-341.

1265. OGG (George). The chronology of the public ministry of Jesus. London, Cambridge Univ. Press, 40, in-8, viii-339 p., 15s. R : W. K. L. Clarke, *Theology*, 41, vol. 42, p. 243-244.

1266. ORCHARD (Bernard). A new solution of the Galatians problem. B. *John Rylands Library*, 44, vol. 28, p. 154-174.

1267. ROCHE (A.). The first monks and nuns. Birmingham, Burns & Oates, 43, in-8, 138 p., 7s. 6d.

1268. SELLERS (R. V.). Two ancient Christologies. A study in the christological thought of the Schools of Alexandria and Antioch in the early history of Christian doctrine. London, S.P.C.K., 40, in-8, xiv-264 p., 16s.

1269. SIMPSON (W. J. S.). St. Augustine's episcopate. London, S.P.C.K., 44, in-8, 160 p., 7s. 6d.

BYZANTINE HISTORY (SINCE JUSTINIAN)

§ 1. Sources

1270. MALALAS (J.). Chronicle : books VIII-XVIII, tr. by M. Spinka and G. Downey. London, Cambridge Univ. Press, 41, in-8, vi-150 p., 9s.

§ 2. General

1271. NERSESSIAN (S. Der). Armenia and the Byzantine empire. London, Oxford Univ. Press, 45, in-8, 170 p., (illus.), 16s. 6d.

§ 3. Special Studies

1272. BEZA (M.). Byzantine art in Roumania. London, Batsford, 40, in- 4, xxii-106 p., (plates), 21s. R : D.T.R., *J. hell. Stud.*, 42 (43), vol. 62, p. 112.

1273. GALANTÉ (A.). Les Juifs de Constantinople sous Byzance. London, Luzac, 40, in-8, 68 p., 6s.

1274. HUSSEY (J. M.). Byzantine monasticism. *History*, 40, vol. 24, p. 56-62.

1275. PEIRCE (H.) and TYLER (R.). Three Byzantine works of art. London, Oxford Univ. Press, 42, in-4, 26 p., (illus.), 21s. (Dumbarton Oaks papers).

HISTORY OF THE MIDDLE AGES

(See also ADDENDA No. 5262-5315).

§ 1. Sources and Criticisms of Sources

1276. AELFRIC. De temporibus anni. Ed. by H. Henel. London, Oxford Univ. Press, 42, in-8, 164 p., (facs.), 21s. (Early Engl. text soc.).

1277. AMBROISE. The crusade of Richard Lion-Heart, ed. by J. L. La Monte, tr. from the Old French by M. J. Hubert. London, Oxford Univ. Press, 42, in-8, 494 p., (illus., map), 20s. (Records of civilization, sources and stud.).

1278. ANDERSON (R. C.). Jal's ' Memoire No. 5 ' and the manuscript ' Fabbrica di galere '. *Mariner's Mirror*, 45, vol. 31, p. 160-167.

1279. ANGUS (W. S.). The Eighth Scribe's dates in the Parker manuscript of the Anglo-Saxon Chronicle. *Med. Ævum*, 41, vol. 10, p. 130-149.

1280. ATKINS (Sir Ivor). Origin of the later part of the Saxon Chronicle. *Eng. hist. R.*, 40, vol. 55, p. 8-26.

1281. BECKERLEGGE (O. A.). An abridged Anglo-Norman version of the *Secretum Secretorum*. *Med. Ævum*, 44, vol. 13, p. 1-17.

1282. BIELER (Ludwig). The problem of ' silua Focluti '. *Irish hist. Stud.*, 43, vol. 3, p. 351-364.

1283. BOND (M. F.). A Farnborough (Kent) court roll of 1408, transcribed by M. F. Bond. *Archaeol. cantiana*, 44, vol. 57, p. 21-25.

1284. BUTLER (H. E.). Notes on the text of the Chronicle of Jocelin of Brakelond. *Med. Ævum*, 41, vol. 10, p. 94-96.

1285. CHAYTOR (Henry John). The medieval reader and textual criticism. *B. John Rylands Library*, 41, vol. 26, p. 49-56.

1286. CHESNEY (K.). The Lumley manuscript of Nicolas de Clamanges. *Med. Ævum*, 40, vol. 9, p. 79-81.

1287. COLGRAVE (Bertram). Two lives of St. Cuthbert: a life by an anonymous monk of Lindisfarne and Bede's prose life; texts, tr. and notes by B. Colgrave. London, Cambridge Univ. Press, 40, in-8, xiv-376 p., 21s. R : R.R.D., *Eng. hist. R.*, 41, vol. 56, p. 156-157.

1288. DAVIES (James Conway) ed. The Welsh assize roll, 1277-1284. Cardiff, Univ. of Wales, 40, in-4, 386 p., 15s. (Bd. of Celtic stud., hist. and law ser., 7). R : F. M. Powicke, *Eng. hist. R.*, 41, vol. 56, p. 491-494. A. Jones, *Archaeol. cambrensis*, 41, vol. 96, p. 103-104.

1289. DAVIES (J. C.). A grant by David ap Gruffydd. *Nat. Library Wales J.*, 43, vol. 3, p. 29-32.

1290. DAVIES (J. C.). A grant by Llewelyn ap Gruffydd. *Nat. Library Wales J.*, 44, vol. 3, p. 158-162.

1291. DEAN (R. J.). A fourteenth-century manuscript of *Le Roman de la Rose* and a fragment of *Le Compot* : Huntington manuscript 902. *Med. Ævum*, 43, vol. 12, p. 18-24.

1292. DOUGLAS (David C.). The Domesday monachorum of Christ Church, Canterbury. London, Roy. Hist. Soc., 44, in-2, 127 p., (facs.), 30s. R : J. Saltmarsh, *Econ. J.*, 45, vol. 55, p. 265-267.

1293. Duchy of Lancaster presentations, 1399-1485, ed. by R. Somerville. *B. Inst. hist. Research*, 40/41, vol. 18, p. 52-76, 122-134.

1294. EDWARDS (John Goronwy) ed. Littere Wallie, preserved in Liber A in the Public Record Office. Cardiff, Univ. of Wales Press Bd., 40, in-4, 302 p., (plates), 15s. (Univ. of Wales, Bd. of Celtic stud., hist. and law ser., 5). R : F. M. Powicke, *Eng. hist. R.*, 41, vol. 56, p. 491-494. E. Davies,

Archaeol. cambrensis, 41, vol. 96, p. 104-107.

1295. FLOWER (C. T.). Introduction to the Curia Regis rolls, 1199-1230 A.D. London, Quaritch, 45, in-8, x-574 p., 52s. 6d.

1296. FLOWER (Robin). William Salesbury, Richard Davies, and Archbishop Parker. *Nat. Library Wales J.,* 41, vol. 2, p. 7-16.

1297. FLOWER (R.). Richard Davies, William Cecil, and Giraldus Cambrensis. *Nat. Library Wales J.,* 43, vol. 3, p. 11-14.

1298. FLOWER (R.) and SMITH (Hugh) ed. The Parker Chronicle and Laws. (Corpus Christi College, Cambridge, MS. 173). London, Oxford Univ. Press, 41, in-2, 118 p., 63s. (Early Engl. text soc.). R : D. Whitelock, *Eng. hist. R.,* 42, vol. 57, p. 120-122.

1299. FORTESCUE (Sir John). De laudibus legum Anglie, ed. and tr. with notes by S. B. Chrimes. London, Cambridge Univ. Press, 42, in-8, cxiv-236 p., 25s. (Cambr. stud. in Engl. legal hist.). R : W. S. Holdsworth, *Eng. hist. R.,* 42, vol. 57, p. 504-506. A. F. Pollard, *History,* 42, vol. 27, p. 155-156. M. Postan, *Econ. Hist. R.,* 42, vol. 12, p. 97.

1300. FOX (Sir Cyril). The Domnic inscribed slab, Llangwyryfon, Cardiganshire. Topographical survey by Sir C. Fox ; epigraphy by Ifor Williams, R. A. S. Macalister and V. E. Nash-Williams. *Archaeol. cambrensis,* 43, vol. 97, p. 205-212 (illus.).

1301. FULCHER OF CHARTRES. Chronicle of the first crusade, tr. from the Latin by M. E. McGinty. London, Oxford Univ. Press, 42, in-8, 100 p., 4s. 6d.

1302. GALBRAITH (V. H.). The making of Domesday book. *Eng. hist. R.,* 42, vol. 57, p. 161-177.

1303. GALBRAITH (V. H.). The St. Edmundsbury chronicle, 1296-1301. *Eng. hist. R.,* 43, vol. 58, p. 51-78.

1304. GALBRAITH (V. H.). Roger Wendover and Matthew Paris. Glasgow, Jackson, 44, in-8, 48 p., 2s. 9d.

1305. GOLDSCHMIDT (E. Ph.). Medieval texts and their first appearance in print. London, Oxford Univ. Press, 43, in-8, 143 p. (Suppl., Bibliographical soc. trans., 16).

1306. GOLLANCZ (Marguerite) ed. Rolls of Northamptonshire sessions of the peace, 1314-1316, 1320. Northampton, Record Soc., 40, in-8, liii-114 p. (Northants. Record Soc., vol. 11). R : H.C.J., *B. Inst. hist. Research,* 41, vol. 19, p. 29-31.

1307. GRAY (Duncan) ed. Newstead priory cartulary, 1344, and other archives, tr. by V. W. Walker. Nottingham, Forman, 40, in-8, viii-262 p., privately printed. (Thornton Soc., record ser., vol. 8). R : C.J., *Eng. hist. R.,* 41, vol. 56, p. 161-162.

1308. HAM (E. B.). A fragment of the *Chanson des Lorrains. Med. Ævum,* 41, vol. 10, p. 86-93.

1309. HOWEL THE GOOD. Cyfreithiau Hywel Dda yn ôl Llyfr Blegywryd (dull Dyfed) : argraffiad beirniadol ac eglurghaol. (The Laws of Howel the Good according to the Book of Blegywryd (the style of Dyfed) : critical ed. by S. J. Williams and J. E. Powell). Caerdydd, Gwasg Prifysgol Cymru, 42, in-8, xlvi-281 p., 15s.

1310. HUGH CANDIDUS. The Peterborough chronicle of Hugh Candidus, tr. by C. and W. T. Mellows, ed. by W. T. Mellows. Peterborough, Nat. Hist. Soc., 41, in-8, 70 p., 2s. 6d. R : C. R. Cheney, *J. archaeol. Assoc.,* 42, vol. 7, p. 70.

1311. HUGHES (M. W.) and JENKINS (J. G.). Calendar of the feet of fines for the county of Buckingham : 7 Richard I to 44 Henry III. Bedford,

Sidney Press, 42, in-8, 138 p., 22s. 6d. (Records, Bucks archaeol. soc., 4). R : C.J., *Eng. hist. R.*, 43, vol. 58, p. 495-496.

1312. HUMPHREYS (W. H.). A register of writs in roll form [of Henry III's reign]. *B. Inst. hist. Research*, 40, vol. 18, p. 1-12.

1313. HUTCHINGS (G.). The *Lancelot* manuscript of Fribourg. *Med. Ævum*, 40, vol. 9, p. 81-83.

1314. HUTSON (A. E.). British personal names in the Historia Regum Britanniae. London, Cambridge Univ. Press, 40, in-8, 160 p., 9s. (Publ. in Engl., vol. 5, no. 1).

1315. JACOB (E. F.). The Book of St. Albans. *B. John Rylands Library*, 44, vol. 28, p. 99-118.

1316. JONES (Thomas) ed. Brut y Tywysogyon, Peniarth MS. 20. (The Chronicle of the Princes, in the National Library of Wales). Cardiff, Univ. of Wales Press Board, 41, in-8, xxiv-255 p., 15s. (Bd. of Celtic stud., hist. and law ser., 6). R : D. Williams, *History*, 41, vol. 26, p. 142-143. J. E. Lloyd, *Archaeol. cambrensis*, 41, vol. 96, p. 208-209. J. G. Edwards, *Eng. hist. R.*, 42, vol. 57, p. 370-375.

1317. KEMPE (Margery). The book of Margery Kempe. Vol. 1, ed. by S. B. Meech ; notes and appendices by H. E. Allen. London, Oxford Univ. Press, 40, in-8, 510 p., (plates), 20s. (Early Engl. text soc., orig. ser., 212). R : B. G. Brooks, *19th Century*, 42, vol. 132, p. 30-32.

1318. KER (Neil R.). Unpublished parts of the *Ormulum*. *Med. Ævum*, 40, vol. 9, p. 1-22.

1319. KER (N. R.). An eleventh-century Old English Legend of the Cross before Christ. *Med. Ævum*, 40, vol. 9, p. 84-85.

1320. KER (N. R.). Medieval libraries of Great Britain : a list of surviving books. London, Royal Hist.

Soc., 41, in-8, xxiii-169 p., 7s. 6d. (Guides and handbooks, 3). R : F. M. Powicke, *History*, 42, vol. 26, p. 297-298. H.H., *Antiq. J.*, 42, vol. 22, p. 148-149. B. Smalley, *Library*, 42, vol. 23, p. 48-49.

1321. KER (N. R.). English MSS. owned by Johannes Vlimmerius and Cornelius Duyn. *Library*, 42, vol. 22, p. 205-207.

1322. KER (N. R.). The migration of MSS. from the English medieval libraries. *Library*, 42, vol. 23, p. 1-11.

1323. KIMBALL (E. G.) ed. Rolls of the Warwickshire and Coventry sessions of the peace, 1377-1397. London, Oxford Univ. Press, 40, in-8, 221 p., 35s.

1324. LAISTNER (M. L. W.) and KING (H. H.). A hand-list of Bede manuscripts. London, Oxford Univ. Press, 43, in-8, 178 p., 18s. 6d.

1325. LEGGE (Dominica) ed. Anglo-Norman letters and petitions from All Souls MS. 182. Oxford, Blackwell, 41, in-8, xxiii-495p., 63s. (Anglo-Norman text soc., texts no. 3). R : H. G. Richardson, *Irish hist. Stud.*, 42, vol. 3, p. 123-124. B. Woledge, *Mod. Language R.*, 42, vol. 37, p. 507-508. H. G. Richardson, *Eng. hist. R.*, 43, vol. 58, p. 222-230. C.H.W., *History*, 43, vol. 28, p. 113-114.

1326. LENNARD (Reginald). A neglected Domesday satellite. *Eng. hist. R.*, 43, vol. 58, p. 32-41.

1327. LE PATOUREL (John). The authorship of the ' Grand Coutumier de Normandie '. *Eng. hist. R.*, 41, vol. 56, p. 292-300.

1328. LEVISON (W.). A combined MS. of Geoffrey of Monmouth and Henry of Huntingdon. *Eng. hist. R.*, 43, vol. 58, p. 41-51.

1329. LEWIS (Henry). Brut Dingestow, ed. by H. Lewis. Caerdydd, Gwasg Prifysgol Cymru, 42, in-8, lviii-328 p., 21s. R : J. Ll. Jones, *Trans. Soc. Cymmr.*, 41 (43), p. 206-210.

1330. MACALISTER (R. A. S.). The Book of Uí Maine, otherwise called ' The Book of the O'Kellys '. Repr. of intr. and indexes. Dublin, Stationery Office, 43, in-8, 65 p., (facs.), 3s. 6d. (Irish MSS. commission). R : E. G. Quin, *Irish hist. Stud.*, 44, vol. 4, p. 106-107.

1331. MACALISTER (R. A. S.). The sources of the preface to the ' Tigernach ' Annals. *Irish hist. Stud.*, 44, vol. 4, p. 38-57.

1332. MICHELS (T. A.). Two corrupt verses in the *Cantilena Super Statum Aegis Alberti*. *Med. Ævum*, 41, vol. 10, p. 102.

1333. MOORMAN (John R. H.). Sources for the life of St. Francis of Assisi. Manchester, Univ. Press, 41, in-8, xvi-176 p., 12s. 6d. R : D. L. Douie, *History*, 41, vol. 26, p. 73-75. M. Deanesly, *Theology*, 41, vol. 43, p. 243-244. W. Gumbley, *Eng. hist. R.*, 42, vol. 57, p. 375-377.

1334. PIGGOTT (Stuart). The sources of Geoffrey of Monmouth, 1 : The pre-Roman King-list, 2 : The Stonehenge story. *Antiquity*, 41, vol. 15, p. 269-286, 305-319.

1335. RATHBONE (E.). Master Alberic of London, ' Mythographus tertius Vaticanus '. *Med. and Renaissance Stud.*, 41, vol. 1, p. 35-40.

1336. RICHARDSON (Helen). A 12th century Anglo-Norman charter (in the Public Record Office, London). *B. John Rylands Library*, 40, vol. 24, p. 168-172.

1337. RICHARDSON (H.). The affair of the lepers. *Med. Ævum*, 41, vol. 10, p. 15-25.

1338. ROGERS (Ralph V.). Manuscript Year Books for 1-10 Edward III (1327-37). *Eng. hist. R.*, 40, vol. 55, p. 562-597.

1339. ROGERS (R. V.). A source for Fitzherbert's ' La Graunde Abridgment '. *Eng. hist. R.*, 41, vol. 56, p. 605-628. (Notes and documents).

1340. SOUTHERN (R. W.). The first life of Edward the Confessor. *Eng. hist. R.*, 43, vol. 58, p. 385-400.

1341. STENTON (Doris M.) and SMITH (Sidney) ed. The Great Roll of the Pipe for the 6th-8th year of the reign of King John, Michaelmas, 1204-1206. London, Pipe Roll Soc., 40, 3 vols. in-8, lii-366, xli-383, xxvii-333 p. (Publ., Pipe Roll Soc., n.s., 18-20). R : F. M. P(owicke), *History*, 41, vol. 26, p. 86-87; 42, vol. 27, p. 85-86; 43, vol. 28, p. 224.

1342. STEVENS (C. E.). Gildas sapiens. *Eng. hist. R.*, 41, vol. 56, p. 353-373.

1343. STOKES (E.) and DRUCKER (L.). Warwickshire feet of fines, abstracted from the originals in the Public Record Office. Vol. 2-3. London, Oxford Univ. Press, 40-43, 2 vols. in-8, ix-237, 286 p., 70s. (Dugdale Soc. publ., 15, 18).

1344. SUMBERG (Samuel L.). The Nuremberg Schembart carnival. London, Oxford Univ. Press, in-8, xi-234 p., 15s. (Columbia Univ., Germanic Stud, n.s., 12). R : M. Beare, *Mod. Language R.*, 43, vol. 38, p. 366-367.

1345. TAYLOR (Mary Margaret). Some sessions of the peace in Cambridgeshire in the 14th century, 1340, 1380-83. Cambridge, Bowes, 42, in-8, lxxii-76 p., 10s. (Cambr. antiq. soc., 8vo publ., 55). R : W. S. Holdsworth, *Eng. hist. R.*, 43, vol. 58, p. 221-222. T. F. T. Plucknett, *Econ. Hist. R.*, 43, vol. 13, 131-132.

1346. THOMAS (A. H.) ed. Calendar of plea and memoranda rolls, preserved among the archives of the Corporation of the City of London at the Guildhall, A.D. 1413-1437. London, Cambridge Univ. Press, 44, in-8, xlii-370 p., 15s.

1347. THOMSON (S. Harrison). The writings of Robert Grosseteste, Bishop of Lincoln, 1235-1253. London, Cambridge Univ. Press, 40, in-8, xv-302 p., (plates), 21s. R : F. M. P(owicke), *B. Inst. hist. Research*, 41, vol. 18, p. 120-121. A. G. Little, *Eng. hist. R.*, 41, vol. 56, p. 306-309. F. J. E. Raby, *Theology*, 40, vol. 41, p. 379-380.

1348. THOMSON (S. Harrison). Unnoticed manuscripts of Wyclyf's *De Veritate Sacre Scripture. Med. Ævum*, 43, vol. 12, p. 68-70.

1349. VERNON (William). A Middlewich chartulary, compiled in the 17th century, ed. by J. Varley. Manchester, Chetham Soc., 41-44, 2 vols. in-8, members only. (Chetham Soc., Remains hist. and lit., n.s., vol. 105). R : C.T.C., *Eng. hist. R.*, 45, vol. 60, p. 407-408.

1350. WADE-EVANS (A. W.). Further remarks on the ' De Excidio '. *Archaeol. cambrensis*, 44, vol. 98, p. 113-128.

1351. WAINWRIGHT (F. T.). The chronology of the ' Mercian Register '. *Eng. hist. R.*, 45, vol. 60, p. 385-392.

1352. WALSH (Paul). The dating of the Irish Annals. *Irish hist. Stud.*, 41, vol. 2, p. 355-375.

1353. WALSH (P.). An Leabhar Muimhneach. *Irish hist. Stud.*, 42, vol. 3, p. 135-143.

1354. WEBB (Clement C. J.). Notes on books bequeathed by John of Salisbury to the cathedral library of Chartres. *Med. and Renaissance Stud.*, 41, vol. 1, p. 128-129.

§ 2. General Works

1355. ANDERSON (R. C.). The oars of northern long-ships. *Mariner's Mirror*, 43, vol. 29, p. 190-195 (plates).

1356. BROOKE (Z. N.). The prospects of medieval history. London, Cambridge Univ. Press, 44, in-8, 32 p., 1s. 6d.

1357. CAM (H. M.). Liberties and communities in medieval England. London, Cambridge Univ. Press, 44, in-8, xiv-268 p., (maps), 15s. R : V. H. Galbraith, *Econ. Hist. R.*, 44, vol. 14, p. 202-203. J. Le P(atourel), *Eng. hist. R.*, 45, vol. 60, p. 124-125.

1358. CARSTEN (F. L.). Slavs in north-eastern Germany. *Econ. Hist. R.*, 41, vol. 11, p. 61-76.

1359. DEANESLY (Margaret). Canterbury and Paris in the reign of Aethelberht. *History*, 41, vol. 26, p. 97-104.

1360. DEANESLY (M.). The court of King Æthelberht of Kent. *Cambridge hist. J.*, 42, vol. 7, p. 101-114.

1361. DEANESLY (M.). Roman traditionalist influence among the Anglo-Saxons. *Eng. hist. R.*, 43, vol. 58, p. 129-146.

1362. GRIERSON (Philip). The relations between England and Flanders before the Norman Conquest. *Trans. Roy. hist. Soc.*, 41, vol. 23, p. 71-112.

1364. LAMB (H.). The Crusades : iron men and saints. New ed. London, Eyre & Spottiswoode, 44, in-8, 319 p., 10s. 6d.

1365. LEEPER (R. W. A.). A history of medieval Austria, ed. by R. W. Seton-Watson and C. A. Macartney. London, Oxford Univ. Press, 41, in-8, 358 p., 21s. R : Z. N. Brooke, *Eng. hist. R.*, 41, vol. 56, p. 651-652.

1366. NEWBOLD (Douglas). The Crusaders in the Red Sea and the Sudan. *Sudan Notes and Records*, 45, vol. 26, p. 213-227.

1367. O'SULLIVAN (M. D.). Old Galway : the history of a Norman colony in Ireland. Cambridge, Heffer, 42, in-8, ix-488 p., (plates, maps), 18s.

1368. ROSE-TROUP (Frances). Exeter vignettes : Clarembald and the miracles of Exeter; Exeter in Norman days; The murder of the precentor. Manchester, Univ. Press, 42, in-8, 57 p., 5s. (Univ. Coll. of S.-W. Engl., Hist. of Exeter research group, monogr. 7). R : J.T., *Eng. hist. R.*, 43, vol. 58, p. 496-497. J. Le P(atourel), *History*, 43, vol. 28, p. 224.

1369. STENTON (F. M.). Anglo-Saxon England. London, Oxford Univ. Press, 43, in-8, 759 p., (maps), 21s. (Oxf. hist. of Engl.). R : P. Grierson, *Eng. hist. R.*, 45, vol. 60, p. 247-249. D. Whitelock, *Mod. Language R.*, 44, vol. 39, p. 293-295.

1370. STRAYER (J. R.) and MUNRO (D. C.). The Middle Ages, 395-1500. London, Appleton, 42, in-8, 750 p., (maps, illus.), 21s. (Century hist. ser.).

§ 3. Political History

1372. BANNARD (Henry E.). A new theory of Cuthwulf's campaign in 571. *19th Century*, 43, vol. 133, p. 274-276.

1373. BARRACLOUGH (G.). Edward I and Adolf of Nassau : a chapter of mediaeval diplomatic history. *Cambridge hist. J.*, 40, vol. 6, p. 225-262.

1374. BAYLEY (C. C.). The campaign of 1375 and the Good Parliament. *Eng. hist. R.*, 40, vol. 55, p. 370-383.

1375. BUENO DE MESQUITA (D. M.). The foreign policy of Richard II in 1397 : some Italian letters. (Notes and documents). *Eng. hist. R.*, 41, vol. 56, p. 628-637.

1376. BUENO DE MESQUITA (D. M.). Giangaleazzo Visconti, Duke of Milan (1351-1402). A study in the political career of an Italian despot. London, Cambridge Univ. Press, 41, in-8, x-408 p., (maps), 21s. C. M. Ady, *Eng. hist. R.*, 41, vol. 56, p. 654-656.

1377. BURNE (A. H.). The battle of Badon : a military commentary. *History*, 45, vol. 30, p. 133-144.

1378. CAMMIDGE (J.). The Black Prince. London, Eyre & Spottiswoode, 43, in-8, 469 p., (illus., maps), 18s.

1379. CARSTEN (F. L.). Medieval democracy in the Brandenburg towns and its defeat in the 15th century. *Trans. Roy. hist. Soc.*, 43, vol. 25, p. 73-91.

1380. DAUNCEY (K. D. M.). The strategy of Anglo-Saxon invasion. *Antiquity*, 42, vol. 16, p. 51-63 (plates).

1381. DAVIES (J. Conway). Some Owen Glyndwr documents. *Nat. Library Wales J.*, 43, vol. 3, p. 48-50.

1382. DENHOLM-YOUNG (N.). A letter from the Council to Pope Honorius III, 1220-1. *Eng. hist. R.*, 45, vol. 60, p. 88-96.

1383. DOUGLAS (David C.). Rollo of Normandy. *Eng. hist. R.*, 42, vol. 57, p. 417-436.

1384. DOUGLAS (D. C.). ' Companions of the Conqueror '. *History*, 43, vol. 28, p. 129-147.

1385. DOUGLAS (D. C.). The ancestors of William fitz Osbern. *Eng. hist. R.*, 44, vol. 59, p. 62-79.

1386. DVORNÍK (F.). The first wave of the *Drang nach Osten*. *Cambridge hist. J.*, 43, vol. 7, p. 129-145.

1387. EDWARDS (Kathleen). The political importance of the English bishops during the reign of Edward II. *Eng. hist. R.*, 44, vol. 59, p. 311-347.

1388. GALBRAITH (V. H.). Good kings and bad kings in medieval English history. *History*, 45, vol. 30, p. 119-132.

1389. GRIFFITH (Margaret C.). The Talbot-Ormond struggle for control of the Anglo-Irish government, 1414-47. *Irish hist. Stud.*, 41, vol. 2, p. 376-397.

1390. HEARNSHAW (F. J. C.). A 13th-century Hitler [Emperor Frederick II]. *National R.*, 42, vol. 119, p. 157-163.

1391. JACOB (E. F.). The collapse of France in 1419-20. *B. John Rylands Library*, 41/42, vol. 26, p. 307-326.

1392. JONES (Sir T. Artemus). Owen Tudor's marriage. *B. Board celtic Stud.*, 43, vol. 11, p. 102-109.

1393. KERR(Wilfred Brenton). Agincourt and Valmont : contrast in the tactics of French and English during Henry V's invasions of France. *J. Soc. Army hist. Research*, 43, vol. 22, p. 66-70.

1394. LARSON (A.). English embassies during the Hundred Years' war. *Eng. hist. R.*, 40, vol. 55, p. 423-431.

1395. OMAN (Sir Charles). A commando raid of 1460. *Army Quar.*, 44, vol. 49, p. 120-123.

1396. POWICKE (F. M.). The oath of Bromholm. *Eng. hist. R.*, 41, vol. 56, p. 529-548.

1397. RICHARDSON (H. G.). The morrow of the Great Charter [with] An addendum. *B. John Rylands Library*, 44, vol. 28, p. 422-443; 45, vol. 29, p. 184-200.

1398. ROWSE (A. L.). The turbulent career of Sir Henry de Bodrugan. *History*, 44, vol. 29, p. 17-26.

1399. RUBINSTEIN (N.). Political rhetoric in the Imperial Chancery during the twelfth and thirteenth centuries. *Med. Ævum*, 45, vol. 14, p. 21-43.

1400. SHAW (P.). The Black Prince. *History*, 40, vol. 24, p. 1-15.

1401. STEEL (Anthony). Richard II. London, Cambridge Univ. Press, 41, in-8, x-320 p., 16s. R : J. Tait, *Eng. hist. R.*, 42, vol. 57, p. 379-383. V. H. Galbraith, *History*, 42, vol. 26, p. 223-239.

1402. STENTON (F. M.). English families and the Norman conquest. *Trans. Roy. hist. Soc.*, 44, vol. 26, p. 1-12.

1403. TREHARNE (R. F.). The significance of the baronial reform movement, 1258-1267. *Trans. Roy. hist. Soc.*, 43, vol. 25, p. 35-72.

1404. WADE-EVANS (A. W.). The Jutish invasion of 514. *Archaeol. cambrensis*, 43, vol. 97, p. 161-168.

1405. WARD (Gordon). The life and records of Eadberht, son of King Wihtred. *Archaeol. cantiana*, 39 (40), vol. 51, p. 9-26.

1406. WILLIAM, Archbishop of Tyre. A history of deeds done beyond the sea, tr. from the Latin, by E. A. Babcock and A. C. Krey. London, Oxford Univ. Press, 44, 2 vols. in-8, 568, 562 p., (maps), 90s. (Columbia Univ., Records of civilization, sources and stud., 35).

§ 4. Jews

1407. GALANTÉ (A.). Les Juifs sous la domination des Turcs seldjoukides. London, Luzac, 42, in-8, 16 p., 5s.

1408. TRACHTENBERG (J.). The Devil and the Jews : the medieval conception of the Jew and its relation to modern anti-semitism. London, Oxford Univ. Press, 43, in-8, 294 p., (illus.), 23s. 6d.

§ 5. Islam

1409. ABBOTT (N.). Aishah : the beloved of Mohammed. London, Cambridge Univ. Press, 43, in-8, xvi-230 p., (plate), 15s.

1409a. BELL (Richard). A Moslem thinker on the teaching of religion : al-Ghazzāli, A. D. 1058-1111. *Hibbert J.*, 43, vol. 42, p. 31-36.

1410. CRESWELL (K. A. C.). Early Muslim architecture. Pt. 2 : Umayyads, early Abbasids, and Tulunids, A.D. 751-905. London, Oxford Univ. Press, 40, in-2, 415 p., (plates), 210s. R : J. W. Crowfoot, *J. asiatic Soc.*, 42, p. 255-258. M. S. Briggs, *Burlington Mag.*, 42, vol. 81, p. 182.

1411. DUNLOP (D. M.). The Dhunnunids of Toledo [&] Notes. *J. asiatic Soc.*, 42, p. 77-96; 43, p. 17-19.

1412. IVANOW (V.). Ismaili tradition concerning the rise of the Fatimids. London, Oxford Univ. Press, 42, in-8, 357, 116 p., 20s. (Islamic research assoc. ser., 10). R : H.A.R.G., *Eng. hist. R.*, 45, vol. 60, p. 423-424.

1413. LÉVI-PROVENÇAL (E.). Something new on Ibn Qūzman. *J. asiatic Soc.*, 44, p. 105-118.

1414. LEWIS (Bernard). The origins of Isma'īlism, a study of the historical background of the Fatimid caliphate. Cambridge, Heffer, 40, in-8, ix-114 p., 8s. 6d. R : D. M. Dunlop, *J. asiatic Soc.*, 45, p. 108-109.

1415. LEWIS (B.). The Islamic guilds in the Middle Ages. *J. central asian Soc.*, 40, vol. 27, p. 462-465.

1416. MINORSKY (V.). The Middle East in western politics in the 13th, 14th and 15th centuries. *J. central asian Soc.*, 40, vol. 27, p. 427-461.

1417. RUNCIMAN (J. S.). Europe and the Turks in the early Middle Ages. *Asiatic R.*, 42, vol. 38, p. 428-431.

1418. SERGEANT (R. B.). Material for a history of Islamic textiles up to the Mongol conquest. London, Luzac, 44, in-4, 39 p., (maps), 4s.

1419. SMITH (Margaret). Al-Ghāzalī, the mystic : a study of the life and personality of Abū Hāmid Muhammad al-Tūsī al-Ghāzalī. London, Luzac, 45, in-8, 247 p., 21s.

1420. STERN (G. H.). Marriage in early Islam. London, Luzac, 40, in-8, vi-198 p., 10s. 6d. (James G. Forlong fund, vol. 18).

§ 6. Vikings

1421. CAMPBELL (A.). Two notes on the Norse kingdoms in Northumbria : 1. The Northumbrian kingdom of Raegnald; 2. The end of the kingdom of Northumbria. *Eng. hist. R.*, 42, vol. 57, p. 85-97.

1422. ELLIS (Hilda R.). Sigurd in the art of the Viking age. *Antiquity*, 42, vol. 16, p. 216-236 (illus.).

1423. GRIMES (W. F.) and RANDALL (H. J.). The earthwork at Vervil near Merthyr Mawr. *Archaeol. cambrensis*, 45, vol. 98, p. 241-247 (illus.).

1424. KENDRICK (T. D.). The Viking taste in pre-Conquest England. *Antiquity*, 41, vol. 15, p. 125-141 (illus.).

1425. MAGOUN (Francis P.). King Alfred's naval and beach battle with the Danes in 896. *Mod. Language R.*, 42, vol. 37, p. 409-414.

1426. SKILBECK (C. O.). Trelleborg. *Antiquity*, 40, vol. 14, p. 272-279 (illus.).

1427. STENTON (F. M.). The Scandinavian colonies in England and Normandy. *Trans. Roy. hist. Soc.*, 45, vol. 27, p. 1-12.

§ 7. History of Law and Institutions

1427a. BALFOUR-MELVILLE(E.W.M.). Burgh representation in early Scottish parliaments. *Eng. hist. R.*, 44, vol. 59, p. 79-87.

1428. BARRACLOUGH (G.). Law and legislation in medieval England. *L.Q.R.*, 40, vol. 56, p. 75-92.

1429. BINCHY (D. A.). The linguistic and historical value of Irish law tracts. London, Oxford Univ. Press, 44, in-8, 36 p., 4s.

1430. CAM (H. M.). From witness of the shire to full parliament. *Trans. Roy. hist. Soc.*, 44, vol. 26, p. 13-35.

1431. CHENEY (Mary). The compromise of Avranches of 1172 and the spread of canon law in England. *Eng. hist. R.*, 41, vol. 56, p. 177-197.

1432. CHEW (Helena M.). The office of escheator in the city of London during the Middle Ages. *Eng. hist. R.*, 43, vol. 58, p. 319-330.

1433. CHEW (H. M.). Mortmain in medieval London. *Eng. hist. R.*, 45, vol. 60, p. 1-15.

1434. CLAY (C. T.). The keepership of the old Palace of Westminster. *Eng. hist. R.*, 44, vol. 59, p. 1-21.

1435. COOPER (Lord). Select Scottish cases of the thirteenth century. Edinburgh, Hodge, 44, in-8, 103 p., 15s. R : H.G.R., *Eng. hist. R.*, 45, vol. 60, p. 424-425.

1436. CURTIS (Edmund). Feudal charters of the De Burgo lordship of Connacht. (Essays and studies presented to Eoin MacNeill, p. 286-295). Dublin, Sign of the Three Candles, 40, in-8, 593 p., 42s. R : E. St. J. Brooks, *Irish hist. Stud.*, 41, vol. 2, p. 440-442.

1437. CUTTINO (G. P.). English diplomatic administration, 1259-1339. London, Oxford Univ. Press, 40, in-8, 195 p., 10s. (Oxf. hist. ser.). R : H. Johnstone, *Eng. hist. R.*, 42, vol. 57, p. 133-135.

1438. DE HAAS (Elsa). Antiquities of bail: origin and historical development in criminal cases to the year 1275. London, Oxford Univ. Press, 40, in-8, 174 p., 11s. 6d. R : W.H.H., *History*, 43, vol. 28, p. 111-112.

1439. DENHOLM-YOUNG (N.). Who wrote ' Fleta ' ? *Eng. hist. R.*, 43, vol. 58, p. 1-12.

1440. DENHOLM-YOUNG (N.). The ' paper constitution ' attributed to 1244. *Eng. hist. R.*, 43, vol. 58, p. 401-423.

1441. DENHOLM-YOUNG (N.). Matthew Cheker. *Eng. hist. R.*, 44, vol. 59, p. 252-257.

1442. EDWARDS (J. G.). Taxation and consent in the Court of common pleas, 1338. *Eng. hist. R.*, 42, vol. 57, p. 473-482.

1443. EDWARDS (J. G.). *Confirmatio Cartarum* and baronial grievances in

1297. *Eng. hist. R.*, 43, vol. 58, p. 147-171, 273-300.

1444. EULAU (Heinz H. F.). Early theories of parliamentarism. *Canad. J. Econ. pol. Sci.*, 42, vol. 8, p. 33-55.

1445. FINBERG (H. P. R.). The early history of Werrington. *Eng. hist. R.*, 44, vol. 59, p. 237-251.

1446. FOX (Levi). The administration of the honor of Leicester in the 14th century. Leicester, Backus, 40, in-8, 92 p., 5s. R : J.H.LeP., *Eng. hist. R.*, 41, vol. 56, p. 161.

1447. GRIERSON (P.). Election and inheritance in early Germanic kingship. *Cambridge hist. J.*, 41, vol. 7, p. 1-22.

1448. HASKINS (G. L.). The King's High Court of Parliament holden at Westminster. *History*, 40, vol. 24, p. 295-310.

1449. HURNARD (Naomi D.). The jury of presentment and the assize of Clarendon. *Eng. hist. R.*, 41, vol. 56, p. 374-410.

1450. JOLIFFE (J. E. A.). Some factors in the beginnings of Parliament. *Trans. Roy. hist. Soc.*, 40, vol. 22, p. 101-139.

1451. JONES (G.). Fjörbaugsgarðr. *Med. Ævum*, 40, vol. 9, p. 155-163.

1452. KANTOROWICZ (Hermann) and SMALLEY (Beryl). An English theologian's view of Roman law : Pepo, Irnerius, Ralph Niger. *Med. and Renaissance Stud.*, 43, vol. 1, p. 237-252.

1453. KUTTNER (S.) and SMALLEY (Beryl). The ' Glossa Ordinaria ' to the Gregorian Decretals. *Eng. hist. R.*, 45, vol. 60, p. 97-105.

1454. LAPSLEY (Gaillard). The interpretation of the Statute of York. 2 pts. *Eng. hist. R.*, 41, vol. 56, p. 22-51, 411-446.

1455. McFARLANE (K. B.). Parliament and ' bastard feudalism '. *Trans. Roy. hist. Soc.*, 44, vol. 26, p. 53-79.

1456. NEWHALL (Richard Ager). Muster and review : English military administration, 1420-1440. London, Oxford Univ. Press, 40, in-8, xii-173 p., 8s. 6d. (Harvard hist. monogr., 13). R : C.H.W., *History*, 44, vol. 29, p. 98. *Army Quar.*, 41, vol. 41, p. 382-383.

1457. ODEGAARD (C. E.). Vassi and fideles in the Carolingian empire. London, Oxford Univ. Press, 45, in-8, 180 p., 6s. (Harvard hist. monogr., 19).

1458. PLUCKNETT (T. F. T.). The origin of impeachment. *Trans. Roy. hist. Soc.*, 42, vol. 24, p. 47-71.

1459. POWICKE (F. M.). The writ for enforcing watch and ward, 1242. *Eng. hist. R.*, 42, vol. 57, p. 469-473.

1460. PROCTER (Evelyn S.). Use and custody of the secret seal (sello de la poridad) in Castille from 1252 to 1369. *Eng. hist. R.*, 40, vol. 55, p. 194-221.

1461. RAYNER (Doris). The forms and machinery of the ' commune petition ' in the 14th century. *Eng. hist. R.*, 41, vol. 56, p. 198-233, 549-570.

1462. REUSCHLEIN (H. G.). Who wrote *The Mirror of Justices?* A note upon the suggestions of Maitland, Pollock and Leadam. *L.Q.R.*, 42, vol. 58, p. 265-279.

1463. RICHARDSON (Henry G.). The English coronation oath. *Trans. Roy. hist. Soc.*, 41, vol. 23, p. 129-158.

1464. RICHARDSON (H. G.). The Oxford law school under John. *L.Q.R.*, 41, vol. 57, p. 319-338.

1465. RICHARDSON (H. G.). Magna Carta Hiberniae. *Irish hist. Stud.*, 42, vol. 3, p. 31-33.

1466. RICHARDSON (H. G.). The Preston exemplification of the *Modus tenendi parliamentum*. *Irish hist. Stud.*, 42, vol. 3, p. 187-192.

1467. RICHARDSON (H. G.). The Irish parliament rolls of the 15th century. *Eng. hist. R.*, 43, vol. 58, p. 448-461.

1468. RICHARDSON (II. G.). Azo, Drogheda, and Bracton. *Eng. hist. R.*, 44, vol. 59, p. 22-47.

1469. RICHARDSON (H. G.). Tancred, Raymond, and Bracton. *Eng. hist. R.*, 44, vol. 59, p. 376-384.

1470. RIESS (Ludwig). The history of the English electoral law in the Middle Ages, tr. by K. L. Wood-Legh. London, Cambridge Univ. Press, 40, in-8, xi-107 p., 7s. 6d. R : H.G.R., *Eng. hist. R.*, 41, vol. 56, p. 339-340.

1471. RODERICK (A. J.). The four cantreds : a study in administration. *B. Board celtic Stud.*, 40, vol. 10, p. 246-256.

1472. ROTHWELL (H.). The confirmation of the charters, 1297. *Eng. hist. R.*, 45, vol. 60, p. 16-35, 177-191, 300-315.

1473. SAYLES (G. O.). Medieval judges as legal consultants. *L.Q.R.*, 40, vol. 56, p. 247-254.

1474. SCHULZ (Fritz). Critical studies on Bracton's Treatise. *L.Q.R.*, 43, vol. 59, p. 172-180.

1475. SCHULZ (F.). Bracton and Raymond de Penafort. *L.Q.R.*, 45, vol. 61, p. 286-292.

1476. SCHULZ (F.). Bracton on kingship. *Eng. hist. R.*, 45, vol. 60, p. 136-176.

1477. SENIGALLIA (Leone Adolfo). Medieval sources of English maritime law. *Mariner's Mirror*, 40, vol. 26, p. 7-14.

1478. SOMERVILLE (R.). The Duchy of Lancaster council and court of duchy chamber. *Trans. Roy. hist. Soc.*, 41, vol. 23, p. 159-177.

1479. STEPHENSON (C. H. S.) and MARPLES (E. A.). Law in the light of history. Book 2 : England in the Middle Ages. London, Williams & Norgate, 40, in-8, xi-316 p., 18s.

1480. Suggett (Helen). An Anglo-Norman return to the inquest of sheriffs. *B. John Rylands Library*, 42, vol. 27, p. 179-181.

1481. Tait (James). Knight-service in Cheshire. *Eng. hist. R.*, 42, vol. 57, p. 437-459.

1482. Taylor (Mary M.). Parliamentary elections in Cambridgeshire, 1332-8. (Select documents, 37). *B. Inst. hist. Research*, 40, vol. 18, p. 21-26.

1483. Ullmann (Walter). Baldus's conception of law as presented by Lucas De Penna. *L.Q.R.*, 42, vol. 58, p. 386-399.

1484. Ullmann (W.). The mediaeval theory of legal and illegal organizations. *L.Q.R.*, 44, vol. 60, p. 285-291.

1485. Ullmann (W.). The influence of John of Salisbury on medieval Italian jurists. *Eng. hist. R.*, 44, vol. 59, p. 384-392.

1485a. Ward (Paul L.). An early version of the Anglo-Saxon coronation ceremony. *Eng. hist. R.*, 42, vol. 57, p. 345-361.

1486. Weinbaum (M. A.). British borough charters, 1307-1660. London, Cambridge Univ. Press, 43, in-8, lxviii-241 p., 21s. R : E. M. Hampson, *Econ. Hist. R.*, 43, vol. 13, p. 118-119.

1487. Whitelock (Dorothy). Wulfstan and the so-called laws of Edward and Guthrum. *Eng. hist. R.*, 41, vol. 56, p. 1-21.

1488. Wigmore (J. H.). Lanfranc, the Prime Minister of William the Conqueror : was he once an Italian professor of law ? A study in historical evidence. *L.Q.R.*, 42, vol 58, p. 61-81.

1489. Wilkinson (Bertie). The Council and the crisis of 1233-4. *B. John Rylands Library*, 43, vol. 27, p. 384-393.

1490. Wilkinson (B.). The government of England during the absence of Richard I on the Third Crusade. *B. John Rylands Library*, 44, vol. 28, p. 485-509.

§ 8. Economic and Social History

1491. Benton (W. A.). The Soham and King's Lynn steelyards. *Trans. Newcomen Soc.*, 38/39 [40], vol. 19, p. 241-248.

1492. Bromberg (Benjamin). The financial and administrative importance of the Knights Hospitallers to the English Crown. *Econ. Hist.*, 40, vol. 4, p. 307-311.

1493. Brooks (F. W.). A medieval brick-yard at Hull. *J. archaeol. Assoc.*, 39 (40), vol. 4, p. 151-174.

1494. Brutzkus (J.). Trade with eastern Europe, 800-1200. *Econ. Hist. R.*, 43, vol. 13, p. 31-41.

1495. Cam (H. M.). The decline and fall of English feudalism. *History*, 40, vol. 25, p. 216-233.

1496. The Cambridge economic history of Europe from the decline of the Roman Empire. Vol. 1 : The agrarian life of the Middle Ages, ed. by J. H. Clapham and E. Power. London, Cambridge Univ. Press, 41, in-8, xviii-650 p., (maps), 30s. R : G.R.C., *Geogr. J.*, 41, vol. 98, p. 48-50. E. F. Jacob, *Economica*, 41, vol. 8, p. 457-459. K. F. Helleiner, *Canad. J. Econ. pol. Sci.*, 43, vol. 9, p. 99-103. H. Burton, *Econ. Record*, 42, vol. 18, p. 105-108. F. M. Powicke, *Econ. Hist. R.*, 42, vol. 12, p. 83-86. R. Lennard, *Econ. J.*, 42, vol. 52, p. 45-53.

1497. Carus-Wilson (E. M.). An industrial revolution of the 13th century. *Econ. Hist. R.*, 41, vol. 11, p. 39-60.

1498. CARUS-WILSON (E. M.). The English cloth industry in the late 12th and early 13th centuries. *Econ. Hist. R.*, 44, vol. 14, p. 32-50.

1499. CRONNE (H. A.). The origins of feudalism. *History*, 40, vol. 24, p. 251-259.

1500. DARBY (H. C.). The medieval Fenland. London, Cambridge Univ. Press, 40, in-8, xvii-200 p., 12s. 6d. R : L. F. Salzman, *B. Inst. hist. Research*, 40, vol. 18, p. 31. E. St. J. Brooks, *19th Century*, 40, vol. 128, p. 101-103. W. G. East, *Economica*, 40, vol. 7, p. 343-344. C. R. Fay, *Econ. J.*, 40, vol. 50, p. 301-303. *National R.*, 40, vol. 114, p. 635-636. C. Fox, *Archaeol. J.*, 39 (40), vol. 96, p. 299-302. W.G.E., *Geogr. J.*, 40, vol. 95, p. 386-387.

1501. DENHOLM-YOUNG (N.). Feudal society in the 13th century : the knights. *History*, 44, vol. 29, p. 107-119.

1502. DEUTSCH (Karl W.). Medieval unity and the economic conditions for an international civilization. *Canad. J. Econ. pol. Sci.*, 44, vol. 10, p. 18-35.

1503. DODWELL (B.). The free tenantry of the Hundred Rolls. *Econ. Hist. R.*, 44, vol. 14, p. 163-171.

1504. EDWARDS (Kathleen). The houses of Salisbury Close in the 14th century. *J. archaeol. Assoc.*, 39 (40), vol. 4, p. 55-115.

1505. FOWLER (G. H.). A household expense roll, 1328. *Eng. hist. R.*, 40, vol. 55, p. 630-634.

1506. Fox (Sir Cyril). A croft in the Upper Nedd Valley, Ystradfellte, Brecknockshire. *Antiquity*, 40, vol. 14, p. 363-376 (illus.).

1507. Fox (Levi). Administration of gild property in Coventry in the 15th century. *Eng. hist. R.*, 40, vol. 55, p. 634-647.

1508. Fox (L.). The early history of Coventry. *History*, 45, vol. 30, p. 21-37.

1509. HILL (Mary C.). Jack Faukes, King's Messenger, and his journey to Avignon in 1343. *Eng. hist. R.*, 42, vol. 57, p. 19-30.

1510. HILTON (R. H.). A 13th-century poem on disputed villein services. *Eng. hist. R.*, 41, vol. 56, p. 90-97.

1511. HOMANS (G. C.). English villagers of the 13th century. London, Oxford Univ. Press, 41, in-8, 493 p., 19s. R : F. M. Powicke, *Eng. hist. R.*, 42, vol. 57, p. 496-502. M. M. Postan, *Econ. Hist. R.*, 45, vol. 15, p. 88-92.

1512. HUSSEY (Arthur). Hythe wills. 3rd and final part. *Archaeol. cantiana*, 39 (40), vol. 51, p. 27-65.

1513. JENKINSON (Hilary) and BROOME (Dorothy M.). An exchequer statement of receipts and issues, 1339-1340. *Eng. hist. R.*, 43, vol. 58, p. 210-216.

1514. LAUGHTON (L. G. Carr). Naval accounts for 1209-1211 : Public Record Office. *Mariner's Mirror*, 42, vol. 28, p. 74-77.

1515. LENNARD (R.). The origin of the fiscal carucate. *Econ. Hist. R.*, 44, vol. 14, p. 51-63.

1516. LENNARD (R.). The destruction of woodland in the eastern counties under William the Conqueror. *Econ. Hist. R.*, 45, vol. 15, p. 36-43.

1517. LENNARD (R.). Domesday plough-teams : the south-western evidence. *Eng. hist. R.*, 45, vol. 60, p. 217-233.

1518. LEWIS (N. B.). The organisation of indentured retinues in 14th-century England. *Trans. Roy. hist. Soc.*, 45, vol. 27, p. 29-39.

1519. MULHOLLAND (Sir M. A.). Early gild records of Toulouse. London, Oxford Univ. Press, 41, in-8, 246 p., 15s.

1520. MURRAY (H. J. R.). The mediaeval games of tables. *Med. Ævum*, 41, vol. 10, p. 57-69.

1521. MYERS (A. R.). The captivity of a royal witch : the household accounts of Queen Joan of Navarre, 1419-1421. *B. John Rylands Library*, 40, vol. 24, p. 263-284; 41/42, vol. 26, p. 82-100.

1522. —— — —— Manchester, Univ. Press, 41, in-8, 24 p., 1s. 6d.

1523. PELHAM (R. A.). The distribution of early fulling mills in England and Wales. *Geography*, 44, vol. 29, p. 52-56.

1524. PIERCE (T. Jones). The growth of commutation in Gwynedd during the 13th century. *B. Board celtic Stud.*, 41, vol. 10, p. 309-330.

1525. PIERCE (T. J.). A note on ancient Welsh measurements of land. *Archaeol. cambrensis*, 43, vol. 97, p. 195-204.

1526. POLLARD (Graham). Mediaeval loan chests at Cambridge. *B. Inst. hist. Research*, 40, vol. 17, p. 113-129.

1527. POOLE (A. L.). Live stock prices in the 12th century. *Eng. hist. R.*, 40, vol. 55, p. 284-295.

1528. POSTAN (M. M.). Some social consequences of the 100 years' war. *Econ. Hist. R.*, 42, vol. 12, p. 1-12.

1529. POSTAN (M. M.). The rise of a money economy. *Econ. Hist. R.*, 44, vol. 14, p. 123-134.

1530. POWER (Eileen). The wool trade in English medieval history. London, Oxford Univ. Press, 41, in-8, vii-128 p., 7s. 6d. (Ford lects.). R : H. M. Cam, *Econ. Hist. R.*, 41, vol. 11, p. 90-92. J. G. Edwards, *Eng. hist. R.*, 42, vol. 57, p. 122-124. J. H. Clapham, *Econ. J.*, 42, vol. 52, p. 62-64. F. M. Powicke, *Economica*, 42, vol. 9, p. 95-97.

1531. REES (William). Ministers' accounts (general series), bundle 1158, mediaeval merchant galleys. *B. Inst. hist. Research*, 42, vol. 19, p. 140-148.

1532. QUENNELL (M. and C. H. B.). A history of everyday things in England. Vol. 1, 1066-1499. New ed. London, Batsford, 43, in-8, 242 p., (illus.), 8s. 6d.

1533. RICHARDSON (H. G.). The medieval plough-team. *History*, 42, vol. 26, p. 287-296.

1534. RICHARDSON (H. G.). Norman Ireland in 1212 [Irish pipe roll of King John]. *Irish hist. Stud.*, 42, vol. 3, p. 144-158.

1535. RUDDOCK (Alwyn A.). The Flanders galleys. *History*, 40, vol. 24, p. 311-317.

1536. RUDDOCK (A. A.). The method of handling the cargoes of mediaeval merchant galleys. *B. Inst. hist. Research*, 42, vol. 19, p. 140-148.

1537. RUDDOCK (A. A.). Historical revision, no. 106 : Italian trading fleets in medieval England. *History*, 44, vol. 29, p. 192-202.

1538. SALTMARSH (John). Plague and economic decline in England in the later Middle Ages. *Cambridge hist. J.*, 41, vol. 7, p. 23-41.

1539. SAYLES (G. O.). Dissolution of a gild at York in 1306. *Eng. hist. R.*, 40, vol. 55, p. 83-98.

1540. SHEEDY (A. T.). Bartolus on social conditions in the fourteenth century. London, King, 43, in-8, 259 p., 16s. 6d.

1541. SHILSON (J. W.). Weighing wool in the Middle Ages. *Antiquity*, 44, vol. 18, p. 72-77.

1542. SMITH (R. A. L.). Marsh embankment and sea defence in medieval Kent. *Econ. Hist. R.*, 40, vol. 10, p. 29-37.

1543. SPILLETT (P. J.), STEBBING (W. P. D.) and DUNNING (G. C.). A pottery kiln site at Tyler hill, near Canterbury. *Archaeol. cantiana*, 42 (43), vol. 55, p. 57-64.

1544. STEBBING (W. P. D.). Hille's or Helle's Court, Ash. *Archaeol. cantiana*, 40 (41), vol. 53, p. 101-108.

1545. STEPHENSON (Carl). Medieval feudalism. London, Oxford Univ. Press, 42, in-8, 126 p., 6s. R : F. M. P(owicke), *Eng. hist. R.*, 43, vol. 58, p. 495.

1546. STEPHENSON (Carl). Commendation and related problems in Domesday. *Eng. hist. R.*, 44, vol. 59, p. 289-310.

1547. VERLINDEN (Charles). The rise of Spanish trade in the Middle Ages. (Studies in sources and bibliography, 7). *Econ. Hist. R.*, 40, vol. 10, p. 44-59.

1548. WARDALE (W. L.). Diocles of Carystos and German popular medicine. *Med. Ævum*, 40, vol. 9, p. 61-78.

§ 9. History of Civilization, Literature and Education

1549. ATKINS (J. W. H.). English literary criticism : the medieval phase. London, Cambridge Univ. Press, 44, in-8, x-212 p., 12s. 6d. R : J. F. Lockwood, *Mod. Language R.*, 44, vol. 39, p. 399-401. F. M. Powicke, *Eng. hist. R.*, 45, vol. 60, p. 111.

1550. BENNETT (H. S.). Science and information in English writings of the 15th century. *Mod. Language R.*, 44, vol. 39, p. 1-8.

1551. BENNETT (J. A. W.). The date of the B-text of *Piers Plowman*. *Med. Ævum*, 43, vol. 12, p. 55-64.

1552. BRYAN (W. F.) and DEMPSTER (G.) ed. Sources and analogues of Chaucer's Canterbury Tales (by) Carleton Brown (and others). London, Cambridge Univ. Press, 41, in-8, xvi-766 p., 60s.

1553. CALLUS (D. A.). Introduction of Aristotelian learning to Oxford. London, Oxford Univ. Press, 44, in-4, 56 p., 7s. R : W. D. Ross, *Philosophy*, 45, vol. 20, p. 278.

1554. CHANEY (Edward F.). François Villon at St. Benoît. *B. John Rylands Library*, 44, vol. 28, p. 58-75.

1555. CHANEY (E. F.). A glimpse of Villon's Paris. *B. John Rylands Library*, 44, vol. 28, p. 340-357.

1556. CHARLES D'ORLÉANS. The English poems of Charles of Orléans, ed. by R. Steele, from Brit. Mus. Harl. 682. London, Oxford Univ. Press, 42, in-8, 300 p., 31s. 6d. (Early Engl. text soc., orig. ser., 215).

1557. CHAYTOR (Henry John). The medieval reader and textual criticism. *B. John Rylands Library*, 41/42, vol. 26, p. 49-56.

1558. CHAYTOR (H. J.). From script to book : an introduction to medieval literature. London, Cambridge Univ. Press, 45, in-8, viii-156 p., 12s. 6d.

1559. CHESNEY (K.). A neglected prose version of the *Roman de Troie*. *Med. Ævum*, 42, vol. 11, p. 46-67.

1560. COULTON (G. G.). Europe's apprenticeship : a survey of medieval Latin with examples. London, Nelson, 40, in-8, 288 p., 8s. 6d. R : B. L. Manning, *Congreg. Quar.*, 41, vol. 19, p. 176-177.

1561. DAVIES (W. Ll.). Some letters of Owen Jones, ' Owain Myvyr '. *Nat. Library Wales J.*, 41, vol. 2, p. 62-68.

1562. DAWKINS (R. M.). The nature of the Cypriot chronicle of Leontios Makhairas. London, Oxford Univ. Press, 45, in-8, 32 p., 2s. (Taylorian lect., 1945).

1563. ELLIS (Hilda R.). Fostering by giants in Old Norse saga literature. *Med. Ævum*, 41, vol. 10, p. 70-85.

1564. ELLIS (H. R.). The road to Hel : a study of the conception of the dead in Old Norse literature. London, Cambridge Univ. Press, 43, in-8, viii-208 p., 12s. 6d. R : N. E. M. Boyce, *Man*, 44, vol. 44, p. 102-103. R. Girvan, *Mod. Language R.*, 44, vol. 39, p. 313-314. H.A., *Queen's Quar.*, 44, vol. 51, p. 476-477.

1565. ENTWISTLE (W. J.). El Conde Dirlos. *Med. Ævum*, 41, vol. 10, p. 1-14.

1566. GALBRAITH (V. H.). Nationality and language in medieval England. *Trans. Roy. hist. Soc.*, 41, vol. 23, p. 113-128.

1567. GALBRAITH (V. H.). John Seward and his circle : some London scholars of the early 15th century. *Med. and Renaissance Stud.*, 41, vol. 1, p. 85-104.

1568. GALWAY (Margaret). Geoffrey Chaucer, J.P. and M.P. *Mod. Language R.*, 41, vol. 36, p. 1-36.

1569. GASELEE (S.). An emendation in *Sacris Sollemniis*. *Med. Ævum*, 41, vol. 10, p. 101.

1570. GOFFIN (R. G.). Quiting by tidings in *The Hous of Fame*. *Med. Ævum*, 43, vol. 12, p. 40-44.

1571. GORDON (I. A.). John Skelton : Poet Laureate. London, Oxford Univ. Press, 44, in-8, 232 p., 12s. 6d. R : J. H. P. Pafford, *Library*, 44, vol. 25, p. 94-95.

1572. GRESHAM (Colin A.). The Book of Aneirin. *Antiquity*, 42, vol. 16, p. 237-257.

1573. GUPPY (Henry). The dawn of the revival of learning. *B. John Rylands Library*, 41/42, vol. 26, p. 206-224, 413-430.

1574. HARVEY (H. G.). The theatre of the Basoche : the contribution of the law societies to French mediaeval comedy. London, Oxford Univ. Press, 42, in-8, 263 p., 12s. 6d. (Stud.

in Romance lang. ser.). R : K. Chesney, *Mod. Language R.*, 42, vol. 37, p. 511-512.

1575. HARVEY (R.). The Provenance of the Old High German *Ludwigslied*. *Med. Ævum*, 45, vol. 14, p. 1-20.

1576. HASKINS (George L.). The University of Oxford and the 'ius ubique docendi'. *Eng. hist. R.*, 41, vol. 56, p. 281-292.

1577. HATTO (A. T.). Gallantry in the mediaeval German lyric. *Mod. Language R.*, 41, vol. 36, p. 480-487.

1578. HILL (Raymond T.) and BERGIN (T. G.). Anthology of the Provençal troubadours; texts, notes, and vocabulary. London, Oxford Univ. Press, 41, in-8, xv-363 p., 22s. 6d. (Yale Romanic stud., 17). R : M. D. Legge, *History*, 42, vol. 27, p. 152-153.

1579. HOLLANDER (L. M.). The Skalds, a selection of their poems. London, Oxford Univ. Press, 45, in-8, 228 p., 18s. 6d.

1580. HUNT (R. W.). Studies on Priscian in the 11th and 12th centuries. *Med. and Renaissance Stud.*, 43, vol. 1, p. 194-231.

1581. JOHNSON (F. C.). Le Grant Ystoire de Monsignor Tristan " Le Bret ". Edinburgh, Oliver & Boyd, 42, in-8, xxiii-166 p., (facs.), 15s.

1582. KANTOROWICZ (Ernst H.). An ' autobiography ' of Guido Faba. *Med. and Renaissance Stud.*, 43, vol. 1, p. 253-280.

1583. KER (N. R.). Medieval libraries of Great Britain, a list of surviving books. London, Roy. Hist. Soc., 41, in-8, xxiii-169 p., 7s. 6d. (Guides and handbooks 3). R : C. Johnson, *Eng. hist. R.*, 43, vol. 58, p. 220-221.

1584. LEVY (H. L.). ' As myn auctour seyth '. *Med. Ævum*, 43, vol. 12, p. 25-39.

1585. LLOYD (J. E.). The Death of Arthur. *B. Board celtic Stud.*, 44, vol. 11, p. 158-160.

1586. MALONE (K.). Notes on Gnomic Poem B of the Exeter Book. *Med. Ævum*, 43, vol. 12, p. 65-67.

1587. MILLER (D. C.). The sequence of the *Waldhere* fragments. *Med. Ævum*, 41, vol. 10, p. 155-158.

1588. MILNE (J. G.) and SWEETING (Elizabeth). Marginalia in a copy of Bartholomaeus Anglicus' *De proprietatibus rerum :* a new version of the Nine Worthies. *Mod. Language R.*, 45, vol. 40, p. 85-89, 237-245.

1589. MOZLEY (J. H.). The collection of mediaeval Latin verse in MS. Cotton Titus D. xxiv. *Med. Ævum*, 42, vol. 11, 1-45.

1590. O'CONNELL (Philip). The schools and scholars of Breiffne. Dublin, Browne & Nolan, 42, in-8, xxxix-669 p., 42s. R : D. Kennedy, *Irish hist. Stud.*, 43, vol. 3, p. 415-416.

1591. ONIONS (C. T.). ' Gaping against an oven '. *Med. Ævum*, 40, vol. 9, p. 86-87.

1592. PASCAL (R.). On the origins of the liturgical drama of the Middle Ages. *Mod. Language R.*, 41, vol. 36, p. 369-387.

1593. POWICKE (F. M.). The compilation of the ' Chronica Majora ' of Matthew Paris. London, Oxford Univ. Press, 44, in-8, 16 p., 1s. 6d.

1594. PROCTER (E. S.). The scientific works of the court of Alfonso X of Castille : the King and his collaborators. *Mod. Language R.*, 45, vol. 40, p. 12-29.

1595. RICHARDSON (H. G.). The schools of Northampton in the 12th century. *Eng. hist. R.*, 41, vol. 56, p. 595-605. (Notes and documents).

1596. RICHEY (M. F.). Essays on the medieval love lyric. Oxford, Blackwell, 43, in-8, vii-115 p., 7s. 6d.

1597. ROBSON (C. A.). The character of Turpin in the *Chanson de Roland*. *Med. Ævum*, 41, vol. 10, p. 97-100.

1598. SCHWARZ (W.). Translation into German in the 15th century. *Mod. Language R.*, 44, vol. 39, p. 368-373.

1599. SEIGNOBOS (C.). The rise of European civilization. New ed. London, Cape, 44, in-8, 377 p., 12s. 6d.

1600. SEVERS (J. B.). The literary relationships of Chaucer's Clerk's tale. London, Oxford Univ. Press, 42, in-8, 383 p., 34s. (Yale stud. in Engl. ser.).

1601. SHEPPARD (L. A.). Printing at Deventer in the 15th century. *Library*, 43/44, vol. 24, p. 101-119.

1602. STEINBERG (S. H.). The *Forma scribendi* of Hugo Spechtshart. *Library*, 40/41, vol. 21, p. 264-278.

1603. STEINBERG (S. H.). Medieval writing-masters. *Library*, 41, vol. 22, p. 1-24 (plates).

1604. STEINBERG (S. H.). A hand-list of specimens of medieval writing-masters. *Library*, 43, vol. 23, p. 191-194.

1605. STRONSKI (S.). La poésie et la réalité aux temps des troubadours. London, Oxford Univ. Press, 43, in-8, 32 p., 2s. R : H. J. Chaytor, *Mod. Language R.*, 44, vol. 39, p. 79.

1606. TANQUEREY (F. J.). Chronologie du *Conte de la Charrette*. *Med. Ævum*, 43, vol. 12, p. 1-17.

1607. THOMSON (S. Harrison). The *Dulcis Jesu Memoria* in Anglo-Norman and Middle French. *Med. Ævum*, 42, vol. 11, p. 68-76.

1608. THORNDIKE (L.). University records and life in the Middle Ages. London, Oxford Univ. Press, 44, in-8, 494 p., 36s. 6d.

1609. URWIN (K.). Pathelin *Chaude Teste* and Guillemette's role in the farce. *Med. Ævum*, 44, vol. 13, p. 18-21.

1610. VINE (Guthrie). Around the earliest Spanish version of Aesop's Fables. *B. John Rylands Library*, 41, vol. 25, p. 97-118.

1611. WEISS (Roberto). Humanism in England during the 15th century. Oxford, Blackwell, 41, in-4, xxiii-190 p., 12s. 6d. (Medium aevum monogr., 4). R : F. J. E. Raby, *Theology*, 41, vol. 43, p. 186-187. S. Gaselee, *Class. R.*, 42, vol. 56, p. 47-48. C. H. Williams, *History*, 43, vol. 28, p. 93-94. J. W. H. Atkins, *Mod. Language R.*, 43, vol. 38, p. 353-354.

1612. WEISS (R.). Leonardo Bruni Aretino and early English humanism. *Mod. Language R.*, 41, vol. 36, p. 443-448.

1613. WEISS (R.). Henry VI and the library of All Souls College (Oxford). *Eng. hist. R.*, 42, vol. 57, p. 102-105.

1614. WEISS (R.). Piero del Monte, John Whethamstede, and the library of St. Albans abbey. *Eng. hist. R.*, 45, vol. 60, p. 399-406.

1615. WHITFIELD (J. H.). Petrarch and the Renascence. Oxford, Blackwell, 43, in-8, 170 p., 12s. 6d. R : C. M. Ady, *Eng. hist. R.*, 44, vol. 59, p. 408-410. R. Weiss, *Mod. Language R.*, 44, vol. 39, p. 310-312.

1616. WILMART (André). Le florilege mixte de Thomas Bekynton. *Med. and Renaissance Stud.*, 41, vol. 1, p. 41-84.

1617. WILSON (R. M.). English and French in England, 1100-1300. *History*, 43, vol. 28, p. 37-60.

§ 10. History of Art

a. GENERAL

1618. BATSFORD (Harry) and FRY (Charles). The greater English church of the Middle Ages. London, Batsford, 40, in-8, 144 p., (illus.), 7s. 6d. (Brit. heritage ser.). R : *National R.*, 40, vol. 115, p. 117-118.

1619. BORENIUS (T.). Italian painting up to Leonardo and Raphael. London, Avalon Press, 45, in-4, 28 p., (illus.), 8s. (Discussions on art ser.).

1620. BUNIM (Miriam Schild). Space in medieval painting and the forerunners of perspective. London, Oxford Univ. Press, 40, in-4, xviii-261 p., (plates), 25s. R : N.P., *Burlington Mag.*, 42, vol. 81, p. 311.

1621. CLARK (Sir Kenneth) ed. Florentine paintings : 15th century. London, Faber, 45, in-4, 28 p., (illus.), 6s. (Faber Gallery ser.).

1622. CONANT (K. J.). Early medieval church architecture. London, Oxford Univ. Press, 43, in-8, 46 p., (plates), 12s.

1623. CROSSLEY (F. H.). English church design, 1040-1540 A.D. London, Batsford, 45, in-8, viii-120 p., (illus.), 12s. 6d.

1624. HENRY (Françoise). Irish art in the early Christian period. London, Methuen, 40, in-8, 739 p., 25s. R : T. D. Kendrick, *Burlington Mag.*, 40, vol. 77, p. 203.

1625. HUTCHINSON (F. E.). The mediaeval architect. *19th Century*, 45, vol. 137, p. 215-220.

1626. KITZINGER (Ernst). Early medieval art in the British Museum. London, Oxford Univ. Press, 40, in-8, 113 p., (illus., plates), 3s. R : F. Saxl, *Burlington Mag.*, 41, vol. 78, p. 101-102.

1627. LEASK (Harold G.). Irish castles and castellated houses. Dundalk, Tempest, 41, in-8, 170 p., (plates), 8s. 6d. R : R. D. Edwards, *Irish hist. Stud.*, 42, vol. 3, p. 232-233. W. D. Simpson, *Archaeol. cambrensis*, 42, vol. 97, p. 131-132.

1628. MENDELL (Elizabeth Lawrence). Romanesque sculpture in Saintonge. London, Oxford Univ. Press, 41, in-4, 213 p., 31s. 6d. (Yale hist. publ., hist. of art, 2). R : *Burlington Mag.*, 44, vol. 85, p. 234.

1629. POST (Chandler R.). A history of Spanish painting. Vol. 8, pt. 1-2 : The Aragonese school in the late Middle Ages. London, Oxford Univ. Press, 41, 2 vols. in-8, 800 p., 358 plates, 63s.

1630. PUGIN (A.). Gothic ornament in England and France. London, Tiranti, 42, in-4, 92 plates, 15s.

1631. RAFTERY (Joseph). Christian art in ancient Ireland. Vol. 2. Dublin, Stationery Office, 41, in-2, 184 p., (plates), 30s. R : C. Fox, Archaeol. cambrensis, 41, vol. 96, p. 209-211. C. A. R. Radford, Antiquity, 42, vol. 16, p. 370-371.

1632. TRISTRAM (E. W.). English medieval wall-painting. London, Oxford Univ. Press, 45, in-4, 178 p., (illus.), 210s.

1633. WHITEHILL (Walter Muir). Spanish Romanesque architecture of the 11th century. London, Oxford Univ. Press, 41, in-8, 352 p., (plates, maps), 63s. R : C.A.R.R., Antiq. J., 42, vol. 22, p. 227-229.

b. MONOGRAPHS

1634. BISHOP (H. E.) and RADFORD (C. A. Ralegh). Bishop Henry Marshall's tomb in Exeter Cathedral. Antiq. J., 41, vol. 21, p. 332-336.

1635. COTT (P. B.). Siculo-Arabic ivories. London, Oxford Univ. Press, 40, 2 vols. in-2, vii-68 p., 80 plates, 105s. (Princeton monogr. in art & archaeol., fol. ser., 3).

1636. CROSSLEY (F. H.) and RIDGWAY (M. H.). Screens, lofts, and stalls situated in Wales and Monmouthshire. 3 pts. Archaeol. cambrensis, 43, vol. 97, p. 135-160; 44, vol. 98, p. 64-112; 45, vol. 98, p. 153-198 (illus.).

1637. DORMAN (B. E.). The story of Ely and its cathedral. Ely, Mason & Dorman, 45, in-8, 76 p., (illus.), 6s.

1638. GARDNER (Arthur). Alabaster tombs of the pre-Reformation period in England. London, Cambridge Univ. Press, 40, in-4, 218 p., (illus.), 21s. R : H. Hope-Nicholson, Burlington Mag., 41, vol. 78, p. 32-33.

1639. HARVEY (John H.). Henry Yevele, architect, and his works in Kent. Archaeol. cantiana, 43, vol. 56, p. 48-53.

1640. HARVEY (J. H.). Henry Yevele, c. 1320-1400 : the life of an English architect. London, Batsford, 44, in-8, viii-86 p., (illus.), 15s.

1641. HEMP (W. J.). Conway Castle. Archaeol. cambrensis, 41, vol. 96, p. 163-174.

1642. HEMP (W. J.). Early timber work at Henblas, Llandderfal and Penarth Fawr, Llanarmon. Archaeol. cambrensis, 42, vol. 97, p. 67-76 (plans, illus.).

1643. HILDBURGH (W. L.). A 12th-century cross from Scania. Antiq. J., 43, vol. 23, p. 48-51 (illus.).

1644. HILDBURGH (W. L.). Some presumably datable fragments of an English alabaster retable, and some assembled notes on English alabaster carvings in Spain. Antiq. J., 44, vol. 24, p. 27-37 (illus.).

1645. KENDRICK (T. D.). Saxon art at Sutton Hoo. Burlington Mag., 40, vol. 77, p. 174-182.

1646. KENDRICK (T. D.) and RADFORD (C. A. Ralegh). Recent discoveries at All Hallows, Barking. Antiq. J., 43, vol. 23, p. 14-18 (illus.).

1647. LONG (Edward T.). Recently discovered wall paintings in England, 1-2. Burlington Mag., 40, vol. 76, p. 124-128, 156-162.

1648. MACLAGAN (Eric). The Bayeux tapestry. London, Penguin, 43, in-8, 32 p., (plates), 2s. (King Penguin ser.).

1649. MANN (James G.). A tournament helm in Melbury Sampford church. *Antiq. J.*, 40, vol. 20, p. 368-379 (illus.).

1650. MANN (J. G.). Two 14th-century gauntlets from Ripon cathedral. *Antiq. J.*, 42, vol. 22, p. 113-122 (illus.).

1651. MANN (J. G.). A late medieval sword from Ireland. *Antiq. J.*, 44, vol. 24, p. 94-99 (illus.).

1652. MORRELL (J. B.). York monuments : the arts and crafts in York. London, Batsford, 44, in-4, viii-131 p., (plates), 63s.

1653. MORRIS (Percy). Exeter cathedral : a conjectural restoration of the 14th-century altar-screen. 2 pts. *Antiq. J.*, 43, vol. 23, p. 122-147; 44, vol. 24, p. 10-21 (illus.).

1654. NEAVERSON (E.). The older building stones of St. Asaph cathedral. *Archaeol. cambrensis*, 45, vol. 98, p. 221-225.

1655. OMAN (Sir Charles C.). English medieval church plate. *Archaeol. J.*, 39 (40), vol. 96, p. 159-177.

1656. O'NEIL (B. H. St. J.). Criccieth Castle, Caernarvonshire. *Archaeol. cambrensis*, 44, vol. 98, p. 1-51 (illus.).

1657. PEATE (J. C.). The double-ended fire-dog. *Antiquity*, 42, vol. 16, p. 64-70 (plates).

1658. PERKINS (J. B. Ward). The Harrington effigy in Cartmel priory. *Antiq. J.*, 43, vol. 23, p. 26-30 (illus.).

1659. RACKHAM (Bernard) and BATY (C. W.). The Jesse window at Llanrhaiadr, Denbighshire. Pt. 1-2. *Burlington Mag.*, 42, vol. 80, p. 62-66, 121-124.

1660. RADFORD (C. A. R.). The early Christian monuments of Scotland. *Antiquity*, 42, vol. 16, p. 1-18.

1661. RUSSELL (Janet). English medieval leatherwork. *Archaeol. J.*, 39 (40), vol. 96, p. 132-141 (illus.).

1662. SEABY (A. W.). Some Berkshire interlacings. *Antiquity*, 44, vol. 18, p. 88-94 (illus.).

1663. SIMPSON (W. Douglas). The castles of Dudley and Ashby-de-la-Zouch. *Archaeol. J.*, 39 (40), vol. 96, p. 142-158.

1664. SIMPSON (W. D.). Castles of ' livery and maintenance '. *J. archaeol. Assoc.*, 39 (40), vol. 4, p. 39-54.

1665. SIMPSON (W. D.). Tonbridge castle. *J. archaeol. Assoc.*, 40 (41), vol. 5, p. 63-72.

1666. THOMAS (W. G. Mackay). Old English candlesticks and their Venetian prototypes. *Burlington Mag.*, 42, vol. 80, p. 145-151 (plates).

1667. VALLANCE (Aymer). Anchor house, Lynsted. *Archaeol. cantiana*, 42 (43), vol. 55, p. 53-56.

1668. WILLIAMS (E. Carleton). Mural paintings of the Three Living and the Three Dead in England. *J. archaeol. Assoc.*, 42, vol. 7, p. 31-40.

1669. WOODFORDE (Christopher). The medieval stained glass in East Harling and North Tuddenham churches, Norfolk. *J. archaeol. Assoc.*, 40 (41), vol. 5, p. 1-32 (plates).

1670. WORMALD (F.). A wall-painting at Idsworth, Hants, and a liturgical graffito. *Antiq. J.*, 45, vol. 25, p. 43-47 (illus.).

1671. YATES (Edward). Notes on medieval church ironwork. *J. archaeol. Assoc.*, 39 (40), vol. 4, p. 175-187.

c. MINIATURES

1672. EGBERT (Donald Drew). The Tickhill psalter and related manuscripts. A school of MS. illumination in England during the early 14th century. London, Quaritch, 40, in-2, 262 p., (plates), 150s.

1673. HERMANNSSON (Halldór). Illuminated MSS. of the Jónsbók. London, Oxford Univ. Press, 40, in-8,

26 p., (plates), 10s. (Cornell Univ. Libr. Islandica, vol. 28). R : F. Wormald, *Burlington Mag.*, 42, vol. 80, p. 104.

1674. HOLLAENDER (Albert). The pictorial work in the ' Flores Historiarum ' of the so-called Matthew of Westminster (MS. Chetham 6712). *B. John Rylands Library*, 44, vol 28, p. 361-381.

1675. KURDIAN (H.). An Armenian MS. with unique Mongolian miniatures. *J. asiatic Soc.*, 41, p. 145-148 (plates).

1676. KURDIAN (H.). An important Armenian MS. with Greek miniatures. *J. asiatic Soc.*, 42, p. 155-162 (plates).

1677. OAKESHOTT (W.). The artists of the Winchester Bible, with 44 reproductions. London, Faber, 45, in-8, 22 p., (illus.), 10s. 6d.

§ 11. History of Music

1678. FARMER (H. G.). Turkish instruments of music in the 15th century. *J. asiatic Soc.*, 40, p. 195-198.

1679. PANUM (Hortense). The stringed instruments of the Middle Ages, their evolution and development. Engl. ed., revised and ed. by J. Pulver. London, Reeves, 41, in-8, ix-511 p., (illus.), 22s. 6d. R : F.B., *Musical Times*, 41, vol. 82, p. 299.

1680. REESE (Gustave). Music in the Middle Ages. With an intr. on the music of ancient times. London, Dent, 41, in-8, 503 p., 25s.

1681. THOMPSON (A. H.). Songschools in the Middle Ages. London, Oxford Univ. Press, 42, in-8, 30 p., 1s. (Church music soc.).

§ 12. History of Philosophy

1682. CALLUS (D. A.). Philip the Chancellor and the *De Anima* ascribed to Robert Grosseteste. ' *Med. and Renaissance Stud.*, 41, vol. 1, p. 105-127.

1683. GILMORE (M. P.). Argument from Roman law in political thought, 1200-1600. London, Oxford Univ. Press, 42, in-8, 156 p., 8s. 6d. (Hist. monogr. ser.).

1684. KLIBANSKY (Raymond). The rock of Parmenides : mediaeval views on the origin of dialectic. *Med. and Renaissance Stud.*, 43, vol. 1, p. 178-186.

1685. KLIBANSKY (R.). Plato's *Parmenides* in the Middle Ages and the Renaissance : a chapter in the history of Platonic studies. *Med. and Renaissance Stud.*, 43, vol. 1, p. 281-330.

1686. LABOWSKY (Lotte). A new version of Scotus Eriugena's Commentary on Martianus Capella. *Med. and Renaissance Stud.*, 43, vol. 1, p. 187-193.

1687. LEGGE (M. D.). John Pecham's *Jerarchie*. *Med. Ævum*, 42, vol. 11, p. 77-84.

1688. MINIO-PALUELLO (L.). The genuine text of Boethius' translation of Aristotle's Categories. *Med. and Renaissance Stud.*, 43, vol. 1, p. 151-177.

1689. SOUTHERN (R. W.). St. Anselm and his English pupils. *Med. and Renaissance Stud.*, 41, vol. 1, p. 3-34.

1690. THOMAS (E. Crewdson). History of the Schoolmen. London, Williams and Norgate, 41, in-8, 677 p., 30s. R : G. F. Nuttall, *Congreg. Quar.*, 41, vol. 19, p. 368. C. C. J. Webb, *Philosophy*, 42, vol. 17, p. 188.

1691. WALZER (Richard). Arabic transmission of Greek thought to medieval Europe. *B. John Rylands Library*, 45, vol. 29, p. 160-183.

§ 13. History of the Church

a. GENERAL

1692. BETTS (R. R.). Jan Hus. *History*, 40, vol. 24, p. 97-112.

1693. CHICHELE (Henry), abp. of Canterbury. The register of Henry Chichele, 1414-43, ed. by E. F. Jacob with the assistance of H. C. Johnson. Vol. 1. London, Oxford Univ. Press, 43, in-8, 480 p., 15s. R : C. Johnson. *Eng. hist. R.*, 44, vol. 59, p. 411-413. N. Sykes, *Theology*, 44, vol. 47, p. 91-93.

1694. ⸺ ⸺ ⸺ Vol. 3. London, Oxford Univ. Press, 45, in-8, 532 p., 15s.

1695. JACOB (E. F.). Englishmen and the General Councils of the 15th century. *History*, 40, vol. 24, p. 206-219.

1696. JACOB (E. F.). Essays in the conciliar epoch. Manchester, Univ. Press, 43, in-8, viii-192 p., 10s. 6d. (Victoria Univ. of Manch., hist. ser., 80). R : C.W.P.O., *Eng. hist. R.*, 44, vol. 59, p. 418-419.

1697. KIDD (B. J.) ed. Documents illustrative of the history of the church. Vol. 3 : c. 500-1500. London, S.P.C.K., 41, in-8, 234 p., 7s. 6d.

1698. MOORMAN (J. R. H.). Church life in England in the 13th century. London, Cambridge Univ. Press, 45, in-8, xxviii-444 p., 25s. R : F. J. E. Raby, *Theology*, 45, vol. 48, p. 253-255.

1699. Ó BRIAIN (Felim). The expansion of Irish Christianity to 1200 : an historiographical survey. 2 pts. *Irish hist. Stud.*, 43, vol. 3, p. 241-266; 44, vol. 4, p. 131-163.

1700. SMALLEY (Beryl). The study of the Bible in the Middle Ages. London, Oxford Univ. Press, 41, in-8, xvi-295 p., 17s. 6d. R : A. G. Little, *Eng. hist. R.*, 42, vol. 57, p. 267-269. M. Deanesly, *Hibbert J.*, 42, vol. 40, p. 198-199. H. H. Rowley, *Baptist Quar.*, 41, vol. 10, p. 458-459.

1701. SPINKA (M.). John Hus and the Czech reform. London, Cambridge Univ. Press, 43, in-8, xiii-82 p., 9s.

1702. TELLENBACH (Gerd). Church, State, and Christian society at the time of the investiture contest, tr. by R. F. Bennett. Oxford, Blackwell, 40, in-8, 220 p., 12s. 6d. (Stud. in mediaeval hist., vol. 3). R : C. Smyth, *Theology*, 41, vol. 42, p. 189-190.

b. HISTORY OF THE POPES

1703. BALDWIN (M. W.). The medieval papacy in action. London, Macmillan, 41, in-8, xiii-113 p., 4s. 6d.

1704. KEMP (E. W.). Pope Alexander III and the canonization of the saints. *Trans. Roy. hist. Soc.*, 45, vol. 27, p. 13-28.

1705. RICHARDSON (H. G.). Clement V and the see of Canterbury. *Eng. hist. R.*, 41, vol. 56, p. 97-103.

1706. STEINBERG (S. H.). A French version of Duranti's prescriptions on the presentation of Papal bulls. *Library*, 42, vol. 23, p. 84-89.

c. HISTORY OF MONASTIC AND OTHER ORDERS

1707. BENNETT (R. F.). Pierre Mandonnet, O.P., and Dominican studies. *History*, 40, vol. 24, p. 193-205.

1708. BOYD (C. E.). A Cistercian nunnery in medieval Italy. London, Oxford Univ. Press, 43, in-8, 202 p., (map), 11s. 6d.

1709. CHAYTOR (H. J.). Statutes of the Confraternity of St. Lazare in Bordeaux. *Med. Ævum*, 41, vol. 10, p. 119-129.

1710. CLARKE (Maude V.). Register of the Priory of the Blessed Virgin Mary at Tristernagh. Dublin, Stationery Office, 41, in-8, xxvi-141 p., 10s. 6d. (Irish MSS. comm.). R : C. J., *Eng. hist. R.*, 42, vol. 57, p. 395-396. A. Gwynn, *Irish hist. Stud.*, 42, vol. 3, p. 216-220.

1711. COTTON (Charles). St. Austin's abbey, Canterbury : treasurers' accounts, 1468-9, and others. *Archaeol. cantiana*, 39 (40), vol. 51, p. 66-107.

1712. CROSBY (S. M.). Abbey of St. Denis, 475-1122. London, Oxford Univ. Press, 42, in-8, 227 p., (illus., maps), 31s. 6d.

1713. DAVIES (J. C.). Ewenny Priory : some recently-found records. *Nat. Library Wales J.*, 44, vol. 3, p. 107-137.

1714. DUNNING (P. J.). The Arroasian Order in medieval Ireland. *Irish hist. Stud.*, 45, vol. 4, p. 297-315.

1715. FINBERG (H. P. R.). The House of Ordgar and the foundation of Tavistock Abbey. *Eng. hist. R.*, 43, vol. 58, p. 190-201.

1716. GRAHAM (Rose). Excavations on the site of Sempringham priory. *J. archaeol. Assoc.*, 40 (41), vol. 5, p. 73-101 (charts).

1717. GRAHAM (R.). The history of the alien priory of Wenlock. *J. archaeol. Assoc.*, 39 (40), vol. 4, p. 117-140.

1718. GRIERSON (P.). Grimbald of St. Bertin's. *Eng. hist. R.*, 40, vol. 55, p. 529-561.

1719. GWYNN (Aubrey). The English Austin friars in the time of Wyclif. London, Oxford Univ. Press, 40, in-8, 295 p., 15s. R : W. A. Pantin, *Eng. hist. R.*, 45, vol. 60, p. 112-114. M. Deanesly, *History*, 41, vol. 26, p. 75-76.

1720. HILL (Rosalind). Bishop Sutton and the institution of heads of religious houses in the diocese of Lincoln. *Eng. hist. R.*, 43, vol. 58, p. 201-209.

1721. JACOB (E. F.). The Brethren of the Common Life. *B. John Rylands Library*, 40, vol. 24, p. 37-58.

1722. JOHNSTONE (Hilda). The chapel of St. Louis, Greyfriars, London. *Eng. hist. R.*, 41, vol. 56, p. 447-450.

1723. KNOWLES (David). The monastic order in England from St. Dunstan to the Fourth Lateran Council, 943-1216. London, Cambridge Univ. Press, 40, in-4, xxiii-764 p., 45s. R : F. M. Powicke, *History*, 41, vol. 25, p. 358-362. E. Hutton, 19*th Century*, 41, vol. 129, p. 509-514. M. Deanesly, *Theology*, 41, vol. 42, p. 181-182. A. H. Thompson, *Eng. hist. R.*, 41, vol. 56, p. 647-651.

1724. KNOWLES (D.). The religious houses of medieval England. London, Sheed & Ward, 40, in-8, viii-167 p., 8s. 6d. R : F. M. Powicke, *History*, 41, vol. 25, p. 358-362. A. H. Thompson, *Eng. hist. R.*, 41, vol. 56, p. 647-651. A.H.T., *Antiq. J.*, 42, vol. 22, p. 76-77.

1725. KNOWLES (D.). The cultural influence of English medieval monasticism. *Cambridge hist. J.*, 43, vol. 7, p. 146-159.

1726. KNOWLES (D.). Some developments in English monastic life, 1216-1336. *Trans. Roy. hist. Soc.*, 44, vol. 26, p. 37-52.

1727. KNOWLES (D.). Revision to lists of medieval religious houses. *Eng. hist. R.*, 45, vol. 60, p. 380-385.

1728. LITTLE (A. G.). Introduction of the Observant Friars into England. London, Oxford Univ. Press, 41, in-8, 14 p., 1s. 6d.

1729. LITTLE (A. G.). Franciscan papers, lists, and documents. Manchester, Univ. Press, 43, in-8, xiii-262 p., 21s. (Victoria Univ. of Manch., hist. ser., 81). R : W. G., *Eng. hist. R.*, 45, vol. 60, p. 125. C. H. Williams, *History*, 45, vol. 30, p. 103-104.

1730. LOVEGROVE (E. W.). Llanthony Priory. *Archaeol. cambrensis*, 43, vol. 97, p. 213-229.

1731. MALDEN (R. H.). Abbeys : their rise and fall. London, Oxford Univ. Press, 44, in-8, 32 p., 1s.

1732. MOORMAN (John R. H.). Early Franciscan art and literature. *B. John Rylands Library*, 43, vol. 27, p. 338-358.

1733. MORGAN (Marjorie M.). Inventories of three small alien priories. *J. archaeol. Assoc.*, 39 (40), vol. 4, p. 141-149.

1734. MORGAN (M. M.). The abbey of Bec-Hellouin and its English priories. *J. archaeol. Assoc.*, 40 (41), vol. 5, p. 33-61.

1735. O'CONNELL (William D.). Cork Franciscan records. Cork, Univ. Press, 42, in-8, 42 p., 2s. 6d. (Hist. and archaeol. papers, 3). R : K. B. Nowlan, *Irish hist. Stud.*, 45, vol. 4, p. 287.

1736. O'NEIL (B. H. St. J.). Talley Abbey, Carmarthenshire. *Archaeol. cambrensis*, 41, vol. 96, p. 69-91.

1737. PETRY (R. C.). Francis of Assisi : apostle of poverty. London, Cambridge Univ. Press, 42, in-8, x-200 p., 18s.

1738. RADFORD (C. A. R.). The Cluniac priory of St. James at Dudley. *Antiq. J.*, 40, vol. 20, p. 449-459 (illus.).

1739. RIOS (Romanus). Subiaco. *B. John Rylands Library*, 44, vol. 28, p. 444-453.

1740. RYAN (John). The abbatial succession at Clonmacnois from the foundation of the monastery to the coming of the Norse (A.D. 545-799). (Essays and studies presented to Eoin MacNeill, p. 490-507). Dublin, Sign of the Three Candles, 40, in-8, 593 p., 42s. R : F. Ó Briain, *Irish hist. Stud.*, 41, vol. 2, p. 463.

1741. SABATIER (P.). The life of St. Francis of Assisi. New ed. London, Hodder, 42, in-8, 346 p., 15s.

1742. SHEPPARD (L. C.). The English Carmelites. Birmingham, Burns & Oates, 43, in-8, 115 p., (illus.), 6s.

1743. SMITH (R. A. Lendon). The financial system of Rochester cathedral priory. *Eng. hist. R.*, 41, vol. 56, p. 586-595. (Notes and documents).

1744. SMITH (R. A. L.). The *regimen scaccarii* in English monasteries. *Trans. Roy. hist. Soc.*, 42, vol. 24, p. 73-94.

1745. SMITH (R. A. L.). The barton and bartoner of Christ Church, Canterbury. *Archaeol. cantiana*, 42 (43), vol. 55, p. 16-25.

1746. SMITH (R. A. L.). Canterbury Cathedral priory : a study in monastic administration. London, Cambridge Univ. Press, 43, in-8, xii-238 p., (map), 15s. (Cambr. stud. in econ. hist.). C. H. Williams, *History*, 45, vol. 30, p. 102-103. F. M. Powicke, *Eng. hist. R.*, 44, vol. 59, p. 405-407. E. Miller, *Econ. Hist. R.*, 44, vol. 14, p. 91-92. R. Lennard, *Econ. J.*, 44, vol. 54, p. 101-103.

1747. SMITH (R. A. L.). The early community of St. Andrew at Rochester, 604-c.1080. *Eng. hist. R.*, 45, vol. 60, p. 289-299.

1748. TACHÉ (Louis). Notes sur l'histoire des exemptions monastiques des origines au 9e siècle. *R. Univ. Ottawa*, 41, vol. 11, sect. spécial, 5*-31*, 149*-177*.

1749. WOODRUFF (C. Eveleigh). Notes on the inner life and domestic economy of the Priory of Christ Church, Canterbury, in the 15th century. *Archaeol. cantiana*, 40 (41), vol. 53, p. 1-16.

d. HAGIOGRAPHY

1750. BOWEN (E. G.). The travels of the Celtic saints. *Antiquity*, 44, vol. 18, p. 16-28 (maps).

1751. DOBLE (G. H.). Saint Iltut. Cardiff, Univ. of Wales Press Board, 44, in-8, 52 p., 5s. R : E. G. Bowen, *Antiquity*, 44, vol. 18, p. 165-166.

1752. DOBLE (G. H.). Saint Congar. *Antiquity*, 45, vol. 19, p. 32-43, 84-95.

1753. FLOWER (Robin). A metrical life of St. Wulfstan of Worcester. *Nat. Library Wales J.*, 40, vol. 1, p. 119-130.

1754. HURLEY (Timothy). St. Patrick and the parish of Kilkeevan. Vol. 1. Dublin, Dollard Printing-house, 44, in-8, xxvii-618 p., 10s. 6d. R : J. F. O'Doherty, *Irish hist. Stud.*, 45, vol. 4, p. 283-284.

1755. LEVISON (Wilhelm). An 8th-century poem on St. Ninian. *Antiquity*, 40, vol. 14, p. 280-291.

1756. LEVISON (W.). St. Alban and St. Albans. *Antiquity*, 41, vol. 15, p. 337-359.

1757. MacDERMOTT (Anthony). St. Brandan the navigator. *Mariner's Mirror*, 44, vol. 30, p. 73-80.

1758. SIMPSON (W. D.). St. Ninian and the origins of the Christian church in Scotland. Edinburgh, Oliver & Boyd, 40, in-8, xii-112 p., (maps), 10s. R : C.A.R.R., *Antiq. J.*, 40, vol. 20, p. 518-519.

1759. WADE-EVANS (A. W.). Vitae Sanctorum Britanniae et genealogiae. Cardiff, Univ. of Wales Press Board, 44, in-8, xx-336 p., 21s. (Board of Celtic stud., Univ. of Wales, hist. and law ser., 9). R : E. D., *Archaeol. cambrensis*, 45, vol. 98, p. 264-266.

1760. WILLIAMS (J. E. Caerwyn). Bucheddau'r Saint : eu cefndir a'n datblygiad fel llen.. (Lives of saints : their background and literary development). *B. Board celtic Stud.*, 44, vol. 11, p. 149-157.

1761. WILSON (R. M.). Some lost saints' lives in Old and Middle English. *Mod. Language R.*, 41, vol. 36, p. 161-172.

e. SPECIAL STUDIES

1762. ANDERSON (Robert Gordon). The biography of a cathedral (Notre Dame de Paris). Toronto, Longmans, 44, in-8, xii-496 p., $4.00. R : P.G.C.C., *Queen's Quar.*, 45, vol. 52, p. 129-130.

1763. ATKINS (Sir Ivor). The church of Worcester from the 8th to the 12th century. Pt. 2 : The Familia from the middle of the 10th to the beginning of the 12th century. *Antiq. J.*, 40, vol. 20, p. 1-38.

1765. BOURQUE (Emmanuel). Les premiers recueils euchologiques. *R. Univ. Ottawa*, 41, vol. 11, sect. spécial, p. 178*-208*.

1766. BROOKE (Z. N. and C. N. L.). Hereford cathedral dignitaries in the 12th century. *Cambridge hist. J.*, 44, vol. 8, p. 1-21.

1767. BROWNE (A. L.). The medieval officials-principal of Rochester. *Archaeol. cantiana*, 40 (41), vol. 53, p. 29-61.

1768. CHENEY (C. R.). English synodalia of the 13th century. London, Oxford Univ. Press, 41, in-8, x-164 p., 10s. R : A. H. Thompson, *Eng. hist. R.*, 43, vol. 58, p. 487-490.

1769. DARWIN (F. D. S.). The English mediaeval recluse. London, S.P.C.K., 44, in-8, 96 p., 6s. R : F. J. E. Raby, *Theology*, 44, vol. 47, p. 279-280.

1770. DEANESLY (Margaret). Early English and Gallic minsters. *Trans. Roy. hist. Soc.*, 41, vol. 23, p. 25-69.

1771. DUDDING (R. C.). The first churchwardens' book of Louth, 1500-1524. London, Oxford Univ. Press, 41, in-8, xx-234 p., 15s. R : E.G.D., *Eng. hist. R.*, 42, vol. 57, p. 529. G.M., *History*, 42, vol. 27, p. 96.

1772. DUNNING (T. P.). Langland and the salvation of the heathen. *Med. Ævum*, 43, vol. 12, p. 45-54.

1773. DUNSTAN (G. R.). A note on the early history of parochial endowments. *Theology*, 43, vol. 46, p. 136-139.

1774. GRAHAM (Rose). Sidelights on the rectors and parishioners of Reculver from the Register of Archbishop Winchelsey. *Archaeol. cantiana*, 44, vol. 57, p. 1-12.

1775. GREEN (V. H. H.). Bishop Reginald Pecock : a study in ecclesiastical history and thought. London, Cambridge Univ. Press, 45, in-8, viii-262 p., 12s. 6d.

1776. GWYNN (Aubrey). Ireland and the English nation at the Council of Constance. Dublin, Hodges, Figgis, 40, in-8, 2s. (Proc., Royal Irish Academy, vol. 45, sect. C, p. 183-233). R : J. F. O'Doherty, *Irish hist. Stud.*, 41, vol. 2, p. 453-454.

1777. HASKINS (George L.) and KANTOROWICZ (Ernst H.). A diplomatic mission of Francis Accursius and his oration before Pope Nicholas III. *Eng. hist. R.*, 43, vol. 58, p. 424-447.

1778. HASSALL (W. O.). Two Papal bulls for St. Mary, Clerkenwell. *Eng. hist. R.*, 42, vol. 57, p. 97-101.

1779. JACOB (E. F.). Petitions for benefices from English universities during the great schism. *Trans. Roy. hist. Soc.*, 45, vol. 27, p. 41-59.

1780. LAUDER (John). St. Andrews formulare, 1541-1546, text transcr. and ed. by G. Donaldson and C. Macrae. Edinburgh, Stair Soc., 42, 2 vols. in-4, 400, xvii-405 p., 42s. (Publ., vol. 7, 9). R : C.J., *Eng. hist. R.*, 43, vol. 58, p. 248-249.

1781. LE PATOUREL (J. H.). Geoffrey of Monthray, Bishop of Coutances, 1049-1093. *Eng. hist. R.*, 44, vol. 59, p. 129-161.

1782. LESLIE (James B.). Raphoe clergy and parishes. Enniskillen,

Ritchie, Fermanagh Times Office, 40, in-8, vii-156 p., 20s. R : S. Ó Domhnaill, *Irish hist. Stud.*, 44, vol. 4, p. 110-112.

1783. LITTLE (A. G.). Theological schools in medieval England. *Eng. hist. R.*, 40, vol. 55, p. 624-629.

1784. LITTLE (A. G.). Personal tithes. *Eng. hist. R.*, 45, vol. 60, p. 67-88.

1785. LLOYD (J. E.). Bishop Sulien and his family. *Nat. Library Wales J.*, 41, vol. 2, p. 1-6.

1786. LYNCH (John). De praesulibus Hiberniae, ed. by J. F. O'Doherty. Dublin, Stationery Office, 44, 2 vols. in-8, v-464, 408 p., 42s. (Irish MSS. comm.). R : A. Gwynn, *Irish hist. Stud.*, 45, vol. 4, p. 275-278.

1787. MACDONALD (A. J. M.). Lanfranc, a study of his life, work and writing. 2nd ed. London, S.P.C.K., 44, in-8, vii-307 p., 12s. 6d. R : G. R. Dunstan, *Theology*, 45, vol. 48, p. 166.

1788. MACDONALD (A. J. M.). Episcopi vagantes in church history. London, S.P.C.K., 45, in-8, 32 p., 1s.

1789. MACDONALD (Inez). A coronation service, 1414. *Mod. Language R.*, 41, vol. 36, p. 351-368.

1790. McFARLANE (K. B.). Henry V, Bishop Beaufort and the red hat, 1417-1421. *Eng. hist. R.*, 45, vol. 60, p. 316-348.

1791. MAJOR (Kathleen). The Lincoln diocesan records. *Trans. Roy. hist. Soc.*, 40, vol. 22, p. 39-66.

1792. MALDEN (R. H.). The growth, building and work of a cathedral church. London, Oxford Univ. Press, 44, in-8, 48 p., 1s. 6d.

1793. MOORMAN (John R. H.). The medieval parsonage and its occupants. *B. John Rylands Library*, 44, vol. 28, p. 137-153.

1794. MORGAN (Marjorie M.). The excommunication of Grosseteste in 1243. *Eng. hist. R.*, 42, vol. 57, p. 244-250.

1795. MORGAN (M. M.). Early Canterbury jurisdiction. *Eng. hist. R.*, 45, vol. 60, p. 392-399.

1796. O'RAHILLY (Thomas F.). The two Patricks, a lecture on the history of Christianity in 5th-century Ireland. Dublin, Inst. for Advanced Stud., 42, in-8, 83 p., 2s. R : J. F. O'Doherty, *Irish hist. Stud.*, 43, vol. 3, p. 323-329.

1797. PANTIN (W. A.). The monk-solitary of Farne : a 14th-century English mystic. *Eng. hist. R.*, 44, vol. 59, p. 162-186.

1798. POTTS (R. U.). St. Mildred's church, Canterbury : further notes on the site. *Archaeol. cantiana*, 43, vol. 56, p. 19-22.

1799. POWICKE (F. M.). Master Simon the Norman. *Eng. hist. R.*, 43, vol. 58, p. 330-343.

1800. ROSS (Woodburn O.). Middle English sermons edited from B.M. MS. Royal 18B, xxiii. London, Oxford Univ. Press, 40, in-8, lxvi-396 p., 30s. (Early Engl. text soc., orig. ser., 209). R : F. J. E. Raby, *Theology*, 41, vol. 42, p. 186-188. M. S. Serjeantson, *Mod. Language R.*, 41, vol. 36, p. 256-257.

1801. SMITH (R. A. L.). The place of Gundulf in the Anglo-Norman church. *Eng. hist. R.*, 43, vol. 58, p. 257-272.

1802. SOMERVILLE (R.). Duchy of Lancaster presentations, 1399-1485. *B. Inst. hist. Research*, 40, vol. 18, p. 52-76.

1803. THOMPSON (Alexander Hamilton). Visitations in the diocese of Lincoln, 1517-1531, ed. by A. H. Thompson. Hereford, Lincoln Record Soc., 40-44, 2 vols. in-4, civ-203, x-263 p., 55s. (Lincoln Record Soc., vol. 33, 35). R : C. R. Cheney, *Econ. Hist. R.*, 41, vol. 11, p. 109-110. A. G. Dickens, *Eng. hist. R.*, 41, vol. 56, p. 313-315. G. F. Nuttall, *Congreg. hist. Soc. Trans.*, 44, vol. 14,

p. 253. G.S.T., *History*, 44, vol. 29, p. 212. A.G.D., *Eng. hist. R.*, 44, vol. 59, p. 419-420. C. R. Cheney, *Econ. Hist. R.*, 44, vol. 14, p. 203-204.

1804. THOMPSON (A. H.). Diocesan organisation in the Middle Ages : archdeacons and the rural deans. London, Oxford Univ. Press, 44, in-8, 44 p., 5s.

1805. THOMPSON (A. H.) and CLAY (Charles). Fasti parochiales. Vol. 2. Leeds, Yorks. Archaeol. Soc., 43, in-8, 12s. 6d. R : H. H. E. C(raster), *Eng. hist. R.*, 44, vol. 59, p. 278-279.

1806. URWIN (Kenneth). The theme of Mary's virginity in 15th-century France. *Mod. Language R.*, 41, vol. 36, p. 105-109.

1807. WHATMORE (L. E.). The sermon against the Holy Maid of Kent and her adherents, delivered at Paul's Cross, November the 23rd, 1533, and at Canterbury, December the 7th. *Eng. hist. R.*, 43, vol. 58, p. 463-475.

1808. WHATMORE (L. E.). A sermon of Henry Gold, vicar of Ospringe, 1525-27, preached before Archbishop Warham. *Archaeol. cantiana*, 44, vol. 57, p. 34-43.

1809. WHITELOCK (D.). Archbishop Wulfstan, homilist and statesman. *Trans. Roy. hist. Soc.*, 42, vol. 24, p. 25-45.

§ 14. **Archaeology, Settlements, Place Names**

1810. BOWEN (E. G.). The settlements of the Celtic saints in South Wales. *Antiquity*, 45, vol. 19, p. 175-186 (maps).

1811. BRENTNALL (H. C.). Wiltshire place-names. *Antiquity*, 41, vol. 15, p. 33-34.

1812. ELLISTON-ERWOOD (F. C.). Notes on bronze objects from Shooters Hill, Kent, and elsewhere, and on the antiquity of ' Jew's harps '. *Archaeol. cantiana*, 43, vol. 56, p. 34-40.

1813. FLETCHER (E. G. M.). Did Hengist settle in Kent? *Antiquity*, 43, vol. 17, p. 91-93.

1814. GOVER (J. E. B.), MAWER (A.) and STENTON (F. M.). The place-names of Nottinghamshire. London, Cambridge Univ. Press, 40, in-8, xlii-348 p., (maps), 21s. (Engl. place-name soc.). R : D. Whitelock, *Mod. Language R.*, 42, vol. 37, p. 81-83. D.C.D., *History*, 41, vol. 26, p. 85-86. F. W. Jessup, *Antiq. J.*, 41, vol. 21, p. 351-352.

1815. GOVER (J. E. B.), MAWER (A.) and STENTON (F. M.). Place names of Middlesex : apart from the City of London. London, Cambridge Univ. Press, 42, in-8, xxxiv-237 p., 18s. (Engl. place-name soc.). R : J.M., *Scottish geogr. Mag.*, 42, vol. 58, p. 77. G.R.C., *Geogr. J.*, 42, vol. 99, p. 202. B. Dowell, *Econ. Hist. R.*, 43, vol. 13, p. 131. D. Whitelock, *Mod. Language R.*, 43, vol. 38, p. 44-45. H.J.R., *Antiq. J.*, 45, vol. 25, p. 86-88.

1816. HANDO (F. J.). The pleasant land of Gwent. Intr. by A. Machen. Newport, Privately printed, 44, in-8, 111 p.

1817. HARDIE (R. P.). The roads of mediaeval Lauderdale. Edinburgh, Oliver & Boyd, 42, in-8, xv-106 p., 7s. 6d. R : W. C. Dickinson, *History*, 42, vol. 27, p. 154-155. C.N.B., *Geogr. J.*, 42, vol. 100, p. 36-37.

1818. HARDMAN (F. W.) and STEBBING (W. P. D.). Stonar and the Wantsum channel. *Archaeol. cantiana*, 42 (43), vol. 55, p. 37-49.

1819. JESSUP (R. F.). Notes on a Saxon charter of Higham. *Archaeol. cantiana*, 42 (43), vol. 55, p. 12-15.

1820. LEEDS (E. T.). A gold ring with runes from central Europe. *Antiq. J.*, 40, vol. 20, p. 329-337 (illus.).

1821. LEEDS (E. T.) and ATKINSON (R. J. C.). An Anglo-Saxon cemetery at Nassington, Northants. *Antiq. J.*, 44, vol. 24, p. 100-128 (illus.).

1822. LLOYD (Sir J. E.). Flintshire notes : Flint and Moed. *Archaeol. cambrensis*, 40, vol. 95, p. 57-64.

1823. LLOYD (Sir J. E.). Dolforwyn (a medieval township in Montgomeryshire). *B. Board celtic Stud.*, 41, vol. 10, p. 306-309.

1824. MACDONALD (Angus). The place-names of West Lothian. Edinburgh, Oliver and Boyd, 41, in-8, xl-179 p., 15s. R : B. G. Charles, *Mod. Language R.*, 41, vol. 36, p. 515-517. D.A.A., *Geogr. J.*, 42, vol. 99, p. 276. W. J. Watson, *Antiquity*, 42, vol. 16, p. 85-87.

1825. MATHIESON (John). Scottish ghost-names and other place-names : some of the difficulties in ascertaining their meaning. *Scottish geogr. Mag.*, 44, vol. 60, p. 1-5.

1826. MYRES (J. N. L.). Cremation and inhumation in the Anglo-Saxon cemeteries. *Antiquity*, 42, vol. 16, p. 330-341.

1827. O'NEIL (B. H. St. J.). The Silchester region in the 5th and 6th centuries, A.D. *Antiquity*, 44, vol. 18, p. 113-122 (illus.).

1828. O'NEIL (B. H. St. J.) and FOSTER-SMITH (A. H.). Montgomery town wall. *Archaeol. cambrensis*, 40, vol. 95, p. 217-228 (illus.).

1829. O'SULLIVAN (M. D.). Old Galway : the history of a Norman colony in Ireland. Cambridge, Heffer, 42, in-8, xiv-488 p., (illus.), 18s. R : H. G. Richardson, *Irish hist. Stud.*, 45, vol. 4, p. 361-367.

1830. PHILLIPS (C. W.). The Sutton Hoo burial ship. *Mariner's Mirror*, 40, vol. 26, p. 345-355.

1831. PHILLIPS (C. W.) and others. The Sutton Hoo ship-burial. *Antiquity*, 40, vol. 14, p. 6-87 (illus.).

1832. REANEY (P. H.). The place-names of Cambridgeshire and the Isle of Ely. London, Cambridge Univ. Press, 43, in-8, lxii-396 p., (maps), 23s. 6d. (Engl., place-name soc., vol. 19). R : H.C.D., *Geogr. J.*, 43, vol. 102, p. 35-37. D. Douglas, *History*, 44, vol. 29, p. 203. S. Potter, *Mod. Language R.*, 44, vol. 39, p. 65-67. E. Miller, *Econ. Hist. R.*, 44, vol. 14, p. 104. F. T. Wainwright, *Antiquity*, 44, vol. 18, p. 211-213. H.J.R., *Antiq. J.*, 45, vol. 25, p. 86-88.

1833. SIMPSON (W. D.). Flint Castle. *Archaeol. cambrensis*, 40, vol. 95, p. 20-26 (illus.).

1834. SIMPSON (W. D.). Harlech Castle and the Edwardian castle-plan. *Archaeol. cambrensis*, 40, vol. 95, p. 153-168 (illus.).

1835. STENTON (F. M.). Historical bearing of place-name studies : the English occupation of southern Britain. *Trans. Roy. hist. Soc.*, 40, vol. 22, p. 1-22. The historical bearing of place-name studies : Anglo-Saxon heathenism. *Trans. Roy. hist. Soc.*, 41, vol. 23, p. 1-24. The historical bearing of place-name studies : the Danish settlement of eastern England. *Trans. Roy. hist. Soc.*, 42, vol. 24, p. 1-24. The historical bearing of place-name studies : the place of women in Anglo-Saxon society. *Trans. Roy. hist. Soc.*, 43, vol. 25, p. 1-13.

1836. WAINWRIGHT (F. T.). Field-names. *Antiquity*, 43, vol. 17, p. 57-66 (illus.).

1837. WARD (Gordon). The Suttons. *Archaeol. cantiana*, 42 (43), vol. 55, p. 1-7.

1838. WARD (G.). The Saxon history of the Wantsum. *Archaeol. cantiana*, 43, vol. 56, p. 23-27.

1839. WARD (G.). The origins of Whitstable. *Archaeol. cantiana*, 44, vol. 57, p. 51-55.

1840. WILLIAMS (Ifor). The Levelinus inscription. *Archaeol. cambrensis*, 40, vol. 95; p. 1-8 (illus.).

1841. WILLIAMS (I.). Rhai enwan lleoedd yn Ninbych. (Some Welsh place-names in Denbighshire). *J. welsh bibliogr. Soc.*, 41, vol. 5, p. 249-261.

1842. WYNESS (F.). Mediaeval Elgin. Aberdeen, W. & W. Lindsay, 44, in-8, 64 p., (illus.), 5s.

K

MODERN HISTORY, GENERAL WORKS

§ 1. General

1843. BARTLETT (H. M.). Great movements in European history, 1660-1919. London, Harrap, 41, in-8, 431 p., 6s. 6d.

1844. COHEN (A.). An Anglo-Jewish scrap book, 1600-1840 : the Jews through English eyes. London, Cailingold, 43, in-8, xxiv-360 p., 12s. 6d.

1845. CONNELL (J. M.). Thomas Paine, a pioneer of democracy. London, Longmans, 40, in-8, 40 p., (illus.), 2s. 6d.

1846. ELTON (mrs. Oliver) ed. Locks, bolts and bars : stories of [British] prisoners in French wars, 1759-1814. London, Muller, 45, in-8, 264 p., 10s. 6d.

1847. FIELDHOUSE (H. N.). Liberalism in crisis. *Canad. hist. Assoc. Rept.*, 44, p. 98-109.

1848. FOOT (Isaac). Oliver Cromwell and Abraham Lincoln : a comparison. London, Simpkin, 45, in-8, 60 p., 2s. 6d.

1849. GOOCH (G. P.). Courts and cabinets. London, Longmans, 44, in-8, 323 p., 12s. 6d. R : C.H.W., *History*, 45, vol 30, p. 113.

1850. GRANT (A. J.) and TEMPERLEY (H. W. V.). Europe in the 19th and 20th centuries (1789-1939) ; with a supplementary section dealing with the years 1938-1939 by L. M. Penson. London, Longmans, 40, in-8, xxiii-716 p., 16s. R : I. M. Massey, *Int. Affairs*, 40, vol. 19, p. 108. *National R.*, 40, vol. 115, p. 238-239.

1851. Have the Americas a common history ? A United States view, by W. C. Binkley; A Canadian view, by G. W. Brown; A Mexican view, by E. O'Gorman; A South American view, by G. Arciniegas. *Canad. hist. R.*, 42, vol. 23, p. 125-156.

1852. HERD (H.). Panorama, 1900-1942. London, Allen & Unwin, 42, in-8, 186 p., 7s. 6d.

1853. HOVDE (B. J.). The Scandinavian countries, 1720-1865 : the rise of the middle classes. Toronto, Ryerson Press, 44, 2 vols. in-8, 823 p., $15.00. R : H.A., *Queen's Quar.*, 44, vol. 51, p. 476-477.

1854. MARRIOTT (Sir John A. R.). Napoleon and Hitler. *Quar. R.*, 42, vol. 278, p. 33-47.

1855. MAZZEI (Philip). Memoirs of the life and peregrinations of the Florentine Philip Mazzei, 1730-1816, tr. by H. R. Marraro. London, Oxford Univ. Press, 42, in-8, 465 p., (plates), 20s.

1856. MOWAT (R. B.) and SLOSSON (P.). History of the English-speaking peoples. London, Oxford Univ. Press, 43, in-8, 590 p., (maps), 21s. R : T.S., *Int. Affairs*, 44, vol. 20, p. 429.

1857. OGG (D.). Europe in the 17th century. Rev. ed. London, Black, 43, in-8, viii-576 p., (map), 20s.

1858. PFEILER (W. K.). War and the German mind. London, Oxford Univ. Press, 42, in-8, 369 p., 16s. 6d.

1859. ROBERTS (M. E.). Outlines of Balkan history. Ilfracombe, Stockwell, 43, in-8, 48 p., 2s.

§ 2. History, by Countries
Afghanistan

1860. SYKES (Sir Percy). A history of Afghanistan. London, Macmillan, 40, 2 vols. in-8, xi-411, viii-414 p., (maps), 50s. R : R. Forbes, *Int. Affairs*, 41, vol. 19, p. 216-217. E. D. Maclagan, *J. asiatic Soc.*, 41, p. 68-70. H. W.-B., *J. central asian Soc.*, 41, vol. 28, p.

92-94. W.F., *Geogr. J.*, 41, vol. 97, p. 260-261. A.E.P., *Queen's Quar.*, 43, vol. 50, p. 100-101.

Africa

1861. Bibliography of current literature dealing with African languages and cultures. *Africa*, 44 , vol. 14, p. 283-287, 358-360, 424-428, 481-484.

1862. LEWIN (E.). Annotated bibliography of recent publications on Africa South of the Sahara, etc. London, Royal Empire Soc., 43, in-8, 104 p., 5s.

1863. CUMMING (D. C.) : The history of Kassala and the province of Taka. Chapter 6. *Sudan Notes and Records*, 40, vol. 23, p. 1-54.

1864. KINGDON (F.D.). The western Nuer patrol, 1927-28. *Sudan Notes and Records*, 45, vol. 26, p. 171-178.

1865. NICHOLLS (G. Heaton). The part of the Union in the development of Africa. *Int. Affairs*, 45, vol. 21, p. 343-354.

1866. WILLIAMS (F. Lukyn). Nuwa Mbaguta, Nganzi of Ankole. *B. Uganda Soc.*, 45, no. 4, p. 3-13.

Albania

1867. ROBINSON (V.). Albania's road to freedom. London, Allen & Unwin, 41, in-8, 135 p., (plates, map), 15s.

Australia

1868. FERGUSON (John Alexander). Bibliography of Australia. Vol. 1, 1784-1830. London ; Sydney, Angus & Robertson, 41, in-8, 540 p., 63s. R : T. Dunbabin, *Austral. Quar.*, 41, vol. 13, no. 3, p. 116-117. G. F. James, *Hist. Stud. Australia N.Z.*, 42, vol. 2, p. 54-56.

1869. FITZHARDINGE (L. F.). Writings on Australian history, 1939-42.

(Bibliography). *Hist. Stud. Australia N.Z.*, 40-41, vol. 1, p. 65-67, 194-195, 275-276; 42, vol. 2, p. 119-121.

1870. BASSETT (Marnie). The Governor's lady : Mrs. Philip Gidley King. An Australian historical narrative. London, Oxford Univ. Press, 40, in-8, 130 p., 10s. 6d. R : K. Fitzpatrick, *Hist. Stud. Australia N.Z.*, 41, vol. 1, p. 283. G. Mackaness, *Austral. Quar.*, 41, vol. 13, no. 1, p. 109-110.

1871. BAVIN (Sir Thomas). Sir Henry Parkes, his life and work. Sydney, Angus & Robertson, 41, in-8, 68 p., 2s. 6d. R : C. H. Currey, *Hist. Stud. Australia N.Z.*, 41, vol. 1, p. 283-284.

1872. CHARLTON (W. K.). Parliament House, Sydney. *Roy. Austral. hist. Soc. J.*, 44, vol. 30, p. 249-258.

1873. DEAKIN (Alfred). The federal story: the inner history of the federal cause. Melbourne, Robertson & Mullens, 44, in-8, xiv-170 p., 12s.6d. R : J. A. McCallum, *Austral. Quar.*, 45, vol. 17, no. 2, p. 113-115. C. H. Currey, *Hist. Stud. Australia N.Z.*, 45, vol. 3, p. 143-145.

1874. DENHOLM (B.). Some aspects of the transition period from war to peace, 1918-1921. *Austral. Quar.*, 44, vol. 16, no. 1, p. 39-50.

1876. GROOM (Jessie). Nation building in Australia : the life and work of Sir Littleton Ernest Groom. Sydney, Angus & Robertson, 41, in-8, 283 p., 12s. 6d. R : T. Dunbabin, *Austral. Quar.*, 41, vol. 13, no. 3, p. 112-115.

1878. O'BRIEN (Eris). Cardinal Moran's part in public affairs. *Roy. Austral. hist. Soc. J.*, 42, vol. 28, p. 1-28.

1879. SHERRARD (Kathleen). The political history of women in Australia. *Austral. Quar.*, 43, vol. 15, no. 4, p. 36-51.

Austria

1880. SELBY (Sir Walford). Austria before the Anschluss and a view of her future prospects. *Int. Affairs*, 45, vol. 21, p. 477-484.

1881. SETON-WATSON (R. W.). The Austro-Hungarian Ausgleich of 1867. *Slavonic Y.B.* (*Slavonic R.*), 40, vol. 19, p. 123-140.

1882. TAYLOR (A. J. P.). The Habsburg monarchy, 1815-1918, a history of the Austrian empire and Austria-Hungary. London, Macmillan, 41, in-8, xii-316 p., (maps), 15s. R : L. Einstein, *History*, 41, vol. 26, p. 83-84. R. W. Seton-Watson, *Eng. hist. R.*, 42, vol. 57, p. 389-392.

Bulgaria

1883. BLACK (C. E.). The establishment of constitutional government in Bulgaria. London, Oxford Univ. Press, 44, in-8, 354 p., 25s. R : W. W. Hall, jr., *Int. R. Missions*, 44, vol. 33, p. 457-458. A. J. P. T(aylor), *Eng. hist. R.*, 45, vol. 60, p. 284.

Canada

1885. INNIS (H. A.). Recent books on the North American Arctic (with) Bibliography. *Canad. hist. R.*, 42, vol. 23, p. 401-407.

1886. TORONTO UNIVERSITY PRESS. Recent publications relating to Canada. *Canad. hist. R.*, 40-45, vol. 21-26.

1887. BAILEY (Alfred G.). The basis and persistence of opposition to confederation in New Brunswick. *Canad. hist. R.*, 42, vol, 23, p. 374-397.

1888. BERTRAND (Camille). Histoire de Montréal, 2 : 1760-1942. Montréal, Frères de Écoles Chrétiennes, 42, in-8, 307 p., $1.25. R : J. I. Cooper, *Canad. hist. R.*, 43, vol. 24, p. 420-421.

1889. BOVEY (Wilfrid). Les Canadiens-français d'aujourd'hui : l'essor d'un peuple, tr. de l'anglais par J.-J. Lefebvre. Montréal, Éd. de l'Action Canad.-Fr., 40, in-8, 419 p.

1890. BREBNER (J. B.). Canadianism. *Canad. hist. Assoc. Rept.*, 40, p. 5-15.

1891. BROWN (George W.) ed. Readings in Canadian history. Toronto, Dent, 40, in-8, xiv-378 p., $2.25. R : D. C. Harvey, *Canad. hist. R.*, 40, vol. 21, p. 418-419.

1892. BROWN (G. W.). Building the Canadian nation. London ; Toronto, Dent, 42, in-8, x-478 p., (illus.), 12s. 6d. R : R.G.T., *Queen's Quar.*, 43, vol. 50, p. 307-309. D. G. Creighton, *Canad. hist. R.*, 43, vol. 24, p. 76.

1893. BROWN (G. W.). Canada in the making. *Canad. hist. Assoc. Rept.*, 44, p. 5-15.

1894. BROWN (G. W.) and CREIGHTON (D. G.). Canadian history in retrospect and prospect : an article to mark the completion of the first 25 years of the ' Canadian Historical Review ', 1920-1944. *Canad. hist. R.*, 44, vol. 25, p. 357-375.

1895. BRUCHÉSI (Jean). Histoire du Canada pour tous. Vol. 2 : Le régime anglais. Montréal, Éd. de l'Action Canad.-Fr., 40, in-8, 364 p., $2.50. (Docs. hist.). R : T. W. L. MacDermot, *Canad. hist. R.*, 40, vol. 21, p. 425.

1896. BRUCHÉSI (J.). De Ville-Marie à Montréal. Montréal, Éd. de l'Arbre, 42, in-8, 154 p., $1.00. R : G. Lanctot, *Canad. hist. R.*, 43, vol. 24, p. 56-57.

1897. BURT (A. L.). A short history of Canada for Americans. Toronto, Gage, 42, in-8, xvi-279 p., $3.50. R : W. P. M(orrell), *Eng. hist. R.*, 44, vol. 59, p. 423-424. A. R. M. Lower, *Canad. hist. R.*, 42, vol. 23, p. 327-328.

1898. —— —— 2nd ed. London, Oxford Univ. Press, 44, in-8, 326 p., (illus., map), 18s. 6d.

1899. COOPER (John Irwin). Montreal, the story of 300 years. Montreal, The Author, Dept. of History, McGill Univ., 42, in-8, 133 p., $1.00. R : G. Lanctot, *Canad. hist. R.*, 42, vol. 23, p. 416-418.

1900. COOPER (J. I.). The political ideas of George Étienne Cartier. *Canad. hist. R.*, 42, vol. 23, p. 286-294.

1901. CORRY (J. A.). The growth of government activities in Canada, 1914-1921. *Canad. hist. Assoc. Rept.*, 40, p. 63-73.

1902. CREIGHTON (Donald Grant). Dominion of the North : a history of Canada. Toronto, Allen, 44, in-8, viii-535 p., $4.50. R : A. B. Corey, *Canad. hist. R.*, 44, vol. 25, p. 432-434.

1903. GLAZEBROOK (G. P. de T.). Canadian external relations : an historical study to 1914. London, Oxford Univ. Press ; Toronto, Univ. Press, 42, in-8, viii-312 p., 12s. 6d. ; $3.00. R : H. M. Clokie, *Canad. J. Econ. pol. Sci.*, 44, vol. 10, p. 104-106. J. W. Dafoe, *Canad. hist. R.*, 43, vol. 24, p. 197.

1904. GOUIN (Léon Mercier). L'idéal patriotique d'Honoré Mercier. *R. Univ. Ottawa*, 41, vol. 11, p. 159-175.

1905. HATCHER (Harlan H.). The Great Lakes. London, Oxford Univ. Press, 45, in-8, xi-384 p., (plates, maps), 16s. R : F. Landon, *Canad. hist. R.*, 45, vol. 26, p. 71.

1906. HUGHES (Everett Cherrington). French Canada in transition. Toronto, Gage, 43, in-8, ix-227 p., (maps, tables), $3.00. R : B. Brouillette, *Canad. hist. R.*, 44, vol. 25, p. 61-63.

1907. —— —— London, Cambridge Univ. Press, 44, in-8, x-228 p., (maps, diagr., tables), 15s. R : A. R. M. Lower, *Canad. J. Econ. pol. Sci.*, 44, vol. 10, p. 99-101.

1908. IRELAND (Willard E.). A further note on the annexation petition of 1869. *Brit. Columbia hist. Quar.*, 41, vol. 5, p. 67-72.

1909. KLINCK (Carl Frederick). Wilfred Campbell, a study in late provincial Victorianism. Toronto, Ryerson Press, 42, in-8, 289 p., $3.50. R : G.H.C., *Queen's Quar.*, 43, vol. 50, p. 96-97.

1910. LAIDLER (George). Long Point, Lake Erie : some physical and historical aspects. *Ontario hist. Soc. Pap.*, 44, vol. 36, p. 48-69.

1911. LANDON (Fred). The Canadian scene, 1880-1890. *Canad. hist. Assoc. Rept.*, 42, p. 5-18.

1912. LAVIOLETTE (Gontran). The Sioux Indians in Canada. Regina, Marian Press, 44, in-8, 138 p., (illus.), $1.50, limited ed. R : K. E. Kidd, *Canad. hist. R.*, 45, vol. 26, p. 203-204.

1913. LEACOCK (Stephen). Montreal, seaport and city. Toronto, McClelland, 42, in-8, xii-340 p., $3.50. R : G. Lanctot, *Canad. hist. R.*, 43, vol. 24, p. 56-57.

1914. LEACOCK (S.). Canada, the foundations of its future. Montreal, Seagram, 42, in-8, xxx-268 p., privately pr. R : A. G. Bailey, *Canad. hist. R.*, 43, vol. 24, p. 306-308.

1915. LONGLEY (Ronald Stewart). Sir Francis Hincks : a study of Canadian politics, railways, and finance in the 19th century. Toronto, Univ. Press, 43, in-8, viii-480 p., $3.00. R : F. H. Underhill, *Canad. hist. R.*, 45, vol. 26, p. 68-69. D. C. M(asters), *Canad. J. Econ. pol. Sci.*, 44, vol. 10, p. 532-533.

1916. LONGLEY (R. S.). Cartier and McDougall, Canadian emissaries to London, 1868-9. *Canad. hist. R.*, 45, vol. 26, p. 25-41.

1917. LOWER (A. R. M.). Two ways of life : the primary antithesis of Canadian history. *Canad. hist. Assoc. Rept.*, 43, p. 5-18.

1918. MACFARLANE (R. O.). Manitoba politics and parties after Confederation. *Canad. hist. Assoc. Rept.*, 40, p. 45-55.

1919. MAHEUX (Arthur). Le nationalisme canadien-français à l'aurore du 20e siècle. *Canad. hist. Assoc. Rept.*, 45, p. 58-74.

1920. MARTIN (Chester) ed. Canada in peace and war : 8 studies in national trends since 1914. Toronto, Oxford Univ. Press, 41, in-8, 244 p., $1.50. R : R. G. Trotter, *Queen's Quar.*, 41, vol. 48, p. 437-438.

1921. MIKEL (W. C.). City of Belleville history. Picton, Ont., Gazette Publ Co., 43, in-8, xiv-322 p., $2.00. R : L. B. Duff, *Canad. hist. R.*, 45, vol. 26, p. 75.

1922. MORTON (W. L.). The extension of the franchise in Canada : a study in democratic nationalism. *Canad. hist. Assoc. Rept.*, 43, p. 72-81.

1923. NUTE (Grace Lee). Lake Superior. Toronto, McClelland, 44, in-8, 376 p., (plates), $4.50. (Amer. lakes ser.). R : M. H. Long, *Canad. hist. R.*, 45, vol. 26, p. 70-71.

1924. ORMSBY (Margaret A.). Prime Minister Mackenzie, the Liberal party, and the bargain with British Columbia. *Canad. hist. R.*, 45, vol. 26, p. 148-173.

1925. PATTERSON (George). More studies in Nova Scotia history. Halifax, Imperial Publ. Co., 41, in-8, 180 p., $2.00. R : E. P. Ray, *Canad. hist. R.*, 42, vol. 23, p. 86.

1926. PECK (A. M.). The pageant of Canadian history. London, Longmans, 44, in-8, 370 p., (illus., map), 15s.

1927. POTVIN (Pascal). Papineau et l'orientation du nationalisme québécois. *Canad. hist. Assoc. Rept.*, 43, p. 35-42.

1928. POULIOT (Léon). La proclamation du gouvernement provisoire de la Rivière-Rouge, 8 décembre 1869. *B. Rech. hist.*, 43, vol. 49, p. 353-358.

1929. POUND (Arthur). Lake Ontario. Toronto, McClelland, 44, in-8, 384 p., (plates), $4.50. (Amer. lakes ser.). R : C. H. J. Snider, *Canad. hist. R.*, 45, vol. 26, p. 322-324.

1930. REID (Robie L.). The inside story of the ' Komagata Maru '. *Brit. Columbia hist. Quar.*, 41, vol. 5, p. 1-23.

1931. RIDDELL (R. G.). A cycle in the development of the Canadian West. *Canad. hist. R.*, 40, vol. 21, p. 268-284.

1932. ROTHNEY (Gordon O.). Nationalism in Quebec politics since Laurier. *Canad. hist. Assoc. Rept.*, 43, p. 43-49.

1933. ROY (P. G.). Reféréncés biographiques canadiennes. *B. Rech. hist.*, 42, vol. 46, p. 97-120, 149-160, 184-187.

1934. ROYAL COMMISSION ON DOMINION-PROVINCIAL RELATIONS. Report. Book 1 : Canada, 1867-1939 ; book 2 : Recommendations; book 3 : Documentation. Ottawa, King's Printer, 40, 3 vols. in-4, 261, 295, 219 p., $1.00. R : D. Ivor, *Economica*, 40, vol. 7, p. 443-446. R. G. Osborne and E. R. Walker, *Econ. R.*, 40, vol. 16, p. 285-259.

1935. RUMILLY (Robert). Histoire de la province de Québec, 1 : G.-É. Cartier. 2 : Le ' coup d'état '. 3 : Chapleau. 4 : Les ' Castors '. 5 : Riel. 6 : Les nationaux. 7 : Taillon. 8 : Laurier. 9 : Marchand. 10 : I.

Tarte. 11 : S.-N. Parent. 12 : Les écoles du Nord-Ouest. 13 : H. Bourasse. 14 : Sir L. Gouin. 15 : Mgr. Bruchési. 16 : Défaite de Laurier. Montréal, Valiquette, 40-45, 16 vols. in-8, 365, 239, 211, 241, 315, 346, 283, 230, 315, 241, 237, 210, 219, 176, 210, 221 p., $1.00 ea. R : J. I. Cooper, *Canad. hist. R.*, 40, vol. 21, p. 426-427; 41, vol. 22, p. 438-440 ; 43, vol. 24, p. 65-67; 44, vol. 25, p. 81-82; 45, vol. 26, p. 72-73.

1936. RYERSON (Stanley B.). French Canada : a study in Canadian democracy. Toronto, Progress Books, 43, in-8, 254 p., $2.00. R : B. K. Sandwell, *Canad. hist. R.*, 44, vol. 25, p. 200-201. A. R. M. Lower, *Canad. J. Econ. pol. Sci.*, 44, vol. 10, p. 529.

1937. SAGE (Walter N.). Where stands Canadian history ? *Canad. hist. Assoc. Rept.*, 45, p. 6-14.

1938. SAGE (W. N.). British Columbia becomes Canadian. *Queen's Quar.*, 45, vol. 52, p. 168-183.

1939. SANDWELL (B. K.). The Canadian peoples. London, Oxford Univ. Press, 41, in-8, 128 p., $1.25. (World to-day). R : R. G. Riddell, *Canad. hist. R.*, 42, vol. 23, p. 328-329.

1940. SANDWELL (B. K.). Political developments around the turn of the century. *Canad. hist. Assoc. Rept.*, 45, p. 49-57.

1941. SAUNDERS (R. M.). History and French-Canadian survival. *Canad. hist. Assoc. Rept.*, 43, p. 25-34.

1942. SISSONS (C. B.). Canadian political ideas in the sixties and seventies : Egerton Ryerson. *Canad. hist. Assoc. Rept.*, 42, p. 94-103.

1943. SKILLING (H. Gordon). The development of Canada's permanent external representation. *Canad. hist. Assoc. Rept.*, 43, p. 82-93.

1944. SPRAGGE (George W.). John Strachan's connexion with early proposals for confederation. *Canad. hist. R.*, 42, vol. 23, p. 363-373.

1945. STACEY (C. P.). The military aspect of Canada's winning of the West, 1870-1885. *Canad. hist. R.*, 40, vol. 21, p. 1-24.

1946. STANLEY (George F. G.). Western Canada and the frontier thesis. *Canad. hist. Assoc. Rept.*, 40, p. 105-117.

1947. UNDERHILL (Frank H.). Political ideas of the Upper Canada reformers, 1867-78. *Canad. hist. Assoc. Rept.*, 42, p. 104-115.

1948. WOOD (William). The historic seaport of Quebec : from immemoriality to the present day. *Canad. hist. R.*, 45, vol. 26, p. 392-400.

Czechoslovakia

1949. KERNER (Robert J.) ed. Czechoslovakia, 20 years of independence. London, Cambridge Univ. Press, 41, in-8, xxi-504 p., (plates, maps), 30s. R : J. Griffin, *Int. Affairs*, 41, vol. 19, p. 341-342.

1950. ODLOŽÍLÍK (Otakar). Components of the Czechoslovak tradition. *Slavonic R.*, 45, vol. 23, p. 97-106.

1951. SELVER (P.). Masaryk. London, Joseph, 40, in-8, 320 p., (illus.), 18s.

1952. SETON-WATSON (R. W.). Twenty-five years of Czechoslovakia. Abbreviated ed. of History of Czechs and Slovaks. London, F. Muller, 45, in-8, 119 p., 7s. 6d.

1953. THOMSON (S. Harrison). Czechoslovakia in European history. London, Oxford Univ. Press, 43, in-8, 398 p., (illus., maps), 25s. R : A. J. P. Taylor, *Eng. hist. R.*, 45, vol. 60, p. 261-264. R. W. Seton-Watson, *Int. Affairs*, 45, vol. 21, p. 276. W. Barker, *Slavonic R.*, 45, vol. 23, p. 173-174.

Denmark

1954. EPPSTEIN (J.) ed. Denmark· London, Cambridge Univ. Press, 45, in-8, viii-90 p., 3s. (Brit. survey handbks. ser.).

Egypt

1955. CRABITÈS (P.). The spoliation of Suez. London, Routledge, 40, in-8, xxviii-276 p., 12s. 6d.

1957. YOUSSEF BEY (Amine). Independent Egypt. London, Murray, 40, in-8, 288 p., 15s. R : E. N. Corbyn, *J. Roy. African Soc.*, 40, vol. 39, p. 282-283. P. G. Elgood, *J. central asian Soc.*, 40, vol. 27, p. 500-502. E.G.S.-H., *Geogr. J.*, 40, vol. 96, p. 60.

Estonia

1958. JACKSON (J. Hampden). Estonia. London, Allen and Unwin, 41, in-8, 248 p., (maps), 8s. 6d. R : H.G.W., *Geogr. J.*, 41, vol. 97, p. 388.

Finland

1959. BORENIUS (Tancred). Field-Marshal Mannerheim. London, Hutchinson, 40, in-8, xv-281 p., 18s. R : J. H. Jackson, *Int. Affairs*, 40, vol. 19, p. 139-140.

1960. MEAD (W. R.). Turku and Helsinki : capital cities of Finland. *Scottish geogr. Mag.*, 43, vol. 59, p. 18-23.

France

1961. B. (C. de). Letters from Paris, 1870-1875, written by a political informant to the head of the London house of Rothschild, tr. by R. Henrey. London, Dent, 42, in-8, 238 p., (illus.), 15s. R : W.T., *History*, 45, vol. 30, p. 113-114.

1962. BRABANT (F. H.). The beginning of the third republic in France : a history of the National Assembly (Feb.-Sept., 1871). London, Macmillan, 40, in-8, xii-556 p., 25s. (Stud. in mod. hist. ser.).

1963. BROGAN (Denis W.). The development of modern France (1870-1939). London, Hamilton, 40, in-8, x-744 p., 21s. R : E. H. Carr, *Int. Affairs*, 40, vol. 19, p. 128. A. L. Rowse, *Pol. Quar.*, 41, vol. 12, p. 223-225.

1964. BRUUN (Geoffrey). Clemenceau. London, Oxford Univ. Press, 44, in-8, 238 p., (illus.), 16s. 6d. R : J.P.T.B., *Eng. hist. R.*, 45, vol. 60, p. 433-434.

1965. BURCKHARDT (C. I.). Richelieu, tr. by E. and W. Muir. London, Allen & Unwin, 40, in-8, 413 p., (illus.), 16s.

1966. COBBAN (Alfred). The influence of the clergy and the ' instituteurs primaires ' in the election of the French constituent assembly, April 1848. *Eng. hist. R.*, 42, vol. 57, p. 334-344.

1967. COBBAN (A.). Local government during the French Revolution. *Eng. hist. R.*, 43, vol. 58, p. 13-31.

1968. COBBAN (A.). The beginning of the French Revolution. *History*, 45, vol. 30, p. 90-98.

1969. COOPER (A. D.). Talleyrand. London, Cape, 43, in-8, 399 p., (plates), 12s. 6d. (Bedford hist. ser.).

1970. DAUDET (Léon). Clemenceau, tr. by E. G. Echlin. London, Hodge, 40, in-8, 296 p., 12s. 6d. R : E. D. Gannon, *Int. Affairs*, 40, vol. 19, p. 128-129.

1971. DU CAMP (Maxime). Paris after the Prussians, tr. by P. A. Wilkins. London, Hutchinson, 40, in-8, 288 p., 15s.

1972. FARMER (P.). France reviews its revolutionary origins. London, Oxford Univ. Press, 44, in-8, 154 p., 15s. 6d.

1973. GLENNIE (M.). The loves of Louis XIV. London, Long, 43, in-8, 160 p., (illus.), 16s.

1974. GUEDALLA (Philip). The two marshals : Bazaine and Pétain. London, Hodder, 43, in-8, 384 p., 10s. 6d. R : *National R.*, 43, vol. 120, p. 509-511. D. Sington, *Int. Affairs*, 44, vol. 20, p. 580.

1975. GUERARD (A.). Napoleon III. London, Oxford Univ. Press, 45, in-8, 360 p., 20s. (Makers of mod. Europe ser.).

1976. HARRISON (M.). Gambler's glory. The story of John Law, of Lauriston, sometime comptroller-general of the finances to King Louis XV. London, Rich, 40, in-8, 391 p., (illus.), 15s.

1977. KUNSTLER (C.). The personal life of Marie-Antoinette, tr. from the French by M. R. Adamson. London, Bell, 40, in-8, xi-345 p., (illus.), 15s.

1978. MOWAT (Robert B.). The Third French republic. *Quar. R.*, 40, vol. 275, p. 190-205.

1979. NEALE (J. E.). The age of Catherine de Medici. London, Cape, 43, in-8, 111 p., 6s.

1980. OMAN (sir Charles). The Lyons mail : the crime of Apr. 27, 1796, and of the trials which followed. A study of personalities and evidence. London, Methuen, 45, in-8, 225 p., 8s. 6d.

1981. PALMER (R. R.). The twelve who ruled [French Revolution]. London, Oxford Univ. Press, 42, in-8, 411 p., 17s.

1982. PETRIE (sir C.). Louis XIV. London, Butterworth, 40, in-8, 320 p., (illus.), 5s. (Keystone ser.).

1983. PREEDY (G. R.). The courtly charlatan : the enigmatic Comte de St. Germain. London, Jenkins, 42, in-8, 208 p., 16s.

1984. SIMON (Yves). La grande crise de la République française : observations sur la vie politique des Français de 1918 à 1938. Montréal, Éd. de l'Arbre, 41, in-8, 237 p. (Problèmes actuels, 4). R : J.-O. Clerc, *Canad. J. Econ. pol. Sci.*, 42, vol. 8, p. 633-634.

1985. SIRICH (J. B.). The revolutionary committees in the departments of France. London, Oxford Univ. Press, 44, in-8, 250 p., 14s.

1986. THOMPSON (J. M.). The French Revolution. Oxford, Blackwell, 43, in-8, xv-536 p., (illus.), 32s. 6d. R : *National R.*, 44, vol. 122, p. 171-172.

1987. WELLMAN (R.). Eugénie. London, Scribner, 42, in-8, 326 p., 15s.

1988. WOODGATE (M. V.). Madame Elizabeth of France. Dublin, Browne & Nolan, 43, in-8, 192 p., 6s.

1989. WRIGHT (Gordon). Raymond Poincaré and the French Presidency. London, Oxford Univ. Press, 43, in-8, 282 p., 21s. 6d. R : V.L.K., *Int. Affairs*, 44, vol. 20, p. 134.

Germany

1990. AUGUSTA, Duchess of Saxe-Coburg-Saalfeld. In Napoleonic days: extracts from the private diary of Augusta, Duchess of Saxe-Coburg-Saalfeld, Queen Victoria's maternal grandmother, 1806-1821, tr. by Princess Beatrice. London, Murray, 41, in-8, vii-237 p., 7s. 6d. R : C.S.B.B., *Eng. hist. R.*, 42, vol. 57, p. 532-533.

1991. BELLER (E. A.). Propaganda in Germany during the Thirty Years' War. London, Oxford Univ. Press, 40, in-4, 49 p., (illus.), 45s.

1992. BRECHT (A.). Prelude to silence : the end of the German republic. London, Oxford Univ. Press, 45, in-8, 176 p., 12s. 6d.

1993. CONZEN (G.). East Prussia, some aspects of historical geography. *Geography*, 45, vol. 30, p. 1-10.

1994. COOLE (W. W.) and POTTER (M. F.) ed. Thus spake Germany : an anthology of German political and racial thought from Frederick the Great to the present day. London, Routledge, 41, in-8, 438 p., 10s. 6d.

1995. CORTI (E. C., count). Ludwig I of Bavaria, tr. from the German by E. B. G. Stamper. New ed. London, Eyre & Spottiswoode, 43, in-8, 422 p., (illus.), 10s. 6d.

1996. DICKINSON (R. E.). The regions of Germany. London, Kegan Paul, 45, in-8, x-176 p., (maps), 10s. 6d. R : G.R.C., *Geogr. J.*, 45, vol. 105, p. 68. E. G. R. Taylor, *Int. Affairs*, 45, vol. 21, p. 541-542.

1997. EBELING (H.). The caste : the political role of the German staff between 1918 and 1938. London, F. Muller, 45, in-8, 60 p., 2s. 6d.

1998. GARDINER (D.). Some travel notes during the Thirty Years' War. *History*, 40, vol. 25, p. 14-24.

1999. GAXOTTE (Pierre). Frederick the Great (tr. by R. A. Bell). London, Bell, 41, in-8, 462 p., 15s. R : M. Goldsmith, *19th Century*, 41, vol. 129, p. 597-598. *Army Quar.*, 41, vol. 42, p. 375-376. B. W., *Eng. hist. R.*, 42, vol. 57, p. 283-284.

2000. GOLDSMITH (Margaret). Frederick the Great. *19th Century*, 40, vol. 127, p. 676-693.

2001. GOLDSMITH (M.). Bismarck and William I. *19th Century*, 40, vol. 128, p. 348-366.

2002. HITLER (Adolf). Speeches, April 1932-August 1939, tr. and ed. by N. H. Baynes. London, Roy. Inst. of Internat. Affairs, 42, 2 vols. in-8, 50s. R : R. C. K. Ensor, *Eng. hist. R.*, 43, vol. 58, p. 246-247. A. L. Rowse, *Econ. J.*, 43, vol. 53, p. 88-91.

2003. JOURDAN (George V.). ' Les Matinées Royales ', a work falsely attributed to Frederick the Great, King of Prussia. *History*, 45, vol. 30, p. 145-158.

2004. MORROW (Ian F. D.). Bismarck. London, Duckworth, 43, in-8, 140 p., 6s. (Great Lives).

2005. ROBERTSON (Sir Charles Grant). The German enigma. *History*, 41, vol. 26, p. 115-122.

2006. SCHWARZ (H. F.). The Imperial Privy Council in the 17th century. London, Oxford Univ. Press, 43, in-8, 492 p., 25s. 6d.

2007. SMITH (G. Burrell). Germany, 1815-1890. London, Arnold, 40, in-8, 206 p., 3s. 6d. R : I. M. Massey, *Int. Affairs*, 40, vol. 19, p. 132-133.

2008. SPIECKER (Karl). Germany : from defeat to defeat, tr. by H. Becker and B. B. Carter. London, Macdonald, 45, in-8, xviii-159 p., 5s. R : H. G. Liddell, *Int. Affairs*, 45, vol. 21, p. 413.

2009. STIRK (S. D.). The Prussian spirit : a survey of German literature and politics, 1914-1940. London, Faber, 42, in-8, 236 p., 12s. 6d. R : L. Woolf, *Pol. Quar.*, 42, vol. 13, p. 219-221. H. G. Atkins, *Mod. Language R.*, 42, vol. 37, p. 399-401.

2010. STRESEMANN (Gustav). Diaries, letters and papers, ed. and tr. by E. Sutton. Vol. 3. London, Macmillan, 40, in-8, v-636 p., 25s. R : *National R.*, 40, vol. 114, p. 755-756.

2011. TAYLOR (A. J. P.). The course of German history : a survey of the development of Germany since 1815. London, Hamilton, 45, in-8, 229 p., 12s. 6d.

2012. TISDALL (E. E. P.). She made world chaos : the intimate story of the Empress Frederick of Prussia. London, Paul, 40, in-8, 288 p., 15s.

2013. TREITSCHKE (H. von). Origins of Prussianism, tr. from German by E. & C. Paul. London, Allen & Unwin, 42, in-8, 163 p., (maps), 7s. 6d.

2014. VALENTIN (Veit). 1848— chapters of German history, tr. by E. T. Scheffauer. London, Allen & Unwin, 40, in-8, 480 p., 12s. 6d. R : E. A. Alport, *Int. Affairs*, 40, vol. 19, p. 133-134. *National R.*, 40, vol. 115, p. 116-117.

2015. WAAS (G. E.). The legendary character of Kaiser Maximilian. London, Oxford Univ. Press, 42, in-8, 235 p., 14s. (Germanic stud. ser.).

Great Britain
(see also **Scotland**)

2016. ABBOTT (Wilbur Cortez). Essays in modern English history in honour of W. C. Abbott. London, Oxford Univ. Press, 42, in-8, 415 p., 15s. R : R. P(ares), *Eng. hist. R.*, 44, vol. 59, p. 433-434.

2017. AIKEN (William A.) ed. The conduct of the Earl of Nottingham : a continuation by several hands of Archdeacon Echard's History of England (1688-1693). London, Oxford Univ. Press, 41, in-4, 192 p., 14s. (Yale hist. publ., MSS. and ed. texts, 17). R : F. E. Hutchinson, *Eng. hist. R.*, 43, vol. 58, p. 237-238.

2018. ARBUTHNOT (Charles). Correspondence, ed. by A. Aspinall. London, Roy. Hist. Soc., 41, in-8, xviii-268 p. (Camden 3rd ser., vol. 65). R : K.G.F., *Eng. hist. R.*, 42, vol. 57, p. 404-405. M. D. George, *History*, 42, vol. 27, p. 88-90.

2019. ARTHUR (Sir G.). Concerning Queen Victoria and her son. London, Hale, 43, in-8, 232 p., (illus.), 12s. 6d.

2020. ASHLEY (M.). Oliver Cromwell. New ed. London, Cape, 40, in-8, 351 p., (illus.), 7s. 6d.

2021. ASPINALL (A.). George IV and Sir William Knighton. *Eng. hist. R.*, 40, vol. 55, p. 57-82.

2022. ASPINALL (A.). Le Marchant's reports of debates in the House of Commons, 1833. *Eng. hist. R.*, 43, vol. 58, p. 78-105.

2023. (ASPINALL A.). Lord Brougham's ' Life and Times '. *Eng. hist. R.*, 44, vol. 59, p. 87-112.

2024. BALSTON (T.). The life of Jonathan Martin, incendiary of York minster. London, Macmillan, 45, in-8, x-147 p., (illus.), 10s. 6d.

2025. BELL (W. G.). Story of London's great fire. London, Lane, 44, in-8, 267 p., 4s. 6d. (Week end libr.).

2026. BELLOC (Hilaire). The last rally, a study of Charles II. London, Cassell, 40, in-8, vii-305 p., 12s. 6d.

2027. BELLOC (H.). Elizabethan commentary. London, Cassell, 42, in-8, 202 p., 7s. 6d.

2028. BENNITT (F. W.). The diary of Isabella, wife of Sir Roger Twysden, baronet, of Royden Hall, East Peckham, 1645-1651. *Archaeol. cantiana*, 39 (40), vol. 51, p. 113-136.

2029. BINDOFF (S. T.). A bogus envoy from James I (Thomas Douglas). *History*, 42, vol. 27, p. 15-37.

2030. BINDOFF (S. T.). The Stuarts and their style. *Eng. hist. R.*, 45, vol. 60, p. 192-216.

2031. BOUSTEAD (Guy M.). The lone monarch (King George III). London, Lane, 40, in-8, 296 p., 15s.

2032. BREARS (Charles). Lincolnshire in the 17th and 18th centuries, compiled from national, county, and parish records. Hull, Brown, 40, in-8, xvi-192 p., 7s. 6d. R : H.J.S., *Scottish geogr. Mag.*, 41, vol. 57, p. 40.

2033. BREBNER (J. B.) and NEVINS (A.). The making of modern Britain : a short history. London, Allen & Unwin, 43, in-8, 243 p., (maps), 7s. 6d. R : L.F., *National R.*, 44, vol. 122, p. 258-259. T.S., *Int. Affairs*, 44, vol. 20, p. 429.

2034. BRETT (S. R.). The Long Parliament. *Quar. R.*, 40, vol. 275, p. 107-117.

2035. BRETT (S. R.). John Pym, 1583-1643 : the statesman of the Puritan revolution. London, Murray, 40, in-8, 307 p., 10s. 6d. R : S.G.L., *Eng. hist. R.*, 40, vol. 55, p. 681-682.

2036. —— —— New ed. London, Murray, 43, in-8, 279 p., 5s.

2037. BROCK (W. R.). Lord Liverpool and Liberal toryism, 1820-1827. London, Cambridge Univ. Press, 41, in-8, 298 p., 8s. 6d. R : A. A(spinall), *Eng. hist. R.*, 43, vol. 58, p. 125-126. A. F. Fremantle, *History*, 42, vol. 27, p. 90-91. D. Thomson, *Econ. J.*, 42, vol. 52, p. 69-70.

2038. BROGAN (D. W.). The English people. London, Hamilton, 43, in-8, 260 p., 10s. 6d.

2039. BROWNING (Andrew). Thomas Osborne, earl of Danby and duke of Leeds, 1632-1712. Vol. 2 : Letters. Glasgow, Jackson, 44, in-8, 620 p., 30s. R : G. N. Clark, *Eng. hist. R.*, 45, vol. 60, p. 408-410.

2040. BRYANT (Arthur). English saga, 1840-1940. London, Collins, 41, in-8, xii-340 p., 10s. 6d. R : E.M.K., *Mariner's Mirror*, 42, vol. 28, p. 255.

2041. BRYANT (A.). The years of endurance, 1793-1802. London, Collins, 42, in-8, 375 p., 12s. 6d. R : *National R.*, 43, vol. 120, p. 171-174.

2042. BRYANT (A.). Years of victory, 1802-1812. London, Collins, 44, in-8, xii-499 p., 12s. 6d.

2043. BUCHAN (John). Oliver Cromwell. New ed. London, Hodder & Stoughton, 42, in-8, 554 p., (maps), 21s.

2044. —— —— New ed. London, Hodder & Stoughton, 44, in-8, 554 p., (maps), 25s.

2045. BUTTERFIELD (H.). The Englishman and his history. London, Cambridge Univ. Press, 44, in-8, x-144 p., 3s. 6d. (Current problems). R : R. Pares, *Econ. Hist. R.*, 45, vol. 15, p. 87-88.

2046. CAVENDISH (Lady Harriet). Hary O : letters of Lady Harriet Cavendish, 1796-1809, ed. by Sir G. Leveson Gower and I. Palmer. London, Murray, 40, in-8, 360 p., 18s.

2047. COUPLAND (Sir Reginald). Wilberforce. New ed. London, Collins, 45, in-8, 447 p., 12s. 6d.

2048. CROMWELL (Oliver). The writings and speeches of Oliver Cromwell, ed. by W. C. Abbott. Vol. 3, 1653-1655. London, Oxford Univ. Press, 45, in-8, 994 p., 28s.

2049. DANGERFIELD (G.). Victoria's heir : the education of a Prince. London, Constable, 42, in-8, 352 p., 15s.

2050. DAWSON (W. H.). Cromwell's understudy : the life and times of general John Lambert, and the rise and fall of the protectorate. New ed. Edinburgh, Hodge, 42, in-8, 464 p., (illus.), 8s. 6d.

2051. DERING (Sir Edward). Parliamentary diary, 1670-1673, ed. by B. D. Henning. London, Oxford Univ. Press, 41, in-8, 178 p., 11s. 6d. (Yale hist. publ.).

2052. D'EWES (Sir Simonds). Journal from the first recess of the Long Parliament to the withdrawal of the King from London, ed. by W. H. Coates. London, Oxford Univ. Press, 42, in-8, 505 p., 27s. (Yale hist. publ., MSS. and ed. texts, 18).

2053. DODD (A. H.). Wales's parliamentary apprenticeship (1536-1625). *Trans. Soc. Cymmr.*, 42 (44), p. 8-72.

2054. DODD (A. H.). North Wales in the Essex revolt of 1601. *Eng. hist. R.*, 44, vol. 59, p. 348-370.

2055. DODD (Alfred). The marriage of Elizabeth Tudor : an exhaustive inquiry into her alleged marriage with the Earl of Leicester and the alleged births of her two sons, Francis Bacon and the Earl of Essex. London, Rider, 40, in-8, xii-188p., 12s. 6d.

2056. DUGDALE (B. E. C.). Arthur James Balfour, K.G., 1848-1930. London, Hutchinson, 40, 2 vols. in-8, 671 p., 9s. 6d.

2057. FALK (Bernard). The Bridgewater millions : a candid family history. London, Hutchinson, 42, in-8, 247 p., 18s.

2058. FIELD (B.). Miledi : the strange story of Emma, Lady Hamilton. London, Constable, 42, in-8, 988 p., (illus.), 18s.

2059. FORRESTER (Eric G.). Northamptonshire county elections and electioneering, 1695-1832. London, Oxford Univ. Press, 41, in-8, viii-166 p., 10s. (Oxf. hist. ser.).

2060. GEORGE III, King of England. Letters from George III to Lord Bute, 1756-1766, ed. with an intr. by R. Sedgwick. London, Macmillan, 40, in-8, 245 p., 18s. (Stud. in mod. hist.). R : *National R.*, 40, vol. 115, p. 246-247. R. Pares, *Eng. hist. R.*, 40, vol. 55, p. 475-479. E. McInnis, *Canad. hist. R.*, 40, vol. 21, p. 327-328.

2061. GIBB (M. A.). The Lord General : a life of Thomas Fairfax. New ed. London, Drummond, 40, in-8, xv-304 p., (illus.), 6s. (Buckingham ser.).

2062. GILMOUR (Margaret). The great lady : a biography of Barbara Villiers, mistress of Charles II. London, Long, 44, in-8, 200 p., 16s.

2063. GORE (John). King George V, a personal memoir. London, Murray, 41, in-8, xx-464 p., (illus.), 18s. R : *National R.*, 41, vol. 116, p. 621-622. R. B.McC., *Eng. hist. R.*, 42, vol. 57, p. 286-287.

2064. GRIGG (Sir Edward). British foreign policy. London, Hutchinson, 44, in-8, 192 p., 7s. 6d. R : D. O. Malcolm, *Int. Affairs*, 45, vol. 21, p. 119-120.

2065. GUEDALLA (P.). Palmerston. New ed. London, Hodder & Stoughton, 42, in-8, 456 p., 7s. 6d.

2066. HALIFAX (George Savile, 1st marq. of). Observations upon a late libel, called ' A letter from a person of quality to his friend, concerning the King's Declaration ', ed. by H. Macdonald. London, Cambridge Univ. Press, 40, in-8, 52 p., 3s. 6d. R : F.E.H., *Eng. hist. R.*, 41, vol. 56, p. 672.

2067. HAMPDEN (John). An 18th-century journal, being a record of the years 1774-1776. London, Macmillan, 40, in-8, 420 p., (illus.), 16s. R : *National R.*, 40, vol. 115, p. 120-121.

2068. HARRIS (S. Hutchinson). Auberon Herbert : crusader for liberty. London, Williams & Norgate, 43, in-8, 382 p., 15s. R : *Quar. R.*, 43, vol. 281, p. 250-251.

2069. HARRISON (G. B.). A Jacobean journal : those things most talked of during 1603-1606. London, Routledge, 41, in-8, xii-406 p., 16s. 6d.

2070. HENDERSON (A. J.). London and the National government, 1721-1742 : a study in politics and the Walpole administration. London, Cambridge Univ. Press, 45, in-8, x-242 p., 18s. R : K.G.C., *Queen's Quar.*, 45, vol. 52, p. 486.

2071. HERBERT (Lord). The Pembroke papers, 1734-1780. London, Cape, 42, in-8, 576 p., (illus.), 21s.

2072. HEXTER (J. H.). The reign of king Pym. London, Oxford Univ. Press, 41, in-8, 253 p., 11s. 6d. (Harvard hist. stud., 48). R : S.G.L., *Eng. hist. R.*, 42, vol. 57, p. 529-530. D. J. McDougall, *Canad. hist. R.*, 43, vol. 24, p. 303-304.

2073. HILL (Christopher) ed. The English Revolution, 1640. Three essays. London, Lawrence and Wishart, 40, in-8, 136 p., 2s. 6d. (Marxist text book ser.). R : G.D., *Eng. hist. R.*, 41, vol. 56, p. 670-671.

2074. HIRST (F. W.). Richard Cobden and John Morley : being the Richard Cobden lecture for 1941. Midhurst, Cobden Club, 41, in-8, 40 p., 1s.

2075. HISTORICAL MANUSCRIPTS COMMISSION. Supplementary Report on MSS. of Robert Graham, Esq., of Fintry, ed. by C. T. Atkinson. London, H.M.S.O., 42, in-8, xvi-227 p., 6s.

2076. HISTORICAL MANUSCRIPTS COMMISSION. Report on MSS. of Lord de l'Isle and Dudley, preserved at Penshurst Place, Kent. Vol. 4, Sidney Papers, 1608-1611, ed. by W. A. Shaw. London, H.M.S.O., 42, in-8, xxxii-395p., 10s. 6d.

2077. HISTORICAL MANUSCRIPTS COMMISSION. Report on the manuscripts of the Rt. Hon. Lord Polwarth, formerly preserved at Mertoun House, Berwickshire, and now in H.M. General Register House, Edinburgh. Vol. 4. London, H.M.S.O., 42, in-8, liv-366 p., 10s. 6d.

2078. HISTORICAL MANUSCRIPTS COMMISSION. Calendar of the MSS. of Maj.-Gen. Lord Sackville, preserved at Knole, Sevenoaks, Kent. Vol. 1, Cranfield papers (1551-1612), ed. by A. P. Newton. London, H.M.S.O., 42, in-8, xxviii-403 p., 10s. 6d.

2079. HOWARD (C.). Lord Randolph Churchill. *History*, 40, vol. 25, p. 25-40.

2080. HUMPHREYS (E. Morgan). David Lloyd George. Llandebie, Llyfrau'r Dryw, 43, in-8, 80 p., 1s. 3d.

2081. HYDE (H. M.). Judge Jeffreys. London, Harrap, 40, in-8, 328 p., (illus.), 12s. 6d.

2082. IMLAH (A. H.). Lord Ellenborough : Edward Law, Governor-General of India. London, Oxford Univ. Press, 40, in-8, 295 p., 20s.

(Harvard hist. stud., 43). R : G.S.G., *Queen's Quar.*, 40, vol. 47, p. 99-100. P.E.R., *Eng. hist. R.*, 40, vol. 55, p. 689-690.

2083. JAMES (Margaret). The political importance of the tithes controversy in the English revolution, 1640-60. *History*, 41, vol. 26, p. 1-18.

2084. JAMESON (E.). Ten Downing Street, the romance of a house. London, Simpkin, 45, in-8, 536 p., 18s.

2085. JASPER (R. C.). Edward Eliot and the acquisition of Grampound. *Eng. hist. R.*, 43, vol. 58, p. 475-481.

2086. JENKINS (Gladys). Ways and means in Elizabethan propaganda. *History*, 41, vol. 26, p. 105-114.

2087. JOHNSTON (Sir Archibald). Diary of Sir A. Johnston of Wariston. Vol. 3, ed. by J. D. Ogilvie. Edinburgh, Scottish Hist. Soc., 40, in-8, lxxxiv-195 p., subscribers only. (Publ., Scottish hist. soc., 3rd ser., vol. 34). R : S.W.C., *J. presb. hist. Soc.*, 41, vol. 7, p. 95.

2088. JOLLIFFE (Michael). List of office-holders in Guy Miege's 'New state of England' and 'Present state of Great Britain'. *B. Inst. hist. Research*, 40, vol. 17, p. 130-138. (Bibliogr. aids to research, 8).

2089. KLINGBERG (F. J.) and HUSTVEDT (S. B.). The warning drum : the British home front faces Napoleon. London, Cambridge Univ. Press, 45, in-8, x-288 p., 24s.

2090. KNICKERBOCKER (F. W.). Free minds : John Morley and his friends. London, Oxford Univ. Press, 45, in-8, 300 p., 16s. 6d.

2091. LANE (Jane). King James the last [James II, King of England]. London, Dakers, 42, in-8, 352 p., 12s. 6d.

2092. LESLIE (Shane). The letters of Mrs. Fitzherbert. London, Burns and Oates, 40, in-8, xxxii-343 p., 15s.

2093. LEVER (Sir Tresham). The life and times of Sir Robert Peel. London, Allen & Unwin, 42, in-8, 320 p., 12s. 6d. R : A. F. Fremantle, *History*, 42, vol. 27, p. 90-91. *National R.*, 42, vol. 119, p. 185-186. L. Woolf, *Pol. Quar.*, 42, vol. 13, p. 341-343.

2094. LLOYD (Sir J. E.) and SCHOLDERER (Victor). Powel's *Historie* (1584). *Nat. Library Wales J.*, 43, vol. 3, p. 15-18 (illus.).

2095. London topographical record, ed. by W. H. Godfrey. Vol. 18. London, Topogr. Soc., 42, in-8, 123 p., members only. R : M.D.G., *Eng. hist. R.*, 43, vol. 58, p. 498-499. M.R.T., *History*, 44, vol. 29, p.98-99.

2096. MACKINNON (James). A history of modern liberty. Vol. 4 : The struggle with the Stuarts, 1647-1689. London, Longmans, 41, in-8, 523 p., 16s. R : G. Davies, *Eng. hist. R.*, 43, vol. 58, p. 233-234.

2097. MADOL (H. R.). The private life of Queen Alexandra. London, Hutchinson, 40, in-8, 291 p., (illus.), 18s.

2098. MARRIOTT (Sir J. A. R.). Castlereagh : the political life of Robert, second Marquess of Londonderry. New ed. London, Methuen, 40, in-8, xv-355 p., (plates), 6s.

2099. MARRIOTT (Sir J. A. R.). England since Waterloo. New ed. London, Methuen, 43, in-8, 558 p., (map), 18s. (Hist. of Engl. ser.).

2100. MASON (A. E. W.). The life of Francis Drake. London, Hodder and Stoughton, 41, in-8, ix-436 p., (maps), 12s. 6d. R : M.A.L., *Mariner's Mirror*, 42, vol. 28, p. 169-172.

2101. MATTINGLY (G.). Catherine of Aragon. London, Cape, 42, in-8, 343 p., 18s. R : W.E.C.H., *Queen's Quar.*, 42, vol. 49, p. 182-185.

2102. MAYNARD (T.). Queen Elizabeth. London, Hollis & Carter, 43, in-8, 398 p., (illus.), 18s. R : A. Peel, *Congreg. Quar.*, 43, vol. 21, p. 369-370.

2103. MOORMAN (J. R. H.). In commemoration of Archbishop Laud executed on Tower Hill, London, January 10, 1645. *B. John Rylands Library*, 45, vol. 29, p. 106-120.

2104. OMAN (Sir Charles). Britain against Napoleon. London, Faber, 42, in-8, 372 p., 12s. 6d.

2105. —— —— New ed. London, Faber, 44, in-8, 372 p., 8s. 6d.

2106. PENSON (Lillian M.). The new course in British foreign policy, 1892-1902. *Trans. Roy. hist. Soc.*, 43, vol. 25, p. 121-138.

2107. PETEGORSKY (David W.). Left-wing democracy in the English civil war. London, Gollancz, 40, in-8, 247 p., 7s. 6d.

2108. PETRIE (Sir Charles). Life and letters of the Rt. Hon. Sir Austen Chamberlain. Vol. 2. London, Cassell, 40, in-8, xi-433 p., 16s. R : Meston, *Int. Affairs*, 40, vol. 19, p. 117-118.

2109. PETRIE (Sir C.). Joseph Chamberlain. London, Duckworth, 40, in-8, 143 p., 2s. 6d. (Great lives ser.).

2110. PITT (William). The war speeches of William Pitt, selected by R. Coupland. Foreword by the Rt. Hon. Winston S. Churchill. 3rd ed. London, Oxford Univ. Press, 40, in-8, xlviii-380 p., 5s.

2111. POLLOCK (sir J.). The Popish plot : a study in the history of the reign of Charles II. New ed. London, Cambridge Univ. Press, 44, in-8, xxvi-380 p., 21s.

2112. PONSONBY (Arthur). Queen Victoria's private secretary : Henry Ponsonby : his life from his letters. London, Macmillan, 42, in-8, xvi-425 p., 21s. R : M. Maxse, *National R.*, 43, vol. 120, p. 80-84.

2113. PRANCE (C. R.). A ' Drake ' mystery. (The Don Pedro de Rada letters in the archives of Spain). *National R.*, 40, vol. 115, p. 221-224.

2114. PRESCOTT (H. F. M.). Spanish Tudor, the life of Bloody Mary. London, Constable, 40, in-8, xv-562 p., 18s. R : W.E.C.H., *Queen's Quar.*, 42, vol. 49, p. 182-185.

2115. RANSOME (Mary). The reliability of contemporary reporting of the debates of the House of Commons, 1727-1741. *B. Inst. hist. Research*, 42, vol. 19, p. 67-79.

2116. READING (Marquess of). Rufus Isaacs, first Marquess of Reading. London, Hutchinson, 42-45, 2 vols. in-8, 290, 384 p., (illus.), 35s.

2117. REDDAWAY (T. F.). The rebuilding of London after the Great Fire. London, Cape, 40, in-8, 336 p., (illus.), 18s. R : A. Robinson, *Econ. J.*, 42, vol. 52, p. 70-73. M. D. George, *Eng. hist. R.*, 41, vol. 56, p. 133-135.

2118. —— —— New ed. London, Cape, 43, in-8, 333 p., (plates), 18s. R : M. Beloff, *Econ. Hist. R.*, 44, vol. 14, p. 95-96.

2119. ROWSE (A. L.). Tudor Cornwall, portrait of a society. London, Cape, 41, in-8, 462 p., 18s. R : A. Peel, *Congreg. Quar.*, 42, vol. 20, p. 79-80. E. G. R. T(aylor), *Geogr. J.*, 42, vol. 99, p. 276-277. C. Morris, *Econ. Hist. R.*, 42, vol. 12, p. 90-91.

2120. SAMUEL (Wilfred S.). Sir William Davidson, royalist (1616-1689) and the Jews. London, Jewish Hist. Soc., 42, in-8, repr. from the Transactions, vol. 14. R : C. Wilson, *Econ. Hist. R.*, 43, vol. 13, p. 136-137.

2121. SARA (M. E.). Life and times of H.R.H. Princess Beatrice. London, Paul, 45, in-8, 160 p., 18s.

2122. SCHENK (Wilhelm). A 17th-century Radical (William Walwyn). *Econ. Hist. R.*, 44, vol. 14, p. 74-83.

2123. SLESSER (Sir H.). History of the Liberal Party. London, Hutchinson, 44, in-8, 172 p., 12s. 6d. R : F. A. v. Hayek, *Economica*, 44, vol. 11, p. 157-158.

2124. SOMERVELL (D. C.). Modern Britain, 1870-1939. London, Methuen, 40, in-8, viii-209 p., (maps), 6s.

2125. STAEBLER (W.). The liberal mind of John Morley. London, Oxford Univ. Press, 43, in-8, 232 p., 23s. 6d.

2126. STUART (Dorothy Margaret). The mother of Victoria. London, Macmillan, 42, in-8, xi-313 p., 15s.

2127. STUART (D. M.). Regency roundabout. London, Macmillan, 43, in-8, xi-175 p., (illus.), 12s. 6d.

2128. SYKES (Norman). Archbishop Wake and the Whig Party, 1716-23, a study in incompatibility of temperament. *Cambridge hist. J.*, 45, vol. 8, p. 93-112.

2129. TAYLER (Henrietta). Jacobite epilogue : a further selection of letters from Jacobites among the Stuart papers at Windsor. London, Nelson, 41, in-8, xx-21-331 p., 15s. R : H. Mangan, *Irish hist. Stud.*, 43, vol. 3, p. 412-414.

2130. TEMPERLEY (Harold) and HENDERSON (Gavin B.). Disraeli and Palmerston in 1857, or, The dangers of explanations in Parliament. *Cambridge hist. J.*, 42, vol. 7, p. 115-126.

2131. THOMAS (W. Jenkin). Some forgotten Welshmen. *Trans. Soc. Cymmr.*, 41 (43), p. 100-114.

2132. TREVELYAN (G. M.). Grey of Fallodon. London, Longmans, 40, in-8, xvi-393 p., (illus.), 6s. (Longmans' ser.).

2133. TREVOR-ROPER (H. R.). Archbishop Laud. London, Macmillan, 40, in-8, 473 p., 21s. R : R. N. Carew Hunt, *19th Century*, 40, vol. 127, p. 486-488. *National R.*, 40, vol. 114,

p. 509-512. G. F. Nuttall, *Congreg. Quar.*, 40, vol. 18, p. 224. *History*, 45, vol. 30, p. 181-190.

2134. TURBERVILLE (A. S.). Aristocracy and revolution : the British peerage, 1789-1832. *History*, 42, vol. 26, p. 240-263.

2135. TURBERVILLE (A. S.). The House of Lords and the advent of democracy, 1837-67. *History*, 44, vol. 29, p. 152-183.

2136. WALDMAN (Milton). Some English dictators. London, Blackie, 40, in-8, 283 p., 12s. 6d.

2137. WALDMAN (M.). Sir Walter Raleigh. London, Collins, 43, in-8, 255 p., (illus.), 12s. 6d.

2138. WALDMAN (M.). Elizabeth and Leicester. London, Collins, 44, in-8, 207 p., (illus.), 12s. 6d.

2139. WALKER-SMITH (D.). Neville Chamberlain. London, Hale, 40, in-8, 413 p., (illus.), 15s.

2140. WILLIAMS (Basil). Carteret and Newcastle : a contrast in contemporaries. London, Cambridge Univ. Press, 43, in-8, viii-240 p., (plates, tables), 15s. R : M. A. Thomson, *History*, 45, vol. 30, p. 192-194.

2141. WILLIAMS (Watkin W.). The life of General Sir Charles Warren. Oxford, Blackwell, 41, in-8, xiii-450 p., (maps), 25s. R : *United Empire*, 42, vol. 33, p. 26.

2142. WILLIAMSON (H. R.). George Villiers [1st Duke of Buckingham, 1592-1628]. London, Duckworth, 40, in-8, 384 p., (illus.), 15s.

2143. WILLIAMSON (James A.). The ocean in English history : being the Ford lectures. London, Oxford Univ. Press, 41, in-8, 208 p., 10s. R : A. T. Milne, *History*, 42, vol. 27, p. 84-85. E. G. R. T(aylor), *Mariner's Mirror*, 42, vol. 28, p. 256. G.R.C., *Geogr. J.*, 42, vol. 99, p. 107. F. R. Salter, *Econ. Hist. R.*, 42, vol. 12, p. 92.

2144. WOODBRIDGE (Homer E.). Sir William Temple : the man and his work. London, Oxford Univ. Press, 40, in-8, xii-361 p., (illus.), 16s. (Mod. lang. assoc., monogr. ser., 12). R : E. S. de B., *History*, 44, vol. 29, p. 99-100. G. Kitchin, *Mod. Language R.*, 41, vol. 36, p. 530-532.

2145. WORMALD (B. H. G.). How Hyde became a royalist. *Cambridge hist. J.*, 45, vol. 8, p. 65-92.

Greece

2146. ALASTOS (D.). Venizelos, patriot, statesman, revolutionary. London, Lund, Humphries, 42, in-8, 304 p., (illus., maps), 12s. 6d. R : F. H. Marshall, *J. hell. Stud.*, 42 (43), vol. 62, p. 114.

2147. BURN (A. R.). The modern Greeks. London, Nelson, 44, in-8, 55 p., (illus.), 5s.

2148. FORSTER (Edward S.). A short history of modern Greece, 1821-1940. London, Methuen, 41, in-8, 237 p., (maps), 12s. 6d. R : *National R.*, 41, vol. 117, p. 569-570. F. H. Marshall, *History*, 42, vol. 26, p. 302-303. *Greece and Rome*, 42, vol. 11, p. 144. P.P.A., *J. hell. Stud.*, 42 (43), vol. 62, p. 114.

Hungary

2149. EPPSTEIN (J.) ed. Hungary. London, Cambridge Univ. Press, 45, in-8, viii-88 p., 3s. (Brit. survey handbks. ser.).

2150. PAGET (John). Diary, 1849. *Slavonic Y.B. (Slavonic R.)*, 40, vol. 19, p. 237-264.

2152. WANKLYN (Harriet). The rôle of peasant Hungary in Europe. *Geogr. J.*, 41, vol. 97, p. 18-35.

Ireland

2153. BRADY (John). The writings of Paul Walsh. *Irish hist. Stud.*, 42, vol. 3, p. 193-208.

2154. CARTY (James). Bibliography of Irish history, 1870-1911. Dublin, Stationery Office, 40, in-8, xviii-320 p., 10s. 6d. R : T. W. Moody, *Irish hist. Stud.*, 44, vol. 4, p. 109-110. B. *Inst. hist. Research*, 43, vol. 19, p. 203.

2155. ASPINALL (A.). The use of Irish secret service money in subsidizing the Irish press. *Eng. hist. R.*, 41, vol. 56, p. 639-646. (Notes and documents).

2156. ASPINALL (A.). The Irish ' proclamation ' fund, 1800-1846. *Eng. hist. R.*, 41, vol. 56, p. 265-280.

2157. BEASLEY (P.). Michael Collins, soldier and statesman. New ed. Dublin, Talbot Press, 41, in-8, 430 p., 5s.

2158. CARNEY (Maura). Agreement between O Domhnaill and Tadhg O Conchobhair concerning Sligo Castle (23 June 1539). *Irish hist. Stud.*, 43, vol. 3, p. 282-296.

2159. CLARKE (Randall). The relations between O'Connell and the Young Irelanders. *Irish hist. Stud.*, 42, vol. 3, p. 18-30.

2160. CREGAN (Donal F.). Daniel O'Neill, a royalist agent in Ireland, 1644-50. *Irish hist. Stud.*, 41, vol. 2, p. 398-414.

2161. CURTIS (Edmund) ed. Calendar of Ormond deeds. Vol. 5 : 1547-84 ; vol. 6 : 1584-1603. Dublin, Stationery Office, 41-43, 2 vols. in-8, xli-396, xix-240 p., 42s. (Irish MSS. comm.). R (Vol. 5) : H. Wood, *Eng. hist. R.*, 43, vol. 58, p. 107-108. D. B. Quinn, *Irish hist. Stud.*, 43, vol. 3, p. 410-411. (Vol. 6) : H. W(ood), *Eng. hist. R.*, 44, vol. 59, p. 420-421. D. B. Quinn, *Irish hist. Stud.*, 44, vol. 4, p. 107-108.

2162. DICKSON (Charles). The life of Michael Dwyer, with some account of his companions. London, Longmans, 44, in-8, 420 p., (map), 15s. R : G. A. Hayes-McCoy, *Irish hist. Stud.*, 45, vol. 4, p. 370-372.

2163. EDWARDS (R. Dudley) and MOODY (T. W.). The history of Poynings' law. Pt. 1 : 1494-1615. *Irish hist. Stud.*, 41, vol. 2, p. 415-424. (Hist. revision, 4).

2164. GRUBB (Isabel). American visitors in Ireland : some reminiscences, 1784-1852. *J. Friends hist. Soc.*, 40 (41), vol. 37, p. 25-30.

2165. HAYES (Richard). Old Irish links with France : some echoes of exiled Ireland. Dublin, Gill, 40, in-8, xii-230 p., 7s. 6d. R : H. Mangan, *Irish hist. Stud.*, 41, vol. 2, p. 456-458.

2166. HAYES-McCOY (G. A.). Index to the Compossicion Booke of Conought, 1585. Dublin, Stationery Office, 42, in-8, 61 p., 3s. 6d. (Irish MSS. comm.). R : D. J. O'Donoghue, *Irish hist. Stud.*, 45, vol. 4, p. 278-279. H.W., *Eng. hist. R.*, 44, vol. 59, p. 421.

2167. IRISH MANUSCRIPTS COMMISSION. Analecta Hibernica. No. 9-15. Dublin, Stationery Office, 40-44, 7 vols. in-8, 142, 302, 174, 187, 77, 249, 458 p., 50s. R (No. 9) : D. J. O'Donoghue, *Irish hist. Stud.*, 45, vol. 4, p. 278-279. (No. 10) : R. D. Edwards, *Irish hist. Stud.*, 42, vol. 3, p. 215-216. (No. 12) : T. P. O'Neill, *Irish hist. Stud.*, 44, vol. 4, p. 199-200. (No. 14) : H. G. Richardson, *Irish hist. Stud.*, 45, vol. 4, p. 352-354.

2168. MCANALLY (Sir Henry). The Government forces engaged at Castlebar in 1798. *Irish hist. Stud.*, 45, vol. 4, p. 316-331.

2169. MCCRACKEN (J. L.). The conflict between the Irish administration and parliament, 1753-6. *Irish hist. Stud.*, 42, vol. 3, p. 159-179.

2170. MCDOWELL (R. B.). United Irish plans of parliamentary reform, 1793. *Irish hist. Stud.*, 42, vol. 3, p. 39-59.

2171. McDowell (R. B.). Irish public opinion, 1750-1800. London, Faber, 44, in-8, 306 p., 21s.

2172. MacLysaght (Edward). Calendar of the Orrery papers, ed. by E. MacLysaght. Dublin, Stationery Office, 41, in-8, xi-396 p., 21s. R : T. W. Moody, *Eng. hist. R.*, 45, vol. 60, p. 256-258.

2173. MacLysaght (E.). The Kenmare manuscripts, ed. by E. MacLysaght. Dublin, Stationery Office, 42, in-8, xiv-517 p., 30s. (Irish MSS. comm.). R : S. Pender, *Econ. Hist. R.*, 44, vol. 14, p. 106. T. W. Moody, *Eng. hist. R.*, 45, vol. 60, p. 256-258.

2174. MacManus (M. J.). Irish cavalcade, 1550-1850. New ed. London, Macmillan, 43, in-8, xx-320 p., 5s.

2175. McNeill (Charles) ed. The Tanner letters : original documents and notices of Irish affairs in the 16th and 17th centuries extracted from the collection in the Bodleian Library, Oxford. Dublin, Stationery Office, 43, in-8, viii-550 p., 42s. R : H.W., *Eng. hist. R.*, 45, vol. 60, p. 127-128.

2176. Mansergh (Nicholas). Ireland in the age of reform and revolution : a commentary on Anglo-Irish relations and on political forces in Ireland, 1840-1921. London, Allen & Unwin, 40, in-8, 272 p., 10s. 6d. R : T. W. Moody, *Irish hist. Stud.*, 42, vol. 3, p. 122-123. W. K. Hancock, *Econ. Hist. R.*, 41, vol. 11, p. 97-99; *Eng. hist. R.*, 41, vol. 56, p. 677-678.

2177. Moody (T. W.). Michael Davitt and the 'pen' letter. *Irish hist. Stud.*, 45, vol. 4, p. 224-253.

2178. Murray (Laurence P.). History of the parish of Creggan in the 17th and 18th centuries, with numerous ancient maps and illustrations. Dundalk, Dundalgan Press, 40, in-8, iv-93 p., 3s. 6d. R : R. D. Edwards, *Irish hist. Stud.*, 43, vol. 3, p. 341-342.

2179. Nicolson (Harold George). The desire to please : a story of Hamilton Rowan and the United Irishmen. London, Constable, 43, in-8, 216 p., 15s. (In search of the past, vol. 2). R : R. B. McDowell, *Irish hist. Stud.*, 45, vol. 4, p. 279-281.

2180. Ó Domhnaill (Seán). Sir Niall Garbh O'Donnell and the rebellion of Sir Cahir O'Doherty. *Irish hist. Stud.*, 42, vol. 3, p. 34-38.

2181. O'Faoláin (Seán). The great O'Neill : a biography of Hugh O'Neill, Earl of Tyrone, 1550-1616. London, Longmans, 43, in-8, 284 p., 15s. R : G. A. Hayes-McCoy, *Irish hist. Stud.*, 44, vol. 4, p. 200-202.

2182. O'Sullivan (T. F.). The young Irelanders. Davis memorial centenary ed. London, Carter & Hussey, 45, in-8, 156 p., 10s. 6d.

2183. Palmer (Norman Dunbar). The Irish land league crisis. London, Oxford Univ. Press, 42, in-8, 350 p., 16s. R : R. C. K. Ensor, *Eng. hist. R.*, 42, vol. 57, p. 275-276. T. W. Moody, *Irish hist. Stud*, 43, vol. 3, p. 329-330.

2184. Quinn (David B.). The early interpretation of Poynings' law, 1494-1534. *Irish hist. Stud.*, 41, vol. 2, p. 241-254.

2185. Quinn (D. B.). Parliaments and Great Councils in Ireland, 1461-1586. *Irish hist. Stud.*, 42, vol. 3, p. 60-77.

2186. Ryan (Desmond). Sean Treacy and the Third Tipperary Brigade. Tralee, Kerryman, 45, in-8, 215 p., 7s. 6d. R : F. O'Donoghue, *Irish hist. Stud.*, 45, vol. 4, p. 376-379.

2187. Salaman (R. N.). The influence of the potato on the course of Irish history. London, Longmans, 44, in-8, 32 p., 2s. 6d.

2188. Shearman (Hugh). Not an inch : a study of Northern Ireland

and Lord Craigavon. London, Faber, 42, in-8, 184 p., 6s. R : R. M. Henry, *Irish hist. Stud.*, 45, vol. 4, p. 281-283.

2189. SHEARMAN (H.). State-aided land purchase under the Disestablishment Act of 1869. *Irish hist. Stud.*, 44, vol. 4, p. 58-80.

2190. SIMINGTON (Robert C.). The Civil survey, A.D. 1654-1656. Vol. 5 : County of Meath, with the returns of tithes for the Meath baronies. Dublin, Stationery Office, 40, in-8, xlviii-410 p., 21s. (Irish MSS. comm.). R : J. Brady, *Irish hist. Stud.*, 45, vol. 4, p. 357-358. H.W., *Eng. hist. R.*, 41, vol. 56, p. 164-165.

2191. —— Vol. 6 : County of Waterford, with appendices. Dublin, Stationery Office, 42, in-8, lxi-557 p., 42s. R : H. W., *Eng. hist. R.*, 44, vol. 59, p. 280-281.

2192. —— Vol. 7 : County of Dublin. Dublin, Stationery Office, 45, in-8, l-317 p., 42s.

2193. SULLIVAN (Maev). No man's man. [Irish nationalist politics, 1890, and T. M. Healy]. Dublin, Browne & Nolan, 43, in-8, vi-295 p., 15s. R : C. C. O'Brien, *Irish hist. Stud.*, 45, vol. 4, p. 375-376.

Italy

2194. BERKELEY (G. F. H.). Some fresh documents concerning the Italian Risorgimento before 1849. London, Oxford Univ. Press, 40, in-8, 23 p., 1s. 6d. (British Acad.).

2195. BERKELEY (G. F. H. and J.). Italy in the making (1 Jan.-16 Nov., 1848). London, Cambridge Univ. Press, 40, in-8, xxvii-489 p., 25s. R : W.M., *Eng. hist. R.*, 42, vol. 57, p. 406-407.

2196. BINCHY (D. A.). Church and state in fascist Italy. London, Oxford Univ. Press, 41, in-8, 784 p., 31s. 6d.

2197. CORRIGAN (Beatrice). D'Annunzio and the Italian state. *Queen's Quar.*, 44, vol. 51, p. 65-71.

2198. DE BEER (E. S.). François Schott's Itinerario d'Italia. *Library*, 42, vol. 23, p. 57-83.

2199. HANCOCK (W. K.). A lonely patriot : Ferdinando Ranalli. London, Oxford Univ. Press, 42, in-8, 28 p., 2s.

2200. RUDMAN (H. W.). Italian nationalism and English letters : figures of the Risorgimento and Victorian men of letters. London, Allen & Unwin, 40, in-8, 444 p., 18s.

2201. SPRIGGE (Cecil J. S.). The development of modern Italy. London, Duckworth, 43, in-8, 216 p., 10s. 6d. R : *National R.*, 44, vol. 122, p. 173-176. A.G.A.W., *Int. Affairs*, 44, vol. 20, p. 289-290.

2202. TOYNBEE (Margaret R.). A royal wedding journey through Savoy in 1684. *History*, 41, vol. 26, p. 36-50.

2203. WHITFIELD (J. H.). Historical revision, no. 105 : New views upon the Borgias. *History*, 44, vol. 29, p. 77-88.

2204. WHYTE (A. J.). The evolution of modern Italy, 1715-1920. Oxford, Blackwell, 44, in-8, vii-275 p., (maps), 18s. R : A. J. Grant, *Eng. hist. R.*, 45, vol. 60, p. 414-416. I. M. Massey, *Int. Affairs*, 45, vol. 21, p.283.

Japan

2205. BORTON (Hugh). Japan since 1931, its political and social developments. London, Allen & Unwin, 41, in-8, xii-149 p., 6s. 6d. (I.P.R. inquiry ser.). R : O. M. Green, *Int. Affairs*, 41, vol. 19, p. 285. G. L. Wood, *Econ. Record*, 41, vol. 17, p. 291-296.

2206. HOWARD (A.) and NEWMAN (E.). The menacing rise of Japan : 90 years of crafty statesmanship in pictures. London, Harrap, 43, in-8, 96 p., (plates), 6s.

2207. NORMAN (E. H.). Japan's emergence as a modern state : political and economic problems of the Meiji period. London, Allen &

Unwin, 40, in-8, 254 p., 10s. (Inst. of Pacific relations inquiry ser.). R : O. M. Green, *Int. Affairs*, 40, vol. 19, p. 147-148. I. F. G. Milner, *Econ. Record*, 40, vol. 16, p. 306-308.

2208. WHITE (Oswald). The development of Japanese aggression. *J. central asian Soc.*, 44, vol. 31, p. 113-125.

2209. WIGHT (Martin). The Tanaka memorial. *History*, 43, vol. 28, p. 61-68.

Jugoslavia

2210. LODGE (Olive). Peasant life in Jugoslavia. London, Seeley, 42, in-8, 332 p., (illus.), 21s.

2211. SETON-WATSON (R. W.). The Yugoslav constitutional position. *Slavonic R.*, 45, vol. 23, p. 85-96.

Latin America

2212. GALDAMES (Luis). A history of Chile, ed. and tr. from the Spanish by I. J. Cox. London, Oxford Univ. Press, 41, in-8, 565 p., 22s. 6d. (Inter-Amer. hist. ser., 4).

2213. HARDING (Bertita). Amazon throne : the story of the Braganzas of Brazil. London, Harrap, 42, in-8, 353 p., 12s. 6d.

2214. LUDWIG (Emil). Bolivar : the life of an idealist. Toronto, Macmillan, 42, in-8, xi-362 p., $4.50. R : J.H.B., *Queen's Quar.*, 42, vol. 49, p. 185-188.

2215. MUNRO (D. G.). The Latin American republics : a history. London, Appleton, 42, in-8, 650 p., (illus.), 21s.

2216. NICHOLS (M. W.). The Gaucho : cattle hunter, cavalryman, ideal of romance. London, Cambridge Univ. Press, 42, in-8, x-152 p., 18s.

2217. ROURKE (T.). Simon Bolívar. London, Joseph, 40, in-8, xiv-386 p., (illus., map), 15s. R : J.P.H.M., *Geogr. J.*, 40, vol. 96, p. 141-142.

2218. ———— New ed. London, Joseph, 42, in-8, 400 p., (illus.), 5s.

2219. WRIGHT (L. A.). A study of the conflict between the republics of Peru and Ecuador. *Geogr. J.*, 41, vol. 98, p. 253-272.

Lithuania

2220. SIMUTIS (A.). The economic reconstruction of Lithuania after 1918. London, Oxford Univ. Press, 42, in-8, 162 p., 7s. 6d.

The Netherlands

2221. LANDHEER (B.) ed. The Netherlands. London, Cambridge Univ. Press, 44, in-8, xxii-464 p., (illus., maps), 30s. (United Nations ser.).

2222. RENIER (G. J.). The Dutch nation : an historical study. London, Allen & Unwin, 44, in-8, 272 p., (map), 15s. R : R.T.C., *Scottish geogr. Mag.*, 44, vol. 60, p. 87-88. A. D. Lindsay, *Int. Affairs*, 45, vol. 21, p. 124-125.

2223. WEDGWOOD (C. V.). William the Silent. William of Nassau, Prince of Orange, 1533-1584. London, Cape, 44, in-8, 256 p., (illus.), 18s.

New Zealand

2224. SCHOLEFIELD (G. H.). Writings on New Zealand history, 1938-1941. *Hist. Stud. Australia N.Z.*, 42, vol. 2, p. 50-53.

2225. Dictionary of New Zealand biography, ed. by G. H. Scholefield. 2 vols. Wellington, Dept. of Internal Affairs, 40, 2 vols. in-4, xxxii-512, vi-571 p., 50s. R : G. F. James, *Hist. Stud. Australia N.Z.*, 41, vol. 1, p. 196-200. W. P. Morrell, *Eng. hist. R.*, 41, vol. 56, p. 662-664.

2226. GRAHAM (George). Te Wi, the massacre there and its consequences as recorded by Tamehana Te Rauparaha, communicated with notes and trans. by G. Graham. *J. polynesian Soc.*, 45, vol. 54, p. 66-78.

2227. MILLAR (F. W.). Women of the public service : their background and future. *J. public Admin. N.Z.*, 44, vol. 6, p. 27-32.

2228. MULGAN (A.). From track to highway : a short history of New Zealand. London, Whitcombe & Tombs, 44, in-8, 128 p., (map), 4s. 6d.

2229. SEWELL (A.) ed. 1840 and after : essays written on the occasion of the New Zealand centenary. London, Whitcombe & Tombs, 40, in-8, 242 p., 6s.

2230. SUTCH (W. B.). The quest for security in New Zealand. London, Penguin, 42, in-8, 160 p., 9d.

2231. WOOD (F. L. W.). New Zealand in the world. Wellington, Dept. of Internal Affairs, 40, in-8, 143 p., 5s. (N.Z. centennial surveys). R : C. A. Sharp, *J. public Admin. N. Z.*, 40, vol. 3, p. 60-61. B.Y., *Int. Affairs*, 40, vol. 19, p. 126-127. J. O. Shearer, *Austral. Quar.*, 40, vol. 12, no. 2, p. 108-110.

Poland

2232. SAWICKI (T.). Rocznik Bibliograficzny : Bibliographical year book. Works in Polish and works relating to Poland published outside Poland, Sept. 1, 1939 to Dec. 31, 1941. Edinburgh, Oliver & Boyd, 42, in-8, 68 p., 3s. 6d.

2233. Cambridge history of Poland, from Augustus II to Pilsudski, 1697-1935, ed. by W. F. Reddaway, J. H. Penson, O. Halecki and R. Dyboski. Vol. 2. London, Cambridge Univ. Press, 41, in-4, xvi-630 p., (maps), 30s. R : *National R.*, 42, vol. 118, p. 95-96. D. Warriner, *Pol.Quar.*, 42, vol. 13, p. 110-112.

2234. GARDNER (M. M.). Kościuszko. New ed. London, Allen & Unwin, 42, in-8, 148 p., 7s. 6d.

2235. KOT (S.). Five centuries of Polish learning : 3 lectures. Tr. by W. J. Rose. Oxford, Blackwell, 41, in-8, v-53 p., 2s.

2236. LASKOWSKI (O.). Jan III Sobieski (King of Poland), 1629-1696. London, Faber, 41, in-8, 344 p., 4s. 6d.

2237. PILSUDSKI (Aleksandra). Memoirs, tr. by J. Ellis. [Biography of Marshal Pilsudski]. London, Hurst and Blackett, 40, in-8, 356 p., 10s. 6d.

2238. PILSUDSKI (J.). Rok, 1920. London, Faber, 41, in-8, 224 p., (maps), 8s. 6d.

2239. ROSE (W. J.). The rise of Polish democracy. London, Bell, 44, in-8, 253 p., 10s. R : J. Balinski-Jundzill, *Int. Affairs*, 45, vol. 21, p. 417. H. J. Paton, *Slavonic R.*, 45, vol. 23, p. 174-175.

2240. RUSSELL (Sir John). Reconstruction and development in eastern Poland, 1930-39. *Geogr. J.*, 41, vol. 98, p. 273-291.

2241. SLOMKA (Jan). From serfdom to self-government : memoirs of a Polish village mayor, 1842-1927, tr. by W. J. Rose. London, Minerva Publ. Co., 41, in-8, 276 p., 8s. 6d.

2242. SZCZEPANOWSKI (S. A.). The Polish nation's struggle for life (in Polish). London, Simpkin & Marshall, 42, in-8, 336 p., (maps), 10s. 6d.

2243. SZWIEJKOWSKI (Zdzislaw). Alexander Swietochowski, 1848-1938. *Slavonic Y.B. (Slavonic R.)*, 40, vol. 19, p. 228-236.

Portugal

2244. THOMAS (Henry). Short-title catalogue of Portuguese books printed before 1601 now in the British Museum, May 1940. London, H.M.S.O., 40, in-8, 43 p., 5s. R : S. Gaselee, *Library*, 40, vol. 21, p. 217-218.

2245. GREENWALL (H. J.). Our oldest ally (Portugal). London, Allen, 43, in-8, 112 p., 7s. 6d. R : E.C.C., *Int. Affairs*, 44, vol. 20, p. 285-286.

Rumania

2246. BURGOYNE (Elizabeth). Carmen Sylva, queen and woman. London, Eyre & Spottiswoode, 41, in-8, xvii-320 p., 12s. 6d.

Scotland

2247. DICKINSON (Gladys). Two missions of Jacques de la Brosse ; affairs of Scotland in the year 1543, and the Journal of the siege of Leith. Edinburgh, Scottish Hist. Soc., 42, in-8, subscribers only. (Publ., 3rd ser., vol. 36). R : A.J.G., *Eng. hist. R.*, 43, vol. 58, p. 249-250.

2248. FYFE (J. G.). Scottish diaries and memoirs, 1746-1843, ed. by J. G. Fyfe. ' Stirling, Mackay, 42, in-8, 603 p., 12s. 6d. R : M.P., *History*, 43, vol. 28, p. 225-226.

2249. GEDDES (Arthur). The foundation of Grantown-on-Spey, 1765. *Scottish geogr. Mag.*, 45, vol. 61, p. 19-22.

2250. GEDDES (A.). Burghs of Laich and Brae [1603 to 1820]. *Scottish geogr. Mag.*, 45, vol. 61, p. 38-45.

2251. McGRAIL (Thomas H.). Sir William Alexander, 1st Earl of Stirling. Edinburgh, Oliver, 40, in-8, xiv-273 p., 10s. 6d. R : J. B. Brebner, *Canad. hist. R.*, 41, vol. 22, p. 65-66.

2252. MACKENZIE (Agnes Mure). Scotland in modern times, 1720-1939. Edinburgh, Chambers, 41, in-8, 432p., 15s.

2253. STUART (Marie W.). The Scot who was a Frenchman : being the life of John Stewart, duke of Albany, in Scotland, France and Italy. London, Hodge, 40, in-8, 327 p., 12s. 6d. R : J.D.M., *History*, 43, vol. 38, p. 115-116.

2254. TAYLER (Alistair N.) and TAYLER (H. A. H.) ed. Jacobite epilogue, a further selection of letters from Jacobites among the Stuart papers at Windsor. London, Nelson, 41, in-8, 331 p., 15s.

2255. TAYLOR (Louise B.). Aberdeen Council letters. Vol. 1 : 1552-1633. London, Oxford Univ. Press, 40, in-8, 488 p., (plates), 30s. R : R. J. Hammond, *Econ. Hist. R.*, 43, vol. 13, p. 135. H.W.M., *Eng. hist. R.*, 43, vol. 58, p. 497-498. W. C. Dickinson, *History*, 43, vol. 28, p. 219-220.

2256. WOOD (Marguerite) ed. Extracts from the records of the burgh of Edinburgh, 1655 to 1665. Edinburgh, Oliver, 40, in-8, 576 p., 21s. R : C. B. Boog Watson, *Scottish geogr. Mag.*, 41, vol. 57, p. 81-84.

South Africa

2257. BAUMANN (G.) and BRIGHT (E. B.). The lost Republic, the biography of a South African land surveyor. London, Faber, 40, in-8, 269 p., 12s. 6d.

2258. COULTER (C. W. A.). The Union of South Africa, 1 : The covenant of union; 2 : The erosion of Empire unity; 3 : Republicanism by gradualness; 4 : The return to sanity. *National R.*, 44, vol. 122, p. 485-500.

2259. PIETERSE (D. J.). Transvaal en Britse Susereiniteit, 1881-1884. *Archives Y.B. South Afr. Hist.*, 40 (41), 3rd year, pt. 1, p. 257-344.

2260. SOWDEN (L.). The South African union. London, Hale, 45, in-8, 200 p., (illus.), 15s.

2261. WALKER (Eric A.). A history of South Africa. New ed. London, Longmans, 40, in-8, 728 p., 16s. R : H. A. Wyndham, *J. Roy. african Soc.*, 41, vol. 40, p. 11-18.

2262. WALKER (E. A.). Britain and South Africa. London, Longmans, 41, in-8, 64 p., 6d. (Pamph. on the Brit. Commonwealth, 2).

Spain

2263. ALVAREZ DEL VAYO (J.). Freedom's battle, tr. from the Spanish by E. E. Brooke. London, Heinemann, 40, in-8, xix-381-viii p., 15s. R : W. H. Carter, *Int. Affairs*, 41, vol. 19, p. 214-215.

2264. ARAQUISTÁIN (Luis). Some survivals of ancient Iberia in modern Spain. *Man*, 45, vol. 45, p. 30-38.

2265. BRENAN (Gerald). The Spanish labyrinth : an account of the social and political background of the Civil War. London, Cambridge Univ. Press, 43, in-8, xx-384 p., (maps), 21s. R : L. Woolf, *Pol. Quar.*, 43, vol. 14, p. 289-290.   C. H. Guyatt, *Int. Affairs*, 44, vol. 20, p. 135-136.

2266. BUCKLEY (H.). Life and death of the Spanish Republic. London, Hamilton, 40, in-8, 432 p., (illus.), 12s. 6d.

2267. GILBERT (E. W.). Richard Ford and his ' Hand-book for travellers in Spain '. *Geogr. J.*, 45, vol. 106, p. 144-151.

2268. HARCOURT-SMITH (S.). Alberoni, or, The Spanish conspiracy. London, Faber, 43, in-8, 244 p., (plates), 15s.

2269. MADARIAGA (S. de). Spain. London, Cape, 42, in-8, 509 p., 25s.

2270. MATTINGLY (Garrett). The reputation of Dr. De Puebla. *Eng. hist. R.*, 40, vol. 55, p. 27-46.

2271. PEERS (E. Allison). Spain in eclipse, 1937-1943 : a sequel to the Spanish tragedy. London, Methuen, 43, in-8, 275 p., 15s. R : *National R.*, 44, vol. 122, p. 86-87.

2272. SENCOURT (R.). King Alfonso. A biography. London, Faber, 42, in-8, 296 p., (illus.), 12s. 6d. R : *Quar. R.*, 42, vol. 279, p. 233-234.

2273. STARKIE (Walter). Grand Inquisitor, being an account of Cardinal Ximenes de Cisneros and his times. London, Hodder, 40, in-8, 492 p., 18s.

2274. WALSH (W. T.). Philip II. New ed. London, Sheed & Ward, 40, in-8, xvi-770 p., (illus.), 10s. 6d.

Sweden

2275. AHNLUND (N.). Gustav Adolf the Great, tr. from the Swedish by M. Roberts. London, Oxford Univ. Press, 40, in-8, 314 p., 14s.

2276. DEWES (S.). Sergeant Belle-Jambe. The life of Marshal Bernadotte, King of Sweden. London, Rich & Cowan, 43, in-8, 168 p., (illus.), 12s. 6d.

2277. SHEPPARD (E. W.). A former invader of Russia : Charles XII of Sweden. *Army Quar.*, 42, vol. 45, p. 86-94 (map).

Turkey

2278. ARGENTI (Philip P.) ed. Chius vincta, or, The occupation of Chios by the Turks (1566) and their administration of the island (1566-1912), described in contemporary diplomatic reports and official documents. London, Cambridge Univ. Press, 41, in-8, cclxxviii-264 p., (plates), 25s.

2279. BAILEY (F. E.). British policy and the Turkish reform movement. London, Oxford Univ. Press, 44, in-8, 326 p., (tables), 20s.

2280. BURTON (H. M.). Development in modern Turkey. *J. central asian Soc.*, 42, vol. 29, p. 17-29.

2281. CASTLE (W. T. F.). Grand Turk. London, Hutchinson, 43, in-8, 170 p., (illus., maps), 10s. 6d. R : A. S. Tritton, *J. asiatic Soc.*, 43, p. 263-264. P. M. Sykes, *J. central asian Soc.*, 43, vol. 30, p. 333.

2282. KOPRULU (F.). Turk Hukuk ve iktisat Tarihi Mecmuasi II, 1932-1939. Revue de l'histoire juridique et economique turque, II. In Turkish, new script. London, Luzac, 40, in-8, 194 p., (illus.), 9s.

2283. MILLER (B.). The Palace school of Muhammad the Conqueror. London, Oxford Univ. Press, 41, in-8, 240 p., 8s. 6d. (Hist. monogr. ser.).

2284. MORISON (W. A.). The revolt of the Serbs against the Turks (1804-1813). London, Cambridge Univ. Press, 42, in-8, xl-181 p., 8s. 6d. R : J.P.P., *Eng. hist. R.*, 42, vol. 57, p. 534.

2285. PARKER (John) and SMITH (Charles). Modern Turkey. London, Routledge, 40, in-8, ix-259 p., 12s. 6d. R : Nestor, *Int. Affairs*, 40, vol. 19, p. 140. A.T.W., *J. central asian Soc.*, 40, vol. 27, p. 477-479. D. Warriner, *Pol. Quar.*, 40, vol. 11, p. 422-423.

2286. WITTLIN (Alma). Abdul Hamid, the shadow of God, tr. by N. Denny. London, Lane, 40, in-8, 296 p., (plates), 12s. 6d. R : L. F. R. Williams, *Asiatic R.*, 41, vol. 37, p. 424-425.

Union of Soviet Socialist Republics

2287. GRIERSON (Philip). Books on Soviet Russia, 1917-1942 : a bibliography and a guide to reading. London, Methuen, 43, in-8, 354 p., 12s. 6d. R : *History*, 45, vol. 30, p. 115.

2288. BADDELEY (J. F.). The rugged flanks of Caucasus. London, Oxford Univ. Press, 40, 2 vols. in-8, 296, 324 p., (plates, maps), 126s.

2289. BATES (Ernest Stuart). Soviet Asia, progress and problems. London, Cape, 41, in-8, 192 p., 8s. 6d. R : G.R.C., *Geogr. J.*, 42, vol. 99, p. 103-104.

2290. BORODIN (G.). Soviet Siberia. London, Hutchinson, 43, in-8, 168 p., (illus.), 15s.

2291. CURTISS (John Shelton). Church and state in Russia (the last years of the Empire, 1900-1917). London, Oxford Univ. Press, 40, in-8, ix-422 p., 26s. 6d. R : N. Zernov, *Int. R. Missions*, 40, vol. 29, p. 546-547.

2292. DURANTY (W.). U.S.S.R. The story of Soviet Russia. London, Hamilton, 44, in-8, 293 p., 15s.

2293. GERHARDI (W.). The Romanovs. London, Rich & Cowan, 40, in-8, 542 p., 30s.

2294. GREENBERG (L.). The Jews in Russia. Vol. 1 : The struggle for emancipation. London, Oxford Univ. Press, 44, in-8, 220 p., 20s. (Yale hist. publ., misc. 45).

2295. LEVIN (A.). The second Duma : a study of the Social-democratic party and the Russian constitutional experiment. London, Oxford Univ. Press, 40, in-8, 414 p., 14s. (Yale hist. publ., misc. 36).

2296. MARSDEN (C.). Palmyra of the North : the first days of St. Petersburg. London, Faber, 42, in-8, 280 p., (illus.), 16s.

2297. MAYNARD (Sir John). The Russian peasant, and other studies. London, Gollancz, 42, in-8, 512 p., 15s. R : C.G., *Int. Affairs*, 43, vol. 19, p. 573-574. L. Woolf, *Pol. Quar.*, 43, vol. 14, p. 205-206. H. J. F[leure], *Geography*, 43, vol. 28, p. 67-68.

2298. PARES (Bernard). Russia. Harmondsworth, Penguin, 41, in-8, 256 p., 6d.

2299. POLOVTSOFF (Alexander). The favourites of Catherine the Great. London, Jenkins, 40, in-8, 288 p., 12s. 6d.

2300. SEMYONOV (Y.). The conquest of Siberia : an epic of human passions, tr. from the German by E. W. Dickes. London, Routledge, 44, in-8, 323 p., (illus., maps), 21s.

2301. STRAUSS (E.). Soviet Russia, anatomy of a social history. London, Lane, 41, in-8, 342 p., 12s. 6d. R : M. Dobb, *Sociol. R.*, 42, vol. 35, p. 106-109. B. Wootton, *Econ. J.*, 42, vol. 52, p. 91-92. J. Maynard, *Pol. Quar.*, 42, vol. 13, p. 100-102. A. Baykov, *Economica*, 42, vol. 9, p. 303-307.

2302. VERNADSKY (G.). Bohdan : Hetman of the Ukraine. London, Oxford Univ. Press, 42, in-8, 168 p., (illus.), 11s. 6d. R : B. H. Sumner, *Eng. hist. R.*, 43, vol. 58, p. 119-120.

2303. YAROSLAVSKY (E.). Twenty-five years of Soviet power. London, Hutchinson, 43, in-8, 80 p., 1s.

United States of America

2304. ABBEY (Kathryn Trimmer). Florida, land of change. London, Oxford Univ. Press, 41, in-8, xii-426 p., (plates, maps), 16s. R : J.E.T., *Eng. hist. R.*, 43, vol. 58, p. 252.

2305. ADAMS (J. T.). The American : the making of a new man. London, Scribner, 43, in-8, ix-404 p., 15s.

2306. ALEXANDER (D. C.). The Arkansas plantation, 1920-1942. London, Oxford Univ. Press, 43, in-8, 118 p., 6s. 6d.

2307. ALINGTON (G.). The growth of America. London, Faber, 40, in-8, 320 p., 12s. 6d.

2308. BARROWS (C. L.). William M. Evarts. London, Oxford Univ. Press, 42, in-8, 600 p., 18s.

2309. BELMONT (Perry). An American democrat : recollections. 2nd ed., rev. and enlarged. London, Oxford Univ. Press, 41, in-8, xvi-729 p., (plates, maps), 18s. 6d. R : D. W. B(rogan), *Eng. hist. R.*, 43, vol. 58, p. 253-254.

2310. BEARD (C. A. and M. R.). The rise of American civilization. New ed. London, Cape, 44, in-8, 1,712 p., 30s.

2311. BIDDLE (G. B.) and LOWRIE (S. D.). Notable women of Pennsylvania. London, Oxford Univ. Press, 42, in-8, 326 p., 14s.

2312. BIRLEY (R.) ed. Speeches and documents in American history. London, Oxford Univ. Press, 42-44, 4 vols. in-8, 312, 336, 320, 344 p., 12s. (World's classics).

2313. CALLCOTT (W. H.). The Caribbean policy of the United States, 1890-1920. London, Oxford Univ. Press, 42, in-8, xiv-524 p., 16s. (Johns Hopkins Univ., W. H. Page school of internat. relations, Shaw lect. on diplomatic hist., 1942). R : H. H .B., *Eng. hist. R.*, 45, vol. 60, p. 284-285.

2314. CARMAN (H. J.) and LUTHIN (R. H.). Lincoln and the patronage. London, Oxford Univ. Press, 43, in-8, 386 p., (illus.), 30s. R : *Eng. hist. R.*, 44, vol. 59, p. 428-429.

2315. CHESTERTON (Cecil). A history of the United States, ed. with intr. by D. W. Brogan. London, Dent, 40, in-8, xxxvii-358 p., 2s. 6d. (Everyman's libr.).

2316. CHITWOOD (O. P.). John Tyler : champion of the Old South. London, Appleton, 40, in-8, xv-496 p., 20s. (Amer. hist. assoc.).

2317. DANIELS (Josephus). The Wilson era. London, Oxford Univ. Press, 45, in-8, 632 p., (illus.), 24s.

2318. Dictionary of American biography, ed. by H. E. Starr. Vol. 21, Suppl. 1. London, Oxford Univ. Press, 44, in-4, 718 p., 52s. 6d. R : T. B(esterman), *J. Documentation*, 45, vol. 1, p. 119.

2319. Dictionary of American history, ed. by J. T. Adams and R. V. Coleman. London, Oxford Univ. Press, 41, 6 vols. in-4, 444, 430, 432, 512, 515, 258 p., 300s. R : D. W. Brogan, *Eng. hist. R.*, 42, vol. 57, p. 143-146. *History*, 42, vol. 26, p. 306-308.

2320. DUNCAN (K.) and NICKOLS (D. F.). Mentor Graham : the man who taught Lincoln. London, Cambridge Univ. Press, 45, in-8, xxx-274 p., 22s. 6d.

2321. FOWLER (D. G.). The Cabinet politician : the Postmasters general, 1829-1909. London, Oxford Univ. Press, 43, in-8, 356 p., 25s.

2322. FRANKLIN (Francis). The rise of the American nation, 1789-1824. Toronto, Progress Publ. Co., 43, in-8, 288 p., (maps), $3.00. (Progress books). R : D. C. Masters, *Canad. hist. R.*, 45, vol. 26, p. 63-64.

2323. GARCEAU (O.). The political life of the American Medical Association. London, Oxford Univ. Press, 42, in-8, 196 p., 10s. 6d.

2324. GLOAG (J. E.). The American nation : a short history of the United States. London, Cassell, 42, in-8, viii-390 p., (maps), 7s. 6d.

2325. HAAS (William H.) ed. The American empire : a study of the outlying territories of the United States. London, Cambridge Univ. Press, 40, in-8, xi-408 p., (plates, maps), 24s. R : A.C.O., *Geogr. J.*, 41, vol. 98, p. 52.

2326. HARMON (George Dewey). Sixty years of Indian affairs ; political, economic, and diplomatic, 1789-1850. London, Oxford Univ. Press, 41, in-8, x-428 p., 22s. 6d.

2327. HAWGOOD (J. A.). The tragedy of German-America : the Germans in the United States of America during the 19th century—and after. London, Putnam, 42, in-8, 334 p., 15s.

2328. HILLDRUP (R. L.). The life and times of Edmund Pendleton. London, Oxford Univ. Press, 40, in-8, 363 p., 16s.

2329. JERNEGAN (C. and R.). Growth of the American people. London, Longmans, 42, in-8, 868 p., (illus.), 12s. 6d.

2330. JONES (V. C.). Ranger Mosby, London, Oxford Univ. Press, 44, in-8, 362 p., (illus.), 21s. 6d.

2332. KROUT (John Allen) and Fox (Dixon Ryan). The completion of independence, 1790-1830. London, Macmillan, 45, in-8, xxiii-487 p.,

20s. (Hist. of Amer. life, vol. 5). R : F. H. Underhill, *Canad. hist. R.*, 45, vol. 26, p. 317-319.

2333. LAWRENCE (A. A.). James Moore Wayne : Southern Unionist. London, Oxford Univ. Press, 43, in-8, 264 p., (illus.), 18s. 6d.

2334. LEECH (Margaret). Reveille in Washington, 1860-1865. London, Eyre & Spottiswoode, 42, in-8, x-483 p., (plates, maps), 18s.

2335. LINK (E. P.). Democratic-Republican societies, 1790-1800. London, Oxford Univ. Press, 42, in-8, 270 p., 14s. (Studies in Amer. culture ser.). R : *Army Quar.*, 43, vol. 45, p. 251.

2336. LONN (Ella). Foreigners in the Confederacy. London, Oxford Univ. Press, 40, in-8, xi-566 p., (plates), 22s. 6d. R : D. W. B(rogan), *Eng. hist. R.*, 43, vol. 58, p. 502.

2337. LUTHIN (R. H.). The first Lincoln campaign. London, Oxford Univ. Press, 45, in-8, 338 p., 20s.

2338. McGILLYCUDDY (J. B.). McGillicuddy, agent : Valentine T. McGillycuddy. London, Oxford Univ. Press, 45, in-8, 304 p., 18s. 6d.

2339. McGLASHAN (C. F.). History of the Donner party, a tragedy of the Sierra. With notes and a bibliography by G. H. and B. M. Hinkle. London, Oxford Univ. Press, 40, in-8, 261 p., 9s.

2340. McKELVEY (B.). Rochester, the water-power city, 1812-1854. London, Oxford Univ. Press, 45, in-8, 400 p., (illus.), 22s. 6d. (Rochester publ. libr., K. Gleason fund publ., 1).

2341. MATHIESSEN (F. O.). American renaissance. London, Oxford Univ. Press, 42, in-8, 704 p., (illus.), 25s.

2342. MEAD (S. E.). Nathaniel William Taylor, 1786-1858 : a Connecticut Liberal. London, Cambridge Univ. Press, 43, in-8, xii-260 p., 15s.

2343. MEADE (Robert D.). Judah P. Benjamin : Confederate statesman. London, Oxford Univ. Press, 44, in-8, 446 p., (illus.), 21s. R : J.E.T., *Eng. hist. R.*, 45, vol. 60, p. 283-284.

2344. MEYNELL (E.). The young Lincoln. London, Chapman & Hall, 44, in-8, 172 p., 12s. 6d. R : L. F., *National R.*, 44, vol. 122, p. 347-348.

2345. MORISON (S. E.) and COMMAGER (H. S.). The growth of the American republic. 3rd rev. ed. London, Oxford Univ. Press, 43, 2 vols. in-8, 884, 826 p., (maps), 42s.

2346. MOWAT (R. B.). The American venture. London, Dakers, 42, in-8, 320 p., 12s. 6d. .

2347. NEVINS (Allan). A brief history of the United States. London, Oxford Univ. Press, 42, in-8, 144 p., (maps), 2s.

2348. NEVINS (A.). The emergence of modern America, 1865-1878, ed. by A. M. Schlesinger and D. R. Fox. New ed. London, Macmillans, 45, in-8, xix-446 p., (illus.), 20s. (Hist. of Amer. life, vol. 8).

2349. NEVINS (A.) and COMMAGER (H. S.). America : the story of a free people. London, Oxford Univ. Press, 42, in-8, 475 p., (maps), 7s. 6d.

2350. NICHOLS (J. P. and R. F.). The republic of the United States, 1493-1942. London, Appleton, 42-43, 2 vols. in-8, 655, 730 p., (maps, illus.), 40s. (Century hist. ser.).

2351. PADOVER (S. K.). Jefferson. London, Cape, 43, in-8, 459 p., (illus.), 21s.

2352. PALMER (G. T.). A conscientious turncoat : John M. Palmer, 1817-1900. London, Oxford Univ. Press, 41, in-8, 308 p., 14s.

2353. PARKMAN (F.). The Oregon trail, ed. by H. S. Commager. London, Oxford Univ. Press, 44, in-8, 288 p., (map), 8s. 6d.

2354. PATTERSON (S. W.). Horatio Gates, defender of American liberties. London, Oxford Univ. Press, 41, in-8, 482 p., 21s.

2355. PEMBERTON (J. C.). Pemberton, defender of Vicksburg. London, Oxford Univ. Press, 42, in-8, 366 p., (illus., maps), 16s.

2356. PHILLIPS (U. B.). The course of the South to secession. London, Appleton, 40, in-8, 176 p., 12s. 6d.

2357. PICKARD (M. F.). The Roosevelts and America. London, Joseph, 42, in-8, 288 p., (illus.), 16s.

2358. PIERCE (Bessie Louise). A history of Chicago. Vol. 2 : From town to city, 1848-1871. London, Knopf, 40, in-8, 547-xxxiii p., 21s. R : D. C. Masters, *Canad. hist. R.*, 41, vol. 22, p. 443-444.

2359. PLASKITT (H.). The United States of America : the people, their history, institutions and way of life. London, Univ. Tutorial Press, 43, in-8, 192 p., (illus.), 3s. 6d.

2360. POTTER (David M.). Lincoln and his party in the Secession crisis. London, Oxford Univ. Press, 42, in-8, 420 p., 17s.

2361. POWELL (J. H.). Richard Rush, republican democrat, 1780-1859. London, Oxford Univ. Press, 43, in-8, 300 p., 16s. 6d.

2362. RICE (H. M.). The life of Jonathan M. Bennett, a study of the Virginias in transition. London, Oxford Univ. Press, 43, in-8, 316 p., 21s. 6d.

2363. ROOSEVELT (F. D.). The public papers and addresses of Franklin D. Roosevelt, ed. by S. I. Rosenman, 1937-40. London, Macmillan, 42, 4 vols. in-8, 731, 719, 675, 772 p., 126s.

2364. SANDBURG (Carl). Storm over the land : from ' Abraham Lincoln, the war years, 1861-1865 '. London, Cape, 42, in-8, 440 p., 12s. 6d.

2365. SCHLESINGER (Arthur M.). Political and social growth of the American people, 1865-1940. London, Macmillan, 41, in-8, xxi-783 p., 16s.

2366. SCHLESINGER (A. M.). The rise of the city, 1878-1898, ed. by A. M. Schlesinger and D. R. Fox. New ed. London, Macmillan, 45, in-8, xvi-494 p., (illus.), 20s. (Hist. of Amer. life, vol. 10).

2367. SHIPLEY (J. S.). Lincoln takes command. London, Oxford Univ. Press, 41, in-8, 334 p., 16s.

2368. SHUTES (M. H.). Lincoln and California. London, Oxford Univ. Press, 43, in-8, 284 p., (plates), 18s. 6d.

2369. SOMERVELL (D. C.). A history of the United States to 1941. London, Heinemann, 42, in-8, 294 p., 10s. 6d.

2370. STEPHENSON (Nathaniel Wright) and DUNN (Waldo Hilary). George Washington, 1732-1799. London, Oxford Univ. Press, 40, 2 vols. in-8, 473, 596 p., 50s.

2371. STICKLES (A. M.). Simon Bolivar Buckner, borderland knight. London, Oxford Univ. Press, 40, in-8, 561 p., 14s.

2372. STRONG (C. F.). The story of the American people. London Univ. Press, 42, in-8, 305 p., (maps) 7s. 6d. R : History, 43, vol. 28, p. 122'

2373. TINKCOM (Harry Marlin). John White Geary : soldier-statesman, 1819-1873. London, Oxford Univ. Press, 40, in-8, 155 p., 8s.

2374. TORRIELLI (Andrew J.). Italian opinion on America as revealed by Italian travellers, 1850-1900. London, Oxford Univ. Press, 41, in-8, vi-330 p., 15s. (Harvard stud. in Romance lang., vol. 15). R : D. W. B(rogan), Eng. hist. R., 44, vol. 59, p. 285. J. H. Whitfield, Mod. Language R., 43, vol. 38, p. 162-163.

2375. TYLER (J. E.). A short history of America. Edinburgh, Chambers, 40, in-8, 264 p., 6s.

2376. VOTO (B. de). The year of decision, 1846. London, Macmillan, 44, in-8, x-538 p., 21s.

2377. WALTERS (R.) jr. Alexander James Dallas. London, Oxford Univ. Press, 44, in-8, 260 p., 15s. 6d.

2378. WARREN (C.). Odd byways in American history. London, Oxford Univ. Press, 42, in-8, 288 p., 12s. 6d. R : D. W. B(rogan), Eng. hist. R., 43, vol. 58, p. 378.

2379. WELLBORN (F. W.), The growth of American nationality, 1492-1865. London, Macmillan, 43, in-8, xvi-1,042 p., (illus.), 21s.

2380. WILLIAMS (David). The contribution of Wales to the development of the United States. Nat. Library Wales J., 42, vol. 2, p. 97-108.

2381. WOODBURN (J. A.), MORAN (T. F.) and HILL (H. C.). Our United States. London, Longmans, 42, in-8, 782 p., (illus.), 10s. 6d.

2382. WRITERS' PROGRAM, U.S.A. Wyoming, a guide to its history, highways and people. London, Oxford Univ. Press, 41, in-8, 490 p., 11s. 6d. (Amer. guide ser.).

§ 3. Discoveries

2383. HEYSE (Th.). Centenary bibliography of publications concerning Henry Morton Stanley. J. Roy. african Soc., 43, vol. 42, p. 91-98.

2384. ALLEN (Bernard M.). Livingstone and Gordon. J. Roy. african Soc., 41, vol. 40, p. 121-127.

2385. BAKER (J. N. L.). Sir Richard Burton and the Nile sources. Eng. hist. R., 44, vol. 59, p. 49-61.

2386. BEAGLEHOLE (J. C.). The discovery of New Zealand. London, Whitcombe & Tombs, 40, in-8, 160 p., 5s. (N.Z. centennial surveys). R : L. F.

Fitzhardinge, *Hist. Stud. Australia N.Z.*, 40, vol. 1, p. 132-133.

2387. BURPEE (Lawrence J.). The fate of Henry Hudson. *Canad. hist. R.*, 40, vol. 21, p. 401-406.

2388. CHISHOLM (Alec H.). Strange new world : the adventures of John Gilbert and Ludwig Leichhardt. Sydney, Angus and Robertson, 41, in-8, 382 p., 12s. 6d. R : C. P. Conigrave, *Roy. Austral. hist. Soc. J.*, 42, vol. 28, p. 48-51.

2389. COLNETT (James). Journal aboard the *Argonaut*, 1789-1791, ed. by F. W. Howay. Toronto, Champlain Soc., 40, in-8, xxxi-328 p., (plates, maps), privately printed. (Publ., 26). R : W. N. Sage, *Brit. Columbia hist. Quar.*, 41, vol. 5, p. 155-156. W. K. Lamb, *Canad. hist. R.*, 41, vol. 22, p. 71-72. J.L.M., *History*, 41, vol. 26, p. 157-158.

2390. COSGRAVE (J. O.). Log of Christopher Columbus's first voyage to America. London, W. H. Allen, 44, in-4, 76 p., (illus.), 12s. 6d.

2391. COUPLAND (Sir Reginald). Livingstone's last journey. London, Collins, 45, in-8, 271 p., 12s. 6d.

2392. CRAFT (Frank A.) and MIT-CHELL (R. Else). In search of Dawes' Mount Twiss. *Roy. Austral. hist. Soc. J.*, 41, vol. 27, p. 245-275.

2393. CRAMP (K. R.). Captain Charles Sturt's expedition into the interior, 1844-46. *Roy. Austral. hist. Soc. J.*, 44, vol. 30, p. 196-214.

2394. CYRIAX (R. J.) and WORDIE (J. M.). Centenary of the sailing of Sir John Franklin with the *Erebus* and *Terror*. *Geogr. J.*, 45, vol. 106, p. 169-197.

2395. DAY (A. Grove). Coronado's quest : the discovery of the south-western states. London, Cambridge Univ. Press, 41, in-8, xvi-418 p., (maps), 15s.

2396. DOWD (B. T.). James Meehan. *Roy. Austral. hist. Soc. J.*, 42, vol. 28, p. 108-118.

2397. DUNCAN (George). The mystery of Henry Hudson. *Queen's Quar.*, 41, vol. 48, p. 115-125.

2398. GLEDHILL (P. W.). The Hawkesbury river, its discovery. *Roy. Austral. hist. Soc. J.*, 41, vol. 27, p. 127-152.

2399. GOULD (R. T.). The charting of the south Shetlands, 1819-28. *Mariner's Mirror*, 41, vol. 27, p. 206-242.

2400. GRAY (Sir J. M.). ' Stanley versus Tippoo Tib '. *B. Uganda Soc.*, 44, no. 2, p. 18-20.

2401. H. (A. R.). The discovery of Torres Strait. *Geogr. J.*, 41, vol. 98, p. 91-102.

2402. HABSHUSH (Hayyim). Travels in Yemen : an account of Joseph Halévy's journey to Najran in the year 1870, ed. by S. D. Goitein. London, Probsthain, 41, in-8, 102-71-138 p., 10s. R : H. Scott, *Geogr. J.*, 42, vol. 99, p. 272-275.

2403. HOBBS (W. H.). Reports of the Greenland expeditions of the University of Michigan, 1926-33. Pt. 2. London, Oxford Univ. Press, 42, in-4, 287 p., (plates, figs.), 21s.

2404. HOWAY (F. W.). Discovery of the Fraser river. *Brit. Columbia hist. Quar.*, 40, vol. 4, p. 245-251.

2405. HOWAY (F. W.) ed. Sailing directions governing the voyage of the vessels ' Captain Cook ' and ' Experiment ' to the northwest coast in the fur trade, A.D. 1786. *Brit. Columbia hist. Quar.*, 41, vol. 5, p. 285-296.

2406. LANCASTER (Sir James). The voyages of Sir James Lancaster to Brazil and the East Indies, 1591-1603. With intr. and notes by Sir W. Foster. New ed. London, Quaritch, 41, in-8, xl-178 p., (illus., maps), 27s.

R : E. G. R. T(aylor), *Mariner's Mirror*, 41, vol. 27, p. 175-176. E.H., *Geogr. J.*, 41, vol. 97, p. 392-393. E. D. Maclagan, *J. asiatic Soc.*, 41, p. 365-366.

2407. LANCTOT (Gustave). Cartier visite la rivière Nicolet en 1535. *Canad. Cath. hist. Assoc. Rept.*, 43-44, vol. 11, Fr. Sect., p. 177-183.

2408. LANCTOT (G.). Cartier's first voyage to Canada in 1524. *Canad. hist. R.*, 44, vol. 25, p. 233-245.

2409. LIVINGSTONE (David). Some letters from Livingstone, 1840-1872, ed. by D. Chamberlin. London, Oxford Univ. Press, 40, in-8, 307 p., 12s. 6d. R : E. W. Smith, *Int. R. Missions*, 40, vol. 29, p. 553-556. W. T. Furse, *J. Roy. african Soc.*, 40, vol. 39, p. 381-382. W. P. M(orrell), *History*, 42, vol. 27, p. 96.

2410. LIVINGSTONE (D.). David Livingstone : the centenary commemoration in London, December 11, 1940. *J. Roy. african Soc.*, 41, vol. 40, p. 108-120.

2411. MCCLYMONT (W. G.). The exploration of New Zealand. Wellington, Dept. of Internal Affairs, 40, in-8, 202 p., 5s. (N.Z. centennial surveys). R : C. A. Sharp, *J. public Admin. N. Zealand*, 40, vol. 3, p. 59-60. J. D. Pascoe, *Hist. Stud. Australia N.Z.*, 40, vol. 1, p. 133-135.

2412. —— —— New ed. London, Whitcombe & Tombs, 43, in-8, 202 p., (illus.), 5s. (N.Z. centennial surveys).

2413. MACKANESS (George). George Augustus Robinson's journey into south-eastern Australia, 1844. *Roy. Austral. hist. Soc. J.*, 41, vol. 27, p. 318-349.

2414. MACKINTOSH (N. A.). The fifth commission of the R.R.S. Discovery II (1929-39). *Geogr. J.*, 41, vol. 97, p. 201-216.

2415. MACNAIR (James I.). Livingstone the liberator. London, Collins, 40, in-8, 382 p., 2s. 6d. (Collins illus. pocket classics). R : E. W. Smith, *Int. R. Missions*, 40, vol. 29, p. 553-556. B. M. Allen, *J. Roy. african Soc.*, 41, vol. 40, p. 79-80. E.H., *Geogr. J.*, 41, vol. 97, p. 128-129.

2416. MASEFIELD (Geoffrey). Livingstone and the Baganda. *B. Uganda Soc.*, 45, no. 4, p. 14-17.

2417. MASSICOTTE (E. Z.). Jacques de Noyon : nouveaux détails sur sa carrière. *B. Rech. hist.*, 42, vol. 48, p. 121-125.

2418. MONTGOMERIE (H. S.). The Morrison myth. *Mariner's Mirror*, 41, vol. 27, p. 69-76.

2419. MORISON (Samuel Eliot). Admiral of the ocean sea : a life of Christopher Columbus. London, Oxford Univ. Press; Toronto, McClelland, 42, in-8, xx-680 p., 21s.; $4.50. R : J. P. Pritchett, *Canad. hist. R.*, 42, vol. 23, p. 415-416. W.E.C.H., *Queen's Quar.*, 43, vol. 50, p. 211-213. J. A. Williamson, *History*, 43, vol. 28, p. 95-98. C.W.W., *Geography*, 43, vol. 28, p. 125.

2420. MORISON (S. E.). Portuguese voyages to America in the fifteenth century. London, Oxford Univ. Press, 42, in-8, 167 p., (maps), 8s. 6d. (Harvard hist. monogr., 14). R : G.H.T.K., *Geogr. J.*, 42, vol. 99, p. 105-106.

2421. MUTCH (T. D.). The first discovery of Australia, with an account of the voyage of the ' Duyfken ' and the career of Willem Jansz. *Roy. Austral. hist. Soc. J.*, 42, vol. 28, p. 303-352.

2422. OAKESHOTT (Walter F.). Founded upon the seas : a narrative of some English maritime and overseas enterprises, 1550-1616. London, Cambridge Univ. Press, 42, in-8, xii-200 p., (plates), 12s. 6d. R : D.B.Q., *History*, 45, vol. 30, p. 108-109. D. J. McDougall, *Canad. hist.*

R., 43, vol. 24, p. 301-302. M.D., *Geography*, 43, vol. 28, p. 96.

2423. PENROSE (B.). Urbane travellers, 1591-1635. London, Oxford Univ. Press, 42, in-8, 261 p., (illus.), 14s. R : W. F., *Geogr. J.*, 42, vol. 100, p. 187-188.

2424. PERHAM (Margery) and SIMMONS (Jack). African discovery : an anthology of exploration. London, Faber, 42, in-8, 280 p., (illus.), 12s. 6d. R : L. P. Mair, *Man*, 43, vol. 43, p. 119. *J. Roy. African Soc.*, 43, vol. 42, p. 88. A. J. Haile, *African Stud.*, 43, vol. 2, p. 217. E. Huxley, *Africa*, 43, vol. 14, p. 97-98. C. Young, *Int. R. Missions*, 43, vol. 32, p. 350-351.

2425. POHL (Frederick J.). Amerigo Vespucci, pilot major. London, Oxford Univ. Press, 45, in-8, 264 p., 20s. R : L. J. Burpee, *Canad. hist. R.*, 45, vol. 26, p. 190-192. E. G. R. Taylor, *Mariner's Mirror*, 45, vol. 31, p. 240.

2426. RICKARD (T. A.). The strait of Anian. *Brit. Columbia hist. Quar.*, 41, vol. 5, p. 161-184.

2427. ROBINSON (Percy J.). Some of Cartier's place-names, 1535-1536. *Canad. hist. R.*, 45, vol. 26, p. 401-405.

2428. ROWLAND (E. C.). The life and work of Lieutenant John Oxley, R.N. *Roy. Austral. hist. Soc. J.*, 42, vol. 28, p. 249-272.

2429. SANCEAU (Elaine). Portugal in quest of Prester John. London, Hutchinson, 43, in-8, 144 p., 10s. 6d.

2430. SEAVER (George). Scott of the Antarctic, a study in character. London, Murray, 40, in-8, 194 p., 10s. 6d.

2431. SIMMONS (Jack). A suppressed passage in 'Livingstone's Last Journals' relating to the death of Baron von der Decken. *J. Roy. African Soc.*, 41, vol. 40, p. 335-346.

2432. SMITH (Sir Andrew). The diary of Dr. A. Smith, director of the 'Expedition for exploring Central Africa', 1834-1836, ed. by P. R. Kirby. Vol. 2. Cape Town, Van Riebeeck Soc., 40, in-8, 342 p., (plates), 16s. R : C. M. D(oke), *Bantu Stud.*, 41, vol. 15, p. 303. W.L.S., *Geogr. J.*, 41, vol. 98, p. 106-107.

2433. SMYTHE (F. S.). Edward Whymper. London, Hodder, 40, in-8, 256 p., (illus.), 21s.

2433a. —— —— New ed. London, Hodder, 42, in-8, 256 p., (illus.), 12s. 6d.

2434. TATE (H. R.). A mediaeval navigator : Vasco da Gama. *J. Roy. African Soc.*, 44, vol. 43, p. 61-65.

2435. TOTHILL (B. H.). Some extracts from the life and travels of Theodore Kotschy. *Sudan Notes and Records*, 42, vol. 25, p. 109-121.

2436. TRIEBEL (L. A.) and BATT (J. C.). French exploration of Australia. Sydney, Éd. du Courrier australien, 43, in-8, 40 p., 2s. R : W. Dizson, *Roy. Austral. hist. Soc. J.*, 43, vol. 29, p. 257-260. H. L. Harris, *Austral. Quar.*, 44, vol. 16, no. 2, p. 124-125.

2437. UREN (Malcolm) and STEPHENS (Robert). Waterless horizons. Melbourne, Robertson & Mullins, 41, in-8, 256 p., (illus., maps), 10s. 6d. R : C. P. Conigrave, *Roy. Austral. hist. Soc. J.*, 42, vol. 28, p. 124-127.

2438. WALLIS (J. P. R.). Thomas Baines, explorer and artist, 1820-1875. London, Cape, 41, in-8, 351 p., 12s. 6d. R : *Scottish geogr. Mag.*, 41, vol. 57, p. 87-88. G.R.C., *Geogr. J.*, 41, vol. 97, p. 190-191.

2439. WILLIAMSON (J. A.). The ocean in English history. Ford lectures, 1939-40. Oxford, Clarendon Press, 41, in-8, 208 p., 10s. R : C. M. MacInnes, *Eng. hist. R.*, 43, vol. 58, p. 490-492. N.P., *Geography*, 43, vol. 28, p. 29.

2440. WITTEK (Paul). The Turkish documents in Hakluyt's 'Voyages'. *B. Inst. hist. Research*, 42, vol. 19, p. 121-139.

§ 4. Naval, Military and Air

2441. WHITE (A. S.) and MARTIN (Ernest J.). A bibliography of volunteering. *J. Soc. Army hist. Research*, 45, vol. 23, p. 2-29.

2442. ADYE (John Miller). The Umbeyla campaign of 1863 and the Bhutan expedition of 1865-66. Contemporary letters, ed. by H. Biddulph. *J. Soc. Army hist. Research*, 40, vol. 19, p. 34-47.

2443. ALBION (Robert Greenhalgh) and POPE (Jennie Barnes). Sea lanes in wartime : the American experience, 1775-1942. London, Allen, 43, in-8, 367 p., 15s. R : A. R. M. Lower, *Canad. hist. R.*, 43, vol. 24, p. 421-422.

2444. ALLIN (Sir Thomas). Journals, 1660-78, ed. by R. C. Anderson. London, Clowes, 40-41, 2 vols. in-8, 318, lii-257 p., 36s. (Publ., Navy Records Soc., vol. 79-80). R : M.A.L., *Mariner's Mirror*, 41, vol. 27, p. 350-352. C.T.A., *Eng. hist. R.*, 41, vol. 56, p. 671-672. M. A. Thomson, *History*, 43, vol. 28, p. 98-99.

2445. ANDERSON (R. C.). The ancestry of the 18th-century frigate. *Mariner's Mirror*, 41, vol. 27, p. 158-165.

2446. ANDERSON (R. C.). Notes on a collection of ship models. *Mariner's Mirror*, 42, vol. 28, p. 92-103.

2447. ANDERSON (R. C.). The two battles of Matapan, 1717 and 1718. *Mariner's Mirror*, 45, vol. 31, p. 33-42.

2448. ARMSTRONG (A. G.) and OMAN (Sir Charles). 'Plus que ça change . . .' 1 : Belisarius and the British (533 and 1943); 2 : Mud on the Garigliano—a winter memory of 1504. *Army Quar.*, 44, vol. 48, p. 100-106.

2449. ARTHUR (Sir G.). From Wellington to Wavell. London, Hutchinson, 42, in-8, 194 p., (illus.), 10s. 6d. R : *Army Quar.*, 42, vol. 44, p. 158-159.

2450. ATKINSON (C. T.). British forces in North America, 1774-81. Pt. 3. *J. Soc. Army hist. Research*, 41, vol. 20, p. 190-192.

2451. ATKINSON (C. T.). The Highlanders in Westphalia, 1760-62, and the development of light infantry. *J. Soc. Army hist. Research*, 41, vol. 20, p. 208-223.

2452. ATKINSON (C. T.). Material for military history in the reports of the Historical Manuscripts Commission. *J. Soc. Army hist. Research*, 42, vol. 21, p. 17-34.

2453. ATKINSON (C. T.). Notes on the Spanish succession war : gleanings from W.O. IV and other sources in the Public Record Office. *J. Soc. Army hist. Research*, 42, vol. 21, p. 83-96.

2454. ATKINSON (C. T.). Brihuega, December, 1710. *J. Soc. Army hist. Research*, 42, vol. 21, p. 112-122.

2455. ATKINSON (C. T.). The army under the early Hanoverians : more gleanings from W.O. IV and other sources in the Public Record Office. *J. Soc. Army hist. Research*, 42, vol. 21, p. 138-147.

2456. ATKINSON (C. T.). Supplementary report of the MSS. of Robert Graham of Fintry. London, H.M.S.O., 42, in-8, xvi-227 p., 6s. (Hist. MSS. comm., 81). R : C. Oman, *J. Soc. Army hist. Research*, 43, vol. 22, p. 36-37.

2457. ATKINSON (C. T.). Foreign regiments in the British army, 1793-1802. Pt. 1. *J. Soc. Army hist. Research*, 42, vol. 21, p. 175-181.

2458. ATKINSON (C. T.). Foreign regiments in the British army, 1793-

1802. Pt. 2-5. *J. Soc. Army hist. Research*, 43, vol. 22, p. 2-14, 45-52, 107-115, 132-142.

2459. ATKINSON (C. T.). British regiments afloat : Cape Passaro and other incidents. *J. Soc. Army hist. Research*, 45, vol. 23, p. 46-53.

2460. ATKINSON (C. T.). The Checquers Court MSS., some extracts relating to the Foot Guards, 1742-48. *J. Soc. Army hist. Research*, 45, vol. 23, p. 114-118.

2461. ATKINSON (C. T.). One of Marlborough's men : Matthew Bishop of Webb's. *J. Soc. Army hist. Research*, 45, vol. 23, p. 157-169.

2462. BACON (R. H.). Lord Fisher. New ed. London, Hodder, 42, 2 vols. in-8, 340, 335 p., (illus.), 15s.

2463. BALLARD (G. A.). British gunvessels of 1875. *Mariner's Mirror*, 40, vol. 26, p. 15-32, 375-387 ; 41, vol. 27, p. 132-146; 42, vol. 28, p. 308-313; 44, vol. 30, p. 65-73.

2464. BALLARD (G. A.). The great brig : H.M.S. Temeraire, 1875. *Mariner's Mirror*, 43, vol. 29, p. 149-162 (plates).

2465. BALLARD (G. A.). Victorian hulks under the white ensign. *Mariner's Mirror*, 45, vol. 31, p. 23-32.

2466. BARRINGTON (Samuel). The Barrington papers, selected letters and papers, ed. by D. Bonner-Smith. Vol. 2. London, Clowes, 41, in-8, xxxi-374 p., 21s. (Navy records soc., publ. 81). R : R.P., *Eng. hist. R.*, 42, vol. 57, p. 401-402. *Mariner's Mirror*, 42, vol. 28, p. 173-174. M. A. Thomson, *History*, 43, vol. 28, p. 98-99.

2467. The battle of Algiers, by a Friend of the National Maritime Museum. *Mariner's Mirror*, 41, vol. 27, p. 324-338.

2468. BERCHIN (Michel) and BEN-HORIN (E.). The Red army. London,

Allen & Unwin, 43, in-8, 242 p., 16s. R : J. Degras, *Int. Affairs*, 44, vol. 20, p. 296-297.

2469. BIDDULPH (H.). Shah Shujah's force (Kabul, 1839). *J. Soc. Army hist. Research*, 41, vol. 20, p. 65-71.

2470. BIDDULPH (H.). Battle of Deig, 13th November, 1804. *J. Soc. Army hist. Research*, 43, vol. 22, p. 71-73.

2471. BIDDULPH (Robert). The expedition to Kertch, 1855 : a contemporary account, ed. by H. Biddulph. *J. Soc. Army hist. Research*, 42, vol. 21, p. 128-135.

2472. BIRD (Sir W. D.). British strategy in Europe, 1803-1814. *Army Quar.*, 40, vol. 40, p. 299-308.

2473. BONNER-SMITH (D.). The abolition of the Navy Board. *Mariner's Mirror*, 45, vol. 31, p. 154-159.

2474. BONNER-SMITH (D.) and DEWAR (A. C.). Russian war, 1854 : Baltic and Black Sea, official correspondence. London, Clowes, 43, in-8, 434 p., 22s. (Publ., Navy Records Soc., vol. 83).

2475. BOTELER (John Harvey). Recollections of my sea life from 1808 to 1830, ed. by D. Bonner-Smith. London, Clowes, 42, in-8, 272 p., 25s. 6d. (Publ., Navy Records Soc., vol. 82). R : G.R.B., *Mariner's Mirror*, 43, vol. 29, p. 127-128. M. A. Thomson, *History*, 43, vol. 28, p. 98-99.

2476. BOURDILLON (Margaret T.). The battle of Cheriton. *Army Quar.*, 44, vol. 48, p. 233-240.

2477. BOWNESS (Edward). The later sailing ships. *Mariner's Mirror*, 43, vol. 29, p. 196-202.

2478. BOXER (C. R.). Admiral João Pereira Corte-Real and the construction of Portuguese East-Indiamen in the early 17th century. *Mariner's Mirror*, 40, vol. 26, p. 388-406.

2479. BRENNAN (Godfrey). The Light Horse and the Mounted Rifle Volunteer Corps. *J. Soc. Army hist. Research*, 42, vol. 21, p. 3-16.

2480. BRITTON (C. J.). Nelson and the River San Juan. *Mariner's Mirror*, 42, vol. 28, p. 213-221.

2481. BRITTON (C. J.). Nelson's statement of his services. *Mariner's Mirror*, 44, vol. 30, p. 18-21.

2482. BRODIE (Bernard). Sea power in the machine age. London, Oxford Univ. Press, 41, in-8, 466 p., 17s. R : H. W. Richmond, *Eng. hist. R.*, 45, vol. 60, p. 416-420.

2483. BROOKS (F. W.). A wage-scale for seamen, 1546. *Eng. hist. R.*, 45, vol. 60, p. 234-246.

2484. BROWNE (D. G.). Private Thomas Atkins, a history of the British soldier from 1840-1940. London, Hutchinson, 40, in-8, 334 p., 7s. 6d.

2485. CABLE (Boyd). The world's first clipper. *Mariner's Mirror*, 43, vol. 29, p. 66-91.

2486. CALLENDER (Sir Geoffrey). Sir John Mennes. *Mariner's Mirror*, 40, vol. 26, p. 276-285.

2487. CALLENDER (Sir Geoffrey) and BRITTON (C. J.). Admiral Benbow, fact and fiction. *Mariner's Mirror*, 44, vol. 30, p. 123-143, 200-219.

2488. CALVIN (D. D.). Ships in Pepys' ' Diary '. *Queen's Quar.*, 44, vol. 51, p. 297-305.

2489. CARMAN (W. Y.). Infantry clothing regulations, 1802. *J. Soc. Army hist. Research*, 40, vol. 19, p. 200-235.

2490. CARMAN (W. Y.). The capture of Martinique, 1809. *J. Soc. Army hist. Research*, 41, vol. 20, p. 1-4.

2491. CARR (H. G.). Pirate flags. *Mariner's Mirror*, 43, vol. 29, p. 131-134.

2492. CAVAGNARI (Sir Louis). Extracts from letters to Lady Cavagnari (1878-1879), ed. by H. L. O. Garrett. *Army Quar.*, 41, vol. 42, p. 322-336.

2493. CHAMIER (J. A.). The birth of the Royal Air Force : the early history and experiences of the flying services. London, Pitman, 43, in-8, 200 p., (illus., maps), 15s. R : *United Empire*, 44, vol. 35, p. 55-56.

2494. CHORLEY (Katharine). Armies and the art of revolution. London, Faber, 43, in-8, 274 p., 12s. 6d. R : C. Garsia, *Int. Affairs*, 44, vol. 20, p. 420-421.

2495. COATES (J. F.). Swansea Bay pilot boats. *Mariner's Mirror*, 44, vol. 30, p. 114-122.

2496. COLBY (E.). Masters of mobile warfare. London, Oxford Univ. Press, 43, in-8, 164 p., (illus.), 13s. 6d.

2497. CONN (Kenneth B.). The Royal Canadian Air Force historical section. *Canad. hist. R.*, 45, vol. 26, p. 246-254.

2498. COOPER (Ernest R.). The Davis back-staff or English quadrant. *Mariner's Mirror*, 44, vol. 30, p. 59-64.

2499. CORSAR (Kenneth Charles). The garrison of Scotland, 1719. *J. Soc. Army hist. Research*, 43, vol. 22, p. 15-19.

2500. COTTON (R. H. A.). English captives in Potsdam in the 18th century. *National R.*, 40, vol. 115, p. 567-575.

2501. COWPER (L. I.) ed. The King's Own, the story of a royal regiment, 1680-1914. Oxford, Clarendon Press, 40, 2 vols. in-8, xii-522, x-450 p., (plates, maps), 42s. R : *Army Quar.*, 40, vol. 41, p. 187-188.

2502. CRUICKSHANK (C. G.). An Elizabethan pensioner reserve. *Eng. hist. R.*, 41, vol. 56, p. 637-639. (Notes and documents).

2503. DAVIES (Godfrey). The formation of the New Model Army. *Eng. hist. R.*, 41, vol. 56, p. 103-105.

2504. DAWSON (R. McGregor). Winston Churchill at the Admiralty, 1911-1915. London, Oxford Univ. Press, 40, in-8, 33 p., 1s. 6d.

2505. DAWSON (R. M.). The cabinet minister and administration : A. J. Balfour and Sir Edward Carson at the Admiralty, 1915-17. *Canad. J. Econ. pol. Sci.*, 43, vol. 9, p. 1-38.

2506. DE BEER (G. R.). The Peninsular war. *Army Quar.*, 43, vol. 46, p. 235-244.

2507. DOUGLAS (Henry Kyd). I rode with Stonewall. London, Putnam, 42, in-8, 401 p., (plates), 25s.

2508. EARLE (Edward Mead). Makers of modern strategy : military thought from Machiavelli to Hitler. Toronto, Ryerson Press, 43, in-8, xii-553 p., $5.50. R : A. E. Prince, *Canad. hist. R.*, 44, vol. 25, p. 202-203. J.E.E., *Army Quar.*, 44, vol. 49, p. 127-128.

2509. ECKENRODE (H. J.) and CONRAD (Bryan). George B. McClellan : the man who saved the Union. London, Oxford Univ. Press, 42, in-8, 310 p., (maps), 16s. R : J.E.E., *Army Quar.*, 43, vol. 46, p. 125-126. D. W. B(rogan), *Eng. hist. R.*, 44, vol. 59, p. 127.

2510. The Elizabethan medical service. *Army Quar.*, 41, vol. 41, p. 300-312.

2511. ELLINGER (W. B.) and ROSINSKI (H.). Sea power in the Pacific, 1936-1941. London, Oxford Univ. Press, 42, in-8, 94 p., 5s.

2512. FARROW (John). The Royal Canadian Navy. *Canad. geogr. J.*, 40, vol. 21, p. 215-256.

2513. FFOULKES (Charles). The tank and its predecessors. *J. Soc. Army hist. Research*, 40, vol. 19, p. 91-98.

2514. FFOULKES (C.). General order book of the Royal Spelthorne Legion, Bedfont : the 'Home Guard' of 1803. *J. Soc. Army hist. Research*, 42, vol. 21, p. 38-48.

2515. FIRTH (C.). The regimental history of Cromwell's army. London, Oxford Univ. Press, 40, 2 vols. in-8, xxxvi-397, 398-768 p., 40s.

2516. FOX (R. M.). History of the Irish citizen army. Dublin, Duffy, 43, in-8, 252 p., 6s.

2517. FRANKLIN (Margaret). Pembroke : the first fortification scheme, 1757-1764. *Mariner's Mirror*, 40, vol. 26, p. 293-301.

2518. FREEMAN (Douglas Southall). Lee's lieutenants : a study in command. London, Scribner, 42-44, 3 vols. in-8, lvi-773, xlv-760, xlvi-862 p., (plates, maps), 67s. 6d.

2519. FULLER (J. F. C.). The decisive battles of the United States. London, Hutchinson, 42, in-8, 283 p., (maps), 18s.

2520. FYFE (Hamilton). 'Combined operations' in 1813 : how Wellington campaigned. *Army Quar.*, 43, vol. 45, p. 199-201.

2521. GANOE (W. A.). The history of the United States army. 2nd rev. ed. London, Appleton, 42, in-8, 640 p., (illus.), 30s.

2522. GRAHAM (G. S.). Fisheries and sea-power. *Canad. hist. Assoc. Rept.*, 41, p. 24-31.

2523. GRAHAM (G. S.). Britain's defence of Newfoundland : a survey, from the discovery to the present day. *Canad. hist. R.*, 42, vol. 23, p. 260-279.

2524. GREEN (Ernest). Corvettes of New France. *Ontario hist. Soc. Pap.*, 43, vol. 35, p. 29-38.

2525. GREENHILL (Basil). The rise and fall of the British coasting schooner. *Mariner's Mirror*, 41, vol. 27, p. 243-259.

2526. GREY (C. G.). A history of the Air Ministry. London, Allen & Unwin, 40, in-8, 319 p., 10s. 6d.

2527. HALL (C. S.). Benjamin Tallmadge, revolutionary soldier. London, Oxford Univ. Press, 43, in-8, 388 p., (illus.), 23s. 6d.

2528. HALL (J. T. S.). The Royal Indian navy. *J. central asian Soc.*, 45, vol. 32, p. 68-79.

2529. HARVEY (D. C.). Nova Scotia and the Canadian naval tradition. *Canad. hist. R.*, 42, vol. 23, p. 247-259.

2530. HAY (I.). The British infantryman : an informal history. London, Penguin, 43, in-8, 224 p., 9d.

2531. HAYES-McCOY (G. A.). Strategy and tactics in Irish warfare, 1593-1601. *Irish hist. Stud.*, 41, vol. 2, p. 255-279.

2532. HITCHCOCK (F. C.). Marshal Saxe. *Army Quar.*, 44, vol. 48, p. 64-67.

2533. HODGSON (Hamilton). The Lincolnshires at Omdurman, September, 1898 : diary, ed. by E. J. Martin. *J. Soc. Army hist. Research*, 42, vol. 21, p. 70-82.

2534. HOOD (D.). The Admirals Hood. London, Hutchinson, 42, in-8, 255 p., (illus.), 18s. R : C.M.R.C., *Mariner's Mirror*, 42, vol. 28, p. 167-169. *National R.*, 42, vol. 118, p. 397-398.

2535. HORNELL (James). A tentative classification of Arab sea-craft. *Mariner's Mirror*, 42, vol. 28, p. 11-40.

2536. HORNELL (J.). Outrigger devices : distribution and origin. *J. polynesian Soc.*, 43, vol. 52, p. 91-100.

2537. JAMES (G. F.). The Admiralty buildings, 1695-1723. *Mariner's Mirror*, 40, vol. 26, p. 356-374.

2538. JAMES (Sir William). Admiral Sir William Fisher. London, Macmillan, 43, in-8, 176 p., 8s. 6d. R : H. G. Thursfield, *National R.*, 43, vol. 121, p. 368-377.

2539. JARVIS (Rupert C.). Cope's march North, 1745. *Eng. hist. R.*, 45, vol. 60, p. 365-379.

2540. KELLY (Fred C.). The Wright brothers. London, Harrap, 44, in-8, 276 p., 10s. 6d.

2541. KING (Cecil). H.M.S. His Majesty's ships and their forbears. London, The Studio, 40, in-8, 328 p., (illus.), 12s. 6d. R : R.C.A., *Mariner's Mirror*, 41, vol. 27, p. 87. N.P., *Geography*, 41, vol. 26, p. 149.

2542. KING (C.). Atlantic charter. [History of the American Navy]. London, The Studio, 43, in-4, xi-232 p., (illus.), 15s.

2543. LAUGHTON (L. G. Carr). Wake or grain. [Interpretation of Commonwealth ' Fighting Instructions ']. *Mariner's Mirror*, 40, vol. 26, p. 339-344.

2544. LAWSON (Cecil C. P.). A history of the uniforms of the British Army. London, Davies, 40-42, 2 vols. in-8, 213, 276 p., (illus.), 30s. R : C. T. A[tkinson], *Eng. hist. R.*, 41, vol. 56, p. 165-166.

2545. LePELLEY (J.). The privateers of the Channel Islands, 1688-1713. *Mariner's Mirror*, 44, vol. 30, p. 22-37.

2546. LePELLEY (J.). The Jacobite privateers of James II. *Mariner's Mirror*, 44, vol. 30, p. 185-193.

2547. LEWIS (Frank R.). John Morris and the Carthagena expedition, 1739-1740. *Mariner's Mirror*, 40, vol. 26, p. 257-269.

2548. LEWIS (Michael A.). British ships and British seamen. London, Longmans, 40, in-8, 52 p., (plates), 1s. (British life and thought 7). R : *Mariner's Mirror*, 41, vol. 27, p. 352.

2549. LEWIS (M. A.). Armada guns : a comparative study of English and Spanish armaments. Section 1-8. *Mariner's Mirror*, 42, vol. 28, 41-73, 104-147, 231-245, 259-290; 43, vol. 29, p. 3-39, 100-121, 163-178, 203-231.

2550. LINDSAY (G. M.). The war on the civil and military fronts : the Lees Knowles lects. on military history for 1942. London, Cambridge Univ. Press, 42, in-8, 112 p., 5s.

2551. LLOYD (C.). A short history of the Royal Navy. London, Methuen, 42, in-8, 134 p., (diagrams), 5s.

2552. LONGSTAFF (F. V.). Esquimalt naval base : a history of its work and its defences. Victoria, B.C., The Author, 41, in-8, 189 p., (plates), $1.50. R : G. Callender, Mariner's Mirror, 42, vol. 28, p. 320. G.S.A., Geogr. J., 42, vol. 100, p. 267-268. G. S. Graham, Canad. hist. R., 43, vol. 24, p. 204-205.

2553. LYMAN (John). The ' Scottish Maid ' as ' the world's first clipper '. Mariner's Mirror, 44, vol. 30, p. 194-199.

2554. McCLINTOCK (M. H.). The queen thanks Sir Howard : the life of Sir Howard Elphinstone. London, Murray, 45, in-8, 273 p., 18s.

2555. MACDONELL (Ranald) and MACAULAY (Marcus). A history of the 4th Prince of Wales's Own Gurkha Rifles, 1857-1937. Edinburgh, Blackwood, 40, 2 vols. in-4, 449, 255 p., 84s. R : Army Quar., 41, vol. 41, p. 364-365.

2556. MACKENZIE-GRIEVE (Averil). The last of the Brazilian slavers, 1851. Mariner's Mirror, 45, vol. 31, p. 2-7.

2557. MARDER (Arthur J.). British naval policy, 1880-1905 : the anatomy of British sea power. London, Putnam, 41, in-8, xix-580-xv p., 31s. 6d. (Bur. of int. research ser.). R : G.S.G., Queen's Quar., 41, vol. 48, p. 420-423.

2558. MARTIN (E. J.). Women's war work with the army : a short account of the dress and badges of the women's auxiliary and nursing services, 1900-1945. J. Soc. Army hist. Research, 45, vol. 23, p. 54-65.

2559. MERRIMAN (R. D.). Captain George St. Lo, R.N., 1658-1718. Mariner's Mirror, 45, vol. 31, p. 13-22.

2560. MILLARD (Victor F. L.). Law and the Florida. Mariner's Mirror, 43, vol. 29, p. 187-190.

2561. MILLARD (V. F. L.). Ships of India, 1834-1934. Mariner's Mirror, 44, vol. 30, p. 144-153.

2562. MILLARD (V. F. L.). Ships of Devon and Cornwall, 1652-1942. Isleworth, Kenilworth Nautical Publ. Co., 45, in-8, 80 p., (illus.), 3s. R : Mariner's Mirror, 45, vol. 31, p. 176.

2563. MIVILLE (Rosaire). Notes sur les puits de Wolfe à Québec. B. Rech. hist., 42, vol. 48, p. 1-12.

2564. MURRAY (Lady Oswyn). The making of a civil servant : Sir Oswyn Murray, G.C.B., Secretary of the Admiralty, 1917-1936. London, Methuen, 40, in-8, xi-212 p., (plates), 10s. 6d.

2565. NAUTICUS. Sir Charles Vinicombe Penrose, Vice-Admiral of the White. Mariner's Mirror, 43, vol. 29, p. 92-99.

2566. NELSON (Horatio, Visct.). The Nelson touch : an anthology of Lord Nelson's letters, compiled by Clemence Dane. London, Heinemann, 42, in-8, 285 p., 15s.

2567. NICKERSON (H.). The armed horde, 1793-1939, a study of the rise, survival and decline of the mass army. London, Putnam, 41, in-8, 427 p., 18s.

2568. NICOLAS (V.). The little ' Indus ' (1833-1837). Mariner's Mirror, 45, vol. 31, p. 210-213.

2569. O'GARA (G. C.). Theodore Roosevelt and the rise of the modern navy. London, Oxford Univ. Press, 43, in-8, 138 p., (illus., tables), 10s. R : H.W.R., Eng. hist. R., 44, vol. 59, p. 285-286.

2570. O'NEIL (B. H. St. J.). Early artillery fortifications at Oslo and Trondheim. *Antiq. J.*, 41, vol. 21, p. 56-61 (illus.).

2571. OSIPOV (K.). Alexander Suvorov, tr. from the Russian by E. Bone. London, Hutchinson, 44, in-8, 207 p., (maps), 15s.

2572. PAFFORD (J. H. P.) ed. Accounts of the parliamentary garrisons of Great Chalfield and Malmesbury, 1645-1646. Devizes, Wilts. Archaeol. and Nat. Hist. Soc., 40, in-8, 112 p., subscribers only. (Records branch, vol. 2). R : E. S. de B., *B. Inst. hist. Research*, 41, vol. 19, p. 31. R. C. Latham, *History*, 43, vol. 28, p. 220-222.

2573. PARKER (W. M.). Rodney and his naval physician. *Army Quar.*, 41, vol. 42, p. 150-164.

2574. PEMBERTON (John C.). Pemberton, defender of Vicksburg. London, Oxford Univ. Press, 42, in-8, xiv-350 p., 16s. R : J.E.E., *Army Quar.*, 43, vol. 46, p. 127.

2575. PENLINGTON (Norman). General Hutton and the problem of military imperialism in Canada, 1898-1900. *Canad. hist. R.*, 43, vol. 24, p. 156-171.

2576. PREEDY (George R.) pseud. The life of rear-admiral John Paul Jones. London, Jenkins, 40, in-8, 312 p., 12s. 6d. R : R.C.A., *Mariner's Mirror*, 40, vol. 26, p. 322.

2577. RATCLIFFE (B.). Marshal de Grouchy and the guns of Waterloo. London, Muller, 42, in-8, 48 p., (map), 5s.

2578. RAWLINSON (H. G.). The history of the 3rd Battalion, 7th Rajput Regiment (Duke of Connaught's Own). London, Oxford Univ. Press, 41, in-4, 324 p., (plates, maps), 42s. R : C. T. A[tkinson], *Eng. hist. R.*, 41, vol. 56, p. 676.

2579. RAWLINSON (H. G.). Our Mediterranean sea-power, how it grew. *National R.*, 44, vol. 122, p. 310-315.

2580. RICHMOND (Sir Herbert W.). Amphibious warfare in British history. London, Wheat (for the Association), 41, in-8, 31 p., 1s. 1d. (Hist. Assoc. pamph., 119). R : *Army Quar.*, 41, vol. 42, p. 378. *Mariner's Mirror*, 41, vol. 27, p. 271-272.

2581. RICHMOND (Sir H. W.). The invasion of Britain : an account of plans, attempts and counter-measures from 1586-1918. London, Methuen, 41, in-8, 86 p., 2s. 6d. R : *Mariner's Mirror*, 41, vol. 27, p. 350.

2582. RICHMOND (Sir H. W.). British strategy : military and economic. A historical review and its contemporary lessons. Toronto ; London, Macmillan, 41, in-8, viii-157 p., $1.10 ; 3s. 6d. (Current problems). R : G.S.G., *Queen's Quar.*, 41, vol. 48, p. 420-423.

2583. RICHMOND (Sir H. W.). Naval history in public education. *History*, 42, vol. 27, p. 1-14.

2584. RUTHERFORD (G.). The capture of the *Ardent* [1779]. *Mariner's Mirror*, 41, vol. 27, p. 106-131.

2585. RUTHERFORD (G.). Sidelights on Commodore Johnstone's expedition to the Cape. Pt. 1-2. *Mariner's Mirror*, 42, vol. 28, p. 189-212, 290-308.

2586. RUTTER (O.). Red ensign : a history of convoy. London, Hale, 43, in-8, 214 p., (illus.), 12s. 6d.

2587. SALTONSTALL (William G.). Ports of Piscataqua : soundings in the maritime history of Portsmouth, N.H., customs district from the days of Queen Elizabeth. London, Oxford Univ. Press, 41, in-4, xii-244 p., (plates, maps), 15s. R : *Mariner's Mirror*, 42, vol. 28, p. 175.

2588. SAUNDERS (H. St. G.). Per Ardua : the rise of British air power,

1911-1939. London, Oxford Univ. Press, 44, in-8, 368 p., (illus., maps), 15s. R : O. Williams, *National R.*, 44, vol. 123, p. 511-517. L. MacLean, *Int. Affairs*, 45, vol. 21, p. 263.

2589. SCOBIE (I. H. Mackay). The Highland independent companies of 1745-47. *J. Soc. Army hist. Research*, 41, vol. 20, p. 5-37.

2590. STANLEY (George F. G.). The Royal Nova Scotia regiment, 1793-1802. *J. Soc. Army hist. Research*, 42, vol. 21, p. 157-170.

2591. STANLEY (G. F. G.). The Canadian militia during the ancien régime. *J. Soc. Army hist. Research*, 43, vol. 22, p. 157-168.

2592. STANLEY (G. F. G.). British operations in the American North-West, 1812-15. *J. Soc. Army hist. Research*, 43, vol. 22, p. 91-106.

2593. STEEL (Watson A.). Captain Henry Steel and the New South Wales Corps, later the 102nd Regiment. *Roy. Austral. hist. Soc. J.*, 43, vol. 29, p. 35-44, 69-87.

2594. STONE (Lawrence). The Armada campaign of 1588. *History*, 44, vol. 29, p. 120-143.

2595. SUETER (Sir Murray). The evolution of the tank : a record of Royal Naval Air Service caterpillar experiments. New, rev. ed. London, Hutchinson, 41, in-8, 408 p., (illus.), 15s.

2596. SUMMERSON (John). The monuments in the Church of St. Nicholas, Deptford. *Mariner's Mirror*, 41, vol. 27, p. 277-289.

2597. SUMNER (Percy). Great wardrobe accounts, 1689 to 1702. *J. Soc. Army hist. Research*, 41, vol. 20, p. 139-153.

2598. TANGYE (Nigel). Britain in the air. London, Collins, 44, in-8, 48 p., (plates), 4s. 6d. (Britain in pictures).

2599. TATE (H. R.). Some early reminiscences of a transport officer : Ashanti field force and Ogaden punitive force. *J. Roy. african Soc.*, 42, vol. 41, p. 101-107.

2600. TEICHMAN (Oskar). The yeomanry as an aid to civil power, 1795-1867. 2 pts. *J. Soc. Army hist. Research*, 40, vol. 19, p. 75-91, 127-143.

2601. TUCKER (Gilbert Norman). The Royal Canadian naval historical section and its work. *Canad. hist. R.*, 45, vol. 26, p. 239-245.

2602. TYLDEN (G.). The permanent colonial forces of Cape Colony. *J. Soc. Army hist. Research*, 40, vol. 19, p. 149-159.

2603. TYLDEN (G.). A South African soldier : Colonel I. P. Ferreira, C.M.G. *J. Soc. Army hist. Research*, 42, vol. 21, p. 96-99.

2604. TYLDEN (G.). Major-General Sir Henry Somerset, 1794-1862. *J. Soc. Army hist. Research*, 43, vol. 22, p. 27-34.

2605. TYLDEN (G.). The commando system in South Africa, 1795-1881. *J. Soc. Army hist. Research*, 45, vol. 23, p. 34-38.

2606. TYLDEN (G.). Lancers. *J. Soc. Army hist. Research*, 45, vol. 23, p. 44-46.

2607. WARD (S. G. P.). The quartermaster-general's department in the Peninsula, 1809-1814. *J. Soc. Army hist. Research*, 45, vol. 23, p. 133-154:

2608. WARDLE (Arthur C.). Mersey-built blockade-runners of the American Civil War. *Mariner's Mirror*, 42, vol. 28, p. 179-188.

2609. WAVELL (Sir Archibald). Allenby, a study in greatness. London, Harrap, 40-43, 2 vols. in-8, 312, xiii-161 p., (maps), 28s. 6d. R (Vol. 1) : J.S.S., *J. central asian Soc.*, 40.

vol. 27, p. 466-469. *National R.*, 40, vol. 115, p. 491-493. *Army Quar.*, 40, vol. 41, p. 188-190. (Vol. 2): N.G.D., *J. central asian Soc.*, 44, vol. 31, p. 212-215.

2610. WEERD (H. A. de). Great soldiers of the two world wars. London, Hale, 43, in-8, 260 p., (illus.), 12s. 6d.

2611. WHITE (Dimitri Fedotoff). The growth of the Red army. London, Oxford Univ. Press, 45, in-8, xiv-486 p., 18s. 6d. R : E.H.W., *Army Quar.*, 45, vol. 51, p. 143.

2612. WILSON (Sir Arnold). Awards for military gallantry. *Quar. R.*, 40, vol. 274, p. 18-26.

2613. WINSTER (Lord). The Admiralty. *Pol. Quar.*, 42, vol. 13, p. 233-247.

2614. WINTON-CLARE (C.). A shipbuilder's war. [War of 1812-15 in North America]. *Mariner's Mirror*, 43, vol. 29, p. 139-148.

2615. WINTRINGHAM (Tom). The War Office. *Pol. Quar.*, 42, vol. 13, p. 117-129.

2616. WRIGHT (L. B.) and MACLEOD (J. H.). The first Americans in North Africa : William Eaton's struggle against the Barbary pirates, 1799-1805. London, Oxford Univ. Press, 45, in-8, 240 p., 20s.

2617. YOUNG (Peter). The Prince of Wales's Regiment of Horse, 1642-46. *J. Soc. Army hist. Research*, 45, vol. 23, p. 107-113.

MODERN RELIGIOUS HISTORY

§ 1. General

2618. ADDISON (William George). Religious equality in modern England, 1714-1914. London, S.P.C.K., 44, in-8, vi-177 p., 8s. 6d.

2619. BATTEN (J. M.). John Dury : advocate of Christian reunion. London, Cambridge Univ. Press, 44, in-8, vi-228 p., 15s.

2620. CLARK (S. D.). Religious organization and the rise of the Canadian nation, 1850-85. *Canad. hist. Assoc. Rept.*, 44, p. 86-97.

2621. CLARKE (W. K. Lowther). Eighteenth century piety. London, S.P.C.K., 44, in-8, 168 p., (illus.), 10s. 6d. R : N. Sykes, *Theology*, 45, vol. 48, p. 134-135.

2622. COLLINS (J. B.). Christian mysticism in the Elizabethan age. London, Oxford Univ. Press, 41, in-8, 267 p., 15s.

2623. FOOTE (Henry Wilder). Three centuries of American hymnody. London, Oxford Univ. Press, 42, in-8, x-418 p., 17s. R : A. Peel, *Congreg. Quar.*, 44, vol. 22, p. 71-72.

2624. HARDYMAN (J. T.). The growth of missionary co-operation in Madagascar. *Congreg. Quar.*, 44, vol. 22, p. 44-50.

2625. LATOURETTE (K. S.). A history of the expansion of Christianity. Vol. 3-6. London, Eyre, 40-45, 4 vols. in-8, 512, 516, 509, 502 p., (maps), 93s. R (Vol. 3) : W. K. L. Clarke, *Theology*, 40, vol. 40, p. 468-469. J. S. Whale, *Int. R. Missions*, 40, vol. 29, p. 274-276. (Vol. 4) : J. S. Whale, *Int. R. Missions*, 41, vol. 30, p. 406-410. A. Peel, *Congreg. Quar.*, 42, vol. 20, p. 359-360.

2626. NORTHCOTT (Cecil). One hundred and fifty years of Christian missions. *Quar. R.*, 43, vol. 280, p. 179-192.

2627. PEASTON (A. Elliott). Nineteenth century liturgies. *Trans. Unitarian hist. Soc.*, 41, vol. 7, p. 215-225.

2628. POWICKE (F. M.). The Reformation in England. London, Oxford Univ. Press, 41, in-8, 144 p., 6s. R : *National R.*, 41, vol. 117, p. 357. J. D. Mackie, *History*, 44, vol. 29, p. 90-93. F.J.S., *J. presb. hist. Soc.*, 42, vol. 7, p. 142. R. N. Carew Hunt, *19th Century*, 42, vol. 131, p. 238-239.

2629. WHITAKER (W. B.). The 18th century English Sunday. London, Epworth Press, 40, in-8, 304 p., 13s. 6d.

2630. WHITNEY (J. P.). The history of the Reformation. London, S.P.C.K., 40, in-8, xv-527 p., 12s. 6d.

2631. WILLOUGHBY (H.). Soldiers' Bibles through three centuries. London, Cambridge Univ. Press, 45, in-8, viii-60 p., 10s. 6d.

2632. WRIGHT (Arthur). The church bells of Monmouthshire. *Archaeol. cambrensis*, 40, vol. 95, p. 36-47, 229-242; 41, vol. 96, p. 49-68, 175-184.

§ 2. Roman Catholicism

a. GENERAL

2633. HUXLEY (Aldous). Grey eminence : a study in religion and politics. London, Chatto & Windus, 41, in-8, 342 p., 15s.

2634. SOMMER (E.). Into exile : the history of the counter-reformation in Bohemia, 1620-1650, tr. by V. Grove. London, New Europe Publ. Co., 44, in-8, 154 p., 8s. 6d.

b. HISTORY OF THE POPES

2635. FERRARA (O.). The Borgia pope : Alexander the sixth, tr. by F. J. Sheed. London, Sheed & Ward, 42, in-8, 448 p., 16s.

2636. HOARE (F. R.). The Papacy and the modern state. London, Burns & Oates, 40, in-8, 427 p., 15s. R : *National R.*, 40, vol. 115, p. 364-365.

2637. PASTOR (L. von). The history of the Popes, tr. by E. Graf. Vol. 30 : Innocent X, 1644-1655. Vol. 31 : Alexander VII, 1655, Clement IX, 1667-1669, Clement X, 1670-1676. Vol. 32 : Innocent XI, 1676-1689, Alexander VIII, 1689-1691, Innocent XII, 1691-1700. Vol. 33-34. London, Kegan Paul, 40-42, 5 vols. in-8, xlvii-467, xii-519, xiv-706, 554, 596 p., 16s. each.

2638. ROPE (Henry E. G.). Benedict XV, the Pope of peace. London, Gifford, 41, in-8, 319 p., 7s. 6d.

c. HISTORY BY COUNTRIES

Australia

2639. ULLATHORNE (William Bernard) abp. of Birmingham. From cabin-boy to archbishop : autobiography. Intr. by Shane Leslie. London, Burns, Oates, 41, in-8, 310 p., 15s.

Canada

2640. LORTIE (Lucien). Bibliographie analytique de l'oeuvre de l'abbé Arthur Maheux, precédée d'une biographie. Québec, 42, in-8, 159 p. R : R.G.T., *Queen's Quar.*, 43, vol. 50, p. 311-312.

2641. ADAIR (E. R.). The church of Saint-Michel de Vaudreuil. *B. Rech. hist.*, 43, vol. 49, p. 38-49, 75-89.

2642. ALFRED (brother). The conversion of Sir Allan MacNab, bart. (1798-1862). *Canad. Cath. hist. Assoc. Rept.*, 42/43, vol. 10, p. 47-64.

2643. BATTLE (Thomas F.). The Rt. Rev. John Farrell, D.D., first bishop of Hamilton. *Canad. Cath. hist. Assoc. Rept.*, 42/43, vol. 10, p. 39-45.

2644. BEAUREGARD (Lucien). La part de M. Isaac-Stanislas Désaulniers à l'introduction du Thomisme au Canada français vers l'époque de la renaissance religieuse de 1840 à 1855. *Canad. Cath. hist. Assoc. Rept.*, 41-42, vol. 9, Fr. Sect., p. 77-87.

2645. CADIEUX (Lorenzo). Fondateurs du diocèse du Sault Ste-Marie. *Canad. Cath. hist. Assoc. Rept.*, 42/43, vol. 10, sect. 2, p. 77-96.

2646. CARON (Ivanhoë). Liste des prêtres séculiers et religieux qui ont exercé le saint ministre en Canada, 1604-1700. *B. Rech. hist.*, 41, vol. 47, p. 76-78, 160-175, 193-201, 225-235, 258-268, 289-299.

2647. CARSON (Victoria Mueller). St. Mary's church, Hamilton : the old cathedral church and its parish. *Canad. Cath. hist. Assoc. Rept.*, 42/43, vol. 10, p. 65-73.

2648. CHARLEVOIX (P. de). La figure la plus populaire : Catherine Tekakwitha. *B. Rech. hist.*, 43, vol. 49, p. 321-338.

2649. CODERE (L. E.). The establishment of St. Patrick's church in Sherbrooke, Quebec; its development and influence throughout a period of 57 years. *Canad. Cath. hist. Assoc. Rept.*, 43-44, vol. 11, Engl. Sect., p. 129-142.

2650. COTE (F. X.). Mgr. de Forbin-Janson, évêque de Nancy et de Toul, et le mouvement religieux du Québec vers 1840. *Canad. Cath. hist. Assoc. Rept.*, 41-42, vol. 9, Fr. Sect., p. 95-118.

2651. EVAN (Richard Xavier). The literature relative to Kateri Tekakwitha, the Lily of the Mohawks, 1656-1680. *B. Rech. hist.*, 40, vol. 46, p. 193-209, 241-255.

2652. GIRARD (Arthur). Monseigneur Joseph-Antoine-Irénée Douville, P.A.V.G., et le séminaire de Nicolet (1838-1918). *Canad. Cath.*

hist. *Assoc. Rept.*, 43-44, vol. 11, Fr. Sect., p. 137-162.

2653. GROULX (Lionel). Le conflit religieux au lendemain de 1760. *Canad. Cath. hist. Assoc. Rept.*, 39/40 (41), vol. 7, Fr. Sect., p. 11-26.

2654. GROULX (L.). La situation religieuse au Canada français vers 1840. *Canad. Cath. hist. Assoc. Rept.*, 41-42, vol. 9, Fr. Sect., p. 51-75.

2655. JOYAL (Arthur). Mgr. F.-X. Cloutier, prophète de Notre-Dame du Cap. Les Trois-Rivières, Imprimerie Saint-Joseph, 40, in-12, 64 p. R : H. Morisseau, *R. Univ. Ottawa*, 41, vol. 11, p. 270.

2656. LUSIGNAN (Lucien). Essai sur les écrits de deux martyrs canadiens [St. Jean de Brebeuf & St. Isaac Jogues]. *B. Rech. hist.*, 44, vol. 50, p. 174-192.

2657. MacLEAN (Alexander D.). The early history of St. Michael's parish, Baddeck, Nova Scotia. *Canad. Cath. hist. Assoc. Rept.*, 43-44, vol. 11, Engl. Sect., p. 109-116.

2658. McNEIL (Evangeline). The importance of the retreat movement in Nova Scotia. *Canad. Cath. hist. Assoc. Rept.*, 42/43, vol. 10, p. 107-115.

2659. MAURAULT (Olivier). La fondation de nouveaux diocèses et l'essor apostolique du Canada français sous Mgr. Bourget. *Canad. Cath. hist. Assoc. Rept.*, 41-42, vol. 9, Fr. Sect., p. 43-49.

2660. MORIN (Victor). La mysticité des fondateurs de Montréal. *Canad. Cath. hist. Assoc. Rept.*, 41-42, vol. 9, Fr. Sect., p. 13-38.

2661. MULLINS (Gladys) and WALSH (T. J.). English-speaking priests who evangelized the Eastern townships ; Pioneer English Catholics in the Eastern townships. *Canad. Cath. hist. Assoc. Rept.*, 39/40 (41), vol. 7, p. 43-70.

2662. OSBORNE (W. J.). The Rt. Rev. William Dollard, D.D., first Bishop of New Brunswick. *Canad. Cath. hist. Assoc. Rept.*, 41-42, vol. 9, p. 23-28.

2663. PACIFIQUE (r.p.). Chroniques des plus anciennes églises de l'Acadie. Montréal, l'Echo de Saint-François, 44, in-8, xx-147 p., $1.00. R : A. G. Bailey, *Canad. hist. R.*, 45, vol. 26, p. 446-447.

2664. POULIOT (Léon). Note sur l'église du Bas-Canada de 1831 à 1833 : l'érection civile des paroisses. *B. Rech. hist.*, 40, vol. 46, p. 289-291.

2665. POULIOT (L.). Le retour des Jésuites au Canada (1842). *B. Rech. hist.*, 42, vol. 46, p. 193-201.

2666. POULIOT (L.). La réaction catholique de Montréal, 1840-1841. Montréal, Imprimerie du Messager, 42, in-8, 121 p. R : R. M. Saunders, *Canad. hist. R.*, 44, vol. 25, p. 76-79.

2667. ROUX (Alphonse). Monseigneur Calixte Marquis et l'érection du diocèse de Nicolet. *Canad. Cath. hist. Assoc. Rept.*, 43-44, vol. 11, Fr. Sect., p. 33-87.

2668. WILSON (F. J.). The Most Rev. Thomas L. Connolly, Archbishop of Halifax. *Canad. Cath. hist. Assoc. Rept.*, 43-44, vol. 11, Engl. Sect., p. 55-108.

France

2669. PALMER (R. R.). Catholics and unbelievers in 18th century France. London, Oxford Univ. Press, 40, in-8, 236 p., 18s.

2670. RABY (F. J. E.). A note on Frédéric Ozanam. *Theology*, 41, vol. 43, p. 332-340.

Great Britain

2671. BLUNDELL (F. O.). Old Catholic Lancashire. Vol. 3. London, Burns, Oates, 42, in-8, 244 p., (illus.), 6s.

2672. GREAVES (R. W.). Roman Catholic relief and the Leicester election of 1826. *Trans. Roy. hist. Soc.*, 40, vol. 22, p. 199-223.

2673. GWYNN (Denis). The second spring, 1818-1852 : a study of the Catholic revival in England. London, Burns, Oates, 42, in-8, 246 p., 9s. R : R. P. McDermott, *Theology*, 43, vol. 46, p. 112-113.

2674. HEENAN (J. C.). Cardinal Hinsley. London, Burns, Oates, 44, in-8, 242 p., (illus.), 8s. 6d.

2675. HUGHES (Philip). Rome and the counter-reformation in England. London, Burns, Oates, 42, in-8, ix-446 p., 12s. 6d. R : G. F. Nuttall, *Congreg. Quar.*, 42, vol. 20, p. 364-365.

2676. LEDDY (J. F.). Newman and his critics : a chapter in the history of ideas. *Canad. Cath. hist. Assoc. Rept.*, 42/43, vol. 10, p. 25-38.

2677. MAY (J. Lewis). Cardinal Newman. London, Bles, 45, in-8, x-230 p., 5s. R : A. C. Scupholme, *Theology*, 45, vol. 48, p. 236.

2678. OLDMEADOW (E.). Francis Cardinal Bourne. London, Burns, Oates, 40-44, 2 vols. in-8, 415, 421 p., (illus.), 34s. R : A. Peel, *Congreg. Quar.*, 44, vol. 22, p. 276-277. I. R. Young, *Theology*, 44, vol. 47, p. 188-189.

2679. POPE (Hugh). A brief history of the English version of the New Testament first published at Rheims in 1582, continued down to the present day. *Library*, 40, vol. 20, p. 351-376; vol. 21, p. 44-77.

2680. VAUGHAN (Herbert, cardinal). Letters to Lady Herbert of Lea, 1867 to 1903, ed. by Shane Leslie. London, Burns, Oates, 42, in-8, xxiii-453 p., 18s. R : A. R. Vidler, *Theology*, 43, vol. 46, p. 20-21.

2681. WIGFIELD (W. M.). Religious statistics concerning recusants of the Stuart period. *Theology*, 40, vol. 41, p. 94-102.

2682. WILLIAMS (W. Gilbert). Recusancy in Caernarvonshire in the time of Charles I. *B. Board celtic Stud.*, 40, vol. 10, p. 271-273.

Ireland

2683. HARTFORD (R. R.). Godfrey Day, missionary, pastor and primate. London, Talbot Press, 40, in-8, 246 p., 7s. 6d. R : J. C. Beckett, *Irish hist. Stud.*, 41, vol. 2, p. 343. H. M. Harriss, *Theology*, 41, vol. 42, p. 313-314.

2684. O'FERRALL (Richard) and O'CONNELL (Robert). Commentarius Rinuccinianus de sedis apostolicae legatione ad foederatos Hiberniae Catholicos per annos 1645-49, ed. by S. Kavanagh. Vol. 4 (1649-51); 5 (1652-66). Dublin, 41-44, 2 vols. in-8, xvii-663, xiv-504 p., 84s. (Irish MSS. comm.). R : D. F. Cregan, *Irish hist. Stud.*, 42, vol. 3, p. 125; 45, vol. 4, p. 273-275.

2685. ROGERS (P.). Father Theobald Mathew, apostle of temperance. Dublin, Browne & Nolan, 43, in-8, 192 p., (illus.), 10s. 6d.

2686. RONAN (M. V.). An apostle of Catholic Dublin, Father Henry Young, 1786-1869. Dublin, Browne & Nolan, 44, in-8, 328 p., (illus.), 15s.

Japan

2687. MEMORIAN-SHEEHY (Rev. Brother). The Catholic church in Japan. *Canad. Cath. hist. Assoc. Rept.*, 41-42, vol. 9, p. 59-64.

United States of America

2688. McAVOY (T. T.). The Catholic Church in Indiana, 1789-1834. London, King, 43, in-8, 219 p., 11s. 6d.

d. HISTORY OF MONASTIC AND OTHER ORDERS

2689. ANSON (Peter F.). The Benedictines of Caldey: the Anglican Benedictines of Caldey and their submission to the Catholic Church. London, Burns, Oates, 40, in-8, xxx-205 p., 7s. 6d. R : H. L. Hubbard, *Theology*, 40, vol. 40, p. 472-473.

2690. BANIM (F. E.). The centenary of the Oblates of Mary Immaculate. *Canad. Cath. hist. Assoc. Rept.*, 41-42, vol. 9, p. 29-23.

2691. BASKERVILLE (G.). English monks and the suppression of the monasteries. London, Cape, 40, in-8, 312 p., 7s. 6d. (Bedford hist. ser., 7).

2692. BRODRICK (James). The origin of the Jesuits. London, Longmans, 40, in-8, vii-274 p., 10s. 6d.

2693. CHADWICK (Hubert). The Scots College, Douai, 1580-1613. *Eng. hist. R.*, 41, vol. 56, p. 571-585.

2694. Les congrégations de femmes au Canada. *B. Rech. hist.*, 44, vol. 50, p. 33-50.

2695. COURCHESNE (Georges). Notes sur m. l'abbé Thomas-Marie-Olivier Maurault (1839-1887). *Canad. Cath. hist. Assoc. Rept.*, 43-44, vol. 11, Fr. Sect., p. 15-32.

2696. DAVIES (J. Conway). Dominicans in Wales. *Nat. Library Wales J.*, 43, vol. 3, p. 50-51.

2697. DUNNE (P. M.). Pioneer Jesuits in northern Mexico. London, Cambridge Univ. Press, 45, in-8, xii-228 p., 18s.

2698. FITZPATRICK (J. D.). Edmund Rice. Dublin, Gill, 45, in-8, xvi-364.p., 8s. 6d.

2699. GAGNON (Onésime). Les Jésuites au début de la colonie [la Nouvelle-France]. *B. Rech. hist.*, 41, vol. 47, p. 3-14.

2700. GOSSELIN (Paul-E.). Mémoire sur l'abbé Louis Ango de Maizerets. *Canad. Cath. hist. Assoc. Rept.*, 42/43, vol. 10, sect. 2, p. 39-45.

2701. KIDD (K. E.). The excavation of Fort Ste. Marie. *Canad. hist. R.*, 41, vol. 22, p. 403-415.

2702. LALLY (T. J.). The excavations of old Fort St. Marie. *Canad. Cath. hist. Assoc. Rept.*, 41-42, vol. 9, p. 15-22.

2703. LANCTOT (Gustave). Un abbé part en guerre contre un Sulpicien. *Canad. Cath. hist. Assoc. Rept.*, 42/43, vol. 10, sect. 2, p. 17-37.

2704. MARIE-IMMACULÉE (Soeur). Monseigneur Joseph-Calixte Marquis et les Soeurs de l'Assomption de la Sainte Vierge. *Canad. Cath. hist. Assoc. Rept.*, 43-44, vol. 11, Fr. Sect., p. 89-111.

2705. MAURAULT (Olivier). Notes sur les Sulpiciens aux alentours de Hamilton au 17e siècle. *Canad. Cath. hist. Assoc. Rept.*, 42/43, vol. 10, sect. 2, p. 11-15.

2706. Les ordres religieux au Canada. *B. Rech. hist.*, 44, vol. 50, p. 3-12.

2707. PAUL-EMILE (Soeur). Les débuts d'une congrégation : les Soeurs Grises de la Croix à Bytown, 1845-1850. *Canad. Cath. hist. Assoc. Rept.*, 42/43, vol. 10, sect. 2, p. 47-76.

2708. ST. PAUL (Mother M.). From Desenzano to 'The Pines' : a sketch of the history of the Ursulines of Ontario, with a brief history of the Order. Toronto, Macmillan, 41, in-8, xviii-387 p., $4.00. R : V. Jensen, *Canad. hist. R.*, 41, vol. 22, p. 444.

2709. WHITE (Newport B.). Extents of Irish monastic possessions, 1540-1541, from MSS. in the Public Record Office, London. Dublin, Stationery Office, 43, in-8, xii-453 p., 21s. (Irish MSS. comm.). R : A. G. Dickens, *Eng. hist. R.*, 45, vol. 60, p. 114-116. D. B. Quinn, *Irish hist. Stud.*, 45, vol. 4, p. 354-357.

e. HISTORY OF MISSIONS

2710. BARABÉ (Paul Henri). Mgr. Adélard Langevin, O.M.I., éducateur. *R. Univ. Ottawa*, 41, vol. 11, p. 338-348, 461-471.

2711. DANAHAR (James R.). The Rev. Richard Jackson, missionary to the Sulpicians. *Canad. Cath. hist. Assoc. Rept.*, 43-44, vol. 11, Engl. Sect., p. 49-54.

2712. KIRISHITO-KI and SAYO-YOROKU. Japanische Dokumente zur Missionsgeschichte des 17. Jahrhunderts. Ins Deutsche übertragen von G. Voss und H. Cieslik. London, Paul, 41, in-4, xii-122 p., (illus.), 12s. 6d. (Monumenta Nipponica monogr.).

2713. LE CHEVALLIER (Jules). Batoche : les missionnaires du Nord-Ouest pendant les troubles de 1885. Montréal, Presse Dominicaine, 41, in-8, 310 p., $1.50. R : W. N. Sage, *Canad. hist. R.*, 42, vol. 23, p. 87-88.

2714. McGUINNESS (Robert J.). The missionary journey of Father Peter De Smet, S.J., in what are now the dioceses of Nelson, B.C., and Calgary, Alberta, and the archdiocese of Edmonton, Alberta, in the years 1845-46. *Canad. Cath. hist. Assoc. Rept.*, 41-42, vol. 9, p. 35-46.

2715. MAYNARD (T.). Apostle of charity : the life of St. Vincent de Paul. London, Allen & Unwin, 40, in-8, 319 p., 7s. 6d.

2716. ROWBOTHAM (A. H.). Missionary and Mandarin : the Jesuits at the Court of China. London, Cambridge Univ. Press, 43, in-8, xii-374 p., (illus.), 18s. R : K. S. Latourette, *Int. R. Missions*, 43, vol. 32, p. 445-446.

2717. VENINI (Bernice). Father Constantine Scollen, founder of the Calgary mission. *Canad. Cath. hist. Assoc. Rept.*, 42/43, vol. 10, p. 75-86.

§ 3. Orthodoxy

2718. ARSENIEV (N.). Holy Moscow, chapters in the religious and spiritual life of Russia in the 19th century. London, S.P.C.K., 40, in-8, 191 p., 4s. 6d. R : *Slavonic Y.B.* (*Slavonic R.*), 40, vol. 19, p. 344-345.

2719. GRAY (Lilian F.). The Bogomils of Yugoslavia. *Hibbert J.*, 41, vol. 39, p. 179-187.

2720. GORODETZKY (Nadejda). The missionary expansion of the Russian Orthodox Church. *Int. R. Missions*, 42, vol. 31, p. 400-411.

2721. TIMASHEFF (N. S.). Religion in Soviet Russia, 1917-1942. London, Sheed, 42, in-8, xii-171 p., 10s. 6d. R : P. J. Thompson, *Theology*, 44, vol. 47, p. 210-213.

§ 4. Protestantism

a. REFORMATION PERIOD

2722. AINSLIE (James L.). The doctrines of ministerial order in the Reformed churches of the 16th and 17th centuries. London, Clark, 40, in-8, x-274 p., 7s. 6d. R : E. J. Price, *Congreg. Quar.*, 40, vol. 18, p. 428-429. R.D.W., *J. presb. hist. Soc.*, 42, vol. 7, p. 143.

2723. BRINKWORTH (E. R.). The study and use of archdeacons' court records : illustrated from the Oxford records (1566-1759). *Trans. Roy. hist. Soc.*, 43, vol. 25, p. 93-119.

2724. CONSTANT (G.). The Reformation in England. Vol. 2 : Introduction of the Reformation into England, Edward VI (1547-1553), tr. by E. I. Watkin. London, Sheed & Ward, 41, in-8, 360 p., 16s.

2725. DAVIES (J. Conway). Original documents, 7 : Letters of admission to the rectory of Whitechurch. *Nat. Library Wales J.*, 45, vol. 4, p. 83-88.

2726. DICKENS (A. G.). Edwardian arrears in augmentations payments and the problem of the ex-religious. *Eng. hist. R.*, 40, vol. 55, p. 384-418.

2726a. DICKENS (A. G.). Archbishop Holgate's Apology. *Eng. hist. R.*, 41, vol. 56, p. 450-459.

2727. DONALDSON (Gordon). Sources for the study of Scottish ecclesiastical organization and personnel, 1560-1600. *B. Inst. hist. Research*, 43, vol. 19, p. 188-203.

2727a. DONALDSON (G.). The Scottish episcopate at the Reformation. *Eng. hist. R.*, 45, vol. 60, p. 349-364.

2728. GRIEVE (Hilda E. P.). The deprived married clergy in Essex, 1553-61. *Trans. Roy. hist. Soc.*, 40, vol. 22, p. 141-169.

2729. HUDSON (W. S.). John Ponet (1516?-1556) : advocate of limited monarchy. London, Cambridge Univ. Press, 43, 2 vols. [in 1], in-8, x-246, 184 p., 27s.

2730. LONGDEN (Henry Isham). Northamptonshire and Rutland clergy from 1500. Vol. 5-15. Northampton, Archer and Goodman, 39-43, 11 vols. in-8, 282, 288, 266, 276, 277, 272, 274, 279, 266, 276, 278 p., 115s. 6d.

2731. MAJOR (Kathleen). Resignation deeds of the diocese of Lincoln. *B. Inst. hist. Research*, 42, vol. 19, p. 57-65.

2732. MELLOWS (W. T.) ed. The foundation of Peterborough cathedral, A.D. 1541. Pt. 2 of Tudor documents. Northampton, Record Soc., 41, in-8, lxxxiii-140 p., 21s. (Publ., vol. 13). C. R. Cheney, *J. archaeol. Assoc.*, 42, vol. 7, p. 71-72.

2733. MOORE (W. G.). The early French Reformation. *History*, 40, vol. 25, p. 48-53.

2734. MOZLEY (J. F.). John Foxe and his Book. London, S.P.C.K., 40, in-8, xii-254 p., 12s. 6d. R : C. S. Phillips, *Theology*, 40, vol. 41, p. 313-315. M. Deanesly, *History*, 41, vol. 26, p. 76-78.

2735. PERCY (Lord Eustace). John Knox. New ed. London, Hodder, 45, in-8, 438 p., 20s.

2736. PERRY (Edith Weir). Under four Tudors : being the story of Matthew Parker, sometime Archbishop of Canterbury. London, Allen & Unwin, 40, in-8, 315 p., (plates), 12s. 6d. R : G.S.T., *History*, 42, vol. 26, p. 319.

2737. PREEDY (George R.) pseud. The life of John Knox. London, Jenkins, 40, in-8, 282 p., 15s.

2738. PRICE (F. Douglas). The abuses of excommunication and the decline of ecclesiastical discipline under Queen Elizabeth. *Eng. hist. R.*, 42, vol. 57, p. 106-115.

2738a. RICE (Garraway). Transcripts of Sussex wills up to 1560. Vol. 4. Lewes, Sussex Record Society, 40, in-8, 21s. R : C. J., *Eng. hist. R.*, 42, vol. 57, p. 396.

2739. SOUTHGATE (W. M.). The Marian exiles and the influence of John Calvin. *History*, 42, vol. 27, p. 148-152.

2740. ZOFF (O.). The Huguenots : fighters for God and human freedom, tr. by E. B. Ashton and J. Mayo. London, Allen & Unwin, 43, in-8, 340 p., (illus.), 16s.

b. ANGLICANISM SINCE 1603

2741. ABELL (A. I.). The urban impact on American protestantism, 1865-1900. London, Oxford Univ. Press, 44, in-8, 286 p., 21s.

2742. ADDLESHAW (G. W. O.). The High Church tradition : a study in the liturgical thought of the 17th century. London, Faber, 41, in-8, 204 p., 7s. 6d.

2743. BAYLDON (Joan). Cyril Bardsley, evangelist. London, S.P.C.K., 42, in-8, vi-216 p., 9s. R : Albert, Bp. of Liverpool, *Theology*, 42, vol. 45, p. 189-190. C. E. Wilson, *Int. R. Missions*, 42, vol. 31, p. 472-473.

2744. BECKETT (J. C.). The Government and the Church of Ireland under William III and Anne. *Irish hist. Stud.*, 41, vol. 2, p. 280-302.

2745. BECKETT (J. C.). William King's administration of the diocese of Derry, 1691-1703. *Irish hist. Stud.*, 44, vol. 4, p. 164-180.

2746. BODEN-WORSLEY (J. F. W.). Memories of Modernists and others, I : Alfred Fawkes (1850-1930). *Theology*, 40, vol. 41, p. 9-15, 74-80, 151-159.

2747. BULLOCK (F. W. B.). The history of Ridley Hall, Cambridge. Vol. 1 : To the end of 1907. Cambridge, Ridley Hall, 41, in-8, 477 p., (illus.), 18s. R : L. E. Elliott-Binns, *Theology*, 41, vol. 43, p. 254-255. N.S., *Eng. hist. R.*, 43, vol. 58, p. 254-255.

2748. CLARKE (C. P. S.). Bishop Chandler, a memoir. London, Mowbray, 40, in-8, 128 p., 3s. 6d. R : R. P. Symonds, *Theology*, 41, vol. 42, p. 253.

2749. CLEMENT (Mary). John Vaughan, Cwrt Derllys, a'i waith (1663-1722). (John Vaughan and his work). *Trans. Soc. Cymmr.*, 42 (44), p. 73-107.

2750. COLLIGAN (J. Hay). William Whittingham and his contemporaries. *J. presb. hist. Soc.*, 41, vol. 7, p. 55-70.

2752. CROSS (F. L.). Darwell Stone, churchman and counsellor. London, Dacre Press, 43, in-8, xxvi-467 p., 30s.

2753. CUMMINGS (H.). Richard Peters. London, Oxford Univ. Press, 44, in-8, 356 p., 18s. 6d.

2754. DARK (S.). Wilson Carlile : the laughing Cavalier of Christ. London, J. Clarke, 44, in-8, 188 p., (illus.), 10s. 6d.

2755. DEARMER (Nancy). The life of Percy Dearmer. London, Cape, 40, in-8, 325 p., 10s. 6d. R : C. Smyth, *Theology*, 40, vol. 41, p. 184-188.

2757. DIXON (H. N.). Religious life in Cambridge in the 80's of the last century. *Congreg. Quar.*, 42, vol. 20, p. 313-317.

2759. DONALDSON (Gordon). The attitude of Whitgift and Bancroft to the Scottish church. *Trans. Roy. hist. Soc.*, 42, vol. 24, p. 95-115.

2760. DUGMORE (C. W.). Eucharistic doctrine in England from Hooker to Waterland. London, S.P.C.K., 42, in-8, 192 p., 7s. 6d. (Norrisian prize essay, Univ. of Camb., 1940).

2761. EMERSON (N. D.). James Bonnell, accountant-general of Ireland, 1653-1699. *Evangelical Quar.*, 40, vol. 12, p. 172-192.

2762. ESDAILE (Katharine A.). St. Martin in the Fields : new and old. London, S.P.C.K., 44, in-8, vii-102 p., (plates), 5s.

2764. FRANCE (W. F.). The oversea episcopate : centenary history of the Colonial Bishoprics Fund. London, Colonial Bishoprics Fund, 40, in-8, 1s. R : J.W.L., *Eng. hist. R.*, 42, vol. 57, p. 288. F. J. Western, *Int. R. Missions*, 42, vol. 31, p. 135-137.

2765. GEGENHEIMER (A. F.). William Smith, educator and churchman, 1727-1803. London, Oxford Univ. Press, 43, in-8, 244 p., 15s. 6d. (Pennsylvania lives, vol. 7).

2766. GEORGE (Dorothy M.). Some caricatures of the clergy in Wales. *Nat. Library Wales J.*, 45, vol. 4, p. 53-56.

2767. GRUBB (Norman P.). Alfred Buxton of Abyssinia and Congo. London, Lutterworth Press, 42, in-8, 173 p., 5s. R : Edward, Bishop of Lichfield, *Int. R. Missions*, 43, vol. 32, p. 454-456.

2768. GWYNNE (Ll. H.). These fifty years, the story of the Old Cairo Medical Mission from 1889 to 1939. London, C.M.S., 40, in-8, 1s. 6d. R : C. C. Chesterman, *Int. R. Missions*, 40, vol. 29, p. 414-415.

2769. HARTFORD (R. R.). William King, the man and his work. *Theology*, 45, vol. 48, p. 55-60.

2770. HUGHES (Edward). The bishops and reform, 1831-3 : some fresh correspondence. *Eng. hist. R.*, 41, vol. 56, p. 459-490.

2771. HUGHES (H. B. L.). The impact on Jamaica of the evangelical revival. *Jamaican hist. R.*, 45, vol. 1, p. 7-23.

2772. JONES (J. J.). The Welsh church periodical press. *Nat. Library Wales J.*, 45, vol. 4, p. 92-94.

2773. JORDAN (W. K.). The development of religious toleration in England. Attainment of the theory and accommodations in thought and institutions (1640-1660). London, Allen & Unwin, 40, in-8, 499 p., 21s. R : A. Peel, *Congreg. Quar.*, 41, vol. 19, p. 74.

2774. LERRY (George). Alfred George Edwards, Archbishop of Wales. Oswestry, Woodall, 40, in-8, 119 p., 4s. 6d.

2775. MASTERS (D. C.). The Nicolls papers : a study in Anglican toryism. *Canad. hist. Assoc. Rept.*, 45, p. 42-48.

2776. NORTHCOTT (C.). Glorious company : 150 years life and work of London Missionary Society, 1795-1945. London, Livingstone Press, 45, in-8, 196 p., (illus., maps), 5s.

2777. OSMOND (P. H.). Isaac Barrow : his life and times. ,London, S.P.C.K., 44, in-8, 240 p., (illus.), 12s. 6d. R : H. F. Stewart, *Theology*, 44, vol. 47, p. 214-215.

2778. PEASTON (A. Elliott). The Prayer book reform movement in the 18th century. Oxford, Blackwell, 40, in-8, xi-115 p., 7s. 6d. R : W.H.B., *Trans. Unitarian hist. Soc.*, 41, vol. 7, p. 243-245.

2780. POLLOCK (Sir John). The Popish plot : a study in the history of the reign of Charles II. Re-issue. London, Cambridge Univ. Press, 44, in-8, xxv-379 p., 21s. R : E. S. de B(eer), *History*, 45, vol. 30, p. 110-112.

2781. RANSOME (Mary). Church and dissent in the election of 1710. *Eng. hist. R.*, 41, vol. 56, p. 76-89.

2782. RECKITT (Maurice B.). Church and society in England from 1800. London, Allen & Unwin, 40, in-8, 266 p., 7s. 6d. (The Church and the world, vol. 3). R : *Theology*, 41, vol. 42, p. 246-247.

2783. RICHARDS (G. C.). William Law, prophet and saint. *Theology*, 40, vol. 41, p. 196-205.

2784. ROBERTS (R. Ellis). H. R. L. Sheppard : life and letters. London, Murray, 42, in-8, 356 p., 15s. R : A. Peel, *Congreg. Quar.*, 42, vol. 20, p. 360-361. L. J. Collins, *Theology*, 43, vol. 46, p. 115-116.

2785. SANDERS (Charles Richard). Coleridge and the Broad Church movement : studies in S. T. Coleridge, Dr. Arnold of Rugby, J. C. Hare, Thomas Carlyle, and F. D. Maurice. London, Cambridge Univ. Press, 42, in-8, viii-308 p., 21s.

2786. SHEPHERD (Robert H. W.). Lovedale, South Africa, 1841-1941. Lovedale, Lovedale Press, 41, in-8, 531 p., (maps), 8s. 6d. R : J.D.R.J., *Bantu Stud.*, 41, vol. 15, p. 53-57. R. Piddington, *Int. Affairs*, 41, vol. 19, p. 282. Clarendon, *Int. R. Missions*, 41, vol. 30, p. 411-412. M. Wrong, *J. Roy. african Soc.*, 41, vol. 40, p. 80-83.

2788. SMYTH (Charles). Simeon and church order : a study of the origin of the evangelical revival in Cambridge in the 18th century. London, Cambridge Univ. Press, 40, in-8, xx-316 p., 16s. (Birkbeck lect., 1937-38). R : H. H. Henson, *Theology*, 40, vol. 41, p. 370-372. M. D. George, *History*, 41, vol. 26, p. 147-149.

2789. SMYTH (C.). The evangelical movement in perspective. *Cambridge hist. J.*, 43, vol. 7, p. 160-174.

2790. STEBBING (W. P. D.). Briefs in St. Leonard's and St. George's parishes in Deal in the 17th and 18th centuries. *Archaeol. cantiana*, 44, vol. 57, p. 26-33.

2791. STRANKS (C. T.). Jeremy Taylor. *Church Quar. R.*, 40, vol. 131, p. 31-63.

2792. SYKES (Norman). The Duke of Newcastle as ecclesiastical minister. *Eng. hist. R.*, 42, vol. 57, p. 59-84.

2793. TAYLOR (A. H.). The clergy of St. John the Baptist, Smallhythe. *Archaeol. cantiana*, 42 (43), vol. 55, p. 26-36.

2794. THEOBALD (Hugh W.). The beginning of the great adventure : the birth of the London Missionary Society. *Congreg. Quar.*, 42, vol. 20, p. 333-340.

2795. TOWERS (Leonard T.). The Bedford Missionary Training College and its connection with the London Missionary Society. *Congreg. hist. Soc. Trans.*, 45, vol. 15, p. 33-40.

2796. TREVOR-ROPER (H. R.). Archbishop Laud, 1573-1645. London, Macmillan, 40, in-8, ix-464 p., (plates), 21s. R : G. Davies, *Eng. hist. R.*, 42, vol. 57, p. 383-384.

2797. WHITING (C. E.). Nathaniel, Lord Crewe, Bishop of Durham, 1674-1721, and his diocese. London, S.P.C.K., 40, in-8, 400 p., 16s. R : N. Sykes, *Theology*, 40, vol. 41, p. 119-120. E. S. de B., *History*, 41, vol. 26, p. 156-157.

2798. WINNINGTON-INGRAM (A. F.). Fifty years work in London (1889-1939). London, Longmans, 40, in-8, 249 p., 10s. 6d. R : L. J. Collins, *Theology*, 40, vol. 41, p. 255-256. *National R.*, 40, vol. 115, p. 243-244.

c. OTHER PROTESTANT CHURCHES

2800. JOHNSON (Thomas H.). The printed writings of Jonathan Edwards, 1703-1758 : a bibliography. London, Oxford Univ. Press, 41, in-8, xii-135 p., 34s. (Princeton Univ. libr. publ.).

2801. ANDERSON (H.). The past 50 years in India and Ceylon of the Baptist Missionary Society, 1892-1942. London, Carey Press, 42, in-8, 36 p., 6d. (Celebrations ser.).

2802. BAKER (G. C.) jr. An introduction to the history of early New England Methodism, 1789-1839. London, Cambridge Univ. Press, 42, in-8, viii-146 p., 18s.

2803. BALLANTYNE (John C.). Origins of Essex Church, Notting Hill Gate, London. *Trans. Unitarian hist. Soc.*, 40, vol. 7, p. 131-138.

2804. BEYNON (E.). Mrs. James, Abergavenny ; her courtship with Howell Harris, and her marriage to George Whitefield. *J. hist. Soc. presb. Church Wales*, 43, vol. 28, p. 10-21.

2805. BEYNON (Tom). Adeiladu capel y Groeswen gan y Methodistiaid yn 1742. (The building of Croeswen chapel, Caerphilly, by the Methodists. With extracts from the diary of Howell Harris). *J. hist. Soc. presb. Church Wales*, 43, vol. 28, p. 22-40.

2806. BEYNON (T.). Llythyran ac adroddiadan Thomas William, Eglwys Ilan, at Howell Harris. (The letters and reports of Thomas William to Howell Harris). *J. hist. Soc. presb. Church Wales*, 44, vol. 29, p. 23-32, 66-75, 129-136.

2807. BEYNON (T.). Howell Harris' visits to Cardiganshire. *J. hist. Soc. presb. Church Wales*, 44, vol. 29, p. 94-101, 119-128.

2809. BROWN (G. K.). Scots theologians and English Unitarians. *Trans. Unitarian hist. Soc.*, 43, vol. 8, p. 5-16.

2810. BURTT (Ruth G.). Records from Nailsworth. *J. Friends hist. Soc.*, 40 (41), vol. 37, p. 31-37.

2811. C. (S. W.). The original MS. of the Westminster confession of faith. *J. presb. hist. Soc.*, 43, vol. 7, p. 151-154.

2812. CADBURY (Henry J.) ed. The Swarthmore documents in America, ed. by H. J. Cadbury. London, Friends' Hist. Society, 40, in-8, 90 p. (Suppl. no. 20 to the Journal of the Friends' hist. soc.).

2813. CADBURY (H. J.). Barbados Quakers, 1683 to 1761 : preliminary list. *J. Barbados Mus.*, 41, vol. 9, p. 29-31.

2814. CARPENTER (M. L.). John Dean : Australian bush preacher. London, Epworth Press, 44, in-8, 100 p., 2s.

2815. CARRUTHERS (S. W.). The scripture proofs of the Westminster confession. *J. presb. hist. Soc.*, 42, vol. 7, p. 102-108.

2816. CARRUTHERS (S. W.). The Westminster Assembly : what it was and what it did. London, Presb. Church of England, 43, in-8, 16 p., 6d. R : R. D. W(hitehorn), *J. presb. hist. Soc.*, 43, vol. 7, p. 178-189.

2817. CARRUTHERS (S. W.). The everyday work of the Westminster Assembly. London, Presbyterian Book Room, 43, in-8, 221 p., 12s. 6d. R : A. J. Grieve, *Congreg. hist. Soc. Trans.*, 44, vol. 14, p. 254-255.

2818. CLARE (A.). The City Temple, 1640-1940. London, Independent Press, 40, in-8, xxiv-288 p., (illus.), 5s.

2819. CLEMENT (Mary). Teulu'r Daltoniaid, Pembre, Sir Gaerfyrddin. (The Dalton family, of Pembry, Carmarthenshire). *J. hist. Soc. presb. Church Wales*, 44, vol. 29, p. 1-12.

2820. COLLIGAN (J. Hay). The metrical psalms in England. *J. presb. hist. Soc.*, 45, vol. 8, p. 56-65.

2821. CONNELL (J. M.). Dickens' Unitarian minister, Edward Tagart. *Trans. Unitarian hist. Soc.*, 44, vol. 7, p. 68-83.

2822. COMPTON (J. E.). Colchester and the missionary movement. *Baptist Quar.*, 42, vol. 11, p. 55-57.

2823. COWELL (Henry J.). Timothy Richard, missionary and mandarin : a centenary tribute. *Asiatic R.*, 45, vol. 41, p. 397-403.

2823a. CRICHTON (A. S.). Annals of a disruption congregation in Aberdeenshire. Aberdeen, Univ. Press, 43, in-8, 68 p., (plates), 1s. 6d.

2824. CRIPPS (Ernest C.). William Allen : Quaker, humanitarian, scientist. *Hibbert J.*, 44, vol. 42, p. 353-358.

2825. CUMBERS (F. H.) ed. Richmond College, 1843-1943. London, Epworth Press, 44, in-8, 190 p., 5s.

2826. CURR (H. S.). Spurgeon and Gladstone. *Baptist Quar.*, 42, vol. 11, p. 46-54.

2827. DAVIES (G. Ll.). Joseph Rowntree Gillett : a memoir. London, Allen & Unwin, 42, in-8, 157 p., 5s.

2828. DAVIES (K. Monica). Lady Huntingdon a Threfecca (Lady Huntingdon and Trevecca College). *J. hist. Soc. presb. Church Wales*, 42, vol. 27, p. 66-75.

2829. DAVIES (W. Lloyd). Early Methodism in Flintshire. *J. hist. Soc. presb. Church Wales*, 45, vol. 30, p. 110-114.

2830. DAY (C. M. Hilton). Whitehaven Presbyterian church : a heritage of 250 years. *J. presb. hist. Soc.*, 45, vol. 8, p. 42-56.

2832. EDWARDS (M.). Methodism and England : a study of Methodism in its social and political aspects during the period 1850-1932. London, Epworth Press, 43, in-8, 252 p., 12s. 6d.

2833. FLOY (Michael). The diary of Michael Floy, jr., Bowery village, 1833-1837, ed. by R. A. E. Brooks. London, Oxford Univ. Press, 41, in-4, xi-269 p., 22s. 6d. R : G. G. van D., *Eng. hist. R.*, 42, vol. 57, p. 535-536.

2834. FOX (William Sherwood). A century of service : a history of the Talbot Street Baptist church, 1845-1945. London, Ont., privately pr. for the Talbot St. Baptist church, 45, in-8, xvi-103 p. R : F. Landon, *Canad. hist. R.*, 45, vol. 26, p. 324-325.

2835. GRAY (W. Forbes). The Westminster Assembly : a tercentenary study (1643-1943). *Hibbert J.*, 43, vol. 42, p. 53-57.

2836. GREEN (J. Brazier). John Wesley and William Law. London, Epworth Press, 45, in-8, 224 p., 12s. 6d.

2837. GRIEVE (Alexander J.). Cavendish church, Suffolk. *Congreg. hist. Soc. Trans.*, 45, vol. 15, p. 7-17.

2838. GRIFFITHS (D. R.). John Leusden's New Testament. *Baptist Quar.*, 44, vol. 11, p. 220-224.

2839. HALL (Lawrence). The Clough Fund. *Trans. Unitarian hist. Soc.*, 40, vol. 7, p. 109-130.

2840. HANKINSON (Frederick). Dissenters' Chapels Act, 1844. *Trans. Unitarian hist. Soc.*, 44, vol. 7, p. 52-57.

2841. HANNEN (Robert B.). Cupar, Fife, 1652-1659. *Baptist Quar.*, 40, vol. 10, p. 45-49.

2842. HANNEN (R. B.). A Scottish Baptist centenary. *Baptist Quar.*, 43, vol. 11, p. 147-151.

2843. HARRIS (Howell). Howell Harris' visits to Kidwelly and district (1743-1770). (Extracts from his diaries). *J. hist. Soc. presb. Church Wales*, 40, vol. 25, p. 10-22, 98-110.

2844. HARRIS (H.). An outline of Howell Harris' journeys in North Wales. Extracts from his journal, transcr. by D. E. Jenkins. *J. hist. Soc. presb. Church Wales*, 40, vol. 25, p. 415-450 ; 41, vol. 26, p. 450-476. (Trevecka MSS. Suppl. 11, 12).

2845. HARRIS (H.). Howell Harris in Carmarthenshire. Extracts from his diaries. *J. hist. Soc. presb. Church Wales*, 41, vol. 26, p. 1-15, 68-81, 102-112, 477-493 ; 42, vol. 27, p. 13-19, 107-116. (Trevecka MSS. Suppl. 12).

2846. HARRIS (H.). A list of the diaries and MSS. of Howell Harris received into the National Library of Wales, May 9, 1941. *J. hist. Soc. presb. Church Wales*, 42, vol. 27, p. 45-60.

2847. HARRIS (H.). Extracts from Howell Harris' diaries : visits to Llanamlet and district. *J. hist. Soc. presb. Church Wales*, 42, vol. 27, p. 165-177.

2848. HARRIS (H.). An outline of Howell Harris' journey in North Wales. Extracts from his journal. *J. hist. Soc. presb. Church Wales*, 43, vol. 28, p. 45-60.

2849. HARRIS (H.). Howell Harris' visits to Birmingham, 1747 and 1763. Extracts from his diaries. *J. hist. Soc. presb. Church Wales*, 44, vol. 29, p. 13-18.

2850. HARRIS (H.). Howell Harris' last two visits to Pembrokeshire and the Fishguard Association, 1770. Extracts from his diaries. *J. hist. Soc. presb. Church Wales*, 44, vol. 29, p. 45-53.

2851. HARRIS (H.). Howell Harris's last journey in North Wales, transcr. by J. Thickens. *J. hist. Soc. presb. Church Wales*, 45, vol. 30, p. 1-20, 33-42, 73-79.

2852. HARRIS (H.). Howell Harris's visits to Cardiganshire. Extracts from his diari ed. by T. Beynon. *J. hist. Soc. presc. Church Wales*, 45, vol. 30, p. 49-62, 100-109.

2853. HARRISON (Frank Mott). John Bunyan and Andrew Gifford. *Baptist Quar.*, 40, vol. 10, p. 139-145 ; 41, vol. 10, p. 376-380.

2854. HARRISON (F. M.). Repudiable ' Bunyan Writings '. *Baptist Quar.*, 44, vol. 11, p. 277-281.

2855. HARRISON (F. M.). The portraiture of John Bunyan. *Baptist Quar.*, 45, vol. 11, p. 337-342.

2856. HERFORD (R. Travers). Joseph Hanson, the weavers' friend. *Trans. Unitarian hist. Soc.*, 43, vol. 8, p. 17-26.

2857. HEWETT (Maurice F.). Early days at Worstead. *Baptist Quar.*, 43, vol. 11, p. 165-174.

2858. HEWETT (M. F.). A 19th century revival in East Anglia. *Baptist Quar.*, 44, vol. 11, p. 233-236.

2859. HEYS (John). Longsight Free Christian Church, Manchester. *Trans. Unitarian hist. Soc.*, 40, vol. 7, p. 163-178.

2860. HEYWOOD (Oliver). Letters of Oliver Heywood and Life of Richard Heywood (1695). *Congreg. hist. Soc. Trans.*, 45, vol. 15, p. 18-32.

2861. HOLT (Felix). The Hincks family. *Trans. Unitarian hist. Soc.*, 44, vol. 7, p. 84-85.

2862. HOPKINS (Charles Howard). The rise of the social gospel in American Protestantism, 1865-1915. London, Oxford Univ. Press, 40, in-8, xii-352 p., 14s. (Yale stud. in relig. educ., 14). R : L. Hodgson, *Theology*, 41, vol. 43, p. 371-372. S. Myers, *Congreg. Quar.*, 42, vol. 20, p. 182-183.

2863. JONES (Idwal). Notes on the ordination controversy, 1809-1810. *J. hist. Soc. presb. Church Wales*, 44, vol. 29, p. 109-119.

2864. JONES (J. Islan). The history of the Presbyterian or Protestant Dissenting Chapel, Hindley, 2 : 1700-1812. *Trans. Unitarian hist. Soc.*, 40, vol. 7, p. 139-162.

2865. JONES (W. G.). John Wesley's chapel in Bristol. *J. hist. Soc. presb. Church Wales*, 41, vol. 26, p. 43-50.

2866. KELLER (C. R.). The second great awakening in Connecticut. London, Oxford Univ. Press, 42, in-8, 287 p., 14s. (Yale hist. publ., misc. 40). R : D. W. B(rogan), *Eng. hist. R.*, 43, vol._58, p. 501.

2867. KENWORTHY (F.). The Unitarian tradition in Liberal Christianity. *Trans. Unitarian hist. Soc.*, 44, vol. 7, p. 58-67.

2868. KLEIN (W. C.). Johann Conrad Beissel, mystic and martinet, 1690-1768. London, Oxford Univ. Press, 42, in-8, 288 p., 10s. 6d. (Penn. lives).

2869. LATHAM (R. C.). Roger Lowe, shopkeeper and Nonconformist. *History*, 41, vol. 26, p. 19-35.

2870. LESLIE (Andrew). Narrative, 1823. *Baptist Quar.*, 42, vol. 11, p. 78-91.

2871. LEWIS (Walter O.). William Staughton. *Baptist Quar.*, 42, vol. 11, p. 74-78.

2872. LORD (F. T.). Achievement : a short history of the Baptist missionary society, 1792-1942. London, Carey Press, 42, in-8, 150 p., 2s. 6d.

2873. McDOUGALL (David). In search of Israel, a chronicle of the Jewish missions of the Church of Scotland. London, Nelson, 41, in-8, 176 p., 2s. 6d. R : C. H. Gill, *Int. R. Missions*, 41, vol. 30, p. 565-566.

2874. McLACHLAN (H.). The religious opinions of Milton, Locke and Newton. Manchester, Univ. Press, 41, in-8, vii-221 p., 7s. 6d. (Theol. ser., 6). R : S. L. Bethell, *Theology*, 41, vol. 43, p. 191-192. A.H., *Trans. Unitarian hist. Soc.*, 41, vol. 7, p. 245-247.

2875. McLACHLAN (H.). New light on the old Unitarian circle. *Trans. Unitarian hist. Soc.*, 42, vol. 7, p. 255-268.

2876. McLACHLAN (H.). Bridgewater Academy, 1688-1756 ? *Trans. Unitarian hist. Soc.*, 45, vol. 8, p. 93-97.

2877. McLEAN (Andrew). The Synod one hundred years ago, ed. by W. B. Shaw. *J. presb. hist. Soc.*, 41, vol. 7, p. 70-79.

2878. MacTAVISH (Duncan C.). Minutes of the synod of Argyll, 1639-1651, 1652-1661, ed. by D. C. Mactavish. Edinburgh, Scottish Hist. Soc., 43-44, 2 vols. in-8, subscribers only. (Publ., 3rd ser.). R : G.D.H., *Eng. hist. R.*, 44, vol. 59, p. 123 ; 45, vol. 60, p. 275.

2879. MELCHER (M. F.). The Shaker adventure. London, Oxford Univ. Press, 41, in-8, 331 p., 14s.

2880. MICKLEWRIGHT (F. H. Amphlett). A footnote to the happy union of 1690. *Trans. Unitarian hist. Soc.*, 43, vol. 8, p. 27-34.

2881. MICKLEWRIGHT (F. H. Amphlett). A new approach to Unitarian history. *Trans. Unitarian hist. Soc.*, 45, vol. 8, p. 122-129.

2882. MONTGOMERY (R. Mortimer). The significance of the Dissenters' Chapels Act of 1844. *Trans. Unitarian hist. Soc.*, 44, vol. 7, p. 45-51.

2883. MORRIS (J. Hughes). Foreign mission centenary (1840-1940). *J. hist. Soc. presb. Church Wales*, 40, vol. 25, p. 41-47.

2884. MURPHY (John). Two notable Scottish centenaries. *Congreg. Quar.*, 43, vol. 21, p. 148-155.

2885. NOTTINGHAM (E. K.). Methodism and the frontier : Indiana proving ground. London, Oxford Univ. Press, 41, in-8, 241 p., 12s. 6d.

2886. NUTTALL (Geoffrey F.). Lyon Turner's ' Original Records ' : notes and identifications. *Congreg. hist. Soc. Trans.*, 40, vol. 14, p. 14-24 ; 43, vol. 14, p. 181-187 ; 45, vol. 15, p. 41-47.

2887. NUTTALL (G. F.). Congregational Commonwealth incumbents. *Congreg. hist. Soc. Trans.*, 43, vol. 14, p. 155-167.

2888. NUTTALL (G. F.). Welbeck Abbey MSS. Woburn Abbey MSS. *Congreg. hist. Soc. Trans.*, 44, vol. 14, p. 218-234.

2889. PAGE (George E.). Some Baptist churches on the borders of Bedfordshire and Huntingdonshire. *Baptist Quar.*, 44, vol. 11, p. 225-232.

2890. PAYNE (Ernest A.). Two Dutch translations by Carey : an Angus library find. *Baptist Quar.*, 42, vol. 11, p. 33-38.

2891. PAYNE (E. A.). 1792 and the ministry to-day. *Baptist Quar.*, 42, vol. 11, p. 65-73.

2892. PAYNE (E. A.). The evangelical revival and the beginnings of the modern missionary movement. *Congreg. Quar.*, 43, vol. 21, p. 223-236.

2893. PAYNE (E. A.). Baptist missionary society history. *Baptist Quar.*, 44, vol. 11, p. 295-298.

2894. PAYNE (E. A.). The Free church tradition in the life of England. London, Student Christian Movement, 44, in-8, 158 p., 6s. R : A. C. Underwood, *Baptist Quar.*, 44, vol. 11, p. 302-304. E. Shillito, *Int. R. Missions*, 45, vol. 34, p. 329-330. *J. presb. hist. Soc.*, 45, vol. 8, p. 71-72. H. Cunliffe-Jones, *Theology*, 45, vol. 48, p. 19-20.

2895. PEEL (Albert). A unique copy of a work of Thomas Cartwright ? *Congreg. hist. Soc. Trans.*, 43, vol. 14, p. 143-154.

2896. PENRY (John). The Notebook of John Penry, 1593, ed. by A. Peel. London, Roy. Hist. Soc., 44, in-8, xxviii-99 p., subscribers only. (Camden, 3rd ser., vol. 67). R : A.F.S.P., *Eng. hist. R.*, 45, vol. 60, p. 272-273. A. J. Grieve, *Congreg. hist. Soc.*

Trans., 45, vol. 15, p. 32. H. Mc-Lachlan, *Trans. Unitarian hist. Soc.*, 45, vol. 8, p. 130. D. W(illiams), *History*, 44, vol. 29, p. 214-215.

2896a. PLUM (Harry Grant). Restoration Puritanism : a study of the growth of English liberty. London, Oxford Univ. Press, 44, in-8, ix-129 p., 15s. 6d. R : C.E.W., *Eng. hist. R.*, 45, vol. 60, p. 427-428. R. C. Latham, *History*, 45, vol. 30, p. 191-192.

2897. PYKE (R.). The early Bible Christians. London, Epworth Press, 41, in-8, 46 p., 1s. 3d. (Wesley hist. lect., 1941).

2898. REID (Adam A.). Benjamin Keach, 1640. *Baptist Quar.*, 40, vol. 10, p. 67-78.

2899. REYNOLDS (W. D.). The past 50 years in the Congo of the Baptist Missionary Society, 1892-1942. London, Carey Press, 42, in-8, 56 p., 6d. (Celebrations ser.).

2900. RICHARDS (Thomas). Eglwys Llanfaches. (Puritanism in Monmouthshire in the 17th century). *Trans. Soc. Cymmr.*, 41 (43), p. 150-184.

2901. ROBERTS (G. T.). Wesley a Harris. *J. hist. Soc. presb. Church Wales*, 45, vol. 30, p. 65-72, 93-99.

2902. ROBERTS (Gomer M.). John Richard, Llansamlet; a pioneer of Welsh Calvinistic Methodism. *J. hist. Soc. presb. Church Wales*, 42, vol. 27, p. 137-159.

2903. ROBERTS (G. M.). Bywyd a gwaith Peter Williams. (The life and work of Peter Williams). Cardiff, University of Wales Press Board, 43, in-8, 228 p., 10s. 6d.

2904. ROBERTS (G. M.). The Rev. David Jones, Llangan : his diary for 1808, transcr. by G. M. Roberts. *J. hist. Soc. presb. Church Wales*, 44, vol. 29, p. 54-65.

2905. ROBSON (R. S.). Presbytery in Newcastle-on-Tyne from the Reformation till the Revolution. *J. presb. hist. Soc.*, 40, vol. 7, p. 3-23; 42, vol. 7, p. 109-134.

2906. ROLLINSON (F. H.). Chipping Norton Baptist church, 1694-1944. *Baptist Quar.*, 44, vol. 11, p. 282-287.

2907. RUSSELL (E.). The history of Quakerism. London, Macmillan, 42, in-8, xiii-586 p., 15s.

2908. SEDDON (John). The Seddon letters. *Trans. Unitarian hist. Soc.*, 42, vol. 7, p. 269-289.

2909. SHEPHERD (T. B.). Methodism and the literature of the 18th century. London, Epworth Press, 40, in-8, 286 p., 10s. 6d. R : R. N. Carew Hunt, *19th Century*, 41, vol. 129, p. 596-597. B. Williams, *Eng. hist. R.*, 41, vol. 56, p. 497-499. M. D. George, *History*, 41, vol. 26, p. 147-149.

2910. SHORT (H. Lismer). The architecture of the old meeting houses. *Trans. Unitarian hist. Soc.*, 45, vol. 8, p. 98-112.

2910a. SMITH (Lilian Adam). George Adam Smith, a personal memoir and family chronicle. London, Hodder, 43, in-8, 272 p., (plates), 8s. 6d.

2911. SWEET (W. W.). Religion on the American frontier, 1783-1850. Vol. 3 : The Congregationalists' collection of source materials. London, Cambridge Univ. Press, 40, in-8, 435 p., 18s.

2912. SWIFT (J. M.). Jehovah's witnesses : a short account of the history, beliefs and methods of a strange and widespread organisation. London, Mowbray, 42, in-8, 16 p., 4d.

2913. UNION OF WELSH INDEPENDENTS. Hanes ac egwyddorion Annibynwyr Cymru. (The history and principles of Welsh Independents). Abertawe, Undeb yr Annibynwyr Cymraeg, 40, in-8, viii-207 p.

2914. WALKER (F. Deaville). A hundred years in Nigeria. London, Cargate Press, 42, in-8, 2s. R : B. D. Gibson, *Int. R. Missions*, 43, vol. 32, p. 351-352.

2915. WALTON (R. C.). Two Baptist pamphleteers [J. E. Bicheno and J. Ovington]. *Baptist Quar.*, 40, vol. 10, p. 209-214.

2916. WATT (Hugh). Thomas Chalmers and the disruption. London, Nelson, 43, in-8, viii-363 p., 12s. 6d. (Chalmers lects., 1940-44). R : W. F. Gray, *Quar. R.*, 43, vol. 281, p. 28-42.

2917. WATTS (G. B.). The Waldenses in the New World. London, Cambridge Univ. Press, 42, in-8, xii-310 p., (illus.), 21s.

2918. WEARMOUTH (R. F.). Methodism and the common people of the 18th century. London, Epworth Press, 45, in-8, 276 p., 12s. 6d.

2919. WHITEHORN (R. D.). The background of the Westminster Assembly. *J. presb. hist. Soc.*, 43, vol. 7, p. 168-173.

2920. WHITLEY (W. T.). The Baptist Annual Register, 1790. *Baptist Quar.*, 40, vol. 10, p. 122-126.

2921. WHITLEY (W. T.). General Ludlow's Baptist comrades. *Baptist Quar.*, 42, vol. 11, p. 39-45.

2922. WHITNEY (J.). John Woolman, Quaker. London, Harrap, 43, in-8, 432 p., (illus.), 21s.

2923. WILLCOCKS (M. P.). Bunyan calling : a voice from the 17th century. London, Allen, 43, in-8, 236 p., 12s. 6d. R : E. A. Payne, *Baptist Quar.*, 43, vol. 11, p. 179-181.

2924. WILLIAMSON (H. R.). The past fifty years in China of the Baptist Missionary Society, 1892-1942. London, Carey Press, 42, in-8, 51 p., 6d. (Celebrations ser.).

2925. WILSON (Charles E.). The B.M.S. and Bible translation. *Baptist Quar.*, 40, vol. 10, p. 97-105, 159-167.

2926. WILSON (H. G.). One hundred years of religious and social work in Birmingham : the Church of the Messiah domestic mission. *Trans. Unitarian hist. Soc.*, 45, vol. 8, p. 113-121.

2927. WINSLOW (O. E.). Jonathan Edwards, 1703-1758 : a biography. London, Macmillan, 40, in-8, xiv-406 p., (illus.), 16s.

2927a. WINTERBOTHAM (F. P.). Kensington Chapel. *Congreg. hist. Soc. Trans.*, 44, vol. 14, p. 241-248.

2928. ZAREK (O.). The Quakers, tr. E. W. Dickes. London, Dakers, 43, in-8, 216 p., 10s. 6d.

§ 5. **Non-Christian Religions and Sects**

2929. ANDERSON (N.). Desert saints : the Mormon frontier in Utah. London, Cambridge Univ. Press, 42, in-8, xx-460 p., (illus., map), 24s.

2930. BARNETT (Lionel D.) ed. Bevis Marks records : contributions to the history of the Spanish and Portuguese Congregation of London, illus. by facsimiles of documents. Pt. 1 : The early history of the Congregation from the beginning until 1800. London, The Congregation, 40, in-4, 62 p., 10s. 6d. R : C. Roth, *B. Inst. hist. Research*, 41, vol. 18, p. 121. C.R., *Eng. hist. R.*, 41, vol. 56, p. 341-342. J. Parkes, *Econ. Hist. R.*, 43, vol. 13, p. 134.

2931. BLOMFIELD (Sara Louisa, Lady). The Chosen highway. London, Bahai Publ. Trust, 40, in-8, x-265 p., 7s. 6d. R : L. D. Barnett, *J. asiatic Soc.*, 41, p. 375-376.

2932. COHEN (Lucy). Some recollections of Claude Goldsmid Montefiore, 1858-1938. London, Faber, 40, in-8, 277 p., 12s. 6d.

2933. CURTISS (John S.). An appraisal of the Protocols of Zion. London, Oxford Univ. Press, 42, in-8, vi-118 p., 6s. 6d. R : C.R., *Eng. hist. R.*, 44, vol. 59, p. 287.

§ 1. General

2934. ADY (C. M.). Morals and manners of the Quattrocento. London, Oxford Univ. Press, 42, in-8, 20 p., 1s. 6d.

2935. ALLEN (D. C.). The star-crossed renaissance : the quarrel about astrology and its influence in England. London, Cambridge Univ. Press, 42, in-8, xii-280 p., 18s. R : U. Ellis-Fermor, Mod. Language R., 42, vol. 37, p. 497-498.

2936. BEARD (C. A. and M. R.). The American spirit : a study of the idea of civilization in America. London, Cape, 42, in-8, 696 p., 21s. (Rise of Amer. civilization, vol. 4).

2937. BLAU (J. L.). The Christian interpretation of the Cabala in the Renaissance. London, Oxford Univ. Press, 44, in-8, 176 p., 15s. 6d.

2938. BURCKHARDT (J. C.). The civilization of the Renaissance [tr. by S. G. C. Middlemore]. London, Allen & Unwin, 44, in-8, 461 p., (illus.), 7s. 6d.

2939. BUSH (D.). The Renaissance and English humanism. London, Oxford Univ. Press, 40, in-8, 139 p., 7s.

2940. CRAWFORD (W. R.). A century of Latin-American thought. London, Oxford Univ. Press, 44, in-8, 328 p., 20s.

2941. FELLOWES (E. H.) and PINE (Edward). The Tenbury letters, selected and ed. by E. H. Fellowes and E. Pine. London, Golden Cockerel Press, 43, in-8, 200 p., 42s.

2942. GRIFFITH (Gwilym O.). Interpreters of man : a review of secular and religious thought from Hegel to Barth. London, Lutterworth Press, 43, in-8, 252 p., 15s.

2943. GRUBBS (Henry A.). Jean-Baptiste Rousseau, his life and works. London, Oxford Univ. Press, 41, in-8, 320 p., 14s. R : L. W. Tancock, Mod. Language R., 45, vol. 40, p. 63-64.

2944. HARRISON (M.). Count Cagliostro. London, Rich & Cowan, 42, in-8, 320 p., (illus.), 18s.

2945. HELLEINER (K. F.). An essay on the rise of historical pessimism in the 19th century. Canad. J. Econ. pol. Sci., 42, vol. 8, p. 514-536.

2946. KLIBANSKY (Raymond). Leibniz's unknown correspondence with English scholars and men of letters. Mediaeval and Renaissance Stud., 41, vol. 1, p. 133-149.

2947. KREJí (Karel). Polish influences on the development of Czech culture. Slavonic Y.B. (Slavonic R.), 40, vol. 19, p. 110-122.

2948. LEE-MILNE (J.) ed. The National trust ; account of 50 years' achievement. London, Batsford, 45, in-8, viii-132 p., (illus.), 15s.

2949. MARTIN (A. von). Sociology of the Renaissance, tr. from the German by L. W. Leukens, ed. by K. Mannheim. London, Routledge, 44, in-8, 100 p., 8s. 6d. (Libr. of sociol.).

2950. NEF (J. U.). The United States and civilization. London, Cambridge Univ. Press, 42, in-8, xviii-422 p., 18s. (C. R. Walgreen found. lect.).

2951. POST (A.). Popular free thought in America, 1825-1850. London, King, 43, in-8, 239 p., 15s.

2952. Soho Centenary, 1844-1944 : a gift from artists, writers and musicians. London, Hutchinson, 44, in-4, 108 p., 21s.

2954. STEWART (Herbert L.). The business morals of the middle class :

what do they owe to the Reformation ?'
Hibbert J., 42, vol. 40, p. 156-165.

2955. TAYLOR (R. E.). No royal
road : Luca Pacioli and his times.
London, Oxford Univ. Press, 43,
in-8, 458 p., (illus.), 24s.

2956. TILLYARD (E. M. W.). The
Elizabethan world picture. London,
Chatto & Windus, 43, in-8, 108 p.,
6s. R : C. Caernarvon, *Theology*, 43,
vol. 46, p. 187-189. H. J. C. Grierson,
Mod. Language R., 44, vol. 39, p. 69-73.

2957. WADE (Ira O.). Voltaire and
Madame du Châtelet, an essay on the
intellectual activity at Cirey. London,
Oxford Univ. Press, 41, in-8, xii-
241 p., 18s. 6d. (Princeton publ. in
Romance lang.). R : A.J.G., *History*,
42, vol. 26, p. 320-321. J. Lough, *Mod.
Language R.*, 42, vol. 37, p. 225-227.

2958. WILLEY (Basil). The eigh-
teenth-century background. London,
Chatto, 40, in-8, 310 p., 15s. R : B.
Blackstone, *Theology*, 40, vol. 40,
p. 457-459.

2959. WILLIAMS (Ifor) and others.
Diwylliant Cymru (Welsh culture).
Trans. Soc. Cymmr., 39 (40), p. 157-
174.

2960. WILSON (T. G.). Victorian
doctor : the life of Sir William Wilde.
London, Methuen, 42, in-8, 338 p.,
15s.

§ 2. Academies, Universities and Educational Institutions

2961. BECKER (C. L.). Cornell
University : founders and the founding. London, Oxford Univ. Press,
44, in-8, 252 p., (illus.), 16s. 6d.

2962. BLOCK (Geoffrey D. M.).
Jewish students at the universities of
Great Britain and Ireland, excluding
London, 1936-1939. *Sociol. R.*, 42,
vol. 35, p. 183-197.

2963. BOARDMAN (F. W.). Columbia ; an American university in peace
and war. London, Oxford Univ.
Press, 44, in-8, 108 p., (illus.), 6s. 6d.

2964. BRITTAIN (F.). A short
history of Jesus College, Cambridge.
Cambridge, Heffer, 40, in-8, 68 p.,
(illus.), 3s. 6d. R : W. K. L. Clarke,
Theology, 41, vol. 42, p. 128.

2965. BUSCOT (W.). The history of
Cotton College, at Sedgley Park, 1763-
1873. London, Burns, Oates, 40,
in-8, xi-308 p., 10s. 6d.

2966. CALVIN (D. D.). Queen's
University at Kingston, 1841-1941.
Kingston, The University, 41, in-8,
321 p., $2.50. R : A.M., *Queen's
Quar.*, 41, vol. 48, p. 317. W. S. Fox,
Canad. hist. R., 41, vol. 22, p. 434-
435.

2967. CAMBRIDGE UNIVERSITY. Historical register of University of Cambridge, supplement 1931-1940. London, Cambridge Univ. Press, 42, in-8,
viii-654 p., 15s.

2968. CHEYNEY (Edward Potts).
History of the University of Pennsyl-
vania, 1740-1940. London, Oxford
Univ. Press, 40, in-8, 461 p., 18s.

2969. COLE (A. C.). A hundred
years of Mount Holyoke College.
London, Oxford Univ. Press, 40, in-8,
426 p., 18s.

2970. COOPER (John Irwin). The
Canada education and home missionary society. *Canad. hist. R.*, 45, vol.
26, p. 42-47.

2971. FURNESS (W.) ed. The centenary history of Rossall school.
Fleetwood, W. Furness, 45, in-8,
386 p., (illus.), 15s.

2972. KNIGHT (G. Wilson). The
dynasty of Stowe. London, Fortune
Press, 45, in-8, 146 p., 10s. 6d.

2973. LYONS (Sir Henry). The
Royal society, 1660-1940 : a history
of its administration under its Charters. London, Cambridge Univ.
Press, 44, in-8, x-344 p., 25s.

2974. McLachlan (H.). Warrington Academy : its history and influence. Manchester, Chetham Soc., 43, in-8, viii-151 p., (plates), members only. (Remains, hist. and literary, n.s., vol. 107). R : R. N. Cross, *Hibbert J.*, 44, vol. 42, p. 379-381. A.D.H., *Trans. Unitarian hist. Soc.*, 44, vol. 7, p. 87-88.

2975. N. (N.). The Jagiellonian university, Cracow. *Slavonic Y.B. (Slavonic R.)*, 40, vol. 19, p. 96-109.

2976. Oman (Sir Charles). Memories of Victorian Oxford, and of some early years. London, Methuen, 41, in-8, 288 p., 15s.

2977. Penrose (Stephen B. L.). That they may have life : the story of the American University of Beirut, 1866-1941. London, Oxford Univ. Press, 42, in-8, 365 p., 17s. R : H. Bowman, *J. central asian Soc.*, 42, vol. 29, p. 254-256. H. S. Coffin, *Int. R. Missions*, 42, vol. 31, p. 467-468.

2978. Queen's University (Kingston, Ontario) : a centenary volume, 1841-1941 [ed. by R. C. Wallace]. Toronto, Ryerson Press, 41, in-8, xi-189 p., (illus.), $2.50, limited ed. R : F. Landon, *Canad. hist. R.*, 42, vol. 23, p. 332. C.A.C., *Queen's Quar.*, 42, vol. 49, p. 280-281.

2979. Salmond (J. B.) and Bushnell (G. H.). Henderson's benefaction : a tercentenary acknowledgment of the University's debt to Alexander Henderson. St. Andrews, Henderson, 42, in-4, 56 p., (plates), 7s. 6d. (Univ. of St. Andrews, Libr. publ., 2). R : H.W.M., *Eng. hist. R.*, 43, vol. 58, p. 118-119.

2980. Stanier (R. S.). Magdalen School (Oxford). Oxford, Blackwell, 40, in-8, xi-252 p., (illus.), 10s. 6d.

2981. Stewart (Herbert L.). The Platonic academy of Florence. *Hibbert J.*, 45, vol. 43, p. 226-236.

2982. Sweetman (E.). History of the Melbourne Teachers' College and its predecessors. London, Oxford Univ. Press, 40, in-8, 144 p., 5s. (Educ. research ser., 157).

2983. Trevelyan (G. M.). Trinity College : an historical sketch. London, Cambridge Univ. Press, 43, in-8, 120 p., (illus.), 6s. R : F. M. P(owicke), *Eng. hist. R.*, 44, vol. 59, p. 434.

2984. Tylecote (M. E.). The education of women at Manchester University, 1883-1933. Manchester, Univ. Press, 41, in-8, ix-150 p., 5s.

2985. Venn (J. A.). Alumni Cantabrigienses : a biographical list of all known students, graduates and holders of office at the University of Cambridge from earliest times to 1900. Pt. 2 : 1752-1900. Vol. 1 : Abbey-Challis; Vol. 2 : Chalmers-Fytche. London, Cambridge Univ. Press, 40-44, 2 vols. in-8, 550, 593 p., 300s. R (vol. 1) : A. B. Emden, *Eng. hist. R.*, 41, vol. 56, p. 507-508. A.R.W., *Antiq. J.*, 41, vol. 21, p. 350-351. (vol. 2) : *Antiq. J.*, 45, vol. 25, p. 88-89.

2986. Vroom (F. W.). King's College (Nova Scotia) : a chronicle, 1789-1939. Collections and recollections. Halifax, N.S., Imperial Publ. Co., 41, in-8, xii-160 p., $2.50. R : W. S. Wallace, *Canad. hist. R.*, 41, vol. 22, p. 435-436.

2987. Wallace (R. C.) ed. Some great men of Queen's (University, Kingston, Ontario) : Grant, Watson, Dupuis, Cappon, Jordan, Shortt. Toronto; Halifax, Ryerson Press, 41, in-8, 133 p., $1.50. R : W. S. Wallace, *Canad. hist. R.*, 41, vol. 22, p. 435-436.

2988. Walls (Robert R.). Innerpeffray : Scotland's first public library (1680). *Scottish geogr. Mag.*, 40, vol. 56, p. 65-69.

2989. Wellard (J. H.). The public library comes of age. London, Grafton, 40, in-8, viii-204 p., 10s. 6d.

2990. WINSTANLEY (D. A.). Early Victorian Cambridge. London, Cambridge Univ. Press, 40, in-8, 472 p., 25s. R : M. G. Jones, *History*, 41, vol. 26, p. 82-83.

§ 3. Education

2991. ALLEN (Carleton Kemp). Forty years of the Rhodes Scholarships. London, Oxford Univ. Press, 44, in-8, 20 p., private distribution.

2992. BERRY (Edmund G.). Bronson Alcott, educational reformer. *Queen's Quar.*, 45, vol. 52, p. 44-52.

2993. BROWN (C. K. F.). The Church's part in education, 1833-1941. London, S.P.C.K., 42, in-8, 192 p., 7s. 6d.

2994. BURR (Nelson R.). Education in New Jersey, 1630-1871. London, Oxford Univ. Press, 42, in-8, 366 p., (illus.), 18s. 6d. (Princeton hist. of New Jersey, vol. 4). R : D. W. B(rogan), *Eng. hist. R.*, 44, vol. 59, p. 421-422.

2995. CAVANAGH (F. A.). State intervention in English education. *History*, 40, vol. 25, p. 143-156.

2996. CLARKE (M. L.). Greek studies in England, 1700-1830. London, Cambridge Univ. Press, 45, in-8, vi-256 p., 18s.

2997. COSTIN (W. C.). William Laud, President of St. John's College and Chancellor of the University of Oxford. Oxford, Blackwell, 45, in-8, 20 p., 2s.

2998. CUNNINGHAM (K. S.), MC-INTYRE (G. A.) and RADFORD (W. C.). Review of education in Australia, 1938. London, Oxford Univ. Press, 40, in-8, 252 p., 8s. 6d.

2999. ELWELL (C. E.). The influence of the enlightenment on the Catholic theory of education in France, 1750-1850. London, Oxford Univ. Press, 44, in-8, 346 p., 20s.

3000. EVANS (Emrys) and others. The Welsh Intermediate Education Act, 1889. *Trans. Soc. Cymmr.*, 39 (40), p. 101-131.

3001. FLETCHER (F. T. H.). Montesquieu and British education in the 18th century. *Mod. Language R.*, 43, vol. 38, p. 298-306.

3002. GORDON (Wilhelmina). Daniel M. Gordon, his life. Toronto, Ryerson Press, 41, in-8, xvii-313 p., $3.50. R : A.E.P., *Queen's Quar.*, 41, vol. 48, p. 429-431. W. S. Wallace, *Canad. hist. R.*, 41, vol. 22, p. 435-436.

3003. GREG (W. W.). 'The English Schoolmaster': Dexter v. Burby, 1602. *Library*, 42, vol. 23, p. 90-93.

3004. HADDOW (A.). Political science in American colleges and universities, 1636-1900, ed. by W. Anderson. London, Appleton, 40, in-8, xiv-308 p., 12s. 6d. (Century pol. sci. ser.).

3005. HAVARD (W. T.) Bp. of St. Asaph. The educational and religious movement in the diocese of St. Asaph in the 18th century. *Nat. Library Wales J.*, 45, vol. 4, p. 35-45.

3006. HIGGINS (M. H.) and DE WINTON (C. F. S.). Survey of education in Portugal. London, Allen & Unwin, 42, in-8, 75 p., 3s. 6d.

3007. JAMET (Albert). Marguerite Bourgeoys, 1620-1700. Montréal, Presse Cath. Panaméricaine, 42, 2 vols. in-8, xiv-398, vi-400 p.

3008. MACK (Edward C.). Public schools and British opinion since 1860. London, Oxford Univ. Press, 42, in-8, 523 p., 18s. 6d.

3009. MAGNAN (C. J.). Educateurs d'autrefois : anciens professeurs à l'École Normale Laval : M. Napoléon Lacasse ; F. E. Juneau ; M. Ernest Gagnon ; M. J.-B. Cloutier ; M. Norbert Thibault. *B. Rech. hist.*, 42, vol. 48, p. 15-19 ; 44-50 ; 86-90 ; 139-145 ; 172-178.

3010. MAKEPEACE (L. M.). Sherman Thacher and his school. London, Oxford Univ. Press, 41, in-8, 217 p., 14s.

3011. MAURAULT (Olivier). Propos et portraits. Montréal, Éd. Bernard Valiquette, 41, in-8, 229 p., $1.25. R : E. R. Adair, Canad. hist. R., 42, vol. 23, p. 83-84.

3012. MONROE (P.). Founding of the American public school system : a history of education in the United States. London, Macmillan, 40, in-8, xiv-520 p., (illus.), 15s.

3013. NEEDHAM (Joseph). The teacher of nations : addresses and essays in commemoration of the visit to England of the great Czech educationalist Comenius, 1641, ed. by J. Needham. London, Cambridge Univ. Press, 42, in-8, vii-99 p., 5s. R : B. Willey, Philosophy, 43, vol. 18, p. 272-273. W. G. Moore, Mod. Language R., 43, vol. 38, p. 374. E. S. de B., History, 44, vol. 29, p. 100.

3014. PATON (John Lewis). The tercentenary of Comenius's visit to England, 1592-1671. B. John Rylands Library, 41/42, vol. 26, p. 149-157.

3015. PELLETIER (Louis-J.). Quelques maîtres d'école de la rive sud. B. Rech. hist., 43, vol. 49, p. 233-242.

3016. REMINGTON (G. C.) and METCALFE (John). The free library movement, 1935-1945. Austral. Quar., 45, vol. 17, no. 2, p. 87-97.

3017. SAVAGE (Roland Burke). A valiant Dublin woman [Teresa Mulally] : the story of George's Hill (1766-1940). Dublin, Gill, 40, in-8, xiv-312 p., 8s. 6d. R : J. Brady, Irish hist. Stud., 45, vol. 4, p. 367-369.

3018. SHIPTON (I.). Arnold of Rugby, 1842-1942. National R., 42, vol. 118, p. 553-558.

3019. SPINKA (M.). John Amos Comenius : the incomparable Moravian. London, Cambridge Univ. Press, 43, in-8, x-178 p., 12s.

3020. SPRAGGE (George W.). Joseph Lancaster in Montreal. Canad. hist. R., 41, vol. 22, p. 35-41.

3021. SPRAGGE (G. W.). John Strachan's contribution to education, 1800-1823. Canad. hist. R., 41, vol. 22, p. 147-158.

3022. STERRY (Sir Wasey). The Eton College register, 1441-1698, alphabetically arranged and ed. with biographical notes. Eton, Spottiswoode, Ballantyne, 43, in-4, xxxviii-414 p., 21s.

3023. TOMPKINS (D. D.). A Columbia College student in the 18th century, ed. by R. W. Irwin and E. L. Jacobsen. London, Oxford Univ. Press, 41, in-8, 85 p., 5s.

§ 4. The Press

3024. COLLINS (Douglas C.). A handlist of news pamphlets, 1590-1610. London, S.-W. Essex Tech. College, 43, in-8, xix-129 p., 10s. 6d. R : G.S.T., History, 44, vol. 29, p. 213. L. Hanson, Library, 45, vol. 26, p. 203-204.

3025. LUNN (Jean). Bibliography of the history of the Canadian press. Canad. hist. R., 41, vol. 22, p. 416-433.

3026. LUNN (Jean). Canadian newspapers before 1821, a preliminary list. Canad. hist. R., 44, vol. 25, p. 417-420.

3027. BAILLIE (James L.) jr. Charles Fothergill, 1782-1840. Canad. hist. R., 44, vol. 25, p. 376-396.

3028. BEVINGTON (M. M.). The Saturday Review, 1855-1868. London, Oxford Univ. Press, 42, in-8, 427 p., 17s. 6d. (Stud. in Engl. and compar. lit.).

3029. ELWIN (Malcolm). The founder of the ' Quarterly Review '— John Murray II. Quar. R., 43, vol. 281, p. 1-15.

3030. FAIRFAX (J. F.). The story of John Fairfax, commemorating the centenary of the Fairfax proprietary of the Sydney Morning Herald, 1841-1941. Sydney, Fairfax, 41, in-8, xix-169 p., 10s. 6d.

3031. FORD (Arthur R.). The Canadian press. *Canad. hist. R.*, 42, vol. 23, p. 241-246.

3032. GOVE (Philip Babcock). Early numbers of 'The Morning Chronicle' and 'Owen's Weekly Chronicle'. *Library,* 40, vol. 20, p. 412-424.

3033. HARVEY (D. C.). Newspapers of Nova Scotia, 1840-1867. *Canad. hist. R.*, 45, vol. 26, p. 279-301.

3034. HATTON (Ragnhild). The 'London Gazette' in 1718 : supply of news from abroad. *B. Inst. hist. Research*, 41, vol. 18, p. 108-111.

3035. HOWE (Ellic). The trade : passages from the literature of the printing craft, 1550-1935, selected by E. Howe. London, Hutchinson, 43, in-8, 151 p., 21s. R : A.F.J., *Library*, 43/44, vol. 24, p. 204-205.

3036. HOWE (E.). Newspaper printing in the 19th century. London, 43, in-8, 43 p., privately printed. R : A.F.J., *Library*, 43/44, vol. 24, p. 205.

3037. HUDSON (Derek). Thomas Barnes of 'The Times', with selections from his critical essays never before printed, ed. H. Child. London, Cambridge Univ. Press, 43, in-8, xii-196 p., (plates), 10s. 6d. R : R. Fulford, *History*, 44, vol. 29, p. 208-209. A.A., *Eng. hist. R.*, 45, vol. 60, p. 282-283.

3038. KIRKCONNELL (Watson). The European-Canadians in their press. *Canad. hist. Assoc. Rept.*, 40, p. 85-92.

3039. LEWIS (Idwal). Welsh newspapers and journals in the United States. *Nat. Library Wales J.*, 42, vol. 2, p. 124-130.

3040. MANSFIELD (F. J.). Gentlemen, the Press ! Chronicles of a crusade—official history of the N.U.J. London, W. H. Allen, 43, in-8, 579 p., 15s. 6d.

3041. MARCHAND (L. A.). The Athenaeum : a mirror of Victorian culture. London, Oxford Univ. Press, 42, in-8, 427 p., 16s.

3042. MARION (Séraphin). Les lettres canadiennes d'autrefois. Tom. 2-3. Ottawa, 40-42, 2 vols. in-8, 196, 208 p., $2.00. R : R. M. Saunders, *Canad. hist. R.*, 41, vol. 22, p. 66-68 ; 43, vol. 24, p. 64-65.

3043. MARTELL (J. S.). Early parliamentary reporting in Nova Scotia, 1817-1837. *Canad. hist. R.*, 40, vol. 21, p. 384-393.

3044. RICHARDS (Thomas) and others. Dinbych a'r wasg Cymraeg (Denbigh and the Welsh press). *Trans. Soc. Cymmr.*, 39 (40), p. 132-156.

3045. WALLACE (W. S.). The journalist in Canadian politics : a retrospect. *Canad. hist. R.*, 41, vol. 22, p. 14-24.

3046. WALLACE (W. S.). The first journalists in Upper Canada. *Canad. hist. R.*, 45, vol. 26, p. 372-381.

§ 5. Philosophy

3047. BARNES (Winston H. F.). Richard Price, a neglected 18th-century moralist. *Philosophy*, 42, vol. 17, p. 159-173.

3048. BIDNEY (David). Psychology and ethics of Spinoza : a study in the history and logic of ideas. London, Oxford Univ. Press, 40, in-8, xv-454 p., 17s. R : A. Wolf, *Philosophy*, 41, vol. 16, p. 331-332.

3049. BORING (E. G.). Sensation and perception in the history of experimental psychology. London, Appleton, 42, in-8, 660 p., (figures), 26s. (Century psych. ser.).

3050. BRINTON (C.). Nietzsche. London, Oxford Univ. Press, 41, in-8, 284 p., 10s. 6d. (Makers of mod. Europe).

3051. BROAD (C. D.). The new philosophy : Bruno to Descartes. *Cambridge hist. J.*, 44, vol. 8, p. 36-54.

3052. BURGH (W. D. de). George Dawes Hicks, 1862-1941. London, Oxford Univ. Press, 42, in-8, 29 p., 3s.

3053. COPLESTON (Frederick). Friedrich Nietzsche. London, Burns, Oates, 42, in-8, xii-213 p., 18s. (Bellarmine ser., 7). R : F. H. Heinemann, *Philosophy*, 44, vol. 19, p. 86-89. B. Wormald, *Theology*, 43, vol. 46, p. 159-160. W. G. de Burgh, *Hibbert J.*, 43, vol. 41, p. 383-384.

3054. FLÜGEL (J. C.). A hundred years of psychology, 1833-1933. New ed. London, Duckworth, 40, in-8, 384 p., 8s. 6d.

3055. GOOCH (G. P.). Hobbes. London, Oxford Univ. Press, 40, in-8, 42 p., 2s. 6d.

3056. GRIFFITH (Gwilym O.). Interpreters of man : a review of secular and religious thought from Hegel to Barth. London, Lutterworth Press, 43, in-8, vii-242 p., 15s.

3057. HODGES (H. A.). Wilhelm Dilthey : an introduction. London, Paul, 44, in-8, 174 p., 10s. 6d.

3058. LOWRIE (W.). A short life of Kierkegaard. London, Oxford Univ. Press, 43, in-8, 284 p., 12s. 6d.

3059. McCOLLEY (Grant). Nicholas Hill and the ' Philosophia Epicurea '. *A. Sci.*, 39 [40], vol. 4, p. 390-405.

3060. McEACHRAN (F.). The life and philosophy of Johann Gottfried Herder. London, Oxford Univ. Press, 40, in-8, 98 p., 7s. 6d.

3061. MACUSE (Herbert). Reason and revolution : Hegel and the rise of social theory. London, Oxford Univ. Press, 41, in-8, xii-431 p., 16s. R : J. Cohn, *Sociol. R.*, 42, vol. 35, p. 101-106. T. M. Knox, *Philosophy*, 42,

vol. 17, p. 264-267. W. G. de Burgh, *Hibbert J.*, 42, vol. 40, p. 299-301.

3062. MITIN (M.). Twenty-five years of philosophy in the U.S.S.R. *Philosophy*, 44, vol. 19, p. 76-84.

3063. MONOD-CASSIDY (Hélène). Un voyageur-philosophe au 18e siècle, l'abbé Jean-Bernard Le Blanc. London, Oxford Univ. Press, 41, in-8, 554 p., 28s. R : J. Lough, *Mod. Language R.*, 43, vol. 38, p. 365-366.

3064. MOSSNER (Ernest Campbell). The forgotten Hume : le bon David. London, Milford, 43, in-8, xv-251 p., 20s. R : J. C. Bryce, *Mod. Language R.*, 44, vol. 39, p. 197-198.

3065. MUIRHEAD (John Henry). Reflections of a journeyman in philosophy on the movement of thought and practice in his time, ed. by J. W. Harvey. London, Allen & Unwin, 42, in-8, xiii-215 p., 15s. R : H. Cook, *Baptist Quar.*, 42, vol. 11, p. 127-128. T. M. Knox, *Philosophy*, 43, vol. 18, p. 89-91. E. de Selincourt, *Hibbert J.*, 43, vol. 41, p. 183-185.

3066. NIKLAUS (Robert). Les *Pensées philosophiques* de Diderot. B. *John Rylands Library*, 41/42, vol. 26, p. 121-148.

3067. RAVEN (C. E.). Synthetic philosophy in the seventeenth century. Oxford, Blackwell, 45, in-8, 24 p., 2s.

3068. STOJANOVIC (Dusan). Dalmatian philosophers. *Hibbert J.*, 40, vol. 38, p. 511-521.

3069. WELLS (Ronald V.). Three Christian Transcendentalists : James Marsh, Caleb Sprague Henry, Frederic Henry Hedge. London, Oxford Univ. Press, 43, in-8, 240 p., 18s. 6d. (Columbia stud. in Amer. culture, 12).

3070. WRIGHT (W. K.). A history of modern philosophy. London, Macmillan, 41, in-8, xvi-633 p., 12s. 6d.

§ 6. Exact, Natural and Medical Sciences

3071. Analytical bibliography of the history of engineering and applied science. *Trans. Newcomen Soc.*, 38/39 [40]-40/41 [44], vol. 19-21.

3072. KARPINSKI (L. C.). Bibliography of mathematical works printed in America through 1850. London, Oxford Univ. Press, 40, in-8, 697 p., 25s.

3073. ROBINSON (A. L.) ed. William McDougall, F.R.S. A bibliography, together with a brief outline of his life. London, Cambridge Univ. Press, 43, in-8, xiv-54 p., 9s.

3074. SMART (John). Bibliography of F. W. Edwards (1888-1940). *J. Soc. Bibl. nat. Hist.*, 45, vol. 2, p. 19-34.

3075. SMART (J.). Bibliography of Enrico Brunetti (1862-1927). *J. Soc. Bibl. nat. Hist.*, 45, vol. 2, p. 35-38.

3076. SMART (J.). Bibliography of Percy H. Grimshaw (1869-1939). *J. Soc. Bibl. nat. Hist.*, 45, vol. 2, p. 39-42.

3077. SMART (J.). Bibliography of E. E. Austen (1869-1938). *J. Soc. Bibl. nat. Hist.*, 45, vol. 2, p. 43-49.

3078. ABRAHAM (J. J.). Lettsom : his life and times. New ed. London, Heinemann, 44, in-8, xx-498 p., (illus.), 15s.

3079. BARWELL (E. H. G.). The death ray man : biography of Grindell Matthews. London, Hutchinson, 43, in-8, 175 p., (illus.), 12s. 6d.

3080. BATEMAN (D.). Berkeley Moynihan; surgeon. London, Macmillan, 40, in-8, xvi-356 p., (plates), 12s. 6d.

3081. BAYON (H. P.). William Harvey, physician and biologist : his precursors, opponents and successors. Pt. 5. *A. Sci.*, 39 [40], vol. 4, p. 329-389.

3082. BOWMAN (A. K.). The life and teaching of Sir William Macewen: a chapter in the history of surgery. Edinburgh, Hodge, 42, in-8, 425 p., 21s.

3083. BRAGG (L.). The history of X-ray analysis. London, Longmans, 43, in-8, 25 p., (illus.), 1s. (Sci. in Britain ser.).

3084. BUTLER (William). The fatality rate of measles : a study of its trend in time. *J. Roy. statist. Soc.*, 45, vol. 108, p. 259-285.

3085. CADELL (Sir Patrick). John Moodie, military medical writer of the 18th century. *J. Soc. Army hist. Research*, 43, vol. 22, p. 148-153.

3086. CALVERT (E. M. and R.T.C.). Serjeant-surgeon John Knight, surgeon-general, 1664-1680. London, Heinemann, 40, in-8, 112 p., (plates), 10s. 6d.

3087. CHAPMAN (S.). Edmond Halley as physical geographer and the story of his charts. London, Roy. Astronomical Soc., 41, in-8, 15 p., (maps, charts), 2s. 6d. (Occasional notes, 9). R : A.R.H., *Geogr. J.*, 41, vol. 98, p. 293-296.

3088. CHESNEY (A. M.). The Johns Hopkins Hospital and the Johns Hopkins University School of Medicine. Vol. 1. London, Oxford Univ. Press, 44, in-8, 336 p., (illus.), 18s. 6d.

3089. CROWTHER (J. G.). Famous American men of science. Vol. 1 : Benjamin Franklin, Joseph Henry. Vol. 2 : T. A. Edison, J. W. Gibbs. London, Penguin, 44, 2-vols. in-8, 191, 159 p., 1s. 6d.

3090. CURIE (E.). Madame Curie, ed. and abridged by P. E. Charvet. London, Cambridge Univ. Press, 42, in-8, viii-180 p., 5s.

3091. CUSHING (H.). The life of Sir William Osler. London, Oxford Univ. Press, 41, in-8, 1417 p., 21s.

3092. DAWSON (W. R.) ed. Sir Grafton Elliot Smith. London, Cape, 40, in-8, 272 p., 7s. 6d. (Academy books).

3093. DEFRIES (R. D.). Development of public health in Canada. Toronto, Canadian Public Health Assoc., 40, in-4, 184 p., $1.25.

3094. DICKINSON (H. W.). The Lewin diary : a link with Rennie. *Trans. Newcomen Soc.*, 38/39 [40], vol. 19, p. 109-117.

3095. DOBBIN (Leonard). The history of the discovery of phosgene. *A. Sci.*, 45, vol. 5, p. 270-287.

3096. DODD (A. H.). The influence of early science on English thought. *Hibbert J.*, 45, vol. 43, p. 216-225.

3097. DODDS (Jackson) and others. The story of the Canadian Red Cross. *Canad. geogr. J.*, 40, vol. 21, p. 283-323.

3098. DUFTON (A. F.). Early application of engineering to the warming of buildings. *Trans. Newcomen Soc.*, 40/41 (43), vol. 21, p. 99-107.

3099. EARNEST (E.). John and William Bartram, botanists and explorers, 1699-1777, 1739-1823. London, Oxford Univ. Press, 41, in-8, 195 p., 9s.

3100. EVE (A. S.) and CREASEY (C. H.). Life and work of John Tyndall. London, Macmillan, 45, in-8, 404 p., (illus.), 21s.

3101. FEATHER (N.). Lord Rutherford. London, Blackie, 40, in-8, xi-195 p., (illus.), 5s.

3102. FLEXNER (A.). Henry S. Pritchett. London, Oxford Univ. Press, 44, in-8, 220 p., (illus.), 16s. 6d.

3103. FRANKLIN (Benjamin). Experiments : a new ed. of Experiments and observations on electricity, ed. by I. B. Cohen. London, Oxford Univ. Press, 41, in-8, xxviii-453 p., (illus.), 17s. R : H. C. Plummer, *Eng. hist. R.*, 42, vol. 57, p. 510-512.

3104. FRASER (Peter). Papers of a pioneer, Sir Pendrill Varrier-Jones, collected by P. Fraser. London, Hutchinson, 43, in-8, 107 p., 6s.

3105. FRENCH (Sidney James). Torch and crucible : the life and death of Antoine Lavoisier. London, Oxford Univ. Press, 42, in-8, ix-285 p., 16s. R : H. C. Plummer, *Eng. hist. R.*, 43, vol. 58, p. 109-111.

3106. GAUL (H. A.) and EIDEMAN (R.). John Alfred Brashear, scientist and humanitarian, 1840-1920. London, Oxford Univ. Press, 41, in-8, 228 p., 10s. 6d. (Pennsylvania lives, 3).

3107. Goodrich collection, 1875 : list of drawings [history of engineering] in the Science Museum, South Kensington, London. *Trans. Newcomen Soc.*, 38/39 [40], vol. 19, p. 249-265.

3108. GRIFFIN (Francis J.). A catalogue of papers concerning the dates of publication of natural history books. 1st suppl. *J. Soc. Bibl. nat. Hist.*, 43, vol. 2, p. 1-17.

3109. HALL (J. K.) ed. One hundred years of American psychiatry. London, Oxford Univ. Press, 44, in-8, 676 p., (illus.), 40s.

3110. HAVARD (W. L.). Sir Paul Edmund de Strzelecki. *Roy. Austral. hist. Soc. J.*, 40, vol. 26, p. 20-97.

3111. JERVIS (James). The Rev. W. B. Clarke, M.A., F.R.S., F.G.S., F.R.G.S., ' the Father of Australian geology '. *Roy. Austral. hist. Soc. J.*, 44, vol. 30, p. 345-457.

3112. KEITH (Sir Arthur). Blumenbach's centenary. *Man*, 40, vol. 40, p. 82-85.

3113. KESTEN (H.). Copernicus and his world, tr. from the German by E. B. Ashton and N. Guterman. London, Secker & Warburg, 45, in-8, x-410 p., 21s.

3114. LaNauze (J. A.). Jevons in Sydney. *Econ. R.*, 41, vol. 17, p. 31-45.

3115. Langton (H. H.). Sir John Cunningham McLennan. London, Oxford Univ. Press, 40, in-8, 123 p., 11s. 6d.

3116. Lavell (Alfred E.). The beginning of Ontario mental hospitals. *Queen's Quar.*, 42, vol. 49, p. 59-67.

3117. Lewis (N. D. C.). A short history of psychiatric achievement with a forecast of the future. London, Chapman & Hall, 42, in-8, 275 p., 12s.

3118. McAllister (E. M.). Amos Eaton, scientist and educator, 1776-1842. London, Oxford Univ. Press, 41, in-8, 603 p., 22s. 6d.

3119. MacArthur (J. S.). A believer in the future life : F. W. H. Myers, 1843-1901. *Hibbert J.*, 43, vol. 41, p. 122-130.

3120. Mantell (Gideon). The journal of Gideon Mantell, surgeon and geologist, 1818-1852, ed. by E. C. Curwen. London, Oxford Univ. Press, 40, in-8, 315 p., 12s. 6d. R : *J. Soc. Bibl. nat. Hist.*, 43, vol. 1, p. 478.

3121. Miller (Norman). Ancestry of modern mathematics. *Queen's Quar.*, 45, vol. 52, p. 22-30.

3122. Millington (E. C.). History of the Young-Helmholtz theory of colour vision. *A.Sci.*, 42, vol. 5, p. 167-176.

3123. Millington (E. C.). Theories of cohesion in the 17th century. *A.Sci.*, 45, vol. 5, p. 253-269.

3124. Mitman (Carl W.). Stevens's ' Porcupine ' boiler, 1804 : a recent study. *Trans. Newcomen Soc.*, 38/39 [40], vol. 19, p. 165-171.

3125. Moorhead (Thomas Gillman). A short history of Sir Patrick Dun's hospital. Dublin, Hodges, Figgis, 42, in-8, 228 p., 7s. 6d. R : T. W. T. Dillon, *Irish hist. Stud.*, 45, vol. 4, p. 287-288.

3126. Naile (F.). The life of Langstroth. London, Oxford Univ. Press, 42, in-8, 215 p., (illus.), 11s. 6d.

3127. Norwood (W. F.). Medical education in the United States before the Civil War. London, Oxford Univ. Press, 44, in-8, 504 p., 36s.

3128. Ó Raghallaigh (Deasmumhan). Three centuries of Irish chemists. Cork, Univ. Press, 41, in-8, 30 p., 2s. 6d. R : K. C. Bailey, *Irish hist. Stud.*, 42, vol. 3, p. 227-228.

3129. Partington (J. R.). The early history of strontium. *A.Sci.*, 42, vol. 5, p. 157-166.

3130. Pearson (C. E.). The history of the hydraulic extrusion process. *Trans. Newcomen Soc.*, 40/41 (43), vol. 21, p. 109-121.

3131. Pulay (E.). Historic events in the light of modern medicine. London, Muller, 43, in-8, 32 p., 2s. 6d.

3132. Rabel (Gabriele). Lamarck : in honour of the 200th anniversary of his birth. *19th Century*, 45, vol. 137, p. 258-264.

3133. Raven (Charles E.). John Ray, naturalist : his life and works. London, Cambridge Univ. Press, 42, in-8, xx-502 p., 30s. R : *Quar. R.*, 43, vol. 281, p. 125-126. A. Peel, *Congreg. Quar.*, 43, vol. 21, p. 69.

3134. Rayleigh (Lord). The life of Sir J. J. Thomson, O.M. London, Cambridge Univ. Press, 42, in-8, viii-299 p., (illus.), 18s. R : *Quar. R.*, 43, vol. 280, p. 241.

3135. Rodgers (A. D.). John Torrey. London, Oxford Univ. Press, 42, in-8, 358 p., 18s. 6d.

3136. Rodgers (A. D.). John Merle Coulter, missionary in science. London, Oxford Univ. Press, 44, in-8, 332 p., (illus.), 25s.

3137. Rodgers (A. D.). American botany, 1873-1892. London, Oxford Univ. Press, 44, in-8, 350 p., 25s.

3138. RUDNICKI (J.). Nicholas Copernicus, tr. from the Polish by B. W. A. Massey. London, Polish Research Centre, 43, in-4, 53 p., (plates), 10s.

3139. RUSSELL (W. L.). New York hospital : a history of the psychiatric service. London, Oxford Univ. Press, 45, in-8, 574 p., (illus.), 50s.

3140. SCHUCHERT (C.) and LE VENE (C. M.). O. C. Marsh, pioneer in paleontology. London, Oxford Univ. Press, 41, in-8, 541 p., 22s. 6d.

3141. SCOTT (E. Kilburn). Smeaton's engine of 1767 at New River Head, London. *Trans. Newcomen Soc.*, 38/39 [40], vol. 19, p. 119-126.

3142. SEABORN (Edwin). The march of medicine in western Ontario. Toronto, Ryerson Press, 44, in-8, xviii-386 p., (illus.), $6.00. R : J.M., *Queen's Quar.*, 45, vol. 52, p. 244-246.

3143. SHERBORN (C. D.). Where is the collection ? An account of the various natural history collections which have come under the notice of the compiler, 1880-1939. London, Cambridge Univ. Press, 40, in-8, 148 p., 3s. 6d.

3144. SMITH (Edgar C.). Samuel Hall and his inventions. *Trans. Newcomen Soc.*, 38/39 [40], vol. 19, p. 87-100.

3145. SMITH (E. C.). The first 20 years of screw propulsion. *Trans. Newcomen Soc.*, 38/39 [40], vol. 19, p. 145-164.

3146. SPRIGGS (Edmund Anthony). John Hunter and his approach to pathology. *A.Sci.*, 42, vol. 5, p. 177-184.

3147. TAYLOR (F. Sherwood). A century of science, 1840-1940. London, Heinemann, 41, in-8, 292 p., 8s. 6d.

3148. TAYLOR (F. S.). The origin of the thermometer. *A.Sci.*, 42, vol. 5, p. 129-156.

3149. TAYLOR (F. S.). The evolution of the still. *A. Sci.*, 45, vol. 5, p. 185-202.

3150. THORNDIKE (Lynn). A history of magic and experimental science. Vol. 5-6. London, Oxford Univ. Press, 41, 2 vols. in-8, xxii-695, xviii-766 p., 66s. 6d. (Hist. of science soc. publ.).

3151. THURSTON (R. H.). A history of the growth of the steam engine. London, Oxford Univ. Press, 40, in-8, 555 p., 14s.

3152. TILANUS (C. B.). Extracts from the diary of C. B. Tilanus. Surgery : a hundred years ago, ed. by Prof. H. T. Deelman, tr. from the Dutch by J. Bles. London, Bles, 40, in-8, 156 p., 6s.

3153. TORY (Henry M.) ed. A history of science in Canada, by F. D. Adams [and others], ed. by H. M. Tory. Toronto, Ryerson Press, 40, in-8, vi-152 p., (illus.), $2.50. R : *Canad. geogr. J.*, 41, vol. 22, p. 109.

3154. VENDRYES (Harry E.). The life of Sir Hans Sloane. *Jamaican hist. R.*, 45, vol. 1, p. 66-75.

3155. WAILES (Rex). Tide mills in England and Wales. *Trans. Newcomen Soc.*, 38/39 [40], vol. 19, p.1-33.

3156. WAILES (R.) and WEBSTER (H. A.). Post mills of the Nord [France]. *Trans. Newcomen Soc.*, 38/39 [40], vol. 19, p. 127-144.

3157. WAYMAN (D. G.). Edward Sylvester Morse. London, Oxford Univ. Press, 44, in-8, 474 p., (plates), 25s. 6d.

3158. WHITE (George). A history of early needle-making. *Trans. Newcomen Soc.*, 40/41 (43), vol. 21, p. 81-86.

3159. ZILBOORG (G.) and HENRY (G. W.). A history of medical psychology. London, Allen & Unwin, 42, in-8, 606 p., (illus., facs.), 28s.

§ 7. **Literature**

a. GENERAL

3160. Cambridge bibliography of English literature, ed. by F. W. Bateson. London, Cambridge Univ. Press, 40, 4 vols. in-8, 147s. R : C. J. Sisson, *Mod. Language R.*, 41, vol. 36, p. 247-249.

3161. MILLER (Edmund Morris). Australian literature from its beginnings to 1935, a descriptive and bibliographical survey, initiated and commenced by the late Sir John Quick. London, Oxford Univ. Press, 41, 2 vols. in-4, 42s.

3162. ARROM (José Juan). Historia de la literatura dramática cubana. London, Oxford Univ. Press, 44, in-8, 132 p., (plates), 12s. 6d. (Yale Romanic stud., 23). R : E. Sarmiento, *Mod. Language R.*, 45, vol. 40, p. 72-73.

3163. BISSON (L.). A short history of French literature from the Middle Ages to the present day. London, Penguin, 43, in-8, 159 p., 9d. (Pelican ser.).

3164. BOAS (F. S.). American scenes, Tudor to Georgian, in the English Literary Mirror. London, Oxford Univ. Press, 44, in-8, 20 p., 2s.

3165. Cambridge history of American literature, in 1 vol. London, Cambridge Univ. Press, 44, in-8, xlii-1,488 p., 18s.

3166. DAICHES (David). The King James version of the English Bible. An account of the development and sources of the English Bible of 1611, with special reference to the Hebrew tradition. London, Cambridge Univ. Press, 41, in-8, 228 p., 15s. R : B. J. Roberts, *Mod. Language R.*, 41, vol. 36, p. 526-529.

3167. DYSON (H. V. D.) and BUTT (John). Augustans and Romantics, 1689-1830. London, Cresset Press, 40, in-8, 318 p., 7s. 6d. (Intr. to Engl. lit., vol. 3).

3168. FRAME (D. M.). Montaigne in France, 1812-1852. London, Oxford Univ. Press, 41, in-8, 320 p., 15s. R : W. G. Moore, *Mod. Language R.*, 42, vol. 37, p. 391-392.

3169. GOLABEK (Jozef). Sorb-Lusatian literature, a survey. *Slavonic Y.B.* (*Slavonic R.*), 40, vol. 19, p. 276-290.

3170. GORDON (George Stuart). Anglo-American literary relations. London, Oxford Univ. Press, 42, in-8, 119 p., 5s. R : *National R.*, 43, vol. 120, p. 84. C. J. Sisson, *Mod. Language R.*, 43, vol. 38, p. 155-156.

3171. HAYCRAFT (H.). Murder for pleasure : life and times of the detective story. London, Davies, 42, in-8, 376 p., 10s. 6d.

3172. LARRABEE (S. A.). English bards and Grecian marbles. London, Oxford Univ. Press, 43, in-8, 324 p., (illus.), 22s. 6d.

3173. LEECHMAN (Douglas). The Indian in literature. *Queen's Quar.*, 43, vol. 50, p. 155-163.

3174. McCORMICK (E. H.). Letters and art in New Zealand. Wellington, Whitcombe and Tombs, 40, in-8, xii-205 p., (plates), 5s. (N.Z. centennial surveys, 10).

3175. MARION (Séraphin). Les lettres canadiennes d'autrefois. Tom. 2-4. Hull, P.Q., Les Ed. ' L'Eclair ', 40-44, 3 vols. in-8, 196, 208, 208 p., $3.00. R (Tom. 2) : R. M. Saunders, *Canad. hist. R.*, 41, vol. 22, p. 66-68. (Tom. 3) : R. M. Saunders, *Canad. hist. R.*, 43, vol. 24, p. 64-65. (Tom. 4) : M. Wade, *Canad. hist. R.*, 44, vol. 25, p. 440-442.

3176. MARRIOTT (sir J. A. R.). English history in English fiction. London, Blackie, 40, in-8, xii-308 p., 8s. 6d.

3177. Mayo (Robert D.). The Gothic short story in the magazines. *Mod. Language R.*, 42, vol. 37, p. 448-454.

3178. Monroe (N. E.). The novel and society. London, Oxford Univ. Press, 42, in-8, 292 p., 14s.

3179. Neff (E.). A revolution in European poetry, 1660-1900. London, Oxford Univ. Press, 40, in-8, 279 p., 15s.

3180. Peyre (H.). L'influence des littératures antiques sur la littérature française moderne. London, Oxford Univ. Press, 42, in-8, 110 p., 9s. (Yale Romantic stud.).

3181. Price (L. M.). Christian Heinrich Schmid and his translations of English drama. London, Cambridge Univ. Press, 42, in-8, lx-122 p., 7s. 6d. (Univ. of Calif. publ. in mod. philol., 26).

3182. Robertson (Jean). The art of letter writing : an essay on the handbooks published in England during the 16th and 17th centuries. Liverpool, Univ. Press, 42, in-8, 80 p., 7s. 6d. R : J. H. P. Pafford, *Library*, 44, vol. 25, p. 99.

3183. Sharp (R. L.). From Donne to Dryden : the revolt against metaphysical poetry. London, Oxford Univ. Press, 40, in-8, 221 p., 14s.

3184. Shuster (G. N.). The English ode from Milton to Keats. London, Oxford Univ. Press, 41, in-8, 324 p., 15s.

3185. Smith (N.). The origin and history of the Association : English Association Chairman's address. London, Oxford Univ. Press, 42, in-8, 12 p., 2s.

3186. Stauffer (D. A.). The art of biography in 18th-century England. London, Oxford Univ. Press, 41, 2 vols. in-8, 588, 303 p., 38s.

3187. Stoll (E. E.). Shakespeare, and other masters. London, Oxford Univ. Press, 41, in-8, 446 p., 19s.

3188. Thorp (Mary). The study of the Nibelungenlied, being the history of the epic and legend from 1755 to 1937. Oxford, Clarendon Press, 40, in-8, vi-196 p., 12s. 6d. (Oxf. stud. in mod. lang. and lit.). R : F. P. Pickering, *Mod. Language R.*, 40, vol. 35, p. 555-556.

3189. Ward (A. C.) ed. Specimens of English dramatic criticism, 17-20th centuries. London, Oxford Univ. Press, 45, in-8, 366 p., 3s. (World's classics).

3190. Wilson (F. P.). English proverbs and dictionaries of proverbs. *Library*, 45, vol. 26, p. 51-71.

3191. Workman (S. K.). Fifteenth century translation as an influence in English prose. London, Oxford Univ. Press, 40, in-8, 210 p., 9s.

b. RENAISSANCE

3192. Aaron (R. I.). The 'Autobiography' of Edward, first Lord Herbert of Cherbury : the original manuscript material. *Mod. Language R.*, 41, vol. 36, p. 184-194.

3193. Adams (H. H.). English domestic or Homiletic tragedy, 1575-1642. London, Oxford Univ. Press, 44, in-8, 240 p., 16s. 6d.

3194. Adams (Joseph Quincy). A new signature of Shakespeare ? *B. John Rylands Library*, 43, vol. 27, p. 256-259.

3195. Adams (J. Q.). The author-plot of an early 17th century play. *Library*, 45, vol. 26, p. 17-27.

3196. Baldwin (C. S.). Renaissance literary theory and practice. Classicism in the rhetoric and poetic of Italy, France and England, 1400-1600. London, Oxford Univ. Press, 40, in-8, 251 p., 14s.

3197. BENTLEY (G. E.). Shakespeare and Jonson : their reputations in the 17th century compared. London, Cambridge Univ. Press, 45, 2 vols. in-8, viii-150, iv-308 p., 45s. R : F. P. Wilson, *Library*, 45, vol. 26, p. 199-202.

3198. BISHOP (Morris). Ronsard, prince of poets. London, Oxford Univ. Press, 40, in-8, 253 p., 16s. 6d.

3199. BOAS (F. S.). Christopher Marlowe : a biographical and critical study. London, Oxford Univ. Press, 40, in-8, x-336 p., (illus.), 15s. R : M. Eccles, *Mod. Language R.*, 42, vol. 37, p. 83-85.

3200. BOAS (F. S.). Aspects of classical legend and history in Shakespeare. London, Oxford Univ. Press, 43, in-8, 28 p., 3s.

3201. BOND (William H.). Two ghosts : Herbert's *Baripenthes* and the Vaughan-Holland portrait of Sidney. *Library*, 43/44, vol. 24, p. 175-181.

3202. BOWERS (F. T.). Elizabethan revenge tragedy, 1587-1642. London, Oxford Univ. Press, 40, in-8, 288 p., 14s. R : U. Ellis-Fermor, *Mod. Language R.*, 41, vol. 36, p. 258-260.

3203. BRADBROOK (M. C.) and THOMAS (M. G. Lloyd). Andrew Marvell. London, Cambridge Univ. Press, 40, in-8, viii-161 p., 7s. 6d. R : L. C. Martin, *Mod. Language R.*, 41, vol. 36, p. 264-265.

3204. BRIDGEWATER (H.). Evidence connecting Bacon with Shakespeare. London, Bacon Soc., 43, in-8, 32 p., 1s.

3205. BUSH (Douglas). English literature in the earlier seventeenth century. London, Oxford Univ. Press, 45, in-8, 630 p., 21s. (Oxf. hist. of Engl. lit., vol. 5).

3206. CAWLEY (Robert Ralston). Unpathed waters : studies in the influence of the voyagers on Elizabethan literature. London, Oxford

Univ. Press, 40, in-8, viii-285 p., 17s. R : J. H. Walter, *Mod. Language R.*, 42, vol. 37, p. 203. E. G. R. T(aylor), *Geogr. J.*, 41, vol. 98, p. 111-112.

3207. CHAMBERS (Sir E. K.). Shakespearean gleanings. London, Oxford Univ. Press, 44, in-8, 156 p., 10s.

3208. CLARKSON (P. S.) and WARREN (C. T.). The law of property in Shakespeare and the Elizabethan drama. London, Oxford Univ. Press, 42, in-8, 374 p., 16s.

3209. CLEMENTS (R. J.). Critical theory and practice of the Pleiade. London, Oxford Univ. Press, 42, in-8, 306 p., (illus.), 12s. 6d. (Stud. in Romance lang. ser.).

3210. COLLINS (B. G.). Shakespeare's religion. *Baptist Quar.*, 45, vol. 11, p. 381-397.

3211. DAWSON (Giles E.). A bibliographical problem in the First Folio of Shakespeare. *Library*, 41, vol. 22, p. 25-33.

3212. DOREN (M. van). Shakespeare. Foreword by Sir Hugh Walpole. London, Allen & Unwin, 41, in-8, 344 p., 12s. 6d.

3213. DUTHIE (G. I.). The ' bad ' quarto of Hamlet. London, Cambridge Univ. Press, 41, in-8, xxii-280 p., 10s.

3214. ENTWISTLE (William J.). Cervantes. London, Oxford Univ. Press, 40, in-8, 191 p., 7s. 6d.

3215. ESPINER-SCOTT (Janet). Some notes on Joachim du Bellay. *Mod. Language R.*, 41, vol. 36, p. 59-67.

3216. GARDINER (Dorothy). Henry Oxinden's authorship. *Archaeol. cantiana*, 44, vol. 57, p. 13-20.

3217. GREG (W. W.). The variants in the First Quarto of ' King Lear ' : a bibliographical and critical inquiry. London, Oxford Univ. Press, 40, in-8, vii-192 p., subscribers only. (Bibliogr. soc. trans., suppl. 15). R :

J. G. McManaway, *Mod. Language R.*, 42, vol. 37, p. 86-88.

3218. GREG (W. W.). The date of ' King Lear ' and Shakespeare's use of earlier versions of the story. *Library*, 40, vol. 20, p. 377-400.

3219. GREG (W. W.). The editorial problem in Shakespeare : a survey of the foundations of the text. London, Oxford Univ. Press, 42, in-8, lv-210 p., 12s. 6d. (Clark lect.). R : G. I. Duthie, *Mod. Language R.*, 43, vol. 38, p. 255-257.

3220. GREG (W. W.). ' The Merry Devil of Edmonton '. *Library*, 44/45, vol. 25, p. 122-139.

3220a. GREG (Walter Wilson). A list of Dr. Greg's writings. *Library*, 45, vol. 26, p. 72-97.

3221. HALL (Vernon). Renaissance literary criticism. London, Oxford Univ. Press, 45, in-8, 270 p., 20s.

3222. HANGEN (E. C.). A concordance to the complete poetical works of Sir James Wyatt. London, Cambridge Univ. Press, 42, in-8, xviii-528 p., 30s.

3223. HARBAGE (Alfred). Elizabethan-Restoration palimpsest. *Mod. Language R.*, 40, vol. 35, p. 287-319.

3224. HARBAGE (A.). Shakespeare's audience. London, Oxford Univ. Press, 42, in-8, 209 p., 11s. 6d. R : G. H. C., *Queen's Quar.*, 42, vol. 49, p. 281-285.

3225. HART (Alfred). Did Shakespeare produce his own plays ? *Mod. Language R.*, 41, vol. 36, p. 173-183.

3226. HART (A.). Stolne and surreptitious copies : a comparative study of Shakespeare's bad quartos. London, Oxford Univ. Press, 42, in-8, xi-478 p., 12s. 6d. R : M. Doran, *Mod. Language R.*, 44, vol. 39, p. 190-193.

3227. HINMAN (Charlton). A proofsheet in the first folio of Shakespeare. *Library*, 42, vol. 23, p. 101-107.

3229. IZARD (Thomas C.). George Whetstone : mid-Elizabethan gentleman of letters. London, Oxford Univ. Press, 42, in-8, viii-297 p., 18s. 6d. R : W.G., *Queen's Quar.*, 43, vol. 50, p. 97-99. J. Robertson, *Mod. Language R.*, 44, vol. 39, p. 73-75.

3230. JONAS (L.). The divine science : the aesthetic of some representative 17th-century English poets. London, Oxford Univ. Press, 41, in-8, 304 p., 15s. (Columbia stud. in Engl. and compar. lit.).

3231. KEATING (L. C.). Studies on the literary salon in France, 1550-1615. London, Oxford Univ. Press, 42, in-8, 180 p., 10s. 6d. (Harvard stud. in Romance lang. ser.). R : H. W. Lawton, *Mod. Language R.*, 42, vol. 37, p. 517-518.

3232. KEEN (Alan). Short account of the recently discovered copy of Edward Hall's ' Union of the Noble Houses of Lancaster and York '. *B. John Rylands Library*, 40, vol. 24, p. 255-262.

3233. KENNEDY (M. B.). The oration in Shakespeare. London, Oxford Univ. Press, 42, in-8, 280 p., 14s.

3234. KING (Arthur H.). The language of satirised characters in ' Poetaster ', a socio-stylistic analysis, 1597-1602. London, Williams and Norgate, 41, in-8, xxxiv-258 p., 20s. (Lund stud. in Engl., 10). R : G. D. Willcock, *Mod. Language R.*, 42, vol. 37, p. 205-207.

3235. LAIRD (John). Shakespeare on the wars of England. *Philosophy*, 43, vol. 18, p. 140-154.

3236. LEWIS (B. R.). The Shakespeare documents : facsimiles, transliterations, translations and commentary. London, Oxford Univ. Press, 42, 2 vols. in-4, 655 p., (illus.), 252s.

3237. LEWIS (D. B. Wyndham). Ronsard. London, Sheed, 44, in-8, xi-340 p., (illus.), 12s. 6d. R : L. A.

Bisson, *Mod. Language R.*, 45, vol. 40, p. 60-63. *National R.*, 44, vol. 123, p. 82-83.

3238. LEWIS (D. B. W.). François Villon. London, Sheed, 45, in-8, 355 p., 12s. 6d.

3239. McGRAIL (T. H.). Sir William Alexander, first Earl of Stirling. London, Oliver & Boyd, 40, in-8, 287 p., 10s. 6d.

3240. McILWRAITH (A. K.). The press-corrections in Jonson's *The King's Entertainment*. *Library*, 43/44, vol. 24, p. 181-186.

3241. MATTHEWS (William). English pronunciation and shorthand in the early modern period. London, Oxford Univ. Press, 43, in-8, 135-214 p., 4s. 6d. (Univ. of Calif. publ. in Engl., vol. 9, no. 3). R : S. Potter, *Mod. Language R.*, 45, vol. 40, p. 317-318.

3242. MILLAR (J. S. L.). The man in the Shakespeare mask. Edinburgh, J. S. L. Millar, 42, in-8, 16 p., 6d.

3243. MORLEY (S. Griswold) and BRUERTON (Courtney). The chronology of Lope de Vega's *Comedias*. London, Oxford Univ. Press, 40, in-8, xiv-427 p., 18s. (Mod. lang. assoc., monogr. ser., 11). R : W. J. Entwistle, *Mod. Language R.*, 41, vol. 36, p, 418-420.

3244. NEWDIGATE (Bernard H.). Michael Drayton and his circle. Oxford, Blackwell, 41, in-8, xv-239 p., 15s. C. J. Sisson, *Mod. Language R.*, 42, vol. 37, p. 372-376. J.E.N., *Eng. hist. R.*, 45, vol. 60, p. 270-271.

3245. NOSWORTHY (J. M.). The Marlowe manuscript. *Library*, 45, vol. 26, p. 158-171.

3246. PARKER (A. A.). The allegorical drama of Calderon. Oxford, Dolphin, 43, in-8, 232 p., 16s.

3247. PEGGRAM (Reed Edwin). The first French and English translations of Sir Thomas More's 'Utopia'. *Mod. Language R.*, 40, vol. 35, p. 330-340.

3248. PHILLIPS (Margaret Mann). Erasmus and propaganda : a study of the translators of Erasmus in England and France. *Mod. Language R.*, 42, vol. 37, p. 1-17.

3249. PROUTY (C. T.). George Gascoigne : Elizabethan courtier, soldier, and poet. London, Oxford Univ. Press, 42, in-8, 363 p., 18s. 6d. R : G.H.C., *Queen's Quar.*, 42, vol. 49, p. 281-285. J. Robertson, *Mod. Language R.*, 43, vol. 38, p. 139-140.

3250. RINGLER (W.). Stephen Gosson : a biographical and critical study. London, Oxford Univ. Press, 43, in-8, 160 p., 13s. 6d.

3250a. ROBERTSON (Jean). The early life of George Chapman. *Mod. Language R.*, 45, vol. 40, p. 157-165.

3251. RUBEL (V. L.). Poetic diction in the English Renaissance from Skelton through Spenser. London, Oxford Univ. Press, 42, in-8, 326 p., 14s. R : E. J. Sweeting, *Mod. Language R.*, 43, vol. 38, p. 354-355.

3252. SAMUEL (E. Webb). Elizabethan literature. *Baptist Quar.*, 40, vol. 10, p. 21-31.

3253. SCHWARZ (W.). The theory of translation in 16th-century Germany. *Mod. Language R.*, 45, vol. 40, p. 289-299.

3254. SPRAGUE (A. C.). Shakespeare and the actors : the stage business in his plays (1660-1905). London, Oxford Univ. Press, 44, in-8, 466 p., (illus.), 28s. R : G.B.H., *Queen's Quar.*, 44, vol. 51, p. 340.

3255. STALKER (Archibald). Is Shakespeare's will a forgery ? *Quar. R.*, 40, vol. 274, p. 248-262.

3256. STEVENSON (Allan H.). Shirley's publishers : the partnership of Crooke and Cooke. *Library*, 44/45, vol. 25, p. 140-161.

3257. Sweeting (Elizabeth J.). Studies in early Tudor criticism, linguistic and literary. Oxford, Blackwell, 40, in-8, xvi-176 p., 12s. 6d. R : J. W. H. Atkins, *Mod. Language R.*, 41, vol. 36, p. 522-524.

3258. Tillotson (Kathleen). Drayton and the Gooderes. *Mod. Language R.*, 40, vol. 35, p. 341-349.

3259. Tillyard (E. M. W.). Shakespeare's history plays. London, Chatto & Windus, 44, in-8, 334 p., 18s.

3260. Wagman (Frederick H.). Magic and natural science in German Baroque literature. London, Oxford Univ. Press, 42, in-8, 186 p., 11s. 6d. (Germanic stud. ser.). R : L. Forster, *Mod. Language R.*, 44, vol. 39, p. 84-86.

3261. Wears (T. M.). Shakespeare's will. *Canad. Bar R.*, 42, vol. 20, p. 53-55.

3262. Wells (H. W.). A chronological list of extant plays produced in or about London, 1581-1642. London, Oxford Univ. Press, 40, in-8, 17 p., 1s. 6d.

3263. Wilson (F. P.). Elizabethan and Jacobean. London, Oxford Univ. Press, 45, in-8, 152 p., 7s. 6d. (Toronto Univ., Alexander lect. in Engl., 1943).

3264. Wilson (John Dover). The origins and development of Shakespeare's *Henry IV*. *Library*, 45, vol. 26, p. 2-16.

c. CLASSICISM

3265. Gore (Philip Babcock). The imaginary voyage in prose fiction : a history of its criticism and a guide for its study, with an annotated check list of 215 imaginary voyages from 1700 to 1800. London, Oxford Univ. Press, 41, in-8, xi-445 p., 23s. 6d. R : G. Jones, *Mod. Language R.*, 42, vol. 37, p. 94-95.

3266. Hazen (A. T.). A bibliography of the Strawberry Hill press, with a record of the prices at which copies have been sold. London, Oxford Univ. Press, 42, in-4, 300 p., (illus.), 66s. 6d. R : P. H. Muir, *Library*, 44, vol. 25, p. 95-98.

3267. Saintonge (Paul F.) and Christ (R. W.). Fifty years of Molière studies, a bibliography, 1892-1941. London, Oxford Univ. Press, 42, in-4, 313 p., 16s. (Johns Hopkins stud. in Romance lit. and lang., extra vol. 19). R : W. G. Moore, *Mod. Language R.*, 44, vol. 39, p. 80.

3268. Schreiber (C. S.). Catalogue of Goethe's works, with the exception of Faust. London, Oxford Univ. Press, 42, in-8, xlii-239 p., 45s. (William A. Speck collection of Goetheana).

3269. Summers (Montague). A Gothic bibliography. London, Fortune Press, 41, in-8, 640 p., (illus.), 42s.

3270. Addison (Joseph). Letters, ed. by W. Graham. Oxford, Clarendon Press, 41, in-8, 564 p., 30s. J. C. Beckett, *Irish hist. Stud.*, 43, vol. 3, p. 320-322.

3270a. Bailey (J.). Dr. Johnson and his circle, ed. by L. F. Powell. New ed. London, Oxford Univ. Press, 44, in-8, 264 p., 3s. 6d. (Home univ. libr.).

3271. Barker (A.). Milton and the Puritan dilemma, 1641-1660. London, Oxford Univ. Press, 44, in-8, 464 p., 17s.

3272. Bithell (J.). Sixty years of Goethe, 1880-1940. *Mod. Language R.*, 41, vol. 36, p. 225-242.

3273. Brittain (Robert E.). Christopher Smart in the magazines. *Library*, 40/41, vol. 21, p. 320-336.

3274. Cawley (R. R.). Milton's literary craftsmanship. London, Oxford Univ. Press, 42, in-8, 115 p., 9s. (Stud. in Engl. ser.).

3275. CHARLES (B. G.). Letters of Hester Lynch Piozzi. *Nat. Library Wales J.*, 41, vol. 2, p. 49-58.

3276. CHASE (I. W. U.) : Horace Walpole, gardenist ; with an edition of his ' The history of modern taste in gardening '. London, Oxford Univ. Press, 43, in-8, 316 p., (plates), 23s. 6d.

3277. CLARK (A. F. B.). Jean Racine. London, Oxford Univ. Press, 40, in-8, 354 p., 15s.

3278. CLIFFORD (James L.). Hester Lynch Piozzi (Mrs. Thrale). London, Oxford Univ. Press, 41, in-8, 505 p., 21s. R : R. N. Carew Hunt, *19th Century*, 41, vol. 129, p. 594-596. G. Jones, *Mod. Language R.*, 41, vol. 36, p. 534-536.

3279. DEARING (Vinton A.). New light on the first printing of the letters of Pope and Swift. *Library*, 43, vol. 24, p. 74-80.

3280. FAIRCHILD (Hoxie Neale). Religious trends in English poetry. Vol. 2 : 1740-1780. Religious sentimentalism in the age of Johnson. London, Oxford Univ. Press, 42, in-8, ix-406 p., 33s. 6d. R : M. S. Serjeantson, *Mod. Language R.*, 44, vol. 39, p. 78-79.

3281. FRENCH (J. M.). Milton in Chancery. London, Oxford Univ. Press, 40, in-8, 428 p., 18s.

3283. GRAFE (L. F.). On the date and idea of Faust's first monologue in Faust II, vv. 4679-4727. *Mod. Language R.*, 45, vol. 40, p. 115-119.

3284. GRIERSON (H. J. C.). Milton and liberty. *Mod. Language R.*, 44, vol. 39, p. 97-107.

3285. HARRISON (Frank Mott). Editions of *The Pilgrim's Progress*. *Library*, 41, vol. 22, p. 73-81.

3286. HARRISON (F. M.). Notes on the early editions of ' Grace Abounding '. *Baptist Quar.*, 43, vol. 11, p. 160-164.

3287. HENNIG (John). Goethe's friendship with Anthony O'Hara. *Mod. Language R.*, 44, vol. 39, p. 146-151.

3288. HENNIG (J.). Simplicius Simplissimus's British relations. *Mod.' Language R.*, 45, vol. 40, p. 37-45.

3289. HILBISH (F. M. A.). Charlotte Smith : poet and novelist, 1749-1806. London, Mitre Press, 42, in-8, 634 p., (plates), 18s.

3290. HODGES (John C.). William Congreve, the man : a biography from new sources. London, Oxford Univ. Press, 43, in-8, 170 p., (illus.), 12s.

3291. HORNE (Colin J.). Dr. William King's ' Miscellanies in prose and verse '. *Library*, 44, vol. 25, p. 37-45.

3292. HUNT (R. N. Carew). John Newton and William Cowper. *19th Century*, 41, vol. 130, p. 92-96.

3293. IRVING (W. H.). John Gay : favourite of the wits. London, Cambridge Univ. Press, 40, in-8, 334 p., (illus.), 21s.

3294. IRWIN (M.). The making of Jonathan Wild. London, Oxford Univ. Press, 41, in-8, 166 p., 10s. (Stud. in Engl. and compar. lit.).

3295. JACKSON (R. Wyse). Swift and his circle. Dublin, Talbot Press, 45, in-8, 112 p., 5s.

3296. KAHRL (G. M.). Tobias Smollett, traveller-novelist. London, Cambridge Univ. Press, 45, in-8, xxiv-166 p., 16s. 6d.

3297. KETTON-CREMER (R. W.). Horace Walpole, a biography. London, Duckworth, 40, in-8, 368 p., (plates), 16s. R : J. W. Goodison, *Burlington Mag.*, 41, vol. 78, p. 65-66.

3298. KINNE (W. A.). Revivals and importations of French comedies in England, 1749-1800. London, Oxford Univ. Press, 40, in-8, 310 p., 15s.

3299. LANCASTER (Henry Carrington). A history of French dramatic literature in the 17th century. Pt. 4 : The age of Racine, 1673-1700. Pt. 5 : Recapitulation, 1610-1700. London, Oxford Univ. Press, 40-43, 2 vols. in-8, 272, 244 p., 90s. R : L. A. Bisson, *Mod. Language R.*, 41, vol. 36, p. 414-418; 44, vol. 39, p. 79-80.

3302. LAWTON (H. W.). The confidant in and before French classical tragedy. *Mod. Language R.*, 43, vol. 38, p. 18-31.

3303. MARTZ (Louis L.). The later career of Tobias Smollett. London, Oxford Univ. Press, 42, in-8, ix-213 p., 18s. 6d. (Yale stud. in Engl., vol. 97). R : J. C. Bryce, *Mod. Language R.*, 44, vol. 39, p. 198-199.

3304. MEAD (Herman R.). Three issues of ' A Buckler against the Fear of Death '. *Library*, 40, vol. 21, p. 199-206.

3305. MILLER (J. R.). Boileau en France au 18me siècle. London, Oxford Univ. Press, 42, in-8, 626 p., 25s. (Johns Hopkins stud. in Romance lit. and lang., vol. 18).

3306. PARKER (William R.). Henry Vaughan and his publishers. *Library*, 40, vol. 20, p. 401-411.

3307. PEGGRAM (Reed E.). A neglected Dutch *Amphitryon* of 1679. *Mod. Language R.*, 41, vol. 36, p. 112-115.

3308. PERSHING (James H.). The different states of the first edition of *Paradise Lost*. *Library*, 41, vol. 22, p. 34-66.

3309. PRICE (L. M.). Christian Heinrich Schmid and his translations of English drama. London, Oxford Univ. Press, 42, in-8, vii-122 p., 7s. 6d. (Univ. of Calif. publ. in mod. philol., vol. 26, no. 1). R : R. Pascal, *Mod. Language R.*, 43, vol. 38, p. 66.

3310. ROBERTSON (Jean). The use made of Owen Felltham's ' Resolves ': a study in plagiarism. *Mod. Language R.*, 44, vol. 39, p. 108-115.

3311. ROSS (M. M.). Milton's royalism. London, Oxford Univ. Press, 43, in-8, 164 p., 15s. 6d.

3312. SAURAT (D.). Milton, man and thinker. New ed. London, Dent, 44, in-8, 291 p., 15s.

3313. SCHLEGEL (A. W.). Lectures on German literature from Gottsched to Goethe, ed. by H. G. Fiedler. Oxford, Blackwell, 44, in-8, 96 p., 10s. R : A. Gillies, *Mod. Language R.*, 45, vol. 40, p. 229.

3314. STAUFFER (Donald A.). The art of biography in 18th-century England. London, Oxford Univ. Press, 41, 2 vols. in-8, xiv-572, x-293 p., 51s. R : G. Jones, *Mod. Language R.*, 42, vol. 37, p. 502-504.

3315. STEELE (Sir Richard). The correspondence of Richard Steele, ed. by R. Blanchard. London, Oxford Univ. Press, 41, in-8, 562 p., 35s. R : B.W., *Eng. hist. R.*, 43, vol. 58, p. 120.

3316. SUTHERLAND (James R.). ' Polly ' among the pirates. *Mod. Language R.*, 42, vol. 37, p. 291-303.

3317. THRALE (Hester Lynch). Thraliana : diary, 1776-1809, ed. by K. C. Balderston. London, Oxford Univ. Press, 42, 2 vols. in-8, 644, 587 p., 63s. R : G. Jones, *Mod. Language R.*, 43, vol. 38, p. 55-57.

3318. TILLOTSON (Geoffrey). Essays in criticism and research. London, Cambridge Univ. Press, 42, in-8, xxx-216 p., 15s.

3319. TREVELYAN (Humphrey). Goethe and the Greeks. London, Cambridge Univ. Press, 41, in-8, xvi-322 p., 18s. R : L. A. Willoughby, *Mod. Language R.*, 43, vol. 38, p. 67-70. A.J.H., *Greece and Rome*, 43, vol. 12, p. 95-96.

3320. WADE (G. I.). Thomas Traherne : a critical biography. London, Oxford Univ. Press, 44, in-8, 280 p., 20s.

3321. WALPOLE (Horace). Correspondence with Madame du Deffand and Wiart, ed. by W. S. Lewis and W. H. Smith. London, Oxford Univ. Press, 40, 6 vols. in-8, 252s. (Yale ed. of H. Walpole's correspondence, vol. 3-8). R : H. Williams, *Mod. Language R.*, 40, vol. 35, p. 543-546.

3322. WALPOLE (H.). Correspondence with George Montagu, ed. by W. S. Lewis and R. S. Brown, jr. London, Oxford Univ. Press, 41, 2 vols. in-4, lvi-418, 560 p., 94s. 6d. (Yale ed. of H. Walpole's correspondence, vol. 9-10). R : H. Williams, *Mod. Language R.*, 43, vol. 38, p. 53-55. M. Maxse, *National R.*, 42, vol. 119, p. 267-270.

3323. WARD (C. E.). The letters of John Dryden : with letters addressed to him. London, Cambridge Univ. Press, 42, in-8, xviii-196 p., (illus.), 18s.

3324. WADE (I. O.). Voltaire and Madame du Châtelet. London, Oxford Univ. Press, 41, in-8, 255 p., 18s. 6d.

3325. WELLS (John Edwin). Thomson's *Spring* : early editions true and false. *Library*, 42, vol. 22, p. 223-243.

3326. WILEY (Autrey Nell) ed. Rare prologues and epilogues, 1642-1700. London, Allen and Unwin, 42, in-8, xlv-358 p., 15s. R : J. H. Walter, *Library*, 42, vol. 23, p. 144-145.

d. ROMANTICISM AND AFTER

(i) General

3327. FEISE (Ernst). Fifty years of German drama : a bibliography of modern German drama, 1880-1930. London, Oxford Univ. Press, 41, in-8, 111 p., 17s. 6d. R : H. G. Atkins, *Mod. Language R.*, 41, vol. 36, p. 558.

3328. ANAND (Mulk Raj). English novels of the 20th century on India. *Asiatic R.*, 43, vol. 39, p. 244-257.

3329. ANCHEN (J. O.). The Australian novel : a critical survey. Melbourne ; Wellington, Whitcombe & Tombs, 41, in-8, 45 p., 3s. 6d. R : G.E.E., *Art in N. Zealand*, 41, vol. 14, p. 94-95.

3330. BENTLEY (P.). The English regional novel. London, Allen & Unwin, 42, in-8, 48 p., 2s. (P.E.N. books).

3331. BROOKS (Van Wyck). New England : Indian summer, 1865-1915. London, Dent, 40, in-8, 557 p., 15s.

3332. BROWN (H. R.). The sentimental novel in America, 1789-1860. London, Cambridge Univ. Press, 42, in-8, x-408 p., 18s.

3333. CHURCH (R.). British authors: a twentieth century gallery. London, Longmans, 44, in-8, 156 p., (portraits), 5s.

3334. DOWNS (Brian W.). Anglo-Danish literary relations, 1867-1900. *Mod. Language R.*, 44, vol. 39, p. 262-279.

3335. EBAN (A. S.). The modern literary movement in Egypt. *Int. Affairs*, 44, vol. 20, p. 166-178.

3336. GEISMAR (Maxwell). Writers in crisis : the American novel between two wars. London, Secker & Warburg, 43, in-8, ix-299 p., 16s.

3337. GODE-VON AESCH (A.). Natural science in German Romanticism. London, Oxford Univ. Press, 41, in-8, 315 p., 15s.

3338. GOHDES (C.). American literature in 19th century England. London, Oxford Univ. Press, 44, in-8, 204 p., 16s. 6d.

3339. GOLDRING (D.). South Lodge: reminiscences of Violent Hunt, Ford Madox Ford and the ' English Review ' circle. London, Constable, 43, in-8, 260 p., (illus.), 15s.

3340. GRIGSON (G.). The Romantics. London, Routledge, 42, in-8, 356 p., 10s. 6d.

3341. HOGG (Thomas Jefferson). The Athenians, being correspondence between T. J. Hogg and his friends Thomas Love Peacock, Leigh Hunt, Percy Bysshe Shelley, and others, ed. by W. S. Scott. London, Golden Cockerel Press, 44, in-4, 86 p., 63s.

3342. HORNADAY (C. L.). Nature in the German novel of the late 18th century, 1770-1800. London, Oxford Univ. Press, 40, in-8, 221 p., 11s. 6d.

3343. HOWARD (L.). The Connecticut wits. London, Cambridge Univ. Press, 43, in-8, xiv-454 p., 27s.

3344. HUNT (Herbert J.). The epic in 19th-century France : a study in heroic and humanitarian poetry from ' Les Martyrs ' to ' Les Siècles Morts'. Oxford, Blackwell, 41, in-8, 446 p., 25s. R : H. F. Stewart, Mod. Language R., 42, vol. 37, p. 97-98.

3345. KAUN (Alexander). Historical sense in Soviet fiction. Slavonic Y.B. (Slavonic R.), 40, vol. 19, p. 55-61.

3346. KETTLER (H. K.). Baroque tradition in the literature of the German enlightenment : studies in the determination of a literary period, 1700-1750. Cambridge, Heffer, 43, in-8, viii-156 p., (illus.), 8s. 6d. R : A. Closs, Mod. Language R., 43, vol. 38, p. 367-368.

3347. LEMAITRE (G.). From cubism to surrealism in French literature. London, Oxford Univ. Press, 42, in-8, 247 p., (illus.), 12s. 6d.

3348. MILLER (E. M.). Australian literature from its beginnings to 1935. London, Oxford Univ. Press, 41, 2 vols. in-8, 1074 p., 42s.

3349. OWEN (Hugh). Llythyrau ychwanegol Morusiaid Môn. (Additional letters of Lewis, Richard, William and John Morris, of Anglesey). J. welsh bibliogr. Soc., 44, vol. 6, p. 49-64.

3350. PEERS (E. Allison). A history of the Romantic movement in Spain. London, Cambridge Univ. Press, 40, 2 vols. in-8, xi-349, xii-470 p., 50s. R : W. C. Atkinson, Mod. Language R., 41, vol. 36, p. 141-142.

3351. QUINLAN (M. J.). Victorian prelude. London, Oxford Univ. Press, 42, in-8, 311 p., 15s. (Stud. in Engl. and compar. lit.).

3352. SADLEIR (Michael). Mr. Michael Sadleir's collection of 19th century fiction. Library, 44/45, vol. 25, p. 105-110.

3353. SMITH (A. J. M.). Colonialism and nationalism in Canadian poetry before Confederation. Canad. hist. Assoc. Rept., 44, p. 74-85.

3354. STRUVE (G.). Twenty-five years of Soviet Russian literature. London, Routledge, 44, in-8, 347 p., 15s.

3355. TAYLOR (F. W.). The economic novel in America. London, Oxford Univ. Press, 42, in-8, 390 p., 18s.

3356. WARD (A. C.). Twentieth-century literature, 1900-1940. 7th ed. London, Methuen, 40, in-8, 304 p., 7s. 6d.

(ii) Individual Writers

3357. BURNETT (Constance Buel). The shoemaker's son, the life of Hans Christian **Andersen**. London, Harrap, 43, in-8, 252 p., 10s. 6d.

3358. TOKSVIG (S.). The life of Hans Christian **Andersen**. London, Macmillan, 40, in-8, xii-290 p., (illus.), 6s.

3359. FYFE (Hamilton). Matthew **Arnold** and the fall of France; with A reply by Sir J. Pollock. Hibbert J., 42, vol. 40, p. 125-131, 355-360.

3360. SCARFE (Francis). **Auden** and after : the liberation of poetry, 1930-1941. London, Routledge, 42, in-8, xvi-208 p., 8s. 6d.

3361. DARGAN (E. P.). and WEIN-BERG (B.). The evolution of **Balzac's** Comédie Humaine. London, Cambridge Univ. Press, 42, in-8, xii-442 p., 30s.

3362. BARRIE (Sir J. M.). Letters of J. M. **Barrie**, ed. by V. Meynell. London, Davies, 42, in-8, 312 p., 15s.

3363. MACKAIL (Denis). The story of J. M. **B(arrie)**. London, Davies, 41, in-8, 736 p., 11s. 6d. R : O. Williams, *National R.*, 41, vol. 116, p. 729-735.

3364. CRAIG (Alec). Outline of a **Baudelaire** bibliography. *J. Documentation*, 45, vol. 1, p. 109-115.

3365. GILMAN (Margaret). **Baudelaire** the critic. London, Oxford Univ. Press, 43, in-8, 274 p., 20s. R : D. Cooper, *Burlington Mag.*, 45, vol. 86, p. 26.

3366. GALLATIN (A. E.). Sir Max **Beerbohm** : bibliographical notes. London, Oxford Univ. Press, 44, in-8, xiii-121 p., (plates), 32s. 6d. (Limited ed.).

3367. MORGAN (A. E.). Edward **Bellamy**. London, Oxford Univ. Press, 45, in-8, 488 p., 33s. 6d.

3368. LARSON (H.). Björnstjerne **Björnson** : a study in Norwegian nationalism. London, Oxford Univ. Press, 45, in-8, 182 p., 13s. 6d.

3368a. GILCHRIST (A.). The life of William **Blake**. London, Dent, 42, in-8, 420 p., 3s. (Everyman's libr.).

3369. LOWERY (Margaret Ruth). Windows of the morning : a critical study of William **Blake's** *Poetical Sketches*, 1783. London, Oxford Univ. Press, 40, in-8, ix-249 p., (plates), 14s. (Yale stud. in Engl., vol. 93). R : G. Tillotson, *Mod. Language R.*, 41, vol. 36, p. 409-410.

3370. MACPHAIL (J. H.). **Blake** and Switzerland. *Mod. Language R.*, 43, vol. 38, p. 81-87.

3371. BRONOWSKI (J.). A man without a mask : William **Blake**, 1757-1827. London, Secker & Warburg, 44, in-8, 153 p., (plates), 8s. 6d.

3372. BRIDGES (Robert) and BRADLEY (Henry). Correspondence, 1900-1923. Oxford, Clarendon Press, 40, in-8, vi-191 p., 7s. 6d. R : C. C. Abbott, *Mod. Language R.*, 41, vol. 36, p. 130.

3373. GUERARD (A.) jr. Robert **Bridges**. London, Oxford Univ. Press, 42, in-8, 348 p., 15s.

3374. THOMPSON (Edward). Robert **Bridges**, 1844-1930. London, Oxford Univ. Press, 45, in-8, 140 p., 7s. 6d.

3375. DODDS (M. Hope). Heathcliff's country ('Wuthering Heights ', by Emily **Brontë**). *Mod. Language R.*, 44, vol. 39, p. 116-129.

3376. RATCHFORD (F. E.). The **Brontës'** web of childhood. London, Oxford Univ. Press, 41, in-8, xviii-293 p., 17s. 6d.

3377. CHARLTON (H. B.). **Browning** as poet of religion. *B. John Rylands Library*, 43, vol. 27, p. 271-307.

3378. SADLEIR (M.). **Bulwer** and his wife. New ed. London, Constable, 45, in-8, 452 p., 9s.

3379. JENSEN (G. E.). The life and letters of Henry Cuyler **Bunner**. London, Cambridge Univ. Press, 40, in-8, 247 p., 18s.

3380. FITZHUGH (Robert T.). Robert **Burns**, his associates and contemporaries : with the journal of the Border tour, ed. by De L. Ferguson. London, Oxford Univ. Press, 43, in-8, 144 p., 18s. 6d.

3381. BONNER-SMITH (D.). **Byron** in the Leeward Islands, 1779. *Mariner's Mirror*, 44, vol. 30, p. 38-48, 81-92.

3382. QUENNELL (Peter). **Byron** in Italy. London, Collins, 41, in-8, 274 p., 12s. 6d.

3383. EVERSON (I. G.). George Henry **Calvert** : American literary pioneer. London, Oxford Univ. Press, 44, in-8, 348 p., 25s.

3384. KLINCK (Carl Frederick). Wilfred **Campbell** : a study in late provincial Victorianism. Toronto, Ryerson Press, 42, in-8, 289 p., $3.50. R : A. J. M. Smith, *Canad. hist. R.*, 44, vol. 25, p. 196-199.

3385. SCUDDER (T.). Jane Welsh **Carlyle.** London, Macmillan, 40, in-8, xii-406 p., (illus.), 18s.

3386. CARLYLE (T.). Journey to Germany, Autumn 1858, ed. by R. A. E. Brooks. London, Oxford Univ. Press, 41, in-8, 222 p., 12s. 6d.

3387. FIEDLER (H. G.). The friendship of Thomas **Carlyle** and Varnhagen von Ense, with a letter hitherto unknown. *Mod. Language R.*, 43, vol. 38, p. 32-37.

3389. WARD (M.). Gilbert Keith **Chesterton.** London, Sheed, 44, in-8, 584 p., (illus.), 21s.

3390. GRIGGS (G. E.) and GRIGGS (E. L.). Letters of Hartley **Coleridge.** London, Oxford Univ. Press, 41, in-8, xv-328 p., 5s. (Oxf. bookshelf ser.).

3391. NETHERCOT (Arthur H.). The road to Tryermaine : a study of the history, background and purposes of **Coleridge's** ' Christabel '. London, Cambridge Univ. Press, 40, in-8, ix-230 p., 18s.

3392. GRIGGS (E. L.). Coleridge Fille, a biography of Sara **Coleridge.** London, Oxford Univ. Press, 40, in-8, 280 p., (plates), 12s. 6d.

3393. PARRISH (M. L.). Wilkie **Collins** and Charles Reade. London, Constable, 40, in-4, x-356 p., (plates), 60s.

3394. CONRAD (Joseph). Letters to Marguerite Poradowska, ed. and tr. by J. A. Gee and P. J. Sturm. London, Oxford Univ. Press, 41, in-8, xxiv-147 p., 12s. 6d.

3395. GORDON (J. D.). Joseph **Conrad,** the making of a novelist. London, Oxford Univ. Press, 41, in-8, 444 p., 17s.

3396. ALLEN (John D.). Philip Pendleton **Cooke.** London, Oxford Univ. Press, 43, in-8, 134 p., (illus.), 12s.

3397. BULLOCK (G.). Marie **Corelli,** the life and death of a best-seller. London, Constable, 40, in-8, 292 p., (illus.), 12s.

3398. DUGDALE (E. T. S.). Madame **D'Arblay.** *Quar. R.*, 40, vol. 274, p. 65-76.

3399. METCALF (J. C.). **De Quincey.** London, Oxford Univ. Press, 40, in-8, 210 p., 8s. 6d.

3400. GUMMER (E. N.). **Dickens's** works in Germany, 1837-1937. London, Oxford Univ. Press, 40, in-8, 200 p., 12s. 6d.

3401. HOUSE (H.). The **Dickens** world. 2nd ed. London, Oxford Univ. Press, 42, in-8, 232 p., 10s. 6d.

3402. POPE-HENNESSY (Una). Charles **Dickens.** London, Chatto, 45, in-8, 476 p., 21s.

3403. LAVRIN (J.). **Dostoevsky.** London, Methuen, 43, in-8, 158 p., 7s. 6d.

3404. PEARSON (H.). Conan **Doyle,** his life and art. London, Methuen, 43, in-8, 193 p., 12s. 6d.

3405. ADAMS (M. Ray). George **Dyer** and English radicalism. *Mod. Language R.*, 40, vol. 35, p. 447-469.

3406. HAIGHT (G. S.). George **Eliot** and John Chapman. London, Oxford Univ. Press, 41, in-8, 279 p., 12s. 6d.

3407. WICKS (Charles Beaumont). Charles-Guillaume **Etienne,** dramatist and publicist (1777-1845). London, Oxford Univ. Press, 40, in-4, 130 p., 7s. 6d. (Johns Hopkins univ. stud. in Romance lit. and lang., vol.

37). R : E. Eggli, *Mod. Language R.*, 42, vol. 37, p. 392-396.

3408. HARRIS (W.). Caroline **Fox.** London, Constable, 44, in-8, 360 p., (illus.), 15s.

3409. FRANKLIN (Miles) and BAKER (Kate). Joseph **Furphy,** the legend of a man and his book. Melbourne, Angus & Robertson, 44, in-8, xiv-190 p., (plates), 10s. 6d. R : A. M. McBriar, *Hist. Stud. Australia N.Z.*, 45, vol. 3, p. 145-148.

3410. ABERDEIN (J. W.). John **Galt.** London, Oxford Univ. Press, 41, in-8, 234 p., 3s. 6d. (Oxf. bookshelf ser.).

3411. ROY (Pierre-Georges). À travers Les anciens canadiens de Philippe-Aubert de **Gaspé**; À travers les Mémoires de Philippe-Aubert de Gaspé. Montréal, Ducharme, 43, 2 vols. in-8, 279, 296 p. R : S. Marion, *Canad. hist. R.*, 43, vol. 24, p. 419-420.

3412. KURTZ (B. J.). Charles Mills **Gayley.** London, Cambridge Univ. Press, 44, in-8, viii-290 p., (plates), 15s.

3413. SHAW (E. P.). Jacques **Gazotte** (1719-1792). London, Oxford Univ. Press, 44, in-8, 146 p. 8s. 6d. R : W. Ll. Bullock, *Mod' Language R.*, 44, vol. 39, p. 306-307.

3415. FLANAGAN (J. T.). James **Hall** : literary pioneer of the Ohio valley. London, Oxford Univ. Press, 42, in-8, 266 p., 11s. 6d.

3416. HALLIBURTON (Richard). Richard **Halliburton,** his story of his life's adventure as told in letters to his mother and father. London, Bles, 41, in-8, 433 p., (illus.), 15s.

3417. BLUNDEN (E.). Thomas **Hardy.** London, Macmillan, 42, in-8, ix-286 p., 7s. 6d. (Engl. men of letters). R : G.H.C., *Queen's Quar.*, 42, vol. 49, p. 394-395.

3418. WEBER (C. J.). **Hardy** of Wessex. London, Oxford Univ. Press, 41, in-8, 314 p., 15s.

3419. HALL (L. S.). **Hawthorne** : critic of society. London, Oxford Univ. Press, 44, in-8, 215 p., 20s.

3420. HAWTHORNE (Nathaniel). The English notebooks of N. **Hawthorne,** based upon the original MSS. in the Pierpont Morgan Library and ed. by R. Stewart. London, Oxford Univ. Press, 41, in-8, 711 p., 27s.

3421. SCHUBERT (L.). **Hawthorne** the artist. London, Oxford Univ. Press, 44, in-8, 194 p., 21s. 6d.

3422. MACLEAN (Catherine Macdonald). Born under Saturn : a biography of William **Hazlitt.** London, Collins, 43, in-8, 652 p., 21s.

3423. WORMLEY (S. L.). **Heine** in England. London, Oxford Univ. Press, 43, in-8, 330 p., 24s.

3424. WITTKE (C.). Against the current : the life of Karl **Heinzen.** London, Cambridge Univ. Press, 45, in-8, x-342 p., 22s. 6d.

3425. EATON (J. W.). **Herder** and Germany. *Queen's Quar.*, 45, vol. 52, p. 8-20.

3426. STAHL (E. L.). Symbolism in **Hölderlin's** early poetry (1784-1800, 1800-1804). *Mod. Language R.*, 44, vol. 39, p. 43-54, 152-166.

3427. PECKHAM (H. H.). Josiah Gilbert **Holland** in relation to his times. London, Oxford Univ. Press, 40, in-8, 220 p., 11s. 6d.

3428. GARDNER (W. H.). Gerard Manley **Hopkins** : a study of poetic idiosyncracy in relation to poetic tradition. London, Secker & Warburg, 44, in-8, 304-ix p., (plates), 25s.

3429. PICK (John). Gerard Manley **Hopkins** : priest and poet. London, Oxford Univ. Press, 42, in-8, 179 p., (illus.), 8s. 6d.

3430. CARTER (John), SPARROW (John), WHITE (William). A. E. **Housman,** an annotated check-list

[with] additions and corrections. *Library*, 40, vol. 21, p. 160-191; 42, vol. 23, p. 31-44.

3431. RICHARDS (Grant). **Housman,** 1897-1936. London, Oxford Univ. Press, 41, in-8, 513 p., 21s.

3432. GRANT (E. M.). The career of Victor **Hugo.** London, Oxford Univ. Press, 45, in-8, 372 p., 20s.

3433. IRVING (W.). The letters of Jonathan Oldstyle, repr. in facs. from the ed. of 1824. Intr. by S. T. Williams. London, Oxford Univ. Press, 41, in-8, 67 p., 8s. (Facs. text soc.).

3435. ASKWITH (Betty). **Keats,** a life. London, Collins, 41, in-8, 288 p., 12s. 6d. R : B. G. Brooks, *19th Century*, 41, vol. 130, p. 194-196.

3436. FORD (G. H.). **Keats** and the Victorians. London, Oxford Univ. Press, 45, in-8, 214 p., 20s.

3437. BROWN (Hilton). Rudyard **Kipling.** London, Hamilton, 45, in-8, 224 p., 10s. 6d.

3438. HOWE (Will D.). Charles **Lamb** and his friends. Toronto, McClelland & Stewart, 44, in-8, 364 p., $4.50. R : L. J. B[urpee], *Queen's Quar.*, 44, vol. 51, p. 224-225.

3439. ELWIN (Malcolm). Savage **Landor.** London, Macmillan, 41, in-8, xxi-498 p., (illus.), 18s.

3440. LAWRENCE (T. E.). Letters, ed. by D. Garnett. New ed. London, Cape, 42, in-8, 896 p., (illus.), 15s.

3441. DAVIDSON (A.). Edward **Lear.** New ed. London, Murray, 40, in-8, xv-280 p., (illus.), 6s. 6d.

3442. MAYNADIER (G. H.). The first American novelist? Mrs. Charlotte **Lennox.** London, Oxford Univ. Press, 40, in-8, 79 p., 6s.

3443. CURRIER (T. F.). Elizabeth **Lloyd** and the Whittiers. London, Oxford Univ. Press, 40, in-8, 146 p., 12s. 6d.

3444. SEDGWICK (W. E.). Herman **Melville.** London, Oxford Univ. Press, 45, in-8, 268 p., 15s. 6d.

3445. CLIFFORD (James L.). Robert **Merry**—a pre-Byronic hero. *B. John Rylands Library*, 42, vol. 27, p. 74-96.

3446. MOORE (George). Letters of George **Moore,** ed. by J. Eglinton. Bournemouth, Sydenham, 42, in-8, 88 p., 10s. 6d.

3447. PARKS (E. W.). Charles Egbert Craddock (Mary Noailles **Murfree**). London, Oxford Univ. Press, 41, in-8, 258 p., 11s. 6d.

3448. NEWBOLT (M., Lady). The later life and letters of Sir Henry **Newbolt.** London, Faber, 42, in-8, ii-426 p., (illus.), 21s. R : *Quar. R.*, 43, vol. 280, p. 240. *National R.*, 43, vol. 120, p. 257-258.

3449. MARCHAND (E. L.). Frank **Norris.** London, Oxford Univ. Press, 43, in-8, 268 p., 18s. 6d.

3450. STARKIE (Enid). A little-known precursor of Baudelaire : the ' Bouzingo ' Philothée **O'Neddy.** *Mod. Language R.*, 44, vol. 39, p. 357-367.

3451. BISSON (L. A.). Amédée **Pichot.** Oxford, Blackwell, 42, in-8, xv-422 p., (plates), 32s.

3452. DUNKEL (W. D.). Sir Arthur **Pinero** : a critical biography with letters. London, Cambridge Univ. Press, 43, in-8, vi-142 p., 9s.

3453. BOOTH (B. A.) and JONES (C. E.). A concordance of the poetical works of Edgar Allan **Poe.** London, Oxford Univ. Press, 41, in-8, 211 p., 25s.

3454. QUINN (A. H.). Edgar Allan **Poe.** London, Appleton, 42, in-8, 810 p., (illus.), 30s.

3455. POWYS (Llewelyn). Letters, ed. by L. U. Wilkinson. London, Lane, 43, in-8, 331 p., 21s.

3456. CORNELL (William K.). Adolphe **Retté** (1863-1930). London, Oxford Univ. Press, 42, in-8, 312 p., 14s. (Romanic stud. ser.).

3457. BUTLER (E. M.). **Rilke** and Tolstoy. *Mod. Language R.*, 40, vol. 35, p. 494-505.

3458. BUTLER (E. M.). Rainer Maria **Rilke**. London, Cambridge Univ. Press, 41, in-8, x-437 p., 21s. R : G. C. Houston, *Mod. Language R.*, 41, vol. 36, p. 550-552.

3459. STARKIE (Enid). On the trail of Arthur **Rimbaud**. *Mod. Language R.*, 43, vol. 38, p. 206-216.

3460. POMEROY (E. M.). Sir Charles G. D. **Roberts** : a biography. London, Hatchards, 43, in-8, 370 p., (plates), 18s. R : G.H.C., *Queen's Quar.*, 43, vol. 50, p. 331-332. A. J. M. Smith, *Canad. hist. R.*, 44, vol. 25, p. 196-199.

3461. EGLINTON (J.). A memoir of A.E. : George William **Russell**. London, Macmillan, 42, in-8, vii-291 p., (illus.), 5s. (Miscellany ser.).

3462. MAHIEU (R. G.). **Sainte-Beuve** aux États-Unis. London, Oxford Univ. Press, 45, in-8, 174 p., 16s. 6d. (Princeton publ. in Romance lang.).

3463. STRAUS (Ralph). **Sala** : the portrait of an eminent Victorian. London, Constable, 42, in-8, xi-309 p., (plates), 18s.

3464. CORSON (James Clarkson). A bibliography of Sir Walter **Scott**; a classified and annotated list of books and articles relating to his life and works, 1797-1940. Edinburgh, Oliver & Boyd, 43, in-8, xv-428 p., 32s.

3465. PARKER (W. M.). More **Scott** marginalia. 3 pts. *Times lit. Supp.*, 41, p. 220, 232, 244.

3466. STRUVE (Gleb). **Scott** letters discovered in Russia. *B. John Rylands Library*, 44, vol. 28, p. 477-484.

3467. GRYLLS (R. G.). Mary **Shelley**. London, Oxford Univ. Press, 41, in-8, 361 p., 3s. 6d. (Oxf. bookshelf ser.).

3468. GLASHEEN (Adaline E. and Francis J.). The publication of ' The Wandering Jew ' [by P. B. **Shelley**]. *Mod. Language R.*, 43, vol. 38, p. 11-17.

3469. LEA (F. A.). **Shelley** and the Romantic revolution. London, Routledge, 45, in-8, 289 p., 12s. 6d.

3470. SCOTT (Walter Sidney). Harriet and Mary : being the relations between Percy Bysshe **Shelley**, Harriet Shelley, Mary Shelley, and Thomas Jefferson Hogg, ed. by W. S. Scott. London, Golden Cockerell Press, 44, in-8, 83 p., 63s.

3471. SILL (E. R.). Around the Horn : a journal, 1861-1862, ed. by S. T. Williams and B. D. Simison. London, Oxford Univ. Press, 44, in-8, 92 p., (illus.), 13s. 6d.

3472. JENKINS (Romilly). Dionysius **Solōmós**. London, Cambridge Univ. Press, 40, in-8, ix-224 p., 8s. 6d. R : F. H. Marshall, *J. hell. Stud.*, 42 (43), vol. 62, p. 113.

3473. SIMMONS (Jack). **Southey**. London, Collins, 45, in-8, 256 p., 12s. 6d. R : O. Williams, *National R.*, 45, vol. 124, p. 514-518.

3474. SOUSA-LEÃO (J. De). **Southey** and Brazil. *Mod. Language R.*, 43, vol. 38, p. 181-191.

3475. STURT (George). The journals of George **Sturt**, ' George Bourne,' ed. by G. Grigson. London, Cresset Press, 41, in-8, 235 p., 8s. 6d.

3476. DODDS (John W.). **Thackeray** : a critical portrait. London, Oxford Univ. Press, 42, in-8, 267 p., 15s.

3477. COSMAN (Max). A Yankee in Canada (Henry D. **Thoreau**). *Canad. hist. R.*, 44, vol. 25, p. 33-37.

3478. HUBBELL (J. B.) ed. The last years of Henry **Timrod**, 1864-1867. London, Cambridge Univ. Press, 41, in-8, xii-184 p., 12s. 6d.

3478a. LAVRIN (J.). **Tolstoy**. London, Methuen, 44, in-8, 167 p., 7s. 6d.

3479. LEON (Derrrick). **Tolstoy** : his life and work. London, Routledge, 44, in-8, 373 p., (illus.), 25s.

3480. McCOURT (Edward A.). **Tolstoi's** *War and Peace. Queen's Quar.*, 42, vol. 49, p. 147-156.

3481. ARMSTRONG (Margaret). **Trelawny,** a man's life. London, Hale, 41, in-8, 379 p., 15s. R : O. Williams, *National R.*, 41, vol. 117, p. 457-463.

3482. TROLLOPE (Anthony). The tireless traveller : 20 letters to the Liverpool Mercury, 1875, ed. by B. A. Booth. London, Cambridge Univ. Press, 41, in-8, 222 p., 12s.

3483. LLOYD (J. A. T.). Ivan **Turgenev.** London, Hale, 43, in-8, 288 p., (illus.), 12s. 6d.

3484. HEMMINGHAUS (E. H.). Mark **Twain** in Germany. London, Oxford Univ. Press, 40, in-8, 70 p., 11s. 6d.

3485. ALLOTT (K.). Jules **Verne.** London, Cresset Press, 40, in-8, 283 p., (illus.), 15s.

3486. BARTLETT (W. I.). Jones **Very** : Emerson's ' Brave Saint '. London, Cambridge Univ. Press, 42, in-8, xvi-238 p., (plates), 18s.

3487. DRUMMOND (Andrew Landale). Blanco **White** : Spanish priest, refugee, celebrity, English clergyman, Unitarian, and sceptic (1775-1841). *Hibbert J.*, 44, vol. 42, p. 263-272.

3488. FAUSSET (H. I'A.). Walt **Whitman.** London, Cape, 42, in-8, 320 p., (plates), 12s. 6d.

3489. BENNETT (W.). **Whittier,** bard of freedom. London, Oxford Univ. Press, 42, in-8, 375 p., (illus.), 16s.

3490. DOUGLAS (A.). Oscar **Wilde** : a summing up. London, Duckworth, 40, in-8, 143 p., 6s.

3491. EVANS (D.). Life and work of William **Williams.** Llandyssul, Gomerian Press, 40, in-8, 372 p., 12s. 6d.

3492. FORSTER (E. M.). Virginia **Woolf.** London, Cambridge Univ. Press, 42, in-8, 28 p., 1s. 6d. (Rede lect., 1941).

3493. WORDSWORTH (Dorothy). Journals of Dorothy **Wordsworth,** ed. by E. de Selincourt. London, Macmillan, 42, 2 vols. in-8, xxv-443, vii-434 p., 36s. R : W. H. Drummond, *Hibbert J.*, 43, vol. 41, p. 178-179.

3494. BROUGHTON (L. N.). Some letters of the **Wordsworth** family, now first published. London, Oxford Univ. Press, 42, in-8, 144 p., 9s. (Cornell stud. in Engl., vol. 32).

3495. MEYER (G. W.). **Wordsworth's** formative years. London, Oxford Univ. Press, 44, in-8, 276 p., 20s.

3496. RALLI (Augustus). **Wordsworth** and his critics. *Queen's Quar.*, 42, vol. 49, p. 101-111.

3497. YEATS (J. B.). Letters to his son W. B. Yeats and others, 1869-1922, ed. with a memoir by J. Hone. London, Faber, 44, in-8, 296 p., 16s.

3498. HONE (J.). W. B. **Yeats,** 1865-1939. London, Macmillan, 43, in-8, ix-504 p., (illus.), 35s.

3499. MENON (V. K. M.). The development of William Butler **Yeats.** Edinburgh, Oliver & Boyd, 42, in-8, xiv-93 p., 8s. 6d.

3500. BATTISCOMBE (Georgina). Charlotte Mary **Yonge.** London, Constable, 43, in-8, 174 p., (illus.), 15s. R : G. Every, *Theology*, 44, vol. 47, p. 17-19.

§ 8. Art and Industrial Art

a. GENERAL

3501. BLUNT (Anthony). Artistic theory in Italy, 1450-1600. London, Oxford Univ. Press, 41, in-8, 168 p., (plates), 7s. 6d. R : T. Borenius, *Burlington Mag.*, 41, vol. 78, p. 101. J. H. Whitfield, *Mod. Language R.*, 42, vol. 37, p. 99-100.

3502. Jacob Burckhardt and England. *Burlington Mag.*, 43, vol. 83, p. 237-241.

3503. COLGATE (William). Canadian art, its origin and development. Toronto, Ryerson Press, 43, in-8, xviii-278 p., $5.00. R : J. Alford, *Canad. hist. R.*, 44, vol. 25, p. 325-327. W.A., *Canad. Art*, 44, vol. 2, p. 43. E.H., *Queen's Quar.*, 44, vol. 51, p. 460-461.

3504. DEUTSCH (O. E.). Sir William Hamilton's picture gallery. *Burlington Mag.*, 43, vol. 82, p. 36-41 (plates).

3505. DOUGLAS (Charles). Artist quarter : reminiscences of Montmartre and Montparnasse in the first two decades of the 20th century. London, Faber, 41, in-8, 354 p., 18s.

3506. GILL (Eric). Eric Gill, an autobiography. London, Cape, 41, in-8, xv-300 p., (illus.), 12s. 6d. R : F. H. A. Micklewright, *Theology*, 41, vol. 42, p. 315-316.

3507. HOFF (U.). Charles I, patron of artists. London, Collins, 42, in-4, 24 p., (plates), 7s. 6d.

3508. KOKOSCHKA (Oskar). An approach to the Baroque art of Czechoslovakia. *Burlington Mag.*, 42, vol. 81, p. 263-268.

3509. MCINNES (G.). A short history of Canadian art. London, Macmillan, 40, in-8, xiv-126 p., (illus.), 8s. 6d. R : D. Duncan, *Canad. hist. R.*, 40, vol. 21, p. 430-431.

3510. PEVSNER (Nikolaus). Academies of art : past and present. London, Cambridge Univ. Press, 40, in-4, xiv-323 p., (plates), 25s. R : H. Read, *Burlington Mag.*, 41, vol. 78, p. 134.

3511. Polish number. The Polish renaissance; Polish renaissance architecture; Renaissance sculpture in Poland. *Burlington Mag.*, 45, vol. 86, p. 3-25.

3512. SITWELL (S.). British architects and craftsmen, 1600-1830. London, Batsford, 45, in-8, ix-196 p., (illus.), 21s.

3513. THORNHILL (Sir James). Sir James Thornhill's collection. *Burlington Mag.*, 43, vol. 82, p. 133-136.

3514. TOLNAY (C. de). The youth of Michelangelo. London, Oxford Univ. Press, 44, in-4, 310 p., (plates), 100s.

3515. WATSON (F. J. B.). On the early history of collecting in England. *Burlington Mag.*, 44, vol. 85, p. 223-228.

3516. WEISBACH (Werner). Spanish baroque art. London, Cambridge Univ. Press, 41, in-8, xi-65 p., 7s. 6d. R : N.P., *Burlington Mag.*, 42, vol. 81, p. 208.

3517. WINKELMAN (B. F.). John G. Johnson : lawyer and art collector. London, Oxford Univ. Press, 42, in-8, 337 p., (illus.), 16s.

b. ARCHITECTURE

3518. AYSCOUGH (Anthony), SITWELL (Sacheverell), and JOURDAIN (M.). Country house baroque : photographs of 18th century ornament, mostly stucco-work, in English and Irish country houses. London, G. H. Hill, 40, in-8, 9 p., 45 plates, 12s. 6d. R : W.A.T., *Burlington Mag.*, 41, vol. 78, p. 34.

3519. BLOMFIELD (Sir Reginald). Richard Norman Shaw, architect, 1831 to 1912. London, Batsford, 40, in-8, 128 p., (illus.), 12s. 6d. R : N. Pevsner, *Burlington Mag.*, 41, vol. 78, p. 202-203.

3520. BLUNT (Anthony). François Mansart and the origins of French classical architecture. London, Warburg Inst., 41, in-8, 82 p., 34 plates, 15s. (Studies, vol. 14). R : *Burlington Mag.*, 42, vol. 80, p. 130.

3521. BRAUN (Hugh). The story of the English house. London, Batsford, 40, in-8, xii-116 p., 10s. 6d.   R : M.S.B., *Burlington Mag.*, 41, vol. 78, p. 66.

3522. DRUMMOND (Andrew L.). A century of chapel architecture, 1840-1940. *Congreg. Quar.*, 42, vol. 20, p. 318-328.

3523. DRURY (J.).   Old Chicago houses. London, Cambridge Univ. Press, 43, in-8, xx-518 p., (illus.), 24s.

3524. FACZYNSKI (J.).   Studies in Polish architecture, tr. from the Polish by P. Jordan. Liverpool, Univ. Press, 45, in-4, 116 p., (illus.), 21s.

3525. FOX (Sir Cyril).   Some south Pembrokeshire cottages. *Antiquity*, 42, vol. 16, p. 307-319 (illus.).

3526. GATER (Sir George) and GODFREY (Walter H.) ed. Survey of London. Vol. 20 : Trafalgar Square and neighbourhood. London, King, 40, in-4, xviii-148 p., 113 plates, 21s. R : A. T. Bolton, *Burlington Mag.*, 41, vol. 78, p. 33-34.

3527. GODFREY (W. H.).   Our building inheritance. London, Faber, 44, in-8, 87 p., (plates), 10s. 6d.

3528. GOODWIN (P. L.) and SMITH (G. E. K.).   Brazil builds : architecture new and old, 1652-1942. London, Allen & Unwin, 44, in-4, 198 p., (illus., plates), 36s. (Museum of modern art ser.).

3529. HAMLIN (Talbot).   Greek revival architecture in America. London, Oxford Univ. Press, 44, in-8, 480 p., (plates, figs.), 42s.   R : N. Pevsner, *Burlington Mag.*, 45, vol. 86, p. 153-154.

3530. HEAL (Sir Ambrose). A great country house in 1623. *Burlington Mag.*, 43, vol. 82, p. 108-116.

3531. HEMP (W. J.) and GRESHAM (Colin).   Park, Llanfrothen, and the unit system. *Archaeol. cambrensis*, 42, vol. 97, p. 98-112 (plates).

3532. JOHNSTON (F. B.) and WATERMAN (T. T.).   The early architecture of North Carolina. London, Oxford Univ. Press, 42, in-4, 316 p., (illus.), 45s.

3533. JONES (Francis).   Wynnstay in 1683-6. *Archaeol. cambrensis*, 40, vol. 95, p. 48-56.

3534. LOUKOMSKI (Georges). Charles Cameron (1740-1812) : monograph on his life and work in Russia, particularly in architecture, interior decoration, furniture design and landscape gardening, adapted into English and ed. by N. de Gren. London, Nicholson, 43, in-4, 102 p., 21s., de luxe ed. 105s.

3535. LUTYENS (Robert). Sir Edwin Lutyens : an appreciation in perspective. London, Country Life, 42, in-8, (illus., diagrams), 8s. 6d.

3536. The problem of the historic country house. *Burlington Mag.*, 43, vol. 83, p. 159-160.

3537. TALLMADGE (T. E.).   Architecture in old Chicago. London, Cambridge Univ. Press, 41, in-8, xvi-218 p., (plates), 18s.

c. SCULPTURE

3538. BURDETT (Osbert) and GODDARD (E. H.).   Edward Perry Warren, the biography of a connoisseur. London, Christophers, 41, in-8, 440 p., (illus.), 18s.

3539. CALLENDER (Sir Geoffrey). The effigy of Nelson in Westminster Abbey. *Mariner's Mirror*, 41, vol. 27, p. 307-313.

3540. ESDAILE (Katharine A.).   Some annotations on John Le Neve's 'Monumenta Anglicana' (1717-19). *Antiq. J.*, 42, vol. 22, p. 176-197.

3541. ESDAILE (K. A.).   Edward Pierce, the sculptor of Milton's bust at Christ's College, Cambridge. *Congreg. hist. Soc. Trans.*, 44, vol. 14, p. 213-217.

3542. FORTUNE (J.) and BURTON (J.). Elizabet Ney. London, Harrap, 44, in-8, 212 p., (illus.), 10s. 6d.

3543. GARDNER (A. Ten Eyck). Yankee stonecutters : the first American school of sculpture, 1800-1850. London, Oxford Univ. Press, 45, in-4, 96 p., 26s. 6d.

3544. HESS (Jacob). Michelangelo and Cordier. *Burlington Mag.*, 43, vol. 82, p. 55-65.

3545. MATHESON (Jean). Old Perth crafts. *Scottish geogr. Mag.*, 42, vol. 58, p. 20-22 (plates).

d. PAINTING

3546. ALFORD (John). The development of painting in Canada. *Canad. Art*, 45, vol. 2, p. 95-103.

3548. BIRKENHEAD (Sheila). Against oblivion : the life of Joseph Severn. London, Cassell, 43, in-8, 244 p., 12s. 6d.

3549. BORENIUS (T.). Later Italian painting, from Titian to Tiepolo. London, Avalon Press, 45, in-4, 28 p., (illus.), 8s. (Discussions on art ser.).

3550. BURY (A.). The life and art of Thomas Collier, R.I. Leigh-on-Sea, Lewis, 44, in-4, 260 p., (illus., plates), 105s.

3551. CAMMAERTS (Emile). The Flemish predecessors of Van Dyck in England. *Burlington Mag.*, 44, vol. 85, p. 303-307.

3552. CÉZANNE (Paul). Letters, ed. by J. Rewald, tr. by M. Kay. London, Cassirer, 41, in-8, 308 p., 15s. R : H. Read, *Burlington Mag.*, 42, vol. 80, p. 52. E. Hoffmann, 19*th Century*, 42, vol. 132, p. 95-96.

3553. CHAPPELL (Edwin). The likenesses of Samuel Pepys, ed. by D. Dale. *Mariner's Mirror*, 41, vol. 27, p. 45-53.

3554. COTMAN (John Sell). Cotman number (1782-1842). *Burlington Mag.*, 42, vol. 81, p. 159-176 (plates).

3555. COWDREY (B.) and WILLIAMS (E. W.) jr. William Sidney Mount, 1807-1868. London, Oxford Univ. Press, 44, in-4, 48 p., (illus.), 33s. 6d.

3556. DALE (Donald). The portraits of Samuel Pepys by John Hayls and Sir Peter Lely. *Mariner's Mirror*, 42, vol. 28, p. 3-10.

3557. The development of painting in Canada, 1665-1945. Toronto, National Gallery of Canada, 45, in-8, 65 p., $1.50. R : M. Barbeau, *Canad. Art*, 45, vol. 2, p. 135-136. A.B., *Queen's Quar.*, 45, vol. 52, p. 121.

3558. DOUGLAS (R. L.). Leonardo da Vinci : his life and pictures. London, Cambridge Univ. Press, 45, in-8, 140 p., (illus.), 24s. R : E. H. Gombrich, *Burlington Mag.*, 45, vol. 86, p. 129-130.

3559. EMMONS (Robert). The life and opinions of Walter Richard Sickert. London, Faber, 41, in-8, xii-327 p., (plates), 25s. R : E. Hoffmann, *Burlington Mag.*, 42, vol. 81, p. 310.

3560. GANZ (Paul). Holbein and Henry VIII. *Burlington Mag.*, 43, vol. 83, p. 269-272.

3561. GAUNT (William). The Pre-Raphaelite tragedy. London, Cape, 42, in-8, 256 p., (illus.), 10s. 6d. R : A. Lawlor, *Austral. Quar.*, 43, vol. 15, no. 2, p. 111-114.

3562. Francesco Guardi and England. *Burlington Mag.*, 43, vol. 82, p. 3-5.

3563. HOLBEIN (Hans). Holbein number. November. *Burlington Mag.*, 43, vol. 83, p. 263-286.

3564. LELY (Sir Peter). Sir Peter Lely's collection. *Burlington Mag.*, 43, vol. 83, p. 185-191 (plates).

3565. LOUKOMSKI (G.). History of modern Russian painting, 1840-1940.

London, Hutchinson, 45, in-4, 184 p., (illus.), 42s.

3566. MACCOLL (D. S.). The life, work and setting of Philip Wilson Steer, with a full catalogue of paintings and list of watercolours in public collections, by A. Yockney. London, Faber, 45, in-8, 240 p., 25s.

3567. MACER-WRIGHT (P.). Brangwyn. London, Hutchinson, 40, in-8, 287 p., (illus.), 10s. 6d.

3568. PANOFSKY (E.). Albrecht Dürer. 2nd ed. London, Oxford Univ. Press, 45, 2 vols. in-4, 326, 234 p., (illus.), 126s.

3569. ROSSETTI (D. G.). Letters to Fanny Cornforth, ed. by P. F. Baum. London, Oxford Univ. Press, 41, in-8, 142 p., 10s. 6d.

3570. SHIRLEY (Hon. Andrew). Bonington. London, Kegan Paul, 41, in-8, 166 p., 157 plates, 31s. 6d. (Engl. master painters).

3571. VINCI (L. da). The notebooks of Leonardo da Vinci, tr. from the Italian by E. MacCurdy. New ed. London, Cape, 44, in-4, 1,296 p., (illus.), 84s.

3572. WALKER (J.) and MACGILL (J.). Great American paintings from Smibert to Bellows, 1729-1924. London, Oxford Univ. Press, 44, in-4, 38 p., (illus.), 42s.

3573. WATERHOUSE (Ellis K.). Reynolds. London, Routledge, 41, in-8, 126 p., 300 plates, 42s. (Engl. master painters). R : T. Borenius, *Burlington Mag.*, 41, vol. 79, p. 94-95.

3574. WELLER (A. S.). Francesco Di Giorgio, 1439-1501. London, Cambridge Univ. Press, 44, in-8, xvi-430 p., (illus.), 60s.

3575. WOOLF (Virginia). Roger Fry, a biography. London, Hogarth; Toronto, Macmillan, 40, in-8, 307 p., (plates), 12s. 6d.; $4.00. R : A. Lawlor, *Art in Australia*, 41, ser. 4,

no. 2, p. 65-66. E.H., *Queen's Quar.*, 41, vol. 48, p. 431-432. T. Borenius, *Burlington Mag.*, 40, vol. 77, p. 100-102.

e. ETCHING AND DRAWING

3576. BARBEAU (Marius). Henri Julien. Toronto, Ryerson Press, 41, in-8, 44 p., (plates). (Can. art ser.). R : A.B., *Queen's Quar.*, 42, vol. 49, p. 171.

3577. FORD (Brinsley). J. F. Lewis and Richard Ford in Seville, 1832-33. *Burlington Mag.*, 42, vol. 80, p. 124-129.

3578. HORNIBROOK (M.) and PETIT-JEAN (C.). Catalogue of the engraved portraits by Jean Morin, c. 1590-1650. London, Cambridge Univ. Press, 45, in-8, viii-56 p., (illus.), 25s.

3579. KEYNES (Geoffrey). New Blake documents : history of the Job engravings. *Times lit. Supp.*, 43, p. 24.

3580. MUIR (P. H.). The Bickhams and their 'Universal Penman'. *Library*, 44/45, vol. 25, p. 162-184 (plates).

3581. OPPÉ (Paul). John Baptist Malchair of Oxford. *Burlington Mag.*, 43, vol. 83, p. 191-197.

3582. ROGER-MARX (Claude). French original engravings from Manet to the present time. London, Imperia, 40, in-2, 130 p., (illus.), 15s.

3583. URZIDIL (J.). Hollar : a Czech emigré in England, tr. by P. Selver. London, Czechoslovak Independent Weekly, 42, in-8, 69 p., 8s. 6d. R : *Burlington Mag.*, 42, vol. 80, p. 103-104.

f. DECORATIVE AND POPULAR ARTS. INDUSTRIAL ART

3584. ANDERSON (L.). The art of the silversmith in Mexico, 1519-1936. London, Oxford Univ. Press, 41, 2 vols. in-4, 468 p., 184 plates, 168s.

3585. BARBEAU (Marius). Old Canadian silver. *Canad. geogr. J.*, 41, vol. 22, p. 150-162.

3586. BENISOVICH (Michael). The history of the *Tenture des Indes*. *Burlington Mag.*, 43, vol. 83, p. 216-225.

3587. EDWARDS (Ralph). Sheraton furniture designs. London, Tiranti, 45, in-8, 12 p., (illus.), 5s.

3588. EDWARDS (R.) and JOURDAIN (M.). Georgian cabinet makers. London, Country Life, 44, in-4, 80 p., (illus.), 42s. R : R. W. Symonds, *Burlington Mag.*, 45, vol. 86, p. 155.

3589. GIBB (G. S.). The white-smiths of Taunton : a history of Reed & Barton, silversmiths. London, Oxford Univ. Press, 44, in-8, 454 p., (illus., figs., map), 20s.

3590. HERNMARCK (Carl). Swedish furniture, 1700-1800. *Burlington Mag.*, 43, vol. 83, p. 305-308.

3591. HONEY (W. B.). Dutch pottery and glass. *Burlington Mag.*, 42, vol. 81, p. 295-300 (plates).

3592. JONES (E. A.). Catalogue of the plate of Magdalen College, Oxford. London, Oxford Univ. Press, 40, in-8, 103 p., (illus., plates), 31s. 6d.

3593. KEYES (F. P.). Queen Anne's lace. London, Eyre & Spottiswoode, 40, in-8, 288 p., 5s.

3594. KURTH (Betty). Some unknown English embroideries of the 15th century. *Antiq. J.*, 43, vol. 23, p. 31-33 (illus.).

3595. LAVER (J.) ed. Nineteenth century French posters. London, Nicholson & Watson, 44, in-8, 18 p , (plates), 5s.

3596. LONGFIELD (Ada K.). Some 18th century Dublin carpet-makers. *Burlington Mag.*, 43, vol. 82, p. 149-152.

3597. MANN (James G.). An embossed visor of Guidobaldo II, Duke of Urbino. *Burlington Mag.*, 43, vol. 82, p. 14-16 (plates).

3598. MASSICOTTE (E. Z.). L'ameublement à Montréal aux 17e et 18e siècles. *B. Rech. hist.*, 42, vol. 48, p. 33-42, 75-86, 202-205.

3599. NANCE (E. Morton). The pottery and porcelain of Swansea and Nantgarw. London, Batsford, 43, in-8, xviii-579 p., 147s. R : A. J. B. Kiddell, *Burlington Mag.*, 43, vol. 82, p. 129.

3600. SCHEURLEER (Th. H. Lunsingh). French 18th-century furniture in Holland. *Burlington Mag.*, 40, vol. 76, p. 8-21.

3601. SYMONDS (R. W.). Masterpieces of English furniture, clocks and barometers. London, Batsford, 40, in-4, 182 p., (plates), 42s. R : F. Davis, *Burlington Mag.*, 40, vol. 77, p. 203-204.

3602. SYMONDS (R. W.). English 18th century furniture exports to Spain and Portugal. *Burlington Mag.*, 41, vol. 77, p. 57-60.

3603. SYMONDS (R. W.). English furniture and colonial American furniture—a contrast. *Burlington Mag.*, 41, vol. 78, p. 183-187.

3604. SYMONDS (R. W.). Domestic furnishing in the time of Charles II. *Burlington Mag.*, 42, vol. 81, p. 218-222 (plates).

3605. SYMONDS (R. W.). The Dutch home and its furniture. *Burlington Mag.*, 42, vol. 81, p. 300-304 (plates).

3606. TODD (T.). A history of British postage stamps. London, Duckworth, 41, in-8, 274 p., (plates), 10s. 6d.

3607. TOKE (N. E.). Swiss stained glass at Temple Ewell. *Archaeol. cantiana*, 39 (40), vol. 51, p. 1-8.

3608. TRAQUAIR (Ramsay). The old silver of Quebec. Toronto, 1940; London, Macmillan, 41, in-4, 180 p., (illus.), $4.00 ; 18s. R : W. Colgate, *Canad. hist. R.*, 41, vol. 22, p. 200-202. E. A. Jones, *Burlington Mag.*, 42, vol. 80, p. 155.

3609. TUNSTALL (Edward A.) and KERR (Antony). The painted room at the Queen's College, Oxford. *Burlington Mag.*, 43, vol. 82, p. 42-46.

3610. WENHAM (E.). Domestic silver of Great Britain and Ireland. London, Oxford Univ. Press, 40, in-8, xxiii-186 p., (illus., plates), 5s. (Oxf. bookshelf ser.).

3611. WILLIAMS (Sydney B.). Antique blue and white Spode. London, Batsford, 43, in-4, xviii-242 p., (plates), 31s. 6d.

§ 9. Music and the Theatre

3612. DAY (Cyrus Lawrence) and MURRIE (Eleanore Boswell). English song-books, 1651-1702 : a bibliography with a first-line index of songs. London, Bibliographical Soc., 40, in-8, xxi-439 p., (plates), 30s., members only.

3612a. DEUTSCH (O. E.). Music bibliography and catalogues. *Library*, 43, vol. 23, p. 151-170.

3613. KING (A. Hyatt). Recent work in music bibliography. *Library*, 45, vol. 26, p. 122-148.

3614. SMITH (W. C.). Catalogue of printed music published before 1801 now in the British Museum. 2nd suppl. June 1940. London, H.M.S.O., 40, in-8, 85 p., 6s. R : H. Claydon, *Library*, 40, vol. 21, p. 223-225.

3615. ADAMS (John Cranford). The Globe Playhouse, its design and equipment. London, Oxford Univ. Press, 42, in-8, 434 p., (illus.), 21s. R : W.A., *Queen's Quar.*, 43, vol. 50, p. 327-330. H. Granville-Barker, *Mod. Language R.*, 44, vol. 39, p. 296-299.

3616. AGATE (James). These were actors : extracts from a newspaper cutting book, 1811-1833, selected and annotated by J. Agate. London, Hutchinson, 43, in-8, 150 p., 10s. 6d.

3617. AGATE (M.). Madame Sarah. London, Simpkin, 45, in-8, 223 p., 9s. 6d.

3618. BACHARACH (A. L.) ed. Beethoven and the romantics. London, Penguin, 43, in-8, 192 p., 9d. (Lives of the great composers, vol. 2).

3619. BACHARACH (A. L.) ed. Brahms, Wagner and their contemporaries. London, Penguin, 43, in-8, 186 p., 9d. (Lives of the great composers, vol. 3).

3620. BAKER (Herschel). John Philip Kemble, the actor in his theatre. London, Oxford Univ. Press, 42, in-8, 424 p., 17s.

3621. BARTLEY (J. O.). The development of a stock character. 1 : The stage Irishman; 2 : The stage Scotsman; 3 : The stage Welshman (to 1800). *Mod. Language R.*, 42, vol. 37, p. 438-447; 43, vol. 38, p. 279-288.

3622. BENTLEY (Gerald Eades). The Jacobean and Caroline stage : dramatic companies and players. London, Oxford University Press, 41, 2 vols. in-8, xx-748 p., 42s. R : G B. Harrison, *19th Century*, 42, vol. 131, p. 186-189. C. J. Sisson, *Mod. Language R.*, 42, vol. 37, p. 88-91.

3623. BIRON (Fernand). Le chant grégorien dans l'enseignement et les oeuvres de Vincent d'Indy. *R. Univ. Ottawa*, 41, vol. 11, p. 42-70, 206-240.

3624. BLOM (Eric). Music in England. London, Pelican, 42, in-8, 220 p., 9d. R : W.R.A., *Musical Times*, 43, vol. 84, p. 23.

3625. BOAS (Frederick S.). The Malvern theatrical festival, 1929-1939. *Queen's Quar.*, 40, vol. 47, p. 219-230.

3626. BOOTH (J. B.). Seventy years of song. London, Hutchinson, 43, in-8, 80 p., (illus.), 1s. 6d. R : O. Williams, *National R.*, 43, vol. 121, p. 233-237.

3627. BOYD (Morrison Comegys). Elizabethan music and musical criticism. London, Oxford Univ. Press, 40, in-8, xi-363 p., 16s. R : H. G., *Musical Times*, 40, vol. 81, p. 261.

3628. BYRD (W.), BULL (J.) and GIBBONS (O.). Parthenia, or, The maydenhead of the first musicke that ever was printed for the virginals. Cambridge, Heffer, 43, in-4, 34 p., 35s. (Harrow replica ser.).

3629. CARNER (Mosco). A study of 20th-century harmony. London, Williams, 42, 2 vols. in-8, 142, 80 p., 12s. R : W.R.A., *Musical Times*, 42, vol. 83, p. 307.

3630. CARSE (Adam). The orchestra in the 18th century. London, Heffer, 40, in-8, 176 p., (illus.), 10s. 6d.

3631. CHURCH-MUSIC SOCIETY. Forty years of cathedral music, 1898-1938, a comparison of the repertories. London, Oxford Univ. Press, 40, in-8, 32 p., 6d. (Occas. papers, 12). R : H.G., *Musical Times*, 42, vol. 83, p. 110-112.

3632. COLLES (H. C.). Walford Davies, a biography. London, Oxford Univ. Press, 42, in-8, 204 p., 10s. 6d.

3633. COOPER (Gerald M.). The chronology of Purcell's works. *Musical Times*, 43, vol. 84, p. 203-205, 236-238, 270-272, 299-301, 331-332, 363-365.

3634. CROSSE (Gordon). Fifty years of Shakespearean playgoing. London, Mowbray, 40, in-8, 159 p., 2s. 6d.

3635. DENT (E. J.). A theatre for everybody : the story of the Old Vic and Sadler's Wells. London, Boardman, 45, in-4, 152 p., 12s. 6d.

3637. DEUTSCH (O. E.). Plea for a British union catalogue of old printed music. *J. Documentation*, 45, vol. 1, p. 41-44.

3638. DISHER (M. Willson). Drury Lane diaries. 1 : Kean and Elliston;

2 : ' The poet Bunn '; 3 : Macready, Munden, Ducrow; 4 : Kean at odds with his public. *Times lit. Supp.*, 41, p. 172, 184, 195-196, 208.

3639. DISHER (M. W.). The century of juvenile drama. *Times lit. Supp.*, 44, p. 108.

3640. ELKIN (R.). Queen's Hall, 1893-1941. London, Rider, 44, in-8, 160 p., (illus.), 21s.

3641. EVANS (M. B.). The passion play of Lucerne. London, Oxford Univ. Press, 43, in-8, 260 p., (illus.), 21s. 6d.

3642. EVANS (Willa McClurg). Henry Lawes : musician and friend of poets. London, Oxford Univ. Press, 42, in-8, 266 p., (illus.), 11s. 6d. R : J. Butt, *Mod. Language R.*, 43, vol. 38, p. 51-52.

3643. FARMER (Henry George). The martial fife : the bi-centenary of its reintroduction. *J. Soc. Army hist. Research*, 45, vol. 23, p. 66-71.

3644. FARMER (H. G.). The Royal Artillery band : fresh light on its history. *J. Soc. Army hist. Research*, 45, vol. 23, p. 90-97.

3645. FELLOWES (Edmund H.). English cathedral music, from Edward VI to Edward VII. London, Methuen, 41, in-8, 268 p., 16s. R : N. Carter, *Congreg. Quar.*, 42, vol. 20, p. 183-184. H.G., *Musical Times*, 42, vol. 83, p. 110-112.

3646. FORBES-WINSLOW (D.). ' Daly's ' : the biography of a theatre. London, W. H. Allen, 44, in-8, 220 p., (illus.), 15s. 6d.

3647. FRENZ (Horst) and CAMPBELL (Louise Wylie). William Gillette on the London stage. *Queen's Quar.*, 45, vol. 52, p. 443-457.

3648. FRICK (C.). The dramatic criticism of George Jean Nathan. London, Oxford Univ. Press, 43, in-8, 179 p., 12s.

3649. GÁL (Hans) ed. Catalogue of manuscripts, printed music and books on music up to 1850 in the library of the music department of the University of Edinburgh (Reid Library). Edinburgh, Oliver & Boyd, 41, in-8, 78 p., 5s.

3650. HANDEL (G. F.). Handel's ' Messiah ' : recent discoveries of early editions. *Musical Times*, 41, vol. 82, p. 427-428.

3651. HARRISON (G. B.). Elizabethan plays and players. London, Routledge, 40, in-8, viii-306 p., 12s.6d.

3652. HUSSEY (D.). Verdi. London, Dent, 40, in-8, xii-355 p., (illus.), 5s. 6d. (Master musicians ser.).

3653. JACOB (Heinrich Eduard). Johann Strauss, a century of light music. London, Hutchinson, 40, in-8, 352 p., 18s. R : H.G., *Musical Times*, 40, vol. 81, p. 412-413. *National R.*, 40, vol. 114, p. 762-763.

3654. JOHNSON (H. E.). Musical interludes in Boston, 1795-1830. London, Oxford Univ. Press, 43, in-8, 384 p., (illus.), 26s. 6d.

3655. KEMP (T. C.). The Birmingham repertory theatre : the playhouse and the man. Birmingham, Cornish Bros., 43, in-8, 151 p., (illus.), 12s. 6d.

3656. KOLODIN (I.). The Metropolitan opera, 1883-1939. 2nd ed. London, Oxford Univ. Press, 40, in-8, 649 p., 20s.

3657. LANCASTER (H. C.). The Comédie française, 1680-1701 : plays, actors, spectators, finances. London, Oxford Univ. Press, 41, in-4, 210 p., 15s. (Johns Hopkins univ. stud. in Romance lit. and lang., extra vol. 17). R : L. A. Bisson, *Mod. Language R.*, 42, vol. 37, p. 109-110.

3658. LEECH (Clifford). The Caroline audience. *Mod. Language R.*, 41, vol. 36, p. 304-319.

3659. LENORMAND (R.). A study of twentieth-century harmony. Vol. 1 : Harmony in France to 1914, tr. from the French by H. Antcliffe. New ed. London, J. Williams, 42, in-8, 142 p., (illus.), 6s.

3660. LEWER (David). The Temple choir in 1842. *Musical Times*, 43, vol. 84, p. 14-16.

3661. LIFAR (S.). Serge Diaghilev, his life, his work, his legend. London, Putnam, 40, in-8, xiv-399 p., (illus.), 21s.

3662. LOEWENBERG (A.). Annals of opera, 1597-1940, compiled from the original sources. Cambridge, Heffer, 43, in-8, xxiv-880 p., 84s.

3663. LOON (H. W. van). The life and times of Johann Sebastian Bach. London, Harrap, 42, in-8, 104 p., (illus.), 6s.

3664. LUDWIG (E.). Beethoven : life of a conqueror, tr. from the German by G. S. McManus. London, Hutchinson, 45, in-8, 270 p., 21s.

3665. MALNICK (Bertha). The origin and early history of the theatre in Russia. *Slavonic Y.B. (Slavonic R.)*, 40, vol. 19, p. 203-227.

3666. MASON (H.). The French theatre in New York. London, Oxford Univ. Press, 40, in-8, 442 p., 18s. 6d.

3667. MASSICOTTE (E. Z.). Le premier Théâtre Royal à Montréal. *B. Rech. hist.*, 42, vol. 46, p. 169-172.

3668. MERRITT (A. F.). Sixteenth-century polyphony. London, Oxford Univ. Press, 40, in-8, 215 p., 12s. 6d.

3669. NETTEL (R.). Music in the five towns, 1840-1914. London, Oxford Univ. Press, 44, in-8, 130 p., (illus.), 8s. 6d.

3670. NEWMAN (Ernest). Life of Richard Wagner. Vol. 3. London, Cassell, 45, in-8, xvi-569-xxxvi p., 30s. R : R. L. Jacobs, *Musical Times*, 45, vol. 86, p. 271-272.

3671. NICOLL (A.). British drama. 3rd rev. ed. London, Harrap, 45, in-8, 332 p., (illus.), 12s. 6d.

3672. ODELL (George C. D.). Annals of the New York stage. Vol. 12-14 : 1882-1891. London, Oxford Univ. Press, 40-45, 3 vols. in-4, 792, 741, 952 p., (illus.), 150s.

3673. ODELL (Mary T.). The Brighton theatre, 1814-1819. Worthing, Aldridge Bros., 45, in-4, 113 p., (illus.), 15s.

3674. ODELL (M. T.). More about the Old Theatre, Worthing : its plays, players and playbills, etc. Worthing, Aldridge Bros., 45, in-4, 194 p., (illus.), 15s.

3675. PASCAL (R.). The stage of the ' Englische Komödianten ' — three problems. Mod. Language R., 40, vol. 35, p. 367-376.

3676. POWER-WATERS (A.). John Barrymore : an authorised biography. London, S. Paul, 42, in-8, 184 p., 12s. 6d.

3677. REYNOLDS (G. F.). The staging of Elizabethan plays at the Red Bull theater, 1605-1625. London, Oxford Univ. Press, 40, in-8, 203 p., (illus.), 9s.

3678. ROBINSON (L.) ed. The Irish theatre ; lectures, Abbey Theatre festival, 1938. London, Macmillan, 40, in-8, xiii-299 p., 7s. 6d.

3679. SAUNDERS (W.). Weber. London, Dent, 40, in-8, ix-291 p., (illus.), 5s. 6d. (Master musicians ser.).

3680. SCHOLES (Percy A.). ' God Save the King ! ' its history and its romance. London, Oxford Univ. Press, 42, in-8, 2s. R : History, 43, vol. 28, p. 117.

3681. SCHOLES (P. A.). The election of a London organist two centuries ago. Musical Times, 42, vol. 83, p. 73-75.

3682. SCHOLES (P. A.). A wonderful new organ of 1754. Musical Times, 42, vol. 83, p. 108-110.

3683. SCOUTEN (A. H.) and HUGHES (Leo). The first season of ' The Honest Yorkshireman '. Mod. Language R., 45, vol. 40, p. 8-11.

3684. SILIN (C. I.). Benserade and his ballets de cour. London, Oxford Univ. Press, 40, in-8, 435 p., 18s.

3685. SISSON (C. J.). Notes on early Stuart stage history. Mod. Language R., 42, vol. 37, p. 25-36.

3686. SMITH (J. Sutcliffe). The story of music in Birmingham. Birmingham, Cornish, 45, in-8, 122 p., 12s. 6d. R : J. Stone, Musical Times, 45, vol. 86, p. 372-373.

3687. STIRLING (Lorna). The development of Australian music. Hist. Stud. Australia N.Z., 44, vol. 3, p. 58-72.

3688. STRONG (L. A. G.). John McCormack, the story of a singer. London, Methuen, 41, in-8, x-291 p., 15s.

3689. TOLLES (W.). Tom Taylor and the Victorian drama. London, Oxford Univ. Press, 40, in-8, 299 p., 17s. 6d.

3690. TOVEY (Sir D. F.) and PARRATT (G.). Walter Parratt : master of the music. London, Oxford Univ. Press, 42, in-8, 121 p., (illus.), 8s. 6d. R : H.G., Musical Times, 42, vol. 83, p. 207-208.

3691. WALDO (L. P.). The French drama in America. London, Oxford Univ. Press, 42, in-8, 288 p., (illus.), 16s.

3692. WHITLEY (W. T.). The first hymnbook in use. Baptist Quar., 41, vol. 10, p. 369-375.

3693. WHITLEY (W. T.). The tune book of 1791. Baptist Quar., 41, vol. 10, p. 434-443.

MODERN ECONOMIC AND SOCIAL HISTORY

§ 1. Political and Social Theory

3694. ANDERSON (D.) and DAVIDSON (P. E.). Ballots and the democratic class struggle. London, Oxford Univ. Press, 43, in-8, 392 p., 24s.

3695. BAUMER (Franklin Le Van). The early Tudor theory of kingship. London, Oxford Univ. Press, 40, in-8, 259 p., 11s. 6d. R : A. F. Pollard, *Eng. hist. R.*, 41, vol. 56, p. 310-313.

3696. BINDOFF (S. T.). Clement Armstrong and his treatises of the commonweal. *Econ. Hist. R.*, 44, vol. 14, p. 64-73.

3697. BUTTERFIELD (H.). The statecraft of Machiavelli. London, Bell, 40, in-8, 167 p., 6s. R : P. Gurney, *19th Century*, 41, vol. 130, p. 129-130. W.K.H., *Eng. hist. R.*, 42, vol. 57, p. 150.

3698. CARLYLE (A. J.). Political liberty : a history of the conception in the Middle Ages and modern times. London, Oxford Univ. Press, 41, in-8, viii-220 p., 12s. 6d. R : C.H.W., *History*, 41, vol. 26, p. 96. *Pol. Quar.*, 41, vol. 12, p. 332-333. F. S. Marvin, *Hibbert J.*, 41, vol. 40, p. 106-108.

3699. CARRITT (E. F.). Liberty and equality. *L.Q.R.*, 40, vol. 56, p. 61-74.

3700. COMMAGER (H. S.). Majority rule and minority rights. London, Oxford Univ. Press, 45, in-8, 96 p., 6s.

3701. CRAIGIE (James). The Basilicon Doron of King James VI. Vol. 1, ed. by J. Craigie. Edinburgh, Scottish Text Soc., 44, in-8, members only. R : D.H.W., *Eng. hist. R.*, 45, vol. 60, p. 426.

3702. CRAVEN (A.). Democracy in American life : a historical view. London, Cambridge Univ. Press, 42, in-8, xii-150 p., 6s.

3703. CREIGHTON (D. G.). Economic nationalism and confederation. *Canad. hist. Assoc. Rept.*, 42, p. 44-51.

3704. HALLER (W.) and DAVIES (G.) eds. The Leveller tracts, 1647-1653. London, Oxford Univ. Press, 44, in-8, 490 p., 44s.

3705. HOFSTADTER (R.). Social Darwinism in American thought, 1860-1915. London, Oxford Univ. Press, 44, in-8, 202 p., 15s. 6d.

3706. LATHAM (R. C.). English revolutionary thought, 1640-60. *History*, 45, vol. 30, p. 38-59.

3707. LEIBHOLZ (H. G.). Nationality in history and politics. *Hibbert J.*, 45, vol. 43, p. 118-125.

3708. LEWIS (H. D.) and THOMAS (J. A.). Y wlanwriaeth a'i hawdurdod. (The state and its authority). Cardiff, University of Wales Press Board, 43, in-8, 132 p. (Cyfres y Brifysgol a'r Werin, 20).

3709. MACKINNON (James). A history of modern liberty. Vol. 4 : The struggle with the Stuarts, 1647-1689. London, Longmans, 41, in-8, 523 p., 16s.

3710. MAVERICK (L. A.). The Chinese and the Physiocrats : a supplement. *Econ. Hist.*, 40, vol. 4, p. 312-318.

3711. MAYER (J. P.). Political thought in France from Sieyès to Sorel. London, Faber, 43, in-8, 148 p., 8s. 6d. R : A. Cobban, *History*, 45, vol. 30, p. 194.

3712. OSBORN (Annie Marion). Rousseau and Burke : a study of the idea of liberty in 18th-century political thought. London, Oxford Univ. Press, 40, in-8, 283 p., 10s. 6d,

3713. SCHLATTER (R. B.). The social ideas of religious leaders, 1660-1688. [In England]. London, Oxford Univ. Press, 40, in-8, vii-248 p., 10s. 6d. R : C.E.W., *Eng. hist. R.*, 41, vol. 56, p. 517-518.

3714. SCOTT (F. R.). Political nationalism and confederation. *Canad. J. Econ. pol. Sci.*, 42, vol. 8, p. 386-415.

3715. SISSON (C. J.). The judicious marriage of mr. Hooker and the birth of ' The laws of ecclesiastical polity '. London, Cambridge Univ. Press, 40, in-8, 220 p., 10s. 6d. R : G.S.T., *History*, 44, vol. 29, p. 213-214. R. N. Carew Hunt, *19th Century*, 41, vol. 129, p. 305-307. P. E. Hallett, *Mod. Language R.*, 41, vol. 36, p. 262-264.

3716. TAWNEY (R. H.). Harrington's interpretation of his age. London, Oxford Univ. Press, 42, in-8, 28 p., 2s. (Raleigh lect. on hist., 1941).

3717. WINSTANLEY (Gerrard). Selections from the works of Gerrard Winstanley, ed. by L. Hamilton. London, Cresset Press, 44, in-8, 198 p., 7s. 6d. R : G. Davies, *Eng. hist. R.*, 45, vol. 60, p. 410-412. R. C. Latham, *History*, 45, vol. 30, p. 38-59. W. Schenk, *Econ. Hist. R.*, 45, vol. 15, p. 101-102.

§ 2. Political Economy

3718. BARNETT (P.). Business cycle theory in the United States, 1860-1900. London, Cambridge Univ. Press, 42, in-8, x-130 p., 6s. (Stud. in business admin. ser.).

3719. BLACK (R. D.). Trinity College, Dublin, and the theory of value, 1832-1863. *Economica*, 45, vol. 12, p. 140-148.

3720. CLARK (Colin). The conditions of economic progress. London, Macmillan, 40, in-8, xii-504 p., 25s. R : J. Plimsoll, *Austral. Quar.*, 41, vol. 13, no. 1, p. 104-109. D. C. MacGregor, *Canad. J. Econ. pol. Sci.*, 45, vol. 11, p. 270-272.

3721. HICKS (J. R.). History of economic doctrine. *Econ. Hist. R.*, 43, vol. 13, p. 111-115.

3722. HONE (Joseph). Richard Cantillon, economist : biographical note. *Econ. J.*, 44, vol. 54, p. 96-100.

3723. LIPSON (E.). A planned economy or free enterprise : the lessons of history. London, Black, 44, in-8, viii-320 p., 15s.

3724. LUTZ (F. A.). History and theory in economics. *Economica*, 44, vol. 11, p. 210-214.

3725. MARSHALL (Alfred). The centenary of the birth of Alfred Marshall, July 26, 1842-July 13, 1942. *Econ. J.*, 42, vol. 52, p. 289-349.

3726. O'CONNOR (M. J. L.). Origins of academic economics in the United States. London, Oxford Univ. Press, 44, in-8, 368 p., 28s.

3727. RIST (Charles). History of monetary and credit from John Law to the present day. Tr. [from the French] by J. Degras. London, Allen & Unwin, 40, in-8, 442 p., 25s. R : E. V. Morgan, *Econ. J.*, 40, vol. 50, p. 282-285. J. K. Horsefield, *Economica*, 40, vol. 7, p. 439-441.

3728. ROLL (E.). A history of economic thought. Rev. ed. London, Faber, 45, in-8, 535 p., 18s.

3729. SPENGLER (J. J.). French predecessors of Malthus, a study in 18th-century wage and population theory. London, Cambridge Univ. Press, 42, in-8, x-398 p., 27s. R : H. M. Robertson, *South African J. Econ.*, 42, vol. 10, p. 295-306.

3730. STARK (W.). The history of economics in its relation to social development. London, Routledge, 44, in-8, viii-80 p., 7s. 6d. (Internat. libr. of sociology and soc. reconstruction). R : J. L. Myres, *Man*, 45, vol. 45, p. 115. J. A. La Nauze, *Econ. R.*, 45, vol. 21, p. 265-267. E. Roll,

Econ. Hist. R., 45, vol. 15, p. 86-87. T. H. Marshall, *Econ. J.*, 45, vol. 55, p. 415-419.

3731. WHITTAKER (Edmund). A history of economic ideas. London, Longmans, 40, in-8, xii-766 p., 25s. (Longmans' econ. ser.). R : H. Burton, *Econ. Record*, 42, vol. 18, p. 94-98. V. W. Bladen, *Canad. J. Econ. pol. Sci.*, 41, vol. 7, p. 100-103. F. A. v. Hayek, *Economica*, 41, vol. 8, p. 104-105.

§ 3. General Economic History

3732. A bibliography of current publications on Canadian economics, prepared by the editorial office of the University of Toronto Press. *Canad. J. Econ. pol. Sci.*, 40-45, vol. 6-11.

3733. GRAS (N. S. B.). List of books and articles on the economic history of the United States and Canada. *Econ. Hist. R.*, 41, vol. 11, p. 114-125.

3734. LARSON (Henrietta M.). List of books and articles on the economic history of the United States and Canada. *Econ. Hist. R.*, 44, vol. 14, p. 113-121; 45, vol. 15, p. 107-112.

3735. MANN (J. de L.). Books and articles on the economic history of Great Britain and Ireland, 1937-1939. *Econ. Hist. R.*, 40, vol. 10, p. 82-87.

3736. ROSENBAUM (E. M.). War economics, a bibliographical approach. *Economica*, 42, vol. 9, p. 64-94.

3737. ARNDT (H. W.). The economic lessons of the nineteen thirties. London, Oxford Univ. Press, 44, in-8, 314 p., 12s. 6d. R : H. Burton, *Econ. R.*, 45, vol. 21, p. 269-270. M.F.W.J., *Int. Affairs*, 45, vol. 21, p. 266-267. F. W. Paish, *Economica*, 45, vol. 12, p. 117-118.

3738. BASCH (Antonin). The Danube basin and the German economic sphere. London, Routledge, 44, in-8, xiv-272 p., 18s. (Internat.

libr. of sociol. and soc. reconstruction). R : H.C.H., *Int. Affairs*, 45, vol. 21, p. 281-282. H. R. G. Greaves, *Pol. Quar.*, 45, vol. 16, p. 182-183. C. Leubuscher, *Economica*, 45, vol. 12, p. 121. J.P.H.M., *Geogr. J.*, 45, vol. 106, p. 154.

3739. BENFIELD (E.). Purbeck shop : a stoneworker's story of stone. Intr. by A. E. Richardson. London, Cambridge Univ. Press, 40, in-8, 186 p., (illus.), 12s. 6d.

3740. BENHAM (Frederic). The muddle of the thirties. *Economica*, 45, vol. 12, p. 1-9.

3741. BERESFORD (M. W.). Lot acres. *Econ. Hist. R.*, 43, vol. 13, p. 74-79.

3742. BEST (R. D.). Brass chandelier : a biography of R. H. Best, of Birmingham. London, G. Allen, 40, in-8, 251 p., (plates), 15s. R : T. S. Ashton, *Econ. Hist. R.*, 43, vol. 13, p. 138.

3743. CLAPHAM (J. H.). Charles Louis, Elector Palatine, 1617-1680 : an early experiment in liberalism. *Economica*, 40, vol. 7, p. 381-396.

3744. COLE (Charles Wolsey). French mercantilism, 1683-1700. London, Oxford Univ. Press, 43, in-8, 364 p., 28s. R : G. N. Clark, *Eng. hist. R.*, 45, vol. 60, p. 412-414. C. R. Fay, *Canad. J. Econ. pol. Sci.*, 45, vol. 11, p. 628-631. E. E. Rich, *Econ. Hist. R.*, 45, vol. 15, p. 96-98.

3745. COMER (J. P.). New York building control, 1800-1941. London, Oxford Univ. Press, 42, in-8, 299 p., 16s. 6d.

3746. CRABBE (Geoffrey). Turkey : a record of industrial and commercial progress in the last quarter of a century. *J. central asian Soc.*, 44, vol. 31, p. 48-63.

3747. CULE (J. E.). Finance and industry in the 18th century : the firm of Boulton and Watt. *Econ. Hist.*, 40, vol. 4, p. 319-325.

3748. CURRIE (A. W.). Canadian economic development. Toronto, Nelson, 42, in-8, v-386 p., $2.00. R : H. A. I(nnis), *Canad. J. Econ. pol. Sci.*, 44, vol. 10, p. 533.

3749. DAY (C.). Economic development in Europe. New ed. London, Macmillan, 42, in-8, xxii-746 p., 18s.

3750. The Economist : a centenary volume, 1843-1943. London, Oxford Univ. Press, 43, in-8, 182 p., (illus.), 7s. 6d. R : A. Robinson, *Econ. J.*, 43, vol. 53, p. 406-408.

3751. FAY (C. R.). English economic history mainly since 1700. Cambridge, Heffer, 40, in-8, vii-253 p., 5s. R : J. M. Keynes, *Econ. J.*, 40, vol. 50, p. 259-261. H. Burton, *Econ. Record*, 41, vol. 17, p. 116-117. V. W. Bladen, *Canad. J. Econ. pol. Sci.*, 41, vol. 7, p. 298-299. W.E.C.H., *Queen's Quar.*, 41, vol. 48, p. 192-194.

3752. FITZPATRICK (Brian). The British empire in Australia : an economic history, 1834-1939. Melbourne, Univ. Press, 41, in-8, xxxii-529 p., 21s. R : F. L. W. Wood, *Hist. Stud. Australia N.Z.*, 41, vol. 1, p. 277-279. G. Greenwood, *Austral. Quar.*, 41, vol. 13, no. 2, p. 106-108. W. P. Morrell, *Econ. Hist. R.*, 42, vol. 12, p. 95-96. W. B. Reddaway, *Econ. J.*, 44, vol. 54, p. 113-115.

3753. FRICKEY (Edwin). Economic fluctuations in the United States : a systematic analysis of long-run trends and business cycles, 1866-1914. London, Oxford Univ. Press, 42, in-8, xxi-375 p., 28s. (Harvard econ. stud., vol. 73). R : T.W., *Int. Affairs*, 45, vol. 21, p. 117-118.

3754. HANCOCK (W. K.). Survey of British Commonwealth affairs. Vol. 2 : Problems of economic policy, 1918-1939. London, Milford, 40-42, 2 vols. in-8, xi-324, xii-355 p., 31s. R (Pt. 1) : A. G. L. Shaw, *Econ. Record*, 42, vol. 18, p. 108-112. H. A.

Innis, *Canad. J. Econ. pol. Sci.*, 42' vol. 8, p. 608-612. W. P. Morrell, *History,* 41, vol. 25, p. 365-367. C. R. Fay, *Econ. Hist. R.*, 41, vol. 11, p. 103-105. H. M. Robertson, *S. African J. Econ.*, 40, vol. 8, p. 477-482. (Pt. 2) : W. P. Morrell, *History*, 42, vol. 27, p. 91-93. A. G. B. Fisher, *Int. Affairs*, 42, vol. 19, p. 382-383. H. A. Wyndham, *J. Roy. african Soc.*, 42, vol. 41, p. 189-194.

3755. HENDERSON (W. O.). British economic activity in the German colonies, 1884-1914. *Econ. Hist. R.*, 45, vol. 15, p. 56-66.

3756. HUGHES (Edward). The English stamp duties, 1664-1764. *Eng. hist. R.*, 41, vol. 56, p. 234-264.

3757. JONES (G. P.) and POOL (A. G.). A hundred years of economic development. London, Duckworth, 40, in-8, 415 p., 18s. (Hundred years ser.). R : E. V. Morgan, *Econ. J.*, 40, vol. 50, p. 308-311. *Economica*, 42, vol. 9, p. 413.

3758. KELSALL (R. Keith). A century of wage assessment in Herefordshire (1666-1762). *Eng. hist. R.*, 42, vol. 57, p. 115-119.

3759. KIEWIET (C. W. de). A history of South Africa, social and economic. Oxford, Clarendon Press, 41, in-8, 292 p., 15s. R : *United Empire*, 41, vol. 32, p. 173. J. C. Beaglehole, *Hist. Stud. Australia N.Z.*, 43, vol. 2, p. 129-140. W. P. Morrell, *Eng. hist. R.*, 42, vol. 57, p. 515-517. L. Fouché, *African Stud.*, 42, vol. 49, p. 228. E. Kahn, *South African J. Econ.*, 42, vol. 10, p. 36-46. C. R. Fay, *Econ. J.*, 42, vol. 52, p. 87-88. H. A. Wyndham, *J. Roy. african Soc.*, 42, vol. 41, p. 129-131. A. I. Richards, *J. Roy. african Soc.*, 42, vol. 41, p. 206-207. W. K. Hancock, *Int. R. Missions*, 42, vol. 31, p. 246-247.

3760. KLEINSORGE (P. L.). The Boulder Canyon project. London,

Oxford Univ. Press, 43, in-8, 344 p., 21s. 6d.

3761. KLOTZ (Edith L.) and DAVIES (Godfrey). The wealth of royalist peers and baronets during the Puritan revolution. *Eng. hist. R.*, 43, vol. 58, p. 217-219.

3762. LEAGUE OF NATIONS, *Economic, financial and transit dept.* Economic fluctuations in the United States and the United Kingdom, 1918-22. London, Allen & Unwin, 42, in-8, 93 p., 6s. R : R. G. Hawtrey, *Economica*, 44, vol. 11, p. 107-108. H. R. Kemp, *Canad. J. Econ. pol. Sci.*, 44, vol. 10, p. 231-232.

3763. LEAGUE OF NATIONS, *Economic, financial and transit dept.* Europe's overseas needs, 1919-20, and how they were met. London, Allen & Unwin, 43, in-8, 52 p., 2s. 6d. R : V. Anstey, *Economica*, 44, vol. 11, p. 151-152. H. R. Kemp, *Canad. J. Econ. pol. Sci.*, 44, vol. 10, p. 233.

3764. LEONTIEF (Wassily W.). The structure of American economy, 1919-1929 : an empirical application of equilibrium analysis. London, Oxford Univ. Press, 42, in-8, 198 p., 10s. 6d. R : K. E. Boulding, *Canad. J. Econ. pol. Sci.*, 42, vol. 8, p. 124-126. E. Rothbarth, *Econ. J.*, 43, vol. 53, p. 213-216.

3765. LEUBUSCHER (C.). Tanganyika Territory : a study of economic policy under mandate. London, Oxford Univ. Press, 44, in-8, x-217 p., 18s. R : A. I. Richards, *Africa*, 45, vol. 15, p. 218-220. G. L. Wood, *Econ. R.*, 45, vol. 21, p. 313-314. A. Pim, *Int. Affairs*, 45, vol. 21, p. 288-289. N. Bentwich, *Pol. Quar.*, 45, vol. 16, p. 269-272. G.F.S., *African Affairs*, 45, vol. 44, p. 89-90. I. G. Thomas, *South African J. Econ.*, 45, vol. 13, p. 60-62. N. F. Hall, *Econ. J.*, 45, vol. 55, p. 434-437.

3766. LEVY (Hermann). The economic history of sickness and medical benefit before the Puritan Revolution.

Econ. Hist. R., 43, vol. 13, p. 42-57 ; 44, vol. 14, p. 135-160.

3767. LOGAN (H. A.). Trends in collective bargaining : a study in casual analysis. *Canad. J. Econ. pol. Sci.*, 43, vol. 9, p. 331-347.

3768. McFADYEAN (Sir Andrew) ed. The history of rubber regulation, 1934-1943, ed. for the International Rubber Regulation Committee. London, Allen & Unwin, 44, in-8, 239 p., 10s. 6d. R : P. T. Bauer, *Econ. J.*, 44, vol. 54, p. 414-416. T. B. Barlow, *Int. Affairs*, 44, vol. 20, p. 566. G. Schneider, *Econ. R.*, 45, vol. 21, p. 118-119.

3769. MARSH (Leonard C.). Canadians in and out of work : a survey of economic classes and their relation to the labour market. Toronto, Oxford Univ. Press, 40, in-8, xxii-503 p., $4.50.

3770. MINVILLE (Esdras). Montréal économique : étude préparée à l'occasion du 3e centenaire de la ville. Montréal, Ed. Fides, 43, in-8, 430 p., $1.50. (Études sur notre milieu). R : J. I. Cooper, *Canad. hist. R.*, 44, vol. 25, p. 435-436.

3771. MULLENDORE (William C.). History of the United States food administration, 1917-19. London, Oxford Univ. Press, 41, in-8, xiv-399 p., 21s. (Hoover libr. on war, revolution, and peace, publ. 18). R : R. J. Hammond, *Eng. hist. R.*, 43, vol. 58, p. 244-246.

3772. NATHAN (Otto) and FRIED (Milton). The Nazi economic system: Germany's mobilization for war. London, Cambridge Univ. Press, 44, in-8, ix-378 p., 24s. R : R. H. Smith, *South African J. Econ.*, 45, vol. 13, p. 58-60. E. H. Stern, *Econ. J.*, 45, vol. 55, p. 104-106.

3773. NEF (John U.). War and economic progress, 1540-1640. *Econ. Hist. R.*, 42, vol. 12, p. 13-38.

3774. NEF (J. U.). Wars and the rise of industrial civilization, 1640-1740. *Canad. J. Econ. pol. Sci.*, 44, vol. 10, p. 36-78.

3775. PEARCE (Brian). Elizabethan food policy and the armed forces. *Econ. Hist. R.*, 42, vol. 12, p. 39-46.

3776. PIM (Sir Alan W.). The financial and economic history of the African tropical territories. London, Oxford Univ. Press, 40, in-8, 244 p., 10s. 6d. R : A. Robinson, *Econ. J.*, 41, vol. 51, p. 115-117. *J. Roy. african Soc.*, 41, vol. 40, p. 176. G.R.C., *Geogr. J.*, 41, vol. 97, p. 189-190. *African Stud.*, 42, vol. 1, p. 155.

3777. PRITCHETT (C. H.). The Tennessee Valley Authority. London, Oxford Univ. Press, 43, in-8, 348 p., (maps, charts), 21s. 6d.

3778. REES (J. F.). Mercantilism. *History*, 40, vol. 24, p. 129-135.

3779. ROBBINS (R. M.). Our landed heritage : the public domain, 1776-1936. London, Oxford Univ. Press, 45, in-8, 462 p., (illus.), 33s. 6d.

3780. ROSENBERG (Hans). Political and social consequences of the great depression of 1873-1896 in central Europe. *Econ. Hist. R.*, 43, vol. 13, p. 58-73.

3781. SHAW (A. G. L.). The economic development of Australia. Melbourne, Longmans, 44, in-8, 193 p., 7s. R : G. V. Portus, *Econ. R.*, 45, vol. 21, p. 267-269.

3782. SHEPHARD (C. Y.). British West Indian economic history in imperial perspective. *J. Barbados Mus.*, 40, vol. 7, p. 59-68, 101-108.

3783. SIMUTIS (A.). The economic reconstruction of Lithuania after 1918. London, Milford, 42, in-8, 148 p., 7s. 6d. R : *Scottish geogr. Mag.*, 43, vol. 59, p. 72.

3784. SNYDER (Carl). Capitalism the creator : the economic foundations of modern industrial society. London, Macmillan, 40, in-8, xii-473 p., 44 charts, 16s. R : E. S. Cooper-Willis, *Econ. J.*, 41, vol. 51, p. 106-107.

3785. STEPHENSON (H. E.) and McNAUGHT (Carlton). The story of advertising in Canada : a chronicle of 50 years. Toronto, Ryerson Press, 40, in-8, xvi-364 p., (illus.), $3.50. R : H. A. Innis, *Canad. J. Econ. pol. Sci.*, 41, vol. 7, p. 109-112.

3786. STOLPER (Gustav). German economy, 1870-1940. London, Allen & Unwin, 40, in-8, xviii-295 p., 7s. 6d. R : W. O. Henderson, *Econ. Hist. R.*, 41, vol. 11, p. 113. D. L. Anderson, *Econ. Record*, 41, vol. 17, p. 289.

3787. TAWNEY (R. H.). The rise of the gentry, 1558-1640. *Econ. Hist. R.*, 41, vol. 11, p. 1-38.

3788. TAWNEY (R. H.). The abolition of economic controls, 1918-1921. *Econ. Hist. R.*, 43, vol. 13, p. 1-30.

3789. TURIN (S. P.). The U.S.S.R. —an economic and social survey. London, Methuen, 44, in-8, 220 p., 16s. R : B. Wootton, *Econ. J.*, 44, vol. 54, p. 391-393.

3790. The United States in the world economy : the international transactions of the United States during the inter-war period. London, H.M.S.O., 44, in-8, viii-216 p., 2s. 6d. R : A. G. B. Fisher, *Int. Affairs*, 44, vol. 20, p. 423.

3791. VLECK (G. W. van). The panic of 1857. London, Oxford Univ. Press, 43, in-8, 138 p., 10s.

3792. WATSON (J. W.). Urban developments in the Niagara peninsula. *Canad. J. Econ. pol. Sci.*, 43, vol. 9, p. 463-486.

3793. WILLIAMS (D. Trevor). The economic development of Swansea and of the Swansea district. Cardiff, Univ. of Wales Press Bd., 40, in-8, 189 p., 1s. 6d. R : E.G.B., *Geography*,

41, vol. 26, p. 148. J. F. Rees, *Economica*, 41, vol. 8, p. 107-109.

3794. WILSON (Pearl). Consumer buying in Upper Canada, 1791-1840. *Ontario hist. Soc. Pap.*, 44, vol. 36, p. 33-40.

3795. WRIGHT (Chester W.). Economic history of the United States. London, McGraw-Hill, 41, in-8, xxviii-120 p., (maps), 21s. (Business and econ. publ.). R : H. A. Innis, *Canad. J. Econ. pol. Sci.*, 42, vol. 8, p. 305-307.

3796. WRIGHT (C. W.). American economic preparations for war, 1914-1917 and 1939-1941. *Canad. J. Econ. pol. Sci.*, 42, vol. 8, p. 157-175.

3797. ZWEIG (Ferdynand). Poland between two wars : social and economic changes. London, Secker & Warburg, 44, in-8, 176 p., 10s. 6d. R : P. E., *Int. Affairs*, 45, vol. 21, p. 279. N. Bentwich, *Pol. Quar.*, 45, vol. 16, p. 180-181. W.J.R., *Slavonic R.*, 45, vol. 23, p. 177-178. N. Momtchilof, *Econ. J.*, 45, vol. 55, p. 431-432.

§ 4. Industry, Mining and Communications

3798. ABBOTT (J. H. M.). The Newcastle packets and the Hunter valley. Sydney, Currawong, 43, in-8, 242 p., (plates), 15s. R : C. H. Bertie, *Roy. Austral. hist. Soc. J.*, 44, vol. 30, p. 83-84.

3799. ALLEN (G. C.). Japanese industry : its recent development and present condition. London, Allen, 40, in-8, x-124 p., 5s. (Inst. of Pacific relations inquiry ser.). R : E. Masey, *Austral. Quar.*, 40, vol. 12, no. 3, p. 113-114.

3800. ALLEN (G. C.), GORDON (M. S.), PENROSE (E. F.). The industrialization of Japan and Manchukuo, 1930-1940 : population, raw materials, and industry, ed. by E. B. Schumpeter. London; Toronto, Macmillan,

41, in-8, xxviii-944 p., 37s. 6d. ; $8.25. (Bur. of internat. research, Harvard Univ. and Radcliffe College, publ.). R : H. F. Angus, *Canad. J. Econ. pol. Sci.*, 42, vol. 8, p. 116-119.

3801. ANDREWS (G. S.). Alaska highway survey in British Columbia. *Geogr. J.*, 42, vol. 100, p. 5-22.

3802. ASPINALL (Sir Algernon). Some roads and their burdens. *J. Barbados Mus.*, 45, vol. 12, p. 61-66.

3803. BALAKRISHNA (R.). Industrial development of Mysore. Bangalore, Bangalore Press, 40, in-8, 305 p., Rs. 5. R : V. Anstey, *Economica*, 41, vol. 8, p. 334-336.

3804. BANNISTER (J. A.). The Houghton iron works. *Ontario hist. Soc. Pap.*, 44, vol. 36, p. 79-82.

3805. BARCLAY-HARVEY (Sir Malcolm). A history of the Great North of Scotland railway. London, Locomotive Publ. Co., 40, in-8, viii-222 p., 10s.

3806. BARD (E. W.). The Port of New York Authority. London, King, 43, in-8, 350 p., (map), 17s. 6d.

3807. BAUER (P. T.). Rubber production costs during the great depression [1929-33]. *Econ. J.*, 43, vol. 53, p. 361-369.

3808. BAUER (P. T.). Some aspects of the Malayan rubber slump, 1929-1933. *Economica*, 44, vol. 11, p. 190-198.

3809. BEACHAM (A.). The Ulster linen industry. *Economica*, 44, vol. 11, p. 199-209.

3810. BEAVER (S. H.). Railways in the Balkan peninsula. *Geogr. J.*, 41, vol. 97, p. 273-294.

3811. BLAKE (John W.). Transportation from Ireland to America, 1653-60. *Irish hist. Stud.*, 43, vol. 3, p. 267-281.

3812. BOOTGEZEL (J. J.). The first dry-dock in the Netherlands. *Trans. Newcomen Soc.*, 38/39 [40], vol. 19, p. 221-226.

3813. BRÓOKE (E. Henry). Chronology of the tinplate works of Great Britain. Cardiff, Wm. Lewis, 45, in-8, viii-177 p., 7s. 6d.

3814. BRUFF (J. G.). Gold rush: the journals, drawings, and other papers of J. Goldsbrough Bruff, ed. by G. W. Read and R. Gaines. London, Oxford Univ. Press, 44, 2 vols. in-4, 718, 684 p., (illus., maps), 100s.

3815. BUCKNALL (Rixon). Our railway history. London, Simpkin, 45, in-8, 148 p., 15s.

3816. BURKE (John F.). Outlines of the industrial history of Ireland. Rev. ed., with a suppl. chapter by M. J. Cryan and M. J. Kennedy. Dublin, Browne and Nolan, 40, in-8, xx-379 p., 4s. 6d. R : W. O'Sullivan, *Irish hist. Stud.*, 42, vol. 3, p. 125-126.

3817. BURN (D. L.). The economic history of steelmaking, 1867-1939 : a study in competition. London, Cambridge Univ. Press, 40, in-8, xi-548 p., 27s. 6d. R : H.W.M., *J. Roy. statist. Soc.*, 40, vol. 103, p. 578-580. G. C. Allen, *Econ. J.*, 41, vol. 51, p. 291-293. A. Birnie, *Eng. hist. R.*, 41, vol. 56, p. 330-332. T. A. Ashton, *Econ. Hist. R.*, 43, vol. 13, p. 126-127. H. L. Beales, *Economica*, 43, vol. 10, p. 200-204. C. R. Fay, *Canad. J. Econ. pol. Sci.*, 42, vol. 8, p. 620-623.

3818. BURNHAM (T. H.) and HOSKINS (G. O.). Iron and steel in Britain, 1870-1930. London, Allen & Unwin, 43, in-8, 252 p., (figs.), 25s. R : A. G. B. Fisher, *Economica*, 44, vol. 11, p. 143. S.H.B., *Geogr. J.*, 44, vol. 103, p. 282-284. S. R. Dennison, *Econ. J.*, 44, vol. 54, p. 123-125. J. Hurstfield, *Econ. Hist. R.*, 45, vol. 15, p. 104-105.

3819. CADBURY'S OF BOURNEVILLE. Industrial record, 1919-1939. London, Pitman, 45, in-4, 84 p., (illus.), 8s. 6d.

3820. CALVIN (D. D.). A saga of the St. Lawrence : timber and shipping through three generations. Toronto, Ryerson Press, 45, in-8, x-176 p., $3.00. R : C. H. J. Snider, *Canad. hist. R.*, 45, vol. 26, p. 322-324 ; *Queen's Quar.*, 45, vol. 52, p. 365-366.

3821. CARROTHERS (W. A.). The British Columbia fisheries. London, Oxford Univ. Press, 41, in-8, xv-136 p., 9s. (Univ. of Toronto, pol. econ. ser., 10). R : W. T. Easterbrook, *Canad. hist. R.*, 42, vol. 23, p. 208-209.

3822. CENTNER (Charles William). Great Britain and Chilian mining, 1830-1914. *Econ. Hist. R.*, 42, vol. 12, p. 76-82.

3823. CHAMBERLIN (Waldo). Industrial relations in Germany, 1914-1939. London, Oxford Univ. Press, 42, in-8, 420 p., 22s. 6d. R : *Economica*, 43, vol. 10, p. 214.

3824. CHAPLIN (W. R.). William Rainsborough (1587-1642) and his associates of the Trinity House. *Mariner's Mirror*, 45, vol. 31, p. 178-197.

3825. CLOW (Archibald and Nan L.). Lord Dundonald [and coal distillation]. *Econ. hist. R.*, 42, vol. 12, p. 47-58.

3826. CLOW (A. and N. L.). Vitriol in the Industrial Revolution. *Econ. Hist. R.*, 45, vol. 15, p. 44-55.

3827. COOPER (Ernest R.). The steelyard at Woodbridge. *Trans. Newcomen Soc.*, 38/39 [40], vol. 19, p. 185-191.

3828. COOPER (E. R.). East coast brigs. *Mariner's Mirror*, 45, vol. 31, p. 148-153.

3829. COURT (W. H. B.). Problems of the British coal industry between the wars. *Econ. Hist. R.*, 45, vol. 15, p. 1-24.

3830. CREECH (E. P.). Similkameen trails, 1846-1861. *Brit. Columbia hist. Quar.*, 41, vol. 5, p. 255-267.

3831. DAVIES (Daniel). Some aspects of mining reform. *Quar. R.*, 41, vol. 276, p. 103-113.

3832. DAVIES (Henry Rees). A review of the records of the Conway and Menai ferries. Cardiff, Univ. of Wales Press Board, 42, in-8, xiv-342 p., 15s.

3833. DEERR (Noel) and BROOKS (Alexander). The evolution of the sugar cane mill. *Trans. Newcomen Soc.*, 40/41 (43), vol. 21, p. 1-9.

3834. DEERR (N.) and BROOKS (A.). The early use of steam power in the cane sugar industry. *Trans. Newcomen Soc.*, 40/41 (43), vol. 21, p. 11-21.

3835. DESSAUER-MEINHARDT (Marie). Monthly unemployment records, 1854-1892. *Economica*, 40, vol. 7, p. 322-326.

3836. DESSAUER-MEINHARDT (M.). Unemployment records, 1848-59. *Econ. Hist. R.*, 40, vol. 10, p. 38-43.

3837. DEVEREUX (R.). John Louden MacAdam. London, Oxford Univ. Press, 40, in-8, xi-184 p., (illus.), 3s. 6d. (Oxf. bookshelf).

3838. DICKINSON (H. W.). Henry Cort's bicentenary. *Trans. Newcomen Soc.*, 40/41 (43), vol. 21, p. 31-47.

3839. DICKINSON (H. W.) and ROGERS (Henry). Origin of gauges for wire, sheets and strip. *Trans. Newcomen Soc.*, 40/41 (43), vol. 21, p. 87-98.

3840. DICKINSON (H. W.) and VOWLES (H. P.). James Watt and the industrial revolution. London, Longmans, 44, in-8, 59 p., 1s. (Sci. in Britain ser.).

3841. DONY (John G.). A history of the straw hat industry. Luton, Gibbs, Bamforth, 42, in-8, 219 p., (plates), 10s. 6d. R : C.E.C., *J. Roy. statist. Soc.*, 43, vol. 106, p. 71. M. Beloff, *Econ. Hist. R.*, 43, vol. 13, p. 134.

C. R. Fay, *Econ. J.*, 43, vol. 53, p. 91-94. C.G.A., *Eng. hist. R.*, 43, vol. 58, p. 502-503.

3842. DRAKE (L. A.). Trends in the New York printing industry. London, Oxford Univ. Press, 41, in-8, 150 p., (charts), 12s. 6d.

3843. ENOCK (A. G.). This milk business : a study from 1895-1943. London, H. K. Lewis, 43, in-8, 296 p., (plates, tables), 18s.

3844. FOENANDER (Orwell de R.). Solving labour problems in Australia : an additional series of essays in the history of industrial relations in Australia. London, Oxford Univ. Press; Melbourne, Univ. Press, 41, in-8, xxxv-168 p., 15s. R : J. W. Davidson, *Econ. Hist. R.*, 45, vol. 15, p. 105-106. A. E. C. Hare, *Hist. Stud. Australia N.Z.*, 42, vol. 2, p. 61-62.

3845. FOSTER (Sir William). A short history of the Worshipful Company of Coopers of London. Cambridge, Coopers Co., 44, in-8, 147 p., 21s. R : M.D.G., *Eng. hist. R.*, 45, vol. 60, p. 271-272. E. S. de B(eer), *History*, 45, vol. 30, p. 108.

3846. GADGIL (D. R.). The industrial evolution of India in recent times. New ed. London, Oxford Univ. Press, 43, in-8, 368 p., 7s. 6d.

3847. GRAVESON (S.) ed. Penny postage centenary : the story of the first postage stamps. London, Postal Hist. Soc., 40, in-4, 144 p., (illus.), 10s. 6d.

3848. —— —— New ed. London, Todd Publ. Co., 42, in-4, 250 p., (illus.), 12s. 6d.

3849. GUTHRIE (John A.). The newsprint paper industry : an economic analysis. London, Oxford Univ. Press, 41, in-8, xxiii-274 p., (maps), 15s. R : C. R. Fay, *Econ. J.*, 44, vol. 54, p. 107-109.

3850. HADDON-CAVE (C. P.). Trends in the concentration of operations of

Australian secondary industries, 1923-1943. *Econ. R.*, 45, vol. 21, p. 65-78.

3851. HADFIELD (E. C. R.). Canals between the English and the Bristol channels. *Econ. Hist. R.*, 42, vol. 12, p. 59-67.

3852. HADFIELD (E. C. R.). The Thames navigation and the canals, 1770-1830. *Econ. Hist. R.*, 44, vol. 14, p. 172-179.

3853. HAMILTON (S. B.). The use of cast iron in building. *Trans. Newcomen Soc.*, 40/41 (43), vol. 21, p. 139-155.

3854. HANNINGTON (W.). Industrial history in wartime, including a record of the shop stewards' movement. London, Lawrence & Wishart, 40, in-8, 112 p., 2s. (Marxist text book ser., 5).

3855. HARRIS (C. M.). Early history of Eastern goldfields from the records of Greaves and Risely, pioneers. *J. West. Austral. hist. Soc.*, 43, vol. 5, p. 46-53.

3856. HARVEY (D. C.). Hopes raised by steam in 1840. *Canad. hist. Assoc. Rept.*, 40, p. 16-25.

3857. HEATON (Herbert). Yorkshire cloth traders in the United States, 1770-1840. Leeds, Thoresby Soc., 43, in-8, 225-287 p., 7s. 6d. (Publ., vol. 37, pt. 3). R : J. de L. Mann, *Econ. Hist. R.*, 44, vol. 14, p. 204-205.

3858. HILL (H. W.). Rowland Hill and the fight for penny post. London, Warne, 40, in-8, 205 p., (illus.), 3s. 6d.

3859. HORST (Sheila T. van der). Native labour in South Africa. London; Cape Town, Juta, 42, in-8, 340 p., 23s. R : J.L., *African Stud.*, 42, vol. 1, p. 227-228. M. Ballinger, *South African J. Econ.*, 42, vol. 10, p. 315-319. F. W. Paish, *Economica*, 42, vol. 9, p. 292-294. R. Hinden, *Pol. Quar.*, 43, vol. 14, p. 110-112.

3860. HOWER (R. M.). The history of an advertising agency, N. W. Ayer & Son at work, 1869-1939. London, Oxford Univ. Press, 40, in-8, 652 p., 17s. (Harvard stud. in business hist., vol. 5).

3861. HUTCHINS (John G. B.). The American maritime industries and public policy, 1789-1914. London, Oxford Univ. Press, 41, in-8, xxi-627 p., 21s. (Harvard econ. stud., vol. 71). R : C. R. Fay, *Econ. J.*, 43, vol. 53, p. 94-96.

3862. INNIS (Harold A.). The cod fisheries, the history of an international economy. Toronto, Ryerson Press, 40, in-8, xviii-520 p., $4.00. (Relations of Canada and the U.S.). R : G. S. G., *Queen's Quar.*, 40, vol. 47, p. 478-481. E.W.G., *Geogr. J.*, 40, vol. 96, p. 137-138. S. A. Saunders, *Dalhousie R.*, 40, vol. 20, p. 255-256. J. Hardouin, *Canad. geogr. J.*, 40, vol. 20, p. xiii. J. L. Morison, *Econ. Hist. R.*, 43, vol. 13, p. 124-125. H. Heaton, *Canad. hist. R.*, 41, vol. 22, p. 60-63. M. Digby, *Econ. J.*, 41, vol. 51, p. 110-112. W. P. Morrell, *Eng. hist. R.*, 42, vol. 57, p. 271-274. J. H. Simpson, *Int. Affairs*, 42, vol. 19, p. 400.

3863. INNIS (H. A.). Essays in transportation in honour of W. T. Jackman, ed. by H. A. Innis. London, Oxford Univ. Press; Toronto, Univ. Press, 41, in-8, xi-236 p., 11s. 6d.; $2.50. R : H. W. Hewetson, *Canad. J. Econ. pol. Sci.*, 42, vol. 8, p. 631-633. J. L. McD., *Queen's Quar.*, 42, vol. 49, p. 95-96.

3864. IRELAND (Willard E.). Early flour-mills in British Columbia. 2 pts. *Brit. Columbia hist. Quar.*, 41, vol. 5, p. 89-110, 191-214.

3865. JENKINS (Rhys). Ironfounding in England, 1490-1603. *Trans. Newcomen Soc.*, 38/39 [40], vol. 19, p. 35-49.

3866. JENKINS (R.). Industries of Suffolk, a historical sketch. *Trans. Newcomen Soc.*, 38/39 [40], vol. 19, p. 173-184.

3867. JOHN (A. H.). Iron and steel on a Glamorgan estate, 1700-1740. *Econ. Hist. R.*, 43, vol. 13, p. 93-103.

3868. JONES (M. J.). Merioneth woollen industry from 1750 to 1820. *Trans. Soc. Cymmr.*, 39 (40), p. 181-208.

3869. KAHN (Ellison). The right to strike in South Africa : an historical analysis. *South African J. Econ.*, 43, vol. 11, p. 24-47.

3870. KEMBLE (John Haskell). England's first Atlantic mail line. *Mariner's Mirror*, 40, vol. 26, p. 33-54.

3871. KHACHATUROV (T. S.). Organization and development of railway transport in the U.S.S.R. *Int. Affairs*, 45, vol. 21, p. 220-235.

3872. KNOWLTON (H.). Air transportation in the United States : its growth as a business. London, Cambridge Univ. Press, 42, in-8, viii-72 p., 7s. 6d.

3873. KUCZYNSKI (Jürgen). A short history of labour conditions in Great Britain and the Empire, 1750 to the present day. London, Muller, 42, in-8, 272 p., 12s. 6d. (Short hist. of labour conditions under industrial capitalism, vol. 1). R : J. Price, *Int. Affairs*, 43, vol. 19, p. 589-590. E. Kahn, *South African J. Econ.*, 43, vol. 11, p. 221-222.

3874. —— —— Repr. London, Muller, 45, in-8, 191 p., 8s. 6d.

3875. KUCZYNSKI (J.). A short history of labour conditions in the U.S.A. from 1789 to the present day. London, Muller, 43, in-8, 228 p., 10s. 6d. (Short hist. of labour conditions under industrial capitalism, vol. 2).

3876. KUCZYNSKI (J.). A short history of labour conditions in Germany under Fascism. London,

Muller, 44, in-8, 239 p., 9s. 6d. (Short hist. of labour conditions under industrial capitalism, vol. 3). R : R. H. Smith, *S. African J. Econ.*, 44, vol. 12, p. 233-234. J. Price, *Int. Affairs*, 44, vol. 20, p. 576-577. F. Schnierer, *Econ. R.*, 45, vol. 21, p. 123-126.

3877. LAMB (W. Kaye). Empress to the Orient. *Brit. Columbia hist. Quar.*, 40, vol. 4, p. 29-50, 79-110.

3878. LANGTON (H. H.). James Douglas, a memoir. Toronto, Univ. Press, 40, in-8, 133 p., privately pr. R : E. S. Moore, *Canad. hist. R.*, 40, vol. 21, p. 427-428.

3879. LEE (Charles E.). Early railways in Surrey. *Trans. Newcomen Soc.*, 40/41 (43), vol. 21, p. 49-79.

3880. LONGLEY (R. S.). Peter Mitchell, guardian of the north Atlantic fisheries, 1867-1871. *Canad. hist. R.*, 41, vol. 22, p. 389-402.

3881. LOWER (J. A.). Construction of the Grand Trunk Pacific Railway in British Columbia. *Brit. Columbia hist. Quar.*, 40, vol. 4, p. 163-181.

3882. MACLAREN (M.). The rise of the electrical industry during the 19th century. London, Oxford Univ. Press, 43, in-8, 258 p., 25s.

3883. MACMULLEN (J.). Paddle-wheel days in California. London, Oxford Univ. Press, 45, in-8, 172 p., (illus.), 18s. 6d.

3884. MASTERS (Donald C.). T. C. Keefer and the development of Canadian transportation. *Canad. hist. Assoc. Rept.*, 40, p. 36-44.

3885. MASTERS (D. C.). Financing the C.P.R., 1880-5. *Canad. hist. R.*, 43, vol. 24, p. 350-361.

3886. MATTHEWS (Harold Evan) ed. Proceedings, minutes and enrolments of the Company of Soapmakers, 1562-1642. Bristol, Record Soc., 40, in-8, 263 p., subscribers only. (Publ., vol. 10). R : S. L. Thrupp, *Econ. Hist. R.*, 41, vol. 11, p. 110-111.

3887. MEIKLE (W. P.). Highway repairs in the 18th century. *Trans. Newcomen Soc.*, 40/41 (43), vol. 21, p. 123-128.

3888. MILBANK (J.) jr. The first century of flight in America. London, Oxford Univ. Press, 43, in-8, 258 p., (illus.), 18s. 6d.

3889. MONAGHAN (John J.). The rise and fall of the Belfast cotton industry. *Irish hist. Stud.*, 42, vol. 3, p. 1-17.

3890. MOORE (E. S.). American influence in Canadian mining. Toronto, Univ. Press, 41, in-8, xxii-144 p., $2.25. R : R. C. Wallace, *Canad. J. Econ. pol. Sci.*, 41, vol. 7, p. 608-609.

3891. MORAZÉ (P.). The treaty of 1860 and the industry of the department of the north. *Econ. Hist. R.*, 40, vol. 10, p. 18-28.

3892. MORRELL (W. P.). The gold rushes. London, Black, 40, in-8, 426 p., 18s. (Pioneer hist.). R : *United Empire*, 40, vol. 31, p. 335-336. A. E. Feavearyear, *Econ. Hist. R.*, 43, vol. 13, p. 122-123. J. L. M(orison), *History*, 41, vol. 26, p. 90-91. T. A. Rickard, *Brit. Columbia hist. Quar.*, 41, vol. 5, p. 237-239. F. W. Howay, *Canad. hist. R.*, 41, vol. 22, p. 205-206. H. A. Innis, *Eng. hist. R.*, 42, vol. 57, p. 392-393. S.W.A., *Geography*, 42, vol. 27, p. 113.

3893. NEAL (Arthur L.). Development of radio communication in Canada. *Canad. geogr. J.*, 41, vol. 22, p. 165-191.

3894. NICOLAY (H.). The bridge of water : the story of Panama and the canal. London, Appleton, 41, in-8, x-295 p., (illus.), 10s.

3895. NOCKOLDS (H.). The magic of a name : history of Rolls Royce. London, G. T. Foulis, 45, in-8, 157 p., 8s. 6d,

3896. OVERTON (Richard C.). Burlington West : a colonization history of the Burlington railroad. London, Oxford Univ. Press, 42, in-8, 603 p., (illus., maps), 19s. R : J. E. Tyler, *Eng. hist. R.*, 42, vol. 57, p. 523-525.

3897. OWEN (Bob). Diwydiannau coll, ardal y ddwy afon, Dwyryd a Glasglyn. (Lost industries of the region of the two rivers Dwyryd and Glaslyn, North Wales). Liverpool, Evans, 43, in-8, 132 p., 5s.

3898. PARSONS (R. H.). The early days of the power station industry. London, Cambridge Univ. Press, 40, in-8, x-217 p., (illus.), 15s. R : W. H. B. Court, *Econ. Hist. R.*, 43, vol. 13, p. 138-139.

3899. PATTERSON (W. J.). The Long Point furnace. *Ontario hist. Soc. Pap.*, 44, vol. 36, p. 70-78.

3900. PICKERING (Arthur J.). The cradle and home of the hosiery trade, (Hinckley, Leic., 1640-1940), ed. by H. W. Chandler. Hinckley, Pickering, 40, in-4, xi-136 p., (illus.), 12s. 6d.

3901. POUNDS (N. J. G.). Population movement in Cornwall, and the rise of mining in the 18th century. *Geography*, 43, vol. 28, p. 37-46.

3902. POUNDS (N. J. G.). Cornish fish cellars. *Antiquity*, 44, vol. 18, p. 36-41.

3903. PRICE (W. W.). The legend of Anthony Bacon [of Cyfarthfa iron works, Merthyr Tydfil]. *B. Board celtic Stud.*, 43, vol. 11, p. 109-112.

3904. RAISTRICK (A.). The South Yorkshire iron industry, 1698-1756. *Trans. Newcomen Soc.*, 38/39 [40], vol. 19, p. 51-86.

3905. RAMSAY (G. D.). The distribution of the cloth industry in 1561-2. *Eng. hist. R.*, 42, vol. 57, p. 361-369.

3906. RAMSAY (G. D.). The report of the Royal commission on the clothing industry, 1640. *Eng. hist. R.*, 42, vol. 57, p. 482-493.

3907. RAMSAY (G. D.). The Wiltshire woollen industry in the 16th and 17th centuries. London, Oxford Univ. Press, 43, in-8, 158 p., 10s. (Hist. ser.). R : C. R. Fay, *Econ. J.*, 44, vol. 54, p. 109-113.

3908. RAWSON (R. Rees). The coalmining industry of the Hawarden district on the eve of the industrial revolution. *Archaeol. cambrensis*, 41, vol. 96, p. 109-135.

3909. REID (K. G.). Overhead administration in the New Zealand government railways. *J. public Admin. N. Zealand*, 42, vol. 4, no. 2, p. 32-44.

3910. RHODES (E. C.). Output, labour and machines in the coal mining industry in Great Britain. *Economica*, 45, vol. 12, p. 101-110.

3911. RICHARDS (C. S.). The iron and steel industry in South Africa : a survey up to July 1939, with an addendum bringing the account up to December 1939. Johannesburg, Witwatersrand Univ. Press, 40, in-4, lxi-471 p., (plates, maps), 25s. R : A. Brady, *Canad. J. Econ. pol. Sci.*, 43, vol. 9, p. 112-113. E. D. McCallum, *Econ. J.*, 41, vol. 51, p. 320-321. F. R. E. Mauldon, *Econ. R.*, 41, vol. 17, p. 111-113. F. A. Fetter, *South African J. Econ.*, 41, vol. 9, p. 235-250.

3912. RIESENBERG (F.) jr. Golden Gate : the story of San Francisco harbour. London, Paul, 42, in-8, 212 p., (illus.), 16s.

3913. ROY (Pierre-Georges). La traverse entre Québec et Lévis; Le pont de glace entre Québec et Lévis; Les canotiers entre Québec et Lévis; Les *horse-boats* entre Québec et Lévis. *B. Rech. hist.*, 42, vol. 46, p. 225-235; 257-271; 289-307; 321-338; 353-357.

3914. ROYDE-SMITH (G.). The history of Bradshaw. London, Blacklock, 40, in-4, 76 p., 3s. 6d.

3915. SAVAGE (Rosemary Lorna). American concern over Canadian railway competition in the North-West, 1885-1890. *Canad. hist. Assoc. Rept.*, 42, p. 82-93.

3916. SCOBIE (I. H. Mackay). The Scottish tartan manufacturers and bonnet makers. *J. Soc. Army hist. Research*, 42, vol. 21, p. 64-70.

3917. SHAW (A. G. L.). The Australian coal industry, 1929-39. *Econ. Record*, 43, vol. 19, p. 46-63.

3918. SIEGFRIED (André). Suez and Panama, tr. by H. H. and D. Hemming. London, Cape, 40, in-8, 400 p., 10s. 6d.

3919. SMITH (R. H.) and BYRON (F. A.). The expansion of industry and the supply of labour. *South African J. Econ.*, 41, vol. 9, p. 251-264.

3920. SMITH (Wilfred). Trends in the geographical distribution of the Lancashire cotton industry. *Geography*, 41, vol. 26, p. 7-17.

3921. STANNARD (Harold). Civil aviation, an historical survey. *Int. Affairs*, 45, vol. 21, p. 497-511.

3922. STEPHENSON (H. E.) and McNAUGHT (Carlton). The story of advertising in Canada : a chronicle of 50 years. Toronto, Ryerson Press, 40, in-8, xvi-364 p., $3.50. R : G. Carter, *Canad. hist. R.*, 40, vol. 21, p. 429-430.

3923. STRUVE (Peter). English tissue-printing in Russia, an episode in Russian economic history. *Slavonic Y.B.* (*Slavonic R.*), 40, vol. 19, p. 303-310.

3924. THURSTON (A. P.). Parker's ' Roman ' cement. *Trans. Newcomen Soc.*, 38/39 [40], vol. 19, p. 193-206.

3925. TINLEY (J. M.). The native labor problem of South Africa. London, Oxford Univ. Press, 42, in-8, xxii-281 p., (maps), 14s. R : S. T. van der Horst, *Economica*, 44, vol. 11,

p. 149-151. J. Lewin, *Africa*, 44, vol. 14, p. 354-355.

3926. TIWARI (R. D.). Railways in modern India. Bombay, New Book Co., 41, in-8, x-284 p., Rs. 10. R : V. Anstey, *Economica*, 42, vol. 9, p. 221-222.

3927. Trade union agreements in Canadian history. Industrial relations section, Queen's University, Kingston, Ontario. Ontario, Queen's Univ., 42, in-8, vi-177 p., $2.00. R : J.L.McD., *Queen's Quar.*, 42, vol. 49, p. 405.

3928. Trebizond and the Persian transit trade. *J. central asian Soc.*, 44, vol. 31, p. 289-301.

3929. VERRAN (W. H.). Shipbuilding at Newquay and notes on local vessels. *Mariner's Mirror*, 45, vol. 31, p. 198-209.

3930. VINCE (Stanley W. E.). The evolution of the port of Harwich. *Geography*, 41, vol. 26, p. 178-186.

3931. WARDLE (Arthur C.). Steam conquers the Pacific : a record of maritime achievement, 1840-1940. London, Hodder, 40, in-8, 208 p., 10s. 6d.

3932. WHITAKER (A. P.). The Huancavelica mercury mine : a contribution to the history of the Bourbon renaissance in the Spanish empire. London, Oxford Univ. Press, 42, in-8, 166 p., 8s. 6d. (Harvard hist. monogr., 16).

3933. WHITTON (Charlotte). A hundred years a' fellin'—some passages from the timber saga of the Ottawa in the century in which the Gillies have been cutting in the Valley, 1842-1942. Ottawa, Runge Press, 43, in-8, xvi-172 p., private distribution only. R : D. C. Masters, *Canad. hist. R.*, 44, vol. 25, p. 208-209 ; *Canad. J. Econ. pol. Sci.*, 44, vol. 10, p. 530.

3934. WILSON (J. H.). Industrial activity in the 18th century. *Economica*, 40, vol. 7, p. 150-160.

3936. WRIGHT (A.). The church bells of Monmouthshire, their inscriptions and founders, with a chapter upon the Chepstow foundry. Cardiff, Lewis, 42, in-8, xii-134 p., (illus., map), 15s.

3937. ZISKIND (D.). One thousand strikes of government employees. London, Oxford Univ. Press, 40, in-8, 279 p., 15s.

§ 5. Commerce

3938. ABEL (D.). A history of British tariffs, 1923-1942. London, Cranton, 45, in-8, 156 p., 9s. 6d.

3939. BAXTER (W. T.). The house of Hancock. London, Oxford Univ. Press, 45, in-8, 350 p., 20s. R : H. M. Robertson, *South African J. Econ.*, 45, vol. 13, p. 326-328.

3940. BROWN (B. H.). The tariff reform movement in Great Britain, 1881-1895. London, Oxford Univ. Press, 44, in-8, 182 p., 16s. 6d. R : A. Redford, *Econ. Hist. R.*, 44, vol. 14, p. 205.

3941. CONDLIFFE (J. B.). The reconstruction of world trade : a survey of international economic relations. London, G. Allen, 41, in-8, 427 p., 12s. 6d. (Prometheus libr.). R : W. H. Hutt, *South African J. Econ.*, 42, vol. 10, p. 73-77.

3942. DALZELL (G. W.). The flight from the flag : the continuing effect of the Civil War upon the American carrying trade. London, Oxford Univ. Press, 41, in-8, 292 p., 16s.

3943. FOSTER (Sir W.). Voyage of Sir Henry Middleton to the Moluccas, 1604-1606. London, Quaritch, 44, in-8, xlii-209 p., (illus., maps), 27s. 6d. (Hakluyt soc., Works, 2nd ser., vol. 88). R : G.R.C., *Geogr. J.*, 44, vol. 103, p. 284. R. O. Winstedt, *J. asiatic Soc.*, 44, p. 202-203. F.W.B., *Eng. hist. R.*, 45, vol. 60, p. 426-427.

3944. GOTTMAN (Jean). Les relations commerciales de la France. Montréal, L'Arbre, 42, in-8, 212 p. R : G.R.C., *Geogr. J.*, 43, vol. 102, p. 266.

3945. GRAHAM (Gerald S.). The origin of free ports in British North America. *Canad. hist. R.*, 41, vol. 22, p. 25-34.

3946. HUMPHREYS (Robin A.) ed. British consular reports on the trade and politics of Latin America, 1824-1826. London, Royal Hist. Soc., 40, in-8, xxii-385 p., privately pr. (Publ., Camden 3rd ser., vol. 63). R : H. F. Peterson, *Econ. Hist. R.*, 44, vol. 14, p. 106-107.

3947. HURSTFIELD (J.). The control of British raw material supplies, 1919-1939. *Econ. Hist. R.*, 44, vol. 14, p. 1-31.

3948. KREIDER (Carl). The Anglo-American trade agreement : a study of British and American commercial policies, 1934-1939. Toronto, Ryerson Press, 43, in-8, xvi-270 p., $6.00. R : G. A. Elliott, *Canad. J. Econ. pol. Sci.*, 44, vol. 10, p. 520-521. E. J. Elliott, *Int. Affairs*, 44, vol. 20, p. 273.

3949. LEAGUE OF NATIONS. Commercial policy in the inter-war period : international proposals and national policies. London, Allen & Unwin, 42, in-8, 164 p., 7s. 6d. R : G. D. A. MacDougall, *Econ. J.*, 43, vol. 53, p. 397-399.

3950. LAWSON (Murray G.). Fur : a study in English mercantilism, 1700-1775. Toronto, Univ. Press, 43, in-8, xxiv-140 p., $1.75. (Univ. of Toronto stud. in hist. and econ., 9). R : L. M. Hacker, *Canad. hist. R.*, 44, vol. 25, p. 205-207. C. R. Fay, *Canad. J. Econ. pol. Sci.*, 45, vol. 11, p. 628-631.

3951. McKEE (Samuel) jr. Canada's bid for the traffic of the Middle West :

a quarter-century of the history of the St. Lawrence waterway, 1849-1874. *Canad. hist. Assoc. Rept.*, 40, p. 26-35.

3952. MACKENZIE-GRIEVE (Averil). The last years of the English slave trade : Liverpool, 1750-1807. London, Putnam, 41, in-8, 332 p., 15s.

3953. McLACHLAN (Jean O.). Trade and peace with old Spain, 1667-1750, a study of the influence of commerce on Anglo-Spanish diplomacy in the first half of the 18th century. London, Cambridge Univ. Press, 40, in-8, xvi-249 p., 15s. R : C. H. Harding, *Econ. Hist. R.*, 44, vol. 14, p. 96-98. R. P(ares), *Eng. hist. R.*, 41, vol. 56, p. 169-170.

3954. MACROSTY (Henry W.). The overseas trade of the United Kingdom, 1930-39. *J. Roy. statist. Soc.*, 40, vol. 103, p. 451-490.

3955. MASON (K.). Notes on the Northern Sea Route. *Geogr. J.*, 40, vol. 96, p. 27-41.

3956. PEEL (George). Imperial preference, 1894-1945. London, Free Trade Union, 45, in-8, 23 p., 6d.

3957. PHILIPS (C. H.). The East India Company, 1784-1834. Manchester, Univ. Press, 40, in-8, vii-374 p., 20s. (Manch. univ. hist. ser., 77). R : Sir C. Fawcett, *Asiatic R.*, 40, vol. 36, p. 849-850.

3958. RADIUS (Walter A.). United States shipping in transpacific trade, 1922-38. London, Oxford Univ. Press, 44, in-8, 220 p., (charts, tables), 21s. 6d. R : S. Thompson, *Int. Affairs*, 45, vol. 21, p. 428-429.

3959. SYMONDS (R. W.). The export trade of furniture to colonial America. *Burlington Mag.*, 40, vol. 77, p. 152-163.

3960. UNDERHILL (Frank H.). Laurier and Blake, 1891-2. *Canad. hist. R.*, 43, vol. 24, p. 135-155.

3961. VILLIERS (sir T.). Mercantile law : history of Cólombo mercantile firms. Ceylon, Author, Adishan, Haputale, 40, in-8, 274 p., Rs. 5.

3962. WILLIAMS (D. T.). The port books of Swansea and Neath, 1709-19. *Archaeol. cambrensis*, 40, vol. 95, p. 192-209.

3963. WILSON (Charles). Anglo-Dutch commerce and finance in the 18th century. London, Cambridge Univ. Press, 41, in-8, xviii-236 p., 15s. R : M. A. Thomson, *Eng. hist. R.*, 43, vol. 58, p. 238-239. S. T. Bindoff, *Econ. Hist. R.*, 42, vol. 12, p. 89-90. E. V. Morgan, *Econ. J.*, 42, vol. 52, p. 76-78.

§ 6. Agriculture and Agricultural Problems

3964. ROTHAMSTED EXPERIMENTAL STATION. Library catalogue of printed books and pamphlets on agriculture, published between 1471 and 1840. 2nd ed. Rothamsted, Experimental Station, 40, in-8, 298 p., 12s.

3965. TATE (W. E.). A note on the bibliography of enclosure acts and awards. *B. Inst. hist. Research*, 41, vol. 18, p. 97-101.

3966. AGRESTI (O. R.). David Lubin, a study in practical idealism. 2nd ed. London, Cambridge Univ. Press, 41, in-8, xviii-372 p., 15s.

3967. ALLSTON (Robert F. W.). The South Carolina rice plantation as revealed in the papers of Robert F. W. Allston, ed. by J. H. Easterby. London, Cambridge Univ. Press, 45, in-8, xxii-478 p., 30s. (Amer. hist. assoc.).

3968. ARNDT (E. H. D.). An experiment in agricultural credit : the Union agricultural credit act of 1926. Pretoria, University Press, 42, in-8, 45 p., 2s. (Pretoria Univ. ser., III, no. 12). R : A.J.B., *South African J. Econ.*, 42, vol. 10, p. 321-322.

3969. ASHBY (A. W.) and EVANS (I. L.). The agriculture of Wales and Monmouthshire. Cardiff, Univ. of Wales, 44, in-8, 300 p., 15s. R : G. E. Fussell, *Econ. Hist. R.*, 45, vol. 15, p. 99-100.

3970. AUSTIN (H. B.). The Merino, past, present, and probable : the history and breeding of the Merino sheep. Sydney, Grahame Book Co., 43, in-8, 248 p., (illus.), 21s.

3971. BAILEY (Joseph C.). Seaman A. Knapp : schoolmaster of American agriculture. London, Oxford Univ. Press, 45, in-8, 324 p., 22s.

3972. BARROW (Bennett H.). Plantation life in the Florida parishes of Louisiana, 1836-1846, as reflected in the diary of B. H. Barrow, ed. by E. A. Davis. London, Oxford Univ. Press, 43, in-8, 474 p., (illus.), 33s. 6d. (Stud. in the hist. of Amer. agric.).

3973. BISSET (C. B.). Water boring in Uganda, 1920-1940. Entebbe, Govt. Printer, 41, in-8, 32 p., 2s. 6d. (Geol. survey, water supply paper 1). R : G.A., *Sudan Notes and Records*, 42, vol. 25, p. 159-160.

3974. COLONIAL OFFICE. Agriculture in the West Indies. London, H.M.S.O., 42, in-8, vi-280 p., 10s. (Colonial No. 182). R : *B. Imp. Inst.*, 42, vol. 40, p. 137-139.

3975. DARBY (H. C.). The draining of the Fens. London, Cambridge Univ. Press, 40, in-8, xix-312 p., 21s. (Cambr. stud. in econ. hist.). R : L. F. Salzman, *B. Inst. hist. Research*, 40, vol. 18, p. 31. E. St. J. Brooks, *19th Century*, 40, vol. 128, p. 101-103. W. G. East, *Economica*, 40, vol. 7, p. 343-344. C. R. Fay, *Econ. J.*, 40, vol. 50, p. 301-303. *National R.*, 40, vol. 114, p. 635-636. C. Fox, *Archaeol. J.*, 39 (40), vol. 96, p. 299-302. J.E.M., *Geography*, 41, vol. 26, p. 42.

3976. DENOON (George). The development of methods of land

registration in South Africa. *South African Law J.*, 43, vol. 60, p. 179-187, 457-467; 44, vol. 61, p. 4-13; 45, vol. 62, p. 458-467.

3977. DERSAL (W. R. van). The American land : its history and its uses. London, Oxford Univ. Press, 43, in-8, 232 p., (illus.), 21s. 6d.

3978. DOBIE (J. F.). The Longhorns. London, Nicholson, 43, in-8, xvi-19-292 p., (plates), 12s. 6d. R : C. R. Fay, *Econ. J.*, 44, vol. 54, p. 109-113.

3979. EDWARDS (Everett E.). Agricultural history as a field of research. *Canad. hist. Assoc. Rept.*, 41, p. 15-23.

3980. FOWKE (V. C.): An introduction to Canadian agricultural history. *Canad. J. Econ. pol. Sci.*, 42, vol. 8, p. 56-68.

3981. FUSSELL (G. E.). English agriculture from Cobbett to Caird (1830-80). *Econ. Hist. R.*, 45, vol. 15, p. 79-85.

3982. GATES (P. W.). The Wisconsin pine lands of Cornell University. London, Oxford Univ. Press, 43, in-8, 278 p., (illus.), 21s. 6d.

3983. HABAKKUK (H. J.). English landownership, 1680-1740. *Econ. Hist. R.*, 40, vol. 10, p. 2-17.

3984. HAYTHORNE (G. V.). Agricultural man-power. *Canad. J. Econ. pol. Sci.*, 43, vol. 9, p. 366-383.

3985. HILL (C.). The agrarian legislation of the interregnum. *Eng. hist. R.*, 40, vol. 55, p. 222-250.

3986. HOPE (E. C.). Agriculture's share of the national income. *Canad. J. Econ. pol. Sci.*, 43, vol. 9, p. 384-393.

3987. HOSKINS (W. G.). The Leicestershire farmer in the 16th century. Leicester, Thornely, 42, in-8, 62 p., repr. from the Trans. of the Leic. archaeol. soc., 1941/42. R : J. Saltmarsh, *Econ. Hist. R.*, 44, vol. 14, p. 196-198.

3988. HOSKINS (W. G.). The reclamation of the waste in Devon, 1550-1800. *Econ. Hist. R.*, 43, vol. 13, p. 80-92.

3989. JONES (Edith B.). South African native land policy. *Bantu Studies*, 40, vol. 14, p. 175-197.

3990. JONES (Robert Leslie). The Canadian agricultural tariff of 1843. *Canad. J. Econ. pol. Sci.*, 41, vol. 7, p. 528-537.

3991. LEAGUE OF NATIONS. *Economic, financial and transit dept.* Agricultural production in continental Europe during the 1914-18 war and the reconstruction period. London, Allen & Unwin, 43, in-4, 122 p., 8s. 6d. R : C. Leubuscher, *Economica*, 44, vol. 11, p. 155. C. W. Guillebaud, *Econ. J.*, 44, vol. 54, p. 410-411. M.D., *Int. Affairs*, 44, vol. 20, p. 575-576.

3992. LORD (Russell). Progress of soil conservation in the United States. *Geogr. J.*, 45, vol. 105, p. 159-169.

3993. McPHAIL (Alexander James). Diary, ed. by H. A. Innis. [History of the Canadian wheat pools]. Toronto, University Press, 40, in-8, 289 p., $2.50. R : F.A.K., *Queen's Quar.*, 40, vol. 47, p. 476-477.

3994. MARTELL (J. S.). The achievements of Agricola and the agricultural societies, 1818-25. *B. Publ. Archives Nova Scotia*, 40, vol. 2, no. 2.

3995. MARTELL (J. S.). From Central Board to Secretary of Agriculture, 1826-1885. *B. Publ. Archives Nova Scotia*, 40, vol. 2, no. 3.

3996. MEEK (C. K.). Land tenure in Mauritius and Fiji. *J. comp. Legisl. int. Law*, 44, vol. 26, pt. 3/4, p. 42-49.

3997. NOBBS (Eric A.). William Duckitt's diary. *Archives Y.B. South Afr. Hist.*, 42 (43), vol. 2, p. 71-90.

3998. NOBBS (E. A.). A note on the history of Karakul breed of sheep in South West Africa. *Archives Y.B.*

South Afr. Hist., 42 (43), vol. 2, p.267-272.

3999. O'DONOVAN (John). The economic history of livestock in Ireland. London, Longmans, 40, in-8, 460 p., 12s. 6d. R : G. E. Fussell, *Econ. Hist. R.*, 41, vol. 11, p. 111-112. J. Johnston, *Irish hist. Stud.*, 41, vol. 2, p. 337-339.

4000. Palestine land transfers regulations. 1. The past history of land sales in Palestine; 2. The new regulations. *J. central asian Soc.*, 40, vol. 27, p. 191-200.

4001. PIERCE (T. J.). An Anglesey crown rental of the 16th century. *B. Board celtic Stud.*, 40, vol. 10, p. 156-176.

4002. RAMSDEN (Eric). James Busby, the prophet of Australian viticulture. Sydney, Author, 40, in-8, 26 p., 2s. 6d. R : J.C.A., *J. polynesian Soc.*, 40, vol. 49, p. 607-608.

4003. SCHMIDT (C. T.). American farmers in the world crisis. London, Oxford Univ. Press, 41, in-8, 359 p., 12s. 6d.

4004. STARR (Arthur J.). 18th century agriculture in Suffolk. *Geography*, 41, vol. 26, p. 116-125.

4005. TATE (W. E.). Members of Parliament and the proceedings upon enclosure bills. *Econ. Hist. R.*, 42, vol. 12, p. 68-75.

4006. TATE (W. E.). Some unexplored records of the enclosure movement. *Eng. hist. R.*, 42, vol. 57, p. 250-263.

4007. TATE (W. E.). A hand-list of English enclosure acts and awards. Pt. 17 : Open fields, commons and enclosures in Kent. *Archaeol. cantiana*, 43, vol. 56, p. 54-67.

4008. TATE (W. E.). The 'Commons' Journals' as sources of information concerning the 18th-century enclosure movement. *Econ. J.*, 44, vol. 54, p. 75-95.

4009. TATE (W. E.). Parliamentary counter-petitions during the enclosures of the 18th and 19th centuries. *Eng. hist. R.*, 44, vol. 59, p. 392-403.

4010. TERRY (Michael). Soil erosion in Australia. *Geogr. J.*, 45, vol. 105, p. 121-129.

4011. TINLEY (J. M.). Control of agriculture in South Africa. *South African J. Econ.*, 40, vol. 8, p. 243-263.

4012. WALKER (Laurie). Irrigation in New South Wales, 1884-1940. *Roy. Austral. hist. Soc. J.*, 41, vol. 27, p. 181-232.

4013. WEBBER (H. J.) and BATCHELOR (L. D.) ed. The citrus industry. Vol. 1 : History, botany and breeding. London, Cambridge Univ. Press, 44, in-8, x-1,028 p., (figs.), 45s.

4013a. WILLAN (T. S.) and CROSSLEY (E. W.). Three 17th-century Yorkshire surveys. Leeds, Yorkshire Archaeological Society, 41, in-8, xxxii-160 p., 12s. 6d. (Record ser., vol. 104). R : M.B., *Eng. hist. R.*, 42, vol. 57, p. 152.

§ 7. Money and Finance

4014. ARNDT (E. H. D.). Peoples banks in South Africa. Pretoria, Univ. Press, 41, in-8, 41 p., 2s. (Publ., ser. 3, no. 10). R : S. H. Frankel, *South African J. Econ.*, 41, vol. 9, p. 312-313.

4015. ASHTON (T. S.). The bill of exchange and private banks in Lancashire, 1790-1830. *Econ. Hist. R.*, 45, vol. 15, p. 25-35.

4016. BARBER (V. A.). A century of deposit banking. London, Waterlow, 44, in-8, 20 p., 6d.

4017. BERRY (T. S.). Western prices before 1861 : a study of the Cincinnati market. London, Oxford Univ. Press, 43, in-8, 666p., (charts), 28s. (Econ. stud. ser.).

4018. BLASER (A. F.) jr. The Federal Reserve Bank of Cleveland. London, Oxford Univ. Press, 42, in-8, 334 p., 17s. 6d.

4019. BOWLEY (A. L.). Studies in the national income, 1924-1938. London, Cambridge Univ. Press, 42, in-8, x-256 p., 15s. (Nat. inst. of econ. and soc. research). R : E. Rothbarth, *Econ. J.*, 43, vol. 53, p. 55-59. J. Robinson, *Pol. Quar.*, 43, vol. 14, p. 112-113. R. Stone, *Economica*, 43, vol. 10, p. 312-315. H. Herzfeld, *South African J. Econ.*, 43, vol. 11, p. 63-64. D. C. MacGregor, *Canad. J. Econ. pol. Sci.*, 45, vol. 11, p. 272-274.

4020. BUTLIN (S. J.). The dollar system in New South Wales and Tasmania, 1822-42. *Hist. Stud. Australia N.Z.*, 41, vol. 1, p. 245-271.

4021. BUTLIN (S. J.). Historical records in Australian banks. *Hist. Stud. Australia N.Z.*, 42, vol. 2, p. 114-118.

4022. BUTLIN (S. J.). Charles Swanston and the Derwent Bank, 1827-50. *Hist. Stud. Australia N.Z.*, 43, vol. 2, p. 161-185.

4023. CLAPHAM (sir John H.). The private business of the Bank of England, 1744-1800. *Econ. Hist. R.*, 41, vol. 11, p. 77-89.

4024. CLAPHAM (sir J. H.). The Bank of England : a history, 1694-1914. London, Cambridge Univ. Press, 44, 2 vols. in-8, x-306, viii-460 p., (plates), 42s. R : J. E. Wadsworth, *History*, 45, vol. 30, p. 60-74. K. R. Bopp, *Canad. J. Econ. pol. Sci.*, 45, vol. 11, p. 616-627. A. G. L. Shaw, *Econ. R.*, 45, vol. 21, p. 128-129. T. S. Ashton, *Econ. J.*, 45, vol. 55, p. 261-265. J. Viner, *Economica*, 45, vol. 12, p. 61-68.

4025. COIT (C. G.). The Federal Reserve Bank of Richmond. London, Oxford Univ. Press, 41, in-8, 156 p., 10s.

4026. COPE (S. R.). The Goldsmids and the development of the London money market during the Napoleonic wars. *Economica*, 42, vol. 9, p. 180-206.

4027. FRANKEL (S. Herbert) and HERZFELD (H.). An analysis of the growth of the national income of the Union in the period of prosperity before the war. *S. African J. Econ.*, 44, vol. 12, p. 112-138.

4028. GEORGE (C. Oswald). British public finance in peace and war. *J. Roy. statist. Soc.*, 41, vol. 104, p. 235-280.

4029. GRUENBAUM (L.). National income and outlay in Palestine, 1936. Jerusalem, Econ. Research Inst., 41, in-8, 112 p. R : S. H. Frankel and H. Herzfeld, *South African J. Econ.*, 43, vol. 11, p. 64-65.

4030. HORSEFIELD (J. K.). The duties of a banker : the 18th century view. *Economica*, 41, vol. 8, p. 37-51.

4031. HORSEFIELD (J. K.). The origins of the Bank Charter Act, 1844. *Economica*, 44, vol. 11, p. 180-189.

4032. HOUSTOUN (H.). Financial policy in wars and slumps. London, King, 44, in-8, 144 p., 10s. 6d. R : W.F.C., *Int. Affairs*, 45, vol. 21, p. 400.

4033. JOHNSON (G. G.). The Treasury and monetary policy, 1933-1938. London, Oxford Univ. Press, 40, in-8, 230 p., 11s. 6d.

4034. JONGH (T. W. de). Monetary and banking factors and the business cycle in the Union. *South African J. Econ.*, 41, vol. 9, p. 138-153.

4035. KING (W. T. C.). The Bank of England. *Econ. Hist. R.*, 45, vol. 15, p. 67-72.

4036. KRISTENSSON (Robert). The consequences of errors in accounting due to inflation, 1914-18. *Econ. Hist.*, 40, vol. 4, p. 371-383.

4037. LAFFER (Kingsley). Taxation reform in Australia. *Econ. Record*, 42, vol. 18, p. 168-179.

4038. LEAGUE OF NATIONS. International currency experience : lessons of the inter-war period. London, Allen & Unwin, 44, in-8, 249 p., 12s. 6d.

4039. LESTER (R. A.). Monetary experiments : early American and recent Scandinavian. London, Oxford Univ. Press, 40, in-8, 316 p., 16s. R : J. Robinson, *Econ. J.*, 40, vol. 50, p. 280-282.

4040. LEVANDIS (J. A.). The Greek foreign debt and the Great Powers, 1821-1898. London, Oxford Univ. Press, 44, in-8, 148 p., 15s. 6d. R : C.W.C., *Eng. hist. R.*, 45, vol. 60, p. 431-432.

4041. LURIE (Richard). The company promotion boom in South Africa, 1933-38 : an analysis of new Johannesburg stock exchange quotations. *South African J. Econ.*, 41, vol. 9, p. 265-273.

4042. McDOUGALL (J. L.). The earning power of Canadian corporate capital, 1934-40. *Canad. J. Econ. pol. Sci.*, 42, vol. 8, p. 557-565.

4043. MARLEY (Joan G.). and CAMPION (H.). Changes in salaries in Great Britain, 1924-1939. *J. Roy. statist. Soc.*, 40, vol. 103, p. 524-533.

4044. MARTELL (J. S.). Nova Scotia's contribution to the Canadian relief fund in the war of 1812. *Canad. hist. R.*, 42, vol. 23, p. 297-302.

4045. MASTERS (D. C.). Toronto vs. Montreal : the struggle for financial hegemony, 1860-1875. *Canad. hist. R.*, 41, vol. 22, p. 133-146.

4046. MEEKINGS (C. A. F.). Surrey hearth tax, 1664. Frome, Surrey Record Soc., 40, in-8, cxxxix-194 p., subscribers only. (Surrey Record Soc., vol. 17, no. 41-42). R : E.H.,

Eng. hist. R., 42, vol. 57, p. 281-282. L.F.S., *History*, 42, vol. 26, p. 320.

4047. MORGAN (E. Victor). Railway investment, Bank of England policy and interest rates, 1844-8. *Econ. Hist.*, 40, vol. 4, p. 329-340.

4048. MORGAN (E. V.). The theory and practice of central banking, 1797-1913. London, Cambridge Univ. Press, 43, in-8, xiv-252 p., (tables, charts), 15s. R : J. K. Horsefield, *Economica*, 43, vol. 10, p. 271. W. W. Rostow, *Econ. Hist. R.*, 44, vol. 14, p. 100-102. R. G. Hawtrey, *Econ. J.*, 44, vol. 54, p. 399-400.

4049. NEALE (E. P.). The growth of New Zealand's general government debt. *Econ. Record*, 45, vol. 21, p. 182-196.

4050. PAISH (F. W.). British floating debt policy (from 1919 to 1939). *Economica*, 40, vol. 7, p. 225-247.

4051. PARKINSON (J. F.). Canadian investment and foreign exchange problems. Toronto, Univ. Press, 40, in-8, xii-292 p., $3.00.

4052. PAYNE (W. F.). Business behaviour, 1919-1922 : an account of post-war inflation and depression. London, Cambridge Univ. Press, 43, in-8, xxii-216 p., 9s.

4053. PLUMPTRE (Arthur F. W.). Central banking in the British Dominions. Toronto, Univ. Press, 40, in-8, xvi-462 p., $4.00. R : D. de Blank, *J. comp. Legisl. int. Law*, 43, vol. 25, p. 91-92.

4054. POOLE (Kenyon E.). German financial policies, 1932-1939. London, Oxford Univ. Press, 40, in-8, xiv-276 p., 15s. R : T. Balogh, *Economica*, 42, vol. 9, p. 98-101.

4055. PREST (Wilfred). Rents in Melbourne [since 1933]. *Econ. Record*, 45, vol. 21, p. 37-54.

4056. ROBERTS (R. O.). Thomas Chalmers on the public debt. *Economica*, 45, vol. 12, p. 111-116.

4057. ROSTOW (W. W.). Explanations of the 'great depression', 1873-96 : an historian's view of modern monetary theory. *Econ. Hist.*, 40, vol. 4, p. 356-370.

4058. SAW (R.). The Bank of England, 1694-1944. London, Harrap, 44, in-8, 164 p., (illus.), 9s. 6d.

4059. SHIRRAS (George Findlay). Federal finance in peace and war, with special reference to the United States and British Commonwealth. London, Macmillan, 44, in-8, xvi-377 p., 21s. R : D. Black, *Economica*, 45, vol. 12, p. 256-257.

4060. SHIRRAS (G. F.) and CRAIG (J. H.). Sir Isaac Newton and the currency. *Econ. J.*, 45, vol. 55, p. 217-241.

4061. SHIRRAS (G. F.) and ROSTÁS (L.). The burden of British taxation (1937/8 and 1941/2). London, Cambridge Univ. Press, 42, in-8, xiv-240 p., 15s. R : H. T. N. Gaitskell, *Econ. Hist. R.*, 44, vol. 14, p. 102-103.

4062. SHORT (L. M.) and TILLER (C. W.). The Minnesota commission of administration and finance, 1925-1939. London, Oxford Univ. Press, 42, in-8, 173 p., 9s.

4063. STAUB (W. A.). Auditing developments during the present century. London, Oxford Univ. Press, 43, in-8, 110 p., 7s. 6d.

4064. STONE (Richard). The national income, output and expenditure of the United States of America, 1929-41. *Econ. J.*, 42, vol. 52, p. 154-175.

4065. TAUS (Esther Rogoff). Central banking functions of the United States Treasury, 1789-1941. London, Oxford Univ. Press, 43, in-8, xii-313 p., 17s. 6d. R : P. B. Whale, *Int. Affairs*, 45, vol. 21, p. 427-428. E. V. Morgan, *Econ. Hist. R.*, 45, vol. 15, p. 102-103. J. K. Horsefield, *Economica*, 45, vol. 12, p. 43-44.

4067. URQUHART (M. C.). Public investment in Canada. *Canad. J. Econ. pol. Sci.*, 45, vol. 11, p. 535-553.

4068. WALKER (Charles H.). Unincorporated investment trusts in the 19th century. *Econ. Hist.*, 40, vol. 4, p. 341-355.

4069. WHALE (P. Barrett). A retrospective view of the Bank Charter Act of 1844. *Economica*, 44, vol. 11, p. 109-111.

4070. WILSON (J. S. G.). The Western Australian basic wage, 1926-42. *Econ. Record*, 43, vol. 19, p. 83-93.

§ 8. Statistics, Migration, Population

4072. BAYKOV (Alexander). A note on the trend of population and the labour problems of the U.S.S.R. *J. Roy. statist. Soc.*, 43, vol. 106, p.349-359.

4073. BORRIE (W. D.). The role of immigrants in population growth in Australia. *Austral. Quar.*, 44, vol. 16, no. 2, p. 17-32.

4074. BORRIE (W. D.). Immigration to New Zealand, 1854-1880. *Roy. Austral. hist. Soc. J.*, 44, vol. 30, p. 299-325.

4075. BREND (William A.). The rise in the German birth rate [since 1919]. *19th Century*, 41, vol. 129, p. 380-390.

4076. Census of Barbados, 1715. *J. Barbados Mus.*, 41, vol. 8, p. 138-143 ; 42, vol. 9, p. 144-151.

4077. CHARLES (Enid). The trend of fertility in Prince Edward Island. *Canad. J. Econ. pol. Sci.*, 42, vol. 8, p. 213-246.

4078. CHARLES (E.). Differential fertility in Canada, 1931. *Canad. J. Econ. pol. Sci.*, 43, vol. 9, p. 175-218.

4079. COATS (R. H.) and MACLEAN (M. C.). The American born in Canada : a statistical interpretation.

Toronto, Ryerson Press, 43, in-8, xxii-176 p., $3.75. (Relations of Canada and the U.S.). R : W. B. Hurd, *Canad. hist. R.*, 43, vol. 24, p. 414-417. W. P. M(orrell), *Eng. hist. R.*, 45, vol. 60, p. 281-282. R. M. Woodbury, *Canad. J. Econ. pol. Sci.*, 44, vol. 10, p. 95-98.

4080. COUZENS (F. C.). Distribution of population of the mid-Derwent basin since the industrial revolution. *Geography*, 41, vol. 26, p. 31-38.

4081. DARKE (W. F.). A short guide to pre-war English outdoor vegetable statistics. *J. Roy. statist. Soc.*, 42, vol. 105, p. 328-335.

4082. Dow (J. C. R.). The inaccuracy of expectations : a statistical study of the Liverpool cotton futures market, 1921/2-1937/8. *Economica*, 41, vol. 8, p. 162-175.

4083. ELDERTON (Sir William) and OGBORN (M. E.). The mortality of adult males since the middle of the 18th century as shown by the experience of life assurance companies. *J. Roy. statist. Soc.*, 43, vol. 106, p. 1-31.

4084. FISH (W. B.). Population trends in France [since 1821]. *Geography*, 40, vol. 25, p. 107-120.

4085. FORSYTH (W. D.). The myth of open spaces : Australian, British and world trends of population and migration. London, Oxford Univ. Press, 42, in-8, xviii-226 p., (maps), 17s. 6d. R : J. Andrews, *Hist. Stud. Australia N.Z.*, 43, vol. 2, p. 207-208. A. M. Carr-Saunders, *Economica*, 43, vol. 10, p. 193-195.

4086. GLASS (D. V.). Population : policies and movements in Europe. London, Oxford Univ. Press, 40, in-8, 496 p., 25s. R : A. L. Bowley, *Pol. Quar.*, 40, vol. 11, p. 411-412. E. Grebenik, *Econ. J.*, 40, vol. 50, p. 488-490.

4087. GREENWOOD (Major). British loss of life in the wars of 1794-1815 and in 1914-1918. *J. Roy. statist. Soc.*, 42, vol. 105, p. 1-16.

4088. GREENWOOD (M.), MARTIN (W. J.) and RUSSELL (W. T.). Deaths by violence, 1837-1937. *J. Roy. statist. Soc.*, 41, vol. 104, p. 146-171.

4089. HANDLEY (James Edmund). The Irish in Scotland (1798-1845). Cork, Univ. Press, 43, in-8, xix-313 p., 10s. 6d. R : W.L.C., *Scottish geogr. Mag.*, 45, vol. 61, p. 28. D. W. Brogan, *Econ. Hist. R.*, 45, vol. 15, p. 98-99.

4090. HANDLIN (O.). Boston's immigrants. London, Oxford Univ. Press, 42, in-8, 305 p., (illus.), 14s. (Harvard hist. stud.).

4091. HANSEN (Marcus Lee). The immigrant in American history, ed. by A. M. Schlesinger. London, Oxford Univ. Press, 40, in-8, xi-230 p., 10s. 6d. R : W. P. M(orrell), *Eng. hist. R.*, 43, vol. 58, p. 374-375.

4092. HANSEN (M. L.) and BREBNER (John Bartlet). The mingling of the Canadian and American peoples. Vol. 1 : Historical. London, Oxford Univ. Press; Toronto, Ryerson Press, 40, in-8, xviii-274 p., (maps), 14s.; $3.50. (Relations of Canada and the U.S.). R : N. Macdonald, W. B. Hurd, *Canad. J. Econ. pol. Sci.*, 41, vol. 7, p. 117-119. W. P. Morrell, *Eng. hist. R.*, 41, vol. 56, p. 315-317. R.G.T., *Queen's Quar.*, 40, vol. 47, p. 369-374. G. deT. Glazebrook, *Canad. hist. R.*, 40, vol. 21, p. 416-418. D. C. H(arvey), *Dalhousie R.*, 40, vol. 20, p. 387-388.

4093. HINDEN (Rita). The fertility and mortality of the population of Palestine. *Sociol. R.*, 40, vol. 32, p. 29-49.

4094. HUTT (W. H.). Two studies in the statistics of Russia. *South African J. Econ.*, 45, vol. 13, p. 18-42.

4095. INSTITUTE OF ACTUARIES. Continuous investigation into the mortality of assured lives : statistics for 15 years, 1924-1938. London, Cambridge Univ. Press, 41, in-2, 36 p., 5s.

4096. KERR (Barbara M.). Irish seasonal migration to Great Britain, 1800-38. *Irish hist. Stud.*, 43, vol. 3, p. 365-380.

4097. MacDOUGALL (G. D. A.). Inter-war population changes in town and country. *J. Roy. statist. Soc.*, 40, vol. 103, p. 30-60.

4098. MARTELL (J. S.). Immigration to and emigration from Nova Scotia, 1815-38. Halifax, Public Archives, 42, in-8, 112 p., $1.00. (Publ. archives of Nova Scotia publ. 6). R : N. Macdonald, *Canad. hist. R.*, 43, vol. 24, p. 315-316.

4099. MASSEY (Philip). The expenditure of 1,360 British middle-class households in 1938-39. *J. Roy. statist. Soc.*, 42, vol. 105, p. 159-196.

4100. PEEL (R. F.). Local intermarriage and the stability of rural population in the English Midlands. *Geography*, 42, vol. 27, p. 22-30.

4101. RADZINOWICZ (L.). English criminal statistics. *L.Q.R.*, 40, vol. 56, p. 483-503.

4102. SHANNON (H. A.) and GREBENIK (E.). The population of Bristol. London, Cambridge Univ. Press, 43, in-8, 92 p., 7s. 6d. (Nat. inst. of econ. and soc. research, occasional papers, 2). R : M.J.E., *J. Roy. statist. Soc.*, 43, vol. 106, p. 69-70. W. D. Forsyth, *Econ. Record*, 43, vol. 19, p. 282-284. R. M. Titmuss, *Econ. Hist. R.*, 43, vol. 13, p. 129-130. A. L. Bowley, *Economica*, 43, vol. 10, p. 259-260.

4103. SHEEHY (Memorian). The Irish in Quebec. *Canad. Cath. hist. Assoc. Rept.*, 43-44, vol. 11, Engl. Sect., p. 35-47.

4104. THORSTEINSSON (Thorsteinn Th.). Saga Íslendinga í Vesturheimi (History of the Icelanders in the Western World). Winnipeg, 40-43,

2 vols. in-8. R : T. J. Oleson, *Canad. hist. R.*, 45, vol. 26, p. 440-444.

4105. TITMUSS (Richard M.). Birth, poverty and wealth : a study of infant mortality. London, Hamilton, 43, in-8, 118 p., 7s. 6d. R : E.G., *J. Roy. statist. Soc.*, 43, vol. 106, p. 171-172.

4106. TRUESDELL (Leon E.). The Canadian born in the United States : an analysis of the statistics of the Canadian element in the population of the United States, 1850 to 1930. London, Oxford Univ. Press, 43, in-8, xviii-263 p., 20s. (Relations of Canada and the U.S.). R : W. B. Hurd, *Canad. hist. R.*, 43, vol. 24, p. 414-417.

4107. WALSHAW (R. S.). Migration to and from the British Isles : problems and policies. London, Cape, 41, in-8, 94 p., 5s. R : H.W.R., *J. Roy. statist. Soc.*, 41, vol. 104, p. 287-288. A. M. Carr-Saunders, *Economica*, 41, vol. 8, p. 328-329.

4108. WILLCOX (Walter F.). Studies in American demography. London, Oxford Univ. Press, 40, in-8, xxx-556 p., (illus.), 21s. R : A. M. Carr-Saunders, *Economica*, 42, vol. 9, p. 101-102.

4109. WILLIAMS (David). Welsh settlers in Russia. *Nat. Library Wales J.*, 43, vol. 3, p. 55-58.

4110. WOODSWORTH (Charles J.). Canada and the Orient. Toronto, Macmillan, 41, in-8, xii-321 p., $3.00. R : A.E.P., *Queen's Quar.*, 43, vol. 50, p. 310. F. E. La Violette, *Canad. J. Econ. pol. Sci.*, 42, vol. 8, p. 314-315.

§ 9. Social History

4111. AITKEN (J.) ed. English diaries of the 19th century. London, Penguin, 44, in-8, 160 p., 9d. (Pelican ser.).

4112. APTHEKER (H.). American negro slave revolts. London, Oxford Univ. Press, 44, in-8, 410 p., 30s.

4113. ARUJA (Endel). Labour legislation and social insurance in Estonia, 1920-1944. *19th Century*, 44, vol. 136, p. 226-232.

4114. ASBURY (Herbert). The underworld of Chicago : an informal history of the Chicago underworld. London, Hale, 42, in-8, 364 p., 18s.

4115. ASPINALL-OGLANDER (Cecil). Admiral's widow : being the life and letters of the Hon. Mrs. Edward Boscawen from 1761 to 1805. London, Hogarth, 43, in-8, 205 p., 12s. 6d. R : *National R.*, 43, vol. 120, p. 342.

4116. ASQUITH (M.). Famine : Quaker work in Russia, 1921-23. London, Oxford Univ. Press, 43, in-8, 70 p., 2s. (Studies in relief problems ser.).

4117. BARNARD (E. A. B.). A seventeenth century country gentleman (Sir Francis Throckmorton, 1640-80). Cambridge, Heffer, 44, in-8, viii-100 p., 10s. 6d.

4118. BELL (E. Moberly). Octavia Hill, a biography. London, Constable, 42, in-8, xvii-297 p., 15s. R : *National R.*, 42, vol. 119, p. 527-529. F. Maurice, *Econ. J.*, 43, vol. 53, p. 98-100.

4119. BELOFF (Max). A London apprentice's notebook, 1703-5. *History*, 42, vol. 27, p. 38-45.

4120. BENTWICH (Norman). Judaea lives again. London, Gollancz, 44, in-8, 189 p., 8s. 6d. R : *J. central asian Soc.*, 44, vol. 31, p. 216-217. J. H. Simpson, *Int. R. Missions*, 44, vol. 33, p. 319-322.

4121. BINDER (Pearl). Russian families. London, Black, 42, in-8, 133 p., (illus.), 7s. 6d.

4122. BIRD (T. H.). Admiral Rous and the English turf, 1795-1877. New ed. London, Putnam, 42, in-8, 332 p., (illus.), 5s.

4123. BLACKTON (C. S.). New Zealand and the Australian anti-transportation movement. *Hist. Stud. Australia N.Z.*, 40, vol. 1, p. 116-122.

4124. BOAN (F.). A history of poor law relief legislation and administration in Missouri. London, Cambridge Univ. Press, 43, in-8, xiv-244 p., 9s.

4125. BOWLEY (M. E. A.). Housing and the state, 1919-1944. London, Allen & Unwin, 45, in-8, 260 p., 15s.

4126. BROOKE (Iris). Western European costume (17th-mid-19th century) and its relation to the theatre. London, Harrap, 40, in-4, 144 p., (illus.), 18s.

4127. BROOKS (F. W.). The vicissitudes of a Lincolnshire manor during the Civil War and the Commonwealth. *Eng. hist. R.*, 43, vol. 58, p. 344-356.

4128. BROWN (J.). The history of public assistance in Chicago, 1833-1893. London, Cambridge Univ. Press, 43, in-8, xvi-183 p., 9s. (Social service monogr.).

4129. BUCKMASTER (H.). Out of the house of bondage : the story of the underground railroad of the American negro slaves. London, Gollancz, 43, in-8, 340 p., 15s.

4130. CAMPBELL (Mildred L.). The English yeoman under Elizabeth and the early Stuarts. London, Oxford Univ. Press, 43, in-8, xiii-453 p., 18s. 6d. (Yale hist. publ., stud., 14). R : W. G. Hoskins, *Econ. Hist. R.*, 44, vol. 14, p. 193-196. G. E. Fussell, *Econ. J.*, 44, vol. 54, p. 103-106. R.V.L., *Eng. hist. R.*, 45, vol. 60, p. 126-127.

4131. CLARK (S. D.). The social development of Canada : an introductory study with select documents. London, Oxford Univ. Press ; Toronto, Univ. Press, 42, in-8, x-484 p., 18s. ; $4.00. R : G. W. Brown, *Canad. hist. R.*, 42, vol. 23, p. 197-198. R.G.T., *Queen's Quar.*, 43, vol. 50, p. 309. E. C. Hughes, *Canad. J. Econ. pol. Sci.*, 43, vol. 9, p. 96-99.

4132. COCHRAN (T. C.) and MULLER (W.). The age of enterprise : a social history of industrial America. London, Macmillan, 43, in-8, x-394 p., 16s.

4133. COLEMAN (J. W.) jr. Slavery times in Kentucky. London, Oxford Univ. Press, 41, in-8, 351 p., 14s.

4134. CONNELY (W.). The reign of Beau Brummell. London, Cassell, 40, in-8, xiv-272 p., 10s. 6d.

4135. CURTIS (Norah) and GILBEY (Cyril). Malnutrition : Quaker relief work in Austria, 1919-24 : Spain, 1936-39. London, Oxford Univ. Press, 44, in-8, 88 p., 2s. R : J. M. Campbell, Int. Affairs, 45, vol. 21, p. 393.

4136. DAKIN (S. B.). A Scotch paisano : Hugo Reid's life in California, 1832-1852. London, Cambridge Univ. Press, 40, in-8, 312 p., 15s.

4137. DAVIES (Clement) and others. Wales and health. Trans. Soc. Cymmr., 39 (40), p. 55-100.

4138. DAWSON (C. A.) and YOUNGE (Eva R.). Pioneering in the Prairie Provinces : the social side of the settlement process. Toronto, Macmillan, 40, in-8, xiv-338 p., $4.50. (Canadian frontiers of settlement). R : S. D. Clarke, Canad. hist. R., 40, vol. 21, p. 336-338. Canad. geogr. J., 40, vol. 20, p. x.

4139. DE BEER (E. S.). The early history of London street-lighting. History, 41, vol. 25, p. 311-324.

4140. DENING (C. F. W.). Old inns of Bristol. Bristol, Wright, 43, in-8, 116 p., (illus.), 12s. 6d.

4141. DU PLESSIS (I. D.). The Cape Malays. Cape Town, Miller, 44, in-8, 95 p., 12s. 6d. R : S. A. Rochlin, African Stud., 44, vol. 3, p. 188-189.

4142. EDWARDS (Isobel E.). Towards emancipation : a study in South African slavery. Cardiff, Univ.

of Wales Press, 42, in-8, 250 p., 15s. (Royal Empire Soc., imperial stud., 9). R : W. P. M(orrell), History, 44, vol. 29, p. 100-101. A. T. Milne, Econ. Hist. R., 45, vol. 15, p. 104. C. W. W. Greenidge, Africa, 43, vol. 14, p. 148-149.

4143. EVANS (E. Estyn). Irish heritage : the landscape, the people and their work. Dundalk, Tempest, 42, in-8, xvi-190 p., 8s. 6d. R : F. T. O'Duffy, Irish hist. Stud., 45, vol. 4, p. 380-384. E. Ettlinger, Man, 44, vol. 44, p. 51-52. G.R.C., Geogr. J., 42, vol. 100, p. 36. T. G. F. Paterson, Geography, 42, vol. 27, p. 112-113. C. Fox, Archaeol. cambrensis, 42, vol. 97, p. 128-129. E. C. Curwen, Antiquity, 42, vol. 16, p. 284-286.

4144. EVANS (Hugh). Cwm Eithin. 3rd ed. Liverpool, Evans, 43, in-8, xvi-236 p., (illus.).

4145. EVANS (Janet) and others. Welsh communities in large cities and a policy for them. Trans. Soc. Cymmr., 39 (40), p. 175-180.

4146. FAUGHT (M. C.). Falmouth, Massachusetts : problems of a resort community. London, Oxford Univ. Press, 45, in-8, 198 p., 18s. 6d.

4147. FAULKNER (H. U.). The quest for social justice, 1898-1914, ed. by A. M. Schlesinger and D. R. Fox. London, Macmillan, 45, in-8, xvii-390 p., (illus.), 20s. (Hist. of Amer. life, vol. 11).

4148. FAYLE (C. Ernest). Charles Wright. London, Allen & Unwin, 43, in-8, 206 p., 8s. 6d.

4149. FISH (C. R.). The rise of the common man, 1830-1850, ed. by A. M. Schlesinger and D. R. Fox. London, Macmillan, 45, in-8, xix-391 p., (illus.), 20s. (Hist. of Amer. life, vol. 6).

4150. FITZPATRICK (E. A.). McCarthy of Wisconsin. London, Oxford Univ. Press, 44, in-8, 326 p., (illus.), 23s. 6d.

4151. FLEURE (H. J.). Guernsey : a social study. *B. John Rylands Library*, 41/42, vol. 26, p. 57-81.

4152. FLOY (Michael) jr. Diary, Bowery village, 1833-1837, ed. by R. A. E. Brooks. London, Oxford Univ. Press, 41, in-4, 282 p., 22s. 6d.

4153. FRANKEN (J. L. M.). 'n Kaapse Huishoue in die 18de Eeu uit von Dessin se Briefboek en Memoriaal. *Archives Y.B. South Afr. Hist.*, 40 (41), 3rd year, pt. 1, p. 1-87.

4154. FRANKLIN (J. H.). The free negro in North Carolina, 1790-1860. London, Oxford Univ. Press, 43, in-8, 282 p., 24s. R : J.E.T., *Eng. hist. R.*, 44, vol. 59, p. 425-426.

4155. FRIEDLANDER (W.) and MYERS (E. D.). Child welfare in Germany before and after Nazism. London, Cambridge Univ. Press, 40, in-8, 273 p., 9s.

4156. GOSSE (Philip). The squire of Walton Hall : the life of Charles Waterton. London, Cassell, 40, in-8, 333 p., 15s.

4157. HALLIDAY (W. R.). A Turkish traveller of the 17th century (Evliya Effendi). *History*, 44, vol. 29, p. 144-151.

4158. HARVEY (Thomas Edmund). The Christian church and the prisoner in English experience. London, Epworth Press, 41, in-8, 79 p., 3s. 6d. (Social service lect., 1941).

4159. HENEY (Helen). Caroline Chisholm—pioneer social worker. *Roy. Austral. hist. Soc. J.*, 43, vol. 29, p. 21-34.

4160. HUGHES (E.). North country life in the 18th century. *History*, 40, vol. 25, p. 113-131.

4161. HUTCHINS (J. H.). Jonas Hanway, 1712-1786. London, S.P.C.K., 40, in-8, 197 p., 8s. 6d. R : C. R. Fay, *Econ. J.*, 40, vol. 50, p. 303-304.

4162. JESSUP (R. F.). Thomas Heron of Chilham. *Archaeol. cantiana*, 43, vol. 56, p. 11-18.

4163. JONES (A. H.). Cheltenham township. London, Oxford Univ. Press, 41, in-8, 173 p., 9s.

4164. JONES (E. D.). The Ottley papers. *Nat. Library Wales J.*, 45, vol. 4, p. 61-74.

4165. JONES (Louis C.). The clubs of the Georgian rakes. London, Oxford Univ. Press, 42, in-8, 270 p., (illus.), 14s.

4166. KEECH (J. M.). Workman's compensation in North Carolina, 1920-1940. London, Cambridge Univ. Press, 42, in-8, x-198 p., 18s.

4167. KIDDLE (Margaret L.). Caroline Chisholm in New South Wales, 1838-46. *Hist. Stud. Australia N.Z.*, 43, vol. 2, p. 186-201.

4168. KIDDLE (M.). Caroline Chisholm and Charles Dickens. *Hist. Stud. Australia N.Z.*, 45, vol. 3, p. 77-94.

4169. KILVERT (Robert Francis). Kilvert's diary, ed. by W. Plomer. Vol. 3. London, Cape, 40, in-8, 461 p., 12s. 6d.

4170. —— —— New ed., ed. by W. Plomer. London, Cape, 44, in-8, 352 p., 10s. 6d.

4171. KNOOP (Douglas) and JONES (G. P.). A short history of freemasonry to 1730. Manchester, Univ. Press, 40, in-8, ix-148 p., 5s. R : L. Morecki, *Econ. Hist. R.*, 43, vol. 13, p. 135-136.

4172. KNOOP (D.) and JONES (G. P.). A handlist of Masonic documents. Manchester, Univ. Press, 42, in-8, viii-56 p., 5s.

4173. KRONENBERGER (Louis). Kings and desperate men : life in 18th-century England. London, Gollancz, 42, in-8, xvi-323 p., 10s. 6d.

4174. LA NAUZE (J. A.). A social survey of Sydney in 1858. *Hist. Stud. Australia N.Z.*, 43, vol. 2, p. 264-268.

4175. LANGUAGE (F. J.). Herkoms en Geskiedenis van die Tlhaping. *African Stud.*, 42, vol. 1, p. 115-133.

4176. LAVER (J.). Fashions and fashion plates, 1800-1900. London, Penguin, 43, in-8, 32 p., (plates), 2s. (King Penguin ser.). R : J. Pope-Hennessy, *Burlington Mag.*, 43, vol. 83, p. 259.

4177. LEVESON-GOWER (I.). The face without a frown : Georgiana, Duchess of Devonshire. London, Muller, 44, in-8, 239 p., (plates), 15s.

4178. LEWIS (W. S.). Three tours through London in the years 1748, 1776, 1797. London, Oxford Univ. Press, 42, in-8, 147 p., (illus., map), 11s. 6d.

4179. LEYBURN (James G.). The Haitian people. London, Oxford Univ. Press, 41, in-8, x-342 p., 18s. (Yale univ., Calvin Chapin mem. publ. fund). R : G.R.C., *Geogr. J.*, 42, vol. 99, p. 279. H.J.F., *Geography*, 42, vol. 27, p. 84.

4180. LOOSLEY (Elizabeth W.). Early Canadian costume. *Canad. hist. R.*, 42, vol. 23, p. 349-362.

4181. Low (Garrett W.). Gold rush by sea. (From his diary), ed. by K. Haney. London, Oxford Univ. Press, 41, in-8, 187 p., 9s.

4182. McPHERSON (J. M.). The Kirk's care of the poor. Aberdeen, Avery, 41, in-8, 218 p., 5s. R : G.D.H., *Eng. hist. R.*, 42, vol. 57, p. 154-155.

4183. MANNHEIM (Hermann). Social aspects of crime in England between the wars. London, Allen & Unwin, 40, in-8, 382 p., 15s. R : C. D. Rackham, *Sociol. R.*, 42, vol. 34, p. 95-98. *Quar. R.*, 41, vol. 276, p. 149-150. E.C.R., *J. Roy. statist. Soc.*, 41, vol. 104, p. 292-293. D. C. Jones, *Economica*, 41, vol. 8, p. 208-210.

4184. MARLBOROUGH (Sarah, Duchess of). Letters of a grandmother, 1732-35 : correspondence with her granddaughter Diana, Duchess of Bedford, ed. by G. S. Thomson. London, Cape, 43, in-8, 184 p., 10s. 6d. R : M. Maxse, *National R.*, 43, vol. 121, p. 471-475.

4185. MARTIN (E. W.). The standard of living in 1860. London, Cambridge Univ. Press, 43, in-8, x-452 p., 27s.

4186. MASSICOTTE (E. Z.). Le costume des voyageurs et des coureurs de bois. *B. Rech. hist.*, 42, vol. 46, p. 235-240.

4187. MASSINGHAM (H. J.). The English countryman : a study of the English tradition. London, Batsford, 42, in-8, viii-148 p., (illus., diagram), 16s.

4188. MAXWELL (Constantia). Country and town life in Ireland under the Georges. London, Harrap, 40, in-8, 396 p., (illus.), 18s. R : E. St. J. Brooks, *19th Century*, 40, vol. 128, p. 310-312. T.W.M., *Eng. hist. R.*, 42, vol. 57, p. 156-157.

4189. MONKSWELL (Lady Mary). A Victorian diarist. Extracts (1873-1895), ed. by E. C. F. Collier. London, Murray, 44, in-8, 284 p., (illus.), 16s.

4190. MORGAN (A. H.). Regional consciousness in the N. Staffs. potteries. *Geography*, 42, vol. 27, p. 95-102.

4191. MORGAN (F. C.). Private purse accounts of the Marquis of Hertford, Michaelmas 1641-2. *Antiq. J.*, 45, vol. 25, p. 12-42.

4192. NUERMBERGER (R. K.). The free produce movement : a Quaker protest against slavery. London, Cambridge Univ. Press, 43, in-8, 148 p., 6s.

4193. NUGENT (Lady). Lady Nugent's journal, ed. by F. Cundall. 3rd ed.

London, West India Committee, 40, in-8, civ-404 p., (illus.), 7s. 6d. (Inst. of Jamaica).

4194. OWEN (G. Dyfnallt). The poor law system in Carmarthenshire during the 18th and early 19th centuries. *Trans. Soc. Cymmr.*, 41 (43), p. 71-86.

4195. PASTON (Lady Katherine). Correspondence, 1603-1627, ed. by R. Hughey. North Walsham, The Secretary, 41, in-8, 152 p., 21s. (to subscribers). (Norfolk record soc., vol. 14).

4196. PIERCE (Lorne). A Canadian people. Toronto, Ryerson Press, 45, in-8, ix-84 p., $1.50. R : R.C.W., *Queen's Quar.*, 45, vol. 52, p. 232.

4197. PIERCE (T. J.). Notes on the history of rural Caernarvonshire in the reign of Elizabeth. *Trans. Caern. hist. Soc.*, 40, p. 35-57.

4198. PLUM (H. G.). Restoration puritanism : a study of the growth of English liberty. London, Oxford Univ. Press, 44, in-8, 139 p., 15s. 6d. R : G. F. Nuttall, *Congreg. Quar.*, 44, vol. 22, p. 373.

4199. POWICKE (F. M.). The murder of Henry Clement and the pirates of Lundy island. *History*, 41, vol. 25, p. 285-310.

4200. QUEENSBERRY (10th Marq. of). The sporting Queensberrys. London, Hutchinson, 42, in-8, 288 p., 15s.

4201. QUENNELL (M. and C. H. B.). A history of everyday things in England, 1851-1942. Vol. 3-4. New ed. London, Batsford, 42-43, 2 vols. in-8, 214, 226 p., (illus., diagram), 18s. 6d.

4202. RADZINOWICZ (L.). The influence of economic conditions on crime, 1 (Poland, 1928-34). *Sociol. R.*, 41, vol. 33, p. 1-36.

4203. REYNOLDS (E. E.). Baden-Powell : a biography of Lord Baden-Powell of Gilwell. London, Oxford Univ. Press, 42, in-8, 283 p., (maps), 12s. 6d,

4204. ROBERT (J. C.). The road from Monticello : a study of the Virginia slavery debate, 1832. London, Cambridge Univ. Press, 41, in-8, x-128 p., 6s.

4205. ROSEN (S. McK.) and ROSEN (L. F.). Technology and society; the influence of machines in the United States. London, Macmillan, 41, in-8, xiv-474 p., 12s. 6d.

4206. ROSS (Dorothy). Class privilege in 17th-century England. *History*, 43, vol. 28, p. 148-155.

4207. ROWNTREE (B. Seebohm). Poverty and progress : a second social survey of York. London, Longmans, 41, in-8, xx-540 p., (plates), 15s. R : E. Grebenik, *Economica*, 42, vol. 9, p. 211-214. .

4208. SCHLATTER (Richard B.). The social ideas of religious leaders, 1660-1688. London, Oxford Univ. Press, 40, in-8, 258 p., 10s. 6d. (Oxf. hist. ser.).

4209. SCHNEIDER (D. M.) and DEUTSCH (A.). The history of public welfare in New York state, 1867-1940. London, Cambridge Univ. Press, 43, in-8, xx-410 p., 21s.

4210. SCOTT (K. J.). The public service association. *J. public Admin. N.Z.*, 43, vol. 6, p. 3-17.

4211. SIMPSON (G. W.). The blending of traditions in western Canadian settlement. *Canad. hist. Assoc. Rept.*, 44, p. 46-52.

4212. SOUTHWORTH (J. G.). Vauxhall Gardens. London, Oxford Univ. Press, 42, in-8, 211 p., (plates), 14s.

4213. SPENCER (Earl). Life at Devonshire House. *Quar. R.*, 42, vol. 279, p. 28-40.

4214. SYPHER (Wylie). Guinea's captive kings : British anti-slavery literature of the 18th century. London, Oxford Univ. Press, 42, in-8, 354 p., 14s. R : R. P(ares), *Eng. hist. R.*, 44, vol. 59, p. 284-285.

4215. THOMAS (A. H.). The rebuilding of London after the Great Fire. *History*, 40, vol. 25, p. 97-112.

4215a. THOMAS (B. B.). Elizabeth Baker and her diary. *Nat. Library Wales J.*, 44, vol. 3, p. 80-101.

4216. THOMSON (Gladys Scott). The Russells in Bloomsbury, 1669-1771. London, Cape, 40, in-8, 384 p., 15s. R : *National R.*, 40, vol. 114, p. 507-509. E.H., *Queen's Quar.*, 40, vol. 47, p. 269-271. A. S. Turberville, *Eng. hist. R.*, 40, vol. 55, p. 469-471.

4217. TORR (V. J.). A Canterbury pilgrimage in 1723. *Archaeol. cantiana*, 44, vol. 57, p. 56-68.

4218. TREVELYAN (G. M.). English social history : a survey of six centuries, Chaucer to Queen Victoria. London, Longmans, 44, in-8, xii-628 p., 21s. R : G. N. Clark, *Eng. hist. R.*, 45, vol. 60, p. 249-252. E. S. de Beer, *History*, 45, vol. 30, p. 99-102.

4219. VESEY-FITZGERALD (B.). Gypsies of Britain : an introduction to their history. London, Chapman & Hall, 44, in-8, 220 p., 15s.

4220. VILLIERS (G. H.). Peter Beckford in Portugal. *National R.*, 43, vol. 121, p. 463-470.

4221. WARNER (Robert Austin). New Haven negroes, a social history. London, Oxford Univ. Press, 40, in-8, xiv-309 p., (plates, maps), 16s. (Yale Univ., inst. of human relations publ.).

4222. WHITNÈY (J.). Elizabeth Fry. New ed. London, Harrap, 45, in-8, 312 p., 12s. 6d.

4223. WILSON (Forrest). Crusader in crinoline : the life of Harriet Beecher Stowe. London, Hutchinson, 42, in-8, 376 p., 18s. R : *National R.*, 42, vol. 119, p. 86-88.

4224. WILLIAMS (Eric). Capitalism and slavery. London, Oxford Univ. Press, 45, in-8, 297 p., 18s. 6d.

4225. WILSON (Sir Arnold) and MACKAY (G. S.). Old age pensions : an historical and critical study. London, Oxford Univ. Press, 41, in-8, 258 p., 16s. R : E. M. Hugh-Jones, *Econ. Hist. R.*, 42, vol. 12, p. 103-104.

4226. WILSON (Sir Duncan). Factory inspection, a 35 years retrospect. *J. Roy. statist. Soc.*, 41, vol. 104, p. 209-234.

4226a. WOODCOCK (Fred). The price of provisions and some social consequences in Worcestershire in the 18th and 19th centuries. *J. Roy. statist. Soc.*, 43, vol. 106, p. 268-272.

4227. WYNNE DIARIES. The Wynne diaries of Mrs. Elizabeth Wynne Fremantle (1779-1857), ed. by A. Fremantle. Vol. 3. London, Oxford Univ. Press, 40, in-8, 408 p., 21s.

4228. YEOMAN (John). The diary of the visits of John Yeoman to London, 1774 and 1777, ed. by M. Yearsley. New ed. London, Watts, 45, in-8, 55 p., 5s.

§ 10. Working Class Movements and Socialism

4229. ALDRED (G. A.). Richard Carlile, agitator : his life and times. Rev. ed. Glasgow, Strickland Press, 41, in-8, 168 p., 1s. 6d.

4230. BAROU (N.). World co-operation, 1844-1944. London, Gollancz, 44, in-8, 52 p., 2s. (Fabian research ser., 87).

4231. BEER (M.). A history of British Socialism. London, Allen & Unwin, 40, in-8, xxxi-451 p., 15s.

4232. BIALIK (M. I.). The co-operative credit movement in Palestine. London, Mitre Press, 41, in-4, 128 p., 10s.

4233. BRAND (C. F.). British labour's rise to power. London, Oxford Univ. Press, 42, in-8, 317 p., 16s. (Hoover libr. ser.).

4234. CARR (H. J.). John Francis Bray. *Economica*, 40, vol. 7, p. 397-415.

4235. COLE (G. D. H.). Chartist portraits. London, Macmillan, 41, in-8, vii-377 p., 15s. R : F.A.K., *Queen's Quar.*, 42, vol. 49, p. 97-98. C. R. Fay, *Econ. J.*, 42, vol. 52, p.66-69.

4236. COLE (G. D. H.). British working class politics, 1832-1914. London, Routledge, 41, in-8, 320 p., 7s. 6d. R : T. Brennan, *Econ. J.*, 41, vol. 51, p. 311-312. Q. Bell, *Pol. Quar.*, 41, vol. 12, p. 231-232.

4237. COLE (Margaret). The Fabian Society. *Pol. Quar.*, 44, vol. 15, p. 245-256.

4238. COLE (M.). Beatrice Webb. London, Longmans, 45, in-8, 197 p., (illus.), 10s. 6d.

4239. CONACHER (W. M.). The first Labour revolt. *Queen's Quar.*, 43, vol. 50, p. 402-406.

4240. CREIGHTON (D. G.). George Brown, Sir John Macdonald, and the 'workingman': an episode in the history of the Canadian Labour movement. *Canad. hist. R.*, 43, vol. 24, p. 362-376.

4241. DAVIES (E.). American labour : the story of the American trade union movement. London, Allen & Unwin, 43, in-8, 100 p., 2s.

4242. DAVIES (W. Lloyd). Notes on Hugh Williams and the Rebecca riots. *B. Board celtic Stud.*, 44, vol. 11, p. 160-167.

4243. DOBB (M.). Trade union experience and policy, 1914-1918. London, Lawrence & Wishart, 40, in-8, 32 p., 6d.

4244. EVATT (H. V.). Australian labour leader : the story of W. A. Holman and the labour movement. 2nd ed. Sydney, Angus & Robertson, 42, in-8, 597 p., 8s. 6d. R : C. H. Currey, *Hist. Stud. Australia N.Z.*, 41, vol. I, p. 202-205.

4245. FITZPATRICK (Brian). A short history of the Australian labor movement. Melbourne, Rawson's Bookshop, 40, in-8, 182 p., 4s. 6d. R : J.M., *Austral. Quar.*, 41, vol. 13, no. 1, p. 116.

4246. GRAVES (S.). A history of socialism. New ed. Letchworth, Hogarth Press, 42, in-8, 302 p., 3s. 6d.

4247. HUTT (A.). British trade unionism : a short history. New ed. London, Lawrence & Wishart, 43, in-8, 160 p., 2s. 6d.

4248. INDEPENDENT LABOUR PARTY in war and peace : a short account of the Party from its foundation to the present day. London, I.L.P., 42, in-8, 64 p., 6d.

4249. JACKSON (J. H.). Jean Jaurès, his life and work. London, Allen & Unwin, 43, in-8, 204 p., 12s. 6d.

4250. LEOPOLD (R. W.). Robert Dale Owen. London, Oxford Univ. Press, 42, in-8, 484 p., (illus.), 25s. 6d. (Harvard hist. stud., vol. 45).

4251. LINDSEY (A.). The Pullman strike : the story of a unique experiment and of a great labour upheaval. London, Cambridge Univ. Press, 43, in-8, xii-386 p., (illus.), 22s. 6d.

4252. LOUGH (J.). D'Argenson and socialistic thought in 18th-century France. *Mod. Language R.*, 42, vol. 37, p. 455-465.

4253. McCONNAGHA (W. A.). The development of the Labour movement in Great Britain, France and Germany. London, Oxford Univ. Press, 42, in-8, 212 p., 11s. 6d.

4254. McPHAIL (Alexander James). Diary, ed. by H. A. Innis. London, Oxford Univ. Press; Toronto, Univ. Press, 40, in-8, xi-289 p., 11s. 6d.; $2.50. R: C. R. Fay, *Canad. hist. R.*, 41, vol. 22, p. 209-211. H. S. Patton, *Canad. J. Econ. pol. Sci.*, 41, vol. 7, p. 122-124.

4255. NIYOGI (J. P.). The co-operative movement in Bengal. London, Macmillan, 40, in-8, 276 p., 10s. 6d. R : V. Anstey, *Econ. Hist. R.*, 43, vol. 13, p. 141. A. H. Tocker, *Econ. Record*, 41, vol. 17, p. 137-138. E. H. D. Arndt, *South African J. Econ.*, 41, vol. 9, p. 85-90. H. Calvert, *J. central asian Soc.*, 41, vol. 28, p. 226-229. V. Anstey, *Economica*, 41, vol. 8, p. 113.

4256. O'DONOGHUE (John G.). Daniel John O'Donoghue, father of the Canadian labor movement. *Canad. Cath. hist. Assoc. Rept.*, 42/43, vol. 10, p. 87-96.

4258. SHINE (H.). Carlyle and the Saint-Simonians. London, Oxford Univ. Press, 41, in-8, 205 p., 10s. 6d.

4259. STURMTHAL (A.). The tragedy of European labour, 1918-1939. London, Gollancz, 44, in-8, 294 p., 7s. 6d. R : J. Price, *Int. Affairs*, 44, vol. 20, p. 434.

MODERN LEGAL AND CONSTITUTIONAL HISTORY

§ 1. General History of Law

4260. ROBERTS (A. A.). A South African legal bibliography, being a bio-bibliographical survey and law finder of the Roman and Roman-Dutch legal literatures in southern Africa with a historical chart, notes on all the judges since 1828 and other appendices. Pretoria, Wallach, 42, in-8, 45s. R : *South African Law J.*, 42, vol. 59, p. 352-353.

4261. SETARO (F.). A bibliography of the writings of Roscoe Pound. London, Oxford Univ. Press, 42, in-8, 202 p., 12s. 6d. (Legal bibliogr. ser.).

4262. BEDWELL (C. E. A.). The Inns of Court. *Queen's Quar.*, 44, vol. 51, p. 273-284.

4263. HOLDSWORTH (Sir W,). The movement for reforms in the law (1793-1832). *L.Q.R.*, 40, vol. 56, p. 33-48, 208-228, 340-353.

4264. POLLOCK (Sir Frederick) and HOLMES (Oliver Wendell). The Pollock-Holmes letters : correspondence, 1874-1932, ed. by M. de W. Howe. London, Cambridge Univ. Press, 42, 2 vols. in-8, xxxiii-275, 359 p., 36s. R : *Quar. R.*, 42, vol. 279, p. 237-238. O. Williams, *National R.*, 42, vol. 119, p. 177-182.

4265. RANKIN (Sir George). Legal problems of Poland after 1918. *Grotius Soc. Trans.*, 40 (41), vol. 26, p. 1-34.

4266. WINDER (W. H. D.). Sir Joseph Jekyll, Master of the Rolls. *L.Q.R.*, 41, vol. 57, p. 512-555.

§ 2. Constitutional Law and History

4267. ADDISON (W. G. C.). The parliamentary oath. *Theology*, 41, vol. 42, p. 217-224.

4268. ASPINALL (Sir Algernon). Constitutional changes in the British West Indies. *J. comp, Legisl. int. Law*, 40, vol. 22, p. 129-135.

4269. BARKER (Sir E.). British constitutional monarchy. London, Oxford Univ. Press, 44, in-8, 24 p., 6d.

4270. BEAGLEHOLE (J. C.) and others. New Zealand and the Statute of Westminster. Wellington, Progressive Publ. Soc., 44, in-8, xx-195 p., 10s. 6d. R : H. L. Harris, *Austral. Quar.*, 45, vol. 17, no. 1, p. 121-123. K. C. Wheare, *Int. Affairs*, 45, vol. 21, p. 538-539. A.Q., *J. comp. Legisl. int. Law*, 45, vol. 27, pt. 3/4, p. 124-125.

4271. BEHRENS (B.). The Whig theory of the constitution in the reign of Charles II. *Cambridge hist. J.*, 41, vol. 7, p. 42-71.

4272. CHURCH (W. F.). Constitutional thought in 16th-century France. London, Oxford Univ. Press, 41, in-8, 370 p., 16s. (Hist. stud. ser.).

4273. CLARKE (Mary Patterson). Parliamentary privilege in the American colonies. London, Oxford Univ. Press, 43, in-8, 316 p., 20s. (Yale hist. publ., misc. 44). R : R. P(ares), *Eng. hist. R.*, 45, vol. 60, p. 274.

4274. CLOKIE (H. McD.). Judicial review, federalism, and the Canadian constitution. *Canad. J. Econ. pol. Sci.*, 42, vol. 8, p. 537-556.

4275. CLOKIE (H. McD.). Basic problems of the Canadian constitution. *Canad. Bar R.*, 42, vol. 20, p. 395-429, 817-840.

4276. CORWIN (Edward S.). The President : office and powers. History and analysis of practice and opinion. London, Oxford Univ. Press, 40, in-8, xiv-476 p., 21s. (N.Y. univ., Stokes foundation, Stokes lect. on politics). R : R. M. Dawson, *Canad. J. Econ. pol. Sci.*, 41, vol. 7, p. 285-289. H. W. Horwill, *Eng. hist. R.*, 41, vol. 56, p. 504-507.

4277. CURREY (C. H.). The Legislative Council of New South Wales, 1843-1943 : constitutional changes, attempted and achieved. *Roy. Austral. hist. Soc. J.*, 43, vol. 29, p. 337-440.

4277a. CUSHMAN (Robert E.). The independent regulatory commissions. London, Oxford Univ. Press, 41, in-8, xiv-780 p., 21s. R : D. W. B(rogan), *Eng. hist. R.*, 42, vol. 57, p. 536-537.

4278. DORR (H. M.) ed. The Michigan constitutional conventions of 1835-1836. London, Oxford Univ. Press, 40, in-8, 626 p., 21s.

4279. DUNHAM (William Huse) jr. The Ellesmere extracts from the ' Acta Consilii ' of King Henry VIII. *Eng. hist. R.*, 43, vol. 58, p. 301-318.

4280. DUNHAM (W. H.) jr. The members of Henry VIII's whole council, 1509-1527. *Eng. hist. R.*, 44, vol. 59, p. 187-210.

4281. FLETCHER (Ruth). The governor as commander-in-chief. *Hist. Stud. Australia N.Z.*, 43, vol. 2, p. 209-223.

4282. FORRESTER (E. G.). Northamptonshire county elections and electioneering, 1695-1832. London, Oxford Univ. Press, 41, in-8, viii-166 p., 10s. (Oxf. hist. ser.). R : *History*, 43, vol. 28, p. 117-118.

4283. FORSEY (Eugene A.). The royal power of dissolution of parliament in the British Commonwealth. Toronto, Oxford Univ. Press, 43, in-8, xx-316 p., $5.00. R : H. McD. Clokie, *Canad. hist. R.*, 43, vol. 24, p. 417-419. R. M. Dawson, *Canad. J. Econ. pol. Sci.*, 44, vol. 10, p. 88-93. J. L. Morison, *Int. Affairs*, 44, vol. 20, p. 570-571.

4284. GARDNER (A. J. A.). Aspects of Dicey's essential condition of federalism. *Hist. Stud. Australia N.Z.*,45, vol. 3, p. 95-110.

4285. HAINES (C. G.). The role of the Supreme Court in American government and politics, 1789-1835. London, Cambridge Univ. Press, 44, in-8, xiv-680 p., 36s.

4286. HAMILTON (Bruce). The Barbados executive committee : an experiment in government. *J. Barbados Mus.*, 44, vol. 11, p. 115-131.

4287. HAWGOOD (John A.). Modern constitutions since 1787. London, Macmillan, 40, in-8, xii-539 p., 16s. R : R. N. Carew Hunt, *19th Century*, 40, vol. 128, p. 516-517.

4288. HOCKETT (H. C.). The constitutional history of the United States, 1826-1876. London, Macmillan, 40, in-8, 405 p., 12s. 6d.

4289. JENNINGS (W. Ivor). The British constitution. London, Cambridge Univ. Press, 41, in-8, xvi-232 p., 8s. 6d. (Engl. institutions).

4290. KAHN-FREUND (O.). The Weimar constitution. *Pol. Quar.*, 44, vol. 15, p. 229-235.

4291. KALTCHAS (Nicholas). Introduction to the constitutional history of modern Greece. London, Oxford Univ. Press, 40, in-8, xvi-187 p., 13s. 6d. R : F.H.M., *History*, 41, vol. 26, p. 92-93.

4292. KEIR (D. Lindsay). The constitutional history of modern Britain, 1485-1937. 2nd ed. London, Black, 43, in-8, viii-568 p., 20s. R : A.M.W., *Queen's Quar.*, 44, vol. 51, p. 97-98.

4293. KEITH (Arthur Berriedale). The constitution of England from Queen Victoria to George VI. London, Macmillan, 40, 2 vols. in-8, lv-485, ix-515 p., 30s. R : *National R.*, 40, vol. 114, p. 380-381. K. Smellie, *Pol. Quar.*, 40, vol. 11, p. 268-271.

4294. KEITH (A. B.). The constitution under strain : its working from the crisis of 1938 down to the present time. London, Stevens, 42, in-8, 72 p., 2s. 6d.

4295. LEWSEN (Phyllis). The first crisis in responsible government in the Cape Colony. *Archives Y.B. South Afr. Hist.*, 42 (43), vol. 2, p. 205-266.

4296. LIPSON (Leslie). The origins of the caucus in New Zealand. *Hist. Stud. Australia N.Z.*, 42, vol. 2, p. 1-10.

4297. LOVEJOY (Allen Fraser). La Follette and the establishment of the direct primary in Wisconsin, 1890-1904. London, Oxford Univ. Press, 41, in-8, 107 p., (maps), 4s. 6d. (Yale univ., Patterson prize essays, vol. 1). R : J.E.T., *Eng. hist. R.*, 43, vol. 58, p. 503-504.

4298. McILWAIN (C. H.). Constitutional history and the present crisis of constitutionalism. *Canad. J. Econ. pol. Sci.*, 41, vol. 7, p. 147-153.

4299. McLINTOCK (A. H.). The establishment of constitutional government in Newfoundland, 1783-1832: a study in retarded colonisation. London, Longmans, 41, in-8, xii-246 p., 15s. (Roy. Empire Soc., imperial stud., 17). R : G. O. Rothney, *Canad. hist. R.*, 42, vol. 23, p. 84-86. H. A. I(nnis), *Eng. hist. R.*, 42, vol. 57, p. 402-403. W. P. Morrell, *Econ. Hist. R.*, 42, vol. 12, p. 102.

4300. MARRIOTT (Sir J. A. R.). An Empire cabinet. *19th Century*, 42, vol. 131, p. 123-128.

4301. NEUENDORFF (Gwendoline). Studies in the evolution of Dominion status : the governor-generalship of Canada and the development of Canadian nationalism. London, Allen & Unwin; Toronto, Nelson, 42, in-8, vi-379 p., 18s.; $6.25. R : R. M. Dawson, *Canad. hist. R.*, 43, vol. 24, p. 61-63.

4302. O'SULLIVAN (Donal). The Irish Free State and its Senate : a study in contemporary politics. London, Faber, 40, in-8, xxxi-666 p., 25s.

4303. PEEKEMA (W. G.). Imperial relations within the kingdom of the Netherlands. *J. comp. Legisl. int. Law*, 42, vol. 24, p. 90-107.

4304. PLUCKNETT (T. F. T.). Ellesmere on statutes. *L.Q.R.*, 44, vol. 60, p. 242-249.

4305. RAMSDELL (C. W.). Laws and joint resolutions of the last session of the Confederate congress (Nov. 7, 1864-March 18, 1865) together with the secret acts of previous congresses. London, Cambridge Univ. Press, 42, in-8, xxviii-184 p., (illus.), 15s.

4306. RAPPARD (W. E.). Switzerland : notes of a lecture. *Grotius Soc. Trans.*, 42 (43), vol. 28, p. 83-85.

4307. RICHARDSON (W. C.). The surveyor of the King's prerogative. *Eng. hist. R.*, 41, vol. 56, p. 52-75.

4308. ROBERTS (M.). The constitutional development of Sweden in the reign of Gustav Adolf. *History*, 40, vol. 24, p. 328-341.

4309. SCOTT (F. R.). Constitutional adaptations to changing functions of government. *Canad. J. Econ. pol. Sci.*, 45, vol. 11, p. 329-341.

4310. SIRES (Ronald V.). Constitutional change in Jamaica, 1834-60. *J. comp. Legisl. int. Law*, 40, vol. 22, p. 178-190.

4311. STRONSKI (S.). The two Polish constitutions of 1921 and 1935. Glasgow, Ksiaznica Polska, 44, in-8, 16 p., 6d.

4312. T. President Roosevelt and the Supreme Court. *South African Law J.*, 42, vol. 59, p. 103-112.

4313. TWISS (B. R.). Lawyers and the constitution, ed. E. S. Corwin. London, Oxford Univ. Press, 42, in-8, 285 p., 15s.

4314. WATKINS (F. M.). The failure of constitutional emergency powers under the German republic. London, Oxford Univ. Press, 40, in-8, 148 p., 8s. 6d.

4315. WEBB (Leicester). Government in New Zealand. Wellington, Dept. of Internal Affairs, 40, in-8, 179 p., 5s. (N.Z. centennial surveys). R : L. Lipson, *J. public Admin. N. Zealand*, 40, vol. 3, p. 62-65.

4316. WHEARE (K. C.). The Statute of Westminster. 2nd ed. London, Oxford Univ. Press, 42, in-8, 344 p., 10s.

4317. WILLSON (David H.). Privy Councillors in the House of Commons, 1604-29. London, Oxford Univ. Press, 40, in-8, ix-332 p., 27s. R : *History*, 43, vol. 28, p. 116-117.

§ 3. Public Law and Institutions Local Government

4318. BARKER (Sir Ernest). The development of public services in western Europe, 1660-1930. London, Oxford Univ. Press, 44, in-8, viii-93 p., 5s. R : A. Cobban, *Int. Affairs*, 45, vol. 21, p. 107-108. C. Leubuscher, *Economica*, 45, vol. 12, p. 56-57.

4319. BERMAN (A. Z.). Municipal enterprise—its history and scope. Cape Town, Juta, 40, in-8, 254 p., 12s. 6d. R : R. J. Randall, *South African J. Econ.*, 40, vol. 8, p. 117-128.

4320. BRECHT (A.) and GLASER (C.). The art and technique of administration in German ministries. London, Oxford Univ. Press, 42, in-8, 205 p., 8s. 6d. (Pol. stud. ser.).

4321. CALDWELL (L. K.). The administrative theories of Hamilton and Jefferson. London, Cambridge Univ. Press, 45, in-8, x-244 p., 21s.

4322. CARTER (A. N.) and DRUMMIE (J. H.). Trends in New Brunswick legislation affecting the executive and governmental agencies. *Canad. Bar R.*, 43, vol. 21, p. 810-825.

4323. COBBAN (Alfred). Administrative centralization in Germany and the new states, 1918-39. *Int. Affairs*, 44, vol. 20, p. 249-264.

4324. COHEN (Emmeline W.). The growth of the British civil service, 1780-1939. London, Allen & Unwin, 41, in-8, 221 p., 10s. 6d. R : *Pol. Quar.*, 41, vol. 12, p. 455-457. M., *J. comp. Legisl. int. Law*, 41, pt. 1, p. 198-199. H. Finer, *Sociol. R.*, 42, vol. 35, p. 98-101.

4325. CORRY (J. A.). Changes in the functions of government. *Canad. hist. Assoc. Rept.*, 45, p. 15-24.

4326. CURTIS (C. A.). Municipal government in Ontario. *Canad. J. Econ. pol. Sci.*, 42, vol. 8, p. 416-426.

4327. DUNDAS (W. C.). The development of local government in counties in Scotland. Edinburgh, Hodge, 42, in-8, 77 p., 5s.

4328. GEORGE (R. H.). Charters granted to English parliamentary corporations in 1688. *Eng. hist. R.*, 40, vol. 55, p. 47-56.

4329. HUGHES (Edward). Civil Service reform, 1853-5. *History*, 42, vol. 27, p. 51-83.

4330. LE PATOUREL (John). Channel Islands institutions—past and future. *History*, 43, vol. 28, p. 171-181.

4331. A list of the department of the Lord Chamberlain of the Household, autumn, 1663. (Select documents, 39). *B. Inst. hist. Research*, 41, vol. 19, p. 13-24.

4332. LOGAN (D. W.). A Civil Servant and his pay. *L.Q.R.*, 45, vol. 61, p. 240-267.

4333. LOMBARDI (J.). Labor's voice in the Cabinet : a history of the Department of Labor from its origin to 1921. London, King, 43, in-8, 366 p., 17s. 6d.

4334. MAINERD (A.). Local government in New South Wales : a review.

Austral. Quar., 45, vol. 17, no. 2, p. 32-43.

4335. MASON (H. G. R.). One hundred years of legislative development in New Zealand. *J. comp. Legisl. int. Law*, 41, pt. 1, p. 1-17.

4336. MATHEWS (Alizon M.). Editions of 'The court and city register', 1742-1813. (Bibliogr. aids to research, 9). *B. Inst. hist. Research*, 41, vol. 19, p. 9-12.

4337. MORTON (W. L.). Direct legislation and the origins of the progressive movement. *Canad. hist. R.*, 44, vol. 25, p. 279-288.

4338. PAPE (T.). The Restoration government and the corporation of Newcastle-under-Lyme. Manchester, Univ. Press, 40, in-8, 64 p., (illus.), 7s. 6d.

4339. PARKER (Robert S.). Public service recruitment in Australia. Sydney, Melbourne Univ. Press, 42, in-8, 296 p., 10s. R : F. B. Stephens, *J. public Admin. N. Zealand*, 42, vol. 5, no. 1, p. 77-81.

4340. PARSLOE (C. G.). The growth of a borough constitution : Newark-on-Trent, 1549-1688. *Trans. Roy. hist. Soc.*, 40, vol. 22, p. 171-198.

4341. PATTERSON (George). The establishment of the county court in Nova Scotia. *Canad. Bar R.*, 43, vol. 21, p. 394-406.

4342. POLLARD (A. F.). A protean clerk of the commons [Robert Ormeston, 16th century]. *B. Inst. hist. Research*, 40, vol. 18, p. 49-51.

4343. POLLARD (A. F.). The growth of the Court of Requests. *Eng. hist. R.*, 41, vol. 56, p. 300-303.

4344. RANSOME (Mary). Division-lists of the House of Commons, 1715-1760. *B. Inst. hist. Research*, 41, vol. 19, p. 1-8.

4345. REDFORD (Arthur) and RUSSELL (Ina Stafford). The history of local government in Manchester. London, Longmans, 39-40, 3 vols. in-8, xvi-392, viii-467, viii-433 p., 63s. R : W. I. Jennings, *Pol. Quar.*, 40, vol. 11, p. 416-419. H. A. Mess, *Econ. J.*, 40, vol. 50, p. 501-502. H. R. G. Greaves, *Econ. Hist. R.*, 44, vol. 14, p. 93-95. E. G. Dowdell, *Eng. hist. R.*, 41, vol. 56, p. 319-323.

4346. RIDDELL (W. A.). Civil Service administration at the provincial, federal and international levels. *J. public Admin. N. Zealand*, 42, vol. 4, no. 2, p. 3-10.

4347. ROBERTS (Glyn). The municipal development of the borough of Swansea to 1900. Cardiff, Univ. of Wales Press Bd., 40, in-8. R : J.F.R., *Eng. hist. R.*, 41, vol. 56, p. 159-160.

4348. SMITH (T. R.). Retirement from the Civil Service. *J. public Admin. N. Zealand*, 42, vol. 4, no. 2, p. 11-23.

4349. STEPHENS (F. B.). The public service—to-day and to-morrow. *J. public Admin. N. Zealand*, 42, vol. 5, no. 1, p. 46-75.

4350. VERNON (R. V.) and MANSERGH (N.) ed. Advisory bodies : a study of their uses in relation to central government, 1919-1939. London, Allen & Unwin, 41, in-8, 520 p., 18s. R : W. A. Robson, *Pol. Quar.*, 41, vol. 12, p. 226-228. C. W. Cohen, *Int. Affairs*, 41, vol. 19, p. 330. *National R.*, 41, vol. 117, p. 124-125. C.T.C., *J. comp. Legisl. int. Law*, 42, vol. 24, p. 76-78.

4351. WEBB (Leicester). Government in New Zealand. Wellington, Whitcombe & Tombs, 40, in-8, 179 p., 5s. (N.Z. centennial surveys 5). R : W. T. G. Airey, *Hist. Stud. Australia N.Z.*, 42, vol. 2, p. 56-58.

4352. WILLCOX (William Bradford). Gloucestershire, a study in local government, 1590-1640. London, Oxford Univ. Press, 40, in-8, xvi-348 p., 14s. (Yale hist. publ., misc. 39).

§ 4. Civil and Penal Law

4353. BEGBIE (Sir Matthew Baillie). Memoirs and documents relating to Judge Begbie, ed. by W. Kaye Lamb. *Brit. Columbia hist. Quar.*, 41, vol. 5, p. 125-148.

4354. BROOKS (A. L.). Walter Clark : fighting judge. London, Oxford Univ. Press, 44, in-8, 288 p., (illus.), 18s. 6d.

4355. COHEN (Maxwell). Habeas corpus cum causa, the emergence of the modern writ, 1, 2. *Canad. Bar R.*, 40, vol. 18, p. 10-42, 172-199.

4356. COHN (E. J.). Legal aid for the poor : a study in comparative law and legal reform. *L.Q.R.*, 43, vol. 59, p. 250-271, 359-377.

4357. DOULL (John). The first Chief Justice of Cape Breton, Richard Gibbons. *Canad. Bar R.*, 45, vol. 23, p. 417-423.

4358. EGERTON (R.). Historical aspects of legal aid. *L.Q.R.*, 45, vol. 61, p. 87-94.

4359. FAIRMAN (C.). Mr. Justice Miller and the Supreme Court, 1862-1890. London, Oxford Univ. Press, 40, in-8, 456 p., 20s.

4360. GOEBEL (J.) and NAUGHTON (T. R.). Law enforcement in colonial New York. London, Oxford Univ. Press, 44, in-8, 908 p., 28s.

4361. GRAHAM (A. D.). The life of the rt. hon. sir Samuel Walker Griffith, G.C.M.G., P.C. London, Sweet & Maxwell, 40, in-8, 105 p., 5s. 6d. (Univ. of Queensland, Macrossan lect., 1938). R : C. H. Currey, *Hist. Stud. Australia N.Z.*, 40, vol. 1, p. 135-136.

4362. GRAY (W. Forbes). The Douglas cause : an unpublished correspondence. *Quar. R.*, 41, vol. 276, p. 69-79.

4363. GRUNHUT (Max). The development of the German penal system, 1920-1932. *Canad. Bar R.*, 44, vol. 22, p. 198-252.

4364. HYDE (Harford Montgomery). Judge Jeffreys. London, Harrap, 40, in-8, 328 p., 12s. 6d. R : E. S. de B., *History*, 41, vol. 26, p. 157.

4365. KEETON (A. A. F.). A historical survey of the limitation of the rights of parents and schoolmasters to inflict corporal punishment on children. *South African Law J.*, 43, vol. 60, p. 430-438.

4366. LALANDE (Léon). The status of organized labour : an outline of the development of the law in Great Britain, the United States and Canada. *Canad. Bar R.*, 41, vol. 19, p. 638-681.

4367. LEWIS (T. H.). Attendances of justices and grand jurors at the courts of quarter sessions, 16th to 18th century. *Trans. Soc. Cymmr.*, 42 (44), p. 108-122.

4368. MAESTRO (Marcello T.). Voltaire and Beccaria as reformers of criminal law. London, Oxford Univ. Press, 42, in-8, x-177 p., 10s. R : A. Paterson, *South African Law J.*, 44, vol. 61, p. 41-44.

4369. MILLAR (Robert Wyness). A septennium of English civil procedure, 1932-1939 (under the rules of the Supreme Court). *Canad. Bar R.*, 41, vol. 19, p. 96-119.

4370. OCKRENT (L.). Land rights : an enquiry into the history of registration for publication in Scotland. Edinburgh, Hodge, 42, in-8, 215 p., 16s.

4371. RADZINOWICZ (L.). International collaboration in criminal science. *L.Q.R.*, 42, vol. 58, p. 110-139.

4372. RADZINOWICZ (L.) and TURNER (J. W. Cecil) ed. Penal reform in England : intr. essays on some aspects of English criminal policy. London, King, 40, in-8, 177 p., 10s. 6d. (Engl. stud. in criminal sci., vol. 1). R : D. C. Jones, *Sociol. R.*, 41, vol. 33, p. 184-185.

4373. RANKIN (Sir G.). Civil law in British India before the codes. *L.Q.R.*, 42, vol. 58, p. 467-482.

4374. RATCLIFF (S. C.) and JOHNSON (H. C.). Quarter sessions indictment book, Easter, 1631 to Epiphany, 1674. Warwick, County Council, 42, in-8, xxxvi-337 p., (plates), 10s. 6d. (Warwick county records, vol. 6). R : A. Peel, *Congreg. Quar.*, 43, vol. 21, p. 58-61.

4375. REITH (Charles). British police and the democratic ideal. London, Oxford Univ. Press, 43, in-8, 279 p., 12s. 6d. R : A. A., *Eng. hist. R.*, 44, vol. 59, p. 427-428. *National R.*, 44, vol. 122, p. 87-88. M. F. P. Herchenroder, *J. comp. Legisl. int. Law*, 44, vol. 26, pt. 3/4, p. 90-91.

4376. RIX (M. S.). Company law, 1844 and to-day. *Econ. J.*, 45, vol. 55, p. 242-260.

4377. ROY (Pierre-Georges). François Marois alias Malouin alias Lafage; Le plaidoyer de Sieur Marois devant le jury. *B. Rech. hist.*, 43, vol. 49, p. 97-102; 150-157.

4378. S. (A.). Law and law courts in Poland, 1919-1939. *Slavonic Y.B.* (*Slavonic R.*), 40, vol. 19, p. 188-202.

4379. WAGER (M.) and DICKSTEIN (P.). A chapter in the development of labour law in the Jewish settlement of Palestine. Tel Aviv, R. Mass, 43, in-8, 192 p. R : N. Bentwich, *J. comp. Legisl. int. Law*, 45, vol. 27, pt. 3/4, p. 116.

4380. WALKER-SMITH (D.) and CLARKE (E.). Life and famous cases of Sir Edward Clarke. London, Eyre & Spottiswoode, 42, in-8, 351 p., 10s. 6d.

4381. WATTS (P. R.). An Elizabethan will. *Austral. Law J.*, 43, vol. 16, p. 353-356.

4382. WISE (Maurice K.). Requisition in France and Italy : the treatment of national private property and services. London, Oxford Univ. Press, 44, in-8, 216 p., 18s. 6d. R : T. L. G. Reid, *Int. Affairs*, 45, vol. 21, p. 398.

§ 5. International Law

4383. ALVAREZ (Don Alejandro). Le développement du droit des gens dans le nouveau monde. *Trans. Grotius Soc.*, 39 [40], vol. 25, p. 169-184.

4384. ANNUAL DIGEST. Annual digest and reports of public international law cases, 1935-37, 1938-40, 1941-42. Ed. by H. Lauterpacht. London, Butterworth, 41-45, 3 vols. in-8, 165s. R (1935-37) : H. A. Smith, *J. comp. Legisl. int. Law*, 42, vol. 24, p. 79-80.

4385. BENTWICH (Norman). Statelessness through the peace treaties after the first World-War. *B.Y.B.I.L.*, 44, vol. 21, p. 171-176.

4386. CALDECOTE (Viscount). International law and neutral rights. *L.Q.R.*, 40, vol. 56, p. 313-319.

4387. CUSTOS. The International Labour Code. *Pol. Quar.*, 42, vol. 13, p. 303-310.

4388. GRAUPNER (R.). British nationality and state succession. *L.Q.R.*, 45, vol. 61, p. 161-178.

4389. HALES (James C.). The creation and application of the mandate system (a study in international colonial supervision). *Trans. Grotius Soc.*, 39 [40], vol. 25, p. 185-284.

4390. HILL (Norman). Claims to territory in international law and relations. London, Oxford Univ. Press, 45, in-8, 256 p., 12s. 6d.

4391. HURST (Sir C. J. B.). The Permanent Court of International Justice. *L.Q.R.*, 43, vol. 59, p. 312-326.

4393. INTERNATIONAL LABOUR OFFICE : The International labour code, 1939 : a systematic arrangement of the conventions and recommendations adopted by the International Labour Conference, 1919-1939. Montreal, The Office, 41, in-4, lvi-920 p., $5.00. R : C.E.A.B., *J. comp. Legisl. int. Law*, 42, vol. 24, p. 78-79. O. de R. Foenander, *Econ. Record*, 42, vol. 18, p. 232-233. I.L.W., *Queen's Quar.*, 42, vol. 49, p. 93-95. H.S., *South African Law J.*, 42, vol. 59, p. 138-139. B.L., *Canad. Bar R.*, 42, vol. 20, p. 477-478.

4394. JENKS (C. Wilfred). Some legal aspects of the financing of international institutions. *Grotius Soc. Trans.*, 42 (43), vol. 28, p. 87-132.

4395. JONES (J. Mervyn). Modern developments in the law of extradition. *Grotius Soc. Trans.*, 41 (42), vol. 27, p. 113-141.

4396. LEAGUE OF NATIONS. League of Nations treaty series : treaties and international engagements registered with the Secretariat. Vol. 200 : 1940/41. London, Allen & Unwin, 42, in-8, 600 p., 15s.

4397. LOEWENFELD (Erwin). The mixed courts in Egypt as part of the system of capitulations after the treaty of Montreux. *Grotius Soc. Trans.*, 40 (41), vol. 26, p. 83-123.

4398. REUT-NICOLUSSI (E.). The reform of the Permanent Court of International Justice. *Grotius Soc. Trans.*, 39 [40], vol. 25, p. 135-149.

4399. TANSILL (Charles C.). The fur-seal fisheries and the doctrine of the freedom of the seas. *Canad. hist. Assoc. Rept.*, 42, p. 71-81.

§ 6. Contemporary Political and Social Movements

a. FASCISM

4400. BINCHY (D. A.). Church and state in Fascist Italy. London, Oxford Univ. Press, 41, in-8, ix-774 p., 31s. 6d. (Roy. inst. of internat. affairs). R : A. Peel, *Congreg. Quar.*, 42, vol. 20, p. 78-79. V. M. Crawford,

Int. Affairs, 42, vol. 19, p. 383. A. L. Rowse, *Pol. Quar.*, 42, vol. 13, p. 225-228. I. M. Massey, *History*, 44, vol. 29, p. 93-94.

4401. CORTESÃO (Armando). Democracy and fascism in Portugal. *Pol. Quar.*, 45, vol. 16, p. 329-341.

4402. MACARTNEY (Maxwell H. H.). One man alone : the history of Mussolini and the Axis. London, Chatto, 44, in-8, vii-183 p., 15s.

4403. MURPHY (James). Mussolini and Bolshevism. *19th Century*, 43, vol. 133, p. 260-268.

4404. SPRIGGE (C. J. S.). Italian Fascism : a retrospect. *19th Century*, 42, vol. 132, p. 163-169.

b. COMMUNISM

4405. DOBB (Maurice). Lenin. *Slavonic Y.B.* (*Slavonic R.*), 40, vol. 19, p. 34-54.

4406. FRÖLICH (Paul). Rosa Luxemburg, her life and work. London, Gollancz, 40, in-8, 336 p., 7s. 6d. R : I. M. Massey, *Int. Affairs*, 40, vol. 19, p. 118-119.

4407. GANKIN (O. H.) and FISHER (H. H.). The Bolsheviks and the World War : the origin of the Third International. London, Oxford Univ. Press, 40, in-8, 856 p., 27s. (Hoover libr. on war, revolution and peace, publ. 15).

4408. HOLLIS (C.). Lenin. New ed. London, Longmans, 40, in-8, viii-285 p., (illus.), 6s.

4409. LENIN (V. I.). [Articles and speeches from Jan. 1916-Mar. 1917, tr. by M. J. Olgin, ed. by A. Trachtenberg]. London, Lawrence, 43, in-8, 463 p., 12s. 6d. (Collected works, vol. 19).

4410. Short history of the Communist Party of the Soviet Union. London, Central Books, 44, in-8, 362 p., 4s. 6d.

4411. WILSON (Edmund). To the Finland station. A study in the writing and acting of history. London, Secker & Warburg, 41, in-8, 509 p., 18s. A. L. Rowse, *Pol. Quar.*, 42, vol. 13, p. 216-219.

c. NATIONAL SOCIALISM

4412. BAYNES (Norman H.). National Socialism before 1933. *History*, 42, vol. 26, p. 264-279.

4413. BUTLER (Rohan D'O.). The roots of National Socialism, 1783-1933. London, Faber, 41, in-8, 310 p., 12s. 6d. R : C. V. Wedgwood, *Int. Affairs*, 41, vol. 19, p. 311-313. *National R.*, 41, vol. 117, p. 468-469.

4414. GUILLEBAUD (C. W.). The social policy of Nazi Germany. London, Cambridge Univ. Press, 41, in-16, viii-134 p., 3s. 6d. (Current problems). R : A. Radomysler, *Economica*, 42, vol. 9, p. 105-107.

4415. HITLER (A.). The speeches of Adolf Hitler, April 1922-August 1939, tr. from German by N. Baynes. London, Oxford Univ. Press, 42, 2 vols. in-8, 1,992 p., 50s. R : *National R.*, 42, vol. 119, p. 364-365. N. Micklem, *Int. Affairs*, 42, vol. 19, p. 485-486.

4416. MICAUD (C. A.). The French right and Nazi Germany (1933-1939) : a study of public opinion. London, Cambridge Univ. Press, 44, in-8, x-256 p., 21s.

P

HISTORY OF COLONIAL, IMPERIAL AND INTERNATIONAL RELATIONS

§ 1. International and Imperial Affairs

a. GENERAL

4417. Canada and foreign affairs (with) Bibliography, by R. O. Mac-Farlane, E. Harrison, G. M. Carter. *Canad. hist. R.*, 41-45, vol. 22-26.

4417a. LEWIN (E.). The Pacific region : a bibliography of the Pacific and East Indian Islands, exclusive of Japan. London, Royal Empire Soc., 44, in-8, 76 p., 4s. (R. E. S. bibliogr., 11).

4418. NASATIR (A. P.). French activities in California : an archival calendar-guide. London, Oxford Univ. Press, 45, in-4, 576 p., 60s.

4419. BELGION (Montgomery). Economic war—with Hitler and with Napoleon. *Quar. R.*, 40, vol. 274, p. 233-247.

4420. BERNSTEIN (H.). Origins of inter-American interest, 1700-1812. London, Oxford Univ. Press, 45, in-8, 136 p., 13s. 6d.

4421. BESSARABIA, Facts and comments concerning, 1812-1940. London, Allen & Unwin, 42, in-8, 63 p., 2s.

4422. BREBNER (John Bartlet). North Atlantic triangle : the interplay of Canada, the United States and Great Britain. Toronto, Ryerson Press, 45, in-8, xxii-386 p., $5.50. (Relations of Canada and the U.S.). R : R. G. T(rotter), *Queen's Quar.*, 45, vol. 52, p. 506-509.

4423. CRANKSHAW (Edward). Russia and Britain. London, Collins, 44, in-8, 128 p., 8s. 6d. (The nations and Britain ser.). R : M. Beloff, *Int. Affairs*, 44, vol. 20, p. 584-585.

4424. CREIGHTON (D. G.). Canada in the English-speaking world. *Canad. hist. R.*, 45, vol. 26, p. 119-127.

4425. DARMSTAEDTER (F.). Germany and Europe, political tendencies from Frederick the Great to Hitler. London, Methuen, 45, in-8, vi-226 p., 12s. 6d. R : I. M. Massey, *Int. Affairs*, 45, vol. 21, p. 544-545.

4426. DULLES (F. R.). The road to Teheran : Russia and America, 1781-1943. London, Oxford Univ. Press, 44, in-8, 288 p., 16s. 6d.

4427. EBENSTEIN (William). The German record, a political portrait. Toronto, Oxford Univ. Press, 45, in-8, 334 p., $3.75. R : R. Flenley, *Int. J.*, 45, vol. 1, p. 84-85.

4428. FLENLEY (R.). Nationalism—the historical approach to the problem in Europe. *Canad. hist. Assoc. Rept.*, 43, p. 63-71.

4429. GAVIN (Catherine). Britain and France : a study of 20th-century relations. London, Cape, 41, in-8, 303 p., 10s. 6d. R : W. M. Jordan, *Int. Affairs*, 41, vol. 19, p. 339.

4430. GEE (H. L.). American England, an epitome of a common heritage. London, Methuen, 43, in-8, 181 p., (illus., map), 7s. 6d.

4431. GOOCH (G. P.). Studies in diplomacy and statecraft. London, Longmans, 42, in-8, vi-373 p., 12s. 6d. R : *Quar. R.*, 42, vol. 279, p. 235-236. *National R.*, 42, vol. 119, p. 272-273. *Pol. Quar.*, 42, vol. 13, p. 457-458. T. P. Conwell-Evans and L. B. Namier, *19th Century*, 43, vol. 133, p. 64-72. F. J. C. Hearnshaw, *J. comp. Legisl. int. Law*, 43, vol. 25, p. 92-93. W. N. Medlicott, *History*, 43, vol. 28, p. 106-108. B. H. Sumner, *Eng. hist. R.*, 44, vol. 59, p. 121-122.

4432. GRAVES (Philip). Briton and Turk. London, Hutchinson, 41, in-8,

260 p., (maps), 12s. 6d. R : A.T.W., *J. central asian Soc.*, 41, vol. 28, p. 368-371.

4433. GREENWOOD (Gordon). Early American-Australian relations from the arrival of the Spaniards in America to the close of 1830. London, Oxford Univ. Press, 44, in-8, 194 p., (illus.), 14s. R : J. A. McCallum, *Austral. Quar.*, 44, vol. 16, no. 3, p. 120-121. A. G. Dorland, *Canad. hist. R.*, 45, vol. 26, p. 447-448.

4434. HODGSON (Sir Robert). Britain and Russia. *J. central asian Soc.*, 43, vol. 30, p. 102-113.

4435. HOWAY (F. W.), SAGE (W. N.) and ANGUS (H. F.). British Columbia and the United States. London, Oxford Univ. Press, 43, in-4, xv-408 p., (maps), 16s. (Relations of Canada and the U.S.). R : W. P. M(orrell), *Eng. hist. R.*, 44, vol. 59, p. 427.

4436. HYAMSON (Albert). The British consulate in Jerusalem in relation to the Jews of Palestine. Pt. 2 : 1862-1914. London, Goldston, 41, in-4, lix-lxxxvii-295-592 p., 21s.

4437. IRELAND (G.). Boundaries, possessions and conflicts in Central and Northern America and the Caribbean. London, Oxford Univ. Press, 42, in-8, 448 p., (map), 19s.

4438. JACKSON (Mabel V.). European powers and South-East Africa : a study of international relations on the south-east coast of Africa, 1796-1856. London, Longmans, 42, in-8, 284 p., 21s. (Roy. Emp. Soc., imperial stud., 18). R : *Quar. R.*, 42, vol. 279, p. 237. E.H., *Geogr. J.*, 42, vol. 100, p. 183. *National R.*, 42, vol. 119, p. 275. F. M. Goadby, *J. comp. Legisl. int. Law*, 43, vol. 25, p. 97-98. J. E. Tyler, *Econ. Hist. R.*, 43, vol. 13, p. 140. H. R. Tate, *J. Roy. African Soc.*, 43, vol. 42, p. 40-41. W. P. Morrell, *History*, 43, vol. 28, p. 99-101. H. M. Robertson, *South African J. Econ.*, 43, vol. 11, p. 283-284.

4439. JERROLD (Douglas). Britain and Europe, 1900-1940. London, Collins, 41, in-8, 195 p., 7s. 6d.

4440. KOHN (Hans). World order in historical perspective. London, Oxford Univ. Press, 42, in-8, xiv-352 p., 12s. 6d. R : H. Lauterpacht, *Int. Affairs*, 43, vol. 19, p. 669-670.

4441. KONOVALOV (Serge). Russo-Polish relations, an historical survey. London, Cresset Press, 45, in-8, 90 p., 4s. R : M. Beloff, *Int. Affairs*, 45, vol. 21, p. 420.

4442. LAMB (F. B.). United States and United Kingdom. London, Harrap, 44, in-8, 244 p., 4s. (Harrap libr.).

4443. LANCTOT (Gustave) ed. Les canadiens français et leurs voisins du sud. Toronto, Ryerson Press, 41, in-8, ix-322 p., $3.00. (Relations of Canada and the U.S.). R : M.T., *Queen's Quar.*, 41, vol. 48, p. 319-320. E. H. Armstrong, *Canad. hist. R.*, 42, vol. 23, p. 75-76.

4444. LOGAN (R. W.). The diplomatic relations of the United States with Haiti, 1776-1891. London, Oxford Univ. Press, 41, in-8, 516 p., 22s. 6d.

4445. McINNIS (Edgar W.). The unguarded frontier : a history of American-Canadian relations. Toronto, McClelland, 42, in-8, viii-384 p., $3.75. R : R. G. T[rotter], *Queen's Quar.*, 44, vol. 51, p. 207-208.

4446. MACKENZIE (Norman). Argentina and Britain. *Pol. Quar.*, 45, vol. 16, p. 124-134.

4447. MARRIOTT (Sir J. A. R.). The Eastern question : an historical study in European diplomacy. 4th ed. London, Oxford Univ. Press, 40, in-8, xii-602 p., (maps), 8s. 6d. R : M. Bryant, *Int. Affairs*, 41, vol. 19, p. 213.

4448. MARRIOTT (Sir J. A. R.). Anglo-Russian relations, 1689-1943. London, Methuen, 44, in-8, 227 p., 8s. 6d. R : M. Beloff, *Int. Affairs*, 44, vol. 20, p. 440.

4449. MONTAGUE (L. L.). Haiti and the United States, 1714-1938. London, Cambridge Univ. Press, 40, in-8, 308 p., 18s.

4450. MOODIE (A. E.). The Italo-Yugoslav boundary, a study in political geography. London, Philip, 45, in-8, viii-242 p., (maps), 8s. 6d. R : H.G.S., *Geogr. J.*, 45, vol. 105, p. 134. A.G., *Geography*, 45, vol. 30, p. 127. R.G.D.L., *Int. Affairs*, 45, vol. 21, p. 546-547. A. J. P. Taylor, *Pol. Quar.*, 45, vol. 16, p. 364-366. *National R.*, 45, vol. 125, p. 347-348. A.G.O., *Scottish geogr. Mag.*, 45, vol. 61, p. 100.

4451. POPPER (Otto). The international regime of the Danube. *Geogr. J.*, 43, vol. 102, p. 240-253.

4452. PRATT (Sir John T.). Far Eastern politics, 1894-1941. *J. central asian Soc.*, 44, vol. 31, p. 126-136.

4453. PRATT (Sir J. T.). China and Britain. London, Collins, 44, in-8, 126 p., (plates, maps), 8s. 6d. (The nations and Britain ser.). R : E. Haward, *Asiatic R.*, 45, vol. 41, p. 109-110. E. Teichman, *Int. Affairs*, 45, vol. 21, p. 136.

4454. RITCHIE (Eric Moore). The unfinished war, the drama of the Anglo-German conflict in Africa in relation to the future of the British Empire. London, Eyre, 40, in-8, 349 p., (maps), 12s. 6d. R : R. N. Lyne, *J. Roy. African Soc.*, 40, vol. 39, p. 216-224.

4455. SFORZA (Count Carlo). Fifty years of war and diplomacy in the Balkans, tr. by J. G. C. Le Clercq. London, Oxford Univ. Press, 41, in-8, 205 p., 14s. R : V. Robinson, *Int. Affairs*, 42, vol. 19, p. 557-558.

4456. SHOTWELL (J. T.) and DEAK (F.). Turkey at the Straits, a short history. London, Macmillan, 40, in-8, xiv-196 p., 8s. 6d.

4457. SHUNZO (Sakamaki). Japan and the United States, 1790-1853. London, Kegan Paul, 40, in-8, 204 p., 8s. 6d. (Trans. of the Asiatic soc. of Japan, Ser. II, vol. 18).

4458. SMITH (Joe Patterson). A United states of North America—shadow or substance ? 1815-1915. *Canad. hist. R.*, 45, vol. 26, p. 109-118.

4459. STECHERT (Kurt). Thrice against England, tr. by E. and C. Paul. London, Cape, 45, in-8, 307 p., 12s. 6d. R : G. M. Routh, *Int. Affairs*, 45, vol. 21, p. 537.

4460. STRONG (C. F.). Dynamic Europe : a background of ferment and change. London, Univ. of Lond. Press, 45, in-8, 472 p., 16s.

4461. SULIMIRSKI (R.). Poland and Germany, past and future. Edinburgh, Oliver & Boyd, 42, in-8, 67 p., (map), 4s.

4462. TANSILL (Charles C.). Canadian-American relations, 1875-1911. London, Oxford Univ. Press; Toronto, Ryerson Press, 44, in-8, 528 p., (map), 23s. 6d.; $4.50. (Relations of Canada and the U.S.). R : A. R. M. Lower, *Canad. hist. R.*, 44, vol. 25, p. 449-451.

4463. TIMPERLEY (H. J.). Japan's southward expansion. *J. central asian Soc.*, 40, vol. 27, p. 408-414.

4464. TROTTER (R. G.). Relations of Canada and the United States. *Canad. hist. R.*, 43, vol. 24, p. 117-134.

4465. VAN ALSTYNE (Richard W.). New viewpoints in the relations of Canada and the United States. *Canad. hist. R.*, 44, vol. 25, p. 109-130.

4466. VAN ALSTYNE (R. W.). American diplomacy in action. London, Oxford Univ. Press, 44, in-8, 776 p., (maps), 30s.

4467. WADE (Mason). Some aspects of the relations of French Canada with the United States. *Canad. hist. Assoc. Rept.*, 44, p. 16-39.

b. BRITISH EMPIRE

4469. Canada and Commonwealth affairs (with) Bibliography, by J. R. Baldwin, R. G. Trotter, H. N. Fieldhouse. *Canad. hist. R.*, 40-45, vol. 21-26.

4470. LEWIN (Evans). Annotated bibliography of recent publications on Africa, south of the Sahara. London, Royal Empire Soc., 43, in-8, 104 p., 5s. (R.E.S. bibliogr., 9). R : H. Drake, *Africa*, 44, vol. 14, p. 356-357.

4471. LEWIN (E.). Best books on the British Empire, a bibliographical guide for students. London, Royal Empire Soc., 43, in-8, 90 p., 2s. 6d. (R.E.S. bibliogr., 10). R : H. Drake, *Africa*, 44, vol. 14, p. 356-357.

4472. —— —— 2nd ed. London, Royal Empire Soc., 45, in-8, 100 p., 4s. (R.E.S. bibliogr., 12).

4473. McDOUGALL (D. J.). Some recent books on the history of Britain and the Empire (with) Bibliography. *Canad. hist. R.*, 42, vol. 23, p. 315-320.

4474. BARKER (Ernest). Ideas and ideals of the British Empire. London, Cambridge Univ. Press, 41, in-8, vii-168 p., 3s. 6d. (Current problems). R : L. Woolf, *Pol. Quar.*, 41, vol. 12, p. 351-352. E.S., *United Empire*, 41, vol. 32, p. 138.

4475. BRADY (A.). Dominion nationalism and the Commonwealth. *Canad. J. Econ. pol. Sci.*, 44, vol. 10, p. 1-17.

4476. Cambridge History of the British Empire, ed. : J. H. Rose, A. P. Newton and E. A. Benians. Vol. 2 : The growth of the new Empire, 1783-1870. London, Cambridge Univ. Press, 40, in-8, xii-1068 p., 50s. R : W. P. Morrell, *History*, 41, vol. 25, p. 324-339. F. Clarke, *Int. Affairs*, 41, vol. 19, p. 271-272. L. Woolf, *Pol. Quar.*, 41, vol. 12, p. 229-230. C. R. Fay, *Econ. J.*, 41, vol. 51, p. 80-91.

E. L. Woodward, 19*th Century*, 41, vol. 129, p. 588-590. H. A. Wyndham, *J. Roy. African Soc.*, 41, vol. 40, p. 273-274. *Army Quar.*, 41, vol. 42, p. 179-183. G.R.C., *Geogr. J.*, 41, vol. 97, p. 63-64. H. A. Innis, *Eng. hist. R.*, 42, vol. 57, p. 512-515. A. G. L. Shaw, *Econ. Record*, 42, vol. 18, p. 242-244.

4477. ELTON (Lord). Imperial commonwealth. London, Collins, 45, in-8, 544 p., (maps), 21s.

4478. EMDEN (Paul H.). Empire days. London, Hutchinson, 42, in-8, 192 p., 9s. 6d.

4479. HEARNSHAW (F. J. C.). Sea power and Empire. London, Harrap, 40, in-8, 291 p., 10s. 6d. R : H.G.L., *Int. Affairs*, 40, vol. 19, p. 127. *National R.*, 40, vol. 115, p. 114.

4480. KNAPLUND (Paul). The British Empire, 1815-1939. London, Hamilton, 42, in-8, 850 p., 18s. R : W.E.C.II., *Queen's Quar.*, 42, vol. 49, p. 406-408. J. C. Beaglehole, *Hist. Stud. Australia N.Z.*, 43, vol. 2, p. 129-140. W. P. Morrell, *Int. Affairs*, 43, vol. 19, p. 591. M. G. Jones, *Econ. Hist. R.*, 44, vol. 14, p. 109-110.

4481. MARTIN (Chester). The British Commonwealth. *Canad. hist. R.*, 44, vol. 25, p. 131-150.

4482. NEWTON (A. P.). A hundred years of the British Empire. London, Duckworth, 40, in-8, 416 p., 15s. R : *United Empire*, 40, vol. 31, p. 335. E. A. Walker, *Int. Affairs*, 41, vol. 19, p. 207-208. W. P. M(orrell), *Eng. hist. R.*, 41, vol. 56, p. 676-677.

4483. —— —— New ed. London, Duckworth, 42, in-8, 416 p., 15s.

4484. SCHUYLER (R. L.). The fall of the old colonial system. London, Oxford Univ. Press, 45, in-8, 332 p., 12s. 6d.

4485. SOMERVELL (D. C.). The British Empire. London, Christopher, 42, in-8, 368 p., (illus., maps), 7s. 6d.

4486. SWEENEY (Joseph). The status of the Irish Free State in the British Commonwealth of nations. *Canad. Bar R.*, 44, vol. 22, p. 183-195.

4487. WALKER (E. A.). The British Empire, its structure and spirit. London, Oxford Univ. Press, 43, in-8, 256 p., 12s. 6d. R : W. P. Morrell, *Int. Affairs*, 43, vol. 19, p. 636-637. Hon. H. A. Wyndham, *J. Roy. African Soc.*, 43, vol. 42, p. 140-144. J. Simmons, *Africa*, 43, vol. 14, p. 221-222.

4488. WILLIAMS (Basil). The British Empire. 2nd ed. London, Milford, 44, in-8, 220 p., 3s. 6d. (Home Univ. libr.). R : W. P. Morrell, *Int. Affairs*, 44, vol. 20, p. 571-572.

4489. WILLIAMSON (James A.). A notebook of Empire history. London, Macmillan, 42, in-8, x-289 p., 10s.

4490. WILLIAMSON (J. A.). A short history of British expansion. 3rd ed. London, Macmillan, 43-45, 2 vols. in-8, xvi-367, xx-470 p., 36s. R (Vol. 2) : W. P. Morrell, *Int. Affairs*, 44, vol. 20, p. 430-431.

4491. WILLIAMSON (J. A.). Great Britain and the Empire, a discursive history. London, Black, 45, in-8, vii-213 p., (maps), 8s. 6d. R : W. P. Morrell, *Int. Affairs*, 45, vol. 21, p. 407.

4492. ZIMMERN (Sir Alfred). From the British Empire to the British Commonwealth. London, Longmans, 41, in-8, 52 p., 6d. (Pamph. on the Brit. Commonwealth, 3).

§ 2. Colonial History and Colonization

a. GENERAL

4493. BEAGLEHOLE (J. C.). The Colonial Office, 1782-1854. *Hist. Stud. Australia N.Z.*, 41, vol. 1, p. 170-189.

4494. BRANDER (J.). Tristan da Cunha, 1506-1902. London, Allen & Unwin, 40, in-8, viii-338 p., (maps),

12s. 6d. R : G. E. R. Deacon, *Geogr. J.*, 40, vol. 96, p. 356-357.

4495. DARLING (A. B.). Our rising Empire, 1763-1803. London, Oxford Univ. Press, 40, in-8, 595 p., 22s. 6d.

4496. DIXON (C. Willis). The colonial administrations of Sir Thomas Maitland. London, Longmans, 40, in-8, viii-274 p., 15s. R : R. P(ares), *Eng. hist. R.*, 41, vol. 56, p. 675.

4497. DOBIE (Edith). The dismissal of Lord Glenelg from the office of Colonial Secretary. *Canad. hist. R.*, 42, vol. 23, p. 280-285.

4498. KNORR (Klaus E.). British colonial theories, 1570-1850. Toronto, Univ. Press, 44, in-8, xix-429 p., $4.00. R : C. R. Fay, *Canad. J. Econ. pol. Sci.*, 45, vol. 11, p. 628-631. H. Burton, *Econ. Record*, 45, vol. 21, p. 115-118. L. F. Horsfall, *Int. Affairs*, 45, vol. 21, p. 405-406. A.E.P., *Queen's Quar.*, 45, vol. 52, p. 100. W. P. Morrell, *Econ. Hist. R.*, 45, vol. 15, p. 94-96. R. Coupland, *Econ. J.*, 45, vol. 55, p. 101-102. C. Leubuscher, *Economica*, 45, vol. 12, p. 261-262. F. Wolfson, *South African J. Econ.*, 45, vol. 13, p. 129-131.

4499. PARRY (J. H.). The Spanish theory of empire in the 16th century. London, Cambridge Univ. Press, 40, in-8, 75 p., 4s. 6d. R : R.T.D., *Eng. hist. R.*, 41, vol. 56, p. 162-163.

4500. PRIESTLEY (H. I.). France overseas through the Old Régime : a study of European expansion. London, Appleton, 40, in-8, xvii-393 p., 25s.

4501. SPECTOR (Margaret M.). The American department of the British Government, 1768-1782. London, Oxford Univ. Press, 40, in-8, 181 p., 12s. 6d. R : W. P. Morrell, *History*, 45, vol. 30, p. 106.

4502. WILLIAMS (E. Trevor). The Colonial Office in the thirties. *Hist. Stud. Australia N.Z.*, 43, vol. 2, p. 141-160.

b. EUROPE

c. ASIA

4503. Calendar of Persian correspondence : letters which passed between some of the Company's servants and Indian rulers and notables. Vol. 7 : 1785-7. Delhi, Govt. of India Press, 40, in-8, 466-xxxvii p., Rs. 20; 31s.

4504. DE SILVA (Colvin R.). Ceylon under the British occupation, 1795-1833. Colombo, Apothecaries Co., 42, 2 vols. in-8, Rs. 14. R : A.F.F., *History*, 43, vol. 28, p. 226. R. P(ares), *Eng. hist. R.*, 45, vol. 60, p. 430-431.

4505. HALL (D. G. E.). English relations with Burma, 1587-1886. *History*, 43, vol. 28, p. 182-200.

4506. JOUVEAU-DUBREUIL (G.). Dupleix. Pondichéry, Imprimerie de la Mission, 41, in-8. R : H. Wilberforce-Bell, *J. central asian Soc.*, 42, vol. 29, p. 148-149.

4507. PARKER (W. M.). A Scoto-Indian administrator [David Anderson]. *Army Quar.*, 44, vol. 48, p. 218-224.

4508. PHILIPS (C. H.). The East India Company, 1784-1834. Manchester, Univ. Press, 40, in-8, vii-374 p., 20s. (Manch. univ., hist. ser., 77). R : P. E. Roberts, *Eng. hist. R.*, 41, vol. 56, p. 143-146.

4509. PHILIPS (C. H.). The New East India Board and the Court of Directors, 1784. *Eng. hist. R.*, 40, vol. 55, p. 438-446.

4510. PHILIPS (C. H. and D.)· Alphabetical list of directors of the East India Company from 1758 to 1858. *J. asiatic Soc.*, 41, p. 325-336.

4511. Poona Residency correspondence. Vol. 7 : Poona affairs, 1801-10, ed. by R. B. Sardesai ; Extra vol. : Selections from Sir C. W. Malet's Letter-book, 1780-84, ed. by R. Sinh.

Bombay, Govt. Central Press, 39-40, 2 vols. in-8, xxxiii-579 p., 13s. ea. R (vol. 7) : P. E. Roberts, *Eng. hist. R.*, 41, vol. 56, p. 659-660 ; (extra vol.) : P. E. R(oberts), *Eng. hist. R.*, 41, vol. 56, p. 674 ; (vol. 7) : C. C. Davies, *J. asiatic Soc.*, 41, p. 378.

4512. REILLY (Sir Bernard). Aden and its links with India. *Asiatic R.*, 41, vol. 37, p. 65-80.

d. AFRICA

4513. EVANS-PRITCHARD (E. E.). A select bibliography of writings on Cyrenaica. *African Stud.*, 45, vol. 4, p. 146-150.

4514. ADAMS (W. J.). The narrative of Private Buck Adams, 7th (Princess Royal's) Dragoon Guards, on the eastern frontier of the Cape of Good Hope, 1843-1848, ed. by A. Gordon-Brown. Cape Town, Van Riebeeck Soc., 41, in-8, xx-316 p., (illus.), 10s. (Publ., 22). R : P. R. Kirby, *African Stud.*, 42, vol. 1, p. 72-74.

4515. ALLEN (Bernard M.). How Khartoum fell. *J. Roy. African Soc.*, 41, vol. 40, p. 327-334.

4516. ARDEN-CLOSE (Sir Charles). The Cross river country in 1895. *Geogr. J.*, 41, vol. 98, p. 189-197.

4517. AXELSON (Eric V.). South-East Africa, 1488-1530. London, Longmans, 40, in-8, xiv-306 p., (plates, maps), 15s. R : W. P. Morrell, *History*, 42, vol. 27, p. 86-87. *J. Roy. African Soc.*, 41, vol. 40, p. 85. G.H.T.K., *Geogr. J.*, 41, vol. 98, p. 50-51. E.P., *Eng. hist. R.*, 41, vol. 56, p. 513-514.

4518. BAGIŃSKI (Henryk). The 60th anniversary of Rogoziński's expedition to the Cameroons. *Geogr. J.*, 44, vol. 103, p. 72-76.

4518a. BLAKE (John W.). Europeans in West Africa, 1450-1560 : documents to illustrate the nature and scope of Portuguese enterprise in West Africa, the abortive attempt of Castilians to create an empire there, and the early English voyages to Barbary and Guinea. London, Quaritch, 42, 2 vols. in-8, xxxvi-461 p., (maps), 42s. (Hakluyt soc., works, 2nd ser., 86-87). R : J.S., *History*, 43, vol. 28, p. 114-115. F.E.D., *Mariner's Mirror*, 43, vol. 29, p. 183-184. H. R. Palmer, *J. asiatic Soc.*, 43, p. 278-280. M. J. Field, *Man*, 43, vol. 43, p. 119. E. G. R. Taylor, *Africa*, 45, vol. 15, p. 38-39.

4519. BRETT (B. L. W.). Makers of South Africa. London, Nelson, 45, in-8, 168 p., (illus.), 10s. 6d.

4520. BREYTENBACH (J. H.). Andries François du Toit, sy Aandeel in die Transvaalse Geskiedenis. *Archives Y.B. South Afr. Hist.*, 42 (43), vol. 2, p. 1-70.

4521. BURNS (Sir Alan C.). History of Nigeria. 3rd ed., revised. London, Allen & Unwin, 42, in-8, 360 p., (maps), 15s. R : L. J. Lewis, *Africa*, 45, vol. 15, p. 98-99. H. Swanzy, *Int. Affairs*, 43, vol. 19, p. 698-700.

4522. CAMPBELL (Alexander). Empire in Africa. London, Gollancz, 44, in-8, 160 p., 6s. R : A. J. Haile, *African Stud.*, 45, vol. 4, p. 47.

4523. CAVENDISH-BENTINCK (F.). Indians and the Kenya highlands. *National R.*, 40, vol. 114, p. 51-58.

4524. COOK (A. N.). British enterprise in Nigeria. London, Oxford Univ. Press, 43, in-8, 342 p., 21s. 6d.

4525. CORY (Sir George E.). The rise of South Africa to 1857. Vol. 6. *Archives Y.B. South Afr. Hist.*, 39 [40], vol. 1.

4526. CROWE (S. E.). The Berlin West-African conference, 1884-1885, ed. by A. P. Newton. London, Longmans, 42, in-8, 249 p., (maps), 15s. (Imperial stud. ser.). R : G.R.C., *Geogr. J.*, 42, vol. 100, p. 138.

National R., 42, vol. 119, p. 530-532. W. O. Henderson, *Econ. Hist. R.*, 43, vol. 13, p. 139. A.E.P., *Queen's Quar.*, 43, vol. 50, p. 431. A. W. Southall, *J. Roy. African Soc.*, 43, vol. 42, p. 86-87. W. P. Morrell, *History*, 43, vol. 28, p. 222-223.

4527. DAVIES (Joan). Palgrave and Damaraland. *Archives Y.B. South Afr. Hist.*, 42 (43), vol. 2, p. 91-204.

4528. EVANS-PRITCHARD (E. E.). The distribution of Sanusi lodges. *Africa*, 45, vol. 15, p. 183-187.

4529. EVANS-PRITCHARD (E. E.). The Sanusi of Cyrenaica. *Africa*, 45, vol. 15, p. 61-79.

4530. GALWAY (Sir Henry L.). West Africa fifty years ago. *J. Roy. African Soc.*, 42, vol. 41, p. 90-100.

4531. GLUCKMAN (Max). Some processes of social change illustrated from Zululand. *African Stud.*, 42, vol. 1, p. 243-260.

4532. GRAY (J. M.). A history of the Gambia. London, Cambridge Univ. Press, 40, in-8, x-508 p., 30s. R : *United Empire*, 40, vol. 31, p. 210-211. Sir H. R. Palmer, *J. Roy. African Soc.*, 40, vol. 39, p. 272-279. M. Perham, *Int. Affairs*, 40, vol. 19, p. 142. L. Woolf, *Pol. Quar.*, 41, vol. 12, p. 118-119. C. R. Fay, *Econ. J.*, 41, vol. 51, p. 113-115. A. P. N(ewton), *Eng. hist. R.*, 42, vol. 57, p. 396-397.

4533. GROBBELAAR (J. J. G.). Die Vrystaatse Republiek en die Basoetoevraagstuk. *Archives Y.B. South Afr. Hist.*, 39 [40], vol. 2.

4534. HALLIDAY (I. G.). Natal and indentured Indian immigration. *South African J. Econ.*, 40, vol. 8, p. 51-59.

4535. HASHIM (Ishag Eff.). The defence of Nyala, 1921, by Ishag Eff. Hashim, M. C. Wordsworth, E. R. Burgess. *Sudan Notes and Records*, 42, vol. 25, p. 81-108.

4536. HATTERSLEY (Alan F.). Portrait of a colony : the story of Natal. London, Cambridge Univ. Press, 40, in-8, 233 p., 8s. 6d. R : *United Empire*, 40, vol. 31, p. 312-313. *J. Roy. African Soc.*, 40, vol. 39, p. 379. W. P. M(orrell), *History*, 41, vol. 26, p. 91-92. C. R. Fay, *Econ. J.*, 41, vol. 51, p. 113-115. A. M. Hamilton, *South African J. Econ.*, 41, vol. 9, p. 90. J. E. Tyler, *Econ. Hist. R.*, 44, vol. 14, p. 107-108.

4537. HATTERSLEY (A. F.). The Natalians. London, Clark, 40, in-8, 200 p., (plates), 10s. 6d. R : E. A. W(alker), *Eng. hist. R.*, 41, vol. 56, p. 349.

4538. HEAD (M. E.). Inter-tribal history through tribal stories. *B. Uganda Soc.*, 44, no. 2, p. 13-17.

4539. HENDERSON (K. D. D.). Survey of the Anglo-Egyptian Sudan, 1898-1941. London, Sudan Govt. Office, 43, in-8, 21 p., 2s. R : P.W.T., *J. central asian Soc.*, 44, vol. 31, p. 223-224.

4540. HOLLIS (Christopher). Italy in Africa. London, Hamilton, 41, in-8, 253 p., (maps), 10s. 6d. R : A. V. Langton, *J. Roy. African Soc.*, 41, vol. 40, p. 364.

4541. HUTCHISON (G. S.). Cecil Rhodes : the man. London, Oxford Univ. Press, 44, in-8, 20 p., (illus.), 2s. 6d.

4542. JOHNSON (F.). Great days: the autobiography of an Empire pioneer. London, Bell, 40, in-8, xix-366 p., 18s.

4543. KUPER (Hilda). The development of a primitive nation (the Swazi from the 16th century). *Bantu Stud.*, 41, vol. 15, p. 339-368.

4544. LEWIN (Julius). The colour bar in the Copper Belt. Johannesburg, S. Afr. Inst. of Race Relations, 41, in-8, 20 p., 6d. (S. Afr. comm. on industr. relations). R : F. A. W. Lucas, *African Stud.*, 42, vol. 1, p. 69.

4545. LONG (B. K.). Drummond Chaplin : his life and times in Africa. London, Oxford Univ. Press, 41, in-8, 388 p., 18s. R : Sir D. O. Malcolm, *J. Roy. African Soc.*, 41, vol. 40, p. 262-272.

4546. LONGRIGG (S. H.). A short history of Eritrea. London, Oxford Univ. Press, 45, in-8, 196 p., 10s. 6d.

4547. McDONALD (J. G.). Rhodes: a heritage. London, Chatto & Windus, 43, in-8, 160 p., (illus.), 8s. 6d.

4548. MARAIS (J. S.). Maynier and the first Boer Republic. Cape Town, Miller, 44, in-8, xvi-162 p., 12s. 6d. R : H. M. Robertson, *S. African J. Econ.*, 44, vol. 12, p. 140-142. E. A. Walker, *Eng. hist. R.*, 45, vol. 60, p. 118-120. P. Lewsen, *African Stud.*, 45, vol. 4, p. 46-47.

4549. MOFFAT (Robert). Visit to Mzilikazi in 1835, ed. by P. R. Kirby. Johannesburg, Witwatersrand Univ. Press, 40, in-8, 38 p., 2s. 6d. (Bantu stud. monogr. ser., 1). R : W. M. Macmillan, *Int. R. Missions*, 41, vol. 30, p 575-576. L.F., *Bantu Stud.*, 41, vol. 15, p. 202-203.

4550. MOFFAT (R.). The Matabele journals of Robert Moffat. Vol. 1. 1829-1854, ed. by J. P. R. Wallis. London, Chatto, 45, in-8, 382 p., 30s. (Oppenheimer ser.).

4551. MOORE (Martin). Fourth shore : Italy's mass colonization of Libya. London, Routledge, 40, in-8, 233 p., 12s. 6d. R : B. Lewis, *Int. Affairs*, 40, vol. 19, p. 61-62. T. Philipps, *J. Roy. African Soc.*, 40, vol. 39, p. 129-133.

4552. MULLER (C. F. J.). Die Geskiedenis van die Vissery aan die' Kaap tot aan die middel van die 18e Eeu. *Archives Y.B. South Afr. Hist.*, 42 (43), vol. 1, p. 1-100.

4553. NADEL (S. F.). A black Byzantium : the kingdom of Nupe in Nigeria. London, Oxford Univ.

Press, 42, in-8, 436 p., (illus., maps), 25s.

4554. NEWMAN (E. W. P.). Britain and North-East Africa. London, Hutchinson, 40, in-8, 286 p., (illus.), 10s. 6d.

4555. PIETERSE (D. J.). Transvaal en Britse Susereiniteit, 1881-1884. *Archives Y.B. South Afr. Hist.*, 40, vol. 1, p. 257-344.

4556. PLESSIS (A. J. du). Die Republiek Natalia. *Archives Y.B. South Afr. Hist.*, 42 (43), vol. 1, p. 101-238.

4557. ROBERTSON (H. M.). The economic development of the Cape under Van Riebeeck. *South African J. Econ.*, 45, vol. 13, p. 1-17, 75-90, 170-184, 245-262.

4558. SCHAPERA (I.). A short history of the Bakgatla baga Kgafela of the Bechuanaland Protectorate. Cape Town, University School of African Studies, 42, in-8, 54 p., 5s. R : A. J. Haile, *African Stud.*, 43, vol. 2, p. 118-119. A. N. Tucker, *Africa*, 43, vol. 14, p. 150.

4559. SCHAPERA (I.). A short history of the BaNgwaketse. *African Stud.*, 42, vol. 1, p. 1-26.

4560. SCHAPERA (I.). Notes on the history of the Kaa. *African Stud.*, 45, vol. 4, p. 109-121.

4561. SCHUTTE (C. E. G.). Dr. John Philip's observations regarding the Hottentots of South Africa. *Archives Y.B. South Afr. Hist.*, 40 (41), 3rd year, pt. 1, p. 89-253.

4562. VANE (Michael). German atrocities in S.-W. Africa. *19th Century*, 40, vol. 128, p. 337-347.

4563. VENTER (P. J.). Landdros en Heemrade (1682-1827). *Archives Y.B. South Afr. Hist.*, 40 (41), 3rd year, pt. 2.

4564. WALKER (Eric A.). The Jameson raid. *Cambridge hist. J.*, 40, vol. 6, p. 283-306.

4565. WALKER (E. A.). Lord Milner and South Africa. London, Oxford Univ. Press, 43, in-8, 26 p., 2s.

4566. WHITEHEAD (G. O.). Mansfield Parkyns and his projected history of the Sudan. *Sudan Notes and Records*, 40, vol. 23, p. 131-138.

e. NORTH AMERICA

(i) UP TO 1763

4567. ADAIR (E. R.). The evolution of Montreal under the French regime. *Canad. hist. Assoc. Rept.*, 42, p. 20-41.

4568. ADAIR (E. R.). France and the beginnings of New France. *Canad. hist. R.*, 44, vol. 25, p. 246-278.

4569. ADAMS (J. T.) ed. Album of American history : colonial period. London, Scribner, 44, in-4, 411 p., 42s.

4570. BARKER (Charles Albro). The background of the Revolution in Maryland. London, Oxford Univ. Press, 40, in-8, x-419 p., 16s. (Yale hist. publ., misc. 38).

4571. BELTING (Natalia Maree). The French villages of the Illinois country. *Canad. hist. R.*, 43, vol. 24, p. 14-23.

4572. BOWES (F. P.). The culture of early Charlestown. London, Oxford Univ. Press, 43, in-8, 166 p., 15s. 6d.

4573. BURT (Alfred Leroy). The frontier in the history of New France. *Canad. hist. Assoc. Rept.*, 40, p. 93-99.

4574. CLARKE (T. W.). The bloody Mohawk. London, Macmillan, 40, in-8, xx-372 p., 12s. 6d.

4575. COMFORT (W. W.). William Penn, 1644-1718 : a tercentenary estimate. London, Oxford Univ. Press, 44, in-8, 196 p., 12s.

4576. DUNAWAY (W. F.). The Scotch-Irish of colonial Pennsylvania. London, Oxford Univ. Press, 45, in-8, 282 p., 18s. 6d.

4577. FAUTEUX (Aegidius). Les Chevaliers de Saint-Louis en Canada. Montréal, Ed. des Dix, 40, in-8, 252 p. R : H. Morisseau, *R. Univ. Ottawa*, 41, vol. 11, p. 130.

4578. FOULCHÉ-DELBOSC (Isabel). Women of New France. *Canad. hist. R.*, 40, vol. 21, p. 132-149.

4579. Fox (Dixon Ryan). Yankees and Yorkers. London, Oxford Univ. Press, 40, in-8, 237 p., 17s. (N.Y. Univ., Stokes foundation, Anson G. Phelps lectureship on early Amer. hist.).

4580. FRÉGAULT (Guy). Le régime seigneurial et l'expansion de la colonisation dans le bassin du Saint-Laurent au 18e siècle. *Canad. hist. Assoc. Rept.*, 44, p. 61-73.

4581. FRÉGAULT (G.). La civilisation de la Nouvelle France (1733-1744). Montréal, Soc. des Ed. Pascal, 44, in-8, 285 p. R : G. Lanctot, *Canad. hist. R.*, 45, vol. 26, p. 319-320.

4582. FRÉGAULT (G.). Iberville le Conquérant. Montréal, Soc. des Ed. Pascal, 44, in-8, 422 p., $3.00. R : B. Brouillette, *Canad. hist. R.*, 45, vol. 26, p. 193-194.

4583. FURNISS (O. C.). Some notes on newly-discovered fur posts on the Saskatchewan river. *Canad. hist. R.*, 43, vol. 24, p. 266-272.

4584. GILBERT (Sir Humphrey). The voyages and colonising enterprises of Sir Humphrey Gilbert, ed. by D. B. Quinn. London, The Society, 40, 2 vols. in-8, xxx+xiv-534 p., (illus., maps), 42s. (Hakluyt Soc., 2nd ser., vol. 83-84). R : *Geogr. J.*, 40, vol. 96, p. 443-444. E. G. R. Taylor, *Mariner's Mirror*, 40, vol. 26, p. 421-423. J. N. L. Baker, *Eng. hist. R.*, 44, vol. 59, p. 116-117.

4585. GIPSON (Lawrence Henry). A French project for victory short of a declaration of war, 1755. *Canad. hist. R.*, 45, vol. 26, p. 361-371.

4586. GODBOUT (Archange). Le Montigny de Schenectady. *B. Rech. hist.*, 43, vol. 49, p. 129-135.

4587. GREENE (L. J.). The negro in colonial New England, 1620-1776. London, King, 43, in-8, 384 p., 22s. 6d.

4588. INNIS (H. A.). Decentralization and democracy. *Canad. J. Econ. pol. Sci.*, 43, vol. 9, p. 317-330.

4589. JEFFERYS (Charles W.). The picture gallery of Canadian history. Vol. 1 : Discovery to 1763. Toronto, Ryerson Press, 42, in-8, xiv-268 p., $2.00. R : M. Barbeau, *Canad. hist. R.*, 43, vol. 24, p. 57-61.

4590. KEMMERER (D. L.). The path to freedom : the struggle for self-government in colonial New Jersey, 1703-1776. London, Oxford Univ. Press, 40, in-8, 384 p., 17s.

4591. LAFORCE (J.-Ernest). Monseigneur Calixte Marquis, colonisateur . . . *Canad. Cath. hist. Assoc. Rept.*, 43-44, vol. 11, Fr. Sect., p. 113-135.

4592. LANCTOT (G.). L'Acadie et la Nouvelle-Angleterre, 1603-1763. *R. Univ. Ottawa*, 41, vol. 11, p. 182-205, 349-370.

4593. LEECHMAN (Douglas). John Rastell and the Indians. *Queen's Quar.*, 44, vol. 51, p. 73-77.

4594. LONG (Morden H.). A history of the Canadian people. Vol. 1 : New France. Toronto, Ryerson Press, 43, in-8, xiv-376 p., $3.50. R : R.G.T., *Queen's Quar.*, 43, vol. 50, p. 307-309. A. R. M. Lower, *Canad. hist. R.*, 43, vol. 24, p. 304-306.

4595. LONN (E.). The colonial agents of the southern colonies. London, Oxford Univ. Press, 45, in-8, 446 p., 30s.

4598. MASSICOTTE (E.-Z.). Agathe de Saint Père, Dame Le Gardeur de Repentigny. *B. Rech. hist.*, 44, vol. 50, p. 202-207.

4599. MILLING (C. J.). Red Carolinians. London, Oxford Univ. Press, 41, in-8, 438 p., 18s.

4600. MORIN (Victor). Le vieux Montréal, fondation, développement, visite. Montréal, Ed. des Dix, 42, in-8, 43 p. R : G. Lanctot, *Canad. hist. R.*, 42, vol. 23, p. 416-418.

4601. MULLETT (Charles F.). James Abercromby and French encroachments in America. *Canad. hist. R.*, 45, vol. 26, p. 48-59.

4602. MURPHY (E. R.). Henry de Tonty, fur trader of the Mississippi. London, Oxford Univ. Press, 41, in-8, 149 p., 9s.

4603. RICH (E. E.) ed.   Minutes of the Hudson's Bay Company, 1671-74, ed. by E. E. Rich.   Toronto, Champlain Soc., 42, in-8, lxviii-276 p., subscribers only.   (Hudson's Bay Co. ser., 5). R : G.R.C., *Geogr. J.*, 43, vol. 102, p. 188-189. J. E. Tyler, *Econ. Hist. R.*, 43, vol. 13, p. 123-124. W. P. M(orrell), *Eng. hist. R.*, 44, vol. 59, p. 281-282. A. S. Morton, *Canad. hist. R.*, 44, vol. 25, p. 68-71. C. R. Fay, *Econ. J.*, 44, vol. 54, p. 109-113.

4604. RICHARD (J.-B.).   Un bourg de la vallée du Richelieu. *B. Rech. hist.*, 43, vol. 49, p. 50-57.

4605. ROY (Pierre-Georges).   Les épidémies à Québec [1640-1854]. *B. Rech. hist.*, 43, vol. 49, p. 204-215.

4606. R O Y (P.-G.).   Armand Laporte de Lalanne. *B. Rech. hist.*, 44, vol. 50, p. 161-169.

4607. ROY (P.-G.). Les officiers de Montcalm mariés au Canada. *B. Rech. hist.*, 44, vol. 50, p. 257-283, 289-302.

4608. SAUNDERS (R. M.). Coureur de Bois : a definition. *Canad. hist. R.*, 40, vol. 21, p. 123-131.

4609. SHIPTON (C. K.).   Roger Conant, a founder of Massachusetts. London, Oxford Univ. Press, 45, in-8, 188 p., (illus., maps), 16s. 6d.

4610. SMITH (E. H.).   Charles Carroll of Carrollton. London, Oxford Univ. Press, 43, in-8, 354 p., (illus.), 21s. 6d.

4611. WALLACE (P. A. W.). Conrad Weiser :   friend of colonist and Mohawk.   London, Oxford Univ. Press, 45, in-8, 662 p., 30s.

4612. WERTENBAKER (Thomas J.). Torchbearer of the Revolution, the story of Bacon's rebellion and its leader. London, Oxford Univ. Press, 41, in-8, 237 p., 11s. 6d.

4613. WERTENBAKER (T. J.).   The golden age of colonial culture. London, Oxford Univ. Press, 42, in-8, 171 p., 12s. 6d. (N.Y. univ., Stokes foundation, A. G. Phelps lect. on early Amer. hist.). R : R. Edwards, *Burlington Mag.*, 43, vol. 82, p. 52. R. P(ares), *Eng. hist. R.*, 43, vol. 58, p. 371-372. E. S. de B(eer), *History*, 43, vol. 28, p. 119-120.

4615. WOOD (R.).   The Pennsylvania Germans.   London, Oxford Univ. Press, 42, in-8, 307 p., 15s.

NORTH AMERICA

(*ii*) 1763-1783

4616. ROOT (Winfred Trexler). The American Revolution in new books and new light (with) Bibliography. *Canad. hist. R.*, 42, vol. 23, p. 308-315.

4617. ALDEN (J. R.).   John Stuart and the southern colonial frontier. London, Oxford Univ. Press, 44, in-8, 400 p., (maps), 22s. 6d.

4618. BOYD (Julian P.).   Anglo-American union : Joseph Galloway's plans to preserve the British Empire, 1774-1788.   London, Oxford Univ. Press, 41, in-8, 185 p., 9s. R : R. P(ares), *Eng. hist. R.*, 45, vol. 60, p. 279.

4619. BOYD (J. P.).   The declaration of independence, the evolution of the text.   London, Oxford Univ. Press, 45, in-4, 50 p., 23s. 6d.

4620. BRENNAN (E. E.). Plural office-holding in Massachusetts, 1760-1780 : its relation to the separation of departments of government. London, Oxford Univ. Press, 45, in-8, 242 p., 18s. 6d.

4621. DAVIDSON (Philip). Propaganda and the American Revolution, 1763-1783. London, Oxford Univ. Press, 41, in-8, xvi-460 p., 18s. R : A. H. Kelly, Canad. hist. R., 41, vol. 22, p. 202-203.

4622. FOSTER (G.). George Washington's world. London, Scribner, 42, in-4, x-348 p., 12s. 6d.

4623. GÉRARD (Conrad Alexandre). Despatches and instructions, 1778-1780 : correspondence of the first French minister to the United States with the Comte de Vergennes. Intr. and notes by J. J. Meng. London, Oxford Univ. Press, 40, in-8, 966 p., 36s. (Inst. fr. de Washington, hist. docs., extra vol.).

4624. GOTTSCHALK (L.). Lafayette and the close of the American Revolution. London, Cambridge Univ. Press, 42, in-8, xiv-458 p., (maps), 27s.

4625. GREENE (E. B.). The revolutionary generation, 1763-1790. London, Macmillan, 44, in-8, xvii-487 p., (illus.), 20s. (Hist. of Amer. life, vol. 4). R : M. Savelle, Canad. hist. R., 44, vol. 25, p. 439-440.

4626. HARPER (Lawrence A.) and ROOT (Winfred Trexler). Mercantilism and the American Revolution; The American Revolution reconsidered. Canad. hist. R., 42, vol. 23, p. 1-41.

4627. HART (F. H.). The valley of Virginia in the American Revolution, 1763-1789. London, Oxford Univ. Press, 42, in-8, 236 p., (plates, maps), 16s.

4628. JOHNSON (Cecil). British West Florida, 1763-1783. London, Oxford Univ. Press, 44, in-8, 270 p., (maps), 20s. R : R. P(ares), Eng. hist. R., 45, vol. 60, p. 277.

4629. KENNEY (James F.). Public records of the old province of Quebec, 1763-91. Trans. Roy. Soc. Canad., 40, 3rd ser., vol. 34, p. 87-133.

4630. KERR (Wilfred Brenton). The maritime provinces of British North America and the American Revolution. Sackville, N.B., Busy East Press, 41, in-8, 172 p., $3.00. R : C. Martin, Canad. hist. R., 42, vol. 23, p. 420-421.

4631. KNOLLENBERG (Bernhard). Washington and the Revolution, a reappraisal. London, Macmillan, 41, in-8, xvii-269 p., 12s. 6d.

4632. LUNDIN (L.). Cockpit of the Revolution : the war for independence in New Jersey. London, Oxford Univ. Press, 40, in-8, 463 p., 17s. R : C.T.A., Eng. hist. R., 42, vol. 57, p. 401.

4632a. MAHEUX (Arthur). Ton histoire est une épopée, 1 : Nos débuts sous le régime anglais. Québec, Charrier & Dougal, 41, in-8, vi-213 p., $1.00. R : A. L. Burt, Canad. hist. R., 41, vol. 22, p. 436-437.

4633. MILLER (J. C.). The origins of the American Revolution. London, Faber, 45, in-8, 372 p., 16s.

4634. NIXON (L. L.). James Burd, frontier defender, 1726-1793. London, Oxford Univ. Press, 41, in-8, 206 p., 9s. (Pennsylvania lives, 4).

4635. PATTERSON (Samuel W.). Horatio Gates, defender of American liberty. London, Oxford Univ. Press, 41, in-8, xiv-466 p., (plates), 21s. R : C.T.A., Eng. hist. R., 42, vol. 57, p. 531. Sir J. E. Edmonds, Army Quar., 42, vol. 43, p. 323-328.

NORTH AMERICA

(iii) AFTER 1783

4636. INNIS (H. A.). Recent books on the North American Arctic. Canad. hist. R., 44, vol. 25, p. 54-60.

4637. ALFRED (brother). The Windham or ' Oak Ridges ' settlement of

French Royalist refugees in York County, Upper Canada, 1798. *Canad. Cath. hist. Assoc. Rept.*, 39/40 (41), vol. 7, p. 11-26.

4638. ARNELL (William). French survivals in the Mississippi valley. *Geography*, 42, vol. 27, p. 89-94.

4639. ARTHUR (Sir George). The Arthur papers, being the papers mainly confidential, private and demi-official of Sir George Arthur, last lieutenant-governor of Upper Canada, in the MS. collections of the Toronto public libraries, ed. by C. R. Sanderson. Pt. 1. Toronto, Univ. Press, 43, in-4, 240 p., $1.00. R : F. Landon, *Canad. hist. R.*, 44, vol. 25, p. 321-323. A.M.W., *Queen's Quar.*, 44, vol. 51, p. 213-215.

4640. AUDET (Francis-J.). Les Députés de Montréal (ville et comtés), 1792-1867. Montréal, Ed. des Dix, 43, in-8, 455p., $2.00. R : E. Fabre-Surveyer, *Canad. hist. R.*, 44, vol. 25, p. 80-81.

4641. BAILEY (T. Melville). Dundurn and Sir Allan MacNab. *Ontario hist. Soc. Pap.*, 44, vol. 36, p. 94-104.

4642. BURT (A. L.). The United States, Great Britain and British North America, from the Revolution to the establishment of peace after the War of 1812. London, Oxford Univ. Press; Toronto, Ryerson Press, 40, in-4, vii-488 p., (maps), 15s.; $4.25. (Relations of Canada and the U.S.). R : *United Empire*, 41, vol. 32, p. 173. G.S.G., *Queen's Quar.*, 41, vol. 48, p. 194-195. R. Pares, *Eng. hist. R.*, 43, vol. 58, p. 240-241.

4643. CARTER (Herbert Dyson). Sea of destiny, the story of Hudson Bay, our undefended back door. London, Hutchinson, 40, in-8, ix-236 p., (plates, maps), 10s. 6d. R : *Geogr. J.*, 41, vol. 98, p. 160-161.

4644. CHILDS (F. S.). French refugee life in the United States, 1790-

1800. London, Oxford Univ. Press, 40, in-8, 229 p., 14s.

4645. CLARK (Mattie M.I.). The positive side of John Graves Simcoe. Toronto, Forward Publ. Co., 43, in-8, 121 p., $1.25. R : D. C. Masters, *Canad. J. Econ. pol. Sci.*, 45, vol. 11, p. 313.

4646. COLNETT (James). Journal aboard the ' Argonaut ' from April 26, 1789 to Nov. 3, 1791, ed. by F. W. Howay. Toronto, Champlain Society, 40, in-8, xxii-328 p., privately pr. (Publ. no. 26).

4647. COREY (Albert B.). The crisis of 1830-1842 in Canadian-American relations. Toronto, Univ. Press, 41; London, Oxford Univ. Press, 42, in-8, 219 p., $3.25; 11s. 6d. R : C. P. Stacey, *Canad. hist. R.*, 42, vol. 23, p. 206-207. S. D. Clark, *Canad. J. Econ. pol. Sci.*, 42, vol. 8, p. 307-311. W. P. M(orrell), *Eng. hist. R.*, 43, vol. 58, p. 253.

4648. COUPLAND (sir Reginald). The Durham report. Abridged ed. London, Oxford Univ. Press, 45, in-8, 256 p., 8s. 6d.

4649. DAVIDSON (Donald C.). Relations of the Hudson's Bay Company with the Russian American Company on the northwest coast, 1829-1867. *Brit. Columbia hist. Quar.*, 41, vol. 5, p. 33-51.

4650. DAWSON (Carl A.) and YOUNGE (Eva R.). Pioneering in the Prairie provinces : the social side of the settlement process. London; Toronto, Macmillan, 40, in-4, xi-338 p., (maps), 20s.; $4.50. (Can. frontiers of settlement, vol. 8). R : C. R. Fay, *Canad. J. Econ. pol. Sci.*, 41, vol. 7, p. 120-122. G. L. Wood, *Econ. Record*, 41, vol. 17, p. 275-278.

4651. DRAPER (W. N.). Pioneer surveys and surveyors in the Fraser Valley. *Brit. Columbia hist. Quar.*, 41, vol. 5, p. 215-220.

4652. ELLIOTT (Sophy L.). The women pioneers of North America. Gardenvale, Quebec, Garden City Press, 41, in-8, xviii-299 p. R : R. M. Saunders, *Canad. hist. R.*, 43, vol. 24, p. 76-77.

4653. FLEMING (C. A.). Pioneer settlers walk 130 miles. *Ontario hist. Soc. Pap.*, 43, vol. 35, p. 14-24.

4654. FLEMING (R. Harvey) ed. Minutes of Council, Northern Department of Rupert Land, 1821-31. Toronto, Champlain Soc., 40, in-8, lxxvii-480 p., subscribers only. (Hudson's Bay Co. ser., 3). R : J. E. Tyler, *Econ. Hist. R.*, 43, vol. 13, p. 123-124. W. P. M(orrell), *Eng. hist. R.*, 42, vol. 57, p. 534-535. C. R. Fay, *Econ. J.*, 42, vol. 52, p. 82-84. W. E. Ireland, *Brit. Columbia hist. Quar.*, 41, vol. 5, p. 307-308. J.L.M., *History*, 41, vol. 26, p. 157-158. G. L. Nute, *Canad. hist. R.*, 41, vol. 22, p. 441-442.

4655. FRASER RIVER GOLD RUSH. Two narratives of the Fraser River gold rush. 1. Extracts from Friesach *Ein Ausglug nach Britisch-Columbien im Jahre* 1858; 2. Letter from Charles G. Major, Fort Hope, Sept. 20, 1859. *Brit. Columbia hist. Quar.*, 41, vol. 5, p. 221-231.

4656. FRIGGE (A. St.-L.). The two Kenelm Chandlers. *B. Rech. hist.*, 43, vol. 49, p. 108-113.

4657. GATES (Lillian F.). The Legislative Council of Upper Canada, 1815-1816. *Ontario hist. Soc. Pap.*, 43, vol. 25, p. 25-28.

4658. GRAHAM (Gerald S.). Sea power and British North America, 1783-1820 : a study in British colonial policy. London, Oxford Univ. Press, 41, in-8, xii-302 p., (maps), 15s. (Harvard hist. stud., vol. 46). R : R.G.T., *Queen's Quar.*, 43, vol. 50, p. 313-315. C. R. Fay, *Econ. J.*, 43, vol. 53, p. 96-98. *Mariner's Mirror*, 42, vol. 28, p. 254. R. Pares, *Eng. hist. R.*, 44, vol. 59, p. 424-425.

4659. HARVEY (D. C.). A blue print for Nova Scotia in 1818, ed. by D. C. Harvey. *Canad. hist. R.*, 43, vol. 24, p. 397-409.

4660. HEAD (Sir Edmund). Memorandum of 1857 on maritime union : a lost confederation document (ed. by A. R. Stewart). *Canad. hist. R.*, 45, vol. 26, p. 406-419.

4661. HOWAY (F. W.), SAGE (W. N.) and ANGUS (H. F.). British Columbia and the United States : the north Pacific slope from fur trade to aviation. London, Oxford Univ. Press, 43, in-8, 424 p., (map), 16s. (Relations of Canada and the U.S.). R : H. A. Innis, *Canad. hist. R.*, 43, vol. 24, p. 311-312. W. T. Easterbrook, *Canad. J. Econ. pol. Sci.*, 43, vol. 9, p. 249-252.

4662. IRELAND (Willard E.). James Douglas and the Russian American Company, 1840. *Brit. Columbia hist. Quar.*, 41, vol. 5, p. 53-66.

4663. IRELAND (W. E.). Preconfederation defence problems of the Pacific colonies. *Canad. hist. Assoc. Rept.*, 41, p. 41-54.

4664. JEFFERYS (C. W.) and McLEAN (T. W.). The picture gallery of Canadian history. Vol. 2 : 1763-1830. Toronto, Ryerson Press, 45, in-8, xviii-271 p., $2.00. R : R. H. Hubbard, *Canad. hist. R.*, 45, vol. 26, p. 451-453. J.F., *Canad. Art*, 45, vol. 2, p. 222-223. *Queen's Quar.*, 45, vol. 52, p. 233.

4665. JENSEN (V.). Lafontaine and the Canadian union. *Canad. hist. R.*, 44, vol. 25, p. 6-19.

4666. JURY (Wilfrid). Old Fairfield on the Thames (Ontario). *Canad. hist. R.*, 44, vol. 25, p. 409-416.

4667. KINCHEN (Oscar A.). The Stephen-Russell reform in official tenure. *Can. hist. R.*, 45, vol. 26, p. 382-391.

4668. KOLEHMAINEN (John Ilmari). Harmony Island : a Finnish Utopian venture in British Columbia. *Brit. Columbia hist. Quar.*, 41, vol. 5, p. 111-124.

4669. LANCTOT (Gustave) ed. The Oakes collection : new documents by Lahontan concerning Canada and Newfoundland. Ottawa, King's Printer, 40, in-8, 78 p., $1.00. (Public archives of Canada).

4670. LANDON (Fred). Western Ontario and the American frontier. London, Oxford Univ. Press, 41, in-8, xiii-305 p., 16s. (Relations of Canada and the U.S.). R : F. H. Underhill, *Canad. hist. R.*, 42, vol. 23, p. 76-78. S. D. Clark, *Canad. J. Econ. pol. Sci.*, 42, vol. 8, p. 307-311. G. Taylor, *Int. Affairs*, 43, vol. 19, p. 687. W. P. M(orrell), *Eng. hist. R.*, 43, vol. 58, p. 373-374.

4671. LANGTON (H. H.). The commission of 1885 to the North-West Territories. *Canad. hist. R.*, 44, vol. 25, p. 38-53.

4672. LAYTON (C. M.). Canadian refugee lands in Ohio. *Canad. hist. R.*, 43; vol. 24, p. 377-380.

4673. LONG (Dorothy E. T.). The elusive Mr. Ellice. *Canad. hist. R.*, 42, vol. 23, p. 42-57.

4674. MACDONELL (Miles). Captain Miles Macdonell's ' Journal of a jaunt to Amherstburg ' in 1801, ed. by W. S. Wallace. *Canad. hist. R.*, 44, vol. 25, p. 166-176.

4675. McDOUGALL (D. J.). Lord John Russell and the Canadian crisis, 1837-1841. *Canad. hist. R.*, 41, vol. 22, p. 369-388.

4676. McINNIS (Edgar W.). The unguarded frontier : a history of American-Canadian relations. Toronto, McClelland, 42, in-8, 384 p., $3.75. R : J. W. Pratt, *Canad. hist. R.*, 43, vol. 24, p. 198-199.

4677. MACLEOD (J. E. A.). Piegan Post and the Blackfoot trade. *Canad. hist. R.*, 43, vol. 24, p. 273-279.

4678. McLINTOCK (A. H.). The establishment of constitutional government in Newfoundland, 1783-1832, a study of retarded colonisation. London, Longmans, 41, in-8, xii-246 p., 15s. (Imperial stud., 17). R : J. L. M(orison), *History*, 41, vol. 26, p. 88-89. J. H. Simpson, *Int. Affairs*, 41, vol. 19, p. 272-273. F. J. C. Hearnshaw, *J. comp. Legisl. int. Law*, 41, pt. 4, p. 203. G.R.C., *Geogr. J.*, 41, vol. 98, p. 161-162. G. Neuendorff, *Economica*, 41, vol. 8, p. 338-339.

4679. McLOUGHLIN (John). Letters from Fort Vancouver to the Governor and Committee (Hudson's Bay Company), ed. by E. E. Rich. Ser. 1-3, 1825-46. Toronto, Champlain Soc., 41-44, 3 vols. in-8, cxxviii-374, xlix-427, lxiii-341 p., subscribers only. (Hudson's Bay Co. ser., 4, 6, 7). R (Ser. 1) : E.W.G., *Geogr. J.*, 43, vol. 102, p. 83-84. J. E. Tyler, *Econ. Hist. R.*, 43, vol. 13, p. 123-124. E. McInnis, *Canad. hist. R.*, 43, vol. 24, p. 203-204. W. P. M(orrell), *History*, 44, vol. 59, p. 125-126. A.M.W., *Queen's Quar.*, 44, vol. 51, p. 457-460. (Ser. 2) : E. McInnis, *Canad. hist. R.*, 45, vol. 26, p. 195-196. W. P. M(orrell), *Eng. hist. R.*, 45, vol. 60, p. 432-433. E.W.G., *Geogr. J.*, 45, vol. 105, p. 216-217. A.M.W., *Queen's Quar.*, 45, vol. 52, p. 484-486.

4680. MAHEUX (Arthur). Durham et la nationalité canadienne-française. *Canad. hist. Assoc. Rept.*, 43, p. 19-24.

4681. Manifestes électoraux de 1792 [in Quebec]. *B. Rech. hist.*, 40, vol. 46, p. 97-103.

4681a. MANNING (Helen Taft). The Civil List of Lower Canada. *Canad. hist. R.*, 43, vol. 24, p. 24-47.

4682. MARION (Séraphin). Les lettres canadiennes d'autrefois, 3 :

1806-1837. Ottawa, Ed. de l'Univ., 42, in-8, 208 p., $1.00.

4683. MARION (S.). La dictature et le Canada français de 1800. *R. Univ. Ottawa*, 41, vol. 11, p. 319-337, 444-460.

4684. MARTIN (Raoul). Le rôle du clergé pendant l'insurrection de 1837. *Canad. Cath. hist. Assoc. Rept.*, 41-42, vol. 9, Fr. Sect., p. 89-93.

4685. MORTON (Arthur S.). Sir George Simpson : overseas Governor of the Hudson's Bay Company. Toronto, Dent, 44, in-8, xii-310 p., $4.50. R : W. L. Morton, *Canad. hist. R.*, 45, vol. 26, p. 321-322.

4686. MURRAY (Elsie McLeod). An Upper Canada ' bush business ' in the fifties. *Ontario hist. Soc. Pap.*, 44, vol. 36, p. 41-47.

4687. PRITCHETT (John Perry). The Red River valley, 1811-1849 : a regional study. London, Oxford Univ. Press, 42, in-8, 317 p., (map), 18s. 6d. (Relations of Canada and the U.S.). A. S. Morton, *Canad. hist. R.*, 43, vol. 24, p. 71-72. W. J. Waines, *Canad. J. Econ. pol. Sci.*, 43, vol. 9, p. 252-254. W. P. M(orrell), *Eng. hist. R.*, 45, vol. 60, p. 280-281.

4688. PRITCHETT (J. P.) and HOROWITZ (Murray). Five ' Selkirk ' letters. (Notes and documents). *Canad. hist. R.*, 41, vol. 22, p. 159-167.

4689. PRITCHETT (J. P.) and WILSON (F. J.). A winter at Hudson Bay, 1811-12. *Canad. hist. R.*, 43, vol. 24, p. 1-13.

4690. ROBINSON (Percy J.). Yonge Street and the North West Company. *Canad. hist. R.*, 43, vol. 24, p. 253-265.

4691. ROME (David). The first two years : a record of the Jewish pioneers on Canada's Pacific coast, 1858-60. Montreal, Caiserman, 42, in-8, 120 p., $1.50. R : W. N. Sage, *Canad. hist. R.*, 43, vol. 24, p. 73-74.

4692. SANDERSON (Charles R.). Some notes on Lord Sydenham. *B. John Rylands Library*, 41, vol. 25, p. 165-188.

4693. SCOTT (W. L.). Glengarry's representatives in the Legislative Assembly of Upper Canada. Pt. 2. *Canad. Cath. hist. Assoc. Rept.*, 39/40 (41), vol. 7, p. 27-42.

4694. SISSONS (C. B.). Four early letters of Egerton Ryerson. *Canad. hist. R.*, 42, vol. 23, p. 58-64.

4695. SISSONS (C. B.). Ryerson and the elections of 1844. *Canad. hist. R.*, 42, vol. 23, p. 157-176.

4696. STANLEY (George F. G.). Documents relating to the Swiss immigration to Red River in 1821. (Notes and documents). *Canad. hist. R.*, 41, vol. 22, p. 42-50.

4697. SUMNER (Elsie Graham). Activities of Canadian patriots in the Rochester district, 1837-1838. *Ontario hist. Soc. Pap.*, 44, vol. 36, p. 28-32.

4698. WALDIE (Jean H.). Pioneer days in Brant county. *Ontario hist. Soc. Pap.*, 43, vol. 35, p. 56-63.

4699. WALLACE (W. S.). The early history of Muskoka. *Queen's Quar.*, 42, vol. 49, p. 247-250.

4700. WOODHOUSE (Thomas Roy). A diary for the year 1827. *Ontario hist. Soc. Pap.*, 44, vol. 36, p. 21-27.

4701. WRIGHT (Esther Clark). The Miramichi : a study of the New Brunswick river and of the people who settled along it. Sackville, N.B., 44, in-8, 79 p., $1.25. R : R. G. T[rotter], *Queen's Quar.*, 44, vol. 51, p. 456-457. A. G. Bailey, *Canad. hist. R.*, 45, vol. 26, p. 74-75.

4702. WRIGHT (E. C.). The settlement of New Brunswick : an advance toward democracy. *Canad. hist. Assoc. Rept.*, 44, p. 53-60.

f. WEST INDIES. CENTRAL AND SOUTH AMERICA

4703. AITON (Arthur S.). Latin-American frontiers. *Canad. hist. Assoc. Rept.*, 40, p. 100-104.

4704. CADBURY (Henry J.). A Quaker account of Barbados in 1718. *J. Barbados Mus.*, 43, vol. 10, p. 118-124.

4705. CROUSE (N. M.). French pioneers in the West Indies, 1624-1664. London, Oxford Univ. Press, 4o, in-8, 294 p., 17s. 6d.

4706. CROUSE (N. M.). The French struggle for the West Indies, 1665-1713. London, Oxford Univ. Press, 44, in-8, 332 p., (illus.), 26s. 6d. R : H. B. L. Hughes, *Canad. hist. R.*, 44, vol. 25, p. 437-438.

4707. Extracts from ' The Barbadian ' newspaper, 1837-1846. *J. Barbados Mus.*, 40-45, vol. 7-12.

4708. Extracts from wills relating to the West Indies recorded in England. *J. Barbados Mus.*, 44-45, vol. 11-12.

4709. FARRAR (P. A.). The Jews in Barbados. *J. Barbados Mus.*, 42, vol. 9, p. 130-133.

4710. Governors' residences. *J. Barbados Mus.*, 43, vol. 10, p. 152-162.

4711. HASKELL (H. N.). Notes on the foundation and history of Harrison College. *J. Barbados Mus.*, 41, vol. 8, p. 186-193; vol. 9, p. 3-15, 59-81.

4712. HENDERSON (Gavin B.). German colonial projects on the Mosquito Coast, 1844-1848. *Eng. hist. R.*, 44, vol. 59, p. 257-271.

4713. HOLLIS (Sir Claud). A brief history of Trinidad under the Spanish crown. Trinidad, Historical Soc., 41, in-8, xiii-108 p., 8s. 4d. (obtainable K. S. Wise, 18 Greenhill, Hampstead, N.W.3). R : *United Empire*, 41, vol. 32, p. 173.

4714. JACOBS (H. P.). The untapped sources of Jamaican history. *Jamaican hist. R.*, 45, vol. 1, p. 92-98.

4715. LUCAS (Nathan). The Lucas manuscript volumes in the Barbados public library. *J. Barbados Mus.*, 42-45, vol. 9-12.

4717. MACGILLIVRAY (J. W.). ' Matters relating to the islands of Barbados and Tobago (1689-1699) '; extracted from publications of the Historical Society of Trinidad and Tobago. *J. Barbados Mus.*, 45, vol. 12, p. 122-125.

4718. McKINSTRY (W. L.). Bowen of Barbados. *J. Barbados Mus.*, 41, vol. 8, p. 47-66.

4719. MADARIAGA (S. de). Hernán Cortés : conqueror of Mexico. London, Hodder & Stoughton, 42, in-8, 554 p., 21s. R : R. C. E. Long, *Man*, 43, vol. 43, p. 23.

4720. MUHLENFELD (August). The Dutch West Indies in peace and war. *Int. Affairs*, 44, vol. 20, p. 81-93.

4721. PAGET (Hugh). The free village system in Jamaica. *Jamaican hist. R.*, 45, vol. 1, p. 31-48.

4722. PARRY (J. H.). The audiencia of New Galicia in the 16th century. *Cambridge hist. J.*, 40, vol. 6, p. 263-282.

4723. PIETERSZ (J. L.). The last Spanish governor of Jamaica. *Jamaican hist. R.*, 45, vol. 1, p. 24-30.

4724. PIETERSZ (J. L.). Spanish documents relating to Jamaica, tr. with notes. *Jamaican hist. R.*, 45, vol. 1, p. 100-115.

4725. POYER (John). John Poyer's Letter to Lord Seaforth. *J. Barbados Mus.*, 41, vol. 8, p. 150-165.

4726. PRITCHETT (John Perry). Selkirk's views on British policy toward the Spanish-American colonies, 1806. *Canad. hist. R.*, 43, vol. 24, p. 381-396.

4727. SHERLOCK (Philip). Jamaica in 1858 : an account of the original MS. journal of a visit. *Jamaican hist. R.*, 45, vol. 1, p. 83-91.

4728. SHILSTONE (E. M.). Some records of the Trent, Carleton, and Cumberbatch families of Barbados. *J. Barbados Mus.*, 41, vol. 9, p. 32-50.

4729. SHILSTONE (E. M.). Barbados in the year 1840. *J. Barbados Mus.*, 40, vol. 8, p. 3-12.

4730. SHILSTONE (E. M.). Nicholas plantation and some of its associations. *J. Barbados Mus.*, 42, vol. 9, p. 120-124.

4731. Some records of the House of Assembly of Barbados. *J. Barbados Mus.*, 43-45, vol. 10-12.

4732. T. (R. W. E.). An historical review of the rainfall of Barbados. *J. Barbados Mus.*, 44, vol. 11, p. 149-156.

4733. WILLIAMS (R. Bryn). Cymry Patagonia. (The Welsh of Patagonia). Aberystwyth, Gwasg Aberystwyth, 42, in-8, 152 p., 4s.

4734. WILLIAMS (James). Dutch plantations on the banks of the Berbice and Canje rivers in the Colony of British Guiana. Georgetown, Daily Chronicle, 40, in-8, 198-xxxiii p. R : J. L. M[yres], *Man,* 44, vol. 44, p. 29.

4735. YOUNG (J. G.). The beginnings of civil government in Jamaica. *Jamaican hist. R.*, 45, vol. 1, p. 49-65.

4736. ZAVALA (Silvio). New viewpoints on the Spanish colonization of America. London, Oxford Univ. Press, 43, in-8, 118 p., 8s. R : W. P. M(orrell), *Eng. hist. R.*, 45, vol. 60, p. 271.

g. AUSTRALASIA

4737. BARNARD (Marjorie F.). Macquarie's world. Sydney, Australian Limited Ed. Soc., 42, in-4, 230 p., 42s., members only. R : C. H. Currey, *Hist. Stud. Australia N.Z.*, 43, vol. 2, p. 202-204.

4738. BURTON (A.). Some early Western Australian diaries. *Hist. Stud. Australia N.Z.*, 40, vol. 1, p. 85-90.

4739. BURTON (A.). Convicts in Western Australia. *J. West. Austral. hist. Soc.*, 43, vol. 5, p. 16-25.

4740. CHURCHWARD (L. G.). Australian-American relations during the gold rush. *Hist. Stud. Australia N.Z.*, 42, vol. 2, p. 11-24.

4741. CLYDE COMPANY. Clyde Company papers : prologue, 1821-1835, ed. by P. L. Brown. London, Oxford Univ. Press, 41, in-8, 260 p., (plates), 8s. 6d.

4742. COWAN (James). Settlers and pioneers. Wellington, Dept. of Internal Affairs, 40, in-8, 153 p., 5s. (N.Z. centennial surveys). R : B., *J. public Admin. N. Zealand*, 40, vol. 3, p. 57. S. R. Smith, *Hist. Stud. Australia N.Z.*, 40, vol. 1, p. 142-143.

4743. DALEY (Charles). A history of South Melbourne to the year 1938. Melbourne, Robertson & Mullens, 40, in-8, xxiii-407 p., (illus.), 12s. 6d. R : G. F. James, *Hist. Stud. Australia N.Z.*, 41, vol. 1, p. 205-207.

4744. DIXSON (Sir William). Madame Rose de Freycinet's visit to Sydney, Nov. 18 to Dec. 26, 1819, tr. by Sir W. Dixson. *Roy. Austral. hist. Soc. J.*, 44, vol. 30, p. 326-339.

4745. DOWD (B. T.). Lake Cargelligo : beginnings of district and village. *Roy. Austral. hist. Soc. J.*, 43, vol. 29, p. 197-215.

4746. DRISCOLL (Frank). Macquarie's administration of the convict system. *Roy. Austral. hist. Soc. J.*, 41, vol. 27, p. 373-433.

4747. ELKIN (A. P.). The place of Sir Hubert Murray in native administration. *Austral. Quar.*, 40, vol. 12, no. 3, p. 23-35.

4748. ELLIOTT (Brian). James Hardy Vaux, a literary rogue in Australia. Adelaide, Wakefield Press, 44, in-8, 28 p., (illus.), 5s. R : L. F. Fitzhardinge, *Hist. Stud. Australia N.Z.*, 45, vol. 3, p. 148-149.

4749. ELLIS (M. H.). Some aspects of the Bigge commission of inquiry into the affairs of New South Wales, 1819-1821. *Roy. Austral. hist. Soc. J.*, 41, vol. 27, p. 93-126.

4750. ELLIS (M. H.). Governor Lachlan Macquarie. *Roy. Austral. hist. Soc. J.*, 42, vol. 28, p. 375-475.

4751. FITZPATRICK (Kathleen). Mr. Gladstone and the Governor, the recall of Sir John Eardley-Wilmot from Van Diemen's Land, 1846. *Hist. Stud. Australia N.Z.*, 40, vol. 1, p. 31-45.

4752. FLETCHER (C. Brunsdon). Australia and the Pacific, 1788 to 1885. *Roy. Austral. hist. Soc. J.*, 42, vol. 28, p. 157-184.

4753. FLETCHER (C. Brunsdon). Australia and the Indian ocean. *Hist. Stud. Australia N.Z.*, 43, vol. 2, p. 255-264.

4754. FOXCROFT (E. J. B.). The New South Wales aborigines' protectorate, Port Phillip district, 1838-50. Pt. 1-2. *Hist. Stud. Australia N.Z.*, 40-41, vol. 1, p. 76-84, 157-167.

4755. FOXCROFT (E. J. B.). Australian native policy : its history especially in Victoria. Melbourne, Univ. Press, 41, in-8, 168 p., 10s. R : A. P. Elkin, *Austral. Quar.*, 41, vol. 13, no. 4, p. 105-107; *Hist. Stud. Australia N.Z.*, 43, vol. 2, p. 274-279.

4756. GODDARD (R. H.). Captain Thomas Raine of the ' Surry ', 1795-1860. *Roy. Austral. hist. Soc. J.*, 40, vol. 26, p. 277-316.

4757. GREENWOOD (Gordon). The contact of American whalers, sealers and adventurers with the New South Wales settlement. *Roy. Austral. hist. Soc. J.*, 43, vol. 29, p. 133-156.

4758. HALL (T. D. H.). Captain Joseph Nias and the Treaty of Waitangi : a vindication. New ed. Wellington, Whitcombe & Tombs, 44, in-8, 96 p., (illus.), 7s. 6d.

4759. HANLIN (Frank). Sidelights on Dr. John Dunmore Lang. *Roy. Austral. hist. Soc. J.*, 44, vol. 30, p. 221-249.

4760. HASLUCK (P.). Black Australians; a survey of native policy in Western Australia, 1829-1897. London, Oxford Univ. Press, 43, in-8, 226 p., (map), 10s. 6d. R : A. P. Elkin, *Hist. Stud. Australia N.Z.*, 43, vol. 2, p. 274-279.

4761. HAVARD (Olive). Lady Franklin's visit to New South Wales, 1839; extracts from letters to Sir John Franklin. *Roy. Austral. hist. Soc. J.*, 43, vol. 29, p. 280-334.

4762. HAVARD (O.). Mrs. Felton Mathew's Journal. *Roy. Austral. hist. Soc. J.*, 43, vol. 29, p. 88-128, 162-195, 217-244.

4763. HENEY (Helen). The first generation of Australians. *Roy. Austral. hist. Soc. J.*, 43, vol. 29, p. 157-161.

4764. JERVIS (James). Alexander Berry, the laird of Shoalhaven. *Roy. Austral. hist. Soc. J.*, 41, vol. 27, p. 18-87.

4765. JERVIS (J.). Settlement in the Picton and The Oaks district (of New South Wales). *Roy. Austral. hist. Soc. J.*, 41, vol. 27, p. 276-298.

4766. JERVIS (J.). Illawarra : a century of history, 1788-1888. *Roy. Austral. hist. Soc. J.*, 42, vol. 28, p.65-107, 129-156, 193-248, 273-303, 353-374.

4766a. JERVIS (J.). Peat's Ferry and the route to the North. *Roy. Austral. hist. Soc. J.*, 43, vol. 29, p. 244-252.

4767. JOYCE (Alfred). A homestead history : the reminiscences and letters of Alfred Joyce of Plaistow and Norwood, Port Phillip, 1843-1864, notes and intr. by G. F. James. London, Oxford Univ. Press ; Melbourne, Univ. Press, 42, in-8, 200 p., 10s. 6d. R : H. L. Harris, *Austral. Quar.*, 42, vol. 14, no. 3, p. 114-115. G. V. Portus, *Hist. Stud. Australia N.Z.*, 42, vol. 2, p. 122-124. W. P. M(orrell), *History*, 43, vol. 28, p. 228.

4768. KIRWAN (Sir John). Early days of the Legislative Council; settlers' difficulties, problems and dangers. *J. West. Austral. hist. Soc.*, 43, vol. 5, p. 6-15.

4769. LETT (Lewis). Papua : its people and its promise, past and future. London, Wadley & Ginn, 45, in-8, 108 p., 7s. 6d.

4770. LUKE (Sir Harry). Britain and the South Seas. London, Longmans, 45, in-8, 72 p., 1s. (Pamph. on the British Commonwealth, 2nd ser., 2). R : M.A., *Geogr. J.*, 45, vol. 106, p. 76-78.

4771. MACKANESS (George). Some private correspondence of the rev. Samuel Marsden and family, 1794-1824. Sydney, The Author, 42, in-4, 79 p., 15s. R : E. Ramsden, *Roy. Austral. hist. Soc. J.*, 42, vol. 28, p. 40-46.

4772. MACKANESS (G.). Some proposals for establishing colonies in the South Seas. *Roy. Austral. hist. Soc. J.*, 43, vol. 29, p. 261-280.

4773. MCKENZIE (N. R.). The Gael fares forth : Waipu and her sister settlements. 2nd ed. Christchurch, Whitcombe & Tombs, 42, in-8, xi-320 p., (plates, maps), 15s.

4774. MATHEW (Felton). The founding of New Zealand : the journals of Felton Mathew, first surveyor-general of New Zealand, and his wife, 1840-1847, ed. by J. Rutherford. Dunedin, Reed, 40, in-8, 267 p., (illus.), 7s. 6d. R : W. P. M(orrell), *Eng. hist. R.*, 41, vol. 56, p. 172.

4775. METCALFE (J. W.). Governor Bourke—or, The lion and the wolves. *Roy. Austral. hist. Soc. J.*, 44, vol. 30, p. 44-80.

4775a. MILLS (Joy E.). The composition of the Victorian parliament, 1856-1881. *Hist. Stud. Australia N.Z.*, 42, vol. 2, p. 25-39.

4776. PARKER (F. L.) and SOMERVILLE (J. D.). The Cooper's Creek controversies. *Hist. Stud. Australia N.Z.*, 43, vol. 2, p. 224-226.

4777. QUIGGIN (Alison Hingston). Haddon the head-hunter : a short sketch of the life of A. C. Haddon. London, Cambridge Univ. Press, 42, in-8, xii-170 p., (plates), 7s. 6d. R : J.L., *Geogr. J.*, 43, vol. 102, p. 88-89. J.H.H., *Man*, 43, vol. 43, p. 70-71.

4778. RABONE (Harold R.). Lord Howe Island, its story from its discovery to the year 1888. *Roy. Austral. hist. Soc. J.*, 40, vol. 26, p. 113-164.

4779. RAFFAELLO (Carboni). The Eureka stockade. Intr. by H. V. Evatt. Sydney, Sunnybrook Press, 42, in-8, xl-144 p., 63s. R : J. Dennis, *Roy. Austral. hist. Soc. J.*, 43, vol. 29, p. 45-61.

4780. RAMSDEN (Eric). James Busby and his work for the Treaty of Waitangi. *Roy. Austral. hist. Soc. J.*, 41, vol. 27, p. 154-165.

4781. RAMSDEN (E.). Busby of Waitangi : H.M.'s resident at New Zealand, 1833-40. Wellington, Reed, 42, in-8, 396 p., 15s. R : J.C.A., *J. polynesian Soc.*, 44, vol. 53, p. 206-210. M. A. Hall-Kenney, *Hist. Stud. Australia N.Z.*, 43, vol. 2, p. 204-207. O. Havard, *Roy. Austral. hist. Soc. J.*, 43, vol. 29, p. 253-257.

4782. ROWLAND (E. C.). Simeon Lord, a merchant prince of Botany Bay. *Roy. Austral. hist. Soc. J.*, 44, vol. 30, p. 157-195.

4783. ROWLEY (C. D.). Clarence River separatism in 1860, a problem of communications. *Hist. Stud. Australia N.Z.*, 41, vol. 1, p. 225-244.

4784. SCOTT (Sir Ernest). Taking possession of Australia—the doctrine of ' Terra Nullius ' (No-Man's Land). *Roy. Austral. hist. Soc. J.*, 40, vol. 26, p. 1-19.

4785. SIMPSON (Helen). The women of New Zealand. Wellington, Dept. of Internal Affairs, 40, in-8, 197 p., 5s. (N.Z. centennial surveys). R : B., *J. public Admin. N. Zealand*, 40, vol. 3, p. 58. S. R. Smith, *Hist. Stud. Australia N.Z.*, 40, vol. 1, p. 142-143. H. Miller, *Austral. Quar.*, 40, vol. 12, no. 2, p. 117.

4786. STEPHENS (Robert). History of the origin of the town of Albany and its street names. *J. West. Austral. hist. Soc.*, 43, vol. 5, p. 43-45.

4787. SUTHERLAND (I. L. G.) ed. The Maori people to-day : a general survey. London, Oxford Univ. Press, 41, in-8, xiii-449 p., (plates, maps), 15s. (Inst. of Pacific relations). R : I. Milner, *Hist. Stud. Australia N.Z.*, 42, vol. 2, p. 58-60.

4788. WARD (L. E.). Early Wellington. New [2nd] ed. London, Whitcombe & Tombs, 42, in-8, 544 p., 12s. 6d.

4789. WILLIAMS (F. W.). Through 90 years : 1826-1916, life and work among Maoris in New Zealand. London, Whitcombe & Tombs, 40, in-8, 360 p., 18s.

4790. WILLIAMS (T.). The Treaty of Waitangi. *History*, 40, vol. 25, p. 237-251.

4791. WOOD (M. E.). First contacts made with Western Australian natives. *J. West. Austral. hist. Soc.*, 43, vol. 5, p. 34-42.

4792. WORMS (Ernest). Aboriginal place names in Kimberley, Western Australia. *Oceania*, 44, vol. 14, p. 284-310.

4793. WYATT (Ransome T.). The history of Goulburn, N.S.W. Goulburn, The Author, 41, in-8, 528 p., (illus.), 10s. R : L. F. Fitzhardinge, *Hist. Stud. Australia N.Z.*, 42, vol. 2,

p. 128. J. Jervis, *Austral. Quar.*, 42, vol. 14, no. 1, p. 115-116.

§ 3. International Affairs from 1500 to 1789

a. GENERAL

b. 1500-1648

4794. CLARK (G. N.). The Barbary corsairs in the 17th century. *Cambridge hist. J.*, 44, vol. 8, p. 22-35.

4795. DODGSON (Campbell). A German-Russian alliance in 1514. *Burlington Mag.*, 40, vol. 76, p. 139-144.

4796. HARBISON (E. Harris). Rival ambassadors at the court of Queen Mary. London, Oxford Univ. Press, 41, in-8, 396 p., 18s. R : J. E. Neale, *Eng. hist. R.*, 44, vol. 59, p. 272-273. G.S.T., *History*, 44, vol. 29, p. 212-213.

4797. MOORE (Sydney H.). The Turkish menace in the 16th century. *Mod. Language R.*, 45, vol. 40, p. 30-36.

4798. WEDGWOOD (C. V.). The thirty years war. New ed. London, Cape, 44, in-8, 544 p., (illus., maps), 12s. 6d. (Bedford hist. ser.).

c. 1648-1789

4799. ABBEY (W. B. T.). Tangier under British rule, 1661-1684. Jersey, Bigwood, 40, in-8, 106 p., 2s. 6d.

4800. CONN (S.). Gibraltar in British diplomacy in the 18th century. London, Oxford Univ. Press, 42, in-8, 329 p., (maps), 14s. R : J. McL., *Eng. hist. R.*, 44, vol. 59, p. 283-284.

4801. HORN (D. B.). British public opinion and the first partition of Poland. Edinburgh, Oliver & Boyd, 45, in-8, viii-98 p., 10s. 6d.

4802. LOEWENSON (Leo). Did Russia intervene after the execution of Charles I ? *B. Inst. hist. Research*, 40, vol. 18, p. 13-20.

4803. ROBITAILLE (Georges). Les préliminaires diplomatiques de la Guerre de Sept Ans. *Trans. Roy. Soc. Canad.*, 40, 3rd ser., vol. 34, p. 91-99.

4804. SAVELLE (Max). The diplomatic history of the Canadian boundary, 1749-1763. London, Oxford Univ. Press; Toronto, Ryerson Press, 40, in-4, xiv-172 p., (maps), 11s. 6d.; $3.25. (Relations of Canada and the U.S.). R : R. P(ares), *Eng. hist. R.*, 42, vol. 57, p. 400.

§ 4. From 1789-1815

4805. AUGUSTA, Duchess of Saxe-Coburg-Saalfeld. In Napoleonic days : extracts from the private diary of Augusta, Duchess of Saxe-Coburg-Saalfeld, Queen Victoria's maternal grandmother, 1806-1821, tr. and selected by Princess Beatrice. London, Murray, 41, in-8, 240 p., 7s. 6d. R : *National R.*, 41, vol. 117, p. 353-354.

4806. CARR (Raymond). Gustavus IV and the British Government, 1804-9. *Eng. hist. R.*, 45, vol. 60, p. 36-66.

4807. CRAWLEY (C. W.). England and the Sicilian constitution of 1812. *Eng. hist. R.*, 40, vol. 55, p. 251-274.

4808. HUGHES (H. B. L.). British policy towards Haiti, 1801-1805. *Canad. hist. R.*, 44, vol. 25, p. 397-408.

4809. KARAL (E. Z.). Halet Efendinin Paris Buyuk elciligi (1802-1806). L'ambassade de Paris de Halet Efendi. In Turkish, new script. London, Luzac, 40, in-8, 136 p., 6s. (Istanbul Universitesi Yayinlari 102).

4810. KNAPTON (E. J.). The origins of the Treaty of Holy Alliance. *History*, 41, vol. 26, p. 132-140.

4811. KNAPTON (E. J.). The Holy Alliance, a retrospect. *Queen's Quar.*, 41, vol. 48, p. 157-166.

4812. KORNGOLD (R.). Citizen Toussaint. London, Gollancz, 45, in-8, 264 p., 7s. 6d.

4813. ROBERTSON (Sir Charles Grant). Great Britain and Napoleon, 1814-15. *History*, 44, vol. 29, p. 27-43.

4814. SHADMAN (S. F.). A review of Anglo-Persian relations, 1798-1815. *J. central asian Soc.*, 44, vol. 31, p. 23-39.

4815. TARLE (Eugene). Napoleon's invasion of Russia. London, Allen & Unwin, 42, in-8, 300 p., (map), 12s. 6d. R : *Quar. R.*, 43, vol. 280, p. 242-243.

§ 5. From 1815 : General

4816. AYERST (D. G. O.). Europe in the nineteenth century. London, Cambridge Univ. Press, 40, in-8, xv-432 p., (illus.), 5s.

4817. COHEN (Victor). The life and times of Masaryk, the President liberator : a history of Central Europe from 1848. London, Murray, 41, in-8, x-262 p., 7s. 6d. R : B. Tufnell, *Int. Affairs*, 41, vol. 19, p. 341. *National R.*, 41, vol. 117, p. 468.

4818. DAVIS (H. J.), DE VANE (W. C.) and BALD (R. C.) ed. Nineteenth century studies. London, Oxford Univ. Press, 41, in-8, 313 p., 14s.

4819. GIBSON (F. W.). The Alaskan boundary dispute. *Canad. hist. Assoc. Rept.*, 45, p. 25-41.

4820. HALL (W. P.) and DAVIS (W. S.). The course of Europe since Waterloo. London, Appleton, 42, in-8, 901 p., (maps, plates), 21s.

4821. LIPSON (E.). Europe in the 19th and 20th centuries, 1815-1939. London, Black, 40, in-8, 800 p., (plates, maps), 18s.

4822. MARRIOTT (Sir J. A. R.). A history of Europe, 1815-1937. New ed. London, Methuen, 43, in-8, xix-615 p., (map), 18s.

4823. NAMIER (L. B.). From Vienna to Versailles. *19th Century*, 40, vol. 127, p. 151-162.

4824. NAMIER (L. B.). After Vienna and Versailles. *19th Century*, 40, vol. 128, p. 463-473.

4825. SOMERVELL (D. C.). Modern Europe, 1871-1939. London, Methuen, 40, in-8, ix-218 p., (maps), 4s.

4825a. —— —— New ed. London, Methuen, 43, in-8, 218 p., (maps), 6s.

4826. YAKOBSON (Sergius). Russia and Africa, 2. *Slavonic Y.B.* (*Slavonic R.*), 40, vol. 19, p. 158-174.

§ 6. From 1815-1890

a. 1815-1871

4827. BROOKES (J. I.). International rivalry in the Pacific islands, 1800-1875. London, Cambridge Univ. Press, 41, in-8, x-454 p., 30s.

4828. DAVIDSON (Donald C.). The war scare of 1854 : the Pacific coast and the Crimean war. *Brit. Columbia hist. Quar.*, 41, vol. 5, p. 243-253.

4829. HENDERSON (Gavin B.). Ralph Anstruther Earle. *Eng. hist. R.*, 43, vol. 58, p. 172-189.

4830. HUMPHREYS (Robin A.). British consular reports on the trade and politics of Latin America, 1824-1826. London, Royal Hist. Soc., 40, in-8, xxii-385 p., privately printed. (Publ., Camden 3rd ser., vol. 63). R : A. A(spinall), *Eng. hist. R.*, 42, vol. 57, p. 405.

4831. LE DUC (Thomas H.). That rumour of Russian intrigue in 1837. *Canad. hist. R.*, 42, vol. 23, p. 398-400.

4832. LIEVEN (Dorothea de, princess) and PALMERSTON (Amelia, visctess.). The Lieven-Palmerston correspondence, 1828-1856, tr. and ed. by Lord Sudley. London, Murray, 43, in-8, 316 p., 18s. R : *National R.*, 43, vol. 120, p. 422-424. A.F.F., *History*, 43, vol. 28, p. 227-228. E.J.P., *Eng. hist. R.*, 44, vol. 59, p. 126-127.

4833. PURYEAR (V. J.). France and the Levant : from the Bourbon restoration to the Peace of Kutiah (1815-1833). London, Cambridge Univ. Press, 41, in-8, xvi-252 p., 15s. (Univ. of Calif., publ. in hist., vol. 27). R : C.W.C., *Eng. hist. R.*, 43, vol. 58, p. 501-502.

4834. PRATT (Julius W.). James K. Polk and John Bull. *Canad. hist. R.*, 43, vol. 24, p. 341-349.

4835. ROBERTSON (W. S.). France and Latin-American independence. London, Oxford Univ. Press, 40, in-8, 626 p., 17s.

4836. SMITH (Goldwin). The Treaty of Washington, 1871 : a study in imperial history. London, Oxford Univ. Press, 41, in-8, xiii-134 p., 12s. R : J. L. Morison, *History*, 41, vol. 26, p. 150-151.

4837. TOMPKINS (Stuart R.). Drawing the Alaskan boundary. *Canad. hist. R.*, 45, vol. 26, p. 1-24.

4838. WEBSTER (Sir C. K.). Britain and the independence of Latin America, 1812-1830. London, Oxford Univ. Press, 44, in-8, 80 p., 4s.

4839. WHITAKER (A. P.). The United States and the independence of Latin America, 1800-1830. London, Oxford Univ. Press, 41, in-8, 652 p., 17s.

b. 1871-1890

4840. HARRIS (D.). Britain and the Bulgarian horrors of 1876. London, Cambridge Univ. Press, 40, in-8, 437 p., 18s. R : B. H. Sumner, *Slavonic Y.B.* (*Slavonic R.*), 40, vol. 19, p. 333-334.

4841. HORNIK (M. P.). Mission of Sir Henry Drummond-Wolff to Constantinople, 1885-87. *Eng. hist. R.*, 40, vol. 55, p. 598-623.

4842. MEDLICOTT (W. N.). Bismarck and the three emperors' alliance, 1881-87. *Trans. Roy. hist. Soc.*, 45, vol. 27, p. 61-83.

4843. RAMM (Agatha). Great Britain and the planting of Italian power in the Red Sea, 1868-1885. *Eng. hist. R.*, 44, vol. 59, p. 211-236.

4844. RUPP (G. H.). A wavering friendship : Russia and Austria, 1876-1878. London, Oxford Univ. Press, 42, in-8, 613 p., 21s. (Harvard hist. stud., vol. 49). R : D. Harris, *Slavonic R.*, 42-43, vol. 21, no. 56, p. 252-254.

§ 7. **From 1890 to 1914**

a. 1890-1914

4845. ASKEW (W. C.). Europe and Italy's acquisition of Libya, 1911-1912. London, Cambridge Univ. Press, 43, in-8, x-318 p., 21s.

4846. BARLOW (Ima Christina). The Agadir crisis. London, Oxford Univ. Press, 40, in-8, 422 p., 18s. R : G. P. G(ooch), *Eng. hist. R.*, 43, vol. 58, p. 255. W. N. Medlicott, *History*, 43, vol. 28, p. 104-105.

4847. FAISSLER (Margareta A.). Austria-Hungary and the disruption of the Balkan league. *Slavonic Y.B. (Slavonic R.)*, 40, vol. 19, p. 141-157.

4848. HALE (O. J.). Publicity and diplomacy (with special reference to England and Germany), 1890-1914. London, Appleton, 40, in-8, xi-486 p., 21s.

4849. HEINDEL (Richard H.). The American impact on Great Britain, 1898-1914 : a study of the United States in world history. London, Oxford Univ. Press, 40, in-8, 439 p., 18s. (Study of the U.S.A. in world hist.). R : F. H. Underhill, *Canad. hist. R.*, 41, vol. 22, p. 77-78. L. Einstein, *History*, 41, vol. 26, p. 151-152. D. W. Brogan, *Eng. hist. R.*, 41, vol. 56, p. 664-667.

4850. HORNIK (M. P.). The Anglo-Belgian agreement of 12 May, 1894. *Eng. hist. R.*, 42, vol. 57, p. 227-243.

4851. KUNO (Yoshi S.). Japanese expansion on the Asiatic continent.

Vol. 2 : A study in the history of Japan, with special reference to her international relations with China, Korea and Russia. London, Cambridge Univ. Press, 40, in-8, xi-416 p., (map), 24s. (Calif. Univ. northeastern Asia seminar, publ.). R : P. J., *Int. Affairs*, 41, vol. 19, p. 218-220. R.H.C., *J. central asian Soc.*, 41, vol. 28, p. 206-209.

4852. SUMNER (B. H.). Tsardom and imperialism in the Far East and the Middle East, 1880-1914. London, Oxford Univ. Press, 42, in-8, 43 p., 2s. 6d. (Brit. Acad., Raleigh lect.).

b. THE ORIGINS OF THE FIRST WORLD WAR

4853. RUMBOLD (Sir Horace). The war crisis in Berlin, July-August 1914, to which is added Despatch from Berlin, April 1933, on the Hitler *régime*. London, Constable, 40, in-8, xvii-372 p., 18s. R : P. Conwell-Evans, *19th Century*, 40, vol. 128, p. 144-153. E. H. Carr, *Int. Affairs*, 40, vol. 19, p. 106-107. *National R.*, 40, vol. 115, p. 360-363.

§ 8. **The First World War**

a. GENERAL

4854. GOOCH (G. P.). British war aims, 1914-19. *Quar. R.*, 43, vol. 280, p. 168-179.

4855. MACKENZIE (Compton). Aegean memories. London, Chatto & Windus, 40, in-8, 419 p., (illus., map), 12s. 6d. R : Lord Meston, *Int. Affairs*, 41, vol. 19, p. 200. *National R.*, 41, vol. 116, p. 498-500. *Army Quar.*, 41, vol. 41, p. 380.

4856. MAURICE (Sir F.). Lessons of allied co-operation, naval, military and air, 1914-1918. London, Oxford Univ. Press, 42, in-8, 203 p., 10s. 6d. R : *National R.*, 42, vol. 119, p. 270-272. C. Hordern, *Int. Affairs*, 42, vol. 19, p. 488-489. *Army Quar.*, 43, vol. 45, p. 253-254.

4857. MOCK (J. R.). Censorship, 1917. London, Oxford Univ. Press, 42, in-8, 262 p., 11s. 6d.

4858. SPERANZA (Gino). Diary: Italy, 1915-1919, ed. by F. C. Speranza. London, Oxford Univ. Press, 41, 2 vols. in-8, 433, 340 p., 30s.

b. WAR ON LAND

4859. BEAN (C. E. W.). The official history of Australia in the war of 1914-1918. Vol. 6 : The A.I.F. in France, May 1918, to the Armistice. London, Angus & Robertson, 42, in-8, lxxvi-1,099 p., (illus., maps), 21s. R : T. Dunbabin, Austral. Quar., 42, vol. 14, no. 4, p. 97-101. Army Quar., 43, vol. 45, p. 255-256.

4860. BUTLER (A. G.). Official history of the Australian army medical services, 1914-1918. Vol. 2-3. Canberra, Austral. War Memorial, 40-43, 2 vols. in-8, 1010, 1103 p., (plates, maps, graphs), 42s. R : J. L. Shellshear, Austral. Quar., 40, vol. 12, no. 3, p. 60-67; 43, vol. 15, no. 3, p. 101-109.

4861. FALLS (C. B.) ed. Official history of the Great War : Military operations, France and Belgium, 1917: German retreat to Hindenburg line and battles of Arras, ed. by C. B. Falls. London, Macmillan, 40, 3 vols. in-8, 628 p., (illus., maps), 12s. 6d., appendices 6s. 6d. ; maps 5s. 6d.

4862. The German defeat in 1918 : how Ludendorff tried to exonerate the army. Army Quar., 41, vol. 41, p. 263-278.

c. WAR ON SEA AND OUTSIDE EUROPE

4863. BELL (Gertrude). The Arab war : confidential information for General Headquarters. Intr. by Sir K. Cornwallis. London, Golden Cockerell Press, 40, in-4, 50 p., 42s. (Limited ed.). R : H.G., J. central asian Soc., 41, vol. 28, p. 98-99.

4864. CORBETT (J. S.). Naval operations. Vol. 3 : May 1915 to

June 1916, including the battle of Jutland. London, Longmans, 40, 2 vols. in-8, 469 p., (maps); text 25s., maps 21s.

4865. HENDERSON (W. O.). The conquest of the German colonies, 1914-18. History, 42, vol. 27, p. 124-139.

4866. HORDERN (Charles). History of the Great War. Military operations: East Africa. Vol. 1 : August 1914-September 1916. London, H.M.S.O., 41, in-8, xl-603 p., (maps), 21s. R : Army Quar., 42, vol. 43, p. 374-379.

4867. PETRIE (Charles). The Mediterranean in two wars. Quar. R., 43, vol. 281, p. 164-175.

4868. TOD (J. K.). The Malleson mission to Trans-Caspia in 1918. J. central asian Soc., 40, vol. 27, p. 45-67.

4869. TUCKER (Gilbert Norman). The organizing of the east coast patrols, 1914-1918. Canad. hist. Assoc. Rept., 41, p. 32-40.

d. WAR IN THE AIR

e. POLITICAL, ECONOMIC AND SOCIAL HISTORY

4870. BAILEY (Thomas A.). The policy of the United States towards the neutrals, 1917-1918. London, Oxford Univ. Press, 43, in-8, 538 p., 21s. 6d. R : W. N. Medlicott, Eng. hist. R., 45, vol. 60, p. 421-422.

4871. BANE (S. L.) and LUTZ (R. H.). Organisation of American relief in Europe, 1918-1919. London, Oxford Univ. Press, 44, in-8, 766 p., (map), 36s.

4872. DEARLE (N. B.). The labour cost of the World War to Great Britain, 1914-22 : a statistical analysis. London, Oxford Univ. Press, 40, in-4, ix-260 p., 10s. 6d. (Carnegie endowment, div. of econ., suppl. vol.). R : H.W.R., J. Roy. statist. Soc., 41, vol. 104, p. 290-292.

4873. GREBLER (Leo) and WINKLER (Wilhelm). The cost of the World War to Germany and to Austria-Hungary. London, Oxford Univ. Press; Toronto, Ryerson Press, 40, in-8, xviii-192 p., 11s. 6d.; $3.00. (Carnegie endowment, econ. and soc. hist. of the World War, suppl. vol.). R : *Army Quar.*, 41, vol. 42, p. 170-172.

4874. HAY (Denys). The official history of the Ministry of Munitions, 1915-1919. *Econ. Hist. R.*, 44, vol. 14, p. 185-190.

4875. HENDERSON (W. O.). The war economy of German East Africa, 1914-1917. *Econ. Hist. R.*, 43, vol. 13, p. 104-110.

4876. MENNE (B.). Armistice and Germany's food supply, 1918-19. London, Hutchinson, 44, in-8, 96 p., 1s.

4877. MOCK (J. R.) and LARSON (C.). Words that won the war: the story of the Committee of Public Information, 1917-1919. London, Oxford Univ. Press, 40, in-8, 372 p., 17s.

4878. MULLENDORE (W. C.). History of the United States food administration, 1917-1919. London, Oxford Univ. Press, 42, in-8, 413 p., 21s. (Hoover libr., 18).

f. DIPLOMATIC HISTORY

4879. HOWARD (Christopher). The Treaty of London, 1915. (Hist. revision). *History*, 41, vol. 25, p. 347-355.

4880. MAURICE (Sir Frederic). The armistices of 1918. London, Oxford Univ. Press, 43, in-8, 112 p., 7s. 6d. R : R.J.C., *Army Quar.*, 43, vol. 47, p. 125. J.H.M.-C., *Int. Affairs*, 43, vol. 19, p. 635-636. W. Arnold-Forster, *Pol. Quar.*, 43, vol. 14, p. 387-388. *B.Y.B.I.L.*, 44, vol. 21, p. 252-253.

4881. SOWARD (F. H.). Sir Robert Borden and Canada's external policy, 1911-1920. *Canad. hist. Assoc. Rept.*, 41, p. 65-82.

4882. WINGATE (Sir Reginald). Libya in the last war: the Talbot mission and the agreement of 1917. *J. Roy. african Soc.*, 41, vol. 40, p. 128-131.

§ 9. From 1918-1939

a. GENERAL

4883. ANTROBUS (George P.). King's messenger, 1918-1940. London, Jenkins, 41, in-8, 250 p., 10s. 6d.

4884. BANE (Suda Lorena) and LUTZ (Ralph Haswell). The blockade of Germany after the armistice, 1918-1919. Selected documents of the Supreme Economic Council, Superior Blockade Council, American Relief Administration and other war-time organizations. London, Oxford Univ. Press, 42, in-8, 882 p., 36s. R : V.L.K., *Int. Affairs*, 44, vol. 20, p. 129. W. N. Medlicott, *Eng. hist. R.*, 45, vol. 60, p. 116-118.

4885. BARTLETT (R. J.). The League to enforce peace. London, Oxford Univ. Press, 44, in-8, 262 p., 15s. 6d.

4886. BIRDSALL (Paul). Versailles twenty years after. London, Allen, 42, in-8, 350 p., 15s. (Prometheus libr.). R : W. M. Jordan, *History*, 43, vol. 28, p. 223-224.

4887. BURNETT (Philip Mason). Reparation at the Paris peace conference. London, Oxford Univ. Press, 40, 2 vols. in-8, 1148, 833 p., 75s. R : A. McFadyean, *Int. Affairs*, 41, vol. 19, p. 203-204.

4888. CARR (Edward Hallett). International relations since the peace treaties. Rev. ed. London, Macmillan, 40, in-8, viii-317 p., 6s. R : J. H. Jackson, *Int. Affairs*, 40, vol. 19, p. 107.

4889. CARR (E. H.). Nationalism and after. London; Toronto, Macmillan, 45, in-8, 74 p., 3s. 6d.; $1.10. R : A.E.P., *Queen's Quar.*, 45, vol. 52, p. 363.

4890. CARTER (Gwendolen M.). Canada and sanctions in the Italo-Ethiopian conflict, 1935. *Canad. hist. Assoc. Rept.*, 40, p. 74-84.

4891. CARTER (G. M.). Some aspects of Canadian foreign policy after Versailles. *Canad. hist. Assoc. Rept.*, 43, p. 94-103.

4892. CECIL OF CHELWOOD (1st Visct.). A great experiment : an autobiography [League of Nations]. London, Cape, 41, in-8, xi-390 p., 16s. R : Sir F. Younghusband, *Asiatic R.*, 42, vol. 38, p. 108-109.

4893. CHURCHILL (W. S.). Step by step, 1936-1939. (New ed.). London, Macmillan, 42, in-8, 358 p., 10s. 6d.

4894. COATES (W. P. and Z. K.). A history of Anglo-Soviet relations. London, Pilot Press, 44, in-8, 816 p., 18s. R : M. Beloff, *Int. Affairs*, 44, vol. 20, p. 438-439.

4895. CURTIS (Monica) ed. Documents on international affairs, 1938. London, Oxford Univ. Press, 42-43, 2 vols. in-8, 536, 368 p., 70s. R : *Pol. Quar.*, 43, vol. 14, p. 390.

4896. DAFOE (J. W.). Canada and the peace conference of 1919. *Canad. hist. R.*, 43, vol. 24, p. 233-248.

4897. DAWES (C. G.). Journal as ambassador to Great Britain. London, Macmillan, 40, in-8, 442 p., (illus.), 25s.

4898. DEÁK (Francis). Hungary at the Paris peace conference. London, Oxford Univ. Press, 42, in-8, 618 p., (map), 27s. 6d. R : V.L.K., *Int. Affairs*, 43, vol. 19, p. 683.

4899. FOOT (M.). Armistice, 1918-39. London, Harrap, 40, in-8, 278 p., 8s. 6d.

4900. Foreign Office. Peace and war : United States foreign policy, 1931-41. The official American document issued by the Dept. of State, Washington. London, H.M.S.O., 43, in-8, 96 p., 1s.

4901. GATHORNE-HARDY (G. M.). A short history of international affairs, 1920-1939. Revised ed. London, Oxford Univ. Press, 42, in-8, 528 p., 12s. 6d.

4902. GLAZEBROOK (G. P. de T.). Canada at the Paris peace conference. London, Oxford Univ. Press, 43, in-8, 164 p., 8s. 6d. R : Sikh, *Int. Affairs*, 43, vol. 19, p. 575-576. H. M. Clokie, *Canad. J. Econ. pol. Sci.*, 44, vol. 10, p. 104-106.

4903. GOODMAN (Paul). The Jewish national home : the second November 1917-1942, ed. by P. Goodman. London, Dent, 43, in-8, xxiv-296 p., 7s. 6d. R : J. W. Parkes, *Int. Affairs*, 44, vol. 20, p. 270.

4904. GUEDALLA (P.). The hundredth year. London, Butterworth, 40, in-8, 311 p., 12s. 6d.

4905. HENDERSON (W. O.). The Peace settlement, 1919. (Historical revision). *History*, 41, vol. 26, p.60-69.

4906. JESSOP (T. E.). The Treaty of Versailles. Was it just ? London, Nelson, 42, in-8, 167 p., 5s.

4907. KING-HALL (Stephen). Our own times, 1913-1939. London, Nicholson, 40, in-8, xi-1204 p., 10s. 6d.

4908. LEAGUE OF NATIONS, *Economic, financial and transit dept.* Relief deliveries and relief loans, 1918-1923. London, Allen & Unwin, 43, in-8, 62 p., 3s. 6d.

4909. LUCKAU (A.). The German delegation at the Paris peace conference. London, Oxford Univ. Press, 41, in-8, 538 p., 25s.

4910. McCALLUM (R. B.). Public opinion and the last peace. London,

Oxford Univ. Press, 44, in-8, ix-214 p., 10s. 6d. R : M. Beloff, *Int. Affairs*, 45, vol. 21, p. 259-260. L. Woolf, *Pol. Quar.*, 45, vol. 16, p. 177-178.

4911. McINNIS (Edgar). The United States and world settlement. *Canad. hist. R.*, 44, vol. 25, p. 151-165.

4912. MARSTON (F. S.). The peace conference of 1919 : organization and procedure. London, Oxford Univ. Press, 44, in-8, xi-276 p., 12s. 6d. (Roy. inst. of internat. affairs). R : H. Nicolson, *Int. Affairs*, 45, vol. 21, p. 258-259. L. Woolf, *Pol. Quar.*, 45, vol. 16, p. 177-178.

4913. MEDLICOTT (W. N.). British foreign policy since Versailles, 1919-39. London, Methuen, 40, in-8, viii-316 p., 8s. 6d. R : E. H. Carr, *Int. Affairs*, 40, vol. 19, p. 50.

4914. —— —— New ed., with appendix 1939-1942. London, Methuen, 42, in-8, viii-344 p., 9s. 6d. R : M. Wight, *Int. Affairs*, 43, vol. 19, p. 591.

4915. MOLSON (Hugh). Years of progress, 1919-1939. *19th Century*, 43, vol. 133, p. 161-166.

4916. NAMIER (L. B.). Conflicts : studies in contemporary history. London, Macmillan, 42, in-8, 223 p., 8s. 6d. R : W.E.C.H., *Queen's Quar.*, 42, vol. 49, p. 417-418. *National R.*, 42, vol. 119, p. 273-274. *Pol. Quar.*, 42, vol. 13, p. 457-458. W. N. M(edlicott), *History*, 43, vol. 28, p. 125-126.

4917. PETRIE (Sir Charles). Twenty years' armistice—and after : British foreign policy since 1918. London, Eyre and Spottiswoode, 40, in-8, 302 p., 7s. 6d.

4918. PETRIE (Sir C.). Twenty years of British foreign policy. *Quar. R.*, 40, vol. 274, p. 1-17.

4919. RAPPARD (W. E.). The quest for peace since the World War. London, Oxford Univ. Press, 40, in-8, 516 p., 17s.

4920. RAYNER (R. M.). The twenty years' truce, 1919-1939. London, Longmans, 43, in-8, 248 p., (map), 12s. 6d.

4921. SCHWARZSCHILD (Leopold). World in trance from Versailles to Pearl Harbour. London, Hamilton, 43, in-8, 286 p., 12s. 6d.

4922. SOWARD (F. H.). Twenty-five troubled years, 1918-1943. London, Oxford Univ. Press; Toronto, Univ. Press, 43, in-8, x-437 p., 15s.; $3.00. R : R. Flenley, *Canad. J. Econ. pol. Sci.*, 44, vol. 10, p. 257-258. A. R. M. Lower, *Int. Affairs*, 44, vol. 20, p. 413-414.

4923. SOWARD (F. H.), PARKINSON (J. F.), MACKENZIE (N. A. M.) and MACDERMOT (T. W. L.). Canada in world affairs : the pre-war years [1935-1939]. Toronto, Oxford Univ. Press, 41, in-8, xiii-343 p., $3.00. R : R. G. Trotter, *Queen's Quar.*, 41, vol. 48, p. 437-438.

4924. TOYNBEE (Arnold J.) and BOULTER (V. M.). Survey of international affairs, 1938. Vol. 1. London, Oxford Univ. Press, 41, in-8, 735 p., 28s. R : L. B. Namier, *19th Century*, 42, vol. 131, p. 137-144. *Pol. Quar.*, 42, vol. 13, p. 115-116.

b. EUROPE

4925. ARON (Raymond). Reflections on the foreign policy of France. *Int. Affairs*, 45, vol. 21, p. 437-447.

4926. AVALISHVILI (Zourab). The independence of Georgia in international politics, 1918-1921. London, Headley, 40, in-8, xxi-286 p., 10s. 6d. R : S. Davidovich, *Int. Affairs*, 41, vol. 19, p. 217-218.

4927. BISSCHOP (W. R.). A commonwealth of European states. *Trans. Grotius Soc.*, 39 [40], vol. 25, p. 1-33.

4928. BLOOD-RYAN (H. W.). The great German conspiracy. London, Drummond, 43, in-8, 276 p., 12s. 6d. R : *National R.*, 43, vol. 121, p. 84-85.

4929. CADOUX (C. J.). The punishing of Germany after the war of 1918-1919. *Hibbert J.*, 45, vol. 43, p. 107-113.

4930. DODD (William Edward). Ambassador Dodd's diary, 1933-1938, ed. by W. E. Dodd, jr., and M. Dodd. London, Gollancz, 41, in-8, 452 p., 12s. 6d. R : I. M. Massey, *Int. Affairs*, 41, vol. 19, p. 333. A. Peel, *Congreg. Quar.*, 41, vol. 19, p. 257-260.

4931. FRAENKEL (Ernst). Military occupation and the rule of law : occupational government in the Rhineland, 1918-1923. London, Oxford Univ. Press, 44, in-8, xi-267 p., 16s. (Inst. of world affairs stud.). R : F. W. Pick, *Int. Affairs*, 45, vol. 21, p. 390.

4932. FRASER (L.). Germany between two wars, a study of propaganda and war-guilt. London, Oxford Univ. Press, 44, in-8, 184 p., 8s. 6d.

4933. GESHKOFF (Theodore I.). Balkan union : a road to peace in south-eastern Europe. London, Oxford Univ. Press, 40, in-8, xvi-345 p., 20s. R : E. Boyle, *Int. Affairs*, 41, vol. 19, p. 213-214.

4934. HADLEY (W. W.). Munich before and after. 2nd ed. London, Cassell, 44, in-8, 184 p., 7s. 6d. R : W. N. Medlicott, *Int. Affairs*, 45, vol. 21, p. 109-110.

4935. HENDERSON (sir N.). Failure of a mission. London, Hodder & Stoughton, 40, in-8, 318 p., 7s. 6d.

4936. HODZA (M.). Federation in Central Europe : reflections and reminiscences. London, Jarrolds, 42, in-8, 236 p., (illus.), 18s.

4937. JORDAN (W. M.). Great Britain, France, and the German problem, 1918-1939 : a study of Anglo-French relations in the making and maintenance of the Versailles settlement. London, Oxford Univ. Press, 43, in-8, xi-235 p., 15s. (Roy. inst. of internat. affairs). R : W. N. Medlicott, *History*, 44, vol. 29, p. 209-211. L. Woolf, *Pol. Quar.*, 44, vol. 15, p. 176-177. T. H. Minshall, *Int. Affairs*, 44, vol. 20, p. 127-128.

4938. KAECKENBEECK (Georges). The international experiment of Upper Silesia : the Upper Silesian settlement, 1922-1937. London, Oxford Univ. Press, 42, in-8, 907 p., 42s. R : C. A. Macartney, *Grotius Soc. Trans.*, 42 (43), vol. 28, p. 169-170. F. A. Mann, *B.Y.B.I.L.*, 44, vol. 21, p. 250-252. W. J. Rose, *J. comp. Legisl. int. Law*, 43, vol. 25, p. 94-95. H. M. Wood, *Int. Affairs*, 43, vol. 19, p. 623-624.

4939. KIRKIEN (L.). Russia, Poland and the Curzon line. Duns, Caldra House, 44, in-8, 62 p., (maps), 3s. R : H. J. Paton, *Int. Affairs*, 45, vol. 21, p. 278.

4940. LIPSON (E.). Europe, 1914-1939. London, Black, 40, in-8, 486 p., (plates, maps), 12s. 6d.

4941. MACKIEWICZ (Stanislaw). Historja Polski, Nov. 11, 1918-Sept. 27, 1939. London, Faber, 41, in-8, 348 p., 8s. 6d.

4942. MACKIEWICZ (S.). Colonel Beck and his policy. London, Eyre & Spottiswoode, 44, in-8, 139 p., 7s. 6d. R : *Int. Affairs*, 45, vol. 21, p. 130-131.

4943. MACKINTOSH (John). The paths that led to war, Europe, 1919-1939. London, Blackie, 40, in-8, 375 p., 10s. 6d.

4944. MAUGHAM (Viscount). The truth about the Munich crisis. London, Heinemann, 44, in-8, 80 p., 5s.

4945. MORGAN (J. H.). Assize of arms : the disarmament of Germany and her rearmament (1919-1939). London, Methuen, 45, in-8, xvii-291 p., 15s. R : J. Menken, *National R.*, 45, vol. 125, p. 256-259.

4946. OFFICIAL DOCUMENTS. Official documents concerning Polish-German and Polish-Soviet relations, 1933-1939. London, Hutchinson, 40, in-8, xiv-222 p., 3s. 6d.

4947. ROUCEK (J. S.). Contemporary Europe : a study of national, international, economic and cultural trends. London, Chapman & Hall, 42, in-8, 670 p., (map), 25s.

4948. SETON-WATSON (H.). Eastern Europe between the wars, 1918-1941. London, Cambridge Univ. Press, 45, in-8, xvi-442 p., (maps), 21s.

4949. STARHEMBERG (Prince). Between Hitler and Mussolini. London, Hodder & Stoughton, 42, in-8, xi-281 p., 15s. R : T. M. Cuninghame, National R., 42, vol. 119, p. 83-86.

4950. STONER (J. E.). S. O. Levinson and the Pact of Paris. London, Cambridge Univ. Press, 43, in-8, xvi-368 p., (plates), 30s.

4951. STRAKHOVSKY (Leonid I.). Intervention at Archangel : allied intervention and Russian counter-revolution in north Russia, 1918-1920. London, Oxford Univ. Press, 44, in-8, 346 p., 20s. R : A. J. P. T(aylor), Eng. hist. R., 45, vol. 60, p. 286-287.

4952. WAMBAUGH (Sarah). The Saar plebiscite, with a collection of official documents. London, Oxford Univ. Press, 40, in-8, vii-489 p., 28s. R : M. S. MacDonnell, Int. Affairs, 40, vol. 19, p. 121.

c. ASIA, AFRICA, AMERICA

4953. BISSON (T. A.). American policy in the Far East, 1931-1940. London, Allen & Unwin, 40, in-8, 162 p., 6s. (Inst. of Pacific relations inquiry ser.). R : O. M. Green, Int. Affairs, 40, vol. 19, p. 148-149. W. G. K. D(uncan), Austral. Quar., 40, vol. 12, no. 3, p. 111-113. P. D. Phillips, Econ. Record, 40, vol. 16, p. 288-289.

4954. A decade of Japanese underground activities in the Netherland East Indies. London, H.M.S.O., 42, in-8, 40 p., 1s. (Netherland Government information bureau).

4955. FRIEDMAN (Irving S.). British relations with China, 1931-1939. London, Allen, 40, in-8, xv-255 p., 10s. (Inst. of Pacific relations inquiry ser.). R : O. M. Green, Int. Affairs, 40, vol. 19, p. 149.

4956. GREW (Joseph C.). Ten years in Japan : a contemporary record drawn from the diaries and private and official papers of the U.S. ambassador to Japan, 1932-1942. London, Hammond, 44, in-8, 480 p., 15s. R : G. S. Moss, Int. R. Missions, 45, vol. 34, p. 98-100. D.B.-B., J. central asian Soc., 45, vol. 32, p. 116-118.

4957. KUNO (Y. S.). Japanese expansion on the Asiatic continent. Vol. 2. London, Cambridge Univ. Press, 40, in-8, 416 p., 24s.

4958. WANG (C. C.). Japan's continental adventure. London, Allen & Unwin, 40, in-8, 224 p., 7s. 6d. R : W. E. L. Shenton, Int. Affairs, 41, vol. 19, p. 220-221.

4959. WOLFF (Serge M.). Mongol delegations in western Europe, 1925-1929. J. central asian Soc., 45, vol. 32, p. 289-298.

Q

ASIA

§ 1. General

4960. CABLE (Mildred). The central Asian Buddhist road to China. *J. central asian Soc.*, 43, vol. 30, p. 275-284.

4961. LAMB (Harold). The march of the Barbarians. [Mongol history]. London, Hale, 41, in-8, 347 p., (maps), 15s. R : D.B.-B., *J. central asian Soc.*, 41, vol. 28, p. 463-464.

4962. MARTIN (H. Desmond). The Mongol army. *J. asiatic Soc.*, 43, p. 46-85.

4963. OLSCHKI (L.). Marco Polo's precursors. London, Oxford Univ. Press, 43, in-8, 110 p., (map), 9s. 6d.

4964. PRAWDIN (Michael) *pseud.* The Mongol empire, its rise and legacy, tr. by E. and C. Paul. London, Allen & Unwin, 40, in-8, 581 p., (maps), 21s. R : P. Hume, *J. central asian Soc.*, 41, vol. 28, p. 379-381.

4965. SAUNDERS (Kenneth). A pageant of Asia : a study of three civilisations. New ed. London, Oxford Univ. Press, 41, in-8, xii-452 p., (plates), 7s. 6d. (Oxf. bookshelf). R : W. Cohn, *Burlington Mag.*, 42, vol. 81, p. 181-182.

4966. TIMPERLEY (H. J.). Some contrasts between China and Japan in the light of history. *Asiatic R.*, 41, vol. 37, p. 104-113.

4967. WALES (H. G. Q.). Archaeological researches on ancient Indian colonization in Malaya. London, Luzac, 41, in-8, 89 plates, (maps), 8s. 6d. (Malayan Br., Roy. Asiatic Soc., Journ., vol. 18, pt. 1).

4968. WALKER (C. C.). Jenghiz Khan. London, Luzac, 40, in-8, 215 p., (maps), 17s. 6d. R : P. M. Sykes, *J. central asian Soc.*, 40, vol. 27, p. 351-353. *Army Quar.*, 40, vol. 40,

p. 188-189. H. D. Martin, *J. central asian Soc.*, 44, vol. 31, p. 220.

4969. YEH (George K. C.). India and China [Buddhism]. *Asiatic R.*, 42, vol. 38, p. 337-351.

§ 2. Western and Central Asia

4970. EDMONDS (C. J.). A bibliography of southern Kurdish, 1937-1944. *J. central asian Soc.*, 45, vol. 32, p. 185-191.

4971. RYAN (M. Lawrance, bishop). Bibliography of the Kurdish press. *J. central asian Soc.*, 44, vol. 31, p. 313-314.

4972. AKSEL (H. Avni). The history of medicine in Turkey. *Asiatic R.*, 44, vol. 40, p. 320-323.

4973. ARBERRY (A. J.). British contributions to Persian studies. London, Longmans, 42, in-8, 44 p., 1s. R : P. M. Sykes, *J. central asian Soc.*, 42, vol. 29, p. 269. R. Landau, *Asiatic R.*, 42, vol. 38, p. 427-428.

4974. BALISTER (Sidney). A great English scholar in Turkey : Sir James Redhouse. *Asiatic R.*, 42, vol. 38, p. 173-176.

4975. BARGER (Evert) and WRIGHT (Philip). Excavations in Swat and explorations in the Oxus territories of Afghanistan. Calcutta, Govt. of India Press, 41, in-8, 67 p., (plates), 8s. 9d. (Mem., Archaeol. survey of India, 64). R : L.D.B., *Eng. hist. R.*, 42, vol. 57, p. 526-527. H. Buchthal, *J. hell. Stud.*, 42 (43), vol. 62, p. 108.

4976. BECKINGHAM (C. F.). The reign of Aḥmad ibn Sa'īd, Imam of Oman. *J. asiatic Soc.*, 41, p. 257-260.

4977. BINYON (Laurence). Examples of Iranian illustrated MSS. in the British Museum. *Asiatic R.*, 41, vol. 37, p. 795-797.

4978. BUCHTHAL (Hugo). Three illustrated Hariri manuscripts in the British Museum. *Burlington Mag.*, 40, vol. 77, p. 144-152.

4979. DODGE (Bayard). The settlement of the Assyrians on the Khabbur [in 1937]. *J. central asian Soc.*, 40, vol. 27, p. 301-320.

4980. ELWELL-SUTTON (L. P.). Modern Iran. London, Routledge, 41, in-8, xii-234 p., (plates, maps), 12s. 6d. R : P. M. Sykes, *J. central asian Soc.*, 42, vol. 29, p. 70-71. J.V.H., *Geogr. J.*, 42, vol. 100, p. 37-38.

4981. EPSTEIN (Eliahu). The Druzes of Palestine. *J. central asian Soc.*, 42, vol. 29, p. 52-63.

4982. FRASER-TYTLER (Sir Kerr). A great North road. *J. central asian Soc.*, 42, vol. 29, p. 129-135.

4983. GRAVES (Philip). The life of Sir Percy Cox. London, Hutchinson, 41, in-8, 350 p., 18s. R : Sir P. Sykes, Sir N. Davidson, *J. central asian Soc.*, 41, vol. 28, p. 362-368. *National R.*, 41, vol. 116, p. 616-617. R. Landau, *Asiatic R.*, 41, vol. 37, p. 679-680.

4984. HABSHUSH (Hayyim). Travels in Yemen : account of J. Halévy's journey to the Najran in 1870, ed. by S. D. Goitien. In San' ani Arabic (Hebrew characters). London, Probsthain, 41, in-8, 102, 5, 138 p., 10s. R : H. St. J. B. Philby, *J. central asian Soc.*, 43, vol. 30, p. 325-327.

4985. HAMZAVI (A. H.). Recent cultural activities in Iran. *Asiatic R.*, 42, vol. 38, p. 420-424.

4986. HAMZAVI (A. H.). Iran's future : some lessons from the past. *J. central asian Soc.*, 44, vol. 31, p. 273-280.

4987. HITTI (Philip K.). History of the Arabs. 2nd ed., revised. London, Macmillan, 40, in-8, xix-767 p., (plates, maps), 31s. 6d. R : H. St. J. B. Philby, *J. central asian Soc.*, 41, vol. 28, p. 457-459.

4988. IBN ER RUMI. Life and works of Ibn er Rumi : 'Ali ibn el-'Abbas, Abu el-Hassan. A Baghdad poet of the 9th century, his life and poetry, ed. by R. Guest. London, Luzac, 45, in-8, 143 p., 12s. 6d.

4989. IBN ISFANDIYAR. Tarikh Tabaristan : history of Tabaristan in Persian. London, Luzac, 42, in-8, 331 p., 15s.

4990. IBN KHALDUN. Prolegomena to history. A summarised translation by Abbas Ammar. *Geography*, 40, vol. 25, p. 57-67.

4991. INGRAMS (Harold). Arabia and the Isles. London, Murray, 42, in-8, xvi-367 p., 18s. R : H. Scott, *J. central asian Soc.*, 42, vol. 29, p. 264-266.

4992. INGRAMS (H.). Political development in the Hadhramaut. *Int. Affairs*, 45, vol. 21, p. 236-252.

4993. JARVIS (C. S.). Arab command : a biography of Lieut.-Col. F. W. Peake Pasha. London, Hutchinson, 42, in-8, 158 p., (plates), 18s. R : F.H., *J. central asian Soc.*, 43, vol. 30, p. 118-119. *National R.*, 42, vol. 119, p. 529-530.

4994. KING (E. H.). Travels in the ancient province of Armenia Minor, 1. *Asiatic R.*, 40, vol. 36, p. 98-111.

4995. LEWIS (Bernard). British contributions to Arabic studies. London, Longmans, 42, in-8, 29 p., 1s. R : D.N.B., *J. central asian Soc.*, 42, vol. 29, p. 264.

4996. MANTSKAVA (I.). The golden age of Georgia. 2 pts. *Asiatic R.*, 41, vol. 37, p. 366-376, 798-809.

4997. MAYER (L. A.). A decree of the Caliph Al-Musta'in billāh [1412]. *Quar. Dept. Antiq. Palestine*, 44, vol. 11, p. 27-29.

4998. MINORSKY (V.). Some early documents in Persian, 1. *J. asiatic Soc.*, 42, p. 181-194.

4999. NERSOYAN (Tiran). The Armenian cathedral of St. James in Jerusalem. *Asiatic R.*, 41, vol. 37, p. 142-153.

5000. PAYANDA (Mohammad). Zindagani Mohammad. Life of Mohammad. In Persian. London, Luzac, 40, 2 vols. in-8, 586 p., (illus.), 25s.

5001. PHILBY (H. St. J. B.). Halévy in the Yaman. *Geogr. J.*, 43, vol. 102, p. 116-124.

5002. PHILBY (H. St. J. B.). Three new inscriptions from Hadhramaut. *J. asiatic Soc.*, 45, p. 124-133.

5003. PRESLAND (John). Deedes Bey: a study of Sir Wyndham Deedes, 1883-1923. London, Macmillan, 42, in-8, xi-360 p., 16s. R : N. Bentwich, *J. central asian Soc.*, 42, vol. 29, p. 260-262. *Quar. R.*, 42, vol. 279, p. 118-119. H. Nicolson, *19th Century*, 42, vol. 132, p. 94-95.

5004. RASID AL-DIN. Geschichte Gazan-Hans, aus dem Ta'rih-i-Mubarak-i-Gazani des Rasid al-Din Fadlallah b. 'Imad al-Daula Abul-Hair. Hrsg. nach den Handschriften von Stambul, London, Paris und Wien. Mit einer Einleitung, kritischem Apparat und Indices, von K. Jahn. Persian text, with foreword, notes in German. London, Luzac, 40, in-8, xliv-387 p., 30s. (E. J. W. Gibb memorial ser.).

5005. SOLTAU (R. H.). Some lessons from the Near East. *History*, 40, vol. 25, p. 1-13.

5006. SOUSA (Ahmed). Irrigation in Iraq, its history and development. London, Luzac, 45, in-8, 54 p., 6d. (Facts and prospects ser.).

5007. STARK (F.). Iraq. *19th Century*, 42, vol. 132, p. 110-117.

5008. STEIN (Sir Aurel). Archaeological notes from the Hindukush region. *J. asiatic Soc.*, 44, p. 5-24 (plates).

5009. TADHKIRAT AL-MULUK. A manual of Safavid administration (circa A.H. 1137=A.D. 1725). Persian text in facsimile, tr. by V. Minorsky. London, Luzac, 43, in-4, xi-218 p., 130 facs., 20s. (E. J. W. Gibb mem. ser., n.s., 16). R : P. M. Sykes, *J. central asian Soc.*, 43, vol. 30, p. 222-223.

5010. TOUKAN (B.). Transjordan : past, present and future. *J. central asian Soc.*, 44, vol. 31, p. 253-264.

5011. WILSON (Sir Arnold). Southwest Persia : a political officer's diary, 1907-14. London, Oxford Univ. Press, 41, in-8, 305 p., 15s. R : H.W.-B., *J. central asian Soc.*, 41, vol. 28, p. 210-212. *National R.*, 41, vol. 116, p. 737-738. J. V. Harrison, *Geogr. J.*, 41, vol. 97, p. 377-382. P. M. Sykes, *J. asiatic Soc.*, 42, p. 59-61.

§ 3. India

5012. SHARMA (S. R.). A bibliography of Mughal India, 1526-1707. London, Luzac, 42, in-8, ix-206 p., 6s.

5013. AHMAD (K. A.). The founder of Pakistan : an appreciation of the historic work of Choudhary Rahmat Ali. London, Luzac, 42, in-8, 33 p., 1s.

5014. AKBARNAMA, The. A history of the reign of Akbar including an account of his predecessors of Abul-Fazl, tr. from the Persian by H. Beveridge. Vol. 3, fasc. 14 (concluding fasc.). Index to vol. 3. London, Luzac, 40, in-8, 5s. (Bibl. Indica, work no. 138, issue no. 1,534, n.s.).

5015. ALLAN (J.), HAIG (Sir T. W.) and DODWELL (H. H.). Cambridge shorter history of India. New ed. London, Cambridge Univ. Press, 43, in-8, xxii-970 p., (map), 18s.

5016. ARUVAMUTHAN (T. G.). Some survivals of the Harappa culture. Bombay, Karnatak Publ. House, 42, in-8, iv-76 p., (illus.). R : S. Rice, *Man*, 43, vol. 43, p. 45-46.

5017. Aziz (Abdul). The imperial treasury of the Indian Mughuls. London, Luzac, 42, in-8, xix-572 p., 16s. (Mughul Indian court and its institutions, 2). R : P. R. Cadell, *J. asiatic Soc.*, 44, p. 96.

5018. Bahadur (Nawab Ali Yavar Jang). The place of the Deccan in Indian history. *Asiatic R.*, 42, vol. 38, p. 385-389.

5019. Banerji (S. K.). Humāyūn Bādshāh. Lucknow, 41, in-8, 306 p., Rs. 8. R : R. Burn, *J. asiatic Soc.*, 42, p. 144-145.

5020. Barton (Sir William). Historical research in India. *Asiatic R.*, 40, vol. 36, p. 541-544.

5021. Batley (C.). The design development of Indian architecture. London, Tiranti, 42, in-2, 52 plates, 12s. 6d.

5022. Beck (H. C.). The Beads of Taxila, ed. by sir J. Marshall. Calcutta, Govt. of India Press, 41, in-8, 8s. 6d. (Mem., Archaeol. survey of India, 65). R : D. MacKay, *Antiquity*, 44, vol. 18, p. 201-204.

5023. Bendrey (V. S.). The study of Muslim inscriptions. Bombay, Karnatak Publ. House, 44, in-8, 197 p., Rs. 7. R : A. S. Tritton, *J. asiatic Soc.*, 45, p. 192.

5024. Bengal past and present. (Journal of the Calcutta Historical Society, vol. 56-57). London, Luzac, 40, in-4, 109, 87 p., Rs. 20.

5025. Bhandarkar (D. R.). Some aspects of ancient Indian culture. London, Luzac; Madras, Univ. Press, 40, in-8, 84 p., 4s. (Sir W. Meyer lect., 1938-39). R : L.D.B., *Eng. hist. R.*, 41, vol. 56, p. 336-337.

5026. Brown (Percy). Indian architecture, pt. 1 : Buddhist and Hindu periods. London, Paul; Bombay, Taraporevala, 42, in-4, xii-212 p., (plates), 38s; Rs. 15. R : K. de B. Codrington, *Burlington Mag.*, 44, vol. 85, p. 234.

5027. —— —— Pt. 2 : Islamic period. London, Paul, 43, in-4, xii-140 p., 100 plates, (maps), 30s.

5028. Brown (W. N.). A pillared hall from a temple at Madura, India, in the Philadelphia Museum of Art. London, Oxford Univ. Press, 40, in-8, 88 p., (illus.), 9s.

5029. Burt (Sir Bryce). India's agricultural progress. *Asiatic R.*, 42, vol. 38, p. 134-151.

5030. Chatterton (Sir Alfred). A century of irrigation in India. *Asiatic R.*, 41, vol. 37, p. 766-784.

5031. Chatterton (Sir A.). Malaria in India. *Asiatic R.*, 41, vol. 37, p. 529-540.

5032. Chintamani (C. Y.). Indian politics since the mutiny. London, Allen & Unwin, 40, in-8, 232 p., 7s. 6d.

5033. Coatman (John). India : the road to self-government (1908-1940). London, Allen & Unwin, 41, in-8, 146 p., 5s. R : Sir F. Younghusband, *Asiatic R.*, 42, vol. 38, p. 218-219. J. Maynard, *Pol. Quar.*, 42, vol. 13, p. 345-346.

5034. Codrington (K. de B.). Portraits of Akbar, the Great Mughal (1542-1605). *Burlington Mag.*, 43, vol. 82, p. 65-67.

5035. Coupland (Sir Reginald). Britain and India, 1600-1941. London, Longmans, 41, in-8, 94 p., 6d. (Pamph. on the Brit. Commonwealth, 1).

5036. Coupland (Sir R.). The Indian problem; Indian politics, 1936-1942; The future of India. Pt. 1-3 of a report on the constitutional problem in India submitted to Nuffield College, Oxford. London, Oxford Univ. Press, 42-43, 3 vols. in-8, 160, 344, 207 p., 20s. R (Pt. 1) : F. Noyce, *Int. Affairs*, 43, vol. 19, p. 603. (Pt. 2) : *National R.*, 43, vol. 120, p. 408. J. Maynard, *Pol. Quar.*, 43, vol. 14,

p. 295-296. W. Paton, *Int. R. Missions*, 43, vol. 32, p. 451-453. (Pt. 2-3) : F. Noyce, *Int. Affairs*, 44, vol. 20, p. 146-147, 300-301. (Pt. 3) : H.E.Ap R.P., *J. central asian Soc.*, 44, vol. 31, p. 208-212. N. Goodall, *Int. R. Missions*, 44, vol. 33, p. 216-220. V. Anstey, *Economica*, 44, vol. 11, p. 48-49.

5037. DARLEY (Sir Bernard). The development of irrigation in India. *Asiatic R.*, 42, vol. 38, p. 14-28.

5038. DASGUPTA (Surendranath). A history of Indian philosophy. Vol. 3. London, Cambridge Univ. Press, 40, in-8, xiii-614 p., 40s. R. : E. J. Thomas, *J. asiatic Soc.*, 41, p. 271-272. E. H. Johnston, *Philosophy*, 41, vol. 16, p. 420-422.

5039. DIGHE (V. G.). Peshwa Bajirao I and Maratha expansion. Bombay, 44, in-8, x-235 p. R : C. C. Davies, *J. asiatic Soc.*, 45, p. 205.

5040. DIKSHITAR (V. R. Ramachandra). War in ancient India. Madras, 44; London, Macmillan, 45, in-8, vii-416 p., 25s. R : L.D.B., *Eng. hist. R.*, 45, vol. 60, p. 267-268.

5041. DIVER (Maud). Royal India : a descriptive and historical study of India's fifteen principal states and their rulers. London, Hodder & Stoughton, 42, in-8, 278 p., 18s.

5042. DUTT (N.). Early monastic Buddhism. Vol. 1. London, Luzac, 41, in-8, viii-340 p., 12s. 6d. (Calcutta Or. ser.).

5043. DUTT (T.). Ancient ballads and legends of Hindustan. Allahabad, Kitabistan, 41, in-8, 300 p., Rs. 2-8.

5044. ELDRIDGE (F. B.). A chapter from the background of eastern seapower. [India, 300 B.C.-1700 A.D.]. *Austral. Quar.*, 42, vol. 14, no. 2, p. 80-90.

5045. GARRETT (H. L. O.). European adventurers of northern India. *Asiatic R.*, 41, vol. 37, p. 785-794.

5046. GEDDES (Arthur). Half a century of population trends in India : a regional study of net change and variability, 1881-1931. *Geogr. J.*, 41, vol. 98, p. 228-253.

5047. GORDINE (Dora). The beauty of Indian sculpture. *J. asiatic Soc.*, 41, p. 42-48 (plates).

5048. GORDON (D. H. and M. E.). Mohenjo-Daro : some observations on Indian prehistory. *Iraq*, 40, vol. 7, pt. 1, p. 1-12.

5049. HAWORTH (Lionel). United India. *19th Century*, 42, vol. 132, p. 229-235.

5050. HOBBS (H.). John Barleycorn Bahadur : old time taverns in India. London, Probsthain, 44, in-8, iii-490 p., 15s.

5051. HORNELL (James). The Chank shell cult of India. *Antiquity*, 42, vol. 16, p. 113-133 (illus.).

5052. HORNELL (J.). Hero memorial-stones of Kathiawar. *Antiquity*, 42, vol. 16, p. 289-300 (illus.).

5053. HUBBACK (Sir John). Orissa, past and present. *Asiatic R.*, 42, vol. 38, p. 351-365.

5054. JOHNSTON (E. H.). Ctesias on Indian manna. *J. asiatic Soc.*, 42, p. 29-35, 249-250.

5055. KIERNAN (V. G.). Metcalfe's mission to Lahore, 1808-1809. Lahore, 43, in-8, 89 p., Rs. 4/12. R : C. C. Davies, *J. asiatic Soc.*, 44, p. 207.

5056. KINCAID (C. A.). Lakshmibai Rani of Jhansi. *J. asiatic Soc.*, 43, p. 100-104.

5057. KING (Cuthbert). Rock drawings on the Indus. *Man*, 40, vol. 40, p. 65-68.

5058. LAW (B. C.). India as described in early texts of Buddhism and Jainism. London, Luzac, 42, in-8, xiii-315 p., (map), 10s.

5059. LE MAY (Reginald). The Bimaran casket. *Burlington Mag.*, 43, vol. 82, p. 116-123.

5060. McCULLY (B. T.). English education and the origins of Indian nationalism. London, King, 43, in-8, 408 p., 22s. 6d.

5061. MAHALINGAM (T. V.). Administration and social life under Vijayanagar. Madras, 40; London, Luzac, 42, in-8, x-476 p., 12s. 6d. (Madras Univ. hist. ser.). R : E. J. Thomas, *J. asiatic Soc.*, 42, p. 67-68. L.D.B., *Eng. hist. R.*, 41, vol. 56, p. 668-669.

5062. MISRA (B. R.). Indian provincial finance, 1919-1939. London, Oxford Univ. Press, 42, in-8, 365 p., 11s. 6d. R : V. Anstey, *Int. Affairs*, 43, vol. 19, p. 650-651. G. F. Shirras, *Economica*, 43, vol. 10, p. 209-212.

5063. MOOKERJI (Radha Kumud). Chandragupta Maurya and his times. Madras, Univ. Press, 43, in-8. R : L.D.B., *Eng. hist. R.*, 44, vol. 59, p. 416-417.

5064. MORELAND (W. H.) and CHATTERJEE (Atul Chandra). A short history of India. 2nd ed., revised. London, Longmans, 45, in-8, xi-548 p., (maps), 21s. R : J. Coatman, *Int. Affairs*, 45, vol. 21, p. 422. K.K., *J. comp. Legisl. int. Law*, 45, vol. 27, pt. 3/4, p. 111. P. R. Cadell, *J. asiatic Soc.*, 45, p. 201.

5065. NAIR (Lajpat Rai). Sir William Macnaughton's correspondence relating to the Tripartite Treaty. Lahore, 42, in-8, 111 p., Rs.2/15. R : C. C. Davies, *J. asiatic Soc.*, 44, p. 207.

5066. NEHRU (J.). Unity of India : collected writings and speeches, 1937-1940. New ed. London, L. Drummond, 42, in-8, 432 p., 12s. 6d.

5067. NOMAN (M.). Muslim India : rise and growth of All India Muslim League. Allahabad, Kitabistan, 42, in-8, 433 p., Rs. 4/8.

5068. O'MALLEY (L. S. S.) ed. Modern India and the West : a study of the interaction of their civilisations. London, Oxford Univ. Press, 41, in-8, 846 p., 36s. R : J. Maynard, *Pol. Quar.*, 41, vol. 12, p. 467-468.

5069. ORR (W. G.). Armed religious ascetics in Northern India. *B. John Rylands Library*, 40, vol. 24, p. 81-100.

5070. PANIKKAR (K. M.). India and the Indian Ocean. London, Allen, 45, in-8, 109 p., 6s. R : Sir H. Richmond, *Asiatic R.*, 45, vol. 41, p. 316-317. H. V. Hodson, *Int. Affairs*, 45, vol. 21, p. 558.

5071. PEAKE (Harold J. E.). A great gap in the archaeological record of India. *Man*, 44, vol. 44, p. 35-38.

5072. PIGGOTT (Stuart). The earliest Buddhist shrines. *Antiquity*, 43, vol. 17, p. 1-10 (illus.).

5073. PIGGOTT (S.). A cylinder-seal from South India. *Antiquity*, 44, vol. 18, p. 98-99 (illus.).

5074. PIGGOTT (S.). Prehistoric copper hoards in the Ganges basin. *Antiquity*, 44, vol. 18, p. 173-182 (illus.).

5075. PRASAD (B.). Origins of provincial autonomy (1861-1920) : the relations between the central governments and the provincial governments in British India. Allahabad, Kitabistan, 41, in-8, 300 p., Rs. 7-8.

5076. PURI (K. N.). Excavations at Rairh. Jaipur, Dept. of Archaeol. and Hist. Research, 41, in-8, iv-73 p., 36 plates. R : S. Piggott, *Antiquity*, 43, vol. 17, p. 106-107.

5077. QURESHI (Ishtiaq Husain). The administration of the Sultanate of Delhi. Lahore, Ashraf, 42, in-8, xvi-288 p., (maps), Rs. 8. R : P. Cadell, *J. asiatic Soc.*, 43, p. 269-270. H.V.L., *J. central asian Soc.*, 43, vol. 30, p. 121-122.

5078. RANDLE (H. N.). The Saurāshtrans of south India. *J. asiatic Soc.*, 44, p. 151-164.

5079. RANKIN (Sir George). Custom and the Muslim law in British India. *Trans. Grotius Soc.*, 39 [40], vol. 25, p. 89-118.

5080. RAO (V. K. R. V.). The national income of British India, 1931-32. London, Macmillan, 40, in-8, 233 p., 10s. 6d. R : V. Anstey, *Economica*, 40, vol. 7, p. 344-345. C. Clark, *Econ. Record*, 40, vol. 16, p. 282-283. G. F. Shirras, *Econ. J.*, 41, vol. 51, p. 325-333. S. D. Neumark, *South African J. Econ.*, 41, vol. 9, p. 96-98.

5081. RAWLINSON (H. G.). India: a short cultural history. New ed. London, Cresset Press, 43, in-8, 452 p., 30s. R : E. S. de B(eer), *History*, 43, vol. 28, p. 108-109.

5082. ROY (Sir Bijoy Prasad Singh). Parliamentary government in India. London; Calcutta, Thacker, 43, in-8, 13s. 6d. R : E. D. Maclagan, *J. asiatic Soc.*, 45, p. 104-105.

5083. RUDRA (A. B.). The Viceroy and Governor-General of India. London, Oxford Univ. Press, 40, in-8, xv-362 p., 15s. R : E.H., *J. central asian Soc.*, 41, vol. 28, p. 224-226.

5084. RUSSELL (Sir Alexander). Forty years' public health progress in India. *Asiatic R.*, 40, vol. 36, p. 474-485.

5085. SCHUSTER (Sir George) and WINT (Guy). India and democracy. London, Macmillan, 41, in-8, xvi-444 p., 12s. 6d. R : J. C. French, *J. central asian Soc.*, 41, vol. 28, p. 446-447. Sir W. P. Barton, *Quar. R.*, 42, vol. 278, p. 99-114. H. Brown, *19th Century*, 42, vol. 131, p. 90-94. Sir P. Cadell, *Asiatic R.*, 42, vol. 38, p. 216-218. H.H.D., *History*, 43, vol. 28, p. 124.

5086. SEN (S. N.). Prachīn Bāngālā Patra Saṅkalan (A collection of Old Bengali letters). Records in Oriental languages. Vol. 1 : Bengali letters. Gen. ed. : S. N. Sen. Calcutta, Univ. Press, 42, in-8, 501 p., (plates). R : E. H. C. Walsh, *J. asiatic Soc.*, 43, p. 270-272.

5087. SHAH (Tribhuvandas L.). Ancient India, from 900 B.C. to 100 A.D. History of ancient India for 1,000 years. London, Probsthain, 40-41, 3 vols. in-4, 386, 444, 506 p., (maps), 59s. 6d. R : A.Y.B., *J. asiatic Soc.*, 41, p. 181-183. R. Burn, *J. central asian Soc.*, 41, vol. 28, p. 105-107.

5088. SHENOY (B. R.). Ceylon currency and banking. London, Longmans, 41, in-8, xi-300 p., 15s. R : E. H. D. Arndt, *South African J. Econ.*, 41, vol. 9, p. 193-198. A. H. Tocker, *Econ. Record*, 42, vol. 18, p. 126-127.

5089. SIGUEIRA (T. N.). The education of India : history and problems. London, Oxford Univ. Press, 40, in-8, 220 p., 4s. 6d.

5090. SINHA (Narendra Krishna). Haidar Ali. Calcutta, Oriental Press, 41, in-8, iv-294 p., Rs. 5. R : P. R. Cadell, *J. asiatic Soc.*, 42, p. 260. P.E.R., *Eng. hist. R.*, 42, vol. 57, p. 530-531.

5091. STEIN (Sir Aurel). A survey of ancient sites along the ' lost ' Sarasvati river. *Geogr. J.*, 42, vol. 99, p. 173-182.

5092. SUBBRAMANIAN (K. R.). Buddhist remains in Andhra and Andhra history : 225-610 A.D. Allahabad, Kitabistan, 43, in-8, 186 p., (illus.), Rs. 2.8.

5093. SUHRAWARDY (S. A. B.). A critical survey of the development of the Urdu novel and short story. London, Longmans, 45, in-8, 316 p., 21s.

5094. TABAQAT-I-AKBARI. A history of India from the early Musulman invasions to the thirty-eighth year of the reign of Akbar of Khwajah Nizamuddin Ahmad, tr. and annotated by B. De, and rev. and ed. by B. Prashad. Vol. 3, pt. 2. London, Luzac, 40, in-8, 10s. (Bibl. Indica, work no. 225, issue no. 1,535, n.s.).

5095. THOMAS (P.). Epics, myths and legends of India : a comprehensive survey of the sacred lore of the Hindus and Buddhists. London, K. Paul, 42, in-4, 231 p., (illus.), 30s.

5096. THOMAS (P. J.). The growth of federal finance in India. London, Oxford Univ. Press, 40, in-8, xi-558 p., 20s. R : F. Noyce, *Econ. J.*, 40, vol. 50, p. 513-515.

5097. THOMAS (P. J.) and SASTRY (N. Sundararama). Commodity prices in south India, 1918-1938. London, Luzac, 40, in-8, 64 p., 2s. (Univ. of Madras, Bull. of the dept. of econ., no. 3).

5098. THOMPSON (Edward). The making of the Indian princes. London, Oxford Univ. Press, 43, in-8, 316 p., 20s. R : H. H. Dodwell, *Eng. hist. R.*, 44, vol. 59, p. 414-415. H.W.-B., *J. central asian Soc.*, 44, vol. 31, p. 98-99. C. C. Davies, *J. asiatic Soc.*, 44, p. 95. J. Coatman, *Int. Affairs*, 44, vol. 20, p. 147.

5099. VATS (M. S.). Excavations at Harappa : archaeological excavations between 1920-1 and 1933-4. Delhi, Manager of Publications, 40, 2 vols. in-8, xv-488 p., 139 plates, 77s. R : V. G. Childe, *Antiquity*, 41, vol. 15, p. 292-295.

5100. VENKATARAMANYYA (N.). The early Muslim expansion in south India. Madras, Univ. Press, 42, in-8, vi-216 p. R : C. C. Davies, *J. asiatic Soc.*, 45, p. 205-206.

5101. VRIDDHAGIRISAN (V.). The Nayaks of Tanjore. Anamalainagar, Anamalai Univ., 42, in-8, xv-197-44 p. (Anamalai univ. hist. ser., 3). R : R. E. Enthoven, *J. asiatic Soc.*, 44, p. 98-99.

5102. WELLESZ (E. F.). An Akbar-namah MS. *Burlington Mag.*, 42, vol. 80, p. 135-141 (plate).

5103. WYNDHAM (Horace). When Napier ruled in India : iron hand in velvet glove. *Army Quar.*, 42, vol. 44, p. 133-142.

§ 4. Indo-China and East Indian Islands

5104. CHRISTIAN (J. L.). Modern Burma : a survey of political and economic development. London, Cambridge Univ. Press, 42, in-8, x-382 p., (map), 18s. (Inst. of Pacific relations ser.).

5105. COLLIS (Maurice). The land of the Great Image : experiences of Friar Manrique in Arakan. London, Faber, 43, in-8, 259 p., 16s. R : E. B. Howell, *J. central asian Soc.*, 43, vol. 30, p. 335-337.

5106. CROSBY (Sir Josiah). The failure of constitutional government in Siam [1932]. *Asiatic R.*, 43, vol. 39, p. 415-420.

5107. FURNIVALL (J. S.). The fashioning of Leviathan : the beginnings of British rule in Burma. London, Probsthain, 40, in-8, 137 p., 5s. (Journ. of the Burma research soc., 29).

5108. FURNIVALL (J. S.). Educational progress in South-East Asia. London, Allen & Unwin, 44, in-8, 186 p., 10s. (Inst. of Pacific relations). R : E. F. Lee, *Int. R. Missions*, 44, vol. 33, p. 228-229.

5109. FURNIVALL (J. S.). Netherlands India. New ed. London, Cambridge Univ. Press, 44, in-8, xxiv-502 p., (maps), 25s.

5110. GORDINE (Dora). A lecture on the sculpture of Indochina, Siam, and Java. *J. asiatic Soc.*, 42, p. 132-138 (plates).

5111. HART (G. H. C.). Recent development in the Netherlands-Indies. *Geogr. J.*, 42, vol. 99, p. 81-102.

5112. HAYDEN (J. P.). The Philippines. London, Macmillan, 42, in-8, 984 p., (illus.), 31s. 6d.

5113. HUTCHINSON (E. W.). Adventurers in Siam in the 17th century. London, Luzac, 40, in-8, xxviii-283 p., (illus., maps), 12s. 6d. (Roy. Asiatic Soc., prize publ. fund, vol. 18). R : W. A. Graham, *J. central asian Soc.*, 41, vol. 28, p. 464-466. R. O. Winstedt, *J. asiatic Soc.*, 41, p. 366-367.

5114. LANDON (Kenneth Perry). Siam in transition : a brief survey of cultural trends in the five years since the revolution of 1932. London, Oxford Univ. Press, 40, in-8, 328 p., 10s. 6d. R : R. Le May, *Asiatic R.*, 41, vol. 37, p. 191-193. W. R. Wheeler, *Int. R. Missions*, 41, vol. 30, p. 292-294. G.G.-B., *Scottish geogr. Mag.*, 41, vol. 57, p. 90.

5115. LE MAY (Reginald). Modern imitations of early stone sculpture from Siam. *Burlington Mag.*, 43, vol. 82, p. 10-14, 197-201 (plates).

5116. MAJUMDAR (R. C.). Kambuja-Deśa, or, An ancient Hindu colony in Cambodia. Madras, Univ. Press, 44, in-8, iv-165 p., Rs. 4. R : R. O. Winstedt, *J. asiatic Soc.*, 45, p. 200-201.

5117. MILLS (Lennox A.). British rule in eastern Asia : a study of comparative government and economic development in British Malaya and Hongkong. London, Milford, 42, in-8, viii-581 p., 25s. (Inst. of Pacific relations internat. research ser.). R : *J. central asian Soc.*, 42, vol. 29, p. 272-275. R. O. Winstedt, *J. asiatic Soc.*, 42, p. 139-140.

5118. MORRELL (Charles M.). The development of Netherlands administration in the East Indies. *Asiatic R.*, 40, vol. 36, p. 137-144.

5119. ROBEQUAIN (C.). The economic development of French Indo-China. London, Oxford Univ. Press, 45, in-8, 410 p., 18s.

5120. STAMP (L. Dudley). Siam before the war. *Geogr. J.*, 42, vol. 99, p. 209-224.

5121. SWETTENHAM (Sir Frank). Footprints in Malaya. London, Hutchinson, 42, in-8, 176 p., (plates), 12s. 6d. R : R. O. Winstedt, *J. asiatic Soc.*, 42, p. 140-141; *Asiatic R.*, 42, vol. 38, p. 333-334.

5122. SWITHINBANK (B. W.). Responsible government in Burma, 1937 to 1941. *Asiatic R.*, 43, vol. 39, p. 153-160.

5123. TWEEDIE (M. W. F.). Prehistory in Malaya. *J. asiatic Soc.*, 42, p. 1-13 (plates).

5124. VANDENBOSCH (Amry). The Dutch East Indies : its government, problems, and politics. 3rd ed. London, Cambridge Univ. Press, 42, in-8, xiv-458 p., 24s. R : A. Muhlenfeld, *J. central asian Soc.*, 42, vol. 29, p. 64-69. J. S. Furnivall, *J. asiatic Soc.*, 42, p. 56-58.

5125. VLEKKE (B. H. M.). Nusantara : a history of the East Indian Archipelago. London, Oxford Univ. Press, 44, in-8, 456 p., (illus., maps), 28s. R : A. L. Warnshuis, *Int. R. Missions*, 44, vol. 33, p. 453-455. R. O. Winstedt, *J. asiatic Soc.*, 44, p. 203-205.

5126. VLEKKE (B. H. M.). The story of the Dutch East Indies. London, Oxford Univ. Press, 45, in-8, 252 p., (illus.), 16s. 6d.

5127. WINSTEDT (Sir Richard O.). A history of Malay literature. London, Luzac; Singapore, Printers, Ltd., 40, in-8, vii-243 p., 8s. 6d.; $3.50. (Roy. Asiatic soc., Malayan br., vol. 17, pt. 3). R : C. O. Blagden, *J. asiatic Soc.*, 41, p. 167-168.

5128. WINSTEDT (Sir R. O.). An undescribed Malay version of the Ramayana. *J. asiatic Soc.*, 44, p. 62-73.

5129. WINSTEDT (Sir R. O.). Indian influence in the Malay world. *J. asiatic Soc.*, 44, p. 186-196.

5130. WINSTEDT (Sir R. O.). Britain and Malaya, 1786-1941. London, Longmans, 44, in-8, 80p., 1s. (Longmans' pamph. on the British Commonwealth, 2nd ser., 1). R : J. Crosby, *J. asiatic Soc.*, 45, p. 94-95. L. C. Finch, *J. central asian Soc.*, 45, vol. 32, p. 113-114.

5131. WINSTEDT (Sir R. O.). Old Malay legal digests and Malay customary law. *J. asiatic Soc.*, 45, p. 17-29.

§ 5. China

5132. BAILEY (H. W.). Kaṇaiska. *J. asiatic Soc.*, 42, p. 14-28.

5133. BINGHAM (W.). The founding of the T'ang dynasty : the fall of Sui and the rise of T'ang. London, Paul, 43, in-8, xiii-183 p., 21s.

5134. BISHOP (C. W.). Beginnings of civilization in eastern Asia. *Antiquity*, 40, vol. 14, p. 301-316.

5135. BURROW (T.). Translation of the Kharosthi documents from Chinese Turkestan. London, Roy. Asiatic Soc., 41, in-8, 157 p., 7s. 6d. (J. G. Forlong Fund). R : M.A.C., *J. central asian Soc.*, 41, vol. 28, p. 378-379.

5136. COHN (William). A Chinese Buddha image of the year 1396. *Burlington Mag.*, 40, vol. 77, p. 14-20.

5137. COHN (W.). Chinese wall-paintings. *Burlington Mag.*, 43, vol. 83, p. 168-174 (plates).

5138. COLLIS (Maurice). The great within. London, Faber, 41, in-8, 350 p., (maps), 21s. R : D. B.-B., *J. central asian Soc.*, 42, vol. 29, p. 276-279.

5139. FITZGERALD (C. P.). The Tower of Five Glories : a study of the Min Chia of Tali, Yunnan. London, Cresset Press, 41, in-8, 280 p., (illus.),

16s. R : G. Reitlinger, *J. central asian Soc.*, 41, vol. 28, p. 237-239. B. Z. Seligman, *Geogr. J.*, 41, vol. 98, p. 156-157.

5140. Fox (G.). British admirals and Chinese pirates, 1832-1869. London, K. Paul, 40, in-8, xiv-227 p., 12s. 6d.

5141. GREEN (O. M.). The foreigner in China. London, Hutchinson, 43, in-8, 190 p., (illus.), 15s. R : P.H.B.K., *J. central asian Soc.*, 43, vol. 30, p. 215-221.

5142. GREEN (O. M.). The story of China's revolution. London, Hutchinson, 45, in-8, 240 p., (illus.), 18s.

5143. HACKNEY (Louise Wallace) and YAU (Chang-foo). A study of Chinese paintings in the collection of Ada Small Moore. London, Oxford Univ. Press, 41, in-2, xvi-279 p., (plates), 168s. R : B. Gray, *J. central asian Soc.*, 41, vol. 28, p. 468-471. *J. asiatic Soc.*, 42, p. 139. W. Cohn, *Burlington Mag.*, 42, vol. 80, p. 10-17.

5144. HIBBERT (Eloise Talcott). K'ang Hsi, Emperor of China. London, Paul, 40, in-8, x-298 p., (illus.), 15s. R : O. M. Green, *Int. Affairs*, 41, vol. 19, p. 348-349. C.H.P., *J. central asian Soc.*, 41, vol. 28, p. 107-109.

5145. HOPKINS (L. C.). Symbols of parentage in archaic Chinese. *J. asiatic Soc.*, 40, p. 351-362.

5146. HOPKINS (L. C.). The bear-skin, another pictographic reconnaissance from primitive prophylactic to present-day panache : a Chinese epigraphic puzzle. *J. asiatic Soc.*, 43, p. 110-117.

5147. HU SHIH. Maker of modern China : the story of Sun Yat-Sen. *Asiatic R.*, 44, vol. 40, p. 302-307.

5148. HUGHES (E. R.). Chinese philosophy in classical times, tr. from the Chinese. London, Dent, 42, in-8, 336 p., 3s. (Everyman's libr.).

5149. Hummel (A. W.) ed. Eminent Chinese of the Ch'ing period : 1644-1912. London, Paul, 44-45, 2 vols. in-8, xi-604, 1103 p., 34s. R (Vol. 1) : W. V. Purcell, *J. asiatic Soc.*, 44, p. 91-92; *Int. Affairs*, 44, vol. 20, p. 592-593.

5150. Jones (F. C.). Shanghai and Tientsin. London, Oxford Univ. Press, 40, in-8, 192 p., 7s. 6d. R : A. F. Algie, *J. central asian Soc.*, 40, vol. 27, p. 361-365.

5151. Kirkpatrick (W. M.). Our understanding of China : past and present. *J. central asian Soc.*, 42, vol. 29, p. 35-42.

5152. Lattimore (Owen). Inner Asian frontiers of China. London, Oxford Univ. Press, 40, in-8, xxiii-585 p., (maps), 25s. (Amer. geogr. soc., research ser., 21). R : J. L. Myres, *Man*, 40, vol. 40, p. 156-157.

5153. Lattimore (Owen and Eleanor). The making of modern China, a short history. London, Allen & Unwin, 45, in-8, 212 p., 8s. 6d. R : C.P.F., *Geogr. J.*, 45, vol. 105, p. 212-213. J. T. Pratt, *Int. Affairs*, 45, vol. 21, p. 423-424. H. St. C. S., *J. central asian Soc.*, 45, vol. 32, p. 219-220. A. E. Armstrong, *Int. R. Missions*, 44, vol. 33, p. 455-457.

5154. Martin (Bernard). Strange vigour : a biography of Sun Yat-sen. London, Heinemann, 44, in-8, xii-248 p., 12s. 6d.

5155. Martin (H. Desmond). The Mongol wars with Hsi Hsia (1205-27). *J. asiatic Soc.*, 42, p. 195-228.

5156. Martin (H. D.). Chinghiz Khan's first invasion of the Chin empire. *J. asiatic Soc.*, 43, p. 182-216.

5157. Mencius. The book of Mencius (abridged), tr. from the Chinese by L. Giles. London, Murray, 42, in-8, 128 p., 3s. 6d. (Wisdom of the East ser.). R : E. B. Howell, *J. asiatic Soc.*, 42, p. 251-252.

5158. Michael (F.). The origin of Manchu rule in China. London, Oxford Univ. Press, 42, in-8, 137 p., 9s.

5159. Mirams (D. G.). A brief history of Chinese architecture. London, Paul, 41, in-8, xxiii-132 p., (illus.), 12s. 6d.

5160. Moule (A. C.). Nestorians in China : some corrections and additions. London, China Society, 40, in-8, 43 p., (illus.), 6s. (Sinolog. ser., 1). R : J. Foster, *Int. R. Missions*, 41, vol. 30, p. 146-147.

5161. Pan Ku. The history of the former Han dynasty, tr. from the Chinese by H. Dubs and P'an Lo-Chi and Jan T'ai. Vol. 2. London, Paul, 45, in-8, 426 p., 30s.

5162. Pratt (Sir John). War and politics in China. London, Cape, 43, in-8, 290 p., 12s. 6d. R : R.H.C., *J. central asian Soc.*, 43, vol. 30, p. 322-323.

5163. Rosinger (Lawrence K.). China's wartime politics, 1937-1944. 2nd ed. London, Oxford Univ. Press, 45, in-8, viii-133 p., 13s. 6d. R : G. E. Hubbard, *Int. Affairs*, 45, vol. 21, p. 558-559.

5164. Seeger (E.). Pageant of Chinese history. London, Longmans, 42, in-8, 386 p., 12s. 6d.

5165. Ssu-Yu Teng. Chang Hsi and the treaty of Nanking, 1842. London, Cambridge Univ. Press, 45, in-8, xii-192 p., 24s.

5166. Sturton (Stephen D.). The site of the Nestorian monastery at Hangchow. *Asiatic R.*, 45, vol. 41, p. 82-85.

5167. Sun Yat-Sen. The international development of China. London, Hutchinson, 44, in-8, 176 p., (maps), 7s. 6d. R : P.H.B.K., *J. central asian Soc.*, 45, vol. 32, p. 114-115.

5168. SZCZEŚNIAK (Bolesław). Notes on the penetration of the Copernican theory into China (17th-19th centuries). *J. asiatic Soc.*, 45, p. 30-38.

5169. THOMAS (F. W.). Sino-Kharoṣṭhī coins. *Numism. Chron.*, 44, 6th ser., vol. 4, p. 83-98.

5170. TSUI CHI. A short history of Chinese civilization. London, Gollancz, 42, in-8, 336 p., (maps, illus.), 12s. 6d.

5171. WANG (S. T.). The Margary affair and the Chefoo agreement. London, Oxford Univ. Press, 40, in-8, 138 p., 7s. 6d. R : F. L., *J. central asian Soc.*, 40, vol. 27, p. 483-485.

5172. WHITE (W. C.). Chinese temple frescoes : a study of 3 wall-paintings of the 13th century. Toronto, Univ. Press, 40, in-4, xvii-230 p., (plates), $4.00. (Roy. Ontario mus. of archaeol., mus. stud., 3). R : A.B., *Queen's Quar.*, 42, vol. 49, p. 171.

5173. WHITE (W. C.) and WILLIAMS (R. J.). Chinese Jews : a compilation of matters relating to the Jews of K'aifeng Fu. London, Probsthain, 43, 3 vols. in-4, (maps, illus.), 72s. (Univ. of Toronto, dept. of Chinese stud.).

5174. WOO (G. H.). Medical progress in China. *Asiatic R.*, 42, vol. 38, p. 179-187.

5175. WU (Aitchen K.). Turkistan tumult. London, Methuen, 40, in-8, 292 p., (plates, maps), 12s. 6d. R : G. Macartney, *J. central asian Soc.*, 40, vol. 27, p. 234-238.

§ 6. Japan (before 1868) and Korea

5176. ANESAKI (M.). The foundation of Buddhist culture in Japan : the Buddhist ideals conceived and implemented by the Prince Regent Shotoku. *Trans. Proc. Japan Soc.*, 41, vol. 37, p. 55-66.

5177. BROMEHEAD (C. N.). Ancient mining processes as illustrated by a Japanese scroll. *Antiquity*, 42, vol. 16, p. 193-207 (illus.).

5178. CASAL (U. A.). The Inro. *Trans. Proc. Japan Soc.*, 41, vol. 37, p. 1-53.

5179. KAJI (R.). Japan : her cultural development. London, Luzac, 40, in-4, vi-74 p., (illus.), 5s.

5180. SADLER (A. L.). A short history of Japanese architecture. Sydney, Angus & Robertson, 42, in-4, xiv-140 p., (plates), 21s.

5181. SINGER (Kurt). Cowrie and baubo in early Japan. *Man*, 40, vol. 40, p. 50-53.

5182. SOPER (A. C.). The evolution of Buddhist architecture in Japan. London, Oxford Univ. Press, 42, in-4, 346 p., (plates), 52s. 6d.

5183. SZCZEŚNIAK (Bolesław). The penetration of the Copernican theory into feudal Japan. *J. asiatic Soc.*, 44, p. 52-61.

5184. TUNG-CHING-CH'ENG. Report on the excavation of the site of the capital of P'o-hai, ed. by Y. Harada and K. Komai. In English, Russian, and Japanese. London, Paul, 40, in-4, xii-140 p., (plates, plans, figs.), 90s. (Archaeol. orientalis, ser. A, vol. 5).

5185. SHAW (C. T.). Archaeology in the Gold Coast [with Select bibliography]. *African Stud.*, 43, vol. 2, p. 139-147.

5186. ARKELL (A. J.). Archaeological research in West Africa. *Antiquity*, 44, vol. 18, p. 147-150.

5187. COOKE (H. B. S.). A preliminary survey of the quaternary period in South Africa. Pretoria, South Africa Bureau of Archaeology, 41, in-8, 60 p., (illus.), 2s. (Archaeol. ser., 4). R : J. L. M(yres), *Man*, 41, vol. 41, p. 135.

5188. COOKE (H. B. S.), MALAN (B. D.) and WELLS (L. H.). Fossil man in the Lebombo mountains, South Africa : the 'border cave', Ingwavuma district, Zululand. *Man*, 45, vol. 45, p. 6-12.

5190. FAGG (Bernard). Preliminary report on a microlithic industry at Rop Rock Shelter, Northern Nigeria. *Proc. prehist. Soc.*, 44, vol. 10, p. 68-69 (illus.).

5191. FAGG (B.). A preliminary note on a new series of pottery figures from Northern Nigeria. *Africa*, 45, vol. 15, p. 21-22.

5192. GOODWIN (A. J. H.). The bored stones of southern Africa. Pt. 1 : Bantu specimens. Cape Town, Univ. Press, 42, in-2, 22 p., 2s. (School of Afr. stud., communications, n.s., 1). R : C. van Riet Lowe, *African Stud.*, 42, vol. 1, p. 232.

5193. GOODWIN (A. J. H.). Notes on archaeological method, with special reference to African conditions. Cape Town, Univ. Press, 42, in-2, 27 p., 2s. 6d. (School of Afr. stud., communications, n.s., 4). R : T. K. Penniman, *Man*, 44, vol. 44, p. 52.

5194. JEFFREYS (M. D. W.). Snake stones. *J. Roy. African Soc.*, 42, vol. 41, p. 250-253.

5195. JOIRE (J.). Archaeological discoveries in Senegal. *Man*, 43, vol. 43, p. 49-52.

5196. LEAKEY (L. S. B.). Stone-age man in East Africa. *B. Uganda Soc.*, 44, no. 2, p. 11-12.

5197. LOWE (C. van Riet). The evolution of the Levallois technique in South Africa. *Man*, 45, vol. 45, p. 49-59.

5198. MEYEROWITZ (Eva L. R.). Four pre-Portuguese bronze castings from Benin. *Man*, 40, vol. 40, p. 129-132.

5199. MEYEROWITZ (E. L. R.). Ancient Nigerian bronzes. 2 pts. *Burlington Mag.*, 41, vol. 79, p. 89-93, 121-126.

5200. MEYEROWITZ (E. L. R.). The stone figures of Esie in Nigeria. *Burlington Mag.*, 43, vol. 82, p. 31-36 (plates).

5201. MEYEROWITZ (E. L. R.). Ancient bronzes in the Royal Palace at Benin. *Burlington Mag.*, 43, vol. 83, p. 248-253.

5202. MURRAY (K. C.). Arts and crafts of Nigeria, their past and future. *Africa*, 43, vol. 14, p. 155-164.

5203. NADEL (S. F.). A black Byzantium : the kingdom of Nupe in Nigeria. London, Oxford Univ. Press, 42, in-8, xiv-420 p., (plates), 25s. (Int. inst. of Afr. lang. and cultures). R : B. Imp. Inst., 43, vol. 41, p. 189-190. H. Vischer, *Int. Affairs*, 43, vol. 19, p. 697-698. A. W. Southall, *J. Roy. African Soc.*, 43, vol. 42, p. 87. M. Gluckman, *African Stud.*, 43, vol. 2, p. 171-173. D. Forde, *Africa*, 43, vol. 14, p. 93-95. C. W. W. Greenidge, *Int. R. Missions*, 43, vol. 32, p. 348-350.

5204. NEWBOLD (Douglas). The history and archaeology of the Libyan desert. *Sudan Notes and Records*, 45, vol. 26, p. 229-239.

5205. O. (F. M.). Contribution to the study of the chronology of African plastic art. *Africa*, 43, vol. 14, p. 183-193 (plates).

5206. PALMER (Sir Richmond). Ancient Nigerian bronzes. *Burlington Mag.*, 42, vol. 81, p. 252-254.

5207. RIET (J. E. M. van der) and BLEEK (D. F.). More rock paintings in South Africa. London, Methuen, 40, in-4, xx p., (plates), 42s. R : J. J. Hawkes, *Archaeol. J.*, 39 (40), vol. 96, p. 302-303. G.C.T., *Proc. prehist. Soc.*, 40, vol. 6, p. 185-186.

5208. SHAW (C. T.). Report on excavations carried out in the cave known as 'Bosumpra' at Abertifi, Kwahu, Gold Coast Colony. *Proc. prehist. Soc.*, 44, vol. 10, p. 1-67 (illus.).

5209. WAINWRIGHT (G. A.). The Egyptian origin of the New Year's sacrifice at Zanzibar. *Man*, 40, vol. 40, p. 164-167.

5210. WAINWRIGHT (G. A.). Early records of iron in Abyssinia. *Man*, 42, vol. 42, p. 84-88.

5211. WAINWRIGHT (G. A.). The coming of iron to some African peoples. *Man*, 42, vol. 42, p. 103-108.

5212. WAINWRIGHT (G. A.). Iron in the Napatan and Meroitic ages. *Sudan Notes and Records*, 45, vol. 26, p. 5-36.

5213. BELLAMY (H. S.). Built before the Flood : the problem of the Tiahuanaco ruins. London, Faber, 43, in-8, 144 p., (illus.), 12s. 6d.

5214. BENNETT (Wendell C.). Chavin stone carving. London, Oxford Univ. Press, 42, in-4, 30 p., 4s. 6d. (Yale anthrop. stud., vol. 3). R : W. L. Hildburgh, *Burlington Mag.*, 45, vol. 86, p. 78.

5215. BENNETT (W. C.) and FORD (J. A.). Archaeological regions of Colombia : excavations in the vicinity of Cali. London, Oxford Univ. Press, 44, in-4, 186 p., (illus.), 16s. 6d.

5216. CLARK (J. G. D.). New World origins. *Antiquity*, 40, vol. 14, p. 117-137 (illus.).

5217. COLEMAN (Arthur P.). The last million years : a history of the pleistocene in North America, ed. by G. F. Kay. London, Oxford Univ. Press, 41, in-8, 216 p., (illus.), 16s.

5218. HAWLEY (F.). Tree-ringing analysis and dating in the Mississippi drainage. London, Cambridge Univ. Press, 41, in-8, xxii-110 p., 9s.

5219. LIPMAN (J.). American primitive painting. London, Oxford Univ. Press, 42, in-4, 172 p., (illus.), 30s.

5220. MARYON (Herbert). Archaeology and metallurgy, 2 : The metallurgy of gold and platinum in pre-Columbian Ecuador. *Man*, 41, vol. 41, p. 124-126.

5221. MEDIONI (G.) and PINTO (M. T.). Art in ancient Mexico. London, Oxford Univ. Press, 41, in-4, 26 p., 259 plates, 42s.

5222. MONTAGU (M. F. Ashley). Genetics and the antiquity of man in the Americas. *Man*, 43, vol. 43, p. 131-135.

5223. NAPIER (Hazel Ballance). Carib petroglyphs in the Virgin island of St. John. *Man*, 43, vol. 43, p. 135-137.

5224. OSGOOD (C.) and HOWARD (G. D.). An archaeological survey of Venezuela. London, Oxford Univ. Press, 44, in-4, 72 p., (plates, figs.), 23s. 6d.

5225. OSGOOD (C.) and ROUSE (I.). The Ciboney culture of Cayo, Redonda, Cuba : archaeology of the Maniabon Hills, Cuba. London, Oxford Univ. Press, 43, in-4, 184 p., (illus., maps), 23s. 6d.

5226. RAINEY (F. G.). Excavations in the Fort Liberté region, Haiti. London, Oxford Univ. Press, 41, in-8, 196 p., (illus.), 16s.

5227. RENAUD (E. B.). The North American tang-knife. *Man*, 42, vol. 42, p. 65-67.

5228. WESLAGER (C. A.). Delaware's buried past : a story of archaeological adventure. London, Oxford Univ. Press, 45, in-8, 184 p., (illus.), 15s. 6d.

5229. ADKIN (G. L.). Former food stores (*pataka*) in Lake Horowhenua. *J. polynesian Soc.*, 42, vol. 51, p. 181-186.

5230. BLACK (Lindsay). Cylcons: the mystery stones of the Darling river valley. Sydney, The Author, 42, in-8, 103 p., (plates), 7s. 6d. R : J. L. M[yres], *Man*, 44, vol. 44, p. 53.

5231. BRADLEY (H. W.). The American frontier in Hawaii : the pioneers, 1789-1843. London, Oxford Univ. Press, 43, in-8, 500 p., (map), 28s. R : G. Greenwood, *Hist. Stud. Australia N.Z.*, 43, vol. 2, p. 272-274.

5232. BUCK (Peter H.). The disappearance of canoes in Polynesia. *J. polynesian Soc.*, 42, vol. 51, p. 191-199.

5233. DUFF (Roger). First records of the *maro* in the New Zealand area. *J. polynesian Soc.*, 43, vol. 52, p. 212-215.

5234. FREEMAN (J. D.). The Seuao cave. *J. polynesian Soc.*, 43, vol. 52, p. 101-109.

5235. FREEMAN (J. D.). The Falemaunga caves. *J. polynesian Soc.*, 44, vol. 53, p. 86-106 (plates).

5236. FREEMAN (J. D.). ' O le Fale o le Fe'e '. *J. polynesian Soc.*, 44, vol. 53, p. 121-144.

5237. FREEMAN (J. D.). The Vailele earthmounds. *J. polynesian Soc.*, 44, vol. 53, p. 145-162 (plates).

5238. GRAHAM (George). Te Aotea: the happenings there, leading to the last intertribal wars of Hauraki. *J. polynesian Soc.*, 45, vol. 54, p. 192-198.

5239. GREENWOOD (William). The upraised hand, or, The spiritual significance of the rise of the Ringatu faith. *J. polynesian Soc.*, 42, vol. 51, p. 1-80.

5240. GRIFFITHS (G.). Discovery and excavation of an old Maori (No. 1) camp near Normanby, Timaru. *J. polynesian Soc.*, 41, vol. 50, p. 211-231.

5241. —— —— No. 2 camp. *J. polynesian Soc.*, 42, vol. 51, p. 115-125.

5242. GRIFFITHS (G.). Discovery of a *moa* egg at Shag river-mouth. *J. polynesian Soc.*, 42, vol. 51, p. 81-85.

5243. HORNELL (James). Was there pre-Columbian contact between the peoples of Oceania and South America? *J. polynesian Soc.*, 45, vol. 54, p. 167-191.

5244. KELLY (Leslie G.). Tapuariki and Raupa, with remarks on Marsden's visit to Hauraki. *J. polynesian Soc.*, 45, vol. 54, p. 199-211.

5245. KNOWLES (Sir Francis H. S.). The manufacture of a flint arrowhead by quartzite hammer-stone. London, Oxford Univ. Press, 44, in-8, 37 p., 5s. (Oxf. Univ., Pitt Rivers mus., occas. papers in technol., 1). R : A. P. Elkin, *Oceania*, 44, vol. 15, p. 168.

5246. LANYON-ORGILL (P. A.). The Easter Island script. *J. polynesian Soc.*, 42, vol. 51, p. 187-190.

5247. LANYON-ORGILL (P. A.). The origin of the Oceanic languages. *J. polynesian Soc.*, 43, vol. 52, p. 25-45 [with Bibliography].

5248. LAYARD (John). Stone men of Malekula : the small island of Vao. London, Chatto & Windus, 42, in-8, 816 p., (plates, maps), 50s. R : *National R.*, 43, vol. 120, p. 255-256.

5249. LEASK (Maurice F.). A kitchen midden in Papua. *Oceania*, 43, vol. 13, p. 235-242.

5250. MITCHELL (J. H.). Takitimu. Wellington, Reed, 44, in-8, 271 p., 22 tables. R : W.G., *J. polynesian Soc.*, 45, vol. 54, p. 87-90, 117-124.

5251. ROLSTON (Richard). Excavations at *pa*-site Lake Horowhenua. *J. polynesian Soc.*, 44, vol. 53, p. 163-174.

5252. ROSE (Frederick). Paintings of the Groote Eylandt aborigines. *Oceania*, 42, vol. 13, p. 170-176 (plates).

5253. RUSSELL (W. E.). Rotuma, its history, traditions and customs. *J. polynesian Soc.*, 42, vol. 51, p. 229-255.

5254. SKINNER (H. D.). A classification of the fish-hooks of Murihiku, with notes on allied forms from other parts of Polynesia. *J. polynesian Soc.*, 42, vol. 51, p. 208-221, 256-286 (plates).

5255. SKINNER (H. D.). The classification of greywacke and nephrite adzes from Murihiku, N.Z. *J. polynesian Soc.*, 43, vol. 52, p. 65-85, 157-190.

5256. STEVENSON (G. B.). Waitaki Maori paintings. *J. polynesian Soc.*, 43, vol. 52, p. 191-198.

5257. VIAL (L. G.). Stone axes of Mount Hagen, New Guinea. *Oceania*, 40, vol. 11, p. 158-163.

5258. WOLFF (Werner). The mystery of the Easter Island script. *J. polynesian Soc.*, 45, vol. 54, p. 1-38.

ADDENDA

G

EARLY HISTORY OF THE CHURCH TO GREGORY THE GREAT

5259. MUCKLE (J. T.). The doctrine of St. Gregory of Nyssa on man as the image of God. *Med. Stud.*, 45, vol. 7, p. 55-84.

5260. PEGIS (A. C.). The mind of St. Augustine. *Med. Stud.*, 44, vol. 6, p. 1-61.

H

BYZANTINE HISTORY (SINCE JUSTINIAN)

5261. LADNER (Gerhart B.). Origin and significance of the Byzantine iconoclastic controversy. *Med. Stud.*, 40, vol. 2, p. 127-149.

I

HISTORY OF THE MIDDLE AGES

5262. BIRD (Otto). The *Canzone d'Amore* of Cavalcanti according to the commentary of Dino del Garbo. [Prints text]. *Med. Stud.*, 40, vol. 2, p. 150-203 ; 41, vol. 3, p. 117-144.

5263. BRIEGER (Peter H.). England's contribution to the origin and development of the triumphal cross. *Med. Stud.*, 42, vol. 4, p. 85-96 (illus.).

5264. BURBACH (Maur). Early Dominican and Franciscan legislation regarding St. Thomas. *Med. Stud.*, 42, vol. 4, p. 139-158.

5265. CHOQUETTE (Imelda). *Voluntas, Affectio* and *Potestas* in the *Liber de Voluntate* of St. Anselm. *Med. Stud.*, 42, vol. 4, p. 61-81.

5266. CUTTINO (G. P.). Henry of Canterbury. *Eng. hist. R.*, 42, vol. 57, p. 298-311.

5267. DENOMY (A. J.). An inquiry into the origin of courtly love. *Med. Stud.*, 44, vol. 6, p. 175-260.

5268. DENOMY (A. J.). *Fin' Amors:* the pure love of the troubadours, its amorality, and possible source. *Med. Stud.*, 45, vol. 7, p. 139-207.

5269. ESCHMANN (Th.). A Thomistic glossary on the principle of the pre-eminence of a common good. *Med. Stud.*, 43, vol. 5, p. 123-166.

5270. ESCHMANN (Th.). ' Bonum commune melius est quam bonum unius ' : a study of the personalist conception in St. Thomas Aquinas. [In German]. *Med. Stud.*, 44, vol. 6, p. 62-120.

5271. FACKENHEIM (Emil L.). The conception of substance in the philosophy of the Ikwan as-Sefa' (Brethren of Purity). *Med. Stud.*, 43, vol. 5, p. 115-122.

5272. FACKENHEIM (E. L.). A treatise on love by Ibn Sina : translated. *Med. Stud.*, 45, vol. 7, p. 208-228.

5273. FLAHIFF (G. B.). Ralph Niger; an introduction to his life and works. *Med. Stud.*, 40, vol. 2, p. 104-126.

5274. FLAHIFF (G. B.). The use of prohibitions by clerics against ecclesiastical courts in England. *Med. Stud.*, 41, vol. 3, p. 101-116.

5275. FLAHIFF (G. B.). The censorship of books in the twelfth century. *Med. Stud.*, 42, vol. 4, p. 1-22.

5276. FLAHIFF (G. B.). The Writ of Prohibition to Court Christian in the thirteenth century. *Med. Stud.*, 44, vol. 6, p. 261-313; 45, vol. 7, p. 229-290.

5277. GORMON (William). Albertus Magnus on Aristotle's second definition of the soul. *Med. Stud.*, 40, vol. 2, p. 223-230.

5278. HENNIG (John). St. Albert, patron of Cashel : a study in the history of diocesan episcopacy in Ireland. *Med. Stud.*, 45, vol. 7, p. 21-39.

5279. KANTOROWICZ (H.). Bractonian problems. Glasgow, Jackson, 41, in-8, 133 p., 4s. (Glasgow univ. publ., 56). R : W. S. Holdsworth, *Eng. hist. R.*, 42, vol. 57, p. 502-504.

5280. KENNEDY (V. L.). The Franciscan *Ordo Missae* in the thirteenth century. *Med. Stud.*, 40, vol. 2, p. 204-222.

5281. KENNEDY (V. L.). The handbook of Master Peter, chancellor of Chartres. *Med. Stud.*, 43, vol. 5, p. 1-38.

5282. KENNEDY (V. L.). The moment of consecration and the elevation of the Host [in the Middle Ages]. *Med. Stud.*, 44, vol. 6, p. 121-150.

5283. KENNEDY (V. L.). Robert Courson on penance. *Med. Stud.*, 45, vol. 7, p. 291-336.

5284. KNOWLES (M. D.). Some aspects of the career of Archbishop Pecham. *Eng. hist. R.*, 42, vol. 57, p. 1-18, 178-201.

5285. LADNER (Gerhart B.). The so-called square nimbus. *Med. Stud.*, 41, vol. 3, p. 15-45 (illus.).

5286. LADNER (G. B.). The symbolism of the medieval corner stone in the medieval West. *Med. Stud.*, 42, vol. 4, p. 43-60.

5287. LADNER (G. B.). An additional note on hexagonal nimbi. *Med. Stud.*, 42, vol. 4, p. 82-84.

5288. LLOYD (John Edward). Geoffrey of Monmouth. *Eng. hist. R.*, 42, vol. 57, p. 460-468.

5289. LYNCH (Lawrence E.). The doctrine of divine ideas and illumination in Robert Grosseteste. *Med. Stud.*, 41, vol. 3, p. 161-173.

5290. McLAUGHLIN (T. P.). The teaching of the Canonists on usury, 4 : Punishment of usurers. *Med. Stud.*, 40, vol. 2, p. 1-22.

5291. McLAUGHLIN (T. P.). The prohibition of marriage against canons in the early twelfth century. *Med. Stud.*, 41, vol. 3, p. 94-100.

5292. MAGOUN (Francis P.) jr. An English pilgrim-diary of the year 990. *Med. Stud.*, 40, vol. 2, p. 231-252.

5293. MAGOUN (F. P.) jr. The pilgrim-diary of Nikulas Munkathvera : the road to Rome. *Med. Stud.*, 44, vol. 6, p. 314-354.

5294. MAGOUN (F. P.) jr. Geographical and ethnic names in the *Nibelungenlied*. *Med. Stud.*, 45, vol. 7, p. 85-138.

5295. MARCIA (M. M.). The Logos as a basis for a doctrine of Providence. *Med. Stud.*, 43, vol. 5, p. 75-101.

5296. MARITAIN (Jacques). L'humanisme de Saint Thomas d'Aquin. *Med. Stud.*, 41, vol. 3, p. 174-184.

5297. MARITAIN (J.). Spontanéité et indépendance. *Med. Stud.*, 42, vol. 4, p. 23-32.

5298. MARITAIN (J.). Sur la doctrine de l'aséité divine. *Med. Stud.*, 43, vol. 5, p. 39-50.

5299. MENUT (Albert J.) and DENOMY (Alexander J.). Maistre Nicole Oresme *Le livre du ciel et du monde* : text and commentary. *Med. Stud.*, 41, vol. 3, p. 185-297; 42, vol. 4, p. 159-297; 43, vol. 5, p. 167-331.

5300. MUCKLE (J. T.). The treatise *De Anima* of Dominicus Gundissalinus. [Prints newly edited text]. *Med. Stud.*, 40, vol. 2, p. 23-83.

5301. MUCKLE (J. T.). Greek works translated into Latin before 1350. *Med. Stud.*, 42, vol. 4, p. 33-42 ; 43, vol. 5, p. 102-114.

5302. MUCKLE (J. T.). The hexameron of Robert Grosseteste : the first twelve chapters of part seven. *Med. Stud.*, 44, vol. 6, p. 151-174.

5303. O'DONNELL (J. Reginald). The *Syncategoremata* of William of Sherwood. [Prints text]. *Med. Stud.*, 41, vol. 3, p. 46-93.

5304. O'DONNELL (J. R.). The philosophy of Nicholas of Autrecourt and his appraisal of Aristotle. *Med. Stud.*, 42, vol. 4, p. 97-125.

5305. O'DONNELL (J. R.). The meaning of ' Silva ' in the commentary on the *Timaeus* of Plato by Chalcidius. *Med. Stud.*, 45, vol. 7, p. 1-20.

5306. POLLARD (A. F.). The clerical organization of Parliament. *Eng. hist. R.*, 42, vol. 57, p. 31-58.

5307. POLLARD (A. F.). Receivers of petitions and Clerks of Parliament. *Eng. hist. R.*, 42, vol. 57, p. 202-226.

5308. POLLARD (A. F.). The Clerk of the Crown. *Eng. hist. R.*, 42, vol. 57, p. 312-333.

5309. RAINE (Angelo). York civic records. Vol. 2 : 1487-1504. Leeds, Yorkshire Archaeological Society, 41, in-8, ix-200 p., 12s. 6d. (Record ser., vol. 103). R : J.T., *Eng. hist. R.*, 42, vol. 57, p. 279-280.

5310. RAND (E. K.). A romantic approach to the Middle Ages. *Med. Stud.*, 41, vol. 3, p. 1-14.

5311. SCOLLARD (R. J.). A list of photographic reproductions of mediaeval manuscripts in the library of the Institute of Mediaeval Studies, Toronto. *Med. Stud.*, 42, vol. 4, p. 126-138; 43, vol. 5, p. 51-74.

5312. SHOOK (L. K.). A technical construction in Old English : translation loans in -tic. *Med. Stud.*, 40, vol. 2, p. 253-257.

5313. SIKES (J. G.). Gulielmi de Ockham opera politica. Accuravit J. G. Sikes, sociis adscitis B. L. Manning, R. F. Bennett, H. S. Offler, R. H. Snape. Vol. 1. Manchester, Univ. Press, 40, in-8, viii-374 p., 36s. R : W. H. V. Reade, *Eng. hist. R.*, 42, vol. 57, p. 377-378.

5314. STEWART-BROWN (R.). The exchequer of Chester. *Eng. hist. R.*, 42, vol. 57, p. 289-297.

5315. WHITING (B. J.). A fifteenth-century English Chaucerian : the translator of *Partonope of Blois*. *Med. Stud.*, 45, vol. 7, p. 40-54.

INDEX OF PERSONS

Dixon (C. Willis), 4496
Dixon (H. N.), 2757
Dixon (Pierson), 1026
Dixson (Sir William), 4744
Dobb (M.), 4243, 4405
Dobbin (Leonard), 3095
Dobbs (Margaret E.), 68
Dobie (Edith), 4497
Dobie (J. F.), 3978
Doble (G. H.), 1751, 1752
Dodd (A. H.), 474, 2053, 2054, 3096
Dodd (Alfred), 2055
Dodd (M.), 4930
Dodd (William Edward), 4930
Dodds (Jackson), 3097
Dodds (John W.), 3476
Dodds (Madeleine Hope), 475, 3375
Dodge (Bayard), 4979
Dodgson (Campbell), 4795
Dodwell (B.), 1503
Dodwell (H. H.), 5015
Dohan (E. H.), 1195
Doke (C. M.), 173, 174
Dollard (William, Bp.), 2662
Donaldson (Gordon), 1780, 2727, 2727a, 2759
Donne Family, 71
Donne (John), 3183
Donner (George), 2339
Dony (John G.), 3841
Doorly (E.), 460
Doren (M. van), 3212
Dorman (B. E.), 1637
Doroshenko (D.), 545
Dorr (H. M.), 4278
Dostoevsky (F. M.), 3403
Douglas (A.), 3490
Douglas (Archibald, 3rd Marq.), 4362
Douglas (Charles), 3505
Douglas (David C.), 1292, 1383-1385
Douglas (Henry Kyd), 2507
Douglas (James), 3878, 4662
Douglas (R. L.), 3558
Douglas (Thomas), 2029
Doull (John), 4357
Douville (Joseph-Antoine-I.), 2652
Douville (Raymond), 309
Dow (J. C. R.), 4082
Dowd (B. T.), 2396, 4745
Downey (G.), 1270

Downs (Brian W.), 3334
Doyle (Sir A. Conan), 3404
Drake (Sir Francis), 2100, 2113
Drake (L. A.), 3842
Draper (A.), 596
Draper (W. N.), 4651
Drayton (Michael), 3244, 3258
Drinkwater (John), 762
Driscoll (Frank), 4746
Driver (G. R.), 89, 399, 967
Drogheda (William of), 1468
Drucker (L.), 1343
Drummie (J. H.), 4322
Drummond (Andrew Landale), 3487, 3522
Drummond-Wolff (Sir Henry), 4841
Drury (J.), 3523
Drusus Julius Caesar, 1148
Dryden (John), 3183, 3323
Dubberstein (W. H.), 61
Du Bellay (Joachim), 3215
Dubs (H.), 5161
Du Camp (Maxime), 1971
Du Châtelet (Mme.), 2957, 3324
Duckitt (William), 3997
Ducrow (Andrew), 3638
Dudding (R. C.), 1771
Du Deffand (Marie Anne, Marq.), 3321
Dudley (D. R.), 1138
Dudley (Harold E.), 878
Dürer (Albrecht), 3568
Duff (Roger), 5233
Dufton (A. F.), 3098
Dugdale (B. E. C.), 2056
Dugdale (E. T. S.), 3398
Dugmore (C. W.), 730, 2760
Dulles (F. R.), 4426
Dunaway (W. F.), 4576
Duncan (George), 2397
Duncan (K.), 2320
Dundas (W. C.), 4327
Dundonald (Earl of), 3825
Dunham (William H.) jr., 4279, 4280
Dunkel (W. D.), 3452
Dunlop (D. M.), 324, 1411
Dunlop (Margaret), 879
Dunn (Waldo Hilary), 2370
Dunne (P. M.), 2697
Dunning (G. C.), 822, 1212, 1543

Hobson (G. D.), 25, 26
Hockett (H. C.), 4288
Hodges (H. A.), 3057
Hodges (John C.), 3290
Hodgson (Hamilton), 2533
Hodgson (Sir Robert), 4434
Hodgson (S.), 27
Hodza (M.), 4936
Hölderlin (Johann Christian F.), 3426
Hoff (U.), 3507
Hofstadter (R.), 3705
Hogg (A. H. A.), 892, 1221
Hogg (Thomas Jefferson), 3341, 3470
Holbein (Hans), 3560, 3563
Holborn (H.), 350
Holdsworth (Sir William), 323, 563, 4263
Hole (Christina), 578
Hole (Willnits J.), 285
Hollaender (Albert), 1674
Holland (Henry), 3201
Holland (Josiah Gilbert), 3427
Hollander (L. M.), 1579
Hollar (Wenceslaus), 3583
Hollis (C.), 4408, 4540
Hollis (Sir Claud), 4713
Holman (W. A.), 4244
Holmes (Oliver Wendell), 4264
Holscher (U.), 944
Holt (Felix), 2861
Homans (G. C.), 1511
Homem (Diogo), 191, 193
Homer, 1082, 1086
Hone (Joseph), 3497, 3498, 3722
Honey (W. B.), 3591
Honorius III (Pope), 1382
Hood (D.), 2534
Hook (S.), 432
Hooker (Richard), 3715
Hope (E. C.), 3986
Hopkins (Charles Howard), 2862
Hopkins (Gerard Manley), 3428, 3429
Hopkins (L. C.), 5145, 5146
Hopper (R. J.), 1068
Hordern (Charles), 4866
Horn (D. B.), 4801
Hornaday (C. L.), 3342
Hornblower (G. D.), 945-947
Horne (Colin J.), 3291
Hornell (James), 433, 914, 948, 949, 2535, 2536, 5051, 5052, 5243

Hornibrook (M.), 3578
Hornik (M. P.), 4841, 4850
Horowitz (Murray), 4688
Horsefield (J. K.), 4030, 4031
Horsfield (A.), 997
Horsfield (G.), 997
Horst (Sheila T. van der), 3859
Hosain (M. H.), 272
Hoskins (G. O.), 3818
Hoskins (W. G.), 3987, 3988
Hotinger (M. D.), 419
House (H.), 3401
Householder (Fred W.), 28
Housman (A. E.), 3430, 3431
Houstoun (H.), 4032
Hovde (B. J.), 1853
Howard (Alexander), 546, 2206
Howard (Christopher), 2079, 4879
Howard (G. D.), 5224
Howard (L.), 3343
Howay (F. W.), 2389, 2404, 2405, 4435, 4661
Howe (Ellic), 3035, 3036
Howe (L. L.), 1160
Howe (M. de W.), 4264
Howe (Will D.), 3438
Howel the Good, 1309
Hower (R. M.), 3860
Howland (A. C.), 344
Howse (W. H.), 476
Hrushevsky (Michael), 547
Hsi Hsia, 5155
Hu Shih, 5147
Hubback (Sir John), 5053
Hubbell (J. B.), 3478
Hubert (M. J.), 1277
Hudson (Derek), 3037
Hudson (Henry), 2387, 2397
Hudson (W. S.), 2729
Hugh Candidus, 1310
Hughes (E. R.), 5148
Hughes (Edward), 2770, 3756, 4160, 4329
Hughes (Everett Cherrington), 1906, 1907
Hughes (G. H.), 71
Hughes (H. B. L.), 2771, 4808
Hughes (Leo), 3683
Hughes (M. W.), 1311
Hughes (Philip), 698, 2675

INDEX OF PLACES

X a